OUT OF THE *SHTETL*

Program in Judaic Studies
Brown University
Box 1826
Providence, RI 02912

BROWN JUDAIC STUDIES

Series Editors
David C. Jacobson
Ross S. Kraemer
Saul M. Olyan

Number 336

OUT OF THE *SHTETL*
Making Jews Modern
in the Polish Borderlands

by
Nancy Sinkoff

OUT OF THE *SHTETL*
Making Jews Modern
in the Polish Borderlands

Nancy Sinkoff

Brown Judaic Studies
Providence

Publication assistance from the Koret Foundation is gratefully acknowledged.

Images reproduced on pages 58–61 are from the Princes' Czartoryski Foundation at the National Museum in Cracow and are used with permission.

The image on page 186 (Feder, Tobias G. *Kol mehatsetsim.* Lemburg, 1875. Title page) is used with permission of the Dorot Jewish Division, The New York Public Library, Astor, Lenox and Tilden Foundations.

The images reproduced on pages 232 and 233 are from the Abraham Schwadron Collection of Jewish Autographs and Portraits, the Joseph Perl papers, JNUL. The image on page 187 is from the Joseph Perl Archive, JNUL. These images are used by permission of The Jewish National and University Library, Jerusalem.

Library of Congress Cataloging-in-Publication Data
Sinkoff, Nancy, 1959-
  Out of the shtetl : making Jews modern in the Polish borderlands / by Nancy Sinkoff.
    p. cm. — (Brown Judaic studies ; no. 336)
  Includes bibliographical references.
  ISBN 1-930675-16-X
  1. Jews— Ukraine— Podillia—Intellectual life— 18th century. 2. Jews—Ukraine—Podillia—Intellectual life—19th century. 3. Zaborz, Mendel ben Yehudah Leyb, 1749-1826. 4. Hasidism. 5. Mitnaggedim. 6. Haskalah. 7. Perl, Joseph, 1773-1839. 8. Jews—Galicia (Poland and Ukraine)—Intellectual life—19th century. I. Title. II. Series.
DS135.U42P637 2003
943.8'6004924—dc22

                                        2003026622

08 07 06 05 04   5 4 3 2 1

Printed in the United States of America
on acid-free paper

IN MEMORY OF MY MOTHER
ALICE B. SINKOFF
(APRIL 23, 1930 – FEBRUARY 6, 1997)

AND MY FATHER
MARVIN W. SINKOFF
(OCTOBER 22, 1926 – JULY 19, 2002)

CONTENTS

ACKNOWLEDGMENTS

I am delighted to acknowledge the individuals and institutions that have assisted me in the completion of this book. This work began as a doctoral dissertation under the guidance of Michael Stanislawski, who was a supportive mentor and teacher throughout my years at Columbia. His scholarship on the Jews of Eastern Europe is the measure by which all of his students gauge themselves. I am grateful for his continued counsel. Yosef Hayim Yerushalmi played a critical role in my graduate education and I will always be indebted to his uncompromising intellectual standards and boundless passion for the Jewish past. During my sojourn as a U.S. historian at Columbia, I benefited greatly from my contact with Professors Eric Foner and the late James Shenton. At the Jewish Theological Seminary of America I was fortunate to study with the late Baruch M. Bokser, whose brilliance as a Talmudist was not lost upon even the most beginning students. Elisheva Carlebach, a teacher and mentor in an informal capacity, was and is always generous with her time. She read and commented on the entire dissertation on which this book is based. Elliot Wolfson's glosses on the material related to Jewish mysticism and Kabbalah in this book that is drawn from my dissertation were critical in saving me from errors.

While doing the archival research for this book in Israel, I participated in the seminar, "Change and Response in Eastern Europe, the 18th-20th Centuries," at the Institute for Advanced Studies at the Hebrew University of Jerusalem, which was an unexpected delight. Since that time, I have benefited greatly from the erudition, as well as the friendship, of the scholars I met there. I mention in particular the discussions with Israel Bartal, Shmuel Feiner, Moshe Rosman, David Sorkin, and Mordechai Zalkin. Professor Rosman, as well, helped me with my initial contacts with Polish archives and also suggested that I send my manuscript to Brown Judaic Studies, fruitful connections in both cases, and a sign of his natural collegiality.

It gives me particular pleasure to thank Jeffrey Shandler, who was a friend before he was a colleague, and whose support through the research and writing of this book has been unwavering. I am indebted to my senior colleague at Rutgers University, Yael Zerubavel, whose mentorship, professionalism, and intelligence make working in the Department of Jewish Studies an honor. She has graciously shepherded me through the many obstacles that lurk in an assistant professor's life. Much of my thinking about Polish and East European Jewry comes from the numerous conversations I have had with my dear friend, Olga Litvak, whose energy for history is only surpassed by her intelligence and wit. Other colleagues have read various drafts of chapters and of the book, making them immeasurably better, including Zachary Braiterman, Paul Clemens, Lois Dubin, Jeremy Dauber, Paul Hanebrink, Rebecca Kobrin, Barbara Mann, and Daniel Unowsky. Rudolph Bell offered me lots of practical advice about how to make a book. Daniel Abrams was only too happy to pore over a piece of manuscript, even one unrelated to the history of Jewish mysticism. Deborah Dash Moore nudged me at just the right time to make the book my own. Mike Siegel of the Rutgers University Geography Department made the excellent maps that illustrate the written argument. Steven Seegal generously took time away from his own research to expedite my receipt of images from the Czartoryski Archive in Cracow. Ulrich Groetsch vetted all of my German translations. I enjoyed discussing the Hebrew employed by the *maskilim* with Reuben Namdar and Donny Inbar, and I thank Shmuel Sandberg and David Szonyi, respectively, for their help in the initial copyediting and index preparation of the book. Arlene Goldstein and Simone Fisch of the Department of Jewish Studies consistently and graciously offered their skills and advice as I completed this project and throughout my time at Rutgers. Steve Siebert of Notabene was unflappable in the face of my many questions and showed me just how elegant and efficient the program can be. David Jacobson of Brown Judaic Studies took great care in guiding this book from its first review to its final manuscript form, and I owe him a great deal of thanks. Gonni Runia expertly formatted the book from its manuscript version and my favorite young historian, Nathan Perl-Rosenthal, enthusiastically read and corrected the page proofs.

The following funding sources supported my work in graduate school and beyond: the Mellon Fellowships in the Humanities, the Center for Israel and Jewish Studies of Columbia University, the President's Fellowship in the Department of History of Columbia University, the Max Weinreich Center for Advanced Jewish Studies, the Jewish Foundation for the Education of Women, the National Foundation for Jewish Culture, the Memorial Foundation for Jewish Culture, the Leo Baeck Institute, the IIE-Fulbright Fellowship, the Interuniversity Program in Jewish Studies, the American Council of Learned Societies, and the Center for Advanced Jewish Studies at the University of Pennsylvania. Publication of this book was made possible by the Koret Foundation, the Research Council of Rutgers University, and the University Seminars of Columbia University. Material in this book was presented to the University Seminar on Israel and Jewish Studies.

The staffs at the libraries of Columbia University, the Jewish Theological Seminary of America, the New York Public Library, the Jewish National and University Library at the Hebrew University, the Central Archives of the Jewish People, and the Czartoryski Library in Cracow were all extremely helpful, and I look forward to working with them again. In particular, I would like to thank the staff of the Department of Manuscripts and Archives of the Jewish National and University Library (JNULA), whose offices became a second home to me during a year in Jerusalem. Its director, Raphael Weiser, recently made sure to expedite my receipt of images from the collection, which arrived in record time. Paweł Prokop gave me invaluable help by xeroxing and sending materials to me from the Czartoryski library. Jerry Schwarzbard, Annette Botnick, and David Wachtel of the library of the Jewish Theological Seminary of America were always forthcoming with assistance.

I could not have completed this work without the support of my friends and family. Susan Oppenheimer's friendship nurtures me constantly, despite a distance of 5,710 miles. Mychal Springer and Suzy Stein have always helped to remind me that the book was only one of many important components of my life. Stuart Schear is the best public relations agent a friend can have, and I thank him for his confidence in my work. My mother-in-law, Serina Dreiblatt, nourished my family throughout my years of study. My three incredible brothers, Martin, Richard, and Jim, have been unflagging sources of intellectual stimulation, support, and love.

Poignantly, my joy and satisfaction in publishing this book is tempered because neither of my parents, Dr. Marvin W. and Alice B. Sinkoff, lived to see it. As models of hard work and individuals of fierce passions, both of them helped me acquire the discipline and drive necessary to make myself into an historian of early modern Polish Jewry. My mother also unwittingly fulfilled a Talmudic injunction by insisting that I learn how to swim, a skill that has served me well over the many years it took to hone my craft. I think I have swum around the world in search of the beginnings of the modern East European Jew. My debt to my late father is even more profound. An American-born, Yiddish-speaking child of Russian-Jewish immigrants, he quite deliberately passed onto me his love of things Jewish and of the life of the mind. Nothing pained me more than having to include the words "in memory" in this book's dedication. I miss him every day.

It is with enormous joy that I thank my three "illuminations," my children, Ezra, Miriam, and Reuben, who got in the way and therefore showed me the way, every day. Their radiance brightens my world immeasurably. I could not have written this book without them, although they may not believe it. Finally, no words can adequately convey the gratitude I feel toward my cherished husband, Gary Dreiblatt. Over all the years of training, research, and writing that it took to complete this book, he has lived with me and the men of the Jewish Enlightenment with few complaints and not one jealous fit, giving unstintingly of his time and love. His devotion, intelligence, and incomparable sense of humor have been constant sources of sustenance and guidance. He is my North Star, without whom I would be lost.

A WORD ABOUT PLACE NAMES

The geographic shifts in the Polish borderlands in the era of partitions make the spelling of place names particularly challenging. For locations in the Polish-Lithuanian Commonwealth before 1772, place names have been rendered throughout the book according to the Polish spelling. Place names in the locations mentioned in the book during the era of partitions and after the final borders were set at the Congress of Vienna in 1815 are rendered in Polish with German equivalents in parentheses, for example, Lwów (Lemberg). The only exceptions to this Polish-centered nomenclature are major European cities, such as Warsaw, Vilna, Cracow, Berlin, and St. Petersburg and the province of Podole, which is rendered as Podolia throughout the book. Individuals whose names bear the locations they are from, such as Jacob Joseph of Połonna (Polonnoye), are named according to the Polish spelling with the familiar English equivalent in parentheses, as above. The Polish spellings are consistent with those found in the *Słownik Geograficzny Królestwa Polskiego i innych Krajów Słowiańskich* (Warsaw, 1885)

LIST OF MAPS AND ILLUSTRATIONS

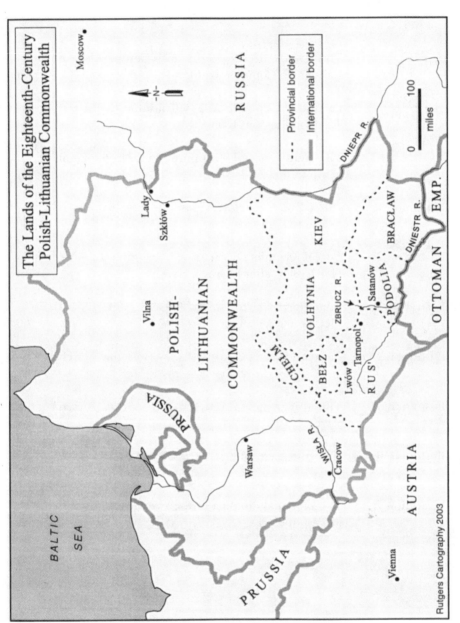

The Lands of the Eighteenth-Century
Polish-Lithuanian Commonwealth

Provincial border
International border

BALTIC
SEA

Moscow

RUSSIA

Lady
Szklów

PRUSSIA

POLISH-
LITHUANIAN
COMMONWEALTH

Vilna

Warsaw

WISŁA R.

Cracow

PRUSSIA

CHEŁM

BEŁZ

Lwów
Tarnopol

R U S'

VOLHYNIA

ZBRUCZ R.

Satanów

PODOLIA

KIEV

BRACŁAW

DNIEPR R.

DNIESTR R.

OTTOMAN EMP.

AUSTRIA

Vienna

0   100
miles

Rutgers Cartography 2003

Map 1

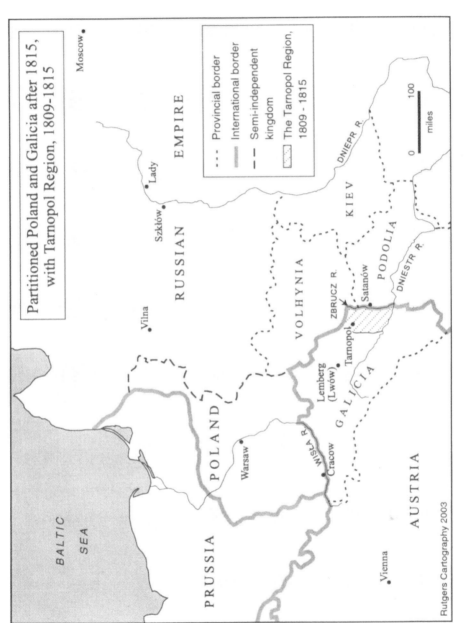

Partitioned Poland and Galicia after 1815, with Tarnopol Region, 1809-1815

Map 2

Ruigers Cartography 2003

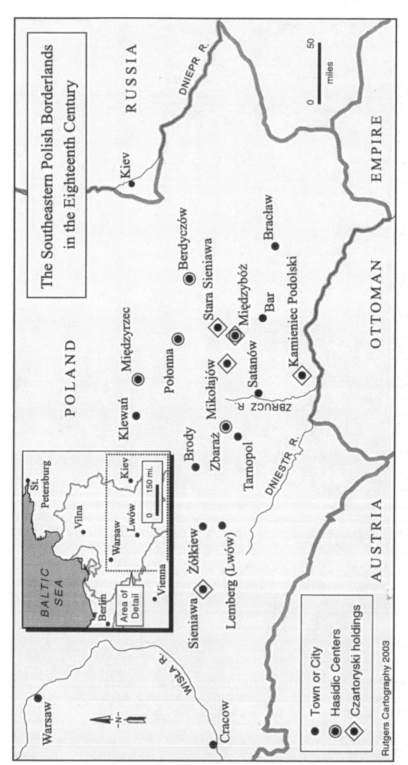

The Southeastern Polish Borderlands in the Eighteenth Century

Map 3

Rutgers Cartography 2003

ENLIGHTENING POLISH JEWS, MODERATING THE JEWISH ENLIGHTENMENT

[In Berlin after 1786] a general mania for innovation took hold. Soon the majority of the people, mocked [by others] as shabby aesthetes, scorned the esteemed Orthodox, the Sages of the Talmud, and the religion. By disdaining this national pride, which was considered evil, they became enlightened solely toward meanness. They were ashamed of their origin, ashamed of their brethren, and, finally, ashamed of their Jewish names. Hirsch was transformed into Herman and into Heinrich, Malkah into Amalie [and into] Mavblume. Moses' prescriptions were examined and found no longer suitable for the spirit of the age. They switched to Deism, to indifference.[1]

Mendel Lefin, unpublished manuscript

Elegy and nostalgia shroud the contemporary image of East European Jewry. Despite perceptions that the destruction of twentieth-century Polish Jewry affirmed a history of unremitting suffering, the contrary is true.[2] Vitality, not travail, distinguished the past of Poland's Jews, who lived relatively unharassed for centuries in the Polish-Lithuanian Commonwealth.[3] Early

---

[1]   The Joseph Perl Archive, JNULA, 4° 1153/134a, 4b–5a. Name changing became a commonplace among acculturated Berlin Jews in the early nineteenth century. Heinrich Heine mocked this practice in his poem, "Jehudah ben Halevy": "So I straightaway/Took a droshky and rushed to the/Court Investigator Hitzig,/Who was formerly called Itzig./Back when he'd been still an Itzig,/He had dreamed a dream in which he/Saw his name inscribed on heaven/With the letter H in front./What did this H mean? he wondered — /Did it mean perhaps Herr Itzig, *Holy* Itzig (for Saint Itzig)?/*Holy*'s a fine title — but not/Suited for Berlin." Cited in Steven M. Lowenstein, *The Berlin Jewish Community: Enlightenment, Family, and Crisis, 1770–1830* (New York: Oxford University Press, 1994), 227, footnote 32. Lefin's use of the term "Orthodox" *(Orthodoxen)* anticipates the mid-century use of the term in the debates between Reform Judaism and Neo-Orthodoxy.
[2]   Gershon David Hundert, "The Conditions in Jewish Society in the Polish-Lithuanian Commonwealth in the Middle Decades of the Eighteenth Century," in *Hasidism Reappraised* (ed. Ada Rapoport-Albert; London: The Littman Library of Jewish Civilization, 1996), 45–50; M. J. Rosman, "Jewish Perceptions of Insecurity and Powerlessness in 16th–18th Century Poland," *Polin* 1 (1986): 19–27; Edward Fram, *Ideals Face Reality: Jewish Law and Life in Poland, 1550–1655* (Cincinnati, Ohio: Hebrew Union College Press, 1997), 15–37.
[3]   See the testimony of historian Salo Baron, historical witness at the trial of Adolf Eichmann. Salo W. Baron, "The Eichmann Trial," in *American Jewish Yearbook* (ed. Morris Fine and Milton Himmelfarb; New York: The American Jewish Commitee and the Jewish Publication Society of America, 1962), 3–53.

modern Polish Jewry, who were nothing less than the demographic source of
all of modern East European Jewry,[4] innovated many of the religious and
cultural movements that shaped Ashkenazic Jewry in the Diaspora throughout the nineteenth and twentieth centuries, including Hasidism, Mitnagged-
ism (the Lithuanian "opponents" to Hasidism), and a variety of casts of
Jewish nationalism.[5] Given the contemporary fascination with mysticism of
all sorts, and with the Kabbalah (Jewish mysticism) in particular, the history
of Hasidism has earned pride of place in both the scholarly and public
realms.[6] But the history of the Polish Jews who consciously chose to embrace
the modern world, the *maskilim* ("enlightened Jews" in the Hebrew terminology of the period) has largely been forgotten, subsumed within a homogeneous narrative of pre-modern Polish Jewry as pious, insular, and anti-
modern, living in exclusively Jewish towns, the much-romanticized *shtetlekh*
(market towns) of Eastern Europe.[7]

---

[4]   In 1700, 51.8 percent of world Jewry was East European. In 1850, East European Jewry
comprised 72 percent of the world's Jews, a result of its extraordinary fecundity and the
practice of early marriage in the eighteenth century. In 1880, it constituted 75 percent of
world Jewry. The percentage decreased to 45.6 percent on the eve of World War II, but that
is simply because of outmigration — the mass influx of East European Jews to the New
World — not to a concomitant growth of Jews in the rest of Europe. The monstrous destruction of European Jewry in the twentieth century signaled an end to the "European era" in
Jewish life, but even more significantly, resulted in the extirpation of a millennium-old
Ashkenazic Jewish culture in Eastern, Central, and Western Europe. On the European era in
Jewish history, see Salo Baron, "The Modern Age," in *Great Ages and Ideas of the Jewish People*
(ed. Leo Schwarz; New York: Modern Library, 1956), 315–390. Data are adapted from
the appendix, "The Demography of Modern Jewish History," in Paul Mendes-Flohr and
Jehuda Reinharz, eds., *The Jew in the Modern World* (Oxford: Oxford University Press, 1995),
701–21.
[5]   On the enduring influence of Polish Jewry on modern Jewish politics, see Ezra Mendelsohn, *On Modern Jewish Politics* (Oxford: Oxford University Press, 1993). For a recent study of
the Lithuanian opponents to Hasidism, see Allan Nadler, *The Faith of the Mithnagdim* (Baltimore, Md.: The Johns Hopkins University Press, 1997).
[6]   The contemporary historiography on Hasidism and Jewish mysticism continues to grow
apace. Recent works include Immanuel Etkes, *Ba'al hashem: haBesht–magyah, mistiqah,
hanhagah* (Jerusalem: Zalman Shazar Center, 2000); Moshe Rosman, *Founder of Hasidism: A
Quest for the Historical Ba'al Shem Tov* (Berkeley: University of California Press, 1996); David
Assaf, *Breslav: bibliografyah mu'eret, R. Naḥman mibreslav, toldotav umorashato hasifrutit: sifrei
talmidav vetalmidei talmidav: ḥasidut Breslav usevivoteihah* (Jerusalem: Zalman Shazar Center,
2000); Mendel Piekarz, *Hahanagah haḥasidut: samkhut ve'emunat tsaddiqim be'aspaklaryat
sifrutah shel haḥasidut* (Jerusalem: Bialik Institute, 2000); Rachel Elior, *Ḥeirut al haluḥot:
hamaḥashavah haḥasidit, meqoroteihah hamistiyyim viyesodoteihah haqabbaliyyim* (Tel Aviv: The
Defense Institute, 1999); and Moshe Idel, *Hasidism: Between Ecstasy and Magic* (Albany: State
University of New York Press, 1995).
[7]   For thoughtful critiques of the image of the *shtetl*, see Barbara Kirshenblatt-Gimblett,
"Introduction," in *Life Is with People* (Mark Zborowski and Elizabeth Herzog; New York:
Schocken Books, 1995), 12–38, Dan Miron, "The Literary Image of the Shtetl," in *The Image
of the Shtetl and Other Studies of Modern Jewish Literary Imagination* (Syracuse, N.Y.: Syracuse

Modernity confronted Polish Jewry already at the end of the eighteenth century when absolutist Russia, Prussia, and Austria partitioned the Commonwealth (1772, 1793, and 1795) and thrust Polish Jewry into an unprecedented relationship with the modern state. The partitions of Poland, as much as the French Revolution, migration, or proto-industrialization, were critical events in the transformation of European Jewry as a whole.[8] The political process of partition resulted in a radically new political and social reality for the Jews of Poland, who nonetheless continued to inhabit the same region they had for centuries. In other words, the state, not the Jews, moved.

The partitions resulted in the "reencounter" of Ashkenazic Jewry (the term denoting the medieval Jewish communities of northern France and German lands) with, and the entry of their Polish-Jewish descendants into, the West European state and its culture. I use the term "reencounter" because the forebears of Polish Jews had been thoroughly expelled from Western Europe from the thirteenth through the fifteenth centuries, after which there were no openly professing Jewish communities in West European lands. The readmission of Western Ashkenazic Jewry into European society began around 1650, after the Thirty Years War, when France acquired the provinces of Alsace and Lorraine, and absorbed an Ashkenazic Jewish population of 20,000, a large, culturally cohesive traditional community whose integration challenged French society.[9] But the numbers of Jews in Alsace and Lorraine paled in comparison to those living in pre-partitioned Poland. Demographics matter. By 1795, the Habsburg Monarchy had acquired a new Jewish population of approximately 260,000. 170,000 Polish Jews became subjects of Prussia after 1795. In that same year, Catherine the Great found herself with 320,000 new subjects, Jews from the *kresy* (the Russian term for the eastern borderlands of the Commonwealth), now under Russian rule.[10]

University Press, 2000), 1–48, and Jeffrey Shandler, "Szczuczyn: A *Shtetl* Through a Photographer's Eye," in *Lives Remembered: A Shtetl Through A Photographer's Eye* (New York: Museum of Jewish Heritage: A Living Memorial to the Holocaust, 2002), 19–27.

[8] Jerzy Lukowski, *The Partitions of Poland, 1772, 1793, 1795* (London: Longman, 1999).

[9] See Jonathan I. Israel, *European Jewry in the Age of Mercantilism, 1550–1750* (Oxford: Clarendon, 1985) for an analysis of the significance of the "early modern period" and the reintegration, what he calls the "economic emancipation," of European Jewry; on the Jews of Alsace and Lorraine, see Zosa Szajkowski, *The Economic Status of the Jews in Alsace, Metz and Lorraine (1648–1789)* (New York: Editions Historiques Franco-Juives, 1954) and Paula E. Hyman, *The Emancipation of the Jews of Alsace: Acculturation and Tradition in the Nineteenth Century* (New Haven, Conn.: Yale University Press, 1991).

[10] Arnold Springer, "Enlightened Absolutism and Jewish Reform: Prussia, Austria and Russia," *California Slavic Studies* 11 (1980): 240. These numbers are only rough estimates; even when more scientific surveys and censuses were taken, the Jewish community eluded them, often in an effort to reduce an increase in taxation. Nonetheless, the numbers indicate the massive size of the Polish Jewish community in the eighteenth century. Moses

While the Congress of Vienna created the semi-independent Congress King-dom of Poland tied to Russia in 1815, most of the former population of Poland's Jews now lived under the rule of three modernizing absolutist states.

The shifting political borders in the era of partitions created the modern "Jewish Question," challenging Europe to define where the Jews should fit in the new, modernizing, putatively secular, state.[11] All of the reform programs and proposals regarding the Jews initiated by the European state between 1772–1815 sought to transform the culture and economic profile of the numerically formidable Ashkenazic population it had absorbed.[12] The "Jew-ish Question" that informed the debates in the French National Assembly during the French Revolution, the Habsburg *Toleranzpatente* for Lower Austria and Galicia, the discussions during the last Polish Parliament (1788–1792), and the edicts of 1804 promulgated by Tsar Alexander I, was, in fact, a question of how to integrate Ashkenazic Jewry, the demographic core of which were the Jews of Poland.[13] In many ways, the vital encounter of Ashkenazic Jewry with the European state in its various national forms through the course of the nineteenth and twentieth centuries informed the history of all of European Jewry from 1772 forward.

The Polish Jewish community not only faced political changes in the eighteenth century, but also encountered the spread of Enlightenment ideas and aspirations that originated in Western Europe. While much of the Polish Jewish community either ignored or rejected the tenets of the Enlighten-ment, an important group of Polish Jewish *intelligenti* embraced ideologies of modernity and articulated programs for the integration, regeneration, and transformation of Polish Jewry already at the end of the eighteenth century. They were the Polish-Jewish exponents of the Jewish Enlightenment

---

Shulvass sees the population shifts in terms of migration, not partition. Moses Shulvass, *From East to West: The Westward Migration of Jews from Eastern Europe during the Seventeenth and Eighteenth Centuries* (Detroit, Mich.: Wayne State University Press, 1971). The case of Viennese Jewry is striking. In 1777, only 520 Jews were legally resident in Vienna, out of an Empire-wide population of 350,000, the majority of whom were the Jews of the new province of Galicia and Lodomeria. See Robert S. Wistrich, *The Jews of Vienna in the Age of Franz Joseph* (New York: Oxford University Press, 1990), 14.

[11] Medieval Christian Europe categorized the Jews and Judaism theologically. The Scien-tific Revolution and the Enlightenment eroded those categories, at least theoretically.

[12] Springer, "Enlightened Absolutism and Jewish Reform," 237–67.

[13] The most illustrative example of the European state's ambivalent attitude toward the integration of Ashkenazic Jewry is the French case. The French state granted Sephardic Jews living in the southwest of France complete political emancipation on January 28, 1790, a full twenty months before it granted the same rights to their Ashkenazic brethren. See Zosa Szajkowski, *Jews and the French Revolutions of 1789, 1830 and 1848* (New York: KTAV, 1970) and M. Diogene Tama, trans., *Transactions of the Parisian Sanhedrim, or Acts of the Assembly of Israelitish Deputies of France and Italy* (New York: University Press of America, 1985).

(Haskalah), whose self-conscious engagement with the foremost intellectual currents of the period challenges the image of a benighted Polish Jewry.[14]

The concerns of the *maskilim* of Poland echoed those of their West European (primarily Prussian) brethren. Enlightened Jews on both sides of the Oder River on Prussia's eastern border sought to balance the relationship between traditional religious obligation and modernity's commitment to individualism and moral autonomy. The hope for full political emancipation and integration inaugurated by the French Revolution challenged the cohesion of early modern Jewish communal life; *maskilim* now had to delineate new social boundaries between Jew and non-Jew.[15] The appeal of the state's vernacular language, while offering new avenues of political access, abetted a decline in literacy and in authority of traditional Jewish texts and languages. Like the *maskilim* of Berlin, Polish *maskilim* adopted the ideals of the European Enlightenment in order to construct a Jewish identity suitable for the modern world. But their conception of modernity differed from that of their Prussian counterparts, who shaped their programs of Enlightenment in the context of an aggressively modernizing nation-state.[16] Polish Jews, whether living in the Austrian or Russian partition of Poland, encountered modernity in Imperial contexts, whose state-building lagged politically, economically, and socially behind Western Europe.[17]

The first four chapters of this book explore the Polish-Jewish response to modernity through an intellectual biography of Mendel Lefin of Satanów (1749–1826), the preeminent personality of the Haskalah in Poland in the period during and after the partitions. While the material and social history

---

[14]   David Fishman's work on the Jewish community of Szkłów, a city in the northeastern region of the Commonwealth, illustrated that Enlightenment ideas penetrated into certain segments of Polish Jewish society soon after the first partition. See David E. Fishman, *Russia's First Modern Jews: The Jews of Shklov* (New York: New York University Press, 1995). Moreover, as several scholars have pointed out, many of the protagonists of the Prussian-Jewish Enlightenment in Berlin and Königsberg were Polish Jews. See Lowenstein, *The Berlin Jewish Community*, 34, and the comments of Abraham Brawer on the "pre-Mendelssohnian" type of Polish *maskil* in A. Y. Brawer, *Galitsyah viyehudeihah: mehqarim betoldot Galitsyah bame'ah hashemoneh-esreh* (Jerusalem: Bialik Institute, 1965), 200. Even Zalkind Hourwitz, who championed the cause of full emancipation for the Jews of France during the Revolution, originally hailed from Lublin. See Frances Malino, *A Jew in the French Revolution: The Life of Zalkind Hourwitz* (Cambridge, Mass.: Blackwell Publishers, 1996).

[15]   Jacob Katz, *Out of the Ghetto: The Social Background of Jewish Emancipation, 1770–1870* (Cambridge, Mass.: Harvard University Press, 1973).

[16]   David Sorkin, *The Transformation of German Jewry, 1780–1840* (New York: Oxford University Press, 1987).

[17]   Andrei Markovits and Frank E. Sysyn, eds., *Nationbuilding and the Politics of Nationalism: Essays on Austrian Galicia* (Cambridge, Mass.: Harvard University Press, 1982). The Polish-Jewish inhabitants of Posen, the Prussian partition of Poland, are the subject of the recent work, Sophia Kemlein, *Die Posener Juden, 1815–1848: Entwicklungsprozesse einer polnischen Judenheit unter preussischer Herrschaft* (Hamburg: Dolling und Galitz, 1997).

of the Jews, their socio-economic profile, communal organization, and ways of life (food, architecture, clothing, burial patterns, demographics, etc.) are important fields of inquiry, I nonetheless maintain that no Jewish community — past or present — has sustained itself without an intellectual or ideological conception of collective selfhood. The revolution of modernity necessitated transformations in communal self-understanding among the Jews of Europe, stimulating them to define themselves in new ways, and the *maskilim* were the first and most articulate spokespersons of the encounter with modernity's challenges. This book thus focuses on the conscious ideological response to modernity articulated by Lefin (and his disciples) within the processes of political, social, and economic change that define "modernization."[18] Dedicated to intellectual-cultural history, this study employs both published and archival literary sources — letters, personal diaries, programmatic essays, political petitions and memoranda, and exegeses and translations of classical Jewish texts — to bring Mendel Lefin's worldview into focus.

Rather than concentrating on the details of Lefin's personal biography, which are fragmentary,[19] I analyze his cultural program for the Jews of

---

[18]   Jürgen Habermas refers to "modernization" as a mixture of several social processes: capitalist and industrial development; increase in the productivity of labor; centralization of political power; urbanization; nationalism; rise of compulsory education; and secularization of values and norms. See Jürgen Habermas, *The Philosophical Discourse of Modernity* (Cambridge, Mass.: MIT Press, 1987). Todd Endelman, Steven Zipperstein and, most recently, Paula Hyman, offer non-ideological models of modernization for the Jews of England, new Russia, and Alsace, respectively. See Todd M. Endelman, *The Jews of Georgian England, 1714– 1830: Tradition and Change in a Liberal Society* (Philadelphia: The Jewish Publication Society of America, 1979); Steven J. Zipperstein, *The Jews of Odessa: A Cultural History, 1794–1881* (Stanford, Calif.: Stanford University Press, 1986); Hyman, *The Emancipation of the Jews of Alsace*. See, too, Mordechai Zalkin, "The Jewish Enlightenment in Poland: Directions for Discussion," in *Qiyyum veshever: yehudei Polin ledoroteihem*, vol. 2 (ed. Israel Bartal and Israel Gutman; Jerusalem: Zalman Shazar Center, 2001), 391–413. On the independence of the ideology of the Enlightenment from social forces, see Derek Beales, "Social Forces and Enlightened Policies," in *Enlightened Absolutism: Reform and Reformers in Later Eighteenth-Century Europe* (ed. H. M. Scott; London: Macmillan, 1990), 37–53.

[19]   General biographical information about Lefin can be culled from the following sources: Lucy Dawidowicz, *The Golden Tradition: Jewish Life and Thought in Eastern Europe* (Boston: Beacon Press, 1967), 24; Samuel Joseph Fuenn, *Qiryah ne'emanah* (Vilna, 1860), 51; Joseph Klausner, *Historyah shel hasifrut ha'ivrit haḥadashah* (Jerusalem: The Hebrew University, 1952), 1:201–22; Raphael Mahler, *Hasidism and the Jewish Enlightenment: Their Confrontation in Galicia and Poland in the First Half of the Nineteenth Century* (Philadelphia: The Jewish Publication Society of America, 1985) and Raphael Mahler, *A History of Modern Jewry, 1780– 1815* (New York: Schocken Books, 1971), 588; Emmanuel Ringelblum, "Hasidism and Haskalah in Warsaw in the Eighteenth Century," *YIVO bleter* 13 (1938): 126; Israel Weinlös, "Mendel Lefin of Satanów: A Biographical Study from Manuscript Material," *YIVO bleter* 1 (1931): 334–57 and Israel Weinlös, "R. Menachem Mendel of Satanów," *Ha'olam* 13 (1925): 39:778–79; 40:799–800; 41:819–20; 42:839–40; Israel Zinberg, *A History of Jewish Literature*

Poland as a way of illuminating the regional diversity in the formulation of the Jewish Enlightenment. While the iconic status of Berlin as the center of the Jewish Enlightenment is well deserved, it is misleading to equate influence with bald imitation. Lefin's efforts to transform Polish Jewry responded to the general cultural trends of the European Enlightenment, but revealed the specific Jewish and Polish contexts in which he lived. He sojourned in the early 1780s among the circle of enlightened Jews in Berlin associated with Moses Mendelssohn (1729–1786), yet did not unreflectively cloak himself in their ideological mantle.[20] He selectively appropriated certain values of the Berlin Haskalah and reshaped them to suit the culture and society of Polish Jewry. His active reinterpretation of the Haskalah for Polish Jewry was *simultaneous* with the ongoing development of the Jewish Enlightenment in Prussia and underscores that there was no one "authentic" Jewish Enlightenment, just as there was no one "authentic" European Enlightenment.[21] Rather there was a broad spectrum of personalities within each national context who constructed different varieties of "Enlightenment," all generally stressing an optimistic belief in human capability as they contemplated the future.[22] Lefin's work, therefore, challenges the trajectory of a unilateral West to East movement of ideas and illustrates that there were several "national" or "regional" paths to becoming a modern European Jew.[23]

(New York: KTAV, 1975), 275. See, too, Hillel Levine, "Menahem Mendel Lefin: A Case Study of Judaism and Modernization" (Ph.D. diss., Harvard University, 1974), although his study did not employ all of the extant documents related to Lefin's life.

[20] The scholarship on the Berlin Haskalah and Moses Mendelssohn is voluminous. Classic studies include Alexander Altmann, *Moses Mendelssohn: A Biographical Study* (Tuscaloosa, Ala.: The University of Alabama Press, 1973); Michael A. Meyer, *The Origins of the Modern Jew* (Detroit, Mich.: Wayne State University Press, 1979); Azriel Shohat, *Im hillufei tequfot* (Jerusalem: The Bialik Institute, 1960); Jacob Katz, *Tradition and Crisis: Jewish Society at the End of the Middle Ages* (trans. Bernard Dov Cooperman; New York: New York University Press, 1993). A newer study is David Sorkin, *Moses Mendelssohn and the Religious Enlightenment* (Berkeley: University of California Press, 1996).

[21] On the reassessment of cultural transmission as an active historical process, see Anthony Grafton, "Introduction: Notes from Underground on Cultural Transmission," in *The Transmission of Culture in Early Modern Europe* (ed. Anthony Grafton and Ann Blair; Philadelphia: University of Pennsylvania Press, 1990), 1–7. See, too, Roger Chartier, *Cultural History: Between Practices and Representations* (trans. Lydia G. Cochrane; Ithaca, New York: Cornell University Press, 1988) for theorization of how different classes, groups, and mileus use varying strategies in response to their environment in order to construct meaning and identity.

[22] Roy Porter, *The Enlightenment* (London: Macmillan, 1990).

[23] The volume, Jacob Katz, ed., *Toward Modernity: The European Jewish Model* (New Brunswick, N.J.: Transaction Books, 1987), is a significant contribution to contextualizing the Haskalah nationally among European Jews at the end of the eighteenth and the beginning of the nineteenth century. For the distinctive encounter of northern Italian Jews with the Haskalah, see Lois C. Dubin, *The Port Jews of Habsburg Trieste: Absolutist Politics and Enlightenment Culture* (Stanford, Calif.: Stanford University Press, 1999); for Anglo-Jewry, see David B.

Lefin's conception of the Haskalah, nurtured in Podole (henceforth, Podolia), a southeastern province of the Polish-Lithuanian Commonwealth, directly influenced its subsequent development in Austrian Galicia and Russian Poland after the partitions.[24] But referring to him as the "Father of the Galician Haskalah," as did historians Raphael Mahler, Israel Weinlös, Isaac Barzilay, and Natan Michael Gelber, is anachronistic and elides the significance of his "Polishness," for lack of a more felicitous term. By "Polishness," I mean that the culture, society, and politics of pre-partitioned Poland, as well as the rich religious culture of medieval and early modern Polish Judaism, informed Lefin's encounter with modernity and his formulation of the Jewish Enlightenment. Except for two important excursions to Berlin and St. Petersburg, Lefin spent the bulk of his years in his native region and moved to Brody and Tarnopol, centers of the Galician Jewish Enlightenment, only at the end of his life.[25] Even after the partitions, he expressed his distinctiveness as a Polish *maskil*. In *Essai d'un plan de réforme ayant pour objet d'éclairer la Nation Juive en Pologne et de redresser par là ses moeurs* (*Essay of a Reform Plan Whose Object is the Enlightenment and Redress of the Morals of the Jews of Poland*, 1791), Lefin urged Polish Jews to study Polish, not German, in the new schools created by the Polish National Education Commission.[26] Lefin

---

Ruderman, *Jewish Enlightenment in an English Key: Anglo-Jewry's Construction of Modern Jewish Thought* (Princeton, N.J.: Princeton University Press, 2000).

[24]   All of the following activists in the Jewish Enlightenment in Galicia and Russia had contact with Lefin and his works: Joseph Perl, Jacob Samuel Bik, Nachman Krochmal, Nachman and Sheindel Pineles, Bezalel Stern, Benjamin Reich, Mordecai Suchostober, Yehudah Leib ben Zevi Hirsch Segal, Eliezer Zweifel, Rashi Fuenn and Isaac Baer Levinsohn. On Fuenn, see Shmuel Feiner, *Mehaskalah lohemet lehaskalah meshammeret: nivḥar mikhtevei Rashi Fin* (Jerusalem: Dinur Center, 1993); on Krochmal, see Jay Harris, *Nachman Krochmal: Guiding the Perplexed of the Modern Age* (New York: New York University Press, 1991); on Isaac Baer Levinsohn, who explicitly referenced Mendel Lefin's writings in his programmatic pamphlet, *Te'udah beyisra'el*, see Isaac Baer Levinsohn, *Te'udah beyisra'el* (ed. Immanuel Etkes; Vilna, 1828), 78 and Michael Stanislawski, *Tsar Nicholas I and the Jews: The Transformation of Jewish Society in Russia, 1825–1855* (Philadelphia: The Jewish Publication Society of America, 1983), 78, 110–20; on the influence of the *maskilim* from Brody on the development of the Haskalah in Odessa, see Zipperstein, *The Jews of Odessa*, 43–54.

[25]   Raphael Mahler dates Lefin's settlement in Brody (Austrian Galicia) at the end of the first decade of the nineteenth century, when Lefin was already fifty-nine years old. Based on conclusions drawn from the *maskil* Meir Letteris's autobiography, Mahler concluded that Lefin made two trips to Berlin, the first between the years 1780–1784, the second in the latter part of the decade. Although Max Erik repeats this assertion, there is no other evidence that Lefin sojourned twice in Berlin. See Meir Letteris, *Zikaron basefer* (Vienna, 1868), 38, Raphael Mahler, *Divrei yemei yisra'el* (Rehavia: Worker's Library, 1956), 1:72, Mahler, *A History of Modern Jewry*, 588–89, and Max Erik, *Etiudn tsu der geshikhte fun der haskole* (Minsk, 1934), 136.

[26]   [Mendel Lefin], *"Essai d'un plan de réforme ayant pour objet d'éclairer la Nation Juive en Pologne et de redresser par là ses moeurs,"* in *Materiały do dziejów Sejmu Czteroletniego* (ed. Arthur Eisenbach et al.; Wrocław: Instytut Historii Polskiej Akademii Nauk, 1969), 414. On dating

also composed his Yiddish translation of Psalms in the dialect specific to the Jews of Podolia (which he called "the Polish-Jewish language"), a decision expressing the regionalism of his formulation of the Haskalah.[27]

Lefin articulated a conception of modern Jewish life that is best described as moderate. He formulated the Haskalah as a temperate response to radicalizing tendencies from both the right, the Hasidic enthusiasm that he personally witnessed, and the left, the streams of Deism and atheism that colored the Berlin Haskalah after the death of Moses Mendelssohn in 1786.[28] Lefin's moderate, enlightened worldview was comprised of several related components that synthesized intellectual exploration of Western, non-Jewish ideas with fidelity to rabbinic culture. He believed in individual intellectual autonomy because it was a gift from God. He sanctioned the pursuit of non-Jewish sciences, particularly natural science, as a means of celebrating God's creative works. He argued for a rationalized attitude toward and practice of Judaism as a bulwark against what he contended was Hasidism's mystification and subversion of the classical rabbinic tradition. He counseled participation in the general body politic without dissolving the autonomous Jewish community. All of these elements, Lefin believed, would protect and revitalize Ashkenazic Jewish culture without weakening the authority of revealed commandment. The Haskalah, for Lefin, was reformist, not revolutionary.

This book's emphasis on Lefin's moderation fits into a historiographic trend within the contemporary field of modern Jewish history to read the

---

the pamphlet, see Alexander Guterman, "The Suggestions of Polish Jews toward the Reforms of Their Legal, Economic, Social and Cultural Status in the Period of the Great Sejm (1788–1792)" (M.A. thesis, The Hebrew University of Jerusalem, 1975), 70. Lefin wrote the pamphlet in French, the language of the European nobility, to reach the widest possible audience.

[27] Simha Katz, "Menachem Mendel Lefin of Satanów's Bible Translations," *Kiryat sefer* 16 (1939): 130. On Lefin's use of the term "Polish-Jewish language" for Yiddish, see the Joseph Perl Archive, JNULA, 4° 1153/67 and 134a, 3b.

My interest in the regional distinctiveness of the Polish-Jewish encounter with modernity reflects a general historiographic commitment to investigate the ideological and national variety among those who espoused and lived Enlightenment ideals. Yet, despite the new awareness of national context in Enlightenment studies, the place of Poland and its Enlightenment (*Oświecenie*) have not been integrated into general historical treatments of either the European or Jewish Enlightenments. Poland is absent in Roy Porter and Mikuláš Teich's important book. See Roy Porter and Mikuláš Teich, eds., *The Enlightenment in National Context* (Cambridge: Cambridge University Press, 1981). The elision of Polish history in the writing of modern European history has also informed the writing of modern Polish-Jewish history, which has often been subsumed under the general rubrics of "East European" or "Russian-Jewish" history.

[28] Lucy Dawidowicz argued that the Haskalah in Eastern Europe fought two opponents, Hasidism and traditional Judaism, missing completely that a *maskil* of Lefin's moderate cast believed that his program would invigorate traditional Jewish culture and life. See Dawidowicz, *The Golden Tradition*, 23.

Haskalah in a conservative key, a trend that parallels the general interest among historians of the European Enlightenment(s) to reconsider the hallmark of the movement: Reason, itself.[29] Edward Breuer, Jay Harris, Shmuel Feiner, and David Sorkin, among others, have redrawn what had been the regnant portrait of the *maskilim* as unrepentant foes of the classical Rabbis of antiquity, of rabbinic tradition in general, and of their contemporary rabbinic authorities.[30] These historians have argued for a more nuanced view of the ways in which the first generation of enlightened Prussian Jews, and subsequent generations of East European Jews, viewed rabbinic tradition. Mendel Lefin's version of the moderate Jewish Enlightenment as a middle path between the dual threat of religious indifference and Hasidic enthusiasm supports a conservative reading of the Haskalah. His worldview thus challenges Jacob Katz's classic interpretation that two movements, Hasidism in the East and Haskalah in the West, led to the dissolution of traditional Ashkenazic Jewish society in the eighteenth century.[31] For Lefin, and for moderate *maskilim* after him, the Haskalah was the solution to, not the cause of, the crisis facing Polish Jewry.

Lefin formulated his conception of the Jewish Enlightenment in the southeastern "Polish borderlands," a term that I employ to convey both a geographic region and a figurative landscape that reflects the demographic, cultural, terminological, and political complexity of Mendel Lefin's life. From 1749, when Lefin was born in Satanów, Poland, to 1826, when he died in Tarnopol, Austrian Galicia, everything — borders, political rule, language, communal organization — changed for the Jews of the southeastern Polish

---

[29] While earlier histories of the Enlightenment in all of its European varieties and of its Jewish counterpart emphasized a direct march toward rationalism, individuality, absolutist politics and the concomitant dissolution of the authority of revealed religion, the bonds of community, and traditional politics, contemporary historians of both the European Enlightenment and of the Haskalah have become increasingly attentive to the conservatism of certain proponents of eighteenth-century Enlightenment values. Many of the journalists, natural philosophers, moralists, doctors, churchmen, and rabbis who were activists in the Enlightenments of Europe staked their worldviews not on Reason, but on experience, and continued to believe that humanity's ability to know the natural and human world empirically was due to divine benevolence. For an older view, see the classic study by Peter Gay, *The Enlightenment: An Interpretation*, 2 vols. (New York: Alfred A. Knopf, 1966). For the revisionist perspective, see the summary in Porter, *The Enlightenment*, 3 and Lois C. Dubin, "The Social and Cultural Context: Eighteenth-Century Enlightenment," in *History of Jewish Philosophy* (ed. Daniel H. Frank and Oliver Leaman; London: Routledge, 1997), 636–59, particularly 637–39.

[30] Sorkin, *Moses Mendelssohn*; Edward Breuer, *The Limits of Enlightenment: Jews, Germans and the Study of Scripture in the Eighteenth-Century* (Cambridge, Mass.: Harvard University Press, 1996); Harris, *Nachman Krochmal*; Shmuel Feiner, "The Early Haskalah among Eighteenth-Century Jewry," *Tarbiz* 67, no. 2 (1998): 189–240.

[31] Katz, *Tradition and Crisis*, 3–4, 9, 195–236.

borderlands.[32] These two cities, separated by a mere 60 kilometers as a bird flies, demarcated a geographic space claimed by various national groups and called by a plethora of names: the Polish-Lithuanian Commonwealth, Rus' Czerwona, Red Rus', western Ukraine, eastern Galicia, "The Kingdom of Galicia and Lodomeria," and Podolia. Today's terminology continues to confound. This region is now called Eastern Europe, at the western edge of independent Ukraine. Until World War I, however, the area west of the Zbrucz River claimed by Maria Theresa in the first partition of Poland was known as Central Europe.[33] The precise geographic stage on which most of this book's narrative unfolds is the territory between the Dniestr and the Dniepr Rivers: the Podolian steppe in Ukraine (literally, "borderlands"). Situated between Poland, Russia, and Austria, caught in the crisis of partition, stuck between the baroque culture of the early modern period and the enlightened culture of modernity, the "borderlands" represent the geographic, political, and cultural liminality of Lefin's region and life.[34] I use the term "Poland" and "Polish-Lithuanian Commonwealth" when referring to the territories within the pre–1772 borders and the terms "Galicia" and "Austrian Galicia" when discussing the new province created by Empress Maria Theresa after the first partition.

The terms referring to the region's Jewish population are equally contested: were they called Polish Jews, *Galizianers* (Yiddish), *Ashkenazim* (Hebrew), or *Ostjuden* (German)? None of these terms is static and all are value-laden; the Jews living east of the Zbrucz River were all of the above.[35] Mendel Lefin was born as a *Podoler* and became a *Galizianer*. He was an Ashkenazic Jew and thought of himself as an enlightened Polish Jew.

---

[32] Paul Robert Magocsi, *Historical Atlas of East Central Europe* (Seattle: University of Washington Press, 1993); Shmuel Ettinger, "The Participation of the Jews in the Settlement of Ukraine (1569–1648)," in *Bein Polin leRusya* (ed. Israel Bartal and Jonathan Frankel; Jerusalem: Zalman Shazar Center, 1994), 107–43; Frank E. Sysyn, *Between Poland and the Ukraine: The Dilemma of Adam Kysil, 1600–1653* (Cambridge, Mass.: Harvard University Press, 1985).

[33] Timothy Garton Ash, "The Puzzle of Central Europe," *The New York Review of Books*, 18 March 1999, 18–23. The Czech Republic, Poland, and Hungary are today often referred to as "East Central Europe." See Piotr S. Wandycz, *The Price of Freedom: A History of East Central Europe from the Middle Ages to the Present* (London: Routledge, 1992) and Miroslav Hroch, "'Central Europe': The Rise and Fall of an Historical Region," in *Central Europe: Core or Periphery?* (ed. Christopher Lord; Prague: Copenhagen Business School Press, 2000), 21–34.

[34] A superb travelogue of the region, Anne Applebaum, *Between East and West: Across the Border Lands of Europe* (New York: Pantheon Books, 1994), conveys a palpable sense of the region's liminality.

[35] The meanings of all of these terms were not unequivocal and depended upon who was doing the naming. See Steven E. Aschheim, *Brothers and Strangers: The East European Jew in German and German Jewish Consciousness, 1800–1923* (Madison: University of Wisconsin Press, 1982) and Scott Ury, "Who, What, When, Where, and Why Is Polish Jewry? Envisioning, Constructing, and Possessing Polish Jewry," *JSS* (new series) 6, no. 3 (2000): 205–28.

After focusing on Lefin's ideology, the last chapter of the book turns to the development of the moderate Haskalah in Austrian Galicia by examining the life and work of Joseph Perl (1773–1839), Lefin's most famous disciple. Although Lefin moved from Podolia to Austrian Galicia some time in the early nineteenth century, his *Weltanschauung*, I argue, never departed from the pre-absolutist context of the Polish-Lithuanian Commonwealth in which he was reared. Perl's self-definition, in contrast, was inextricably rooted in the new, post-partition context of the modernizing absolutist Austrian state. I end the book with Perl because his efforts to further the moderate Haskalah, which he believed to be continuous with his teacher's vision, took place in the same locale inhabited by Lefin. That is, the new province of Galicia and Lodomeria, a political region imposed on partitioned Poland by the Habsburgs, was not created *ex nihilo*. It was comprised of the western and southern sections of the eastern borderlands of the Polish-Lithuanian Commonwealth, and its Jewish residents were the very same Polish Jews whose transformation Lefin had aspired to. Throughout the nineteenth century, *maskilim* living in the borderlands (both under Austrian and Russian rule) still confronted the "Polishness" of the Jews they hoped to transform. Pitching his new enlightened school effort in Austrian Galicia forty years after the first partition, Perl complained that "everyone knows that the current state of Jewish education among Polish Jews . . . is not only useless, but also harmful for the body and soul."[36] Perl's comment illustrates the tenacity and continuity of Polish-Jewish cultural identity in Austrian Galicia well after the dismemberment of the Commonwealth.

Perl's activism on behalf of the moderate Haskalah, however, in contrast to Lefin's, was met with sharp opposition by Galicia's traditional Jewish population, in great part because of his political and cultural alliance with the absolutist state. The fifth chapter, "After Partition: The Haskalah in Austrian Galicia," thus underscores the impact of the partitions on Polish Jewry due to the new form of state that suddenly controlled their lives, and underlines the key premise of the first four chapters. Just as Lefin's life and ideology cannot be understood outside the context of the Polish-Lithuanian Commonwealth, the history of post-partition, Galician Jewry must be anchored in the history of Poland that preceded it. My work thus assumes the centrality of the so-called periphery, the southeastern provinces of the Polish-Lithuanian Commonwealth, both before and after the partitions, for understanding the varied national and ideological shadings within the Jewish Enlightenment in particular, and within modern East European Jewish history in general.

---

[36] Published in the first appendix in Philip Friedman, "Joseph Perl as an Educational Activist and His School in Tarnopol," *YIVO bleter* 31–32 (1948): 188.

While the Holocaust looms as the defining event for modern Diaspora Jewry, and casts a particularly long shadow over the Polish-Jewish past, this book asserts that the ways in which Jews negotiate and understand their relationship to the state — and how that relationship informs their shaping of tradition and culture — is even more crucial.[37] By focusing on the lives of Mendel Lefin and Joseph Perl, I hope to illuminate the centrality of Poland to modern East European Jewish history. I also aim, by unhinging the Polish-Jewish past from its teleological trajectory toward catastrophe, to recover the voices that articulated a moderate, enlightened future for Polish Jews already in the last quarter of the eighteenth century. In their embrace of European culture, *maskilim* like Lefin and Perl represented the first efforts of Polish Jews to leave the *shtetl*. In their commitment to the continuity of rabbinic Judaism, they remained firmly planted in Polish-Jewish culture. The tension between these two aspirations still resonates with many of the most fundamental concerns of contemporary Ashkenazic Jewish life in the Diaspora.

---

[37] On the centrality of the state in defining the emancipatory process, Pierre Birnbaum and Ira Katznelson aptly observed, "It is clear that as Jews managed to map and travel the pathways of emancipation, *the nature of the state they confronted proved pivotal,* shaping the character of anti-Semitism, the qualities of economic development, the contours of the class structure, the development of the public arena, and the constitution of civil society." Emphasis is mine. Pierre Birnbaum and Ira Katznelson, "Emancipation and the Liberal Offer," in *Paths of Emancipation: Jews, States, and Citizenship* (ed. Pierre Birnbaum and Ira Katznelson; Princeton, N.J.: Princeton University Press, 1995), 36. The volume's sophisticated treatment of the various national forms of emancipation, however, does not include Polish or Galician Jewry.

CHAPTER ONE

IN THE PODOLIAN STEPPE

The contents [of Mendel Lefin's *Der ershter khosed* (*The First Hasid*)] are obvious from the title. It investigates the origins of Hasidism, which was rooted in the cities of Podolia from the very beginning. Who knows what we lack in losing this book? He undoubtedly informed us truthfully [about Hasidism] because he was its contemporary, both in *time* and *place*.[1]

Abraham Baer Gottlober (1885)

The Polish-Lithuanian Commonwealth

In 1569, in an act of state known as the Union of Lublin, the Kingdom of Poland and the Duchy of Lithuania came together to form the Polish-Lithuanian Commonwealth. The new state was one of the largest in Continental Europe, stretching from the Dvina in the north to the Black Sea in the south and from beyond the Dniepr in the east to Silesia and West Prussia in the west. The two parts of the Commonwealth shared a common king, parliament (*Sejm*), political structure, and foreign policy, but had distinct law codes, armies, and administrations. The Commonwealth's republicanism was unique in Europe, but severely delimited by the social structure of the state, the majority of whose denizens were peasants. Known as the "Noble Republic," the Commonwealth boasted one of the largest noble classes in Europe. Free from taxation, with almost unrestrained power in the Polish *Sejm* to enact legislation and elect the king, the Polish *szlachta* (nobility) enjoyed a high level of political rights compared to their noble peers in the rest of Europe. The Polish nobility regarded itself as descendants of a race of "heroic Sarmatians" who had defeated Rome. Central to their identity was an assumption of national uniqueness; believing the Polish-Lithuanian Commonwealth to be the apotheosis of liberty, the *szlachta* defined themselves in opposition to other European nobilities and stubbornly mythologized their liberties, privileges, religion, culture, and economic structure. They gave pride of place to their independence from the Polish king.[2] Economically,

---

1 Emphasis in the original. Abraham Baer Gottlober, "R. Isaac Baer Levinsohn and His Time–Memoirs of the History of the Russian-Jewish Haskalah," *He'asif* (Warsaw, 1885), 7. Cited by Avraham Rubinstein in [Joseph Perl], *Über das Wesen der Sekte Chassidim* (ed. Avraham Rubinstein; Jerusalem: Publications of the Israel Academy of Sciences and Humanities, 1977), 5, footnote 28.

2 The nobility alone had a voice in the *Sejm*; clergy, burghers, and peasants had no repre-

the nobility was similarly empowered, although the greatest wealth was concentrated in the hands of about twenty magnate families, and not distributed equally among the *szlachta*. For example, in the 1770s, 1.9 percent of the *szlachta* controlled 75 percent of the nobles' wealth in Lithuania. The eastern lands of the Commonwealth, in Podolia, Volhynia, and Ukraine, were dominated economically by the huge *latifundia* (agricultural plantations) of a few magnate families.[3]

Characteristic of the Commonwealth was its ethnic and religious heterogeneity. Home to Poles, Germans, Ukrainians, Lithuanians, Belorussians, Ruthenians, Letts, Estonians, Turks, Armenians, Italians, Scots, and Jews, the Commonwealth tolerated Protestanism, Greek and Armenian Orthodoxy, Ukrainian Catholicism, Islam, and Judaism.[4] This diversity was even more pronounced in the private cities of the eastern and southeastern part of the state. For example, in sixteenth-century Zamość, Scots, Jews, Italians, Hungarians, Germans, Greek Orthodox, and Armenians comprised the forty-four home owners in the city.[5] The childhood memoirs of Jacob Frank, the eighteenth-century messianic pretender, relate that when the *shamash* (beadle) of the Jewish community of Korolówka knocked on the doors of the Jews to rouse them for penitential prayers in the month before the New Year, he also knocked on the doors of Polish Christians and Armenians, attesting to the heterogeneity of the town.[6] Yet, the implicit religious tolerance of the Commonwealth would be sorely tested, as with so much else, in the political crisis that began in the seventeenth century.[7]

Poland suffered numerous foreign incursions and wars during the seventeenth century, including a series of Cossack rebellions (beginning in 1591 and culminating with the notorious Chmielnicki revolt in 1648–1649), the Northern War (1655–60), the invasion of Muscovy in 1654, the Turkish invasion of 1671, which resulted in the Ottoman acquisition of almost one-third of Commonwealth territory, and the wars with Sweden (1700–1721).

---

sentation. See Jerzy Lukowski, *Liberty's Folly: The Polish-Lithuanian Commonwealth in the Eighteenth Century, 1697–1795* (London: Routledge, 1991), 20–22, 77, and 222–23 and Jerzy Jedlicki, *A Suburb of Europe: Nineteenth-Century Polish Approaches to Western Civilization* (Budapest: Central European University Press, 1999), 1–3.

[3]   Jerzy Lukowski, *The Partitions of Poland, 1772, 1793, 1795* (London: Longman, 1999), 10–15 and Lukowski, *Liberty's Folly*, 14.

[4]   Frank E. Sysyn, *Between Poland and the Ukraine: The Dilemma of Adam Kysil, 1600–1653* (Cambridge, Mass.: Harvard University Press, 1985), 6.

[5]   Edward Fram, *Ideals Face Reality: Jewish Law and Life in Poland, 1550–1655* (Cincinnati, Ohio: Hebrew Union College Press, 1997), 20.

[6]   Chone Shmeruk, "Investigations into Jacob Frank's Childhood Memoirs," *Gal-Ed* 15–16 (1997): 39.

[7]   In 1733, for example, non-Catholics were barred from civil office. See Lukowski, *Liberty's Folly*, 22.

One Polish historian has argued that the ruin resulting from the wars of the mid-seventeenth to mid-eighteenth century was "as devastating to Poland as the Black Death, which missed Poland, was for western Europe."[8] The unremitting assault on Poland's sovereignty continued in the eighteenth century, culminating in the three partitions in 1772, 1793, and 1795 by Austria, Russia, and Prussia.

Jewish Settlement in the Noble Republic

All peoples tend to embellish the longevity of their settlement in a region, as if to secure their rightful claim of residence and belonging. The Jews of Poland were no different. The "Khazar theory of origins," a Polish-Jewish etiology tale that gripped the imaginations of medieval and modern Jews alike, posited that the Khazar kingdom in the region of the Black Sea was the *Ur*-community of East European Jews.[9] Pressure from the tenth-century Kievan state dissolved Khazaria, whose king and inhabitants had converted to Judaism in the middle of the eighth century, but its Jewish population remained in eastern Europe, the legend goes, settling communities throughout the Slavic world. There is little evidence to support this account as the basis of Jewish settlement in Eastern Europe. More credible is the analysis that the Jews of early modern Poland are the descendants of German Jews who migrated eastward, beginning in the eleventh century, and became a significant stream simultaneous with German migration to Poland in the thirteenth through fifteenth centuries. Because Muscovy and Prussia were barred to the Jews, the Polish-Lithuanian Commonwealth became the most important area of Jewish settlement in Europe. Immigration rose in the second half of the fifteeenth century when Jews were expelled from the lands of Germany, Austria, Silesia, and Bohemia. By the end of the century, there were between 10,000 and 15,000 Jewish souls in Poland.[10]

---

[8]   Ibid., 14.

[9]   The most famous example is *Sefer hakuzari* (first printing, 1506) by the poet and philosopher Judah Halevi (before 1075–1141), in which the converted Khazar king conducts a philosophical religious dialogue with representatives of Islam, Christianity, Judaism, and Aristotelian philosophy. Modernizing Jews turned to Halevi's work throughout the eighteenth and nineteenth centuries, both as an expression of religious tolerance and ardor for Hebrew poetry. See Shmuel Werses, "Judah Halevi in the Mirror of the Nineteenth Century," in *Megammot vetsurot besifrut hahaskalah* (Jeruselem: Magnes Press, 1990), 50–89. Ovadiyah ben Pesakhiyah, the protagonist of Joseph Perl's satire, *Bohen tsaddiq*, relates with amazement the "truth" of the existence of the Jewish kingdom of Khazaria, which is confirmed during his travels to the region of the Caspian Sea. See [Joseph Perl], *Bohen tsaddiq* (Prague, 1838), 89–90.

[10]   Bernard Weinryb, *The Jews of Poland* (Philadelphia: The Jewish Publication Society of America, 1976), 3–32.

The Jewish population rose dramatically with the geographic expansion of Poland that took place after the Union of Lublin. The Commonwealth encompassed Poland, Lithuania, Ukraine (including Podolia and Volhynia), and Rus' (Ruthenia or Red Rus'), the area that came to be called East Galicia (see map 1). These southeastern regions became particularly hospitable to Jewish settlement as a burgeoning economy based on grain grew with the expansion of noble holdings in the steppe.[11] The vast plateau of the Ukraine, known for its mineral-rich, black soil, became the breadbasket of Europe as raw materials were shipped on Poland's many rivers north and northwest. To maximize production, Polish magnates turned their estates into agricultural plantations, which, from the sixteenth century onward, were worked by enserfed peasants who were legally bound to the land and to weekly labor duties *(corvée* or *robot)*. The magnates, who sought to exercise complete control over their estates and to restrict the privileges of the burghers, stunted urban development. Yet *szlachta* hostility to urban life created a huge obstacle to their desire for economic growth.[12] They needed managers and administrators to oversee their affairs and hence turned to Jewish intermediaries to manage their holdings, in the process encouraging Jewish settlement in their towns. From the mid-sixteenth century onward, Jews were an essential component in the Polish colonization of the Ukrainian provinces of Volhynia, Podolia, Bracław, and Kiev; indispensable to the management of the newly acquired magnate lands, the Jewish population of Ukraine increased thirteen-fold between 1569–1648.[13] By 1765, more than half of the Polish-Lithuanian Commonwealth's Jewish population (750,000) lived in private, noble-owned towns.[14] This economic interdependence between magnate and Jew had a portentous effect on the region in general and on the Jewish community in particular.

---

[11] Sysyn, *Between Poland and Ukraine,* 24; Shmuel Ettinger, "The Participation of the Jews in the Settlement of Ukraine (1569–1648)," in *Bein Polin leRusya* (ed. Israel Bartal and Jonathan Frankel; Jerusalem: Zalman Shazar Center, 1994), 107–43; Adam Żółtowski, *Border of Europe: A Study of the Polish Eastern Provinces* (London: Hollis & Carter, 1950), 2.

[12] Maria Bogucka, "Polish Towns between the Sixteenth and Eighteenth Centuries," in *A Republic of Nobles: Studies in Polish History to 1864* (ed. J. K. Federowicz; Cambridge: Cambridge University Press, 1982), 138–56.

[13] Ettinger, "The Participation of the Jews in the Settlement of Ukraine (1569–1648)," 107–43 and Shmuel Ettinger, "The Role of the Jews in the Settlement of the Ukraine in the Sixteenth and Seventeenth Centuries," in *Bein Polin leRusya* (ed. Israel Bartal and Jonathan Frankel; Jerusalem: The Zalman Shazar Center, 1994), 143–49.

[14] M. J. Rosman, *The Lords' Jews: Magnate-Jewish Relations in the Polish-Lithuanian Commonwealth during the Eighteenth Century* (Cambridge, Mass.: Harvard Ukranian Research Institute, 1990), 39.

Although since the thirteenth century Jewish immigrants had been subject
to the direct authority of the Polish king, by the mid-sixteenth century they
became subject to the local lord. The *Sejm* of 1539 granted owners of private
towns the exclusive right to place obligations on their Jewish populations,
which, in turn, freed the Jews from royal authority and opened up enormous
administrative and economic opportunities for them.[15] Denied settlement in
royal towns in the western part of the state, and subject to competition from
Christian burghers and guilds, the Jewish community looked east toward the
private towns of the Polish nobility, where they were welcomed with favorable privileges, including the right of municipal residency and self-government. In private Polish towns the Jewish community enjoyed a special economic relationship with the local lord, in contrast to the native townsmen, who
were hampered in their efforts to encourage urban industry. For example,
native burghers were forbidden to export any of Poland's raw materials on
the Wisła River, except for cattle and oxen, while Jewish middlemen virtually
dominated all other commercial activity on the river.[16] From the sixteenth
century onward, the Jews of Poland were increasingly concentrated in noble
lands and had turned away from collecting taxes for the king and toward a
variety of economic roles associated with the nobles' *latifundia*. Jews collected
taxes on private estates, ran inns and taverns, extended credit, and were
involved with both foreign and domestic trade.[17]

The Jews were an essential feature of the landscape of southeastern early
modern Poland. As William Coxe, an early nineteenth-century British
traveller in the borderlands remarked, "In stating the different classes of inhabitants the Jews must not be omitted. This people date their introduction
into Poland about the time of Casimir the Great, and as they enjoy privileges
which they scarcely possess in any other country, excepting England and
Holland, their numbers have surprisingly increased."[18] So, too, were they an
integral component of Polish urban life. At the time of the census of 1764,
there were Jewish communities established in at least 823 private towns.[19]

---

[15] Jacob Goldberg, "The Privileges granted to Jewish Communities of the Polish Commonwealth as a Stabilizing Factor in Jewish Support," in *The Jews in Poland* (ed. Chimen Abramsky, Maciej Jachimczyk, and Antony Polonsky; London: Basil Blackwell, 1986), 31–54; Adam
Teller, "The Legal Status of the Jews on the Magnate Estates of Poland-Lithuania in the
Eighteenth Century," *Gal-Ed* 15–16 (1997): 41–63.

[16] Lukowski, *Liberty's Folly*, 20–22, 77; Gershon Hundert, "Some Basic Characteristics of
Jewish Life in Poland," *Polin* 1, no. 1 (1986): 31; Rosman, *The Lords' Jews*, 39–40.

[17] Judith Kalik, *Ha'atsulah hapolanit viyehudeihah bemamlekhet Polin-Lita bere'i hatehiqqah bat
hazeman* (Jerusalem: Magnes Press, 1997) and Ettinger, "The Participation of the Jews in the
Settlement of Ukraine (1569–1648)."

[18] William Coxe, *Travels in Poland and Russia* (London, 1802; repr. New York: Arno, 1970),
118–19.

[19] Lukowski, *Liberty's Folly*, 77–80 and Artur Eisenbach, *The Emancipation of the Jews in*

Concentrated in the private towns of the Polish nobility, the Jews were legally free, neither juridically bound by the authority of the Christian magistrates nor subject to municipal taxes. This singular status of Polish Jewry, which by the mid-eighteenth century constituted at least half of the Polish urban population and was the principal component of the middle class, engendered deep animosity on the part of the beleaguered native burgher class.[20]

Traditional Ashkenazic Jewish Culture in the Eighteenth Century

The Jews of early modern Poland were *Ashkenazim*. This Hebrew term, appropriated by medieval Jews to designate the Jewish communities of northern Europe (France and German lands), came to include all of their descendants who had migrated eastward to the Polish-Lithuanian Commonwealth.[21] The Ashkenazic Jews of early modern Poland shared a cultural world with their German and French ancestors, including a religious-legal culture centered around study of the Talmud, extensive adherence to customary law (*minhag*), as opposed to codified law (*halakhah*), and a language, medieval German, which later developed into what is commonly known as Yiddish.[22] The world of Ashkenazic Jewry was not homogenous; there were subdivisions between those communities that followed the liturgy of France and the Netherlands and those that followed the regional traditions of Bohemia and, later, Lithuania. Nonetheless, before the age of the Enlightenment, Polish Jews and German Jews were more similar to one another than to other Jewish subcultures. As with so many other aspects of Polish Jewish life, it was the eighteenth century that transformed what had been an unselfconscious bond between German Jews and Polish Jews into a complex, often ambivalent, relationship.[23]

Poland, 1780–1870 (ed. Antony Polonsky and trans. Janina Dorosz; London: Basil Blackwell, 1991), 28.
[20] Gershon Hundert, "Jewish Life in the Eighteenth-Century Polish-Lithuanian Commonwealth," in *Qiyyum veshever: yehudei Polin ledoroteihem* (ed. Israel Bartal and Israel Gutman; Jerusalem: Zalman Shazar Center, 1997), 226.
[21] Hundert, "Some Basic Characteristics of Jewish Life in Poland," 30. Today, the divide between the descendants of Iberian Jewry, the *Sephardim*, and the descendants of northern European Jewry, the *Ashkenazim*, still exists, although each group has spawned a transnational diaspora of its own.
[22] On the role of customary law in Ashkenazic Jewish life, see Haym Soloveitchik, "Religious Law and Change: The Medieval Ashkenazic Example," *AJS Review* 12, no. 2 (Fall 1987): 205–21; Israel Ta-Shma, "Law, Custom, and Tradition among Ashkenazic Jews in the Eleventh and Twelfth Centuries," *Sidra* 3 (1987): 85–161. The medieval Jews of Ashkenaz, Ta-Shma writes, believed that "ancestral custom (*minhag avoteinu*) is Torah." Cited in Ta-Shma on 92 and 98. See, too, the discussion of *minhag* in Chapter Five.
[23] Steven M. Lowenstein, "The Shifting Boundary Between Eastern and Western Jewry," *JSS* (new series) 4, no. 1 (Fall 1997): 61–78; Israel Bartal, "The Image of Germany and

To speak of a normative traditional culture of early modern Polish Jewry is to risk oversimplification and generalization. Nonetheless, in order to understand what self-conscious modernizing Polish Jews like Mendel Lefin wanted to safeguard, we need to describe the contours of Polish rabbinic culture before the onslaught of Sabbatianism, Frankism, and Hasidism in the seventeenth and eighteenth centuries.

Traditional Jewish religious thinking, both in the past and today, is fundamentally ahistorical. The rabbinic leadership of antiquity saw itself as the authoritative recipients of an unbroken chain of tradition leading back to the original Revelation at Sinai, a tradition whose authority and binding obligatory power is not subject to the vicissitudes of time.[24] Rabbinic Jews see themselves as the "true" inheritors of Biblical Israel, the authoritative ajudicators of Jewish legal tradition. The biblical verse, "If there arise a matter too hard for you to judge, between blood and blood . . . [and there be] controversy within your gates: then you should arise and go up to the place that your God will choose, and you shall come to the priests, the Levites, *and to the judge that shall be in those days, and inquire*" (Deut 17:8–13), became the definitive proof of any given generation's rabbinic leadership, from the earliest documented rabbinic texts, the Mishnah and the Talmuds, and is still adduced today.[25] The teachings of the first generations of Mishnaic and Talmudic Sages were viewed as either a) encoded in the original biblical revelation and then transmitted by the Sages or b) an authoritative legal expression of divine intent. Rabbinic legislation, therefore, was viewed as immutable. Jews were obligated to obey the decisions of the Sages in perpetuity because God's command is the locus of the Sages' power.[26]

The representatives of religious authority in medieval Ashkenaz were rabbis, or sages, learned men who were schooled in the vast corpus of Jewish religious texts and derived authority from their students and the larger Jewish community. The medieval rabbi had two central functions, a) heading an institution, or school, of higher learning (a yeshivah), and b) overseeing a rabbinical court, the locus for the ajudication of Jewish law. In medieval

---

German Jewry in East European Jewish Society During the Nineteenth Century," in *Danzig: Between East and West* (ed. Isadore Twersky; Cambridge, Mass.: Harvard University Press, 1985), 1–17; Steven E. Aschheim, *Brothers and Strangers: The East European Jew in German and German Jewish Consciousness, 1800–1923* (Madison: University of Wisconsin Press, 1982).

[24] Yosef Hayim Yerushalmi, *Zakhor: Jewish History and Jewish Memory* (Seattle: University of Washington Press, 1982).

[25] Emphasis is mine.

[26] See the elegant exposition in Michael Berger, *Rabbinic Authority* (New York: Oxford University Press, 1998), particularly 3–39, and Jacob Katz, "Rabbinical Authority and Authorization in the Middle Ages," in *Studies in Medieval Jewish History and Literature* (ed. Isadore Twersky; Cambridge, Mass.: Harvard University Press, 1979), 41–56.

times, the rabbi, and his authority, was independent of the organized Jewish community; his authority derived not from appointment or salary, but from his ability to master, disseminate, and rule on the central texts of Jewish religious life. In order to be authoritative, the medieval Ashkenazic rabbi had to have students who viewed his credentials as impeccable.

The canonical corpus of rabbinic texts for ajudicating Jewish law in medieval Ashkenaz included the *Sefer mordekhai*, written by Mordechai ben Hillel ha-Kohen, a late thirteenth-century German scholar, *Sefer mitsvot hagadol*, by Moses of Coucy, a French Tosafist, *Sefer mitsvot haqatan*, by Isaac ben Joseph of Corbeil and *Pisqei harosh*, a code penned by Asher ben Yehiel (1250–1327, and known by his acronym as the "Rosh") in the early four-teenth century. Asher's third son, Jacob ben Asher, the *dayyan* (judge) of Toledo in the first half of the fourteenth century, organized his own code in four subcategories, which he called "columns" (*turim*), comprising the whole of Jewish life. This work, subsequently known as the *Arba'at haturim*, became so influential that it was the second Hebrew book to be printed (1475) after the commentary of Rashi on the Pentateuch.[27] These texts were considered guides to the Babylonian Talmud, the original source of rabbinic law, which all learned sages and rabbinic figures had to master in order to execute Jewish jurisprudence.

Heir to the legal and cultural tradition of medieval Ashkenazic Jewry, Polish rabbinic culture began to distinguish itself from its French and German roots by the mid-sixteenth century, which, in turn, informed a change in the relationship of the Ashkenazic rabbi to the Jewish community. These changes were manifest both in terms of the library of traditional Ashkenazic Judaism, the texts considered to be the cultural inheritance of rabbinic Jewry, its institutions, i.e. how that culture was disseminated, and the relation-ship of the two to the thorny question of rabbinic authority. The sixteenth-century was marked by the introduction of Sephardic homiletic, exegetical, and legal texts into the canon of Ashkenazic Jewry, the efflorescence of codification, itself a product of the printing revolution, and the controversy over *pilpul* (from the Hebrew word for "pepper," and meaning a sharp-witted method of argumentation), a method of Talmud instruction, and its role in the curriculum of the Ashkenazic yeshivah.[28]

The rise of *pilpul* as a central feature of yeshivah education as an end in itself, rather than as an intellectual means to prepare the elite rabbinic

---

[27] Elchanan Reiner, "The Yeshivas of Poland and Germany during the Sixteenth and Seventeenth Centuries and the Debate over *Pilpul*," in *Keminhag Ashkenaz uFolin: sefer yovel leChone Shmeruk* (ed. Israel Bartal, Chava Turniansky, and Ezra Mendelsohn; Jerusalem: Zalman Shazar Center, 1993), 21.
[28] Ibid., 30 and 45.

student to use medieval guides and the Talmud to ajudicate law, sparked a
controversy among prominent Ashkenazic rabbis in the sixteenth century. At
the same time, the printing of the *Shulḥan arukh (The Set Table,* 1564), which
contained the exposition of the *Arba'at haturim* by Joseph Karo (1488–1575),
a Spanish refugee, and the glosses of Moses Isserles (1525 or 1530–1572), a
wealthy rabbinic figure from Cracow (Kraków in Polish), on Karo's decisions,
furthered the trend toward *pilpul.*[29] Isserles's "tablecloth" (*hamappah* in
Hebrew), covering Karo's "table", made the *Shulḥan arukh* a living code of
Jewish law for East European Jewry. Able to rely on the decisions penned in
the *Shulḥan arukh* for the daily conunudrums of Jewish life, yeshivah students
in Poland bent their intellectual muscle not on investigating the sources of
Jewish law, but on proving their scholarly breadth. Although study of the
Talmud was still important, exploration and harmonization of the commentaries of the Tosafists increasingly preoccupied the sixteenth-century Polish
yeshivah student.

Simultaneous with the growth of *pilpul* was the efflorescence and penetration of the study of the Jewish mystical tradition. Elite groups of devotees
of Jewish mysticism joined *kloizim,* small voluntary groups devoted to the
study of mystical texts.[30] Less intellectually-inclined Jews were exposed to
kabbalistic ideas through the popularization of the practical kabbalah. Books
devoted to both the performance of the commandments and ethical
behavior based on mystical techniques and ideas became an important staple
of Polish Jewry's library in the seventeenth and early eighteenth centuries.[31]
It needs to be underscored that this description of traditional rabbinic
Judaism as it was lived in early modern Poland was categorically male. Men
were the figures of rabbinic authority, the audience to whom rabbinic and
mystical texts were aimed, the ajudicators of rabbinic law, and they comprised the laity, who increasingly determined the life of the Jewish community. Jewish women had access to rabbinic spirituality and creativity through
their husbands and fathers, and through the popularization of both rabbinic
and mystical texts into Yiddish. While numerous women's prayers, called

[29]   Isadore Twersky, "The Shulhan 'Aruk: Enduring Code of Jewish Law," in *The Jewish Expression* (ed. Judah Golden; Bantam: New York, 1970), 322–43; Menachem Elon, *Hamish-pat ha'ivri: toldotav, meqorotav, eqronotav* (Jerusalem: Magnes Press, 1973), 1087–138; Joseph Davis, "The Reception of the Shulhan 'Arukh and the Formation of Ashkenazic Jewish Iden-tity," *AJS Review* 26, no. 2 (November 2002): 251–76.
[30]   Elchanan Reiner, "Wealth, Social Status and *Talmud Torah*: The *Kloiz* in the East European Jewish Community in the Seventeenth and Eighteenth Centuries," *Zion* 58, no. 3 (1993): 287–328. For the *kloiz* in Brody, see N. M. Gelber, *Arim ve'imahot beyisra'el: Brody* (Jerusalem, 1955), 62.
[31]   Moshe Rosman, *Founder of Hasidism: A Quest for the Historical Ba'al Shem Tov* (Berkeley: University of California Press, 1996), 19–21.

tekhines, are extant from early modern Poland, it is important to note that most, if not all, of them were written by men for women, and not authored by women themselves. So, too, many Yiddish texts — although introduced with the obligatory apology that the works were intended for women — were read avidly by men unlearned in Hebrew and the rabbinic corpus.[32]

This overview of early modern Polish rabbinic culture does not mean that Polish Jews of the eighteenth century were a homogeneous group. Within the parameters of traditional Ashkenazic Jewish culture, there was a rabbinic elite devoted to *pilpul*, Talmudic study, and esoteric mysticism; practitioners of practical kabbalah; rabbinic appointees to the leadership of the kahal (the administrative body of the Jewish community) whose authority derived not from erudition, but from political and economic connections to the magnate class; and popular preachers and makers of amulets, called *ba'alei shem*, who travelled the countryside in search of a clientele. Yet there was still a hegemony to rabbinic culture within early modern Polish Jewish life, one that has been characterized as "baroque," valorizing the exclusive study of the Talmud and its commentators, disregarding the grammar and philology of the Hebrew language and distrusting non-Jewish sources of knowledge.[33] By the mid-eighteenth century, however, several important controversies would shake the authority of the traditional rabbinate to its very core. In particular, the ground shifted in the southeastern borderlands.

The Sabbatian and Frankist Challenge

The region of Podolia, originally part of medieval Rus' but annexed to Poland in the fifteenth century, and "Right Bank" Ukraine (the provinces of Kiev and Bracław) fell to the Ottoman Empire in 1672 according to the terms of the Treaty of Buczacz. The Polish-Lithuanian Commonwealth recovered Podolia, however, by the Treaty of Karlowitz in 1699. Prior to the

---

[32] Recent work on Jewish women's spirituality in Eastern Europe can be found in Chava Weissler, *Voices of the Matriarchs: Listening to the Prayers of Early Modern Jewish Women* (Boston: Beacon Press, 1998). For a critique of misreading Yiddish texts solely in terms of their presumed female audience, see Michael Stanislawski, "The Yiddish *Shevet Yehudah*: A Study in the 'Ashkenization' of a Spanish-Jewish Classic," in *Jewish History and Jewish Memory: Essays in Honor of Yosef Hayim Yerushalmi* (ed. Elisheva Carlebach, John M. Efron, and David N. Myers; Hanover, N.H.: Brandeis University Press, 1998), 134–49. An analysis of the historiography that interprets Hasidism as liberatory for women can be found in Ada Rapoport-Albert, "On Women in Hasidism, S. A. Horodecky and the Maid of Ludmir Tradition," in *Jewish History: Essays in Honour of Chimen Abramsky* (ed. Ada Rapoport-Albert and Steven J. Zipperstein; London: Peter Halban, 1988), 495–525.

[33] On the "baroqueness" of early modern Polish Jewish culture, see David Sorkin, "From Context to Comparison: The German Haskalah and Reform Catholicism," *Tel Aviver Jahrbuch für Deutsche Geschichte* 20 (1991): 23–58.

treaty, the regional rabbinic center of Podolia was in Lwów. After the conclusion of the Turkish wars, the Podolian Jewish community gained its own independent regional administration, and in 1713 a regional rabbi was appointed in Satanów.[34] Kamieniec Podolski, an island fortress, was Podolia's capital city, but Jews living there were subject to frequent expulsions; settlement thus grew in the neighboring towns of Międzybóż and Satanów, private holdings of the Sieniawski-Czartoryski families. Although Podolia was hit particularly hard by the Chmielnicki revolt in 1648–1649, Podolia's magnates managed to reconstitute their estates after the devastating effects of the constant warfare of the seventeenth century. Moshe Rosman argues, in fact, that Podolia was on a trajectory different from the rest of the country, and that the magnates' profitable export of grain was not interrupted by the Northern War in the first two decades of the eighteenth century.[35] The head tax calculated in 1577 for the Podolian Jewish communities show Międzybóż and Satanów among the top kehillot (communities) in southeastern Poland, with the former paying 230 zlotys and the latter ninety zlotys per year.[36] By 1774, Międzybóż could be counted among one of the fifteen largest Jewish communities in the Commonwealth, and at the time of the census in 1764, the Jewish population in Podolia totalled 40,000, constituting six percent of the Jewish population of Poland, a figure that contradicts the regnant view of the severe depression chracterizing Podolia's kehillot in the eighteenth century.[37] In that same year, the poll tax for Satanów was 1,369 zlotys.

Podolia's distinctiveness also lay in the affinity of its denizens, whether Polish, Ruthenian, or Jewish, for a popular mystical culture that assumed the existence and power of the supernatural world. Miracle workers were not unique to the Jewish population, but considered part of the general fabric of Podolian life.[38] Majer Bałaban cites a Stephen Bonczewski who noted, "There is no people among whom magicians and witches have so multiplied as they have here in Poland, particularly in the mountains, in Rus', in Lithuania, in Ukraine, [and] in the heart of Wallachia."[39] Sectarianism and mysticism of all kinds flourished in eighteenth-century Podolia, including the sect of Old Believers, a schismatic Russian-Orthodox group, and the Starchy sect,

---

34   Majer Bałaban, *Letoldot hatenu'ah hafranqit* (Tel Aviv: Devir, 1934), 116–17.
35   Rosman, *Founder of Hasidism*, 53 and 61.
36   Bałaban, *Letoldot hatenu'ah hafranqit*, 20.
37   Moshe Rosman, "Międzybóż and R. Ba'al Shem Tov," *Zion* 52 (1987): 181 and Rosman, *Founder of Hasidism*, 61. See, too, Jacob Leczinski, "The Condition of Ukrainian Jewry at the End of the Eighteenth and the Beginning of the Nineteenth Centuries," *He'avar* 7 (1960): 6–14.
38   Rosman, *The Lords' Jews*, 20.
39   Bałaban, *Letoldot hatenu'ah hafranqit*, 90.

an offshoot of the Old Believers.[40] Moreover, eighteenth-century Podolia was fertile ground for both Sabbatianism and Frankism, a heretical sectarian offshoot of the former that combined Christian, Muslim, and Jewish beliefs. Their legacy in Podolia had an enormous impact on the perceptions by *maskilim* and *mitnaggedim* (the rabbinic opponents of Hasidism) of the dangers of mysticism.

The emergence of Sabbatianism, belief in the messianic aspirant Sabbatai Zevi (1626–1676) as a harbinger of the messianic era, spawned a tremendous penitential movement throughout the Jewish Diaspora in the mid-seventeenth century. Spurred on by the belief in the imminence of redemption, Jews in Italy, German lands, the Balkans, and the Polish-Lithuanian Commonwealth engaged in voluntary self-flagellations and other acts of penance; businessmen liquidated their enterprises in anticipation of the coming of the Messiah; women packed their bags and kept them on their beds in anticipation of being transported to the Land of Israel. The activism of Sabbatai Zevi's messianic claim threatened the traditional rabbinate, whose worldview and liturgy encoded a quiescent hope for messianic redemption.[41] Moreover, Sabbatai Zevi and his followers exhibited antinomian behavior, some of which was sexual, and also challenged the traditional rabbinic authorities by tampering with the Jewish calendar. Sabbatians regularly ate on fast days and many celebrated the Sabbath in the middle of the week. The overt flouting of Jewish law led to swift opposition on the part of the traditional rabbinic leadership, who placed Sabbatai and his followers in *ḥerem* (excommunication). The rabbinic opponents of Sabbatianism were hopeful that Sabbatai's imprisonment in Gallipoli in August 1666 and subsequent conversion to Islam in September of that year would end the episode of the false messiah, even though they knew that restoring the faith of the former believers could be a daunting task. After all, despair was a normal response to hopes thwarted. As the German-Jewish memorist, Glückl of Hameln, recalled:

> About this time people began to talk of Sabbatai Zevi. But "woe unto us that we have sinned" (Lam 5:16) and never lived to see what we had heard and nigh believed. When I think of the 'repentence done' by young and old my pen fails me — but the whole world knows of it! Oh Lord of All Worlds, hoping as we did that Thou hadst shown compassion on Israel and redeemed us, we were like a woman who sits in labour and suffers mighty pangs, and thinks once her suffering is over she shall be blessed with a child; but it was only hearkening after a wind. (Isa 26:18)[42]

---

40   Rosman, *Founder of Hasidism*, 58.
41   Gershom G. Scholem, "Towards an Understanding of the Messianic Idea," in *The Messianic Idea in Judaism* (New York: Schocken Books, 1971), 1–36.
42   Glückl of Hameln, *The Memoirs of Glückl of Hameln* (trans. Marvin Lowenthal; New York: Schocken Books, 1977), 45–46.

But rabbinic hopes for the restitution of traditional authority were dashed when the apostasy, justified as theologically necessary by Nathan of Gaza, Sabbatai's prophet, engendered a clandestine heretical Sabbatian movement that remained a powerful force within Jewish society for the next two centuries. Many believers refused to accept the verdict of history, unwilling to admit that their faith had been an illusion, and continued to believe in Sabbatai even though he had donned the turban. Nathan of Gaza's new theology, which was deeply indebted to the spread of kabbalistic ideas in the sixteenth and seventeenth centuries, justified Sabbatai's conversion as a necessary precondition to redemption. Sabbatai had entered the kabbalistic realm of the "husks" (*qelippot*) in order to reintegrate them into the realm of holiness. Antinomian behavior was thus a prerequisite for hastening the advent of the Messianic Age.[43]

The spread of heretical Sabbatianism to Poland is still a subject of scholarly dispute. We know that in 1722, four rabbinic figures, Issacar Ber ben Joshua Heschel of Cracow, Shmuel ben Zevi Hirsch of Cracow, Yitzhak Eisik ben Elazar of Lwów, and Mordecai ben Shemariyah Shmerl of Lublin, signed a writ of excommunication against Sabbatians that was binding throughout Podolia.[44] Gershom Scholem, and others, argued that in the years 1725–1726, itinerant Sabbatians — often members of the "secondary intelligentsia," preachers, peddlers, kosher slaughterers, and cantors — disseminated their views in southeastern Poland and Ukraine, which were geographically contiguous with Ottoman Turkey, and had been lost by the Poles in 1672. At the same time, radical Sabbatian followers of Baruchiah Russo, the leader of the Dönmeh sect in Salonika and Constantinople, created links with Sabbatians in Podolia, and sent emissaries to Prague, Fürth, Berlin, and Mannheim.[45] Moses Hagiz (1671–1751), the most important protagonist in the eighteenth-century rabbinic anti-Sabbatian controversies, devoted his energies to gathering testimony against these itinerant Sabbatians and, in 1725, tried to convince the Council of Four Lands, the most prestigious rabbinic body in Poland, to enact a ban against them. This effort failed, but Hagiz did not waver in his pursuit of the suspected heretics, and in the 1730s

---

[43]   On Sabbatianism, see Gershom G. Scholem's magesterial biography, Gershom Scholem, *Sabbatai Sevi: The Mystical Messiah, 1626–1676* (trans. R. J. Werblowsky; Princeton, N.J.: Princeton University Press, 1973) and Gershom G. Scholem, "Redemption Through Sin," in *The Messianic Idea in Judaism* (New York: Schocken Books, 1971), 78–141.

[44]   Menahem Nahum Litinski, *Sefer qorot Podolyah veqadmoniyyut hayehudim sham* (Odessa: A. Belinson, 1895), 65–55.

[45]   Gershom Scholem, "The Sabbatian Movement in Poland," in *Mehqarim umeqorot letoldot hashabta'ut vegilguleihah* (Jerusalem: The Bialik Institute, 1974), 68–140, particularly 102–5, and Gershom G. Scholem, "The Crypto-Jewish Sect of the Dönmeh," in *The Messianic Idea in Judaism* (New York: Schocken Books, 1971), 142–66.

turned his attention to the vilification of Moses Hayim Luzzatto (1707–1747), a brilliant Italian kabbalist whom he suspected of harboring and teaching Sabbatian doctrine. In this later effort, Hagiz solicited the aid of Jacob Emden, whose father, Hakham Zevi, had supported Hagiz in his first controversy against Nehemiah Hayon in Amsterdam. Emden endorsed Hagiz's bans against Luzzatto's writings and then included the young Italian in his list of Sabbatian precursors in his anti-Sabbatian tract, *Torat haqena'ot* (*Scroll of Zeal*). Emden became a tireless anti-Sabbatian polemicist, publishing numerous tracts, many on his own printing press, to expose the dangers of the illicit sect. He became the central figure in the Sabbatian controversy with Jonathan Eybeschütz in 1750, an event that shook all of European Jewry and resulted in further undermining the status of the traditional rabbinate.[46]

Coupled with the anti-Sabbatian controversies of the early eighteenth century was the eruption in mid-century of the public disputation between Judaism and Frankism. Jacob Frank (1726–1791), the founder of the eponymous heretical movement, was born in a village called Bereżanka or Berczana, and then moved with his family to Korolówka on the Polish-Turkish border, where, historians speculate, there were connections with members of the Dönmeh. On January 17, 1756, Frank attracted the attention of the Jewish authorities when he, along with a group of Jews in Lanckaroń (Landskron), were arrested for crimes of a sexual and heretical nature. The rabbi of Lanckaroń turned to the rabbi in Satanów, who was the chief religious authority of the region of Podolia at that time, to investigate the charges. Due to the illness of the rabbinic head in Satanów, Eleazar Lipmann of Smoszczić, the son-in-law of the rabbi from Lanckaroń, carried out the investigation and forwarded the results to the regional rabbinic seat. Like many Podolian cities, Lanckaroń was under the authority of the Catholic bishop in Kamieniec Podolski, Mikołaj Dembowski. On February 5, 1756, Dembowski demanded a full report of what had occurred in Lanckaroń and set March 31, 1756 as the date to hear the evidence. The case never went to trial because none of the rabbinic authorities appeared. The Jewish super-

---

[46] Elisheva Carlebach, *The Pursuit of Heresy: Rabbi Moses Hagiz and the Sabbatian Controversies* (New York: Columbia University Press, 1990), 172, 191, and 245–51. Emden's anti-Sabbatian oeuvre includes *Torat haqena'ot* (1752); *Sefat emet uleshon zeḥorit* (1752); *Aqizat aqrav* (1753); *Edut beya'aqov* (1756); *Shevirat luḥot ha'even* (1756); *Petaḥ einayim* (1756); *Qitsur tsitsat novel tsevi* (1757); *Sefer hashimush* (1758–1762); *Sefer hitavqut* (1762–69) *Mitpaḥat sefarim* (1768); *Megillat sefer* (first published only in 1896). See Jacob Joseph Schacter, "Rabbi Jacob Emden: Life and Major Works" (Ph.D. diss., Harvard University, 1988).

Debate continues to rage about the penetration of Sabbatianism in the seventeenth-century Commonwealth and there is still no consensus. Note Weinryb's comments, "If we take literally the heresy-hunter Jacob Emden and those who follow his 'conspiracy theory,' most of Podolia and some other parts of Poland were supposedly infested with Sabbatians. But this is far from the truth." Weinryb, *The Jews of Poland*, 234.

communal organization, the *va'ad* of the region of Lwów, meeting on May 10, 1756, then ordered the chief rabbi in Satanów to reinvestigate the incident. Only some of the participants appeared at the investigation, but the results spurred the members of the regional *va'ad* meeting in Brody and Konstantynów, including Hayim ha-Cohen Rapoport (1700–1771), an eminent figure within the rabbinic leadership of Polish Jewry who would be the central defender of Judaism in the 1759 disputation with the Frankists, to excommunicate the accused.[47] The writ of excommunication was sent throughout Poland in June 1756 and affirmed in Lwów, Busk, Łuck, Lanckaroń, Jezierzany, and Ofoczna. Frank, who was considered a citizen of the Ottoman Empire, was never tried, but the other participants were sentenced to hard labor.[48]

Because the Frankists practiced an admixture of Judaism and Christianity, Catholic authorities, too, viewed the group with suspicion. Bishop Dembowski, who was personally hostile to rabbinic Judaism, compelled the Jewish community to debate the Frankists in a theological disputation in Kamieniec Podolski in June 1757 in order to clarify the doctrine of Frank and his followers. All of the leaders of Podolian Jewry were invited to participate, including individuals from Międzybóż, Bar, Satanów, Lanckaroń, Balin, Jezierzany, Husiatyn, and Jagielnica. The Frankists hailed from Satanów and Zbaraż, as well as from Busk. At the Satanów investigation, the Frankists had enumerated nine principles of their faith. The third principle directly attacked the authority and sanctity of the Oral Law; they claimed that the Talmud was riddled with lies and fundamentally opposed to Scripture. This charge struck a painful chord among the Jews present at the disputation because Polish hostility to the Talmud had been well attested in the previous century. The rabbinic participants of the investigation in Kamieniec Podolski therefore went to great lengths to show that the Talmudic category of *akum* (idolaters) only applied to the pagans of antiquity and not to eighteenth-century believers in the three monotheistic faiths. As they argued, the [monotheistic] Gentiles "believe in the creation of the world, in the exodus from Egypt, in God, the Creator of the heavens and the earth, and in the

---

[47] Hayim ha-Cohen Rapoport established a study house in Słuck in his youth and was appointed to the rabbinate in Zitel in 1729. From 1730, he was the head of the rabbinical court in Słuck, and from 1740, head of the rabbinical court in Lwów; in 1763, Adam Kazimierz Czartoryski appointed Rapoport as chief rabbi of all of *medinat rusiya*, the most eastern regions of the Commonwealth. In 1761, he signed a ban against Jonathan Eybeschütz, but later repented of his action and refused involvement in the Eybeschütz affair. See Meir Wunder, *Entsiqlopedyah lehakhmei Galitsyah* (Jerusalem: Institute for Commemoration of Galician Jewry, 1986), 991–94. See, too, Solomon Buber, ed., *Anshei shem: ge'onei yisra'el, adirei torah, rabbanim asher shimshu baqodesh ba'ir Lwów mishenat 1500 ve'ad 1890* (Cracow, 1895), 236–38.

[48] Bałaban, *Letoldot hatenu'ah hafranqit*, 68, 118–19, 127.

power of God's divine words. Thus, not only is it not forbidden to save them, but we must also pray to God for their wellbeing, etc."[49] The efforts of the rabbinic figures notwithstanding, the disputation resulted in a full exoneration of the Frankists and in a condemnation of the Talmud. The bishop's ruling demanded that the Jewish community turn over all Jewish books forbidden by the Church, sentenced individual Jews to corporal punishment, and required that the rabbinic Jewish community compensate the exculpated Frankist Jews of Satanów and Lanckaroń. Worried about the implications of this decision, the Jewish community notified both Hayim ha-Cohen Rapoport and Jacob Emden and inquired regarding the possibility of their interceding with the authorities in Warsaw and Amsterdam. Dembowski's sudden death temporarily stayed the escalation of the crisis.[50]

On June 16, 1758, Jacob Frank, who had fled to Turkey after the disputation, received a letter from the Polish King, August III, permitting him and his group to return to Poland. Soon thereafter, a group of these Frankists approached the Archbishop in Lwów with a request to convert to Christianity. The second public disputation between the Frankists and the Polish-Jewish rabbinical establishment was held in Lwów in the late summer of 1759. Once again, the Frankists enumerated a series of doctrinal beliefs outside the pale of traditional rabbinic culture, but they stunned their opponents by invoking the blood libel, the charge that Jewish law requires Christian blood for the preparation of unleavened bread on the holiday of Passover. A string of blood libels (1728, Lwów; 1722 and 1738, Gniszewo [Gniesen]; 1736–40, Poznań; 1747, Zasław; 1748, Dunajgród; 1753, Żytomierz [Zhitomir]; 1756, Jampol) voiced in eighteenth-century Poland made the traditional Jewish community particularly sensitive to charges of the Talmud's alleged hostility to Christians.[51] The Lwów disputation included seven public meetings, in which over thirty rabbinic Jews and ten Frankists participated. An eyewitness to the trial, Dov Ber of Bolechów (1723–1805), a prominent Polish-Jewish wine merchant renowned for his command of languages, was asked to be the Polish-Yiddish interpretor for the trials. His memoirs are valuable testimony to the spread of popular anti-Jewish views in the eighteenth-century Commonwealth:

> The priest, Jacob Radliński, canon of Lublin, wrote much on this matter [the well-known Christian-Jewish debate over the meaning of the verse, "The sceptre shall not depart

---

[49]   Cited in ibid., 144.
[50]   Ibid., 190–91.
[51]   Bałaban, *Letoldot hatenu'ah hafranqit,* 101. *The Talmud of the Jewish Belief,* first published in 1610 in Cracow, became the source for the entry in the first Polish encyclopedia on the blood libel. See Zenon Guldon and Jacek Wijaczka, "The Accusation of Ritual Murder in Poland, 1500–1800," *Polin* 10 (1997): 99–140.

from Judah . . . until Shiloh come," (Gen 49:10)][52] in a book, full of lies, entitled *Rab Shemuel*, in Polish "Samuel Rabin."[53] This book abounds in mistakes and shameful falsehoods, which are not worth writing down or quoting to reasonable people. The third edition of it appeared at Lublin in 1753 of the Christian Era. In the same year it came into my hands, and I read it. Besides this book, "Samuel Rabin," I read also some more of their theological writings dealing with the Jews, in which they malign and slander the Jewish people and our holy Oral Law, which we have by tradition. All these books I read with grief in my heart, but I acquired much knowledge of their doctrines. I discerned in their arguments great errors and obduracy. Moreover, I became acquainted with all the fables and miracles in which they believed, things which never really existed. The reward of my labour in that distasteful study was given to me and to the whole of Israel on the occasion of the great and famous dispute that took place in Lemberg between all Israel, on the one side, and the evil sect of the believers in Shabbetai Zebi, may his name be extinguished, on the other side.[54]

Hayim ha-Cohen Rapoport, then the head of the rabbinical court in Lwów, became the leading voice on the side of the traditional Jewish community. The Frankists taunted him during the trial by alluding to the blood libel: "Hayim, here is 'blood for blood'. You have spoken in a way that allows our blood to flow, so here is blood in exchange for blood."[55] Rapoport gave the concluding argument against the Frankist charges on August 28, 1759, in which he relied on the evidence adduced in a recent Catholic work surveying Scripture and the Talmud, Humphrey Prideaux's *The Old and New Testament connected in the history of the Jews and neighbouring nations, from the declension of the kingdoms of Israel and Judah to the time of Christ* (London, 1716–18), to show that there was no evidence for the blood libel in Jewish sources.[56] Rapoport's testimony conclusively refuted the blood libel charge, but this victory was

---

[52]   This verse was at the center of the Barcelona Disputation between Nachmanides and the apostate Pablo Christiani in 1263, in which Christiani adduced the Talmud to attest to Christ's divinity and used Gen 49:10 to prove God's abandonment of the Jews. See Hyam Maccoby, ed., *Judaism on Trial: Jewish-Christian Disputations in the Middle Ages* (Rutherford, N.J.: Fairleigh Dickinson Press, 1981).

[53]   Jacob Paul Radliński, priest, theological writer, poet and historian published *Prawda chrześcijańska, to jest list Rabina Samuela do Rabina Izaka przekład z łacińskiego z dodatkami tłumacza*, which became an important source for anti-Jewish pamphleteers, in Lublin in 1732; a second and third edition were published in 1733 and 1753.

[54]   Ber Bolechów, *The Memoirs of Ber Bolechow, (1723–1805)* (ed. and trans. M. Vishnitzer; New York: Oxford University Press, 1922; repr. Arno, 1973), 180–81. Bolechów called his account of the disputation *Divrei binah*, selections of which were published in A. Y. Brawer, *Galitsyah viyehudeihah: mehqarim betoldot Galitsyah bame'ah hashemoneh-esreh* (Jerusalem: Bialik Institute, 1965). An original manuscript of *Divrei binah* was held in the Joseph Perl Archive until the 1980s, but is no longer extant.

[55]   Cited by Chimen Abramsky, "The Crisis of Authority within European Jewry in the Eighteenth Century," in *Studies in Jewish Religious and Intellectual History* (ed. Siegfried Stein and Raphael Loewe; Tuscaloosa, Ala.: The University of Alabama Press, 1979), 16.

[56]   D. Valentin Ernst Loescher translated the English text into German, with the title *Alt und Neu Testament in eine Connexion mit der Juden und benachbarten Völker Historie gebracht vom Verfall der Reiche Israel und Juda an bis auf Christi Himmelfahrt*, in 1726.

soon forgotten with the mass conversion to Christianity of Frank and one thousand of his followers.[57]

What had started as a sectarian offshoot of radical Sabbatianism ultimately resulted in a huge public renunciation of Judaism in the context of a Christian-Jewish polemic over the veracity of the Talmud. Despite Polish Jewry's material security, it still harbored deep fears and insecurities about its place in Polish Christian society.[58] The Frankists' public embrace of Christianity and disparagement of Judaism, which was wrapped in the mystical vocabulary of heretical Sabbatianism, confirmed the worst fears of the traditional Jewish community still reeling from the Sabbatian controversies of the earlier part of the century. It is not surprising, therefore, that the traditional Jewish community in Podolia responded with swift denunciations of new forms of Jewish worship that appeared later in the century. As Elisheva Carlebach has argued, the rabbinic campaigns against crypto-Sabbatianism in the early eighteenth century, which embodied the effort to bolster the authority of the crisis-ridden traditional rabbinate, created the ideological framework, tactics, and vocabulary for the rabbinic polemics against Hasidism in the later part of the century. The *mitnaggedim* drew a direct analogy between Sabbatianism and Hasidism, perceiving both as fundamental threats to traditional sources of authority in the Jewish community. Their anti-Hasidic tactics included writs of excommunication, gathering evidence, and efforts to prohibit the publication of kabbalistic works, the very same strategies employed by the opponents of Sabbatianism a half-century earlier.[59]

An extensive body of scholarship has been devoted to describing and explaining the relationship between Sabbatianism and Hasidism, focusing on geographic, chronological, personal, literary, doctrinal, and sociological similarities between the two movements.[60] Yet, what concerns us here is not whether or not there are Sabbatian foundations within Hasidism, or even whether there are individuals who might be linked with the two movements,

---

[57]   Bałaban, *Letoldot hatenu'ah hafranqit*, 209–76.
[58]   M. J. Rosman, "Jewish Perceptions of Insecurity and Powerlessness in 16th–18th Century Poland," *Polin* 1 (1986): 19–27.
[59]   Carlebach, *The Pursuit of Heresy*, 277–78.
[60]   The classic accounts are Bałaban, *Letoldot hatenu'ah hafranqit*, 67–68; Benzion Dinur, *Bemifneh hadorot* (Jerusalem: The Bialik Institute, 1955); Jacob Katz, "Regarding the Connection of Sabbatianism, Haskalah, and Reform," in *Studies in Jewish Religious and Intellectual History* (ed. Siegfried Stein and Raphael Loewe; Tuscaloosa, Ala.: University of Alabama Press, 1979), 83–101; Shimon Dubnow, *Toldot hahasidut* (Tel Aviv: Devir, 1930), 1:24–34; Heinrich Graetz, *Geschichte der Juden* (Leipzig, 1900), 95–98; Yehudah Liebes, "New Light on the Matter of the Besht and Sabbatai Zevi," *Mehqerei yerushalayim bemahashevet yisra'el* 3 (1983): 564–69; Scholem, "The Sabbatian Movement in Poland." See, too, Michael Silber's map of the spread of Hasidism in Eviatar Friesel, *Atlas of Modern Jewish History* (New York: Oxford University Press, 1990), 50.

but rather how the Podolian legacy of Sabbatianism, and of Frankism in particular, affected the ways in which *maskilim* like Mendel Lefin perceived Hasidism.

By 1850 Hasidism was triumphant throughout most of Eastern Europe (save a small pocket in Lithuania) and had thoroughly transformed Polish-Jewish society, but its success was by no means assured in the eighteenth century.[61] Although there were sporadic attempts to combat Hasidism in the early part of the century, a more concrete, centralized opposition only took shape when Hasidism began to infiltrate the northern regions of Poland in the 1770s. The years 1772–1815 were marked by the struggle between *mitnaggedim* and Hasidim.[62]

The first official published record of the opponents of Hasidism was the publication of *Zemir aritsim veharavot tsurim* (*The Song of Tyrants and Flint Knives*)[63] in 1772, although the community of Szklów issued anti-Hasidic measures a year earlier.[64] Throughout the seven documents that comprise *Zemir aritsim veharavot tsurim* charges recur against Hasidic practices, such as changing the time of established prayers, using polished knives for kosher slaughtering, and praying in small, separate prayer groups, which threatened the communal fabric of traditional Jewish society. Opponents of Hasidism were afraid that the renewal movement would cause an irreparable fissure in the Jewish community, as had the Karaites, or worse, could lead to the heresies of Sabbatai Zevi and Jacob Frank. This connection appears in the *herem* (ban) issued by the community of Cracow in 1786: "And who knows whereto these things [Hasidic customs] will lead, or of the magnitude of the obstacle that is likely to derive from this, as has already happened in the world; many did as these people did, who by their own mouths were called Hasidim, and in the end they performed a deed like that of [the biblical figure] Zimri and became idolaters."[65] A symmetrical analogy between Sabbatianism and

---

[61]   Raphael Mahler, *Hasidism and the Jewish Enlightenment: Their Confrontation in Galicia and Poland in the First Half of the Nineteenth Century* (Philadelphia: The Jewish Publication Society of America, 1985), 25 and Dubnow, *Toldot hahasidut*, 1:37.

[62]   For the primary sources, see Mordecai Wilensky, *Hasidim umitnaggedim: letoldot hapulmus shebeineihem bashanim 1772–1815* (Jerusalem: The Bialik Institute, 1970). See, too, Mordecai Wilensky, "Hasidic-Mitnaggedic Polemics in the Jewish Communities of Eastern Europe: The Hostile Phase," in *Tolerance and Movements of Religious Dissent in Eastern Europe* (ed. Béla K. Király; New York: Columbia University Press, 1975), 89–113; Norman Lamm, "The Phase of Dialogue and Reconciliation," in *Tolerance and Movements of Religious Dissent in Eastern Europe* (ed. Béla K. Király; New York: Columbia University Press, 1975), 89–113; Immanuel Etkes, "Hasidism as a Movement: The First Stage," in *Hasidism: Continuity or Innovation* (ed. Bezalel Safran; Cambridge, Mass.: Harvard University Press, 1988), 1–26.

[63]   The title is a combination of Isa 25:5 and Josh 5:2.

[64]   Wilensky, *Hasidim umitnaggedim*, 1:63.

[65]   Published in ibid., 1:138. On Zimri, see 1 Kgs 17:9–20.

Hasidism is likewise reflected in the edicts of the community of Mohylew, Lithuania, against the Hasidim, which were promulgated roughly around 1778. A direct connection, not merely a metaphoric one, appears in a document composed in 1800 by Avigdor of Pinsk and presented to Tsar Paul I, in which the author named three heirs of Sabbatianism: Israel of Międzybóż (Medzibozh), Dov Ber of Międzyrzec (Mezhirech), and Jacob Joseph of Połonna (Polonnoye). David of Maków (1741?–1814/5), the zealous anti-Hasidic publicist, saw Hasidism as another link in the chain of a heretical past leading back to the Zadokites of the Second Temple period. Even German rabbis, such as Joseph Steinhart, the rabbi of Fürth, saw a direct connection between Hasidism and Sabbatianism after receiving the anti-Hasidic pamphlet, *Zemir aritsim*.[66]

An itinerary of Mendel Lefin's life shows that he lived in proximity to the important centers of Hasidism in Podolia.[67] His knowledge of Hasidism was thus due to close contact with the new form of spirituality, rather than to rumor or second-hand accounts. Acutely aware of both the Frankist debacle and of the efflorescence of Hasidism, Lefin's self-understanding as a *maskil* was a product of the region in which he matured and lived for most of his

---

[66] Litinski, *Sefer qorot Podolyah*, 28 and 32; Wilensky, "Hasidic-Mitnaggedic Polemics," 103–04; Shmuel Werses, *Haskalah veshabta'ut: toldotav shel ma'avaq* (Jerusalem: Zalman Shazar Center, 1988), 99–102; Wilensky, *Ḥasidim umitnaggedim*, 1:34, 44–46, 67, footnote 32, and 241.

[67] Documentary evidence corroborates Lefin's itinerary as follows: 1791, *Międzybóż* (see Abraham Baer Gottlober, *Zikhronot umasa'ot* [ed. Reuben Goldberg; Jerusalem: The Bialik Institute, 1976], 174–75 and Israel Halpern, "R. Levi Isaac of Berdyczów and the Decrees of the Government in His Time," in *Yehudim veyahadut bemizraḥ eiropah: mehqarim betoldoteihem* [ed. Israel Halpern; Jerusalem: Magnes Press, 1963], 344–45); 1788–1792, *Warsaw*, (see *Materiały do dziejów Sejmu Czteroletniego*); 1794, *Sieniawa*, (see manuscript 2253, the Czartoryski Library, Cracow and Israel Weinlös, "Mendel Lefin of Satanów: A Biographical Study from Manuscript Material," *YIVO bleter* 1 [1931]: 348); 1797, *Sieniawa*, (see Majer Bałaban, "Mendel Lewin i książę Adam Czartoryski," *Chwila*, no. 5313–14 [7–8 stycznia 1934]: 10–12); 1803–4, *St. Petersburg*, (see Czartoryski MS EW 3267, Adam Jerzy Czartoryski to Adam Kazimierz Czartoryski, 10 August 1803, the Czartoryski Library, Cracow); 1805, *Mikołajów*, (see the Joseph Perl Archive, JNULA, 4° 1153/8); 1806–8, *Mikołajów*, (with a trip to *Annopol*, (see the Abraham Schwadron Collection, and the Joseph Perl Archive, JNULA, 4° 1153/appendix); 1815, *Sieniawa*, (see the Joseph Perl Archive, JNULA, 4° 1153/appendix); 1817, *Tarnopol*, (see Franz Kobler, *Jüdische Geschichte in Briefen aus Ost und West* [Vienna: Im Saturn-Verlag, 1938], 147–48 and the Joseph Perl Archive, JNULA, 4° 1153/129); 1818, *Tarnopol*, (see the Joseph Perl Archive, JNULA, 4° 1153/2 and 4° 1153/6); 1821–1825, *Tarnopol*, (see the N. M. Gelber Archive, letters from Sheindel Pineles to Moses Inländer, July 17, 1821; July 21, 1822; February 19, 1824; September 30, 1824; February 3; and March 3, 1825, The Central Archives of the Jewish People). I am grateful to Tamar Schechter, author of a master's essay at Bar-Ilan University on Sheindel Pineles, Joseph Perl's daughter, for sharing these letters with me. The only evidence for Lefin's stay on the estate of Joshua Zeitlin is S. J. Fuenn's account; see Samuel Joseph Fuenn, *Qiryah ne'emanah* (Vilna, 1860), 272. In 1808, Lefin was still in Podolia; we cannot be precise as to when he settled in Brody.

life. Like the *mitnaggedim* who were his contemporaries, Lefin, too, believed there was a direct link connecting Sabbatianism, Frankism, and Hasidism.[68]

The Heartland of Hasidism

From its beginnings, Podolia was the hub of Hasidism, with Międzybóż as its epicenter. Born in 1700 in Okopy, a small town in Podolia, Israel ben Eliezer Ba'al Shem Tov, the man later called the "Besht," moved to Międzybóż, Podolia in 1740, and remained there until his death in 1760. In Międzybóż, the Besht attracted a group of followers, including Jacob Joseph of Nemirov (later called Jacob Joseph of Połonna [Polonnoye]), Judah Leib, the *mokhiah* (preacher) of Połonna, Nahman Kosover, Isaac of Drohobycz, Wolf Kozis, David Purkes, and Dov Ber of Międzyrzec (Mezherich). Międzybóż was one of the largest cities in the Ukraine, more than half the size of neighboring Bar, and an important link in the trade routes leading to Volhynia and Kiev. The city's Polish magnate owners, the Czartoryskis, built a castle in its center. There was also a garrison of soldiers stationed there, helping to ensure the security of merchants doing business between the West and East. One of the fifteen wealthiest Jewish communities in the Polish-Lithuanian Commonwealth, Międzybóż did not suffer under the burden of enormous communal debt in the 1730s and 1740s that plagued many kehillot. It appears that the Besht moved to Międzybóż precisely because of its prosperity, lived in a house owned by the Jewish communal administration next to the synagogue, and was thoroughly integrated into the fabric of the communal life of the city.[69] After the Besht's death, Międzybóż declined both economically and as a Hasidic center, and the movement shifted to new centers in Volhynia, which influenced Reisen (the region of Szkłów) and Lithuania.[70] Later in the eighteenth century, Międzybóż would regain some of its original importance under the domineering personality of the Besht's grandson, Barukh of Międzybóż (Medzibozh).

---

[68] These analogies had long literary lives in the southeastern Polish borderlands. See the story, "The First Hasidim," in Samuel Joseph Agnon's collection of short stories about his hometown of Buczacz in Austrian Galicia. Shmuel Joseph Agnon, *Ir umelo'ah* (Jerusalem: Schocken Books, 1986), 526.

[69] Rosman, "Międzybóż and R. Ba'al Shem Tov," 177–89.

[70] Dubnow, *Toldot haḥasidut*, 1:77. In the spring of 1772, the *ga'on* of Vilna signed a ban against the Hasidim under pressure from the community of Szkłów, which felt under siege both by the penetration of Hasidism and by the first partition of Poland, which severed the community from the central Jewish institutions in Poland. In 1787, a regional meeting of communal leaders and rabbis was held in Szkłów and a series of edicts were passed against the Hasidim. David E. Fishman, *Russia's First Modern Jews: The Jews of Shklov* (New York: New York University Press, 1995), 11–15.

The first stage in the emergence of Hasidism coincides with the earliest years of Mendel Lefin's life, from his birth in Satanów in 1749 to his trip to Berlin in 1780, underscoring the specific Podolian context for both his turn to and shaping of the Jewish Enlightenment. Unfortunately, we have almost no documentary evidence to shed light on these formative years, but we do know that Lefin's father was born in Zbaraż, a town to the northwest of Satanów.[71] Zbaraż already had a Jewish presence at the end of the fifteenth century and, typical of the towns in the region, was administered by Jewish arrendators. Suffering during both the Chmielnicki revolt in the mid-seventeenth century and from the attacks of the Haidamaks in the eighteenth, Zbaraż's Jewish population nonetheless continued to grow.[72] The city was known for its prominent rabbinate and, as we saw above, was also home to the Frankist heresy. Until his trip to Berlin in 1780, we hear nothing of Lefin, and in his numerous writings he provides little personal information about those years.[73] Even Abraham Baer Gottlober, the Russian *maskil* who is the source of most of the biographical information that we have about Lefin, complained about the difficulty in correctly assessing his date of birth. In his memoirs, Gottlober does not provide any substantial biographical information about Lefin's early years, but describes him, in classic maskilic fashion, as a Talmudic protegé who fortuitously discovered the world beyond traditional Jewish study through a classic work of seventeenth-century Jewish science, Joseph Solomon Delmedigo's *Sefer elim*.[74] In Gottlober's view, Lefin

---

[71] Jacob Samuel Bik, one of Lefin's disciples, remarked in an outline for his biography of Lefin: "His father was a learned man, fluent in *gemara* (Talmud), and his mother was very chaste. They educated him with their knowledge until he became an expert." Cited in A. M. Haberman, "Toward a History of Menachem Mendel Lefin of Satanów," in *Sefer Klausner* (Tel Aviv: The Jubilee Committee and the Society "*Omanut*", 1937), 461.

[72] D. Dombrovska, Abraham Wein, and Aharon Vais, eds., *Pinqas haqehillot. Polin: entsiqlopedyah shel hayishuvim hayehudiyyim lemin hivasdam ve'ad le'aḥar sho'at milḥemet ha'olam hasheniyyah, Galitsyah hamizraḥit* (Jerusalem: Yad Va-Shem, 1980), 199–200.

[73] I assume that Lefin remained in Satanów prior to his trip to Berlin in 1780, thus coming of age simultaneously with the efflorescence of Hasidism in Podolia. Mahler reports that Lefin moved to Mikołajów after his marriage and prior to his trip to Berlin. Raphael Mahler, *Divrei yemei yisra'el* (Rehavia: Worker's Library, 1956), 1:72.

[74] Abraham Baer Gottlober, "Russia," *Hamaggid* 17 (1873): 348. Reading *Sefer elim* undoubtedly galvanized the young Lefin to see the possibility of harmonizing secular learning with rabbinic Judaism in his own time. Moreover, Delmedigo's critique of his Polish-Jewish contemporaries' all-embracing commitment to Talmudic casuistry, which he observed while living in Poland from 1620–1624/5, making them "enemies of rational learning. . . . God, they say, has no need of . . . grammarians, rhetoricians and logicians, nor of mathematicians or astronomers . . . all [of] their wisdom . . . [is] foreign and drawn from impure sources," surely resonated with Lefin's historical experience. Cited in Isaac Barzilay, *Yoseph Shlomo Delmedigo (Yashar of Candia): His Life, Works and Times* (Leiden: E. J. Brill, 1974), 67. See, too, the influence of *Sefer elim* on the Russian *maskil*, Mordecai Aharon Günzberg, in Israel Bartal, "Mordecai Aaron Günzberg: A Lithuanian Maskil Faces

was so intoxicated with this new world that he devoured whatever secular books he could find in the study house and, in the process, damaged his eyes. Lefin's ostensible curative journey to Berlin, the center of the Jewish Enlightenment at the end of the eighteenth century, is thus cast as a happy coincidence born of illness. This reading of Lefin's journey to Berlin as an explanation for his commitment to the Haskalah is not sufficient.

The most recent work on the origins of the Haskalah has looked at eighteenth-century figures, such as Ezekiel Feivel of Palanga (1756–1834), Israel Zamość (c. 1700–1772), and Barukh Schick (1740–1812?), an enlightened rabbinic Jew from Szkłów, as Jewish representatives of the "early Enlightenment."[75] Shmuel Feiner, for example, has defined a type of *maskil*, which included Jewish medical students who travelled to Frankfurt-on-the-Oder, merchants, rabbinic figures, and autodidacts, who were all deeply rooted in traditional Jewish culture. These individuals sought to expand its horizons through actively pursuing all branches of knowledge, studying and publishing in the fields of Hebrew grammar and language, reviving the medieval philosophic tradition, and cultivating new aesthetic values while emphasizing God's role as master of a creative and purposeful world. The dominant features of their ideology were common to the European *Frühaufklärung*. As a disparate group, with slim, but discernible contacts with one another, these men were suspicious of both atheism and pietism. What distinguished them from the previously hegemonous rabbinic elite was the creation of a new social type: the secular intellectual.[76] This view of the *maskil* was already

---

Modernity," in *From East and West: Jews in a Changing Europe, 1750–1870* (ed. Frances Malino and David Sorkin; London: Oxford University Press, 1990), 126–47, and on Judah Leib Mieses in Judah Leib Mieses, *Sefer qinat ha'emet* (Vienna: Anton von Schmid, 1828), 25.

[75] Shmuel Feiner, "The Early Haskalah among Eighteenth-Century Jewry," *Tarbiz* 67, no. 2 (1998): 189–240 and David Sorkin, "The Early Haskalah," in *New Perspectives on the Haskalah* (ed. Shmuel Feiner and David Sorkin; London: Littmann Library, 2001), 9–26. Feiner and Sorkin both reject Immanuel Etkes's earlier work describing the eighteenth-century exponents of the Haskalah as "precursors" or "harbingers" of the late, or mature Haskalah, which flourished in Austrian Galicia in the 1820s and in Imperial Russia in the 1840s. Immanuel Etkes, "The Question of the Precursors of the Haskalah in Eastern Europe," in *Hadat vehahayim: hahaskalah be'eiropa hamizrahit* (ed. Immanuel Etkes; Jerusalem: Zalman Shazar Center, 1993), 29. See, too, Immanuel Etkes, "Immanent Factors and External Influences in the Development of the Haskalah Movement in Russia," in *Toward Modernity: The European Jewish Model* (ed. Jacob Katz; New Brunswick, N.J.: Transaction Books, 1987), 13–32.

[76] While agreeing with Feiner on many points regarding the origins and radicalization of the Haskalah, David Sorkin nonetheless asserts that the Haskalah's essential feature was not the creation of a secular intellectual. His work, in fact, defines the Jewish Enlightenment within the European "Religious Enlightenment," thereby minimizing its transformative break with traditional Jewish life. Radicalization, when it occurred, was not inherent to the Haskalah, which had focused on transforming Judaism. Rather, it was the addition of a social agenda that emphasized transforming the Jews themselves that transfigured the ideology of the early *maskilim*. Seeing the shift in generational terms, Sorkin argues that the

suggested many years ago by Jacob Katz, although he defined himself as a social historian and focused on the economic and political changes in European and Jewish society that gave rise to the new social types rather than on the cultural-intellectual features of their new conception of the world.[77] Feiner's work aptly describes a kind of eighteenth-century Jew and his modern intellectual and cultural predilections, but what is more difficult to ascertain is the cause of the shift in these individuals' consciousness and self-definition. In other words, Lefin fits the category of the early *maskil*, but we still lack a precipitous cause for his journey to Berlin.

What were the events or trends in late eighteenth-century Polish-Jewish life that spurred individuals to look toward the West and to justify their appetite for its ideas in the Jewish medieval rationalist tradition? In the case of many of these early figures the appearance of a bold new pietism that did not seek validation by the traditional power structure in the Jewish community — what came to be known first as Beshtianism and then as Hasidism — in the heartland of Ashkenazic Jewry, the Polish-Jewish Commonwealth, was a sufficient cause for many of them to turn toward the Enlightenment as a means of saving traditional rabbinic culture. Several additional factors specific to Podolian Jewish society in the eighteenth century, including the openness of Polish society to West European intellectual and cultural currents, the Frankist legacy, and the pentration of Jacob Emden's anti-Sabbatian polemics created the context in which a small group of traditional rabbinic Polish Jews forged a new vision of Jewish identity that they called the Haskalah.

The dearth of information about the first forty years of Lefin's life (the pre-Berlin years and those immediately after) begs the question of what

---

Haskalah under the watch of *maskilim* born in the mid-eighteenth century, such as Marcus Herz, Herz Homberg, David Friedländer, and Solomon Maimon, in contrast to the enlightened Jews born early in the century, represented by Moses Mendelssohn and Naftali Herz Wessely, became radicalized and politicized in the context of the enlightened absolutist state. See Sorkin, "From Context to Comparison," 33, footnote 2 for the generational chart, David Sorkin, "The Case for Comparison: Moses Mendelssohn and the Religious Enlightenment," *Modern Judaism* 14 (1994): 121–38, and David Sorkin, *Moses Mendelssohn and the Religious Enlightenment* (Berkeley: University of California Press, 1996).

[77] Jacob Katz, *Tradition and Crisis: Jewish Society at the End of the Middle Ages* (trans. Bernard Dov Cooperman; New York: New York University Press, 1993). In his survey of modern Hebrew literature, Joseph Klausner depicted the reconciliation of the Haskalah and religion as a product of the Galician and Italian period of Hebrew letters (circa 1830–1850). His periodization and categorization of the Haskalah into rigid "Rationalist" and "Romantic" categories, slights, if not ignores, the phenomenon of a religiously informed enlightenment in German lands in the late eighteenth century and the simultaneous emergence of a religiously moderate Haskalah in Eastern Europe. See Joseph Klausner, *Historyah shel hasifrut ha'ivrit haḥadashah* (Jerusalem: The Hebrew University, 1952), 289–90.

compelled him to go to Berlin. Unfortunately, we lack documents penned by
Lefin before his sojourn in Berlin, so we cannot compare, as David Fishman
has done in the case of Barukh Schick, Lefin's pre- and post-Berlin years.[78]
Surely, as Gottlober argued, Lefin's lifelong struggle with eye disease, which
gave special meaning to the well-worn Enlightenment metaphor of bringing
the light of reason to the darkness of fanaticism and irrationality, was, in
part, the impetus for his pilgrimage in Berlin in 1780. So, too, knowledge of
the intellectual vitality of Berlin, elements of which had already permeated a
thin stratum of Polish-Jewish society,[79] must have provided an equally strong
magnet for an individual of Lefin's temperament. Contrary to the image of
backward eighteenth-century Poland in general and the region of Podolia in
particular, not all of its towns were tiny, parochial enclaves impenetrable to
the influence of new ideas. Although Międzybóż was the largest kehillah
(Jewish community) in the region, with approximately 2039 Jews in 1766,
Lefin's birthplace, Satanów, home to 1625 Jews in that same year, was an
important economic center in eighteenth century Podolia, and served, as did
other border towns, as a point of contact for merchants travelling between
the West and the East, and as a conduit for the spread of ideas.[80] Merchants
in Satanów exported lumber and grain to Danzig and had contact with their
counterparts bringing goods from the fairs in Leipzig and Frankfurt-on-the-
Oder.[81] Satanów's centrality also lay in its having served as the seat of the
regional rabbinate of Podolia since 1713. By the mid-eighteenth century,
Satanów was hardly impervious to western influences.[82]

In fact, Isaac Satanów (1732–1804), the *maskil* whose surname derived
from his place of birth, preceded Lefin's journey to Berlin by nine years.

---

[78]   David Fishman, "A Polish Rabbi Meets the Berlin Haskalah: The Case of R. Barukh
Schick," *AJS Review* 12 (1987): 95–121.

[79]   Israel Bartal, "'The Second Model': France as a Source of Influence in the Processes of
Modernization of East European Jewry, 1772–1863," in *Hamahppekhah hatsarfatit verishumah*
(ed. Richard Cohen; Jerusalem: Zalman Shazar Center, 1991), 275.

[80]   On the significance of border cities, see Michael Stanislawski, *Tsar Nicholas I and the Jews:
The Transformation of Jewish Society in Russia, 1825–1855* (Philadelphia: The Jewish Publication Society of America, 1983), 56, and Fishman, *Russia's First Modern Jews*. Late eighteenth-
century Berlin and Trieste displayed many of the same features of Polish towns on the
border, but on a much larger scale: rapid urban growth, exemption from taxation or duties,
and burgeoning mercantile activity. See Steven M. Lowenstein, *The Berlin Jewish Community:
Enlightenment, Family, and Crisis, 1770–1830* (New York: Oxford University Press, 1994); Lois
C. Dubin, *The Port Jews of Habsburg Trieste: Absolutist Politics and Enlightenment Culture*
(Stanford, Calif.: Stanford University Press, 1999); Lois Dubin, "Researching Port Jews and
Port Jewries: Trieste and Beyond," ed. David Cesarani, *Jewish Culture and History* 4, no. 2
(Winter 2001): 47–58.

[81]   Weinlös, "Mendel Lefin of Satanów: A Biographical Study," 336.

[82]   Bałaban, *Letoldot hatenu'ah hafranqit,* 116–17 and Rosman, *The Lords' Jews*, 213–14.

Settling in the Prussian capital in 1771 or 1772, Isaac Satanów wrote numerous maskilic works and was director of the printing press of the Berlin *Freischule*, called the "Society for the Education of Youth," from its founding in 1783 until 1788. An important institution for the dissemination of Enlightenment publications, the press issued Lefin's first major publication, the pamphlet *Moda levinah* (*Insight to Understanding*, Berlin, 1789), which contained examples from his *Iggerot hahokhmah* (*Letters of Wisdom*, in *Hame'assef*, 5, 1789) and *Sefer refu'at ha'am* (*The Book of Popular Healing*, Żółkiew, 1794).[83] Lefin clearly believed that there was an audience among the traditional Jews in Satanów and other towns in Podolia for his Enlightenment works, for he informed the readers of *Moda levinah* that to assure receipt of his new works they could send advance subscriptions to Leszniów, "where there are merchants from Międzyrzec," to Satanów, or to Międzybóż and Berdyczów, "where there are merchants from Mi ędzybóż and Satanów."[84] Lefin also suggested to those readers who wanted to purchase *Sefer refu'at ha'am* to contact a Meir of Satanów. Later in the century, other maskilic works attracted subscribers from Satanów, including three for *Besamim rosh* (*The Best Spices*), two for *Sefer hamiddot* (*Ethics*), one for *Melekhet mahashevet hahodesh* (*Tool for Calculating the Cycles of the Moon*), three for *Mishlei assaf* (*Collected Fables*), and one for *Te'udah beyisra'el* (*Testimony in Israel*).[85]

The rabbinical establishment in late eighteenth-century Satanów, too, was open to the ideals of the early Haskalah. In 1788 Lefin received an approbation from Alexander Sender (Zevi) Margoliot (1720–1802), the head of the rabbinical court in Satanów and the former head of the rabbinical court in Zbaraż, for his Yiddish translation of Ecclesiastes.[86] Margoliot also gave his approval to Lefin's *Moda levinah* in 1789 and to the 1794 publication of *Sefer refu'at ha'am*. Lefin also turned to other members of the rabbinical establishment in Satanów, such as Mordecai Margoliot (1752/8–1818), Alexander Sender's son, who had replaced his father as the head of the rabbinical court, and to Joshua Zelig Bloch, the *dayyan* of the community, when he sought an approbation in 1808 for his book, *Sefer heshbon hanefesh* (*Moral Accounting*). Mordecai Margoliot also gave his approval to Lefin's Yiddish translation of Proverbs, which appeared in 1814.[87] Traditional rabbinic Jews

---

83   The two *maskilim* from Satanów must have known each other, sharing both Berlin as a destination and David Friedländer as a friend. On Isaac Satanów and the *Freischule* press, see Alexander Altmann, *Moses Mendelssohn: A Biographical Study* (Tuscaloosa, Ala.: The University of Alabama Press, 1973), 351–54.
84   Mendel Lefin, *Moda levinah* (Berlin, 1789).
85   Berl Kagan, *Sefer haprenumeranten* (New York, 1975), 191.
86   Lefin's translation of and commentary to Ecclesiastes will be discussed in Chapter Four.
87   [Lefin], *Sefer mishlei shelomo im perush qatsar veha'ataqah hadashah bilshon Ashkenaz leto'elet aheinu beit yisra'el be'artsot Polin* (Tarnopol, 1814).

living in eighteenth-century Satanów who were interested in the literary products of the European Enlightenment could thus acquire books and Enlightenment writings at fairs or through other mercantile routes, and at the same time garner intellectual nourishment from the medieval Jewish rationalist tradition.

As we have explored above, the Frankist legacy in Podolia had a profound effect on traditional rabbinic Jews and on their perception of the vulnerability of traditional rabbinic authority and life in early modern Poland. While the Frankist debacle and the efflorescence of Hasidism in Podolia did not *necessarily* propel Lefin toward the Haskalah, these forces certainly made a decisive stamp on the moderate shading of his program, just as similar expressions of enthusiasm within Christian circles had spurred a turn toward rational and critical rethinking of Christian religious tradition. Michael Heyd has argued that Protestant ministers in England and on the Continent, threatened by enthusiasts and Deists, incorporated the new Science and the faculty of human reason into their study of Scripture.[88] Shmuel Feiner has demonstrated that early *maskilim*, such as Shelomo Chełm, Yehudah Horowitz, Barukh Schick, and Yehudah Leib Margoliot, among others, reacting negatively to the spread of pietistic behavior among eighteenth-century Jews, showed interest in the medieval rationalist tradition and the world of contemporary Enlightenment thought in order to bolster traditional rabbinic authority.[89] The power of enthusiastic pietism to wreak havoc on the traditional Jewish community was felt acutely in southeastern Poland, where the rabbinic authorities already felt vulnerable. The geographic and historical proximity of the Frankist disputations, the burning of the Talmud, and the mass conversion of Frank's followers planted profound doubts in the mind of a Podolian *maskil* like Mendel Lefin regarding the nature of Hasidism. As well, Lefin imbibed the anti-Sabbatian polemics of Moses Hagiz and Jacob Emden and adduced from them the analogies between the perils of Sabbatianism and Frankism and those of Hasidism.[90]

One of the essential features of Lefin's critique of Hasidism was the deviance the new pietists displayed, in his view, regarding age-old Ashkenazic

---

[88]   Michael Heyd, *'Be Sober and Reasonable': The Critique of Enthusiasm in the Seventeenth and Early Eighteenth Centuries* (New York: E. J. Brill, 1995), 189–90.

[89]   Feiner, "The Early Haskalah," 228–29.

[90]   It is not surprising that Emden's works were seen as authoritative by Polish Jews. He had intimate family ties to Poland in general and to the southeastern borderlands in particular. Two of his sons lived in Poland and were part of the rabbinical establishment. The first, Meir, was the head of the rabbinical court in Stary Konstantynów from 1759–1780, and the younger, Meshullam Zalman, was the head of the rabbinical court in Podhajce, and then in Brody. His daughters, too, were well-connected to Polish rabbinical families. See Dinur, *Bemifneh hadorot*, 85, footnote 10.

custom.[91] Within the cultural world of Polish Jewry, customary law had always had preeminent authority. Hasidism, with its myriad new rituals and customs, threatened the known fabric of Jewish religious practice in Poland. In light of the Sabbatian and Frankist flaunting of rabbinic law, the proliferation of Hasidic customs — even if they accompanied the fulfillment of traditional commandments — appeared to be dangerously deviant, and *mitnaggedim* and *maskilim* alike recoiled from them. Regarding the Hasidic custom of celebrating the third meal of the Sabbath with extended singing and eating, Lefin immediately drew an analogy to both Sabbatianism and Frankism, and looked toward the tactics of his rabbinic precursors to combat the new movement:

> [Jacob] Frank, may his name be blotted out, also began his sect with joyous activities, such as dancing and songs at the third meal of the Sabbath, which led to carnal acts performed according to the secret (*sod*) (perhaps he revealed the meaning of the phrase "in her foundation" that is in the Sabbath eve song, "I Will Sing with Praises," to them).[92] We are all obligated to thank and praise God, may he be blessed, that their dough swiftly and publicly became *hamets* [prohibited leavening] . . . and that the sages of that generation denounced them quickly, cleansing Israel of their [the Frankists'] evil with much less damage than that which Sabbatai Zevi caused. May God, blessed be he, protect us once more. They hastened again (through the zeal of our teacher, the great R. Moses Hagiz) to suppress R. Moses Hayim Luzzatto's sect, which began to spread through kabbalistic works and through his new *Zohar* [*Zohar tinyana*] that had already led many astray, even his teacher, R. Isaiah Bassan,[93] because in his time the damage [caused by] Sabbatai Zevi was not yet forgotten.[94]

---

91   The seemingly endless explosion of Hasidic custom that diverged from traditional Jewish law as it had been practiced in Poland alarmed subsequent generations of *maskilim* in Eastern Europe, including Lefin's disciple, Joseph Perl, and members of his circle in Tarnopol. See Chapter Five.

92   Although Lefin does not mention the Hasidim by name in this section of the manuscript, he used the example of the Frankists' licentiousness, which he believed they had justified based on the phrase *uvisoda dilah* ("in her [the female aspect of the Divine's] foundation") of the kabbalistic poem, "I Will Sing with Praises," in which the union between God and the Divine Presence (*shekhinah*) is described with sexual imagery, as proof of the dangers inherent in the popularization and spread of kabbalistic teachings. Joseph Perl knowingly translated this line in a coarse, explicit manner devoid of symbolism in his German anti-Hasidic pamphlet, *Über das Wesen der Sekte Chassidim* (*Regarding the Essence of the Hasidic Sect*), in an effort to discredit the Hasidim. See [Joseph Perl], *Über das Wesen*, 44, footnote 50.

93   Isaiah ben Israel Hezekiah Bassan (died 1739), one of eighteenth-century Italy's most eminent rabbinic figures, instructed Moses Hayim Luzzatto in his youth and ardently defended him against Moses Hagiz's accusations of the kabbalist's alleged Sabbatianism. Lefin may have read about Hagiz's pursuit and Bassan's defense of Luzzatto in Jacob Emden's *Torat haqena'ot*, in which Luzzatto was listed as one of the most significant forerunners of Jonathan Eybeschütz's Sabbatianism. Carlebach, *The Pursuit of Heresy*, 217–51.

94   The Joseph Perl Archive, JNULA, 4° 1153/72, 1b, and published in N. M. Gelber, "Mendel Lefin of Satanów's Proposals for the Improvement of Jewish Community Life presented

Mendel Lefin was well acquainted with anti-Sabbatian rabbinic writings and frequently mentioned Emden's work as a source for his own perspective on the links between the dating of the Zohar (The Book of Splendor), the spread of Sabbatianism, the eruption of Frankism, and the emergence of Hasidism.[95] In the same manuscript, he evoked Emden and warned about the dangers of popularizing the esoteric mystical tradition:

> God chose us due to the merit of our holy ancestors and distinguished us from those who err. He gave us the holy Torah with an explicit revelation, as it is written: "From the beginning, I have not spoken in secret," (Isa 48:16) a revealed Torah with a clear explanation "that is not in Heaven" (b. Eruvin 55a). [It is] explained for all who seek it. Its secrets and allusions were only transmitted secretly to designated men. Therefore, several hundred years passed in which they kept the Zohar hidden . . . and they forbade showing it even to the great men of Israel of antiquity, may their memories be blessed. We saw what happened afterwards when the manuscript of the Zohar was revealed in the time of R. Isaac of Acco,[96] and after R. [Isaac] Delattes was permitted to print it.[97] Barely a few years passed when, due to our many sins, the actions of Satan succeeded in misleading several thousands in Israel and capturing them in the webs of secrets (sodot)

---

to the Great Sejm (1788–1792)," in The Abraham Weiss Jubilee Volume (ed. Samuel Belkin; New York: Shulsinger Brothers, 1964), 283, footnote 33.

[95] Emden's Sefer hashimush, for example, was the main source of information about the allegations against Frank in the community of Satanów. See Scholem, "The Sabbatian Movement in Poland," 122. For Lefin's references to Emden, see the Joseph Perl Archive, JNULA, 4° 1153/5, 4° 1153/72, 1b and 2a, and 4° 1153/130, 71; Mendel Lefin, "Elon moreh," Hamelits (1867): 6–8; [Mendel Lefin], "Essai d'un plan de réforme ayant pour objet d'éclairer la Nation Juive en Pologne et de redresser par là ses moeurs," in Materiały do dziejów Sejmu Czteroletniego (ed. Arthur Eisenbach et al.; Wrocław: Instytut Historii Polskiej Akademii Nauk, 1969), 411. On the dating of the Zohar, see Isaiah Tishby, ed., The Wisdom of the Zohar (London: Oxford University Press, 1989), 1:40, and on the debate about its authority among East European maskilim, see Werses, Haskalah veshabta'ut, 103–06, Shmuel Werses, "Hasidism in the Perspective of Haskalah Literature: From the Polemics of Galician Maskilim," in Megammot vetsurot besifrut hahaskalah (Jerusalem: Magnes Press, 1990), 97, and Shmuel Werses, "Regarding the Lost Pamphlet, Maḥkimat peti," in Megammot vetsurot besifrut hahaskalah (Jerusalem: Magnes Press, 1990), 319–23. Werses rightly criticizes Hillel Levine who dismissed Lefin's fear of the Sabbatian underpinnings to Hasidism in his discussion of the anti-Hasidic polemic embedded in Lefin's Sefer ḥeshbon hanefesh. See Hillel Levine, "Between Hasidism and Haskalah: On a Disguised Anti-Hasidic Polemic," in Peraqim betoldot hahevrah hayehudit biymei habeinayim uva'et haḥadashah (ed. Immanuel Etkes and Joseph Salmon; Jerusalem: Zalman Shazar Center, 1980), 190, and Werses's comment in Werses, Haskalah veshabta'ut, 103, footnote 22. In his unpublished dissertation on Lefin, Levine made little of the Frankist legacy in Podolia, except to say that Lefin, "at the tender age of seven," was aware of the controversy in Lwów. See Hillel Levine, "Menahem Mendel Lefin: A Case Study of Judaism and Modernization" (Ph.D. diss., Harvard University, 1974), 11.

[96] The only evidence of the publication of the Zohar comes from the diary of Isaac of Acco that was printed in Abraham Zacuto's Sefer yuḥasin. A kabbalist and author of Me'irat einayim, a commentary on Nahmanides, Isaac of Acco tells of seeing the Zohar in Spain at the beginning of the fourteenth century. Tishby, The Wisdom of the Zohar, 1:13–17.

[97] Isaac Delattes supervised the printing of one part of the Zohar, to which he appended an introduction, in Mantua in 1558.

in which the evildoers of Israel, Sabbatai Zevi, [Nehemiah] Hayon, etc. had steeped their venom. Indeed, now, in our generation, they have flourished and flooded the country. Their books are widely disseminated, filling the houses of villagers and commoners. They have betrayed "the secret (*sod*) of God to those who fear him" (Ps 25:14), openly sharing the [esoteric] books with Gentiles. I, myself, have seen the books of *Ets ḥayim* (*Tree of Life*),[98] *Pardes* [*rimonim*] (*Orchard of Pomegranates*),[99] *Berit menuḥah* (*Covenant of Repose*),[100] *Zohar*, etc. in Gentile homes, some of whom study them with the heretics of Israel, due to our many sins.[101] They [the Gentiles] seek the secrets (*sodot*) of their own faith in them and connect [the esoteric exegeses], as well, to the abominations of the idolatrous secrets of the Persians and Greeks. . . . R. Jacob Emden did a wonderful job of investigating that then (in R. Shimon bar Yochai's period), no book was called by the term *ḥibbur* (publication) until many generations after the Talmud (and certainly [the terms] "forewords" (*hapetiḥot*) and "introductions" (*hahaqdamot*) were only innovated in the period . . . after the "Rif",[102] may his memory be blessed). . . . [But,] his [Emden's] proof regarding the profligacy of the generation who spent so much money copying these secrets, and his other suggestions regarding the style of concretizing kabbalistic secrets, made no difference.[103]

Lefin relied on Emden's research in *Mitpaḥat sefarim* (*Covering of the Scrolls of the Law*), which attacked the antiquity of the *Zohar*, for his own purposes. Emden's attack on the *Zohar* was ambivalent. His zealous pursuit of Sabbatianism forced him to impugn a book whose sanctity — as well as that of the kabbalistic tradition as a whole — he affirmed.[104] Lefin showed no respect for the *Zohar* and discredited the mystical work because of his campaign

---

[98] *Ets ḥayim* was one of the most important kabbalistic works of the great Kabbalist, Hayim b. Joseph Vital (1542–1620); it contained most of his writings elaborating on the teachings of Isaac Luria and circulated in manuscript form until the late eighteenth century.

[99] *Pardes rimonim* was written by Moses b. Jacob Cordovero (1522–1570), the most important kabbalist in Safed prior to Isaac Luria.

[100] Attributed to Abraham Sephardi of the fourteenth century, *Berit menuḥah* was first published in 1648.

[101] In 1819, Jacob Samuel Bik wrote to Lefin regarding a Polish translation of *In Praise of the Ba'al Shem Tov* that was causing a stir in Polish noble homes. There is no evidence of a Polish version of *Shivḥei haBesht*. Moshe Rosman, and others, speculate that Bik's letter to Lefin, written when Bik still considered himself a *maskil*, was a deliberate parody alluding to the plot line of Perl's *Megalleh temirin* (1819), which revolved around the Polish nobility's reading of an exposé of Hasidism. For Bik's letter to Lefin, see Philip Friedman, "The First Battles between the Haskalah and Hasidism," *Fun noentn ovar* 4 (1937): 260–61. See, too, Rosman, *Founder of Hasidism*, 210.

[102] Isaac b. Jacob Alfasi (1013–1103), known by the acronym Rif, was the author of the most important code of Jewish law, *Sefer hahalakhot*, prior to Maimonides's *Mishneh torah*.

[103] The Joseph Perl Archive, JNULA, 4° 1153/72, 1a and 2a.

[104] On Emden's contribution to critical scholarship on the Zohar, see Tishby, *The Wisdom of the Zohar*, 1:41–43. Mendelssohn, perhaps misreading Emden's attack on the Zohar as consonant with his own distrustful views of the Kabbalah, praised him for unmasking the dangers inherent in the influence of the kabbalistic tradition on Sabbatianism. See Katz, "Regarding the Connection," 95 and Yehuda Friedlander, "The Struggle of the Mitnagedim and Maskilim against Hasidism: Rabbi Jacob Emden and Judah Leib Mieses," in *New Perspectives on the Haskalah* (ed. Shmuel Feiner and David Sorkin; London: The Littman Library of Jewish Civilization, 2001), 103–12.

against mysticism in general. Lefin also believed that the *Zohar* provided dangerous fodder for contemporary mystical movements (the Hasidim) and for Christian anti-Jewish polemics. In the manuscript cited above, as well as in his anonymously published French pamphlet, *Essai d'un plan de réforme ayant pour objet d'éclairer la Nation Juive en Pologne et de redresser par là ses moeurs* [1791], Lefin turned to unilateral censorship of kabbalistic works, targeting the *Zohar* in particular, as a means of stemming the spread of Hasidism.

Taken together, therefore, the Frankist legacy, the impact of Emden's anti-Sabbatian polemics, and the direct contact with Beshtian Hasidism created the context for the response of a small group of traditional rabbinic Jews in Podolia to seek solutions to what they perceived to be insidious and dangerous changes occuring in Polish Jewish society. Mendel Lefin was not alone among his generation to feel that Hasidism would lead Polish Jewry down the inexorable path of heresy and conversion.[105] The letters of Lefin's correspondents, including Israel Bodek, Meir ha-Cohen Reich, and Hayim Malaga, attest to their shared perception of Hasidism's perils.[106] Already critical of the "baroqueness" of early modern Ashkenazic Jewish culture, Lefin believed that the insularity of the new pietists was deepening the subversion of historical Ashkenazic Jewish piety. Polish Jews were increasingly living in a circumscribed world in which "the study of wisdom and science and the rest of the sciences is considered apostasy."[107] Lefin's childhood and maturation in Podolia prior to 1780 thus prompted him to journey to Berlin and informed his response to the Berlin Haskalah. This response, in turn, helped to shape the parameters of the maskilic program that he brought back to Podolia and then to Austrian Galicia. Despite the partitions, the

---

[105] Certainly Lefin's mitnaggedic contemporaries held such suspicions. Even bearing in mind the polemical context of his words and, thus, their hyperbole, David of Maków, citing the *ga'on* of Vilna, argued that the Maggid of Kozienice's custom of mediating the prayers of his Hasidim was "complete idolatry." Cited in Wilensky, *Hasidim umitnaggedim,* 2:44–45.

[106] The Joseph Perl Archive, JNULA, 4° 1153/8, 4° 1153/70, 4° 1153/129, 4° 1153/130, and 4° 1153/135. Abraham Schwadron Collection of Jewish Autographs and Portraits, JNULA, Mendel Lefin papers. See, too, Meir ha-Cohen Reich's letter to his son, Benjamin Reich, in the personal diary of Jacob Samuel Bik, 39b. This manuscript belongs to the municipal library in Frankfurt-on-the-Main, Bibliotheca Merzbacheriana Monacensis, 64, Ms. Hebrew folio 11; a microfilm is available in the Department of Microfilmed Hebrew Manuscripts, JNULA, film number 26448. Lefin was, however, acutely aware that he and his maskilic friends were a tiny minority among Eastern European Jewry. Writing from Austrian Galicia in the second decade of the nineteenth century, he remarked, "A small group of enlightened men still lives here. Scorned and hated by the mob of course, they are still tolerated as writers and copyists for all legal matters, such as for the promissory and settlement notes presented to all the German authorities." Joseph Perl Archive, JNULA, 4° 1153/134a, 5b.

[107] Lefin's comment was published in his *Liqqutei kelalim* (*Selections of Rules*) in Gelber, "Mendel Lefin of Satanów's Proposals," 300.

economic and political reality of Polish Jewry in the late eighteenth and early nineteenth centuries remained shaped by the political and economic life of the Commonwealth, and provided the context for Lefin's commitment to a moderate program of Haskalah. Selective appropriation of the ideas of the West European Enlightenment and the Berlin Haskalah, and their seamless adaptation into a program of moderate Enlightenment especially constructed for Polish Jewry, became Lefin's lifework.

East Meets West: Mendel Lefin's Encounter with the Berlin Haskalah

For a period of two to four years, Lefin lived in Berlin where he befriended Moses Mendelssohn, David Friedländer (1750–1834), and Simon Veit, Mendelssohn's son-in-law, and was welcomed by a broad circle of *maskilim*. In Gottlober's words, "When Mendelssohn heard about him [Lefin], he welcomed him with open arms and was his dear friend for the entire time he stayed in Berlin. Lefin stayed in Berlin for two years and his soul, too, cleaved to that of Mendelssohn, until he [Lefin] felt that he [Mendelssohn] had become his rabbi and teacher."[108] Unlike Isaac Satanów and Solomon Maimon, two other Polish Jews who had made the pilgrimage to Berlin, Lefin did not settle there permanently. He returned to his native land, bringing with him a singular program of Haskalah that was not only a product of what he had encountered in Berlin, but also an active creation of his own views of the best way to enlighten traditional Polish Jewry.

Lefin left Berlin sometime in 1784, returned to Podolia, and soon settled in Mikołajów, a private town between Międzybóż and Satanów.[109] He never explained his reasons for leaving Berlin when he did, but his disciples clearly believed, projecting backwards, that the rapid pace of change occurring in the Prussian capital after the deaths of Moses Mendelssohn and Frederick the Great in 1786 were decisive in compelling Lefin to depart.[110] As Abraham Baer Gottlober conjectured:

> Mendel Lefin also settled in Berlin, where his soul was filled with wisdom, reason, and pleasant thoughts, which he heard from Mendelssohn's noble mouth, *but the great and*

---

[108] Gottlober, "Russia," *Hamaggid* 17 (1873): 348. Other accounts of Lefin's life mention his staying in Berlin for three or four years, until 1783 or 1784, but we have no evidence to corroborate fully when he left German lands. See N. M. Gelber, *Aus zwei Jahrhunderten* (Vienna: R. Löwit, 1924), 41, who says that Lefin returned to Poland in 1783 and Raphael Mahler, *Divrei yemei yisra'el*, 1:72, for the four-year account.

[109] Lefin signed his 1789 contribution to *Hame'assef* "Mendel of Satanów," which may indicate either that he had returned to his place of birth or that he was already living in Mikołajów, but refering to himself by his place of birth.

[110] On the rapid change of Jewish life in Berlin at the end of the eighteenth century, see Lowenstein, *The Berlin Jewish Community*.

strong spirit that split mountains and turned everything upside down did not damage him. Lefin left Berlin as whole as he had been when he came, whole in Torah and faith, his soul sated with wisdom's luminescence.[111]

The historical conditions that made Berlin a center of the Enlightenment, both Jewish and general, after the Seven Years War, and produced an accelerated modernization among its Jewish elite have been studied by Steven Lowenstein. The consequences of this rapid modernization included an increase in out-of-wedlock births, conversions, and public denunciations of rabbinic culture and authority. Between 1790–1794, the Haskalah journal, *Hame'assef* (*The Gatherer*), which had begun publication in 1783 under the stewardship of Isaac Satanów, published Aaron Wolfsohn-Halle's *Siḥah be'erets haḥayim* (*Dialogue in the Afterlife*), a fierce attack on rabbinic Judaism that so alienated its readership that the journal completely lost its audience and stopped publishing. This events were universally decried by *maskilim* like Lefin, who defined the Haskalah as an intellectual movement distinct from the social processes of modernization. Yet, in the 1780s, Lefin continued to contribute to *Hame'assef*, published *Moda levinah* under the auspices of the "Society for the Education of Youth" and *Sefer refu'at ha'am* with approbations from Mendelssohn and Dr. Marcus Herz (1747–1803), and maintained personal ties with David Friedländer.[112] Perhaps Gottlober and Jacob Samuel Bik (1770–1831) — the latter from personal contact — knew that Lefin was already privately dismayed with behavior he had witnessed in Berlin upon his departure, even though he may have been reluctant to put his grievances into print. In an unpublished poem that Lefin sent to David Friedländer after the appearance of *Moda levinah* in 1789, he attested to his continued loyalty to Friedländer and to the hostility that erupted after Friedländer's support of the anonymous publication of *Mitspeh yoqte'el* (Berlin, 1789) by the Prussian *maskil* Saul Berlin (1740–1794). Berlin's work, which mercilessly attacked the glosses of Raphael Cohen (1722–1803), rabbi of the united communities of Altona, Hamburg, and Wandsbeck, to the *Shulḥan arukh*, immediately set off a controversy within Berlin Jewry about the boundaries of acceptable criticism of rabbinic culture. The first stanza of Lefin's poem intoned, "Noble Friedländer!\Everyone thanks you\Although they curse you publicly, within the recesses of their hearts they are jealous of you\To their distress, you exist; they will not seek you in vain\You deserve honor for your deeds and the beauty of your wisdom."[113]

---

[111] Gottlober, "Russia," *Hamaggid* 17 (1873): 355. The emphasis is mine. See, too, the opinion of Jacob Samuel Bik, cited in Haberman, "Toward a History of Menachem Mendel Lefin of Satanów," 462.

[112] Lefin, *Hame'assef* 5 (Kislev, 1789): 81–92 and (Shevat, 1789): 136–144.

[113] Published in Haberman, "Toward a History of Menachem Mendel Lefin of Satanów," 463.

While Lefin may have brought a distrust and distaste for religious extremism to Berlin with him, he began to express his disenchantment with the Berlin Haskalah only with the publication of the 1791 French pamphlet that he wrote for the Four-Year *Sejm* (1788-1792):

Mendelssohn defined an era in Berlin. He cleared the path indicated by Maimonides, and trained children according to the ideas that [Maimonides] had of the ceremonial law in order to educate them to become enlightened and honest men. He published a beautiful translation of the Five Books of Moses and of the Psalms for their use. He soon found imitators who put him in fashion; soon, other translations were issued, even of the prayerbook. They began to work on useful journals, but those who continued them believed that they were more enlightened [than their predecessors, yet they] were deficient in their own personal conduct, publicly attacking the backwardness of the rabbis in their journal. (This journal finally degenerated altogether). They soon incurred the general contempt of the people through this [behavior]. In the end, they became more intolerant than the ordinary devoted people whom they vilified.[114]

In a later manuscript Lefin reflected on the rapidity of change that had occurred in Jewish Berlin once ignorance of German no longer posed a barrier to acculturation, "Now, however, since this past [prejudice] has been dispelled, everything proceeds very quickly. Advance subscribers and helpful hands in the group [of *maskilim*] were immediately found for everything that they wanted to undertake solely for the benefit of the Enlightenment. No wonder that they soon became dizzy from this haste."[115]

The distinguishing feature of Lefin's conception of the Jewish Enlightenment was its moderation. Despite his critique of the radicalization of the Berlin Haskalah, Lefin never wavered in his commitment to a moderate Jewish Enlightenment as an antidote to the extreme poles of Hasidism on the one hand and to the radical acculturation, what many *maskilim* referred to as the "false" Enlightenment, taken up by a segment of Berlin Jewry, on the other.[116] In a letter to Israel Bodek, Lefin admitted that "the sickness of the imagination of a falsely enlightened (*allzuaufgeklärten*) friend here, together with the untimely efforts of petty opportunities to prepare eulogies for the former [the Enlightenment] there, could have easily instilled some bitterness in me," but in fact had not.[117] Lefin believed that a moderate Haskalah

---

[114] See [Lefin], *"Essai d'un plan de réforme,"* 413.

[115] The Joseph Perl Archive, JNULA, 4° 1153/134a, 4b–5a.

[116] See Lowenstein, *The Berlin Jewish Community*, 72, on the concern among some *maskilim* about what they called the "superficial" or "false" Enlightenment among their fellow Berliners who "'misinterpreted' the liberation of new thinking to mean personal license." See, too, Shmuel Feiner, "The Pseudo-Enlightenment and the Question of Jewish Modernization," *JSS* (new series) 3, no. 1 (Fall 1996): 62–86.

[117] Unsigned and undated letter to (Friend) Bodek, the Joseph Perl Archive, JNULA, 4° 1153/6, 1a. The original is *"Die Imaginationskrankheit eines allzuaufgeklärten Freunds hier, nebst der unzeitigen Bemühungen kleinlichen gelegenheiten Lobreden anzudichten jenes dort: könnten mir*

could balance between what he perceived to be two corrosive forces — mysticism and atheism — and steer Polish Jewry back to the rational tradition embodied by the work of the medieval Jewish philosopher, Moses Maimonides.[118] Maimonides's famous harmonization of the Aristotelian "golden mean" with a life lived by the dictates of the Torah served as an exemplary construct for Lefin's conception of a moderate, authentic Jewish Enlightenment.

Lefin's Enlightenment commitments to transform the particular culture of Polish Jewry did not emerge in a hermetically-sealed Jewish context. Born in the mid-eighteenth century, his turn to the Jewish Enlightenment was shaped by Jewish life in Podolia and by the political events rocking Poland and Europe at the end of the century. Just as his cultural program of the Haskalah was deeply informed by the turmoil within the Podolian-Jewish community, so, too, Lefin's politics were shaped by pre-absolutist political configurations of the Polish-Lithuanian Commonwealth. Lefin's lifelong relationship with the Polish magnate Adam Kazimierz Czartoryski, one of the most powerful representatives of the pre-partitioned Polish-Lithuanian Commonwealth, was a crucial influence on both Lefin's specific suggestions for reforming the Jews of Poland and his practical ability to write and publish works of the Haskalah. The impact of this formative relationship in Lefin's life underscores the importance of analyzing rigorously the specific historical circumstances in which the Haskalah emerged and the ways in which those circumstances shaped its development. While depictions of Lefin as an important "forerunner" of the Haskalah movement in Russia, or as the "Father of the Galician Haskalah" may be historically true, these *ex post facto* evaluations of Lefin's contribution to the dissemination of the Jewish Enlightenment in Eastern Europe disregard the specific historical context in which his commitment to the Haskalah developed. Unlike later generations of *maskilim* in Eastern Europe, whose politics and cultural programs were intimately related to the emergence of the centralized, enlightened absolutist state,[119] Lefin remained oriented toward the Polish variety of the traditional conception of the "royal alliance," appealing to his magnate patron,

---

vielleicht einige Bitterkeit abgenötiget haben." I attribute this unsigned document to Lefin because of its explicit moderation and its citing of Claude-Adrien Helvétius, the French psychologist whom Lefin quoted in several other writings. See Chapter Three.

[118] Lefin's identification with Maimonides will be explored fully in Chapter Three. For an analysis of the early Haskalah's use of Maimonides, see James Lehmann, "Maimonides, Mendelssohn, and the *Me'assfim*: Philosophy and Biographical Imagination in the Early Haskalah," *LBIYA* 20 (1975): 87–108 and Werses, "Hasidism in the Perspective of Haskalah Literature," 106.

[119] Raphael Mahler advanced the most extensive argument for the intrinsic link between absolutism and the Haskalah. See Chapter Five.

rather than to the absolutist state, throughout his life.[120] Lefin brought his traditionalist politics to the debates about reforms of the Jewish community that took place during the fateful last years of the Commonwealth's independent existence (1772–1795) and to the negotiations that produced the 1804 Edicts on Jewish status in Russia.

---

[120] For the classic discussion of the "royal alliance," see Yosef Hayim Yerushalmi, *The Lisbon Massacre and the Royal Image in the Shebet Yehudah* (Cinncinnati, Ohio: Hebrew Union College Press, 1976). Jewish political strategy in Poland aimed at forging alliances with the nobility, in particular with the great magnate families who gained political power in the decentralized Commonwealth. See Gershon Hundert, "Jews, Money, and Society in the Seventeenth-Century Polish Commonwealth: The Case of Kraków," *JSS* 43 (1981): 161–74.

CHAPTER TWO

THE *MASKIL* AND THE PRINCE:
PRIVATE PATRONAGE AND THE DISSEMINATION OF THE JEWISH ENLIGHTENMENT IN EASTERN EUROPE

> After having been received in Połtawa in a truly touching manner by Adam Waleńzki, I am in your estates, my dear, where I delight heart and soul in all of the love and recognition that you have here. In entering your lands I have been received by several thousand people, Jews and Christians, minor nobles, burghers, the old and the young, who presented me with bread and salt, raising their hands to the sky and crying, "God bless our Prince and Princess, their children and grandchildren." I resisted none of their pure effusions; thereupon I began to cry from the bottom of my heart, having only the desire to see you here.[1]
>
> Izabela Fleming Czartoryska to Adam Kazimierz Czartoryski, Stara Sieniawa, Podolia, September 1, 1804.

The "Polishness" of Mendel Lefin's Podolian background shaped his vision of the Jewish Enlightenment, which he proffered as a remedy to eighteenth-century Polish Jewry's deepening spiritual malaise. Encouraged and challenged by his trip to Berlin, Lefin returned to Podolia in the 1780s, hoping to continue his participation in the Haskalah as it developed in German lands and to formulate an ideological and educational program suitable for his Polish brethren. Yet, just as the historiography on the Haskalah in Eastern Europe has bypassed the Podolian stage of its development, most historians have assumed that the Polish environment offered no stimulus to the Haskalah.[2] Yet, when Lefin returned to Podolia, he settled in Mikołajów, a private town between Międzybóż and Satanów under the authority of Prince Adam Kazimierz Czartoryski (1734–1823), the patriarch of one of Poland's most important magnate families. Czartoryski was not only General of Podolia, one of the wealthiest magnates in Poland, holding estates in Central Poland, Lithuania, Przemyśl, and Podolia, but also a leading supporter of

---

[1] 6030 III, EW 623. The Czartoryski Family Archive. The letter is dated with both 1804 and 1805, but archival notations affirm 1804 as the accurate date because the letter mentions Seweryn Potocki, who died in March 1805.

[2] Michael A. Meyer, *Response to Modernity: A History of the Reform Movement* (New York: Oxford University Press, 1988), 155.

the Polish Enlightenment that had begun to flourish under the reign of King Stanisław Poniatowski, his cousin.[3] Czartoryski's active and personal patronage of Lefin enabled the latter to become a major figure in the emergence of the Haskalah in Eastern Europe.

At some point soon after Lefin's settlement in Mikołajów — we don't know exactly when — he met Czartoryski. Gottlober's version of their meeting relates that Czartoryski, whose permanent home was in the family castle in Międzybóż, was touring his estates and fortuitously chanced upon a small shop run by Lefin's wife. Once in the shop, Czartoryski noticed on the counter a mathematical text by Christian Wolff, the German Enlightenment philosopher and mathematician known for his belief in the compatibility of reason and revelation, and whose works enjoyed wide currency among enlightened circles in Poland and among Prussian *maskilim*.[4] Startled to see such a learned German book in a small Jewish store, he inquired after the proprietor, and thus began the friendship between the Polish magnate and the enlightened Jew. In Gottlober's words:

> The prince was shocked [to see Wolff's book] and asked the Jewish woman: "Whose book is this?" She answered, "My husband investigates it night and day, and sometimes when he comes here he cannot separate from it and brings it with him to the store, too." . . . R. Mendel Lefin came and stood before the prince. Now Mendel Lefin was neither attractive nor fit, and his face was covered with pimples. However, when he opened his mouth to speak, his words were filled with grandeur and glory. Wisdom, understanding, and reason hovered upon his lips, which were filled with grace. The prince spoke with him and heard his vast wisdom. When the Prince learned that Lefin was a disciple and friend of the great sage, [Moses] Mendelssohn, who had already left his mark on the world among the respected thinkers of Germany, and whom the Prince revered, from that time forward, he [Czartoryski] supplied R. Mendel Lefin with all of the needs for permanently maintaining a house from the Czartoryski treasury. [Czartoryski] also [gave Lefin] monthly supplies of beer and whisky that were so abundant that his wife was able to sell the extra spirits. Czartoryski also gave him unlimited golden ducat[s] to withdraw

---

[3]   When Adam Kazimierz Czartoryski's father, August Aleksander Czartoryski, married Maria Zofia Sieniawska Denhoffow in 1731, he acquired the Sieniawski estates, which were the second largest in the Polish-Lithuanian Commonwealth, and ensured his family's prominence in Polish politics for the next two centuries. W. H. Zawadzki, *A Man of Honour: Adam Czartoryski as a Statesman of Russia and Poland, 1795–1831* (Oxford: Clarendon Press, 1993), 8.

[4]   On the receptivity of Christian Wolff's philosophy in Poland, see Mieczysław Klimowicz, "Polnische Literatur und Kunst im Zeitalter der Aufklärung," in *Polen und Deutschland im Zeitalter der Aufklärung* (ed. Rainer Riemenschneider; Braunschweig: Georg-Eckert-Institut für Internationale Schulbuchforschung, 1981), 98. For Lefin's interest in mathematics, see the Joseph Perl Archive, 4° 1153/130, 21–22, 44–46, and the Abraham Schwadron Collection of Jewish Autographs and Portraits, Mendel Lefin papers; on Christian Wolff and the Haskalah, see David Sorkin, "From Context to Comparison: The German Haskalah and Reform Catholicism," *Tel Aviver Jahrbuch für deutsche Geschichte* 20 (1991): 23–58.

from his treasury, and Lefin saved all of this money in order to give it as charity to the
poor in their time of need.[5]

The hagiographic and apocryphal tone of Gottlober's account notwithstanding, we know that Prince Adam Kazimierz Czartoryski became Lefin's patron
sometime in the 1790s, first hiring him to tutor his sons in mathematics and
philosophy and later helping to publish his political and literary works.
Czartoryski provided Lefin with a lifelong stipend and made great efforts to
ensure that his beneficiary found comfortable lodgings in which to work, as
is attested in the following deposition written by Czartoryski to Tomasz
Bernatowicz, the administrator of his Podolian estates:

> Honorable Gentleman Bernatowicz, *Stolnik*[6] of Lithuania: Disburse five golden ducats to
> the Jew, Mendel Lefin, each month beginning from March 1, 1797 until I give you
> different orders. Second, I stipulate that he be given a house in which to stay (if there is
> something in reserve) and if, unfortunately, there is nothing, [a house should] be built
> for him quickly in proportion to his needs, but comfortable enough for him to live in
> during the winter. While the erection of such a building is taking place, I am obliged to
> consider accomodating him in Mikołajów.
>
>   Submitted in Sieniawa, March 10, 1797.
>   Adam X [Kazimierz] Czartoryski.[7]

As a generalization, the definitive influence of the German cultural sphere
on the Haskalah in Eastern Europe cannot be denied, but Czartoryski's
patronage of Lefin suggests that in individual cases the Polish nobility was

---

5   Abraham Baer Gottlober, "Russia," *Hamaggid* 17 (1873): 356. Gottlober, who never met
Lefin personally, received the physical description of Lefin from Mordecai Suchostober,
Lefin's disciple who helped edit his translation of the *Guide of the Perplexed* and taught in the
rabbinical seminary in Żytomierz (Zhitomir). The contrast between Mendelssohn's physical
ugliness and his spiritual beauty owes much to the paradoxical image shaped by Isaac
Euchel (1756–1804) in his biography of Mendelssohn published in *Hame'assef* in 1789: "He
[Mendelssohn] was not handsome; nonetheless, all who regarded him found him pleasing
because wisdom illuminated his face." Cited in Shmuel Feiner, *Haskalah vehistoryah: toldotav
shel hakarat-ever yehudit modernit* (Jerusalem: Zalman Shazar Center, 1998), 87.
6   A title denoting a mid-level bureaucrat or steward.
7   Published in Majer Bałaban, "Mendel Lewin i książę Adam Czartoryski," *Chwila*, no.
5313–5314 (7–8 stycznia 1934): 10. Tomasz Bernatowicz was a graduate of the National
Cadets School founded by Czartoryski and Poniatowski, and became employed by the
Czartoryskis as administrator of their Podolian estates sometime after 1782. See Adam Jerzy
Czartoryski, *Pamiętniki i Memoriały Polityczne, 1776–1809* (ed. Jerzy Skowronek; Warsaw:
Instytut Wydawniczy Pax, 1986), 92. He figures large in the Czartoryski correspondence,
both between Czartoryski *fils* and his father, Adam Kazimierz, as well as between Izabela
Czartoryska and her husband. See, for example, 6338 IV, EW 1503, 28 June, 1802, 93; 6338
IV, EW 1503, 3 July, 1802, 147; 6338 IV, MS EW 1503, 19 March 1803, 187-190; 16 May, 1803,
199; 26 May, 1803, 205, etc. On July 27, 1809, Adam Kazimierz expressed concern to Adam
Jerzy that they might lose the services of Bernatowicz. See Czartoryski, *Pamiętniki i Memoriały
Polityczne*, 397.

interested in connections with enlightened Jews and that elements of enlightened Polish noble culture influenced certain *maskilim*.[8] Here it is important to emphasize that Lefin continued to live in Podolia with Czartoryski's support, spending time in Międzybóż and Mikołajów, until the end of the first decade of the nineteenth century. He visited the Prince on his estates in Puławy and Sieniawa, areas under Austrian rule after the first partition, and was in Warsaw during the Four-Year *Sejm* (1788–1792) at Czartoryski's behest. Lefin also travelled to St. Petersburg with the young Prince Adam Jerzy Czartoryski in the early years of the first decade of the nineteenth century. When Lefin left Podolia for Austrian Galicia — sometime in the second decade of the nineteenth century — he was still supported by the Polish magnate. The Czartoryski-Lefin patronage relationship suggests that a small group of Jews and Christians had common cultural and intellectual concerns and interests, at least for a brief period of time, in the last years of the Polish-Lithuanian Commonwealth.

The continuity of the Czartoryski Family's patronage of Lefin into the nineteenth century speaks to the abiding "Polishness" of the southeastern borderlands after the partitions.[9] The territories of Podolia and western Ukraine ruled by Russia after the third partition were unequivocally Polish, a status recognized by Poles and Russians alike, the latter referring to those areas as "gubernii acquired from Poland." The feudal character of the southeastern Polish borderlands posed innumerable problems for the new rulers, not the least of which was the tradition of noble republicanism, with its well-defined rights and privileges that had distinguished the Polish *szlachta*. Russia was not a feudal society, but an autocracy that dictated its subjects'

---

[8]   Israel Bartal, "'The Heavenly City of Germany' and Absolutism à la Mode d'Autriche: The Rise of the Haskalah in Galicia," in *Toward Modernity: The European Jewish Model* (ed. Jacob Katz; New Brunswick, N.J.: Transaction Books, 1987), 14–32 and Israel Bartal, "'The Second Model': France as a Source of Influence in the Processes of Modernization of East European Jewry, 1772–1863," in *Hamahppekhah hatsarfatit verishumah* (ed. Richard Cohen; Jerusalem: Zalman Shazar Center, 1991), 271–85.

[9]   Throughout the nineteenth century, Polish irredentism in Galicia and in the southeastern borderlands posed formidable challenges to both Imperial Russia and Austria. Revolutionary insurrection only erupted against Russian rule, but Polish national consciousness was cultivated by the *intelligenti* who remained in the partitioned lands and by emigré patriots who found refuge in London and Paris. See Stanislaus Blejwas, *Realism in Polish Politics: Warsaw Positivism and National Survival in Nineteenth Century Poland* (Yale Russian and East European Publications; New Haven, Conn.: Yale Concilium on International and Area Studies, 1984); Andrzej Walicki, *The Enlightenment and the Birth of Modern Nationhood: Polish Political Thought from Noble Republicanism to Tadeusz Kosciuszko* (Notre Dame, Ind.: University of Notre Dame Press, 1989); Peter Brock, "Polish Nationalism," in *Nationalism in Eastern Europe* (ed. Peter Sugar and Ivo Lederer; Seattle: University of Washington Press, 1969), 310–72.

status from above, without any recourse to a medieval legal tradition.[10] Unwilling to manage the social consequences of the peasant (or, better, the serf) question, which would have required expropriating the ruling elite, the Russian tsars maintained the socio-economic status quo and the dominance of the Polish nobility in the newly acquired *kresy*.[11] Thus, the feudal character of the southeastern borderlands persisted until mid-century, when the peasant question exploded throughout the region (in 1846 in Austrian lands, in the European-wide revolutions in 1848, and, finally, in Russia, in 1861 with the emancipation of the serfs).[12]

The relationship of the Polish nobility to "its" Jews and serfs likewise endured into the new century, a relationship that was predicated on the traditional feudal economic and political structure of the Commonwealth.[13] Lefin looked to Czartoryski, not to the Russian or Austrian state, as a source of political authority. Despite his interest in the cultural program of the *Toleranzpatent* (Edict of Toleration), Lefin expressed reservations about absolutism as a whole and about Joseph II's political agenda, particularly with regard to military conscription of the Jewish community.[14] Although he participated in the debates over the reform of the Jews, first in the Four-Year

---

10   Gregory L. Freeze, "The *Soslovie* (Estate) Paradigm and Russian Social History," *American Historical Review* 20 (1986): 11–26 and Michael Stanislawski, "Russian Jewry, the Russian State, and the Dynamics of Jewish Emancipation," in *Paths of Emancipation: Jews, States and Citizenship* (ed. Pierre Birnbaum and Ira Katznelson; Princeton, N.J.: Princeton University Press, 1995), 264–65.

11   Zawadzki, *A Man of Honour*, 86.

12   Stefan Kieniewicz, *The Emancipation of the Polish Peasantry* (Chicago: University of Chicago Press, 1969) and J. Leskiewicz, "Land Reforms in Poland (1764–1870)," *Journal of European Economic History* 1 (1972): 435–48.

13   See Andrei S. Markovits, "Introduction: Empire and Province," in *Nationbuilding and the Politics of Nationalism: Essays on Austrian Galicia* (ed. Andrei S. Markovits and Frank E. Sysyn; Cambridge, Ma.: Harvard University Press, 1982), 2. Although flawed by its overdependence on Marxist theory, see Artur Eisenbach, *The Emancipation of the Jews in Poland, 1780–1870* (ed. Antony Polonsky and trans. Janina Dorosz; London: Basil Blackwell, 1991), for a discussion of the emancipation of the Jews of Poland in the context of the disintegrating social system of the Polish-Lithuanian Commonwealth and under the rule of the three partitioning powers.

14   Between 1781–1789, Emperor Joseph II issued a series of *Toleranzpatente* (Edicts of Toleration) for the provinces under his rule. On December 18, 1788, he extended the obligations of conscription to the Monarchy's Jewish community. Certain exceptional communities, such as the Jews of Mantua and Trieste, were not conscripted. See Lois C. Dubin, *The Port Jews of Habsburg Trieste: Absolutist Politics and Enlightenment Culture* (Stanford, Calif.: Stanford University Press, 1999), 148–52 and Eisenbach, *The Emancipation of the Jews in Poland*, 55. The *Toleranzpatent* for Lower Austria on January 2, 1782, is the most well-known of the edicts and promised religious tolerance in return for the abolition of Jewish communal autonomy. Joseph II's toleration edict for Galicia will be discussed in detail in Chapter Five.

Sejm in Warsaw and later as a behind-the-scene advisor to Adam Jerzy Czartoryski, who was on the "Unofficial Committee" involved with Imperial Russian legislation on the Jewish question, the issue of the reciprocity (the quid pro quo) between internal Jewish reform and emancipation that characterized the Haskalah in German lands is completely absent from Lefin's writings.[15] Mendel Lefin's identity as a *maskil* was bound to the late eighteenth-century Polish-Lithuanian Commonwealth, and to the culture of private patronage that had flourished in the private towns of the Polish nobility and had granted the Jews extensive communal, religious, and cultural autonomy.

The Czartoryski-Lefin relationship was that of patron and protégé, defined by the mutual dependence between the Polish magnates and the Jews living on their private lands.[16] There was no economic parity between Lefin and Czartoryski and no broad societal consequences of their friendship.[17] Yet, the relationship served the interests of both men. Czartoryski's interest in Lefin was part of the prince's extensive commitment to the cultivation and dissemination of the Enlightenment while Lefin's connection to Czartoryski allowed him to gain access to the arena in which Polish reformers debated reform programs for the Jewish community. The two men shared a common vocabulary of "rationality," "Enlightenment," and the

---

[15]   On the quid pro quo implicit in the emancipatory struggle in Prussian lands, see David Sorkin, *The Transformation of German Jewry, 1780–1840* (New York: Oxford University Press, 1987) and Steven M. Lowenstein, *The Berlin Jewish Community: Enlightenment, Family, and Crisis, 1770–1830* (New York: Oxford University Press, 1994).

[16]   M. J. Rosman, *The Lords' Jews: Magnate-Jewish Relations in the Polish-Lithuanian Commonwealth during the Eighteenth Century* (Cambridge, Mass.: Harvard Ukranian Research Institute, 1990).

[17]   Although the Lefin-Czartoryski relationship evokes the famous friendship between the Berlin *maskil*, Moses Mendelssohn, and the German *Aufklärer*, Gottfried Ephraim Lessing, there were substantive differences between them. The Lessing-Mendelssohn relationship was between intellectual and social peers on the "neutral" ground of a new society in the making. See Alexander Altmann, *Moses Mendelssohn: A Biographical Study* (Tuscaloosa, Ala.: The University of Alabama Press, 1973), 36–50; Michael A. Meyer, *The Origins of the Modern Jew* (Detroit, Mich.: Wayne State University Press, 1979), 18, 54–55; on the term "neutral society," see Jacob Katz, *Tradition and Crisis: Jewish Society at the End of the Middle Ages* (trans. Bernard Dov Cooperman; New York: New York University Press, 1993). For a qualification of the term as "semineutral," see Jacob Katz, *Out of the Ghetto: The Social Background of Jewish Emancipation, 1770–1870* (Cambridge, Mass.: Harvard University Press, 1973), 42–56, particularly page 54. The Czartoryski-Lefin relationship also invites comparison with the Court Jews and their royal patrons. But, Lefin provided no financial expertise to the Czartoryskis. The only "service" he provided for the prince was tutoring his sons and setting an example of an "enlightened" Jew among his cultural circle. On the Court Jews, see F. L. Carsten, "The Court Jews: A Prelude to Emancipation," *LBIYA* 3 (1958): 140–56 and Jonathan I. Israel, *European Jewry in the Age of Mercantilism, 1550–1750* (Oxford: Clarendon, 1985).

"rights of Man," as well as a commitment to reforming the Jewish community in Poland. Yet, Adam Kazimierz Czartoryski and Mendel Lefin's motivations for the reform of the Jewish community of Poland exhibited a dissonance between patron and protégé. As a moderate *maskil*, Lefin was preeminently concerned with the internal transformation and spiritual reorientation of Polish Jewry. Czartoryski, on the other hand, was preoccupied with reforming Polish society in order to protect its liberties and sovereignty from the assaults of the partitioning powers. His fundamental concern regarding the Jews reflected the need to reform the Jewish community as part of an overall strategy to prevent further attacks on what was left of the Polish-Lithuanian Commonwealth.

As with all of the debates over the reform, transformation, *régénération*, and civic and political emancipation of the Jews that raged throughout Europe between the French and Russian Revolutions, there existed a wide spectrum of views — both among Jewish and Gentile proponents of change, as well as among its opponents — in the Polish-Lithuanian Commonwealth during the period of partitions and reforms.[18] Most of the historiography on this epochal period has not taken into account the Polish arena, even though it was due to the partitions that eastern Ashkenazic Jews — arguably the very members of the Jewish community that European society deemed in need of reform and transformation — were thrust within the borders of absolutist Europe. Although little known, debates over the condition of Jewish society and the question of inclusion of the Jews into a reformed Poland took center stage in the Four-Year *Sejm* (1788–1792), preceding, and then simultaneous with, the contentious debates over Jewish status in the French National Assembly. The arguments and counter-arguments about Jewish participation in the Polish body politic, and even more specifically, in the municipalities, took place simultaneously with the French debates, and illuminate the influence of West European ideas on Polish society, the existence of an important, if small, group of Jewish activists interested in the Enlightenment, and the particular drama of the partitioned Commonwealth in the throes of survival, reform, and tentative modernization. The Czartoryski family was central to all of these currents.

---

[18]   For important works on reform and transformation in Prussia, Habsburg Trieste, France, and Imperial Russia, see Sorkin, *The Transformation of German Jewry*; Dubin, *The Port Jews of Habsburg Trieste*; John Doyle Klier, *Russia Gathers Her Jews: The Origins of the 'Jewish Question' in Russia, 1772–1825* (Dekalb, Ill.: Northern Illinois University Press, 1986); and Michael Stanislawski, *Tsar Nicholas I and the Jews: The Transformation of Jewish Society in Russia, 1825–1855* (Philadelphia: The Jewish Publication Society of America, 1983).

"The Family" and Pre-Partition Reform

The Czartoryski princes traced their lineage back to Gedymin, the Grand Duke of Lithuania. The marriage of Prince Kazimierz Czartoryski (1674–1741), the Vice-Chancellor of Lithuania, to Izabela Morsztyn (1671–1758) marked the beginning of the Polish nobility's intoxication with French culture. Their daughter, Konstancja (1696–1759), married Stanisław Poniatowski (1676–1762); one of the sons of that union would become King Stanisław August Poniatowski (1734–1798), Poland's last sovereign. When Prince Kazimierz and Izabela's son August Alexander wed Maria Zofia Denhoffow in 1731, he acquired the Sieniawski estates, the second largest landed fortune in the Polish-Lithuanian Commonwealth. Adam Kazimierz Czartoryski was their first son; his wealth was so great that when he divided his estates in 1812, they included twenty-five towns and townships and 450 villages, which were valued at almost fifty million zlotys. These unions of money, power, and culture ensured the dominance of the Czartoryskis, who were known for two centuries simply as "The Family," in Polish politics.[19]

"The Family" had been associated with political reform since the 1720s, advocating various programs to modernize Poland, such as remedying the constitutional imbalance by abolishing legislation by consensus (the notorious *liberum veto* that held a virtual stranglehold over the parliamentary process) and strengthening the crown, ensuring longer, more regular meetings of the *Sejm*, prohibiting Confederacies (the nobility's well-protected right of armed rebellion) and reducing the power of the military office of *Hetman*. But other magnate interests, particularly that of the Potocki family, stymied such reform efforts, no doubt because they suspected that a reformed Poland modeled after the Czartoryski plan would secure the political hegemony of "The Family." Attempting to interest a strong foreign power in their reform efforts, the Czartoryskis sent Adam Kazimierz to St. Petersburg in 1762 to ask Catherine II for help. This turn toward Russia, inspired by a genuine desire for reform but coupled with a bid for power, proved to be the first step in the slow and steady Russian subjugation of Poland from mid-century, through the era of partition, and well into the nineteenth century. Catherine II rejected "The Family's" choice of Adam Kazimierz as the next king of Poland, choosing Stanisław Poniatowski, Czartoryski's cousin, instead. When Poniatowski was elected to the Polish throne, which he ascended at the Coronation *Sejm* of December 1764, he did so beholden to Russia.

---

[19] William Fiddian Reddaway, et al., *Cambridge History of Poland* (New York: Octagon, 1971), 21.

Illustration 1

Dzieci Żydowskie (*Jewish Children*) by Jean-Pierre Norblin (1745–1830)
(The Princes' Czartoryski Foundation at the National Museum in Cracow, Poland)

Illustration 2

Adam Kazimierz Czartoryski, by Josef Kapeller (1761–1806)
after J. Grassi, Warsaw
(The Princes' Czartoryski Foundation at the National Museum in Cracow, Poland)

Illustration 3

Adam Jerzy Czartoryski, by A. Geiger after J. Abel, Vienna.
(The Princes' Czartoryski Foundation at the National Museum in Cracow, Poland)

Illustration 4

Izabela Fleming Czartoryska, by Giuseppe Marchi (1735–1808), London
(The Princes' Czartoryski Foundation at the National Museum in Cracow, Poland)

The Polish Enlightenment and Adam Kazimierz Czartoryski

Stanisław August Poniatowski's election in 1764 marked the beginning of a new cultural era in Poland. The king keenly felt a sense of urgency to transform Poland's moribund political structures given that the six *Sejmy* (parliaments) prior to his coronation had been stymied by the ill-famed *liberum veto*, the Sarmatian principle by which one man could block the unanimity necessary to effect legislation in the *Sejm*. He hoped, despite the Commonwealth's dependence on Russia, to institute moderate reforms that would encourage constitutionalism and his unpublished "*Anecdote historique*" outlined a program to strengthen the executive and legislative branches of the Polish government through hereditary election of the king and institution of majority rule in the *Sejm*, which would be in permanent session.[20] Many of Poniatowski's proposed reforms reflected the influence of the Enlightenment — in its most generic European-wide meaning — on Poland and the growth of an indigenous Polish Enlightenment since 1764.[21] Contemporaneous with its Western European counterparts, the Polish Enlightenment drew on the writings of the German *Aufklärer* and the French *lumières* while addressing specific Polish problems, such as the *liberum veto*, the moribund state of the nation's cities, and the dissoluteness of the impoverished serfs. Unlike the West European movements, the Polish Enlightenment was borne by the nobility and the king, not by the educated middle classes.[22] King Stanisław August Poniatowski and Prince Adam Czartoryski were two of the most important patrons of the movement. Drawing on the influence of new ideas — such as Wolffian philosophy — spread by Poles educated in foreign universities during the reign of his predecessor, August III, the new king set about creating a center in the royal court for the cultivation of Enlightenment ideas with specific emphasis on the criticism and rejection of the old, antiquated myths and ways of life that had led to the country's

---

[20]   Richard Butterwick, "The Enlightened Monarchy of Stanisław August Poniatowski (1764–1795)," in *The Polish-Lithuanian Monarchy in European Context, c. 1500–1795* (ed. Richard Butterwick; New York: Palgrave, 2001), 193–218.

[21]   West European enlighteners, particularly *les lumières*, became fascinated with the events in the "East," resulting in several important enlightenment works on Poland, including Marat's *Adventures of the Young Count Potowski*, *Polish Letters*, and *Foreign Interest in Poland*, as well as Rousseau's *Considerations on the Government of Poland*, penned in 1772. See Larry Wolff, *Inventing Eastern Europe: The Map of Civilization on the Mind of the Enlightenment* (Stanford, Calif.: Stanford University Press, 1994).

[22]   Klimowicz, "Polnische Literatur und Kunst im Zeitalter der Aufklärung," 97 and Mieczysław Klimowicz, "Die Frühaufklärung der Jahre 1733–1763 und die Aufklärung der Periode des Königs Stanisław August im Lichte der deutsch-polnischen literarischen Beziehungen," in *Frühaufklärung in Deutschland und Polen* (ed. Karol Bal, Siegried Wollgast, and Petra Schellenberg; Berlin: Akademie Verlag, 1991), 163–73.

stagnation.[23] He also helped to found a school and a school commission, and promoted the journal, *Monitor* (1765–1785), all of which became institutional expressions of the new, "enlightened" spirit.

In 1765, Poniatowski helped to establish the Knights' School (also called the Cadet Corps) to educate qualified officers and public servants along the lines of the best innovations of the Piarist educator, Stanisław Konarski. In 1740, Konarski had started the *Collegium Nobilium,* a high school for the sons of gentlemen, as a direct challenge to Jesuit domination of education. His school's curriculum focused on modern languages, mathematics, and science, and introduced riding, outdoor games, and French drama as part of the curriculum. Spreading the ideas of Bacon, Descartes, Leibniz, Locke, and Wolff in a campaign against the old scholastic curriculum, the Piarist movement also turned to classics of the Polish renaissance, particularly the work of Copernicus, to anchor the beginnings of the Polish Enlightenment in its own national past.[24] Faith in the liberalizing power of education extended to a criticism of Poland's political structure. Konarski's pamphlet, "On the Means to Successful Government" (Warsaw, 1760–1763), located the roots of Poland's problems in the *liberum veto,* as well as on the nobility's selfishness. A similar combination of a progressive critique of the educational and political systems with a desire to protect the noble republicanism of the Commonwealth informed the new Knights' School.

Adam Kazimierz Czartoryski was a generous benefactor of the new Cadet Corps and served as the school's first commandant. He supplied the library with its core 10,000 volumes and was instrumental in bringing John Lind from England to be the school's first director. The Knights' School taught classical and modern literature, geography, history, and law. No formal religious instruction was provided, although mass was performed. Secular morality was the guiding principle of the school, underscored by the Enlightenment trio of reason, utility, and obligation to the state and to one's fellow man. Polish was the language of instruction. The Knights' School's explicit emphasis on the duty to the state, as opposed to the individual (in this case

---

23   Klimowicz, "Polnische Literatur und Kunst im Zeitalter der Aufklärung," 98.
24   William J. Rose, *Stanislas Konarski: Reformer of Education in Eighteenth-Century Poland* (London: Jonathan Cape, 1929); Henryk Hinz, "The Philosophy of the Polish Enlightenment and its Opponents: The Origins of the Modern Polish Mind," *Slavic Review* 30, no. 2 (June 1971): 344; *Cambridge History of Poland,* 82–86. This turn to Polish Renaissance classics underscores the distinctive national coloring of the Enlightenment in Poland, a feature shared with the Haskalah, as well. In contrast to Peter Gay's analysis of the *philosophes'* appropriation of Greco-Roman classics to shape their supposed non-national, universalist Enlightenment, Polish exponents of the Enlightenment, while translating and reading ancient classics, "returned" not to ancient Greece and Rome, but to Poland's "Golden Age," the sixteenth century. For treatment of the Enlightenment as a return to universal paganism, see Peter Gay, *The Enlightenment: An Interpretation* (New York: Alfred A. Knopf, 1966).

noble) interest, found its most famous representative in Tadeusz Kościuszko (1746–1817), the republican insurrectionist who, after fighting in the American Revolutionary war, returned to Poland and attempted to defy the Commonwealth's third, and final, partition.[25]

Adam Kazimierz Czartoryski also fostered his commitment to the Enlightenment through the important role he played in the National Education Commission (*Komisja Edukacji Narodowej*), which, founded in 1773 with monies from the recently dissolved Jesuit order, was Europe's first modern ministry of education.[26] The Commission created a network of secular middle schools with the goal of instilling Enlightenment values into the next generation and was responsible for overseeing Poland's two great universities in Vilna and Cracow. With Czartoryski's help and financial assistance, some of Europe's most distinguished intellectuals, such as the French physiocrat Pierre-Samuel Dupont de Nemours (1739–1817) and the Swiss mathematician, Simon L'Huillier, were brought to Poland to advise the Commission, as well as to tutor the young Czartoryski sons.[27]

Adam Kazimierz Czartoryski's interest in the Enlightenment extended to the literary realm, which he nurtured through patronage and in his own writings. In 1763, he co-founded (with Poniatowski's help) the moral weekly, *Monitor*, which, modelled after Britain's *Spectator*, published essays, letters, articles, and reportage in a semi-scholarly vein. Its objective, like that of its English exemplar (and, notably, of Moses Mendelssohn's Hebrew moral weekly, *Qohelet musar*), was popular education: to bring new ideas to the literate public.[28] *Monitor* was renewed in 1765 with the support of his cousin, the king, and, in fact, became the main voice of royal support for reform. Appearing twice weekly until December 1785, *Monitor*'s articles aimed their moralistic barbs at irresponsible and uncivil *szlachta* behavior (drunkenness, arrogance, and deceit). The weekly also reflected Poniatowski's and Czartoryski's interest in physiocracy and published numerous articles on agriculture and new methods of cultivation. A few issues even boldly suggested that serfdom be abolished. The moralistic essays still left room for articles on

---

[25] Jerzy Lukowski, *Liberty's Folly: The Polish-Lithuanian Commonwealth in the Eighteenth Century, 1697–1795* (London: Routledge, 1991), 222–23.

[26] School reform in the Habsburg Monarchy and in Prussia was also galvanized by the dissolution of the Jesuit order. In Austria, Pope Clement XIV ceded all of the Jesuit schools, colleges, houses and other property — which equalled over 13 million florins — to Maria Theresa, who established a commission to reform the Austrian education system. See James Van Horn Melton, *Absolutism and the Eighteenth-Century Origins of Compulsory Schooling in Prussia and Austria* (Cambridge: Cambridge University Press, 1988), 210.

[27] Zawadzki, *A Man of Honour*, 17.

[28] On the flourishing of moral weeklies modelled after *Spectator* in the Russian Empire, see G. Gareth Jones, "Novikov's Naturalized *Spectator*," in *The Eighteenth Century in Russia* (ed. J. G. Garrard; Oxford: Clarendon Press, 1973), 149–65.

translation theory, the refinement of the Polish language, and reviews of contemporary theater.[29] Czartoryski himself published theater criticism and theory under the pseudonym *Teatralski*. *Monitor* also fostered a literary link between the West European and Polish Enlightenments by bringing translations of classics of medieval and early modern thought, as well as new writings by the *philosophes*, to its reading public. The journal cultivated a new spirit of intellectual creativity and restlessness that advanced Polish culture and literature.[30]

Unfettered by the demands of the crown (a political position that he did not want) and blessed with a huge personal fortune, Czartoryski enjoyed the life of a renaissance intellectual. He cultivated knowledge of eighteen languages, and was interested in literature, history, the arts, natural sciences, chemistry, political economy, and military strategy. He travelled extensively, particularly in England, and nourished his own private "republic of letters" with the works of many of Europe's greatest eighteenth-century luminaries, many of whom, like himself, were freemasons. Adam Kazimierz Czartoryski, and later his son, Adam Jerzy, belonged to the Parisian Lodge, Les Neuf Soeurs, whose membership included Dupont de Nemours, G. B. Mably, F. Wonsowicz, Joachim Heinrich Campe, Johann Heinrich Pestalozzi, A. Strzecki, and Tadeusz Kościuszko. Benjamin Franklin was elected "Venerable" of the lodge in 1781.[31] These personal connections proved useful to Czartoryski as he cultivated a private "enlightened" court on his lands. Puławy, the Czartoryski estate on the Wisła River about 110 kilometers south of Warsaw, became one of Poland's most vital cultural and intellectual centers in the late eighteenth century under the direction of both Adam Kazimierz Czartoryski and his wife, Izabela Czartoryska, even competing with

[29]   Lukowski, *Liberty's Folly*, 220.

[30]   Klimowicz, "Polnische Literatur und Kunst im Zeitalter der Aufklärung," 99–100 and Hinz, "The Philosophy of the Polish Enlightenment and its Opponents," 341.

[31]   Many members of the lodge were Philanthropists, including Campe and Pestalozzi, and their interest in educational reform and Czartoryski's respect for Franklin influenced the former's choice of the civic catechism for the new Polish Knights' School. See Ernst A. Simon, "Pedagogic Philanthropism and Jewish Education (Hebrew Section)," in *Jubilee Volume in Honor of Mordecai Kaplan* (ed. Moshe Davis; New York, 1953), 149–87; and Nicholas Hans, "UNESCO of the Eighteenth Century: *La Loge des Neuf Soeurs* and its Venerable Master, Benjamin Franklin," *Proceedings of the American Philosophical Society* 97 (1953): 513–24. For an important study on the relationship of freemasonry to the Enlightenment, see Margaret Jacob, *Living the Enlightenment: Freemasonry and Politics in Eighteenth-Century Europe* (Oxford: Oxford University Press, 1991); on the catechism for the Cadets School, see Jean Fabre, *Stanislas-Auguste Poniatowski et l'Europe des Lumières* (Strasbourg: Publications de la Faculté des Lettres de l'Université de Strasbourg, 1952), 147, 156. Several members of Alexander I's "Unofficial Committee" were also masons, underscoring the progressive bent of freemasonry at the end of the eighteenth and beginning of the nineteenth century.

Stanisław August Poniatowski's royal court.[32] Drawing some of Europe's
greatest minds to their estate in order to instruct their sons, the Czartoryskis
transformed Puławy into a rural, noble "salon." The residence and employment of such a vast army of tutors for the Czartoryski boys was typical of the
eighteenth-century Polish magnate estate, where one could always count "a
vast number of residents," as Julian Ursyn Niemcewicz, the poet, novelist,
and translator brought to Puławy as a religious tutor later commented in his
memoirs.[33] Adam Jerzy Czartoryski's tutors included Colonel Stanisław
Ciesielski and Józef Koblanski for history, Franciszek Kniaznin for Polish
literature, Grzegorz Piramowicz, co-founder of the National Education Commission, Józef Szymanowski, a poet, lawyer, and official in the government
Treasury Commission, and Niemcewicz. The French artist, Jean-Pierre Norblin (1745–1830), was also invited to Puławy, becoming the Czartoryski's
court painter.[34]

Deriving great satisfaction from his role as patron, Czartoryski surrounded
himself with talented and brilliant men, such as François Sapieha, Domi-
nique Radziwiłł, Józef Szymanowski, Edward Dembowski, Jan Jawornicki, a
liberal estate commissioner, and Feliks Bernatowicz, a novelist and play-
wright. When his protégés left Puławy, Czartoryski's patronage did not cease.
Instead, the prince sent them on European study journeys, which he generously financed. As one scholar has written: "His [Czartoryski's] solicitousness
followed them [the protégés] from destination to destination, making provision at each of them for a sojourn at a boarding house, such as at the lovely
Parisian residence and greenhouse of the engraver, Wille, where so many
young Poles, like Kościuszko, spent happy years, offering thanks to Prince
Adam, the protective god of these places."[35] Bernatowicz is a case in point.
After studying in Vilna, he was sent by his uncle Tomasz, the *stolnik* in

---

[32]   Even prior to Poniatowski, the royal court was a center for international culture in
Poland. See Emanuel Rostworowski, "Polens Stellung in Europa im Zeitalter der Auf-
klärung," in *Polen und Deutschland im Zeitalter der Aufklärung* (ed. Rainer Riemenschneider;
Braunschweig: Georg-Eckert-Institut für Internationale Schulbuchforschung, 1981), 19 and
Barbara and Stanisław Jedynak, "Die philosophische und gesellschaftlichen Anschauungen
Stanisław Leszczyńskis," in *Frühaufklärung in Deutschland und Polen* (ed. Karol Bal, Siegfried
Wollgast, Petra Schellenberger; Berlin: Akademie Verlag, 1991), 229–47.
[33]   Cited in Witold Molik, "Residenten als ein Relikt der Magnatenklientel auf polnischen
Boden im 19tn Jahrhundert," in *Patronage und Klientel: Ergebnisse einer polnisch-deutschen
Konferenz* (ed. Hans-Heinrich Nolte; Cologne: Böhlen Verlag, 1989), 85. See, too, Fabre,
Stanislas-Auguste Poniatowski et l'Europe des Lumières, 146–47.
[34]   Uwe Westfehling, *Jean-Pierre Norblin: ein Künstler des Revolutionszeitalters in Paris und
Warschau* (Cologne: Wallraf-Richartz-Museum, 1989). After the partitions, Norblin, who had
lived in Poland for thirty years, corresponded with Adam Kazimierz Czartoryski and
expressed his hope that Poland's sovereignty would be restored. See Zygmunt Batowski, ed.,
Z korespondencyi Norblin (Lwów, 1911), 8–10.
[35]   Cited in Fabre, *Stanislas-Auguste Poniatowski et l'Europe des Lumières*, 148.

Witebsk (Vitebsk), to a lyceum in Krzemieniec, where he rigorously studied Latin, French, and Polish literature, knowledge that proved indispensable for securing a position as Czartoryski's secretary for French and Polish correspondence. In residence at Czartoryski's estate in Sieniawa, Bernatowicz made frequent trips abroad — to Vienna, Munich, and Dresden — in order to expand his intellectual interests, all at the prince's recommendation and expense. He began to write in Sieniawa, turning first to translations and then to comedies and novels, becoming a significant cultural figure in his own right.[36]

On the Eve of the First Partition

Despite Poniatowski's interest in reforming the Commonwealth in the spirit of an enlightened monarchy with a strong noble-led legislature, he was unsuccessful at convincing a majority of the nobility that reform, which required attenuation of their privilege, was necessary for the stability of the country. Critically important to Poland's defense was the abolition of the *liberum veto* to prevent legislative quagmire and the raising of a strong, standing army. The *szlachta*, however, increasingly paranoid about Enlightenment rhetoric that included a social program, resisted reform and allowed their xenophobia to prohibit civil tolerance of non-Catholics at the *Sejm* of 1764. Catherine, positioning herself as a protector of dissidents, used the religious issue to impose more control on Poniatowski, and thwarted the Czartoryskis' reform efforts in 1768 by forcing the Polish Parliament to accept a Russian guarantee of Polish liberties and to extend rights to non-Roman Catholic Christian dissenters (Russian Orthodox and Protestants). The Polish nobility, always zealous in the defense of its privileges and liberties, organized against Russia in the Confederation of Bar (1768–1772), with the concomitant goal of deposing Poniatowski, whom they viewed as Catherine's pawn. Although Adam Kazimierz Czartoryski had supported earlier reform initiatives, he could not fail to sympathize with the Confederates who sought to throw off the Russian yoke. Adam Kazimierz Czartoryski secretly supported the Confederation of Bar, as did his father and uncle. His support for the Confederates illustrates the paradox of Polish republicanism: defense of Poland's liberty meant protection of noble privilege and could easily be wed to resistance to political reform.[37]

The confederates' rebellion alarmed Poland's powerful neighbors, Turkey, Austria, and Prussia, and resulted in the First Partition, with Poland being stripped of almost one-third of its territory and over one-third of its

---

[36]   *Polski słownik biograficzny*, 1 (Cracow: Komitet redakcyjny, 1935), 463.
[37]   Walicki, *The Enlightenment and the Birth of Modern Nationhood*, 10.

population.[38] Prussia received 5 percent of the territory and approximately 580,000 people; Russia took 12.7 percent of the territory and 1,300,000 people; Austria acquired 11.8 percent of the territory and 2,130,000 people. The treaty of partition was signed on July 25/August 5 (Julian calendar/Gregorian calendar), 1772.[39]

Catherine's new, post-partition ambassador to Poland, Otto Magnus Stackelberg, did his utmost to keep Poland quiescent, but reform-minded *szlachta* were aware that the partition of 1772 was an ominous warning that if they did not begin to address Poland's political problems, its belligerent neighbors would be only to happy to carve up the remaining sections of the former Commonwealth among themselves.[40] The Czartoryskis' clandestine support of the Confederation of Bar led them to become the mainstay of the opposition party to the king after 1775. This party (alternatively called the Opposition, the Magnate Party, and the Ministerial Party) was a heterogeneous group of progressive enlighteners and traditional magnate republicans; of the latter, most were hostile to any kind of political reform. What bound them together was their hostility to Russia's control of Poland. A series of reform measures was passed at the *Sejm* of 1775–1776, which included reforming the judiciary and creating a Permanent Council that was supposed to strengthen the executive. Yet, soon thereafter, Catherine insured that Poniatowski's opponents would be elected to the Permanent Council and the five *Sejmy* that met between 1778–1786 did almost nothing. A law codification project spearheaded by Andrzej Zamoyski never came to fruition and the standing army's numbers rose only pitifully, from 16,100 in 1778 to 18,300 by 1786, compared to Prussia's ranks, numbering 190,000, and Russia and Austria with much more. By 1788, the Opposition had organized sufficiently to win over forty percent of the deputies to the *Sejm.* Hostile to the Permanent Council and to the king, their leadership, including Adam Kazimierz Czartoryski, Kazimierz Nestor Sapieha, Ignacy Potocki, Michał Oginski, and Karol Radziwiłł, turned to the new Prussian king, Frederick William II, who was eager to challenge Russia's control of Poland, and convinced other members of the Diet to undo the Russian system that had ruled Poland since 1775. Flexing their muscles, the Opposition demanded full Russian withdrawal from southeastern Poland and in January 1789 voted for the abolition of the Permanent Council in favor of a Parliamentary Committee.[41] Debate ensued and what had begun as a regular meeting of

38   Lukowski, *Liberty's Folly*, 189–203 and Zawadzki, *A Man of Honour*, 14–16.
39   Norman Davies, *God's Playground: A History of Poland* (New York: Columbia University Press, 1984), 1:521.
40   Hinz, "The Philosophy of the Polish Enlightenment and its Opponents," 341.
41   Daniel Stone, *Polish Politics and National Reform, 1775–1788* (New York: Columbia University Press, 1976), 13–79.

the *Sejm* stretched into the Four-Year *Sejm* (1788–1792), which also became known as the "Great" *Sejm*, culminating in the promulgation of the Constitution of May 3, 1791.

Reforming Poland, Reforming Poland's Jews

Scholarly discussions of the debates over inclusion of the Jews in the new body politic at the end of the eighteenth century have been dominated, until recently, by the French model. In France, as has been recounted many times, the French National Assembly spent over two years discussing whether or not to include the Jews in the new republic, a debate that was spurred by an economic crisis and peasant unrest in Alsace, a province heavily populated by poor, traditional Ashkenazic Jews much like their Polish brethren to the east. After many months of debate, the Assembly emancipated the Sephardic Jews of southwest France, who in many ways had already been integrated *de facto* into French society; twenty months later, all of the Jews of France were given full political rights, a decision reached as a necessary result of the adoption of the new Constitution, which formalized the separation of church and state and granted religious freedom implied by the promulgation of the "Declaration of the Rights of Man as a A Citizen."[42] It is important to recall, however, that inclusion of the Jews as individuals in the new France was not uncontested, both by Jews and Gentiles alike. The debates that raged during the National Assembly included those who argued for the immutability of the Jewish condition and, thus, for their inadmissability into French society. Even ardent proponents of Jewish emancipation, like the Jacobin priest Abbé Grégoire, hoped that the dissolution of societal obstacles to Jewish integration would pave the way to total Jewish self-annihilation: conversion to Christianity, in other words.[43]

---

[42] The classic analysis of the inexorability of the political emancipation of the Jews during the French Revolution is in Salo Baron, "Ghetto and Emancipation," *The Menorah Journal* 14 (June 1928): 515–26. See, too, Zosa Szajkowski, *Jews and the French Revolutions of 1789, 1830 and 1848* (New York: KTAV, 1970); Frances Malino, *The Sephardic Jews of Bordeaux: Assimilation and Emancipation in Revolutionary and Napoleonic France* (Tuscaloosa, Ala.: University of Alabama Press, 1978); Paula E. Hyman, *The Emancipation of the Jews of Alsace: Acculturation and Tradition in the Nineteenth Century* (New Haven, Conn.: Yale University Press, 1991).

[43] Abbé Grégoire's complex posture toward the regeneration of the Jews, non-whites, and women as a condition of their inclusion into French society has recently been explored by Alyssa Goldstein Sepinwall, "Regenerating France, Regenerating the World: the Abbé Grégoire and the French Revolution, 1750–1831" (Ph.D. diss., Stanford University, 1998). See, too, Arthur Hertzberg, *The French Enlightenment and the Jews* (New York: Columbia University Press, 1968) and Pierre Birnbaum, "Between Social and Political Assimilation: Remarks on the History of Jews in France," in *Paths of Emancipation: Jews, States, and Citizenship* (ed. Pierre Birnbaum and Ira Katznelson; Princeton, N.J.: Princeton University Press, 1995), 94–127.

The Polish debates over inclusion of the Jews into Polish society, which took place during the Great *Sejm* simultaneously with the discussions underway in the French National Assembly, did not result in the emancipation of the Jews. The term "emancipation," which has come to mean "political emancipation," the extension of full political rights to the Jews as individuals, was not on the agenda of Poland's reformers at the end of the eighteenth century for the reason that Poland, like Imperial Austria and Imperial Russia — the societies in which most of the world's Jews in the eighteenth century actually lived — were not engaged in nation-state building, which required the total dissolution of medieval corporate bodies, religious, legal and economic. Moreover, the revolution in human consciousness in which human "rights" were considered "self-evident" because of the separation of society into a civil/public realm and a confessional/private realm protected by a "neutral" state apparatus and encoded in law, had not occurred.[44] The social organization of Polish society, its tenaciously feudal socio-economic structure, the reluctance of its noble class either to cede any of its power to the crown or to the other estates or to cultivate a native burgher class, and the unique relationship between the magnate class and the Jewish population thus defined and delimited the parameters of the Enlightenment proposals offered by enlightened Poles and Jews alike at the Four-Year *Sejm*. It is, therefore, far more accurate to speak of "inclusion" of the Jews, and not their "emancipation," in the Polish context.[45]

The triumph of the Opposition Party, dominated by the nobility, led to the municipalities' demand for political participation in the life of the Republic. The degenerate state of Poland's towns was inextricably linked to *szlachta* desire for complete control of and hostility to urban life. But no discussion of reform could proceed without recognition of the claims of the urban classes and of the municipalities themselves. Because at least two-thirds of the Republic's town dwellers were Jews, any discussion of the extension of

---

[44]   See Lynn Hunt, ed. and trans., *The French Revolution and Human Rights: A Brief Documentary History* (Boston: Bedford, 1996). As Lois Dubin writes about the Habsburg context: "But in contrast to the emancipation proferred French Jews in 1790–91, the Habsburg process was partial and incremental: the enlightened absolutist state never struck the eventual bargain of emancipation — full integration and citizenship in exchange for relinquishment of communal autonomy — with its Jewish subjects. It was anticorporatist, but again, only to a degree. . . . Its own state-building was not sufficiently extensive or thoroughgoing to do away with corporate bodies; at most it succeeded in coopting and weakening them." Dubin, *The Port Jews of Habsburg Trieste*, 195.

[45]   Pierre Birnbaum and Ira Katznelson have argued, persuasively, that the French model of emancipation be seen as exceptional, not normative or prescriptive, for the eighteenth century. See Pierre Birnbaum and Ira Katznelson, "Emancipation and the Liberal Offer," in *Paths of Emancipation: Jews, States, and Citizenship* (ed. Pierre Birnbaum and Ira Katznelson; Princeton, N.J.: Princeton University Press, 1995), 4.

political rights to the burgher estate could not but provoke a debate regarding the Jews, their place (or lack thereof) in the estate system, and their inner reform.[46] It is not surprising, therefore, that discussion of the Jewish question emerged with the opening of the Four-Year *Sejm* on October 6, 1788.

The debates at the Four-Year *Sejm* regarding the Jewish question were conducted in the context of a European-wide discussion about Jewish emancipation, both civic and political. Civic emancipation, in contrast to political emancipation, meant the abolition of the innumerable laws discriminating against the Jews while retaining the latter's formal corporate separateness. Reformers and conservatives alike were well aware of the Prussian Jewry Ordinance (April 17, 1750) and the Austrian *Toleranzpatent* (January 2, 1782). Christian Wilhelm Dohm's influential pamphlet, *Über die bürgerliche Verbesserung der Juden*, the very title of which implied that the condition of Jewish life needed improvement, appeared in a Polish adaptation in Warsaw in 1783.[47] As well, members of the Polish intelligentsia, and some Jewish petitioners, knew of the debates raging in France.[48] Between November 1788 and January 1790, at least fifteen pamphlets, of which thirteen were published, were written dealing with the Jewish question.

In Poland, discussion over reform of the Jews took place in the midst of rising tensions between Christian burghers and their Jewish competitors in Poland's royal towns. The 1768 *Sejm*'s decision to restrict Jewish privileges and rights to earn a living through trade had led to mass Jewish migrations from Lublin, Vilna, Warsaw, Cracow, Poseń, Przemyśl, Opatów, Torn, and Bidgość. Although the animosity between burghers and Jews was not new, it escalated after the 1768 *Sejm*. In Warsaw, these tensions culminated in a riot in May 1790, which brought to the fore one of the pronounced triangles of economic hostility in the Commonwealth: noble-Jews-townspeople.[49] Initially

---

[46]   Daniel Stone, "Jews and the Urban Question in Late Eighteenth Century Poland," *Slavic Review* 50, no. 3 (Autumn 1991): 531–41.

[47]   The press in Warsaw displayed interest in the debates over the civic emancipation of the Jews in Prussia and Austria and Dohm's pamphlet appeared in Polish translation in 1783 as *Pamiętnik historyczno-polityczny*, edited by Piotr Switkowski. Besides summarizing Dohm, Switkowski advocated military conscription for the Jews. See Eisenbach, *The Emancipation of the Jews in Poland*, 53 and Alexander Guterman, "The Suggestions of Polish Jews toward the Reforms of Their Legal, Economic, Social and Cultural Status in the Period of the Great Sejm (1788–1792)" (M.A. thesis, The Hebrew University of Jerusalem, 1975), 22–23.

[48]   The degree of interest in France among Polish reformers, both Gentile and Jewish, is disputed among scholars. Eisenbach, Cygielman, and Etkes all deemphasize the knowledge of the French debates in the Warsaw press, while Israel Bartal and Guterman point to connections between the French and Polish discussions of Jewish reform. For a full discussion, see Bartal, "'The Second Model': France as a Source of Influence."

[49]   On the riot, see Shmuel Cygielman, "Regarding the Suggestions of Mateusz Butrymowicz, a Representative of the Great *Sejm*, for the Reform of the Jewish Community of Poland

focused on the issue of membership in the municipality, the Four-Year *Sejm*
debates grew to encompass discussion of Jewish attire, taxation, lease holding
on breweries and taverns, and communal autonomy.[50] Although many of the
proposals written by Christian Poles for the *Sejm* about the reform of Jewish
communal life shared the generic Enlightenment assumption that inclusion
of the Jews in the body politic was contingent on the quid pro quo of their
inner transformation into "useful" citizens, there was no consensus of
opinion about how to effect this transformation.

   Andrzej Zamoyski, a conservative nobleman, brought a petition to the
Sejm in 1788 about the burghers and peasants that touched on the Jewish
question. Seeking to limit Jewish and Polish contact and to reduce economic
competition between Poles and Jews, Zamoyski felt that the right of residence for Jews in Polish cities should be curtailed. The Jews, he argued,
should be forbidden to employ Christian domestics and any individual Jew
who could not show that he was either a tradesman with property valued at at
least 1,000 zlotys or an *arendar* (leesee), artisan, or farmer should leave
Poland. His proposals garnered the support of the conservative clergy, but
were rejected by the *Sejm*.[51] Other conservative voices in the *Sejm* vigorously
defended the feudal system and noble prerogative and either ignored or
anathemetized the Jews.[52] On the opposite end of the spectrum, Father
Stanisław Staszic, an important Enlightenment ideologue who was critical of
noble republicanism and a champion of the burgher estate, advocated in his
Warnings for Poland that Jews be subjected to the general law of the municipalities. His conclusions regarding the civic integration of the Jews,
however, were predicated on a virulent anti-Semitic view of Jewish economic
behavior. Ignoring the nobility's involvement in distillery and brewing,
Staszic offered an alarmist argument to the effect that peasant drunkenness

---

and Lithuania at the End of the 1780s and R. Hershel Józefowicz of Chełm's Response," in
Bein yisra'el la'amim: sefer mugash leShmuel Ettinger (ed. Shmuel Almog; Jerusalem: Zalman
Shazar Center, 1987), 92–93 and Krystyna Zienkowska, "'The Jews have killed a Tailor:' The
Socio-political Background of a Pogrom in Warsaw in 1790," *Polin* 3 (1988): 78–102. An
earlier conflict in Warsaw erupted between Jewish and Christian burghers in 1775 when the
former, given permission by August Sulkowski, Marshal of the Permanent Council, established a settlement ("New Jerusalem") on the outskirts of the city. Another marshal, Lubo-
mirski, ordered the razing of the settlement which, he argued, was in violation of the
sixteenth-century statute prohibiting Jewish settlement in Warsaw. See Stone, *Polish Politics
and National Reform, 1775–1788*, 18.
50   Prior to 1768, Jews, Protestants and Greek Catholics (Uniates) were excluded from
municipal membership, although the Jewish kahal functioned as a parallel, second
municipality to the Christian one.
51   Guterman, "The Suggestions of Polish Jews toward the Reforms," 22 and S. M. Dubnow,
History of the Jews in Russia and Poland (Philadelphia: The Jewish Publication Society of
America, 1916), 271, 281–82.
52   Eisenbach, *The Emancipation of the Jews in Poland*, 76.

was due entirely to Jewish dominance of the liquor trade, referring to the Jews as "locusts."[53]

Hugo Kołłątaj (1750–1812), an advocate of the burgher movement and active exponent of the standardization and rationalization of national life in Poland, wrote, in his *Anonymous Letters*, "O nation! If merciful Providence permits you to stand on the threshold of true liberty . . . be bold to write one code for all men and one legal procedure for all provinces."[54] He displayed a tolerant attitude toward the Jews, arguing in *Political Right of the Polish Nation* that "the human rights of Jews are to be respected no less than the rights of any other human beings."[55] Kołłątaj was particularly sensitive to the anomalies of Jewish economic life in Poland (the perennial competition with the burghers and the Jews' unenviable role of middlemen between the peasants and the nobility) that fueled anti-Jewish resentment. It was Kołłątaj, then Vice Chancellor of the *Sejm*, who intervened on behalf of the Jews during the May riot and expressed to Stanisław Małachowski, the speaker of the *Sejm*, that the perpetually seething tension between Jews and Poles would erupt if reforms were not promulgated. Yet, despite Kołłątaj's open-minded attitude toward expanding the civil rights of the Jews, his commitment to the French model of integration meant that he favored abolition of the kahal and the compulsory prohibition of traditional Jewish garb as the means to further the rapprochement between Jews and Poles.[56]

In 1789, Mateusz Butrymowicz reissued, in revised form, an anonymous 1785 pamphlet (*The Jews, or the Urgent Necessity of a Reform amongst the Jews in the Lands of the Republic*), now entitled *How to Turn Polish Jews into Citizens Useful for the Country*, which did not go as far as Kołłątaj's suggestions for incorporation of the Jews into the burgher estate. Butrymowicz advocated a change in the legal and residential status of the Jews, arguing for their inclusion into a "state citizenship," but he remained unprepared to support the abolition of the feudal structure. His pamphlet discussed the "condition" of the Jews, implying their potential for change if the social forces of their oppression were relieved. He advocated Polonization of the Jews through the abolition of the kahal, abandonment of Yiddish, prohibition of the importation of Hebrew books and of Jewish traditional dress, and "productivization" through the redirection of Jewish economic activity away from trade and commerce toward handicrafts and agriculture. Recognizing the Jews'

---

53 On Staszic's political thought, see Walicki, *The Enlightenment and the Birth of Modern Nationhood*, 38–62. See, too, Jacob Goldberg, "The Changes in the Attitude of Polish Society toward the Jews in the Eighteenth Century," *Polin* 1 (1986): 41.
54 Cited in Walicki, *The Enlightenment and the Birth of Modern Nationhood*, 72.
55 Cited in Goldberg, "The Changes in the Attitude of Polish Society," 44.
56 Eisenbach, *The Emancipation of the Jews in Poland*, 74–75.

human rights, Butrymowicz argued against the state's interference in Jewish religious life, but implicitly called for the transformation of Judaism, with its cultural-national foundations, into a "confession." Thus, despite his good intentions, Butrymowicz, too, felt that an almost complete vitiation of Jewish cultural and religious distinctiveness had to precede integration into Polish life.[57]

There was an occasional voice among the debators, like that of Józef Pawlikowski, which articulated the position of preserving Jewish culture with integration into the life of the state. Pawlikowski argued, "We have agreed to be tolerant of their religion. By what logic, then, shall we now interfere with it, with its holidays, with its fasts? Why should we be towards them like the Spaniards of old?[58] Let us not force them to change their garb! Let us instead act towards them so as to make them feel not aggrieved but happy with being Poles."[59] Pawlikowski's position was singular also in that he blamed the impoverishment of the towns on peasant misery, rather than on Jewish exploitation, and focused on the nobility's role in the subjugation of the serfs.[60] On the whole, however, the main current of Polish discussion regarding reform of the Jews called for a state-initiated limitation of Jewish communal autonomy and culture, an effort which could not but be perceived by the majority of Poland's Jews as a threat to the very existence of Jewish life.

Although the issue of how to reform Jewish life had been raised as early as 1775, it was the 1790 Warsaw riot mentioned above that forced the question of the Jews onto the agenda of the Great *Sejm*. On May 19, 1790, Jacek Jezierski (1722–1805), Castellan of Łuków, suggested that a "Commission for Jewish Reform" be appointed. The Commission was composed of three Senators and six members of the *Sejm*, including Kołłątaj and Tadeusz Czacki (1765–1813), a liberal reformer who recognized the civic rights of the Jews.[61] Kehillah representatives, as well as enlightened Jews like Lefin, had been

---

[57] Cygielman, "Regarding the Suggestions of Mateusz Butrymowicz," 90–91; Eisenbach, *The Emancipation of the Jews in Poland*, 77; Dubnow, *History of the Jews in Russia and Poland*, 279–81.

[58] Pawlikowski was referring to fifteenth-century Spain, which "offered" the Jews a choice between conversion or death as a means to "integrate" them into Spanish society.

[59] Cited in Goldberg, "The Changes in the Attitude of Polish Society," 42.

[60] Eisenbach, *The Emancipation of the Jews in Poland*, 79.

[61] On Czacki's attitudes toward the Jews, see Adam Żółtowski, *Border of Europe: A Study of the Polish Eastern Provinces* (London: Hollis & Carter, 1950): 80 and Israel Halpern, "The Partition of Poland in Krochmal's Historical Thought," in *Yehudim veyahadut bemizraḥ eiropah: meḥqarim betoldoteihem* (Jerusalem: Magnes Press, 1963), 405–07. His writings and person were known to *maskilim*, who viewed him as sympathetic to their struggles for civic recognition. See, for example, Isaac Baer Levinsohn, *Te'udah beyisra'el* (ed. Immanuel Etkes; Vilna, 1828), 9.

involved from the beginning with the *Sejm* debates on the relationship of the Jews to the burgher estate, the right of Jewish domicile in Polish cities and the level of Jewish taxes. The Commission itself felt obligated to pay attention to current Jewish opinion and eleven Jews, Dr. Eliasz Ackord, Dr. Jacques Calmanson, Zalkind Hourwitz (via a Polish adaptation of his French *Apologie*), Dr. Solomon Polonus, Dr. Moshe Markuse, Mendel Lefin, Avraham Hirszowicz, Pesach Haymowicz, Shimon Wolfowicz, Joshua Herszel ben Joseph (Józefowicz), and Zevi Hirsch ben Shaul (Shaulowicz), presented petitions to the Commission. Lefin's participation was assured by his relationship to Prince Adam Czartoryski.[62]

The petitioners, ten of whom were born within the boundaries of the Commonwealth (Solomon Polonus was born in Amsterdam, the son of a Jew from Vilna) represented the intelligentsia of Polish Jewry: four doctors, one factor, two literary men (Lefin the fortunate one with a noble benefactor, Hourwitz living impoverished in Paris), one royal administrator, one syndic (royal representative) in the Warsaw Jewish kahal, and two rabbis.[63] As in France, the eleven petitions ranged in opinion among those which championed the full, unlimited integration of the Jews into Polish society, those which urged the civic emancipation of the Jews, but resisted the complete dissolution of Jewish communal autonomy, and those which rejected any reform of Jewish life whatsoever.[64]

Little is known about Ackord, except that, born in Mohylew, he made his way to Berlin, where he earned a degree in medicine in 1783. He must have had contact with Mendelssohn and the *maskilim* in Prussia for the former helped to get Ackord appointed to the Berlin academy. He then came to Warsaw, where he worked as a women's doctor, and then translated the anonymous pamphlet employed by Butrymowicz into German, dedicating it to the king. The pamphlet regarded the condition of the Jews sociologically, not unlike Dohm's treatise, positing that hostile Gentile legislation had played the decisive role in shaping the condition of the Jews. Their reform, therefore, was predicated on being included in the burgher estate. The pamphlet, however, did not call for the abolition of the feudal system.

---

[62] N. M. Gelber, "Mendel Lefin of Satanów's Proposals for the Improvement of Jewish Community Life presented to the Great *Sejm* (1788–1792)," in *The Abraham Weiss Jubilee Volume* (ed. Samuel Belkin; New York: Shulsinger Brothers, 1964), 275.
[63] On the category of "maskilic physician," a Jewish doctor who, indebted to Enlightenment categories and analysis of the condition of the Jews, advocated their reform, focusing specifically on the connection between the physical regeneration of their "diseased" condition and their improved social, civil, and political status, see John Efron, *Medicine and the German Jews: A History* (New Haven, Conn.: Yale University Press, 2001): 64–104.
[64] The discussion below is indebted to Guterman, "The Suggestions of Polish Jews toward the Reforms."

Ackord's decision to translate the pamphlet into German suggests that his audience was not Poland or its reformers, but Western Europeans. Born in Chrobishów, near Zamość, Jacques Calmanson studied in France, Germany, Turkey, and Russia, and trained as a doctor. He returned to Poland and settled in Warsaw, where he cultivated contacts with both royal and noble circles. At the end of his life he was a freemason. In 1784, Calmanson wrote a pamphlet to the king regarding taxes that the Jews were allegedly hiding from the royal court and then in 1791 translated a Hebrew text into Polish, which invited the representatives of the kehillot (Jewish communities) to come to Warsaw to meet with the king with the implicit suggestion that the Jews could help pay off the royal debt. Given Castalan Scypion Piattoli's intense negotiations to relieve the king of his debt through an annual tribute paid by the Jewish communities that, in turn, would be granted a form of emancipation into Polish society, it is reasonable to assume that Calmanson and Piattoli were in contact with one another.[65] Calmanson also had ties to the Czartoryskis, perhaps through masonic circles. In 1786, when Warsaw was under Prussian rule, he published his *Essai sur l'état actual des Juifs de Pologne et leur perfectibilité* and dedicated it to Hoym, the adminstrator of Prussian Poland. Later, Calmanson translated the pamphlet into Polish and dedicated to Tsar Alexander I, who, in gratitude, sent Calmanson a gift of cigarettes through the mediation of Adam Jerzy Czartoryski.[66] The pamphlet is notable for Calmanson's description of Hasidism, which he saw as an obstacle to the transformation of the Jewish community: "This sect in Poland was not known at all twenty years ago. It originated in Międzybóz in Podolia and its founder was an enthusiastic rabbi who exploited the ignorance of the people, who are in love with miracles. It therefore dawned on him to pretend to be a prophet."[67]

Zalkind Hourwitz, the Jewish co-winner of the famous Metz Essay Contest of 1785 in which contestants were asked to respond to the question, "Are there means of rendering the Jews more useful and more happy in France?" did not petition the Polish *Sejm* directly. His essay, *Apologie des Juifs en réponse à la question: est-il des moyens de rendre les Juifs plus heureux et plus utiles en France?*, penned in 1787, appeared in Poland in Polish translation in December 1789, only ten months after it was published in France. Born outside

---

[65] N. M. Gelber, "Ksiądz Piattoli a Sprawa Żydowska na Sejmie Wielkim," *Nowe Życie* 1, no. 6 (Grudzień 1924): 321–33.

[66] Eisenbach believes the translation was done by J. Czechowicz, as *Uwagi nad stanem niniejszym Żydów polskich i ich wydoskonaleniem* (*Remarks on the Present Condition of the Polish Jews and on their Perfectibility*, Warsaw, 1797). See Eisenbach, *The Emancipation of the Jews in Poland*, 533, footnote 172.

[67] Cited in Guterman, "The Suggestions of Polish Jews toward the Reforms," 38. See, too, Shimon Dubnow, *Toldot haḥasidut* (Tel Aviv: Devir, 1930), 2:218–19.

Lublin in 1751, Hourwitz, like other self-conscious modernizing Polish Jews, had made his way to Berlin, where he was a tutor. In 1774, he travelled to Metz and then settled in Paris.[68] Hourwitz's French pamphlet was notable for its uncompromising demand that Jews be granted equal rights, without any appeals for retention of corporate status and rabbinic prerogative. He rejected outright the quid pro quo so prominent in debates over Jewish rights, rejecting any calls for the inner transformation of the Jews as a prerequisite for their inclusion in the nation-state. The Polish rendition of the *Apologie* differed from the original, which was strongly anti-clerical in tone. Despite its criticism of the rabbinate, the Polish version defended the Talmud.

Little biographical information exists about Avraham Hirszowicz. His memo, entitled *Projekt do reformy i poprawy obyczajów starozakonnych mieszkanców Królestwa polskiego* (*Project for the reform and improvement of the customs of the Jewish ["Old Testament"] residents of the Kingdom of Poland*), directly appealed to the king, urging a top-down approach toward the reform of the Jews. His suggestions pointed to Jewish economic behavior as the primary cause of the Jews' condition and encouraged the king to make the Jews useful to the state by forbidding early marriages, redirecting them away from commerce and trade and toward agriculture, enacting sumptuary laws, and using royal funds to create employment.

Pesach Haymowicz, too, was close to the royal court, and his suggestions for the reform of the Jews reflect his position. From Opatów, Haymowicz arrived in Warsaw in 1754, where he was appointed as a syndic — there were five in Warsaw until the end of the Republic — of the Jews. His responsibilities included raising taxes, ajudicating cases in the royal court, and monitoring Jewish employment and residence in the city, in short, keeping an eye on the Jewish community for the king. Eventually, Haymowicz was removed from his position, but wrote his petition, *Project for the organization of Jewish courts, to Mysłkowski, the burgrave of the city of Płock, according to suggestions offered by a man of the Old Testament, Pesach Haymowicz, the former syndic of the Jews of Warsaw*, in the spirit of one still in the king's inner circle. Its primary aim was to reduce Poniatowski's debt, and Haymowicz was undoubtedly cultivated by Piattoli for that purpose.

Shimon Wolfowicz, born in 1755 to a wealthy Jewish family in Vilna, was educated in Polish law. By 1785, when a new rabbi was to be appointed to the Vilna kahal, Wolfowicz emerged as one of the chief opponents of the candidate, Shmuel ben Avigdor, and of the kahal. A social conflict within the Vilna community raged for almost thirty years, known as *Maḥloqet harav* (*The*

---

68 Frances Malino, "The Right to be Different: Zalkind Hourwitz and the Revolution of 1789," in *From East and West: Jews in a Changing Europe, 1750–1870* (ed. Frances Malino and David Sorkin; London: Basil Blackwell, 1990), 86.

Dispute over the Rabbi). Wolfowicz contended that the kahal leadership was insensitive to the plight of poorer members of the community and that the kahal's extensive debt was particularly burdensome to the lower social classes. The conflict escalated, involving the *woyewoda* (the *palatine* of a province with responsibility over its Jewish communities) of Vilna, the magnate Karol Radziwiłł, and in 1786 Wolfowicz was arrested and imprisoned. Shmuel ben Avigdor became the rabbi of Vilna. While in prison (on Radziwiłł lands), Wolfowicz wrote *Więzień w Nieświeżu do Stanów Sejmujących o potrzebie reformy Żydów (A Prisoner in Nieśwież to the present Sejm regarding the need to reform the Jews*, 1789–90). The pamphlet was dominated by Wolfowicz's conviction that the kahal was incompatible with modernization and reform. He urged its dissolution and the separation of Church and State. Upon Wolfowicz's release from prison, Shmuel ben Avigdor was then ordered by Radziwiłł to resign his position, illustrating Wolfowicz's influence on the magnate.

Joshua Herszel ben Joseph (Józefowicz), the rabbi of Chełm, responded directly to Butrymowicz's reissuing of the anonymous pamphlet in February 1789 with *Myśli stosowane do sposobu informowania Żydów polskich w pożtecznych Krajowi obywateli (Thoughts regarding the means of reform of the Jews of Poland into useful citizens of the state)*, whose title echoed Butrymowicz's, as did its content. Józefowicz's work challenged all of Butrymowicz's assumptions about the alleged debased condition of the Jews, rejecting the Polish reformer's contention that the Jews *as they were* were harmful to the state.[69] With regard to Jewish economic activity, Józefowicz illustrated how contemporary Jewish economic activity was both productive and varied, and repudiated the claim that Jewish religious behavior — particularly Sabbath and holiday rest — led to idleness. The Polish nobility, not the Jews, were responsible for the oppression of the peasantry. Defending the Jews against charges of misanthropy, a common canard directed at the Talmud, he argued that Jewish law encouraged morality and discipline and was compatible with a Christian state. Józefowicz defended distinctive Jewish dress, although he conceded that there was no Torah law that commanded a particular Jewish costume. He cavilled against the prohibition on importation of foreign Jewish books into Polish territory on the grounds that they encouraged broader cultural and economic horizons, beneficial to all. Józefowicz accused Butrymowicz of blaming the entire Jewish community for the faults of individuals and, finally, expressed his view that any reform of Jewish religion would assault the basis of Judaism. Józefowicz's pamphlet was a full defense of traditional Polish-Jewish life and a rejection of the assumption that a change in Jewish civil status has to be anteceded by a reform of Judaism and of the Jews

---

69 See Cygielman, "Regarding the Suggestions of Mateusz Butrymowicz."

themselves. He continued to advocate on behalf of his traditionalist position even after the Declaration of the Constitution of May 3, 1791, urging the king to see that the Constitution placed the Jews at the mercy of the burgher class, who despised them. This appeal underscores Józefowicz's traditional political posture; the rabbi preferred an alliance with the king that preserved Jewish communal autonomy to changes that may have afforded Jews individual freedoms, but left them without either royal or noble protection.

Zevi Hirsch ben Shaul (Shaulowicz) came from a family with connections to the Polish royal family. His grandfather, Meir Margoliot, the head of the rabbinical court of Ostróg (Ostraha), was selected by the king as the chief rabbi of Ukraine and Podolia in 1777.[70] Meir's son, Shaul, then head of the rabbinical academy in Zbaraż, inherited the position, and went on to become the rabbinical authority in Komarno and Lublin.[71] His son, Zevi Hirsch ben Shaul, made a traditional appeal to Poniatowski on September 13, 1791 that he not promulgate any new legislation regarding the Jews without consulting the rabbinic leadership. He also assured the king that the Jewish community, in exchange for preservation of their communal autonomy, was not reluctant to offer him financial assistance. Zevi Hirsch's "Thanks to Stanisław August on January 17, 1792 (the king's nameday)," penned in Hebrew, but which appeared in Polish translation, echoed the long-standing political posture of the traditional rabbinate: the Jews preferred feudal Polish rule to the unknown, be it Austrian, Prussian, or Russian rule.[72]

Solomon Polonus, born in Amsterdam to a Polish-Jewish family, was trained as a doctor, and belongs, like Hourwitz, Markuse and Lefin, to a group of modernized Polish Jews who were well aware of the French debates over emancipation. Polonus himself translated several documents from French into Polish between August 3, 1789 and October 21, 1791, intending them for publication. He wrote *Projekt względem reformy Żydów* (*Project regarding the reform of the Jews*) defending the "usefulness" of Polish Jewry. His pamphlet urged religious tolerance that would allow the Jews to practice Judaism freely, and argued that the bestowal of civil rights upon the Jews, including the end to all residential restrictions and the right to purchase land, would be beneficial to the state. His proposal also recognized the oligarchical structure of the contemporary kahal and suggested that future elections

[70] Menahem Nahum Litinski, *Sefer qorot Podolyah veqadmoniyyut hayehudim sham* (Odessa: A. Belinson, 1895), 65–66.

[71] D. Dombrovska, Abraham Wein, and Aharon Vais, eds., *Pinqas haqehillot. Polin: entsiqlopedyah shel hayishuvim hayehudiyyim lemin hivasdam ve'ad le'ahar sho'at milḥemet ha'olam hasheniyyah, Galitsyah hamizraḥit* (Jerusalem: Yad Va-Shem, 1980), 199. On the Margoliot family, see Meir Wunder, *Entsiqlopedyah lehakhmei Galitsyah* (Jerusalem: Institute for Commemoration of Galician Jewry, 1986), 3:904–49.

[72] Eisenbach, *The Emancipation of the Jews in Poland*, 122.

should be predicated on education; only Polish-speaking Jews should be enfranchised. The reformed rabbinate and kahal should be supervised by the King's minister of police, a position equivalent to a minister of the interior. On the hotly contested issue of military conscription, Polonus came down firmly on the side of the quid pro quo: five years of military service should be sufficient to guarantee the full receipt of civic rights. Polonus's proposal reflected his wish for full civic emancipation of the Jews within the confines of the feudal Polish republic with the king still at the head. He continued to hold this position during Poland's last days, supporting the Kościuszko rebellion and criticizing the Russians in a speech he gave in a Vilna synagogue on May 17, 1794.

Moses Markuse, born in Słonim in the northeast of Poland in 1743, began his medical studies in Berlin, with the famed Marcus Herz, and then moved to Königsberg in 1766, where he married. He returned to Poland in 1774. There he was a physician to the King and to some members of the Crown Treasury Commission between 1782–1790. During the Four-Year *Sejm*, Markuse penned his *Seyfer refues haniqra 'Ezer yisroel'* (*The Book of Remedies that is called 'The Help of Israel'*), the first modern Yiddish book written explicitly for East European Jews. Its subtitle, "for the classrooms in the country of Poland (*lehadarim bemedinas folin*)," designated its audience. A free adaptation of the Swiss physician Samuel-August Tissot's *Avis au Peuple sur sa Santé* (Paris, 1761), *Seyfer refues* was published in 1790 with the assistance of Michał Bobrowski, a Polish nobleman.[73] Markuse's book, although devoted to the dissemination of popular medicine and to a campaign against medical quackery, was also preoccupied with Jewish economic life, whose concentration in petty trade he blamed on traditional Jewish education, which kept children indoors and valorized study over physical labor. Reform of Jewish education could remedy the Jews' idleness and lack of productivity. Markuse also attacked the reliance of traditional Polish Jewry on medical charlatans, the *ba'alei shem* (amulet makers) that traversed the Polish countryside. Unlike Calmanson, however, Markuse's critique of *ba'alei shem* was not directed at Hasidism as such, but derived from his ambition to professionalize the state of Jewish medicine, much as had Tissot in his original work.[74] The

---

[73] Biographical information on Markuse can be found in Chone Shmeruk, "Moses Markuse from Słonim and the Source of His Book, *Ezer yisroel*," in *Sifrut yidish befolin: mehqarim ve'iyyunim historiyyim* (Jerusalem: Magnes Press, 1981), 185–202 and Chone Shmeruk, "Moses Markuse and his Book, *Ezer yisroel*," in *Sifrut yidish: peraqim letoldoteihah* (Tel Aviv: The Porter Institute for Poetics & Semiotics, 1978), 187–97. The Polish translation of Tissot's *Avis* was published in Warsaw in 1774 and then again in 1785. See, too, Antoinette Emch-Dériaz, *Tissot: Physician of the Enlightenment* (American University Series; New York: Peter Lang, 1992).

[74] Markuse directed his wrath most hysterically toward midwives, not toward *ba'alei shem*.

significance of *Seyfer refues* lies less in its direct effect on the debates over Jewish status in the *Sejm* than as testimony to the influence of general Enlightenment ideas on Jewish exponents of reform during the Commonwealth's last days. Bobrowski's financial support of Markuse also attests to the dependence *maskilim* had upon the patronage of reform-oriented Poles.

Mendel Lefin wrote a variety of works, both published and unpublished, which bear on the civic reform of the Jews and the Jewish community: *Essai d'un plan de réforme ayant pour objet d'éclairer la Nation Juive en Pologne et de redresser par là ses moeurs* (*Essay of a Reform Plan Whose Object is the Enlightenment and Redress of the Morals of the Jews of Poland*),[75] *Liqqutei kelalim* (*Selections of Rules*),[76] "*Teshuvah*" (*Responsum*),[77] and *Entwurf eines Rabinersystems in den Gutern Ihrer Durchlaucht des Fursten Adam Czartoryski, General von Podolien* (*Outline of a Rabbinic System in the Estates of Your Highness, Prince Adam Czartoryski, Prince of Podolia*).[78] Linguistically diverse (French, Hebrew, German), all of the materials are informed by Lefin's relationship to the Czartoryskis.[79]

The prince's interest in Lefin as a Jew should be understood as a consequence of the dense Jewish settlement in the southeastern Polish border-

---

On his quest to professionalize the practice of medicine in Poland, see Efron, *Medicine and the German Jews*, 77–92.

[75] [Mendel Lefin], "*Essai d'un plan de réforme ayant pour objet d'éclairer la Nation Juive en Pologne et de redresser par là ses moeurs*," in *Materiały do dziejów Sejmu Czteroletniego* (ed. Arthur Eisenbach et al.; Wrocław: Instytut Historii Polskiej Akademii Nauk, 1969), 409–21.

[76] In 1964, Gelber published *Liqqutei kelalim*, Mendel Lefin's Hebrew text reflecting on the deliberations at the Polish *Sejm*, as an appendix to his article on Lefin's reform proposals for the Great *Sejm*. Lefin apparently did not finish the work. Only one chapter with sixty-nine sections (sections six and sixty-five are missing) is extant in manuscript. See Appendix 2 in N. M. Gelber, "Mendel Lefin of Satanów's Proposals for the Improvement of Jewish Community Life presented to the Great *Sejm* (1788–1792)," in *The Abraham Weiss Jubilee Volume* (ed. Samuel Belkin; New York: Shulsinger Brothers, 1964), 271–301. All subsequent references to *Liqqutei kelalim* will be marked by the author's name and the page number of the appendix on which the citation appears.

[77] The Joseph Perl Archive, JNULA, 4° 1153/72.

[78] Mss. 2253, the Czartoryski Family Archive and Library, Cracow, Poland. It is dated Sieniawa, April 4, 1794, and prefaced by the Polish phrase, "*Myśli Mendla względem ustanowienia Rabinów*" ("Mendel's Thoughts regarding the Rabbinate").

[79] Lefin, encouraged by Moses Mendelssohn, also embarked on a translation of Tissot's work. In the 1780s, he began a Hebrew translation, excerpts of which first appeared in *Moda levinah* (*Insight to Understanding*, Berlin, 1789), but the full rendition, entitled *Sefer refu'at ha'am* (*The Book of Popular Healing*), was only published in Żółkiew in 1794, four years after Markuse's Yiddish version saw the light of day. Unable to secure enough pre-subscribers for the publication of *Sefer refu'at ha'am* in the 1780s, it was only Czartoryski's later financial support that made the book's completion possible. See Shmeruk, "Moses Markuse from Słonim," 192. Czartoryski's interest in Tissot is attested in the fact that his physician, a Dr. Wolff, recommended the Swiss doctor to King Poniatowski, who invited him to Poland to become his personal physician. Tissot declined the offer. See Emch-Dériaz, *Tissot*, 100.

lands. Central to the colonization efforts of the Polish nobility from the mid-sixteenth century onward, more than 30,000 Jews lived on Czartoryski holdings by 1765, playing an essential role in the *latifundia* economy.[80] Any change in Poland's political and economic structure would have an enormous impact on this large "estate," as well as for magnates like the Czartoryskis, who were economically dependent upon the middle-class acumen of Jews living on their holdings. Adam Kazimierz Czartoryski's involvement with Lefin thus underscores the tie between the Polish magnate class and "its" Jews on the eve of the Commonwealth's last chance for internal reform.

Czartoryski's relationship with Lefin gave him direct access to the Jewish community, whose opinions he was interested in hearing as he formulated reform plans for Poland. He endeavored to cultivate other enlightened Jews besides Lefin, although the latter was his most successful and consistent Jewish protégé. On April 23, 1800, Heinrich Gotfried Bertschneider, the librarian of the University of Lwów (Lemberg), wrote to Friedrich Nikolai in Berlin at Czartoryski's request. The prince, wrote Bertshneider, "inquires after Solomon Maimon, whose autobiography was published by [Karl Phillip] Moritz. I believe the Prince has philanthropic intentions regarding this man. If you, yourself, were willing to write to the Prince through me, he would be very satisfied to correspond with you at this opportunity."[81] Czartoryski may also have been the silent voice behind the Enlightenment efforts of Dr. Eliasz Ackord.[82] Moreover, Czartoryski's interest in the Jews extended to curiosity about the amuletic and alchemic practices of contemporary Jewish mystics. When in London in 1772, Adam Kazimierz Czartoryski met with Samuel Falk, the Ba'al Shem of London — as had the recently deposed King of Corsica — perhaps seeking aid for Poland after the first partition.[83]

Finally, Czartoryski's devoted patronage of Mendel Lefin was a product of the prince's active cultivation of a group of unknown European writers and

[80] Rosman, *The Lords' Jews*, 214.

[81] The letter to Nikolai is cited in Raphael Mahler, *Divrei yemei yisra'el* (Rchavia: Worker's Library, 1956), 1:72.

[82] Czartoryski's connection to Ackord is speculative, but suggestive. Recounting the prince's fortuitous meeting with Lefin in Mikołajów, A. B. Gottlober mentioned a Dr. Akelschmidt who accompanied Czartoryski on his tour of the Jewish communities in his lands. But, Jacob Shatzky argued that there was no doctor by that name in Poland at the time and that Gottlober, notoriously sloppy with names and times, confused the name of Akelschmidt with that of Eliasz Ackord. See Jacob Shatzky, "Recensions: Review of A. Friedkin's *Avraham Baer Gottlober un zayn epokhe*," *Pinkas* 1 (1927–28): 162–68.

[83] Michal Oron, "Mysticism and Magic in Eighteenth-Century London: Samuel Falk, the 'London Ba'al Shem'," in *Sefer Yisra'el Levin* (ed. Re'uven Zur and Tova Rosen; Tel Aviv: The University of Tel Aviv, 1995), 2:19, footnote 57. On Samuel Falk, see Cecil Roth, "The Cabalist and the King," in *Essays and Portraits in Anglo-Jewish History* (Philadelphia: The Jewish Publication Society of America, 1962), 139–64.

intellectuals, without regard to national origin or religious confession, whose ability to create and thus to gain artistic and literary renown was entirely due to his beneficence.[84] Lefin's productivity was directly related to Czartoryski's patronage, which was an indispensable component of the beginnings of the Haskalah in Eastern Europe. As in Berlin and Szkłów, the existence of a group of wealthy benefactors or even of a single well-endowed patron made all the difference in whether or not aspiring *maskilim* could devote their energies to writing. Members of the Jewish community who directed their literary aspirations toward a transformation of Jewish life needed a livelihood to support their cultural work, particularly because their writings fell beyond the purview of traditional Jewish literary creativity. Early *maskilim* like Solomon Maimon, Joel Brill Loewe, Salomon Dubno, Herz Homberg, and Israel Zamość travelled to Berlin, where they became private tutors in the homes of eighteenth-century upper-class households, particularly for the children of wealthy Berlin Jews.[85] Joshua Zeitlin, a prosperous Russian Jew, turned his estate of Ustia in Mohylew, near Szkłow, into an oasis for a variety of turn-of-the-nineteenth-century Jewish intellectuals, including Barukh Schick and Lefin himself.[86] While the later Haskalah in Prussia would be buttressed by the emergence of a cultivated middle class interested in the Enlightenment and committed to funding its institutions — printing presses, journals and schools — the system of private patronage was essential for the support of the East European Haskalah and the Polish Enlightenment.

Lefin became acquainted with members of the Czartoryski cultural circle while spending time on the Czartoryski estate in Sieniawa, and was cultivated by Izabela Czartoryska, Adam Kazimierz's wife, a patron in her own right. Izabela's estate in Puławy was a magnet for European culture and she was an important collector of both artistic people and their creations. Lefin held Izabela Czartoryska in special regard, attested by this panegyric he wrote to her on behalf of the Jews of Mikołajów in 1805:

---

[84] Czartoryski's masonic lodge, Les Neuf Soeurs, accepted, at least theoretically, all nations and creeds. See Hans, "UNESCO of the Eighteenth Century," 314. Nonetheless, Katz illustrated that the Christian roots of freemasonry made admittance of Jews into most lodges problematic for much of the eighteenth century. See Jacob Katz, *Jews and Freemasons in Europe, 1723–1939* (trans. Leonard Oschry; Cambridge, Mass.: Harvard University Press, 1970).

[85] Lowenstein, *The Berlin Jewish Community*, 39, and 209, footnote 26. Christian *intelligenti* were also employed as tutors in wealthy magnate homes; Scypion Piattoli, for example, was a tutor for both the Potockis and the Lubomirskis. Gelber, "Ksiądz Piattoli a Sprawa Żydowska na Sejmie Wielkim," 321.

[86] David E. Fishman, *Russia's First Modern Jews: The Jews of Shklov* (New York: New York University Press, 1995), 58 and Samuel Joseph Fuenn, *Qiryah ne'emanah* (Vilna, 1860), 271–73.

Words of Thanks

We have lived and been sustained by the generosity of your hands for many days and years. Far away, you have been hidden from our eyes. We have only thanked your name and your memory. Indeed, we have been jealous even of those who only see your image on a tablet, an inchoate substance impossible to stir [even] with all the rams of Nevayot. (Isa 60:7)

Come please, now, your Highness, accept all of these yearning hearts that offer words of good will before you. Accept now the reward for your justness to Israel from the Lord their God. Take delight in these eyes, which regard you and are filled with love, issuing honor and emitting song, gladness, and joy for you. Regard these whispering tongues and their silent lips and see us standing, all of us, mute statues, awed and silenced now, from our abundant joy in you.

Remember these servants among the myriads of our brethren, the House of Israel, who are close to you, so they will be able to appear before you, worthy to be your favored [subjects] upon whom you bestow your mercy. But we, in this unforeseen hour, only need to quench the thirst of our eyes in the glory of your face in order to engrave the likeness of your image on our hearts as a memorial for all the days of our lives.[87]

Izabela was not unmoved by this display of gratitude and remarked to her husband, "I am at the end of my travels in Ukraine and Podolia. I arrived here [Mikołajów] yesterday with a cacophany of song [by] Jews and Christians, as in all of your lands, my dear, where I have been received in a manner that I will never forget."[88]

Lefin's reform proposals were influenced by the Haskalah in Berlin and by the French Enlightenment, but his keen awareness of the specific conditions of Polish Jewry — the relationship of the Jews to the magnate class, his sensitivity to age-old Christian hostilities to Judaism, and his perception of Polish Jewry's spiritual crisis — shaped his writings at all times. Lefin's suggestions for reform of the Polish-Jewish community were not merely reactive proposals, but constructive suggestions for the renewal of a rational, but traditional, Jewish life in Poland. This can been seen already in his first published work on the reform of the Jewish community of Poland, *Essai d'un plan de réforme ayant pour objet d'éclairer la Nation Juive en Pologne et de redresser par là ses moeurs*, which appeared anonymously in Warsaw in 1791.[89]

Written for the National Education Commission on which Adam Kazimierz Czartoryski served, the *Essai d'un plan de réforme* reflected Lefin's moderate conception of the Haskalah; it also illustrated his sensitivity to the

---

87 The Joseph Perl Archive, JNULA, 4° 1153/8. The poem is dated 2 Elul [August 27], 1805.

88 Izabela Fleming Czartoryska to Adam Kazimierz, September 16, 1805, Mikołajów. 6030 III, EW 623.

89 On dating the pamphlet, see Guterman, "The Suggestions of Polish Jews toward the Reforms," 70.

external pressures bearing upon the Jewish community of Poland. Although the *Essai d'un plan de réforme* was written with Czartoryski's patronage, Lefin was not a mouthpiece for the prince. Lefin's *Essai d'un plan de réforme* can be read as a rejoinder to a kind of modern public disputation — in the medieval meaning of a staged dialogue between the representatives of Judaism and Christianity — over the character of the Jews and Judaism taking place at the Four-Year *Sejm*. Acutely aware of the animosity toward the Jews that informed much of the Polish discussion of the "Jewish Question," as well as of the historic hostility of the Polish Church to the Talmud, Lefin penned the *Essai d'un plan de réforme* both as an apologia on behalf of Judaism and as a proposal for the reform of the Jewish community.[90] He revealed in an unpublished manuscript entitled *"Teshuvah"* that he composed the French pamphlet in response to deputy Hugo Kołłątaj's order and the National Education Committee's agreement (later slightly modified by Father Scypion Piattoli) for all Jewish men to shave their beards.[91] Prior to the eighteenth century, most Jewish men — although there were differences in style between East and West European Jews — wore beards in fulfillment of the biblical commandment, "You shall not round off the side-growth on your head or destroy the side growth of your beard" (Lev 19:27), and, if they shaved, did so only with a permissible tool, a pair of scissors, not with a razor. In the course of the eighteenth century, when being clean-shaven became marked as "modern," or "Western," the Jewish beard, a metonym for the

---

[90] Literary hostility to the Talmud was well attested in Poland already by the seventeenth century. Authors such as Mojecki (*Jewish Cruelties*), Hobicki, Micźniski, and Szleskobski published tracts criticizing the Oral Law. *The Talmud of the Jewish Faith* (1610, Cracow) became the source for the first Polish encylopedia's (1745) entry "proving" the commonplace belief that the Talmud required Jews to use Christian blood on Passover. Between 1547–1787, there were eighty-one cases of ritual murder accusation in Poland, and the blood libel loomed large in the Frankist disputation in Lwów in 1759. See Majer Bałaban, *Letoldot hatenu'ah hafranqit* (Tel Aviv: Devir, 1934), 160–61; Goldberg, "The Changes in the Attitude of Polish Society," 41; Klier, *Russia Gathers Her Jews*, 175–77; Zenon Guldon and Jacek Wijaczka, "The Accusation of Ritual Murder in Poland, 1500–1800," *Polin* 10 (1997): 99–140. One of the central anti-Talmud texts employed by Polish writers of the eighteenth century was Johann Andreas Eisenmenger's *Entdecktes Judenthum*, which cited the Talmud as the source for the Jews' poisoning community wells during the Black Death. See Cygielman, "Regarding the Suggestions of Mateusz Butrymowicz," 88–89 on the anti-Jewish stereotypes employed by Mateusz Butrymowicz in his pamphlet.

[91] The Joseph Perl Archive, JNULA, 4° 1153/72, 2b. Kołłątaj's order read: "All the Jews living or domiciled in the States of the Republic, with no exception, must shave off their beards and stop wearing the Jewish dress; they should dress as the Christians in the States of the Republic do." Quoted in Eisenbach, *The Emancipation of the Jews in Poland*, 96. See, too, my "Strategy and Ruse in the Haskalah of Mendel Lefin of Satanów (1749–1826)," in *New Perspectives on the Haskalah* (ed. Shmuel Feiner and David Sorkin; London: Littman Library of Jewish Civilization, 2001), 86–102.

Jewish male himself, became scrutinized and contested by Jews and Gentiles.[92] Kołłątaj's order struck at the heart of the aesthetic and sexual codes of
modernization. Lefin, distrustful of any political changes that would dissolve
Jewish corporate and religious autonomy, reacted strongly against Kołłątaj's
decree and penned his pamphlet as a defense of Jewish religious practice.

Many Polish reformers saw rabbinic Judaism, and particularly the Talmud,
as an obstacle to the integration of the Jews into Polish life, and the pamphlet literature circulating in Warsaw at the time of the Great *Sejm* was full of
these attitudes. Lefin countered this assault upon Jewish religious life with a
discussion of the historical development of Judaism and its fundamental
compatibility with an enlightened Polish state. He began the *Essai d'un plan
de réforme* with a bold assertion of the centrality of religion in Jewish life and
an equally dauntless claim of the Talmud's universalism:

> Religion is the most powerful and the most active motive of the Jewish nation, and one
> can draw essential advantages even from its prejudices; that is why it is very important for
> every political reformer to know them [the prejudices] thoroughly. The Talmud, which
> places the love of one's fellow man as the foundation of its entire system, is its [the Jewish
> nation's] principle code of law.[93]

Acknowledging that much of the Talmud was concerned with fine legal discussions about how to fulfill Jewish ceremonial law, and acutely aware that
Christian polemical literature had historically viewed the Talmud as the
source of Jewish separatism and alleged misanthropy, Lefin insisted that its

---

[92]   Elliot Horowitz, "The Early Eighteenth Century Confronts the Beard: Kabbalah and
Jewish Self-Fashioning," *Jewish History* 8 (1994): 95–115. By the end of the eighteenth century, many westernized Jews viewed the beard as a sign of the cultural and aesthetic backwardness of their East European brethren from whom they sought to distance themselves. Max
Lilienthal, a German *maskil* who travelled to Russia on behalf of the Russian government,
remarked that the Russian-Jewish *maskilim*, were "Dirty, *bearded* Jews who are barely touched
by the rays of enlightenment." Cited in Steven J. Zipperstein, *The Jews of Odessa: A Cultural
History, 1794–1881* (Stanford, Calif.: Stanford University Press, 1986), 52. Emphasis is mine.
In his *Autobiography*, Solomon Maimon viewed his decision to shave his beard as a sign of his
modernity and rationality, symbols that were not lost upon the traditional chief rabbi of
Hamburg, who said in dismay upon meeting Maimon: "You also are not unknown to me; I
examined you as a boy several times, and formed high expectations of you. Oh! is it possible
that you have altered so' (*Here he pointed to my shaven beard*). To this I replied that I also had
the honour of knowing him, and that I remembered his examinations well. My conduct
hitherto, I told him, was as little opposed to religion properly understood, as it was to
reason. 'But,' he interrupted, '*you do not wear a beard*, you do not go to the synagogue: is that
not contrary to religion?'" Solomon Maimon, *An Autobiography* (trans. J. Clark Murray;
Urbana: University of Illinois Press, 1954), 261. Emphases are mine. Being clean-shaven was
a precondition for Jews seeking admission to the Berlin Lodge (*Grosse National- Mutterloge zu
den drei Weltkugeln*) at the end of the eighteenth century. See Katz, *Jews and Freemasons in
Europe, 1723–1939*, 22. Scores of other examples exist.
[93]   [Lefin], "*Essai d'un plan de réforme*," 410.

many "sound maxims" touched upon Jewish morals, and that "even the ceremonial laws have a relationship to morals and are only different aspects of "the [commandment to] love one's fellow man [as oneself]."[94] Lefin's words reflected the eighteenth-century's preoccupation with universal morality and his own commitment to the defense of traditional rabbinic Judaism and its main text, the Talmud, against charges of immorality and religious parochialism.

Throughout the *Essai d'un plan de réforme* Lefin described Judaism in a manner that he believed would be palatable to his Polish readers, but his words also reflected his perception that the rational rabbinic Judaism inherent in the Talmud had been diverted and debased by mysticism and irrationality. Although Lefin acknowledged that a legitimate esoteric tradition existed within the Talmud, he insisted that the internal censoring mechanism of the tradition protected this elite teaching from abuse by the ignorant. He wrote:

> It [the Talmud] was very selective about the choice of those that it believed worthy of being initiates; it demanded very pure morals, a penetrating mind, formidable erudition, and an advanced age, etc. Most of those men who penetrated it [the esoteric tradition] often retreated from it with a fearful respect. [The prohibition against entering the *PaRDeS* (the "paradise" or "orchard" of the esoteric tradition)] is repeated many times in the Talmud.[95]

In Lefin's view, Moses Maimonides was the next link in the great chain of tradition after the Talmud. But the Maimonides he presented to his readers was not the codifier of the *Mishneh torah*; rather, he was the philosopher of *The Guide of the Perplexed*. Lefin argued that Maimonides understood correctly that metaphysics was equivalent to the esoteric tradition of the Talmud. Using his great intelligence, the philosopher was able to develop systematic, concrete and "reasonable" foundations for most of the ceremonial law. Moving on to a discussion of the subsequent perversion of the true spirit of the Talmud, Lefin pointed to the philosophic sectarians of the post-Maimonidean period who "took infinitely more from Greek scholars than from Jewish scholars, started to allegorize everything, denied the resurrection of the dead, and ended up becoming atheists."[96] The extremism of these sectarians

---

[94] Ibid., 418, footnote 1.

[95] Ibid., 419, footnote 2. *b. Hagigah 14b* relates the story of four men (Ben Azzai, Ben Zoma, *Aḥer*, and R. Akiba) who entered a *pardes* (orchard), of which only one, R. Akiba, left unharmed. By the thirteenth century, the Talmudic narrative and the word *pardes* had been transformed into an acronym denoting four methods of Torah exegesis: P (*peshat*, literal or plain sense), R (*remez*, allusive), D (*derash*, homiletic) and S (*sod*, esoteric). See Gershom G. Scholem, *On the Kabbalah and Its Symbolism* (New York: Schocken Books, 1969), 53.

[96] [Lefin], *"Essai d'un plan de réforme,"* 410. In his own lifetime, Maimonides was compelled to defend his belief in resurrection of the dead. See his "The Essay on Resurrection" in Moses Maimonides, *Crisis and Leadership: The Epistles of Maimonides* (ed. David Hartman and

made Maimonides's philosophic work — and the interest in non-Jewish sciences — suspect among the Jewish community as a whole. In Lefin's view, the rejection of philosophy and of non-Jewish learning proved disastrous to the course of Polish Jewish history. Vulnerable in the wake of the Maimonidean controversy, the Jews found comfort and refuge in the "pious ignorance" of Talmudic casuistry and mysticism. These religious streams — excessive Talmudism and foolish mysticism — were the extreme foils to Lefin's conception of a moderate, rational Talmudic Judaism purged of its kabbalistic element. Both extremist tendencies resulted in a kind of collective irrationality. Decrying Polish Jewry's overzealous attention to the minutiae of the ceremonial law and its belief in the miraculous at the expense of "rational" behavior, Lefin wrote:

> The most corrupt men, who nonetheless perform many ceremonial laws with fervor, pass for just and honest [men], whereas men with integrity are regarded as impious if they fail [to fulfill the ceremonial law] one time. [For example,] during a winter night, two young men were thrown into a granary filled with hay. The house caught on fire, the wind blew very severely and terribly, and [these young men] battled the fire and were engulfed in flames and suffocating smoke for a long time . . . until they saved the village from certain destruction. These two generous young men were forgotten the next day, during which time someone was discovered who piously took a secret bath in cold water and whose devotion is believed to have saved the city.[97]

Lefin placed the greater part of the blame for the irrationality of his brethren on the influence of the mystical tradition, which he believed had been revitalized with the appearance of the kabbalistic text, the *Zohar*, and had spawned the Hasidic movement of his own day. He argued that the staunch conservatism and low cultural level of Polish Jewry was due to the hegemony of misguided kabbalistic influence. Lefin did not mince words when criticizing Hasidism to a non-Jewish audience, believing that Polish reformers shared his contempt for mysticism.[98] *Essai d'un plan de réforme* derided Hasidic enthusiasm and its embrace of simple faith and mocked its

---

trans. Hillel Halkin; Philadelphia: The Jewish Publication Society of America, 1985), 220–35. On the Maimonidean controversy, see Yitzhak Baer, *A History of the Jews in Christian Spain* (Philadelphia: The Jewish Publication Society of America, 1978), 1:96–110.

[97]   [Lefin], *"Essai d'un plan de réforme,"* 418, footnote 1.

[98]   To that end, Lefin recommended in the second part of *Essai d'un plan de réforme* that the National Commission of Education should confer a prize upon the individual who wrote the best practical treatise critiquing mystical writings, including the *Zohar*, the *Zenda vesta* (hymns from Zarathustra) and the works of Emmanuel Swedenborg (1688–1772), in order to expose their irrationality, thus drawing their "credulous readers away from these works." Such critical works would, in Lefin's words, "move the torch of reason away from from the magical lantern of their imaginations." See [Lefin], *"Essai d'un plan de réforme,"* 417. For Lefin's critique of the faculty of imagination, see Chapter Three.

hermeneutic techniques.[99] Lefin disparaged the Hasidic preoccupation with
miracles,[100] but reserved his greatest contempt for the leaders of contemporary Hasidism (the zaddikim), and their aura of putative sanctity. Citing Jean
La Bruyère, the French essayist whose *Les Dialogues Sur Le Quietism* had
attacked religious enthusiasm and extreme pietism, Lefin wrote:

> They [the Hasidim] believe prophecy and donation [*le don*] effect miracles, which they
> attribute to the leaders of their sect as an article of faith. "By virtue of his assuring that he
> has seen a marvel, a man of the people falsely persuades others that he has seen a
> marvel," [says] La Bruyère. It is actually [considered] a meritorious deed [among their
> disciples] if one contributes to their [*les chefs de leur secte*] amusement in such a manner as
> to give them the right disposition in which to receive inspiration from [their] higher
> knowledge, or at least if one takes an interest in praising them as much as is possible to
> ensure their reputation. . . . Making the elaboration of their fame a religious duty and
> belief in them, above all, an article of faith, is an ingenious tactic that serves the great
> Lamas of this sect. . . . This is why they [the zaddikim] pretend to serve their proselytes
> and are enriched considerably by their donations. Their faithful disciples have frequent
> occasions to convince themselves of their leaders' great merit by contemplating their
> numerous courts comprised of rich pilgrims who visit them from many places, as well as
> by the elegance of their tables laden with silver dishes and with the most exquisite foods.
> Just as these great men know how to ennoble themselves through these earthly pleasures,
> they are believed to obtain the remission of sins more surely than the ancient laws that
> command tears and lamentations.[101]

The charismatic authority of the zaddikim was, Lefin believed, suspect. He
was particularly enraged by their claim to an exclusive, even prophetic,
relationship with God. Recoiling from what he believed was Hasidic contempt for traditional rabbinic Jews, Lefin wrote:

> These ones [the zaddikim] care even less in their allocation of souls [than Shimon bar
> Yochai did].[102] They regard the knowledge of ceremonies, which motivated the Rabbis,
> as a base measure worthy of a peasant. Instead, the real proprietors of the souls [i.e. the
> zaddikim], [who have] secret qualities and are above ordinary conceptions, have the
> good fortune to be regarded as God's confidantes. . . . The true souls consist of a web of
> instantaneous feelings of truth and exalted senses, which is infinitely above the twaddle,
> called *investigations and reasons* of the other, false souls. . . . [They believe that] these

---

[99]   [Lefin], "*Essai d'un plan de réforme*," 411 and 415.

[100] The rejection of Hasidic miracles, particularly of miraculous births, became an important feature in the later Galician and Russian Haskalahs. Benjamin Rivlin's *taqqanah*
(communal edict) in Szkłów from 1787, which concluded that miracles were a contradiction
to natural science, was an exceptional early example of a mitnaggedic critique of Hasidic
miracles. See Fishman, *Russia's First Modern Jews*, 120–21.

[101] [Lefin], "*Essai d'un plan de réforme*," 411 and 419, footnotes 5 and 6. On La Bruyère's influence on Lefin, see Hillel Levine, "Between Hasidism and Haskalah: On a Disguised Anti-
Hasidic Polemic," in *Peraqim betoldot haḥevrah hayehudit biymei habeinayim uva'et haḥadashah*
(ed. Immanuel Etkes and Joseph Salmon; Jerusalem: Zalman Shazar Center, 1980), 186.

[102] Earlier in the *Essai* Lefin asserted that Shimon bar Yochai, the ancient rabbinic figure to
whom the *Zohar* is traditionally attributed, had denied a soul to non-Jews. See [Lefin], "*Essai
d'un plan de réforme*," 411.

noble souls [the zaddikim], like aspects of the divine essence, have an active influence on
everything that is intended by creation.[103] In their opinion, even miracles, which they
perform daily, are but a natural consequence of the "association of their ideas."[104]

Compared to the zaddikim, whose claims to leadership and power were
based solely on false charisma and manipulation of the Jewish public,
particularly of its youth, the Talmudic casuistry belabored by Poland's rabbinic elite should be, in Lefin's view, "deeply blessed."[105] Lefin's comment
illustrates that though East European *maskilim* like himself criticized what
they believed to be the insular, or "baroque," tradition of early modern Polish Jewry, they did not reject the rabbinic culture of Ashkenaz in its entirety.
Lefin's conception of the Jewish Enlightenment, as well as that of his
moderate disciples, strove to restore the past glory of Polish Jewry, which had
been ossified by its exclusive intellectual engagement with commentary on
the Talmud, and was being further subverted by Hasidism.

For Lefin, who believed not only in the permissibility of studying Gentile
sciences, but also in their efficacy in renewing Jewish faith, one of the most
deplorable aspects of contemporary Hasidism was its scorn for non-Jews and
non-Jewish knowledge. In his reading of Jewish history, Lefin argued that the
suspicion of philosophy after the Maimonidean controversy had caused the
Jewish community to reject all Gentile knowledge as heresy and to find
refuge in the Zoharic view that no non-Jew deserved to be called a human
being.[106] The cultivation on the part of the Hasidim of a sense of superiority
and exclusivity through their rejection of non-Jewish learning struck Lefin as
a contradiction of the universalism inherent in creation itself. He wrote:
"Man is particularly beloved by God. God created him after his divine image.
He created all of mankind from Adam alone so that no one would derive
from a particular origin, etc."[107]

---

[103] Here Lefin is criticizing the Hasidic belief in the theurgic power of the zaddik, whose
actions in the mundane world, his followers believed, were capable of influencing the
supernal realm. The zaddik's ability to cleave to the Godhead enabled him to stimulate the
Divine's efflux upon his followers. See Ada Rapoport-Albert, "God and the Zaddik as the
Two Focal Points of Hasidic Worship," in *Essential Papers on Hasidism* (ed. Gershon David
Hundert; New York: New York University Press, 1991), 299–329. On theurgy, see Moshe Idel,
Kabbalah: New Perspectives (New Haven, Conn.: Yale University Press, 1988).

[104] [Lefin], *"Essai d'un plan de réforme,"* 411–12. The phrase "association of ideas" will be
discussed in Chapter Three.

[105] Ibid., 412.

[106] The Zoharic belief in the divine origin of the human soul implicitly excluded Gentiles
as recipients of the Godhead's emanation. The *Zohar* stated that non-Jews only had a *nefesh*
ḥayah (a temporal, animal soul) and not a *neshamah*, a supernal soul. On the theory of the
soul in the *Zohar*, see Isaiah Tishby, ed., *The Wisdom of the Zohar* (London: Oxford University
Press, 1989), 677–807, particularly 725, 727.

[107] [Lefin], *"Essai d'un plan de réforme,"* 415. Lefin is freely interpreting the phrase *nivra*
adam yeḥidi (man [*Adam*] was created alone) that appears in *m. Sanhedrin 4:5, t. Sanhedrin*

The second half of *Essai d'un plan de réforme* lay the foundation for Lefin's detailed reform proposals, which focused on the creation of a state-appointed rabbinate, the establishment of a Polish Normal School, and the cultivation of literary works that would expose the folly of Hasidism. The most characteristic feature of Lefin's proposals is their emphasis on moderation and the use of positive incentives rather than external compulsion for change.[108] Lefin wrote, "In general, one needs, as much as possible, to use attractive resorts for engaging the people in the observation of the [state's] law. . . . It is appropriate to blend the repugnant, but salutary, medications furtively with the exquisite tidbits for it [the Jewish people]."[109]

Lefin's commitment to moderation was both ideological and tactical. In fact, the theme of moderating between two extremes was a leitmotif of all of Lefin's work — it appears most starkly in his *Sefer heshbon hanefesh* (*Moral Accounting*, 1808) — and is reiterated in the *Essai d'un plan de réforme* to propose specific ways through which to redirect the Polish Jewish community away from the poles of mysticism and rote Talmudic casuistry toward the rational rabbinic path paved by Maimonides. Yet, Lefin also penned his proposals with tactical considerations in mind. He was fully aware that the traditional Polish Jewish community absorbed by the Habsburgs after the first partition had responded with fear and suspicion to Joseph II's decrees in the *Toleranzpatent*. Moreover, he distrusted the "well-intentioned" proposals of most Polish reformers. Lefin thus wrote the French pamphlet, emphasizing the centrality of religion for the Jewish community of Poland, as a means of urging the Polish authorities to refrain from interfering in internal Jewish affairs and to design reforms compatible with traditional Jewish rabbinic culture.

Lefin's defense of communal autonomy was not only a response to Gentile intervention into internal Jewish life. It was also a strategy to protect the Jewish communal authority from the alternative form of Jewish leadership represented by the Hasidim.[110] Throughout *Essai d'un plan de réforme*, Lefin emphasized the need to engage the traditional Polish-Jewish rabbinate in the

---

8:4, and *b. Sanhedrin 37a*, "Why was man [*Adam*] created alone? So that the zaddikim would never say, "*We* are the descendants of a zaddik [to the exclusion of others]." Emphasis is mine. Lefin defended rabbinic writings that used the word "man" to mean Jew, not Gentile, by arguing that such writings only applied to commandments that were obligatory for Jews alone. Joseph Perl mentioned Lefin's opinion in one of the former's unpublished writings on the Talmud. See Heb. 38.7075, "Notes to Joseph Perl's Literary Work," and the Joseph Perl Archive, JNULA, 4° 1153/72, 3b.

[108] Mahler, *Divrei yemei yisra'el*, 1:79 and Gelber, "Mendel Lefin of Satanów's Proposals," 273–74.

[109] [Lefin], "*Essai d'un plan de réforme*," 416.

[110] Shmuel Werses, *Haskalah veshabta'ut: toldotav shel ma'avaq* (Jerusalem: Zalman Shazar Center, 1988), 105.

struggle against Hasidism and considered it, despite its obvious failings, a necessary ally against the new mystical group. For example, a strong, traditional rabbinate supported by the state and secure in its power could even encourage productive work among the followers of the Hasidim by rewarding those who cultivated wheat for *matsah* (unleavened bread for Passover) and kosher hemp for clothes.[111] This would have the added benefit of diversifying Jewish economic activity. In *Liqqutei kelalim*, he suggested that the Jewish community "spin, weave, and prepare its clothes from the products of Jewish craftsmen, so that the people will see that these crafts sustain the artisans."[112]

While Lefin championed moderate reform of the Jewish community, the authority he wished to confer upon the state-appointed rabbinate was immoderate, even authoritarian. Lefin believed the state-appointed rabbinate should exercise complete control in the realm of culture. He argued that the rabbinate should have the power to censor books; the primary goal of the state rabbis' censorship campaign should be the suppression of the *Zohar* and all its commentaries. This rabbinate should also distribute copies of Jacob Emden's *Mitpaḥat sefarim* (*Covering of the Scrolls of the Law*), which challenged the antiquity of the *Zohar*, and issue a new edition of *The Guide of the Perplexed* that could "be understood by the simplest people."[113] Lefin also suggested that the National Education Commission should establish a Jewish Normal School in Warsaw, in which Polish would be the language of instruction, and whose graduates would be allowed — to the exclusion of all others — to receive approbations from the state-rabbinate for their publications. The texts at this school would include Polish translations of Scripture, which, he argued, would enable Polish Jews to appreciate the "sublime poetry of their ancestors that they have [until now] never understood."[114] Reading Hebrew through Polish would force the Jewish community to admit that they owed the discovery of the beauty of their own religious poetry to a non-Jewish language, challenging the Hasidic rejection of non-Jewish culture as inherently heretical. Last, Lefin proposed that satires and comedies be written about the Hasidim to expose the foolishness of their commentaries,

---

[111] [Lefin], "*Essai d'un plan de réforme*," 417. Lefin's reference to "kosher" hemp pertains to the biblical prohibition of wearing a garment made of a wool and linen mixture (*sha'atnez*).

[112] Lefin, *Liqqutei kelalim*, in Gelber, "Mendel Lefin of Satanów's Proposals," 298–99. On Lefin's economic critique of Polish Jewry, see Derek Jonathan Penslar, *Shylock's Children: Economics and Jewish Identity in Modern Europe* (Berkeley: University of California Press, 2001), 81–82.

[113] [Lefin], "*Essai d'un plan de réforme*," 414. Lefin himself embarked on such a translation, which was only published posthumously. See Moses Maimonides, *Sefer moreh nevukhim* (trans. Mendel Lefin; Żółkiew, 1829).

[114] [Lefin], "*Essai d'un plan de réforme*," 414.

advice which he later followed by writing *Making Wise the Simple* (*Maḥkimat peti*) and *The First Hasid* (*Der ershter khosed*), two anti-Hasidic satires that are no longer extant. He hoped that these critical works of parody would challenge the Hasidim to defend themselves in writing, which, in turn, would spur the creation of "reasonable and eloquent writings, which the nation absolutely lacks."[115]

Lefin had a clear sense of audience in the *Essai d'un plan de réforme*. According to his comments in "*Teshuvah*," the deputies of the National Education Commission — here Czartoryski's hand can be felt — urged Lefin to write the pamphlet anonymously and in such a manner as to disguise its Jewish provenance.[116] Lefin continues to explain that he crafted the *Essai d'un plan de réforme* to appear as neutral as possible, with no special pleading on behalf of the Jews. He learned this strategy, he explains, from a Talmudic story in *b. Me'ilah*.[117] The Talmud describes the case of a certain Reuben, the son of Istroboli, who disguised himself as a Roman in order to thwart three anti-Jewish decrees (i.e., violating the Sabbath, proscribing circumcision, and compelling transgression of the laws governing sexual relations). The Romanized Reuben, no longer recognized as a Jew, posed three carefully constructed questions to his antagonistic audience so that each response would require the lifting of the respective hostile edict. The ruse worked until Reuben was unmasked, relates the Talmud, and the Romans "came to know that he was a Jew, and [the decrees] were reinstituted."[118] Lefin's literary tactics — penning it in French, the cultured language of the Polish magnate class, and publishing it anonymously — he hoped, would allow its "objective" admission into the debate over the Jews. If the reformers discussing the future of the Jews suspected its Jewish source, Lefin reasoned, they would in all likelihood dismiss its contents as particularistic and reject the *Essai d'un plan de réforme*'s claims of the reasonableness of Judaism and its compatibility with the modern state.

Lefin's tactics in writing the *Essai d'un plan de réforme* in French and without personal attribution underscores the polemical nature of the debates over the Jews at the Four-Year *Sejm*. He clearly felt that conscious dissimulation was necessary to defend traditional Ashkenazic Jewish culture, particularly

---

[115] Ibid., 415.
[116] Anonymity was also a feature of Lefin's Yiddish translation of Proverbs (Lemberg, 1814) and of an anonymous anti-Hasidic Yiddish comedy, *Di genarte velt* (*The Duped World*), which probably appeared in the second decade of the nineteenth century and relied on Yiddish translations of Proverbs that are very close to those innovated by Lefin. Meir Wiener believed that Lefin himself had written the book. See Meir Wiener, *Tsu der geshikhte fun der yidisher literatur in nayntsnt yorhundert* (Kiev, 1940), 38.
[117] The Joseph Perl Archive, JNULA, 4° 1153/72, 3a.
[118] *b. Me'ilah 17a.*

the Talmud. As he relates in *"Teshuvah,"* Lefin deliberately cited contempo-rary non-Jewish political and social theorists in the *Essai d'un plan de réforme* to bolster the pamphlet's authority and "objectivity." Reaching eastward, far outside standard Jewish defenses of the Talmud, Lefin cited the maxims of Confucius in defense of ceremonial law, "You should never dispense with that which the ceremonial prescribes . . . however minute, however incon-venient and unnecessary they appear to you."[119] He even went so far as to quote great writers "who are haters of Israel."[120] On the last page of the essay, directly below the citation from Confucius, Lefin cited Voltaire, arguably the eighteenth century's most towering intellectual figure and a man known by his contemporaries, including the *maskilim*, as a foe of the Jews.[121] The title of Lefin's *Essai d'un plan de réforme* included the "redressing of Jewish mo-rals," a subtle allusion, perhaps, to Voltaire's own *Essai sur les Moeurs* (*Essay on Morals*), in which the French *philosophe* criticized alleged Jewish greed, misanthropy, and fanaticism. Lefin, of course, repudiated the Voltairian belief in the fundamental incompatibility of Judaism and the modern state, but, in keeping with the pamphlet's artful dissimulation, allowed a non-Jewish writer to articulate his point of view. Bookending the *Essai d'un plan de réforme*, and earning pride of place on its front cover, was a citation from Montesquieu, the eighteenth-century French enlightener perceived both as a moderate voice within the chorus of the Enlightenment and as Voltaire's ideological opposite on the Jewish question.[122] *Essai d'un plan de réforme* boldly defends religion by citing Montesquieu's most famous work, *De l'Esprit des Lois* (*The Spirit of Laws*), on its frontispiece, "One must pay great attention to the disputes of theologians, but it is necessary to conceal it [that atten-tion] as much as possible. . . . Religion is always the best guarantee that one can have of men's morals." In the notes that follow the body of the *Essai d'un plan de réforme*, Lefin quoted Montesquieu again in order to inveigh against the use of legislation as a means to transform culture. The example he cited, Montesquieu's well-known censure of Tsar Peter I's 1698 edict requiring the Muscovites to shorten their beards and clothing, was carefully chosen, a

---

[119] [Lefin], *"Essai d'un plan de réforme,"* 417.

[120] The Joseph Perl Archive, JNULA, 4° 1153/72, 3a.

[121] On Voltaire's attitudes toward the Jews, see Hertzberg, *The French Enlightenment and the Jews*, 10, 286–87, 290, 297 and Frank E. Manuel, *The Broken Staff: Judaism through Christian Eyes* (Cambridge, Mass.: Harvard University Press, 1992), 193–201. On Voltaire as the blem-ish in the image of the Revolution for enlightened Jews who advocated political emancipa-tion, see Shmuel Feiner, "'The Rebellion of the French' and 'The Freedom of the Jews': The French Revolution in the Image of the Past of the East European Jewish Enlightenment," in *Hamahppekhah hatsarfatit verishumah* (ed. Richard Cohen; Jerusalem, 1991), 240.

[122] On Montesquieu's moderation in general, see Henry F. May, *The Enlightenment in America* (New York: Oxford University Press, 1976), 40; on his moderation regarding the Jews, see Hertzberg, *The French Enlightenment and the Jews*, 10, 287–90.

barely veiled allusion to Kołłątaj's decree ordering Jewish men to shave their beards.[123] While Lefin cited Voltaire as part of a strategy to disguise his authorship of the *Essai d'un plan de réforme*, his use of Montesquieu revealed his true beliefs about reforming the Jewish community of Poland. If the educational changes initiated by the National Education Commission were implemented with respect for traditional rabbinic Judaism, then the *"Jewish nation will fulfill its obligation or, rather, effect its wellbeing — that it has yet to understand — on its own."*[124] A moderate plan of reform based on "attractive resorts," not on compulsion, would be the only means to assure the successful transformation of the Jews and their integration into a modern Polish state.

In all of his writings, Lefin underscored his commitment to a moderate process of change initiated internally by the Jewish community by maintaining the importance of the kahal and traditional rabbinic prerogative against suggestions by Polish reformers and other *maskilim* for their abolition. Yet, the decentralized political situation of pre-partition Poland, in which the nobility — particularly the magnate aristocrats — held enormous political and economic power, created a two-tiered (and competitive) system of political authority for Poland's Jews. Thus, when Lefin argued for the protection of the kahal, he was doing so against the combined assault of the king, the national *Sejm*, and the *Sejm*'s representatives, whose political authority extended to royal (free) towns. But the relationship of the Jewish community in private noble towns to "their" lords was far less autonomous than Lefin's words to the *Sejm* suggest. His proposals for the reform of the Jewish community, both in *Liqqutei kelalim* and in the later work, *Entwurf eines Rabinersystems*, an unpublished German manuscript on the rationalization of the rabbinate, reflect a much more dependent, symbiotic relationship with the magnate class. Lefin wrote both *Liqqutei kelalim* and *Entwurf eines Rabinersystems* in the general context of that relationship and within the particular parameters of his personal bond with Czartoryski.

In the private towns of the Polish nobility, both the kahal and the Christian municipality were subject to the magnate, who had the authority to review their respective operating budgets and courts.[125] Thus, the "autonomous" Jewish courts in the estates of the Czartoryskis were an integral part of the owner's court system. Even criminal matters and appeals between Jews were directed to his court.[126] While the Jewish kahal represented autonomy

---

[123] [Lefin], *"Essai d'un plan de réforme,"* 420.

[124] Ibid., 414. Emphasis in the original.

[125] Adam Teller, "The Legal Status of the Jews on the Magnate Estates of Poland-Lithuania in the Eighteenth Century," *Gal-Ed* 15–16 (1997): 41–63.

[126] Rosman, *The Lords' Jews*, 56.

and the abiding power of Jewish tradition for the Jews, it merely served as a convenient institution for the collection of taxes, the preservation of order, and the administration of one group of subjects for the magnate. Because the magnate class generally viewed the *Sejm*-imposed Jewish head tax as siphoning off the limited resources of the Jewish community living under its jurisdiction, they tried, as much as they could, to reduce the kahal-imposed taxes on their Jewish subjects. The magnates, therefore, viewed the kahal as competitor for their personal authority and strove to have absolute control over it. The lord either intervened directly and dictated kahal affairs or rendered the kahal powerless by bypassing its authority and dealing instead with individual Jews. Typically, the non-Jewish authority confirmed kahal election results and supervised Jewish communal authorities.[127]

Even the venerable institution of the communal rabbi was dependent upon and subject to the magnate's authority. The kahal rabbi fulfilled a number of functions: adjudicating Jewish law, chairing the rabbinical court, officiating at weddings and divorces, and providing religious instruction to the community in the form of sermons and classes. He was on the kahal payroll, but augmented his earnings through gifts and fees charged for specific functions. Although the privileges extended to the Jews of Poland-Lithuania by the magnates included the right to select a rabbi, the nobles sought to control these appointments by turning the rabbinic office into an *arenda*, a lease held by the highest bidder. The individual who won the nobles' *konsens* (rabbinic license) was granted the rabbinic office and the right to accept the kahal's salary and the additional gifts and commissions. In Moshe Rosman's words, "By the eighteenth century . . . the rabbi was not a salaried employee of the *kehillah*, who owed them his livelihood and hence his loyalty. He was a lessee whose lease was the magnate's to give and to enforce."[128]

The dependence of the kahal rabbi on the authority of the magnate is starkly evident throughout *Liqqutei kelalim* and *Entwurf eines Rabinersystems*. In *Liqqutei kelalim*, Lefin repeatedly refers to the "Prince" and his support for reform of the Jewish community.[129] For example, if an accused party wanted to appeal the adjudication of the Jewish court, his only recourse should be to appeal to the state rabbi, whose authority derived from the "Prince's [Czartoryski's]" appointment. Final arbitration of such a dispute, therefore, rested with a rabbinical figure both part of but separate from the community. Furthermore, Lefin wrote: "The kahal's register (*pinqas*) must be brought to

---

127 Ibid., 70, 188, and 191.
128 Ibid., 201 and Teller, "The Legal Status of the Jews," 57–59.
129 Lefin, *Liqqutei kelalim*, in Gelber, "Mendel Lefin of Satanów's Proposals," 293–95 and 297–300.

the *"Prince's court,* may His Honor be blessed, once a year and read in its entirety there. Any legitimate and equitable suggestions made by the Prince, may His Honor be blessed, should be appended and affixed to the register, which will be authorized by the court's seal, as a law in perpetuity."[130]

In *Liqqutei kelalim,* Lefin made suggestions for the reform of the kahal following extensive analysis of the causes of its corruption, such as abuse in the election of communal representatives, corruption in the administration of the public treasury, and concentration of economic life in trade and leasing. Writing in Hebrew, Lefin did not restrain his criticism, which was pointed, even bitter. Many of his words echoed those of non-Jewish critics. But, unlike Polish reformers who advocated abolition of the kahal, Lefin sought to maintain and reform Jewish communal autonomy. Key for Lefin was the cultivation of a modern, non-Hasidic rabbinate whose affective and spiritual authority derived from the Jewish community, but whose communal power derived from the Gentile rulers.

Lefin's view of the power that should be bestowed upon this state-rabbinate underscored the specific East European context of his proposals. Unlike many of his maskilic peers in Berlin, Lefin did not advocate the disbanding of the Jewish community's medieval corporate status as part of a reform program predicated on the assumption of all local prerogatives by the centralized absolutist state in its monopoly on power. Rather, he believed the rabbinate, reformed and appointed by the state, should retain its power to excommunicate. In *Liqqutei kelalim,* Lefin recalled a disagreement he had had with Moses Mendelssohn over the appropriate degree of the non-Jewish authorities' involvement in the internal life of the Jewish community.[131] Mendelssohn's uncompromising commitment to individual moral, ethical, and religious autonomy led him to the conclusion that only total civic freedom, which allowed for the untrammeled expression of religious conviction, could liberate the individual. Matters of conscience had to be separated from the state, and from any form of compulsion, in order for religion to retain its ideal purity. In contrast to Christian Wilhelm Dohm, who had argued in favor of the retention of Jewish courts and their powers, Mendelssohn believed Jews should be evaluated by Jewish law, but in the courts of the

---

[130] Ibid., 292. Emphasis in the original.

[131] Lefin wrote, "I also discussed this matter with the sage, R. Moses from Dessau [Mendelssohn], and except for one thing that annoyed him greatly, meaning, *that according to him the general burden of this business should be placed upon the Ruler, may His Honor be blessed,* he did not make any suggestions, except regarding some small details in a general way. *But I do not want to be involved with them* [the non-Jewish authorities], except to be free to publish publications and good advice, for if not, I must worry lest jealousy and hatred, which spoils everything and destroys all benefit for the Jews, God forbid, rise up against me." See ibid., 287. Emphasis in the original.

state, and he opposed the writ of excommunication (*herem*) on the grounds that true religious beliefs could not be coerced. Although Mendelssohn himself rejected the equation that full Jewish participation in European society was contingent upon the community's regeneration, he supported the state-building efforts of enlightened absolutism. He therefore urged the disbanding of the traditional Jewish communal municipality and dissolution of the rabbinic prerogative of excommunication.[132] Lefin did not. Because the full political emancipation of the Jews, as opposed to the alleviation of their civic status, was never on the agenda of the Polish reformers, Lefin never felt pressured to argue for the political dismemberment of Jewish communal autonomy as a prerequisite to the granting of Jewish rights. The quid pro quo, implicit in so many of the exchanges on the emancipation of the Jews of Prussia, was absent in Lefin's writings.

Suspicious of the intentions of Polish reformers advocating dissolution of the kahal, Lefin nonetheless readily conceded that the kahal was riddled with corruption and mismanagement, which had led to Jewish communal indebtedness and to a debasement of Jewish morality. Discussing the inner decay of the Polish-Jewish community in medical terms, Lefin began with a plea for moderation:

> An experienced physician who wishes to supervise the care of old wounds that have been festering in a sick body for a long time will be extremely circumspect and reluctant to use aggressive medications to close the wounds hastily . . . So, too, when the leader of the community needs to make fences and restrictions before the breaches of the age, he should be forbidden to make use of punitive edicts. On the contrary, he should guide [the community] by very gentle reforms, [gradually] persuading it to adhere to them.[133]

Echoing the comment in "*Teshuvah*" that the non-Jewish authorities did not know what was ultimately beneficial for the Jewish community, Lefin negatively compared the techniques of "integration" of medieval Christian Spain to the enlightened agenda of Emperor Joseph II:

> The kings of Spain thought of themselves as just and righteous, [believing] their abundant humility filled them with mercy. They tortured Israel grievously in order to admit them [the Jews] — through forced conversion — into the Christian paradise. Even Emperor Joseph II should be distrusted; he wanted to subjugate the Sons of Israel and force them to become tradesmen for his own benefit.[134]

Lefin's emphasis on moderate solutions, however, did not prevent him from vigorously attacking the causes of corruption and decadence that he believed

---

[132] David Sorkin, *Moses Mendelssohn and the Religious Enlightenment* (Berkeley: University of California Press, 1996), 115–25.
[133] Lefin, *Liqqutei kelalim*, in Gelber, "Mendel Lefin of Satanów's Proposals," 287.
[134] Ibid., 287.

had weakened the Jewish community. The first part of *Liqqutei kelalim* excoriates kahal elections and the management of the public treasury. In Lefin's view, the election process was inherently biased in favor of the upper classes, who controlled the candidate selection process and engaged in nepotism. Other forms of corruption included buying influence and increasing local taxes to pander to the Gentile authorities.[135] The deficiencies in the management of the public treasury included haste, haphazardness, and arbitrariness, in short, irrationality. In lieu of a careful accounting of revenues and expenditures, vague estimates fell prey to intimidation and nepotism, and led to an unfair allocation of the taxes necessary for running communal institutions. This internal corruption caused numerous disputes and, in turn, exacerbated existing class divisions within the Jewish community, in which the poor fell victim to the whims of the wealthy.[136]

Lefin outlined several ways to root out corruption in the systems of communal representation and taxation. The rationalization (i.e. the organization, standardization, and formalization) of the process of legislating *taqqanot* (communal edicts), of raising money, and of distributing funds from the communal treasury, Lefin believed, would result in greater accountability of communal representatives, greater representation in the communal institutions, and a more upright way of life among his brethren. Nodding toward the idealized vision of Lithuanian Jewry held by many *maskilim*, with the towering intellect of the *ga'on* of Vilna at its helm, Lefin suggested that all reforms of the Polish-Jewish kehillot be based on the internal edicts "of Vilna and Grodno, those [communities] renowned for reason and justice."[137]

In order to preserve the Jewish community's internal autonomy, which protected its cultural integrity, Lefin insisted upon Jewish selection of its communal supervisors *with* Gentile oversight of the process. The first step for improving the accountability of the communal representatives in their adjudication of public needs, Lefin concluded, was the creation of a permanent communal register, "a special book [in which] all of the details of the public events, appointments, decisions, accounts, taxes [would be enumerated]. . . . [This record] will show the later generations how their ancestors acquitted themselves in every difficult matter; even the lists of minor taxes

---

135 Ibid., 288. See, too, Edward Fram, *Ideals Face Reality: Jewish Law and Life in Poland, 1550–1655* (Cincinnati, Ohio: Hebrew Union College Press, 1997), 56.

136 Lefin, *Liqqutei kelalim*, in Gelber, "Mendel Lefin of Satanów's Proposals," 289–90.

137 Ibid., 287 and 292. Vilna, the capital city of Lithuania, was the home to the *ga'on*, Elijah, around whom the rabbinite struggle against Hasidism in the eighteenth century centered. See Immanuel Etkes, "The Vilna Gaon and the Haskalah: Image and Reality," in *Peraqim betoldot hahevrah hayehudit biymei habeinayim uva'et hahadashah* (Jerusalem: Magnes Press, 1980), 192–217.

for immediate needs will be listed and saved in the public book.[138] Apparently, communal *pinqasim* had not been adequate in preventing corruption.

Second, the group of communal representatives, to be called the "committee," would meet at least once a week to supervise the needs of the community. Their meetings would take place in a special, closed chamber, opened only for the purpose of their meetings, and in which "the public account registers and account books would be stored." Before a representative could enter the inner sanctum of the committee's chamber he would have to take two oaths, "an oath of public trust" that he would not be biased [in his adjudication of law] and "an oath of secrecy" that he would not disclose any information about the process taking place inside the chamber. In contrast to what Lefin perceived to be the raucous and chaotic manner in which communal reforms of the past had been legislated, the atmosphere in the committee's chamber would be one of "permanent calm and quiet." He wrote: "It should be forbidden to speak of impertinent matters or engage in any individual or secret discussions. If someone transgresses this law, the guards at the door will drag him outside in shame, in addition to [the other representatives' imposing] a financial fine toward the charitable coffer [upon him]."[139]

Third, although the public was forbidden entry into the committee's chamber, Lefin hoped to democratize the running of the Jewish community by making at least a symbolic overture to public participation in the process. The closed committee chamber, therefore, would have one small window through which "any common man" could "extend his request on a letter." This window would be the avenue of communication between the Jewish public and their representatives during the discussion, voting, and signing into law of the reforms. Moreover, "one whose suggestion letter was accepted in the public register three times, even if he was not from among the nominees [to the committee from his occupational group, would be] nominated immediately and welcomed into the committee without hesitation," provided he was at least twenty-five years old and literate. Lefin stressed the importance of formalizing and standardizing this procedure. After a fixed amount of time for discussion, a secret vote would be taken on color-coded ballots indicating support or rejection of the proposed measure. Majority rule would decide the outcome. Lefin hoped that secrecy, a careful counting of ballots, and a formal, collective oath taken by the representatives renouncing any prior predilections or commitments would guard against "guile and deceit." The entire process would be transcribed into the public register by

---

[138] Lefin, *Liqqueti kelalim,* in Gelber, "Mendel Lefin of Satanów's Proposals," 291.
[139] Ibid., 291.

the speaker of the kahal, the law stamped into the book with the committee's seal.[140]

The second series of suggestions for reform in *Liqqutei kelalim* was devoted to reform of the management of the communal treasury. Lefin directed his comments to rooting out corruption in the kahal's economic life by making the tax burden on all segments of the Jewish community more equitable. His comments were theoretical because the autonomous collection of taxes by the elders of the Jewish community had been annulled by the *Sejm* of 1764. The 1764 Parliament had "reformed" the structure of taxation of the Jewish community by swelling the obligatory head tax to two zlotys for both sexes (thereby limiting the discretion of the kahal elders who in the past had allotted the tax burden according to the various communities' ability to pay) and forbidding the regular conventions of the Council of the Four Lands, the national, super-kahal of Poland-Lithuania.[141] "If the collection of taxes were still transmitted to us," wrote Lefin:

> Then we [would be] obligated to simplify it through any type of effort and strategy, in any case, because we [unlike the non-Jewish authorities] know the true economic status of our brethren. . . . When we find the poor oppressed due to [their requirement to] pay a large sum in one fell swoop, then we could exchange the head tax for the meat tax or for the tax on bread, [or] for the money required for wood, [and exchange] the house-holder's tax for the candle tax . . . without changing the government's commands. In any case, we will have lightened the burden of our poor brethren and protected ourselves from the complaints and grumbling associated with these [burdensome taxes].[142]

Taxation from within the community was necessary to protect against abuse by the Gentile authorities. An equitable allocation of taxes required, in Lefin's view, a rationalization and standardization of the procedure. Ridding the process of the imposition of taxes for an unexpected need (i.e. the fortification of the walls of a synagogue or the creation of a new charity fund for the disabled poor) of the haste and arbitrariness that characterized the process in the past would place the new tax structure on a fair and just basis. Moreover, the need for the new taxes and their apportionment should be made public by the reformed administrative committee detailed above.[143]

As he had suggested in the *Essai d'un plan de réforme*, Lefin extended the need for rationalization and standardization to the rabbinate. He suggested that the provincial rabbis keep meticulous records of their revenues (e.g. from writing writs of divorce) and expenses that would be evaluated collectively with the state rabbinate every three years. As individuals they would be

---

[140] Ibid., 291–92.
[141] Dubnow, *History of the Jews in Russia and Poland*, 109–11, 180, 194, and 198.
[142] Lefin, *Liqqutei kelalim*, in Gelber, "Mendel Lefin of Satanów's Proposals," 293.
[143] Ibid., 294.

taxed appropriately and without bias, and any transgressor would be fined accordingly. Taking aim at those rabbis who might be disposed toward the Hasidic practice of having large meals with their disciples in exchange for *pidyonot* (donations), Lefin suggested that "every kind of expenditure . . . that is not for the general good should be cancelled and all *group meals* and *feasts* on public disbursements should be forbidden."[144]

The dependent nature of Jewish communal authority is even more starkly evident in *Entwurf eines Rabinersystems*, which Lefin bestowed upon Czartoryski as a parting gift on April 4, 1794, when the prince left Sieniawa to fight in the Kościuszko Insurrection, the Commonwealth's last stand against final dismemberment. Lefin penned *Entwurf eines Rabinersystems* at the beginning of the rebellion, hoping it would be successful, restore order to Poland, and allow Czartoryski to effect his reform plan. *Entwurf eines Rabinersystems* was Lefin's direct appeal to Czartoryski for help in reforming the corrupt rabbinate on the magnate's estates.

As he had concluded in *Liqqutei kelalim*, Lefin explained to Czartoryski that the degenerate condition of the rabbinate was due to the election process, the uncertainty of rabbinic income, the sad state of the judiciary, the widespread custom of rabbinic gifts, and, implicitly, the competition for the *konsens*, which led to corruption. Lefin believed Czartoryski's appointment of "virtuous" chief rabbis, who would in turn select righteous subordinate rabbis, would be the first step toward reform of the rabbinate. He next reiterated his proposal for the creation of a formal rabbinic fees book to prevent arbitrary fluctuations in rabbinic salaries. All of the subordinate rabbis should be required to keep a careful book of receipts. Any transgression, such as a bribe or undocumented receipt, should be immediately punished by the chief rabbi.[145] A formal procedure for meting out fines, as well as one for hearing appeals, should be a permanent part of the *konsens*. The authority of the district rabbis, who should be men of unimpeachable integrity, would be strengthened by awarding them a ten-year license, and their rent (*konsens*) to the Prince should be reduced for their travel expenses. The subordinate rabbis' rent could be reduced if they proved their honesty by passing an examination.[146]

The suggestions in *Entwurf eines Rabinersystems* presuppose a commonality of interests between Lefin and his Polish patron, but they also exhibit the same awareness of audience that characterized Lefin's suggestions in the *Essai d'un plan de réforme*. In *Entwurf eines Rabinersystems*, Lefin assumed that Czartoryski would support his proposals for the rationalization of rabbinic

---

[144] Ibid., 295. Emphasis in the original.
[145] Lefin, *Entwurf eines Rabinersystems*, 30.
[146] Ibid., 31.

selection, the standardization of rabbinic salaries and fees, and the selection of district rabbis. Why? Lefin knew that as men of the Enlightenment, both he and Czartoryski shared a commitment toward rationalizing state and estate institutions. Second, Lefin believed Czartoryski could not but accept suggestions that would make life on his estates more orderly, and a standardization of rabbinic fees would ensure that the magnate receive as high a fee for the rabbinic *konsens* as he could. Cleaning the rabbinic house and resolving a source of internal Jewish communal discord could only be in Czartoryski's interest, and Lefin cleverly addressed those concerns in the first part of *Entwurf eines Rabinersystems*.

Yet Lefin's preoccupation with Hasidism and his profound distrust of the movement remained central to all of his writings, including these specific proposals for reform. Assuming that enlightened members of the Polish magnate class such as Czartoryski shared his negative view of mysticism, Lefin used *Entwurf eines Rabinersystems* to advance his anti-Hasidic agenda, but only in a footnote at the end of the pamphlet. Lefin not only made specific suggestions to Czartoryski about individuals suitable for the position of district rabbi, but also urged the prince to empower his administrator, Tomasz Bernatowicz, to support the new rabbis against the Hasidim:

> I know of a small number of competent district rabbis, such as Rabbi Beerish Rapoport, the former Międzybóż rabbi, and also the current Klewań and Międzyrzec rabbi. The first [Rapoport] is to be particularly recommended on account of his mature age, his general valued moral conduct, and his venerable origin [i.e. his *yikhes*, rabbinic lineage]. In addition, his considerable assets of several 1000 # [a kind of currency] can guarantee his incorruptibility in the future. Meanwhile, Sir von Bernatowicz's masterful skill will be required to protect Rabbi Rapoport against the settled Międzybóż nest of zealots, particularly against their cunning general.[147]

This footnote from *Entwurf eines Rabinersystems* reveals that Lefin's choice of district rabbi had to be an individual with irreproachable qualities: impeccable rabbinic lineage, authority and experience, maturity, financial independence, and, most importantly, assured anti-Hasidic leanings. Rabbi [Dov] Beerish Rapoport (1737–1803), a scion of one of the great Polish-Jewish rabbinic families, was a fitting choice. Dov Beerish's paternal grandfather was none other than Hayim ha-Cohen Rapoport, whose stand against the Frankists earned him an enduring name in later maskilic polemics against Hasidism because of the ideational connection *maskilim* drew linking Sabbatianism, Frankism, and Hasidism.[148] His son, Aryeh Leibush Rapoport (1720–1759), was head of the yeshivah of Lwów, but died early, leaving two sons,

---

147 Ibid., 32.
148 See [Joseph Perl], *Boḥen tsaddiq* (Prague, 1838), 113 and Werses, *Haskalah veshabta'ut*, 106.

Moshe Simha, who became head of the rabbinical courts in Bolechów and Jericzów, and Dov Beerish.

In 1754, Dov Beerish Rapoport married Miriam, the granddaughter of Jacob Emden, the noted anti-Sabbatian polemicist. In 1771, Rapoport became head of the rabbinical court in Międzybóż and Lefin undoubtedly became acquainted with him from the time he spent living in the Czartoryski castle there. The two men later participated in a meeting held in Berdyczów in 1809, in response to the Tsar's order expelling the Jews from Russian villages.[149] Lefin hoped that a rabbi of the character of Dov Beerish Rapoport supported by the Prince's administrator would be a match for the "cunning general" of the Międzybóż Hasidim, who could be none other than Barukh of Międzybóż (Medzibozh), the grandson of the Besht and a central figure in Podolian and Volhynian Hasidism between 1780 and 1811. Barukh was known for his awe inspiring and arrogant bearing by Hasidim and anti-Hasidim alike.[150]

The footnote also demonstrates, albeit obliquely, Lefin's belief that Hasidism, particularly the leadership of the zaddik, whose position of authority rested on the support of his followers and not upon his being awarded the *konsens* by the Polish lord, posed a threat to Czartoryski's control of the Jews on his lands. Lefin hoped that by appealing to Czartoryski's interest in maintaining the magnates' control of the traditional rabbinate he had found a strong ally in his maskilic battle with the Hasidim. As he had articulated in "*Teshuvah*," Lefin believed that the Hasidim welcomed the efforts of those Polish reformers who wanted to weaken the traditional rabbinate: "Thus they [the Polish reformers] really wanted to annul the power of excommunication . . . (and the sectarians already rejoiced about this and agreed with this opinion wholeheartedly)."[151] Lefin's comments in the *Essai d'un plan de réforme* and *Entwurf eines Rabinersystems* showed how defensive and defenseless the traditional rabbinate had become by the 1790s against the charismatic power of the Hasidim. In the *Essai d'un plan de réforme,* he stated that the Hasidim had "shattered" and "humiliated" the traditional rabbis who, "formerly intolerant, have become gentle as lambs and only hope for a refuge

---

[149] Wunder, *Entsiqlopedyah leḥakhmei Galitsyah,* 984–89; Menachem Mendel Biber, *Mazkeret legedolei Ostrahah* (Berdyczów: Hayim Jacob Sheftil, 1907), 295–96; Israel Halpern, "R. Levi Isaac of Berdyczów and the Decrees of the Government in His Time," in *Yehudim veyahadut bemizraḥ eiropah: meḥqarim betoldoteihem* (Jerusalem: Magnes Press, 1963), 344.

[150] Arthur Green, *Tormented Master: A Life of Rabbi Nahman of Bratslav* (Tuscaloosa, Ala.: The University of Alabama Press, 1979), 95–98 and Dubnow, *Toldot haḥasidut,* 2:208–13 and 312, where Dubnow calls Barukh the "general of the army of Hasidim in Podolia" with regard to the latter's conflict with Shneur Zalman of Lady (Liady) over the collection of money for Jews expelled from Russian villages in 1808.

[151] The Joseph Perl Archive, JNULA, 4° 1153/72, 3a.

from the persecution of their adversaries [the Hasidim]."[152] Thus, while Moshe Rosman has argued that the magnates' systematic intervention into the kahal may have been one of the forces that led to the disintegration of the Polish-Jewish community in the eighteenth century and also "indirectly encouraged the development of Hasidism, which was based on a charismatic leadership operating independently of the autonomy structures,"[153] Lefin's comments in *Entwurf eines Rabinersystems* suggest that certain members of the Jewish community hoped the magnates' intervention into the kahal at the end of the eighteenth century would protect it *from* the onslaught of Hasidism.

Lefin believed that he and Czartoryski shared certain Enlightenment beliefs. But he no doubt understood that their motives for reforming the rabbinate derived from different sources. Lefin did not dwell on those differences. Rather, he closed the pamphlet with a flowery coda invoking their shared interests:

> Your Highness, keep this document as a memento of Your worthy convictions (for never yet has a great man in Poland affirmed so truthfully, and with deeds, the right of mankind, as well as [the rights] of the Jewish nation): May the God of the oppressed increase Your noble pleasures — soon in this war, Your Highness — with a renewed brilliance of fortune and honor, as well as with the implementation of this plan in its place.[154]

All of the works above illustrate that Lefin's determination to reform the Jewish community in Poland was related to, but not dependent upon, the national debate in the Commonwealth on the Jewish question. Lefin continued to appeal to Czartoryski for help in reforming the rabbinate even after the disappointing declarations of the Constitution of May 3, 1791, which, hindered by the magnates' unwillingness to challenge Poland's feudal structure, offered no new solutions for the problems facing the Jews or the serfs.[155] Despite its limitations, the Constitution was greeted with euphoria, even by the Jews, but had little chance to be implemented, as conservative magnates, known as the Targowica Confederates, banded together to oppose it. Adam

---

[152] [Lefin], "*Essai d'un plan de réforme,*" 413.

[153] Rosman, *The Lords' Jews,* 205–06. Rosman's later work, and that of Shmuel Ettinger, shows, however, that Hasidim often became part of the communal structure. See Moshe Rosman, *Founder of Hasidism: A Quest for the Historical Ba'al Shem Tov* (Berkeley: University of California Press, 1996) and Shmuel Ettinger, "Hasidism and the *Kahal* in Eastern Europe," in *Hasidism Reappraised* (ed. Ada Rapoport-Albert; London, 1996), 63–75.

[154] Lefin, *Entwurf eines Rabinersystems,* 36.

[155] The Constitution's declaration of principles established a hereditary monarchy, made the ministers of state accountable to the *Sejm,* abolished the *liberum veto,* and proclaimed all armed associations (the Confederacies) illegal. It made no real steps toward the emancipation of the serfs. Stone, *Polish Politics and National Reform, 1775–1788,* 82.

Kazimierz and Adam Jerzy Czartoryski, both of whom had shown unequivocal support for Poland's "gentle revolution" of 1791, a phrase coined by
Kołłątaj to distinguish support for moderate change using Poland's existing
institutions from the violence of the French Revolution, refused to join the
conservatives. Catherine II supported the Confederates and attacked Poland
in late May 1791, quickly forcing the ill-equipped Polish army to surrender.
The territorial concessions of the Second Partition were ratified with Russia
on July 22, 1793 and with Prussia on September 26, 1793. The Kościuszko
Insurrection, the Commonwealth's last and most extensive military campaign in the era of the partitions, involved the participation of almost all
strata within Polish society, including Jews and peasants. But the patriots
were no match for the partitioning powers. The Polish troops capitulated on
November 9, 1794, and the final agreements marking the end of independent Poland were completed from January to March 1797 with Russia and
Austria gaining the most new territory.[156] Adam Jerzy Czartoryski, who had
played an important role in the military campaigns against the partitioning
powers, left Poland for England, returning to his homeland later as intercessor with Alexander I, Catherine II's successor to the Russian throne.[157]

The political dismemberment of Poland, however, did not spell the end of
the feudal estate structure of the Commonwealth. Although the Russian Tsar
and not the Polish king now embodied the highest political authority in the
lives of the Jews of the former southeastern lands of the Polish-Lithuanian
Commonwealth, the absolutist Russian Empire had as little interest as the
Polish nobility had had in radically transforming the socio-economic structure of society. For the Jews of Russian Poland living in private, noble towns,
Poland's magnates still comprised the Gentile political authority under
whose protection they lived. Lefin's views of how to effect reform within the
Jewish community did not shift dramatically with the new political reality. He
continued to advocate moderate civic reform of his people through his
relationship with the Czartoryskis and their involvement with the new
Russian legislation on the Jewish question.

Adam Jerzy Czartoryski, Lefin, and the Russian Legislation of 1804

Historians interested in Mendel Lefin have generally viewed the Constitution
of 3 May's disappointing treatment of the Jewish question as the end of his
involvement with the civic reform of the Jews.[158] Yet, Lefin's long-term

---

Lukowski, *Liberty's Folly*, 256–63.
Charles Morley, "Czartoryski as a Polish Statesman," *Slavic Review* 30, no. 3 (September
1971): 606–14.
N. M. Gelber, *Aus zwei Jahrhunderten* (Vienna: R. Löwit, 1924), 56–57.

relationship with the Czartoryskis allowed him indirect influence on the Russian Legislation of 1804, Tsar Alexander I's attempt to cope with the huge Jewish population he had inherited with the partitions of Poland. Lefin endeavored, through Adam Jerzy Czartoryski, to infuse the legislation with the spirit of moderation that characterized his earlier reform writings (*Essai d'un plan de réforme, Liqqutei kelalim, "Teshuvah,"* and *Entwurf eines Rabiner-systems*).

The treaty of January 26, 1797 marking the end of Poland's existence required the former Polish nobility to choose one of the partitioning rulers as its sovereign. Catherine II had seized most of the Czartoryski's estates in the third partition and threatened to sell them if Prince Adam Kazimierz would not swear loyalty to her. Because of his extensive holdings in the territories west of the Zbrucz River, now known as the Kingdom of Galicia and Lodomeria, Adam Kazimierz Czartoryski had become an Austrian Field Marshal.[159] Determined not to lose his eastern lands, Adam Kazimierz sent his two sons to St. Petersburg in 1795 with the hope of appeasing Catherine's demands. The mission was successful: the trip ensured that the Czartoryski estates would not be expropriated, as were the lands of other Polish nobles in August 1795, and the Czartoryski sons became Gentlemen of the Russian Court. Although the much cherished liberty of the Polish *szlachta*, which was so intimately bound to national sovereignty, was smashed with the final partition, the nobility, including the Czartoryskis, retained much of their economic power and legal status until the mid-nineteenth century.[160]

The ascension of Tsar Alexander I to the Russian throne in 1801, after the short reign of his unfortunate brother Paul, opened the possibility of introducing enlightened reforms into the Empire. The Jewish question became part of the general reform considerations because the third partition resulted in Russia's acquisition of 320,000 Jewish souls from the former southeastern borderlands of the Polish-Lithuanian Commonwealth.[161] Alexander I formed his "Unofficial Committee," comprised of Nicholas Nivosiltsev, Count Paul Stroganov, Count Victor Kochubey, the minister of internal affairs, and Prince Adam Jerzy Czartoryski, in June of that year to advise him on administrative, peasant, legal, educational, and Jewish reform. The young advisors shared a conservative commitment to reform that looked to rationalization, not democratization, as the cure for Russia's ills, and they never

---

[159] Zawadzki, *A Man of Honour*, 31–34. The Austrian *Feldmarschall* was equivalent, at least after 1848, to a five-star general of the U.S. army. See István Deák, *Beyond Nationalism: A Social and Political History of the Habsburg Officer Corps, 1848–1918* (New York: Oxford University Press, 1992), 15, table 1.3 for ranks in the Habsburg army.

[160] Zawadzki, *A Man of Honour*, 32–40.

[161] Arnold Springer, "Enlightened Absolutism and Jewish Reform: Prussia, Austria, and Russia," *California Slavic Studies* 11 (1980): 241.

seriously addressed restructuring or abolishing serfdom.[162] Becoming a close friend of Alexander I, Adam Jerzy Czartoryski attempted to work within the context of Russian control of Poland to maintain some of pre-partition Poland's liberty throughout the first three decades of the nineteenth century. Between 1802 and 1806, he was appointed foreign minister. In October 1802, he became curator of the University of Vilna. Between 1813 and 1815, he played a prominent role in Russian-Polish affairs in the semi-independent "Congress Kingdom" of Poland.[163] Czartoryski's presence on the committee was a link between the Polish Enlightenment and the debates of the Great *Sejm* and the reforming impulse of Alexander I's reign. Concern for improving the legal status of Russia's new Jewish population, all of whom lived on former Polish territory, was a hallmark of Adam Jerzy Czartoryski's efforts in Russia.[164]

On November 9, 1802, Alexander I convened a special committee for the "Amelioration of the Jews" with Gabriel Derzhavin (the minister of justice who had suggested in 1800 that the Jews be expelled from villages in western Russia and resettled in southern Ukraine), Kochubey, Count V. A. Zubov, Mikhail Speransky, and two Polish nobles, Adam Jerzy Czartoryski and Seweryn Potocki. The committee consulted with several Poles, including Tadeusz Czacki who was known for his liberal attitude toward the Jews, and with the Jews themselves. Abraham Peretz, Nota Notkin, and Judah Leib Nevakhovich of Szkłów (the author of the *The Lament of the Daughter of Judah*), enlightened Jewish businessmen living in St. Petersburg, appealed to the committee to introduce reforms for the Jews of the Russian Empire.[165] Representatives from several kehillot also travelled to St. Petersburg, suspicious of the intentions of the committee, to make their voices heard.

Mendel Lefin, too, was in St. Petersburg at the time of the deliberations of the "Committee for the Amelioration of the Jews." He was there both as a friend of the Czartoryskis and as a tutor to Zevi Hirsch Peretz, the grandson of Joshua Zeitlin, on whose estate near Szkłów he wrote *Sefer ḥeshbon hanefesh*. Lefin had been recommended to Zevi Hirsch's father, Abraham Peretz, by David Friedländer.[166] Lefin contributed to the Committee as a behind-the-scene advisor to Adam Jerzy Czartoryski, undoubtedly at the behest of his

---

[162] Nicholas Riasanovsky, *A Parting of the Ways: Government and the Educated Public in Russia, 1801–1855* (Oxford: Clarendon, 1976), 67–71.

[163] Morley, "Czartoryski as a Polish Statesman."

[164] Zawadzki, *A Man of Honour*, 2–3, 46, and 59 and Jolanta Pekacz, "To What Extent did Prince Adam Czartoryski Influence Alexander I's 'Jewish' Statute of 1804?" *The Polish Review* 40, no. 4 (1995): 403–41.

[165] Fishman, *Russia's First Modern Jews*, 124–28.

[166] Yehuda Leib Gordon, *Voskhod*, "K Istorii Poselenia Evreev V Peterburge," 1:2 (1881): 29–47. Olga Litvak graciously translated this Russian article for me.

patron, Adam Kazimierz Czartoryski, who, in March 1803, advised his son that "Mendel is the most suitable *(najzdatniejszy)* man to give his thoughts regarding the arrangements for the Jews. Write to [Tomasz] Bernatowicz to ask him if he [Mendel] is healthy enough to make the trip. [If so], then it will be necessary to provide transportation and housing for him, and I will write to Bernatowicz."[167] Lefin's deep-seated commitment to reforming and transforming his people through moderate reforms generated from within the Jewish community surely affected his patron's son. In 1803, Adam Jerzy wrote to his father, with whom he was in regular correspondence about the subject of the Jews and other reform issues:

> Soon a translation of this ukase [about the creation of an advanced seminary for the catholic priesthood attached to the University of Vilna] will come to you, my dear father. Soon, too, I expect that the new arrangements regarding the Jews will be successful. *Mendel is already here.* As much as possible we are trying to let moderation, justice and the good of the Jews themselves influence these arrangements.[168]

He confirmed his commitment to reform of the Jews in a letter to his mother in March 1804:

> I have also spoken [to my father] about the Committee of the Jews, a subject discussed in the papers that you have sent to me, my dear mother, on my father's behalf. I will profit from them and as a member of the Committee I will endeavor to do as much as possible for this class of men and make them as useful as they can be for society.[169]

A long project entitled "Thoughts on Improving the Civic Position of the Jews" found in the Czartoryski family archive may also have been written by Adam Jerzy Czartoryski. The content of the pamphlet echoes many of Lefin's reforms. For example, the project suggests that the Jews themselves be consulted on the reform of their community and that unemployed Jews be placed in workhouses. The pamphlet in the Czartoryski archive also urged that Jews attend schools with either Russian or German as the language of instruction, but that the state should not tamper with any aspect of their religious instruction.[170] In *Liqqutei kelalim*, Lefin had emphasized that any reform of the Jewish community should come from its internal edicts and in the *Essai d'un plan de réforme* he made the specific suggestion that the district

---

[167] Adam Kazimierz Czartoryski to Adam Jerzy Czartoryski, Kraków, March 19, 1803. The original letter, 6285 EW 1046, 265–268, reads, "Mendel najzdatniejszy jest człowiek do dania swoich myśli względem urządzenia Żydów," while the copy, 6338 IV, MS EW 1503, 187–190, omits the word "urządzenia."

[168] Adam Jerzy Czartoryski to Adam Kazimierz Czartoryski, August 10, 1803. Czart. MS EW 3267. Emphasis is mine. The last sentence of the letter is cited in Zawadzki, *A Man of Honour*, 59.

[169] Adam Jerzy Czartoryski to Izabela Czartoryska, March 2, 1804. Czart. MS EW 3267.

[170] Zawadzki, *A Man of Honour*, 59.

rabbis should be empowered "to forbid the support of (through a misunderstood commiseration with) the idle poor who are capable of working, and even to use their power of excommunication to oblige them to yield to the workhouses that have been established."[171]

Moderation, the use of positive incentives, was a central feature of the committee's deliberations on how to acculturate the Jews. The liberal cast of the deliberations owed much to Adam Jerzy Czartoryski's participation and familiarity with the range of debates about the Jews that had occupied the Four-Year *Sejm*.[172] A journal entry of the Committee on September 20, 1803 read:

> Transformations brought about by governmental force will generally not be stable and will be especially unreliable in those cases where this force struggles against centuries-old habits, with ingrained errors, and with unyielding superstition; it would be better and more opportune to direct the Jews toward improvement, to open the path to their own benefit, overseeing their progress from afar and removing anything that might lead them astray, not employing any force, not setting up any particular institution, not acting in their place, but enabling their own activity. As few restrictions as possible, as much freedom as possible. This is a simple formula for any organization of society! In the calculation of the variables determining human action, the basic foundation ought always to rest on private gain, the internal principle which never stops anywhere, and which evades all laws that are inconvenient. . . . Everywhere that governments thought merely to command, there appeared only the phantom of success, which was maintained for awhile in the air, and then disappeared together with the principles that gave birth to it. In contrast to every undertaking carried out insensitively are those generated by private gain, freely maintained, and only patronized by the government, which were shown to be maintained by an internal force, a firm basis established by time and by personal benefit.
>
> In every respect the Jews should be encouraged toward education, preferably by means of quiet encouragement, organized by their own activity.[173]

Although Lefin's influence on the committee cannot be directly traced, the journal's emphasis on moderation resounds with the tone of the *Essai d'un plan de réforme*, *Liqqutei kelalim*, and *Entwurf eines Rabinersystems*. In fact, Shmuel Ettinger has argued that the entry cited above was nothing more than a translation from Montesquieu's *De l'Esprit des Lois*, Book 19, chapter 14.[174] Lefin had cited the very same chapter and verse in his *Essai d'un plan de réforme*. While Montesquieu's ideas had spread among liberal sectors of both

---

[171] Lefin, *Liqqutei kelalim*, in Gelber, "Mendel Lefin of Satanów's Proposals," 292 and [Lefin], "*Essai d'un plan de réforme*," 417.

[172] Daniel Beauvois, "Polish-Jewish Relations in the Territories Annexed by the Russian Empire in the First Half of the Nineteenth Century," in *The Jews in Poland* (ed. Chimen Abramsky, Maciej Jachimczyk, and Antony Polonsky; London: Basil Blackwell, 1986), 81 and Louis Greenberg, *The Jews in Russia: The Struggle for Emancipation* (New Haven, Conn.: Yale University Press, 1944), 1:9.

[173] Cited in Klier, *Russia Gathers Her Jews*, 129–30.

[174] Shmuel Ettinger, "The Edicts of 1804," *He'avar* 22 (1977): 101, footnote 51.

Russian and Polish society, it is still highly probable that Lefin's respect for
Montesquieu's moderate position on changing culture influenced the
Committee — through Adam Jerzy Czartoryski's intercession — to cite the
French *philosophe* and stress reform of the Jews through positive incentives.[175]
    Although the Russian state was ultimately unwilling to address the socio-
economic problems of the southeastern borderlands and to integrate the
Jews into the Empire, the Imperial Statute Concerning the Jews, promulgated on December 9, 1804, was liberal and enlightened compared to the
legislation of Tsar Nicholas I (1825–1855), which later had a decisive effect
on the transformation of Russian Jewry.[176] The 1804 decrees maintained the
existence of the Jewish muncipality and its responsibilities for raising taxes;
limited the terms of kahal elders and required that they learn either Russian,
German or Polish; admitted Jews to municipal councils and general courts of
justice; allowed the Jewish community to maintain its own network of
elementary schools provided they incorporate the use of general languages;
and did not mandate the compulsory resettling of the Jews.[177] The most
punitive aspect of the decrees was clause thirty-four, which prohibited the
Jews from holding the leases on taverns, drinking houses and inns, and
forbade them from selling liquor. The Polish landlords who tried to circumvent the law were to be subject to fines, but, in fact, it was in the interest of
both the Jews and their Polish lords to retain these traditional Jewish occupations.[178] As a result of this commonality of interest — and of Russian
reluctance to tackle the problem of the serfs directly — there was no
fundamental change in the socio-economic structure of Jewish communal
life within Russian lands until Tsar Nicholas I's reign. The government also
stepped back from any internal involvement with intra-Jewish politics, and
allowed the establishment of non-kahal supervised prayer groups, "[in cases
of communal conflict in which] one group among the Jews will not want to
participate in the other group's synagogue."[179] In practice, this meant that
there were no obstacles to the flourishing of Hasidic *minyanim* (prayer
quorums).[180]
    Clause thirty-four, however, also stipulated — in relation to Jewish involve-
ment with liquor arendas — that from January 1, 1807, no Jews were to be

---

[175] On the influence of Montesquieu's political thought on Polish reformers, see Jerzy
Lukowski, "Recasting Utopia: Montesquieu, Rousseau and the Polish Constitution of 3 May
1791," *The Historical Journal* 37, no. 1 (March 1994): 65–87.
[176] Stanislawski, *Tsar Nicholas I and the Jews*.
[177] Salo W. Baron, *The Russian Jew under Tsars and Soviets* (New York: Schocken Books,
1987), 20 and Ettinger, "The Edicts of 1804," 100.
[178] Klier, *Russia Gathers Her Jews*, 141–47.
[179] Clause fifty-three of the edict, published in Ettinger, "The Edicts of 1804," 109.
[180] Fishman, *Russia's First Modern Jews*, 21.

allowed to live in the villages of Astrakhan, the Caucasus, Little and New Russia. This aspect of the edict, which was formalized in February 15, 1807 at Derzhavin's urging, had the disastrous result of initiating an expulsion of Jews from villages, which alarmed the representatives of the Jewish communities, who attempted to stay the ruling. An inadvertent result of the harsh measure was the momentary unity of the conflicting groups within the Jewish community. Sometime in 1809, a diverse group of Jews, including Barukh of Międzybóż (Medzibozh), Levi Isaac of Berdyczów and other Ukrainian Hasidim, Dov Beerish Rapoport, Joshua Herszel Józefowicz, Mendel Lefin, and Tobias Gutmann Feder (a *maskil* who would later attack Lefin's Yiddish writings), all met in Berdyczów to discuss ways to contravene the expulsion edict.[181] Their negotiations were ineffective, but the chaos that ensued in the wake of the Napoleonic Wars meant that the expulsions ceased. When the final boundaries between the Congress Kingdom of Poland and the Pale of Settlement were drawn on June 9, 1815, Jewish life in the southeastern borderlands settled back into its older patterns.

For Lefin, the 1804 legislation had two important effects. First, it sanctioned in law what had occurred in practice: the triumph of Hasidic separatism in most of Eastern Europe, and the retreat of the Russian authorities — for the time being — from direct involvement in internal Jewish cultural politics. Second, the 1804 edicts ended Lefin's political involvement with the non-Jewish authorities in his campaign against Hasidism. Schooled in the politics of the pre-absolutist "Noble Republic," Lefin could no longer appeal to the Czartoryskis, now dependent upon the Tsar and the Austrian Emperor, to intervene in the culture wars of the Jewish community. Rather, Lefin followed his own advice and continued his struggle against Hasidism on the literary battlefield. From his perspective, the work of changing the spiritual course of Polish Jewry had just begun. Returning to Mikołajów, Lefin endeavored to effect that change by creating a body of literature for East European Jewish youths, including original satires and philosophical essays, translations of Scripture, and adaptations of West European travelogues and American Enlightenment thought, and infusing them with his anti-Hasidic agenda.

---

[181] Halpern, "R. Levi Isaac of Berdyczów," 342–44. On Feder, see Chapter Four.

CHAPTER THREE

THE BATTLE AGAINST HASIDISM AND THE STRUGGLE FOR THE ADOLESCENT SOUL

> Hasidism did not strive to reform the principles of religion or its customs, but [strove for] a deeper reform, for reform of the *soul*. Through the means of powerful psychological influence, Hasidism created a type of *believer* for whom emotion was more important than external custom, communion with God [*devequt*] and religious ardor [*hitlahavut*] more important than inquiry into and study of Torah.[1]
>
> Simon Dubnow, *Toldot hahasidut* (1930)

From its very beginnings, opponents of Hasidism struggled to understand its appeal.[2] But it was not until the last quarter of the eighteenth century, when the third generation of Hasidic devotees had so thoroughly transformed a spiritual revolution into a religious movement, that the Ashkenazic rabbinic authorities voiced their opposition through a series of public bans.[3] Despite these denunciations from the region's highest rabbinic authorities, Hasidism continued to spread, and soon captured the hearts and souls of much of East European Jewry. Lefin's earliest published work, *Essai d'un plan de réforme ayant pour objet d'éclairer la Nation Juive en Pologne et de redresser par là ses moeurs*, attested to the spread of Hasidism by the 1790s:

> They [the Hasidim] have already totally inundated the Ukraine, where they have hired a number of rabbis to combat the others [the traditional rabbinate]. . . . They have

---

[1]   Simon Dubnow, *Toldot hahasidut* (Tel Aviv: Devir, 1930), 1:35. Emphasis in the original.

[2]   Classic works, including the studies of Benzion Dinur, Raphael Mahler, and Mendel Piekarz, looked to the social underpinnings of Hasidism and argued that class conflict explained the movement's appeal. In this reading, the Hasidim represented the downtrodden Jewish masses, who rose up against the hegemony of both the rabbinic elite and the Gentile state. See Benzion Dinur, *Bemifneh hadorot* (Jerusalem: The Bialik Institute, 1955), 81–227; Raphael Mahler, *Hasidism and the Jewish Enlightenment: Their Confrontation in Galicia and Poland in the First Half of the Nineteenth Century* (Philadelphia: The Jewish Publication Society of America, 1985); Mendel Piekarz, *Biymei tsemihat hahasidut: megammot ra'ayoniyyot besifrei derush umusar* (Jerusalem: Magnes Press, 1978).

[3]   Mordecai Wilensky, *Hasidim umitnaggedim: letoldot hapulmus shebeineihem bashanim 1772-1815* (Jerusalem: The Bialik Institute, 1970) and Mordecai Wilensky, "Hasidic-Mitnaggedic Polemics in the Jewish Communities of Eastern Europe: The Hostile Phase," in *Tolerance and Movements of Religious Dissent in Eastern Europe* (ed. Béla K. Király; New York: Columbia University Press, 1975), 89–113.

resolutely taken hold in Podolia, which is their motherland, the same in Volhynia and Lithuania. . . . A considerable niche exists here, too, in Warsaw, which is often visited by its leaders, who sometimes bleed them [their followers] well.[4]

While there were many areas within eighteenth-century Polish-Jewish life — communal authority and administration, kosher slaughtering, prayer, and religious leadership — that were disputed between Hasidism and its opponents, the structure of the human soul and its ability to subdue and conquer evil — as Dubnow concluded in the 1930s — was their most contested battleground. Lefin devoted a large part of his *oeuvre* to the human soul because he believed that an understanding of the soul was the key to comprehending, and improving, the human condition. Analysis of the soul would unlock the mysteries of knowledge, both of the physical and of the metaphysical worlds; moreover, knowlege of the soul's faculties could lead to controlling its appetites. Comprehending the soul was, for Lefin, as well as for many eighteenth-century thinkers, the key to knowing the self. Mastery of the map of the soul was essential to Lefin's specific historical battle against Hasidism, a struggle that encompassed efforts to challenge Hasidic social organization, techniques for expiating sin, patterns of prayer, and methods of attracting Jewish youth to its camp. All of his philosophical, psychological, and ethical works were part of Lefin's overarching effort to safeguard traditional Ashkenazic piety and structures of religious authority from what he believed to be Hasidic subversion. Lefin directed his anti-Hasidic efforts specifically at the Jewish youth of Eastern Europe, the group whom he felt to be most vulnerable to the seductions of Hasidism. He did so through both a selective appropriation of the terminology and methods of eighteenth-century natural philosophy, particularly the science of the mind, what he called *ḥokhmat haneshamot* ("science of the souls"), and an appeal to the medieval Jewish rationalist tradition.

Mendel Lefin's Psychology

The natural philosophers of the eighteenth century, Mendel Lefin among them, saw no contradiction between belief and science. Asserting that the world of metaphysics was fundamentally unknowable, they bracketed it off from critical inquiry. In so doing, they protected faith from the period's relentless drive to investigate the realms of the knowable world of nature, including the fields of physics, physical astronomy, chemistry, biology,

---

4   [Mendel Lefin], *"Essai d'un plan de réforme ayant pour objet d'éclairer la Nation Juive en Pologne et de redresser par là ses moeurs,"* in *Materiały do dziejów Sejmu Czteroletniego* (ed. Arthur Eisenbach et al.; Wrocław: Instytut Historii Polskiej Akademii Nauk, 1969), 410 and 420, footnote 7.

physiology, and psychology. Indebted to an Aristotelian dualism that presupposed a mind/body divide, eighteenth-century natural philosophers assumed humanity's distinctiveness based on the existence of an immaterial and immortal soul, which could be studied empirically. Psychology, they believed, should begin with the "solid facts" of a natural science based on observation.[5] Phenomena preceded principles that could be drawn only from the results of empirical perception.[6]

Lefin's psychological thought reflected a familiarity and engagement with contemporary European psychological theory. Although he does not directly cite John Locke's *Essay Concerning Human Understanding* (1690), which claimed that the mind was an "empty cabinet" capable of passive perception of the outside world, all of Lefin's psychological writings are indebted to Lockian conceptions.[7] Locke's sensationalism, the formulation that all human knowledge was derived from the external environment, became the basis for the psychological thought of Christian Wolff, Charles Bonnet, Guillaume-Lambert Godart, Johann Gottlob Krüger, David Hartley, Claude-Adrien Helvétius, Etienne Bonnot de Condillac, George Berkeley, and Voltaire, and can also be found in Lefin's work.[8] Equally important to Lefin was Locke's conception of the "association of ideas," which provided an explanation of how the mind, evoking one discrete idea, could simultaneously recall other ideas connected to it and thus conjoin individual sense impressions or ideas to one another.[9] Lefin appears, however, to have been

---

5   Gary Hatfield, "Remaking the Science of the Mind: Psychology as Natural Science," in *Inventing Human Science* (ed. Christopher Fox, Roy Porter, and Robert Wokler; Berkeley: University of California Press, 1995), 184–231.
6   Ernst Cassirer, *The Philosophy of the Enlightenment* (Boston, Mass.: Beacon Press, 1962), 7–8, 21–23.
7   John Locke, *An Essay Concerning Human Understanding* (ed. Alexander Campbell Fraser; New York: Dover, 1959). On Locke, see Peter Gay, *The Enlightenment: An Interpretation* (New York: Alfred A. Knopf, 1966), 1:167–80.
8   On Locke's influence on these European thinkers, see Hatfield, "Remaking the Science of the Mind," 197–200. Lefin specifically mentioned Leonhard Euler, Benjamin Franklin, and Helvétius by name in his writings. For Lefin's reference to Euler, see the Joseph Perl Archive, JNULA, 4° 1153/56, which was Lefin's personal journal. On the journal's front page Lefin mentioned that a friend had borrowed the first volume of Euler's letters [*Letters to a German Princess* (1770)] from him on 3 Av (August 6), 1826; to Franklin, see the Abraham Schwadron Collection of Jewish Autographs and Portraits, JNULA, Mendel Lefin papers, document b, and Israel Weinlös, "R. Menachem Mendel of Satanów," *Ha'olam* 13 (1925): 800; to Helvétius, see the Abraham Schwardron Collection of Jewish Autographs and Portraits, JNULA, Mendel Lefin papers, documents b, d and e, and the Joseph Perl Archive, JNULA, 4° 1153/6 and 4° 1153/128d. Moreover, we should not discount the possibility that Christian Wolff's psychological writings — so central to the growth of empirical psychology on the Continent — influenced Lefin, although he does not cite Wolff in any of his writings.
9   Locke used the "association of ideas" only to explain cognitive error, such as a child's correlation of darkness with goblins or a pagan's association of God with corporeality, but

directly influenced by the work of David Hartley (1705–1757), a physician by training, who, in his *Observations on Man, His Frame, His Duty, and His Expectations* (1749), developed Locke's conception of the "association of ideas" by grounding it in Newtonian physiology. Drawing on Newton's *Principia* for information about the structure of the nervous system and its reception of external stimuli, Hartley posited a physiological basis for human understanding, what Peter Gay called a "physiological psychology."[10] In Hartley's vocabulary of human understanding, all ideas derived from simple sense perceptions, which were received by the vibration of the nerves and then conducted to the brain:

> The white medullary substance of the brain, spinal marrow, and the nerves proceeding from them, is the immediate instrument of sensation and motion. . . . External objects impressed upon the senses occasion, first in the nerves on which they are impressed, and then in the brain, vibrations of the small, and as one may say, infinitesimal, medullary particles. . . . The vibrations mentioned in the last proposition are excited, propagated, and kept up, partly by the äther, i.e. by a very subtle and elastic fluid, and partly by the uniformity, continuity, softness, and active powers of the medullary substance of the brain, spinal marrow, and nerves.[11]

Simple sense perceptions became complex ideas through the "association of ideas," the connection of discrete perceptions to one another.

Lefin's theory of the soul began with faculty psychology, and he divided the soul's powers into three faculties (sensual, imaginative or pictorial, and rational).[12] The imaginative faculty was strongest among children, who could respond physiologically to external stimuli, but were incapable of organizing those stimuli into clear thoughts when they were very young. In a German fragment from Lefin's *Nachlaß eines Sonderlings zu Abdera* (*The Literary Estate of a Crank from Abdera*),[13] which he dedicated to Izabela Czartoryska, Lefin used

---

other European thinkers expanded the concept. See Locke, *An Essay Concerning Human Understanding*, 1: 529–35.

[10]   The centrality of the vibrations of the nerves can also be found in the work of Johann Gottlob Krüger (*Versuch einer Experimental Seelenlehre*, 1756), Christian Wolff, and Charles Bonnet (*Essai analytique sur les facultés de l'âme*, 1760). See Gay, *The Enlightenment*, 2: 181–84 for the term "physiological psychology."

[11]   David Hartley, *Observations on Man, His Frame, His Duty and His Expectations* (London: T. Tegg & Son, 1834), 5 and 8. The term "äther" is from Newton.

[12]   The Abraham Schwadron Collection of Jewish Autographs and Portraits, papers of Mendel Lefin (1749–1826), and the Joseph Perl Archive, JNULA, 4° 1153/127d, entitled *Ma'amar olam hagemul* (*Essay on the Afterlife*) [lit. *Essay on The World of Reward*], 1b.

[13]   Israel Weinlös, who had access to the Perl library in Tarnopol during the interwar years, saw two editions of Lefin's *Nachlaß*, a philosophic work on Kantian philosophy that is no longer extant. Lefin began the first version, consisting of 242 folios, in 1794 in Sieniawa, and completed it in 1806 in Mikołajów, which is confirmed by the appendix to the Perl Archive compiled by Phillip Koffler. Lefin completed the second edition, consisting of 248 folios, and readied it for publication, in 1823. See Israel Weinlös, "Mendel Lefin of Satanów: A

the word *sensuousness* to describe the capacity of a child's nervous system to perceive external stimuli, but hastened to explain that this meant "nothing more than to have the ability *to connect* the components of sensations or images."[14] The sensual and imaginative faculties could only respond to impressions and record them; they were not capable of judgment. The rational soul, on the other hand, could arrange impressions according to a set order.[15] Summing up the distinctions among the three faculties, Lefin wrote:

> The conceptions that constantly preoccupy the consciousness of our soul are either (1) *Sensual.* This means they originate directly from the physical world. For example, I have the chance to get a glimpse of the aeloic harp, to hear its voice, or to feel the sting of an electric spark. All [three examples] transmit a vibration of the nerves. (2) *Pictorial,* [that which is] drawn from the inner memory reservoir of former impressions; I remember having seen, heard, or felt this or that. Or, finally, (3) *Rational,* meaning, [conceptions] that are neither impressions from objects of the physical world, nor mere copies from [the impressions of the objects of the physical world], but represent copies conceptualized by the mind. The mind itself selects several pictorial conceptions about the material (e.g. abstraction, combination, conclusion, or simple hypothesis) in order to fashion a kind of conception completely dissimilar to them.[16]

The external world provided concrete stimuli that "pushed themselves involuntarily into the soul from the outside, forcefully motivating the soul more than the other [types of] conceptions," wrote Lefin.[17] In *Sefer ḥeshbon hanefesh* (*Moral Accounting,* Lemberg, 1808), Lefin's work of moral self-reform that will be explored in detail below, he implicitly evoked Hartley's theory of vibrations to explain how the inner world of the soul, which he called *olam haqatan* (literally, "the small world"), received information from the external world (*olam hagadol,* "the large world"). Because Lefin's conception of the soul equated the world of the senses with the "bestial soul," he argued that sensual perception was within its province:

Biographical Study from Manuscript Material," *YIVO bleter* 1 (1931): 334–57. Roughly twenty fragmentary pages survived the transfer of the Joseph Perl archive to Jerusalem from Tarnopol. The extant fragments from *Nachlaß* include those in the Abraham Schwadron Collection of Jewish Autographs and Portraits, Mendel Lefin papers and in the Joseph Perl Archive, JNULA, 4° 1153/128, which contains five discrete fragmentary essays, four of which are from *Nachlaß*. Notes to *Nachlaß* also appear in Lefin's unpublished journal, the Joseph Perl Archive, JNULA, 4° 1153/130, 139.

14   The Joseph Perl Archive, JNULA, 4° 1153/128b, paragraph 2. Emphasis in the original. See, too, Weinlös, "R. Menachem Mendel of Satanów," 800 for an outline of the chapters of *Nachlaß*; the fourth chapter of the first section was entitled "*Sinnlicht, Animalität, und Verstand* (Sensuous[ness], Animalness, and Reason)."

15   Mendel Lefin, *Sefer ḥeshbon hanefesh* (Lemberg, 1808), paragraph 79.

16   The Joseph Perl Archive, JNULA, 4° 1153/71a, 1a.

17   The Joseph Perl Archive, JNULA, 4° 1153/127d, 1b.

A man's bestial soul [receives stimuli and] dispatches [information] to the whole body through the *tubes of the brain* (*tsinurot hamohim*), the branches of white threads that leave the brain and spinal chord and diffuse vitality and feeling upon the body (like the capillaries that leave the heart to carry the nourishment in the blood to all of the limbs). Their principle feeling is in their membranes, and when one channel [neuron] ceases [to respond] or its membrane hardens or weakens too much, then the existence and vitality of its [corresponding] limb is nullified.[18]

In another fragment, Lefin was even more explicit about the influence of the concept of nerve vibrations: "Each one of the active or passive, intentional or involuntary, vibrations of the nerves *produces* an idea in our soul. Each of the ideas generally reproduces a long-discarded earlier idea from the stores of memory, with which it associates or joins in some way."[19] So, too, was Lefin indebted to associationism, calling it *hilluf harayonot, mehalekh hamahashavot, mehalekh harayonot*, and *qishur harayonot* (all of which translate to "the association of ideas" or "association of thoughts") in several places in his writings.[20] Lefin believed that the process of aging stiffened and therefore diminished the sensitivity of the nerves; the condition of the human understanding was, thus, subject to a process of development, with infancy representing the point of the nerves' highest sensitivity, middle-age exemplifying a balance between the nerves' sensual acuity and rationality, and old age, concluding with death, signalling the end of all sensual experience.[21] Lefin adduced scriptural support for the rupture from sensual experience that death wrought in his Hebrew commentary on Eccl 12:7: "The spinal cord will harden, the skin will burst open, the brain will split in half, and the veins and arteries will shrink ([the text uses] an allegory of a vessel in a well that breaks, the pulley runs backwards, and the cord shortens and winds around itself); then the body will turn into an inanimate object, and the soul will return to Heaven."[22]

Lefin, however, was not a pure sensationalist. He believed, like Locke and Hartley before him, in the capacity of the mind to retain the simple ideas it had received from the senses, which he referred to as the imaginative faculty of human understanding. But, he placed even greater emphasis on the

---

[18] Lefin, *Sefer ḥeshbon hanefesh*, paragraph 67 with its footnote and paragraph 78. See, too, Mendel Lefin, "*Elon moreh*," *Hamelits* (1867): 12.

[19] The Abraham Schwadron Collection of Jewish Autographs and Portraits, JNULA, Mendel Lefin Papers, document c, paragraph 25.

[20] Lefin, *Sefer ḥeshbon hanefesh*, paragraphs 78, 81–82, 96, footnote to paragraph 97. See, too, the Joseph Perl Archive, 4° 1153/130, 38–39, and 56, and 4° 1153/127d, 2a and Harris Bor, "Enlightenment Values, Jewish Ethics: The Haskalah's Transformation of the Traditional *Musar* Genre," in *New Perspectives on the Haskalah* (ed. Shmuel Feiner and David Sorkin; Oxford: The Littman Library of Jewish Civilization, 2001), 54–5.

[21] The Joseph Perl Archive, JNULA, 4° 1153/71a, 2a. See, too, the Joseph Perl Archive, JNULA, 4° 1153/128a.

[22] Mendel Lefin, *Sefer qohelet im targum yehudit uvi'ur* (Odessa, 1873).

mind's active, rational capacity.[23] Lefin's interest in sensationalism reveals his use of contemporary psychological theory, but his rejection of the prevailing wisdom that human understanding was but a passive response to external stimuli illuminates his conscious interpretation of ideas from the West European Enlightenment. Stated differently, Lefin's response to contemporary psychological theories was never a blind imitation of them. He sought to appropriate West European ideas in order to use those that suited his purpose: revivification of Polish-Jewry based on the medieval Jewish rational tradition and its emphasis on the activity of the rational faculty. It was self-evident for Lefin that the mind had the capacity to conceptualize ideas independently of sense perceptions. Like Mendelssohn, Lefin believed that the senses presented a disorderly mass of impressions to the brain, which could not untangle them without the skill of the rational faculty.[24] To illustrate his point, he contrasted the control exerted by the rational faculty of a mature, sentient adult to the unbridled exercise of the imaginative faculty during sleep. While sleeping, the faculties of sense perception and rationality shut down, giving the imaginative capacity of the mind (and its confused "association of ideas") free rein. Lefin explained:

> Because sensory thoughts are dormant [when we are asleep], [we create] a just and serious world out of our fantasies. We relax during good dreams, and have worries, anxieties, and fears during bad dreams. For example, a simple Jew can dream that he is sitting in the Land of Israel, which he sees [and feels]. His mind and reason do not deny the dream. [Still dreaming, and] believing that he is now joyously living in the Land of Israel, he takes back his donation from the official emissary [who raises funds for Jews living in the Land of Israel]. . . . At the time of deep sleep . . . all three eyes ["faculties"] are shut. The only one that may be open is the middle eye [of the imaginative faculty]. In such a way, the process of dreams begins, like Satan's games of disguise and confusion. However, soon the sensory and rational thoughts both awaken, the entire delusion falls away, and the "process of ideas" returns again to its habitual course (according to sensation and reason).[25]

The rational faculty of the mind was, unlike the sensory and imaginative faculties, capable of controlling and guiding the "association of ideas," which Lefin compared to the unceasing, undulating motion of waves and running

---

[23] See Locke, *An Essay Concerning Human Understanding*, 1:193–95; Hartley, *Observations on Man*, 2; Lefin, *Sefer ḥeshbon hanefesh*, paragraphs 50, 53, and 55, on memory and the mind's power to retain and recall previous sense perceptions.

[24] On Mendelssohn's rejection of pure sensationalism, see Alexander Altmann, *Moses Mendelssohn: A Biographical Study* (Tuscaloosa, Ala.: The University of Alabama Press, 1973), 658–59.

[25] The Joseph Perl Archive, JNULA, 4° 1153/127d, 3a–3b. See, too, Lefin, *Sefer ḥeshbon hanefesh*, paragraph 78, Hartley, *Observations on Man*, 29, and Leonhard Euler, *Letters of Euler on Different Subjects in Physics and Philosophy addressed to a German Princess* (trans. Henry Hunter; London: Murray & Highley, 1802), 1:359 on sleep as a condition in which sensual stimuli could not be perceived. On Euler, see Gay, *The Enlightenment*, 1:126–44.

water. The ability of the rational faculty to order the tumultuous "process of ideas" ("the ability to connect ideas with intention") was the quality of the mind that distinguished men from animals. The existence of the rational faculty made human language and speech possible; thus, it could also be called the faculty of speech.[26] Because the rational faculty was weak in infants and non-existent in animals, both groups lacked language. Sensory impressions alone defined the "association of ideas" in children's and animals' "knowledge" of the world. As we shall see below, Lefin's faculty psychology and conception of the developmental powers of the soul provided the intellectual arsenal in his battle against the Hasidic conception of human understanding.

Limiting Reason in the East European Jewish Enlightenment

The eighteenth-century preoccupation with epistemology was intimately bound up with a concern to elucidate its parameters. The emphasis on what the mind could know through the senses, rather than what might have been previously considered innate to the faculty of human understanding, underscored the limitations of human apprehension of the natural world. Nature, and its study through biology and physiology, usurped the centrality of mathematics and physics. Reason became a tool to help guide humanity in understanding its relationship to the empirical world. However, interest in natural science and the empirical quality of sense perception did not necessarily mean the abandonment of traditional, religious metaphysics, and many natural philosophers used their interest in the natural world to support their belief in a creative, benevolent God.[27]

Tracing the precise literary influences of the celebration of natural science in the West European and Polish Enlightenments on Lefin's thought is difficult because he only rarely mentioned his sources. We can surmise that his connections with *maskilim* in Berlin and with the Czartoryskis' enlightened circles gave Lefin entrée — both direct and indirect — to British, German, and French ideas.[28] The Czartoryskis' extensive travel on

---

[26] Lefin, *Sefer ḥeshbon hanefesh*, footnote to paragraph 97. Maimonides called the second faculty of the soul the *nefesh medabberet* ("the speaking soul"), which distinguished man from all other sublunar beings. See the discussion of Maimonides's philosophical terminology in Israel Efros, *Philosophical Terms in the Moreh Nebukim* (Columbia University Oriental Studies; New York: AMS Press, Inc., 1966), 86–87.

[27] Cassirer, *The Philosophy of the Enlightenment*, 13, 65–68, and 93. See, too, Gay, *The Enlightenment*, 2:160.

[28] W. H. Zawadzki, *A Man of Honour: Adam Czartoryski as a Statesman of Russia and Poland, 1795–1831* (Oxford: Clarendon Press, 1993), 17, 19, and 31; Joseph Klausner, *Historyah shel hasifrut ha'ivrit hahadashah* (Jerusalem: The Hebrew University, 1952), 1:15; Roderick Weir Home, "Scientific Links Between Britain and Russia in the Second Half of the Eighteenth

the Continent and to England, in particular, made them particularly receptive to a broad swath of ideas, an eclectic array of which — Wolffianism, Cartesianism, Newtonianism, empiricism, and sensationalism — found their way to the Commonwealth.[29] Conscious of his traditional audience and dedicated to the continuity of traditional rabbinic observance, Mendel Lefin felt compelled to justify his interest in natural science by adducing scriptural and rabbinic support. In his *Iggerot haḥokhmah* (*Letters of Wisdom*), Lefin posited that scientific investigation of the natural world must sensitize the observer to the greatness and purposefulness of God's creative power. Although man could not perceive the distinctiveness of an individual grain of sand or of a sesame seed without the aid of a microscope, God's infinite knowledge could fathom the essence of the largest and smallest of creatures. Citing the saying of Rabbi Yohanan recited at the conclusion of the Sabbath (*b. Megillah 31a*), "Where you find the greatness of the Holy One, blessed is he, there you find his humility," Ps 113:5–6 ("Who is like the Lord our God, who is enthroned on high, and yet looks far down to behold the things that are in Heaven, and on the earth!"), and Ps 92:6 ("How great are your works, O Lord, how very subtle are your designs!"), Lefin concluded that the study of natural science led inexorably to the recognition of God's unique design for the natural world. This diverse universe, home to eighteen different kinds of ants, twenty-four types of lice, more than twenty-four varieties of spiders, eighty-seven kinds of crabs, more than one hundred kinds of gnats and over one hundred types of flies, all coexisting and serving a role in the natural order, had to be the work of a purposeful God.[30] His mention of the microscope (invented in 1660) and the citation of the long taxonomic list reveals Lefin's conservative interest in scientific inventions and discoveries. His paramount concern was not recent scientific innovation, but the investigation of natural science as a stimulus to traditional rabbinic piety. With that

---

Century," in *Electricity and Experimental Physics in Eighteenth-Century Europe* (ed. Roderick Weir Home; Hampshire: Variorum, 1992), 212–13.

[29] Richard Butterwick, *Poland's Last King and English Culture: Stanisław August Poniatowski, 1732–1798* (Oxford: Oxford University Press, 1998), 40.

[30] The letter was originally published in *Iggerot haḥokhmah*, which was included in Lefin's *Moda levinah* (Berlin, 1789) and later reprinted at the beginning of all the post-1845 editions of *Sefer ḥeshbon hanefesh*. The letter does not appear in the edition of *Sefer ḥeshbon hanefesh* published in Lefin's lifetime. The Talmud uses the word *gevurato* (might or power), while Lefin's text has *gedulato* (greatness) to refer to God's omnipotence and omniscience. On this point, see, too, Lefin's unpublished "The Variability of the Standard of Human Life or for the Name Day of His Austrian Imperial Monarch, [His] Majesty's General Field Marshal, [His] Highness the Prince Adam Czartoryski, the 24th of December, 1814, a Serious but Edifying Consideration," Joseph Perl Archive, JNULA, 4° 1153/128a, paragraphs 5 and 6. The Koffler appendix confirms Lefin's authorship of this essay, but cites 1815 as its date of composition. See the Joseph Perl Archive, JNULA, 4° 1153/appendix.

goal in mind, the study of natural science should be encouraged among his contemporary Polish Jews.[31]

Like other early modern Ashkenazic Jews interested in the physical world, Lefin looked specifically to medieval Jewish precedents to sanction his study of nature. David Ruderman has argued that rabbinic leaders of the early modern period, such as Moses Isserles (1525 or 1530–1572) and Judah Loewe of Prague (1525–1609), circumscribed the role of science in order to create a permissible and autonomous realm for its study that coexisted with traditional fields of knowledge, rabbinic and mystical literature. Isserles and Loewe themselves turned to Bahya ibn Pekuda (second half of the 11th century), a passionate supporter of the religious obligation to study nature, to validate their pursuit of physical science. In his *Hovot halevavot* (*Duties of the Heart*, 1080), arguably one of the most influential texts of medieval *musar* (ethics), Bahya ibn Pakuda affirmed the primacy of studying nature, "Contemplate, therefore, God's creatures, from the largest of them to the smallest, and reflect on those matters which are at present hidden from you . . . and because these marks of divine wisdom vary in created things, it is our duty to study them and meditate on them until the whole matter becomes established in our souls and abides in our consciousness."[32] Both modernizing and traditional Jews in the eighteenth century employed *Hovot halevavot*, published over thirty times in Eastern Europe during the seventeenth and eighteenth centuries, as support for their respective concerns.[33] Lefin, explicitly referring to the first chapter in *Hovot halevavot*, "The Gate of God's Unity," concluded that the extraordinary complexity of the natural world illustrated God's greatness and was proof of the existence of a good and purposeful God:

> Letter 1, Section 15: Thus it is clear from natural science that God, may he be exalted, imprinted all of creation with his power: a) [Creation] is an illuminated mirror through which to see his completeness. In the created world, his infinite greatness and his humility can be found in the same place. His wisdom, dominion, compassion, and devotion to his creatures are revealed eternally in his created world. b) [The Sages] concluded that the goal of creation was two-fold: *to reveal his completeness and to please his creatures.* Section 16: a) [God's power] astonishes us with his ordered creation of all kinds of trees and plants in a [systematic] relationship to one another, like that of nations and

---

[31]   See Hillel Levine, "Menahem Mendel Lefin: A Case Study of Judaism and Modernization" (Ph.D. diss., Harvard University, 1974), 67,106–109.

[32]   David B. Ruderman, *Jewish Thought and Scientific Discovery in Early Modern Europe* (New Haven, Conn.: Yale University Press, 1995), 22. See, too, 56–99. Barukh Schick constructed his anatomy treatise, *Tiferet adam* (Berlin, 1777), as a commentary on the fifth chapter of *Hovot halevavot*. On Schick, see David Fishman, "A Polish Rabbi Meets the Berlin Haskalah: The Case of R. Barukh Schick," *AJS Review* 12 (1987): 95–121.

[33]   Allan Nadler, *The Faith of the Mithnagdim* (Baltimore: The Johns Hopkins University Press, 1997), 78 and 216, footnote 5.

tribes, families and clans, species [kingdom, phylum, class, order, family]; all of them have roots, stems, branches, leaves, buds, and flowers. Not one of them was created in vain. They can reproduce themselves eternally. . . . b) [God's creative power is] even more [evident] in the creation of animals, which required complex, powerful [biological] designs, channels and vessels, thin cavities and even thinner cavities, limitless and unfathomable forms [of creation].[34]

Maimonides's love of the natural world also lent support to Lefin's interest in studying natural science as a path to piety. In the *Mishneh torah*, Laws of the Foundation of the Torah (2:2 and 4:2), Maimonides concluded that contemplation of God's "great and wondrous works and creatures" would lead to love and fear of the Divine. In the conclusion of his translation of Maimonides's *Guide of the Perplexed* into mishnaic Hebrew, Lefin reiterated his conviction that God's omnipotence was revealed in his creation of the diametrically opposed worlds of the most exalted creations (the planets) and the most humble (the insect world), and in the incomparable complexity of the natural world.[35] Lefin frequently referred to investigating God's creatures in order to apprehend God's greatness as the fundamental responsibility of a self-conscious Jewish life. He considered it self-evident that man "must examine God's creatures, be observant of Creation according to his ability, and behold the stamp of the Creator on everything, blessed is he, for his glory and perfection is inscribed in it."[36] The capacity of human beings to respond actively to the external world of the senses was God's greatest gift to humanity, a sign of their being beloved to him. Following Maimonides again, Lefin interpreted the term *betselem* ("in [God's] image") that appears in Gen 1:26 and Gen 9:6 as "in reason,"[37] positing that the possession of reason was unique to the human species, making it superior to animals, but inferior to the "separate intellects" (the heavenly hosts). Reason, God's "additional love" (*ḥibbah yeterah*),[38] enabled man to be conscious of God:

---

34 Lefin, *Hame'assef* 5 (1789): 83–84. Emphasis in the original. See, too, Lefin's letter to his uncle on the purpose of his book, *Moda levinah*, as "praises to God, may he be blessed, from 'the gate of reflection [in Bahya's *Ḥovot halevavot*]' in order to recognize the power of his deeds, wisdom, and lovingkindness that is revealed in living creatures." The Joseph Perl Archive, JNULA, 4° 1153/130, 21 and 55.

35 Conclusion to Moses Maimonides, *Sefer moreh nevukhim* (trans. Mendel Lefin; Żółkiew, 1829). On Maimonides's interest in the natural world, see Ruderman, *Jewish Thought and Scientific Discovery in Early Modern Europe*, 29.

36 Lefin, *Hame'assef* 5 (1789): 85.

37 In this interpretation of *betselem* the phrase *betselem elohim bara oto* (Gen 1:26) reads: "In (or "with") reason [God] created him." See the discussion of *tselem* as "intellectual apprehension" in Moses Maimonides, *The Guide of the Perplexed* (trans. Shlomo Pines; Chicago: University of Chicago Press, 1963), 1:1.

38 *m. Avot 3:18*, "An additional love [*ḥibbah yeterah*] is granted to him [man] because he was created in [God's] image, as it is written, "in [God's] image [he] created man." (Gen 9:6)

Even though God bestowed lovingkindness (*rahamim*) upon all kinds of creatures through their limbs and wonderful powers for survival and self-protection, such blessed creatures are not aware of themselves, and certainly not aware of their Creator's love. This is not so with divine reason (*tselem*). Man recognizes the preciousness of this gift and the fact of God's love, for through this wonderful spark man can peek into the small breach between himself and the breadth of the firmament to speculate about the great power and distance of the exalted hosts that are immeasurably far away. Man knows that human beings are nothing compared to the smallest of them, and since all of them are separate intellects, certainly their power, reason, and justice — according to their greatness, exaltedness, lucidity, and eternity — are much greater than ours, for they constantly tell of God's honor and glory.[39]

Lefin's view of the role of the study of natural science as a handmaid in the effort to encourage traditional piety was consonant with the scientific understanding of eighteenth-century natural philosophy, whose practitioners saw no contradiction between scientific empiricism and belief in a benevolent God.[40] Harmonious with natural religion, natural philosophy held as commonplace the existence of a purposeful God who had endowed humanity with the rational capacity to explore the natural world (which God had meticulously created and ordered), God's providence over humanity, and the immortality of the soul in Heaven, or in the world-to-come. Many practitioners of eighteenth-century natural philosophy popularized the results of their scientific experimentation, believing in the utility of these findings for understanding the ways of Providence and improving society.[41] Lefin's varied *oeuvre*, which consisted of adaptations of German travelogues into Hebrew, Yiddish biblical translations, political petitions, and original philosophical excursuses, fit the worldview of eighteenth-century natural philosophers, who eschewed specialization in favor of broad general knowledge. He was not alone among Polish Jews in his broad interest in the natural world. Another Polish-Jewish *maskil* who conformed to this type was Abraham Jacob Stern (1762–1842), a brilliant mathematician known in his time for his practical inventions, such as the adding machine that received a patent from the Austrian government in 1815. Stern also wrote Hebrew poetry and was active in the public life of Polish Jewry.[42]

---

[39] Lefin, "*Elon moreh*," 1 and "Key to the Pamphlet, *Elon moreh*," the Joseph Perl Archive, 4° 1153/23.

[40] Cassirer, *The Philosophy of the Enlightenment*, 43 and Gerald R. Cragg, *Reason and Authority in the Eighteenth Century* (Cambridge: Cambridge University Press, 1964), 28–61.

[41] J. L. Heilbron, "Franklin as an Enlightened Natural Philosopher," in *Reappraising Benjamin Franklin: A Bicentennial Perspective* (ed. J. A. Leo Lemay; Cranbury, N.J.: Associated University Presses, 1993), 196–220.

[42] Ephraim Kupfer, "From Far and Near," in *Sefer zikaron mugash leDr. N. M. Gelber leregel yovelo hashivim* (ed. Israel Klausner, Raphael Mahler, and Dov Sadan; Tel Aviv: Olameinu, 1963), 218.

Although Lefin never wrote a discrete scientific treatise and was not engaged in first-hand scientific experimentation, as were *maskilim* like Stern and a rabbinic figure like Barukh Schick, he was aware of the impact of the Copernican Revolution on the scientific and intellectual community of his day. A hint of Lefin's position can be found in his comment on Josh 10:12–13 ("Sun, stand still upon Giv'on and moon, in the valley of Ayyalon; and the sun stood still, and the moon stayed, until the people had avenged themselves upon their enemies"), which, if read literally, could be adduced as a prooftext for the validity of geocentrism.[43] In his journal, Lefin interpreted the verse:

> It is apparent that the sun was never in Giv'on and the moon was never in the valley of Ayyalon. "A generation *goes* (*halakh*) and a generation *comes* (*ba*)" (Eccl 1:4), etc., meaning, it goes "*à fonds perdue*," not literally walking [from the root "*halakh*"] in place, thus "the earth *stands* (*omedet*) eternally, etc.," in Eccl 1:4, means "*exists*" [not stands], such as "and he established (*ya'amid*) them forever and ever." (Ps 148:6)[44]

Lefin read the biblical Hebrew root *amad* (lit. "to stand"), which appears in the verses in both Joshua and Ecclesiastes, contextually as "to exist" and "to establish," indicating an openness to contemporary scientific theories, even to those which were viewed by many of his traditional contemporaries as opposed to Scripture.[45] Lefin resolved the conflict between science and faith implied by the verse in Joshua by relying on a non-literal translation of the verb "to stand," a hermeneutic technique that he had learned, in part, from his close study of the first chapters of Maimonides's *Guide of the Perplexed*.

---

[43] On Jewish attitudes toward the Copernican Revolution, see Hillel Levine, "Paradise Not Surrendered: Jewish Reactions to Copernicus and the Growth of Modern Science," in *Epistemology, Methodology, and the Social Sciences* (ed. Robert S. Cohen and Marx W. Wartofsky; Dordrecht, Holland: D. Reidel Publishing Company, 1983), 203–25.

[44] The Joseph Perl Archive, 4° 1153/130, 21. Emphasis is mine.

[45] Tobias Katz (1652–1729), a Polish-Jewish doctor who had studied at the University of Padua and authored a popular scientific handbook for Polish Jews, *Ma'aseh tuviyah* (*Tobias's Account*) in 1707, rejected Copernicus on the grounds that his views contradicted Scripture. Yet, Joseph Solomon Delmedigo, whose *Sefer elim* may have had a formative influence on Lefin and contemporary *maskilim* such as Aaron Wolfsohn-Halle (1754–1835), supported the Copernican position. Wolfsohn–Halle criticized Phinehas Elijah Hurwitz (1765–1821) in the pages of *Hame'assef* for his reluctance to accept Copernicus in his *Sefer haberit* (*Book of the Covenant*), an encyclopedic survey of natural science presented in harmonious conjunction with the Kabbalah. Hurwitz relied on Tycho Brache's theory that held that all the planets, except the earth, revolved around the sun. See *Hame'assef* (Berlin, 1809): 68–75. On *Sefer haberit*, see Ira Robinson, "Kabbala and Science in *Sefer haberit*: Modernization Strategy for Orthodox Jews," *Modern Judaism* 9, no. 3 (October 1989): 275–88, although Robinson's use of the term "Orthodox" is anachronistic and his conclusion that Hurwitz was a *maskil* problematic. Hurwitz's interest in science displayed none of the features of modernity (for example, interest and trust in Gentile writings) characterized by the Haskalah.

Lefin's disciple, Joseph Perl, continued on the path paved by his mentor regarding the compatibility of studying natural science as a way of honoring the Creator when he included a story by one of his students, Bezalel Stern, entitled "God Does Everything at its Appointed Time" (Eccl 3:11), which celebrated the seasons and God's providence over the laws of nature, in his 1813 *luaḥ* (calendar). The calendars, entitled *Tsir ne'eman* (*Faithful Messenger*), included discrete sections on natural science, called "natural investigations" (*beḥinot hateva*), illustrating the compatibility of the moderate Haskalah as it developed in Austrian Galicia with the empirical study of nature.[46]

Investigation of the natural world affirmed the worldview of the eighteenth-century natural philosopher. The limitlessness and intricacy of God's created world was, tautologically, proof of God's existence and study of his created world posed no threat to this unassailable "fact." Penetration of the mysteries of metaphysics, a realm beyond sensory perception, however, posed difficult challenges, not the least of which was the lack of concrete, sensual evidence for this realm beyond nature. Lefin, like Isserles and Loewe before him, separated the realm of metaphysics from human speculation, underscoring the conservativism of the Ashkenazic encounter with scientific thought in the early modern period. As in his psychology, Lefin's conclusions about the limitations of human apprehension illustrate his selective use of Western European ideas and his dependence upon the thought of medieval Jewish rationalists, particularly Maimonides.

Locke's psychological and epistemological thinking reigned authoritative for the first half of the eighteenth century. In the *Essay Concerning Human Understanding*, Locke affirmed that he would consider his writings a success if they helped the "busy mind of man" to stop "meddling with things exceeding its comprehension."[47] The senses could accurately respond to the material world and were created by God in order to enable humanity to function in that world. An understanding of the finite capacities of the senses would lead to the recognition of God and of humanity's religious duty, but not to "a perfect, clear, and adequate knowledge" of life, which, "perhaps, is not in the comprehension of any finite being."[48] Man should be content with the

---

46   The 1813 calendar was never published, but remained in manuscript. See the Joseph Perl Archive, 4° 1153/96b, 1a–2a. See, too, Joseph Perl, *Tsir ne'eman* (Tarnopol: Nachman Pineles, 1814). Bezalel Stern was a student in Perl's school in Tarnopol and later became a leader in the newly-established Jewish community in Odessa. On Stern, see Michael Stanislawski, *Tsar Nicholas I and the Jews* (Philadelphia: The Jewish Publication Society of America, 1983), 58, 78, 93–94; Steven J. Zipperstein, *The Jews of Odessa: A Cultural History, 1794–1881* (Stanford, Calif.: Stanford University Press, 1986), 44, 56–63; N. M. Gelber, "The History of the Jews of Tarnopol," in *Entsiqlopedyah shel galuyyot: Tarnopol*, vol. 3 (ed. Phillip Krongruen; Jerusalem, 1955), 91.
47   Locke, *An Essay Concerning Human Understanding*, 1:28.
48   Ibid., 1:28 and 1:402.

parameters of his knowledge, which were limited to the temporal world. Helvétius also took the position that the accuracy and rationality of the perceptual capacity of the senses was defined by the empirical world. "God said to man," he wrote, "I endow thee with sensibility, the blind instrument of my will, that, being incapable of penetrating into the depth of my views, thou mayest accomplish all my designs."[49]

Despite his debt to Locke and interest in Helvétius, Lefin identified the work of Immanuel Kant (1724–1804) as the source for his views on the limitations of human knowledge. He described his *Nachlaß* as "Reveries of a Fifty-year-old Disciple of Kantian Metaphysics, consisting in eight essays," the first of which was entitled "*Gesichtskreis des menschlichen Verstandes*" (*The Boundary of Human Reason*).[50] Kant's revolutionary epistemology rejected the passivity of the sensationalist model of human apprehension. His philosophical method, which he called "transcendental," assumed the mind's active, *a priori* ability to apprehend empirical reality. Without the mind's activity, there could be no objective reality.[51] Kant, who sought to find and explain the existence of a universal structure of knowledge, argued that sensationalism was particularistic by necessity. Only an *a priori* structure of human understanding could meet the test of universality and objectivity. The details of nature, for example, could only be observed and sensed if the mind was *a priori* subject to universal laws of understanding. The same held true for all sense perception. For Kant, therefore, the individual mind, also called "human understanding" or "reason," was the beginning and end of all cognition. A human being could only understand the perceptions of his senses because of the activity of the mind, and the parameters of the activity of the mind only extended to what it could empirically cognize. While sense perception alone was not sufficient to explain human apprehension, supra-

---

49 Claude-Adrian Helvétius, *De l'Esprit or Essays on the Mind and its Several Faculties* (trans. William Mudford; New York: Albion, 1810), 249.

50 Published in Weinlös, "R. Menachem Mendel of Satanów," 800. Lefin's interest in Kant was shared by other *maskilim*, such as Solomon Maimon, Lazarus Bendavid, and Marcus Herz. In his *Essai d'un plan de réforme*, Lefin mentioned the effort on the part of *maskilim* in Berlin to issue a new translation of Maimonides's *Guide of the Perplexed* with a commentary based on Kant's philosophy. Isaac Euchel, who was Kant's student at the University of Königsberg, published Solomon Maimon's *Givat hamoreh* (*The Guide's Height*) in 1791. Kant's influence on Euchel can be seen in the latter's programmatic article on the necessity of studying history, "A Word to the Reader about the Use of Ancient History and the Knowledge that is Connected to It," published in *Hame'assef* 1 (1784): 9–14. Lefin may also have penned a French essay on Kant, dedicating it to Adam Jerzy Czartoryski. See [Lefin], "*Essai d'un plan de réforme*," 420. See, too, Meir Letteris, *Zikaron basefer* (Vienna, 1868), 40 and Shmuel Feiner, *Haskalah vehistoryah: toldotav shel hakarat-ever yehudit modernit* (Jerusalem: Zalman Shazar Center, 1998), 40.

51 Ernst Cassirer, *Kant's Life and Thought* (trans. James Haden; New Haven, Conn.: Yale University Press, 1981), vii–xviii.

sensible perception or traditional metaphysics was entirely beyond human apprehension, even given the mind's activity. Kant thus concluded that human knowledge was inherently limited by empiricism and could not make any claims to metaphysical knowledge. Since metaphysical assumptions were not provable, Kant redefined metaphysics as the science of outlining the limits of human reason.[52] In one of his earliest works, *Dreams of a Spirit-Seer* (1766), Kant defined metaphysics as "a science of the limits of human reason. . . . [Therefore] the reader . . . can excuse himself from all vain inquiries with regard to a question the data for which are to be found in a world other than the one in which he perceives himself to be."[53] Kant's epistemology was both objective, in that it was subject to universal laws, and subjective, in that it was grounded in the mind of the individual.

Despite Lefin's self-definition as a Kantian, scrutiny of his writings demonstrates that he was also dependent upon a selective reading of Maimonides. In his epistemology, Lefin sought to harmonize the views of the towering Gentile intellectual of his period with the monumental intellectual achievement of his medieval forebear. In the *Guide of the Perplexed*, Maimonides presented his epistemology, but did so in a complex often contradictory manner, a feature of the work as a whole, which he acknowledged in the introduction.[54] The *Guide* both set very narrow limits on human apprehension and posited that man's ultimate goal was intellectual perfection and apprehension of the Divine. On the one hand, Maimonides postulated that the human intellect could comprehend terrestrial physics, which formed a coherent, knowable system based on sense perception, but could not apprehend celestial physics and metaphysics, a more extensive system which concerned the Divine. In most cases in the *Guide*, Maimonides argued that God and the celestial beings were not intrinsically knowable and that the corporeality of human beings inherently delimited their epistemological capacities.[55] On the other hand, the explicit goal of the *Guide* was intellectual apprehension of God, which meant penetration of metaphysical truths, the last of Maimonides's four stages of perfection. Lefin adopted the first reading of Maimonides's definition of the parameters of human knowledge, either ignoring or rejecting (without a frank admission of this rejection) the statements in the *Guide* that urged the select capable few of striving to apprehend the Divine. In the fourth chapter of *Elon moreh*, Lefin's introduction to his comprehensive translation into mishnaic Hebrew of Ibn Tibbon's Hebrew

---

52   Ibid., 83, 101–02, 157, and 166.
53   Cited in ibid., 95.
54   Herbert A. Davidson, "Maimonides on Metaphysical Knowledge," *Maimonidean Studies* 3 (1992): 49–103.
55   Maimonides, *The Guide of the Perplexed*, 1:31, 1:68, and 3:9.

translation of the *Guide*,[56] he faithfully translated all of *Guide* 1:31, in which
Maimonides stated uncategorically that there are "existents and matters that,
according to its [the human intellect's] nature, it is not capable of appre-
hending in any way or through any cause; the gates of apprehension are shut
before it" to illustrate his support for the medieval's view of the limits of
human knowledge.[57]

Lefin not only assumed a limited Maimonidean epistemology, but also
adopted his "negative theology," arguing that God could only be known
through his attributes of action.[58] In the *Guide* 1:58, Maimonides stated that
only a negative description of God's essence could be correct because any
positive definition would imply a gap between God's subject and the predi-
cate of his behavior, thereby implying that God's essence was complex, not
unified. God's pure unity was a Maimonidean principle not to be violated.
Lefin concurred, writing in *Elon moreh* that human understanding sometimes
functioned only as negative knowledge, such that human beings recognize
that they can never know precisely how many stars are in the sky, but accept
that there cannot be "less than" a specific number: "In every case where it is
impossible to apprehend the essence of the thing that we are considering, we
are satisfied with what it is *not*."[59] Lefin concluded his "Key to *Elon moreh*" by

---

56   Lefin began the translation in 1785, following in Euchel's footsteps. He never fully
completed the translation, but two parts of it were published posthumously in 1829 by two of
his disciples, Mordecai Suchostober and Jacob Samuel Bik, who were aided by Izak Ozer
Rotenberg and Isaiah Meir Finkelstein. The third section was issued by Solomon Rubin in
Hakarmel. *Elon moreh* was later published as a supplement to the Russian-Jewish Hebrew
periodical, *Hamelits*. See Lefin, *"Elon moreh,"* Klausner, *Historyah shel hasifrut*, 1:220–21, and
Weinlös, "R. Menachem Mendel of Satanów," 838. See, too, the correspondence between
Joseph Perl and Solomon Judah Rapoport about Lefin's translation in Weinlös, "Mendel
Lefin of Satanów: A Biographical Study," 354–55. As well, Lefin inquired of his young friend,
Benjamin Reich, as to whether or not his father, Meir ha-Cohen Reich, was able to obtain a
copy of Johannes (II) Buxtorf's Latin translation of Samuel ibn Tibbon's Hebrew translation
of the *Guide*, published in 1689. See The Joseph Perl Archive, JNULA, 4° 1153/130, 20, and
his comments on the translation and on *Elon moreh*, 31, 52, 54, and 67. A manuscript of *Elon
moreh* that differs from the published version, including a "Key to the Treatise *Elon moreh*," is
still extant. See the Joseph Perl Archive, JNULA, 4° 1153/23.
57   Maimonides, *The Guide of the Perplexed*, 1:65 and 1:67. Naftali Herz Wessely, a maskilic
contemporary of Mendelssohn's who contributed to his Torah commentary also expressed
reservations about those who extrapolated expertise in metaphysics from their knowledge of
natural science. For Wessely's conservative epistemology, see Edward Breuer, *The Limits of
Enlightenment: Jews, Germans and the Study of Scripture in the Eighteenth Century* (Cambridge,
Mass.: Harvard University Press, 1996), 139.
58   Shlomo Pines, "The Limitations of Human Knowledge According to Al-Farabi, Ibn
Bajja, and Maimonides," in *Studies in Medieval Jewish History and Literature* (ed. Isadore
Twersky; Cambridge, Mass.: Harvard University Press, 1979), 98–100. See, too, Moses
Maimonides, *Mishneh torah*, The Book of Knowledge, Laws of the Foundations of the Torah
(1:10).
59   Lefin, *"Elon moreh,"* 20.

citing the scriptural incident (Exod 3:6) in which Moses hides his face from
seeing God in the burning bush in order to underscore his conviction that
human apprehension is limited to the temporal world. Job, argued Lefin, in
contrast to Moses, could not accept the limitations of his knowledge, and
wanted, to his detriment, to understand God's attribute of judgment fully.
Better, Lefin urged his readers, to accept that "human apprehension is
sufficient for us to recognize just a tiny bit of God's honor (*kevodo*), may he
be blessed. We will merit blessing and success in two worlds [if we do] not
stubbornly investigate that which covers God, as it is written: 'And Moses
turned away his face lest he see God' (Exod 3:6)."[60] While man should not
attempt to perceive God's glory, study of God's attributes of action,
particularly by examining the products of his creativity (the natural world),
would lead to recognition of God's existence and greatness.

In his effort to legitimize his conscious borrowing of Kant's epistemology,
yet anchoring the program of the moderate Haskalah in the medieval Jewish
rational tradition, Lefin read Maimonides through Kant. By focusing on
their epistemology, and not on their ethics, Lefin diffused the differences
between the two philosophers.[61] Kant's rejection of the validity of heteronomous legislation was a clear threat to traditional rabbinic culture and had
little in common with Maimonides's ethics, which, although subordinate to
the goal of intellectual perfection outlined in the *Guide*, were a fundamental
concern of his in the *Eight Chapters* and the *Mishneh torah*.[62] While Lefin
disregarded the threat, other modernizing Jews engaged in the debates
published in the journal literature of the Hebrew Haskalah felt the Kantian
challenge to Jewish law clearly. Samuel David Luzzatto (1800–1865), for
example, believed that Kant's argument, which defined a moral action as

---

[60]   The Joseph Perl Archive, JNULA, 4° 1153/23, 12. Maimonides cited Exod 3:6 in the
Guide 1:5 and expanded on the difference between Moses' seeking to know God's way
(*derekh*), which was revealed to him, in contrast to God's glory (*kavod*), which was withheld,
in *Guide*, 1:54. Davidson notes that Maimonides's view of Exod 33:18 and Exod 33:23, in
which Moses seeks to see God's face, accords with Onkelos' Aramaic translation, which
distinguishes between the ability of humanity to cognize the existence, but not the essence,
of God. On Maimonides's interpretation of this verse in the *Guide*, see Herbert Davidson,
"The Middle Way in Maimonides' Ethics," *PAAJR* 54 (1987): 73.
[61]   Mendelssohn, too, grappling with the Maimonidean intellectual inheritance, read his
medieval predecessor differently than did Lefin. Mendelssohn rejected philosophical speculation and apprehension of God as the highest goal of a sentient life, and strove to distance
his thought from Maimonides, relying more extensively on Nachmanides in his Torah
commentary. See David Sorkin, *Moses Mendelssohn and the Religious Enlightenment* (Berkeley:
University of California Press, 1996), xxiii and 62–65 and James Lehmann, "Maimonides,
Mendelssohn, and the *Me'assfim*: Philosophy and Biographical Imagination in the Early
Haskalah," *LBIYA* 20 (1975): 87–108.
[62]   Davidson, "The Middle Way in Maimonides' Ethics."

one that was performed autonomously and freely by an individual out of a rational sense of duty, not out of submission to revealed authority, was categorically perilous for traditional Judaism. He rightly sensed that Kant's "moral theology" secularized ethics and rendered divine commandment invalid, if not completely meaningless. Luzzatto expressed his repudiation of Kant through the wordplay of an acronym; KaNT (*kaf, nun, tav*) was the opposite of *TaNaKh*, the acronym for the Jewish literary canon (*Torah, Nevi'im, Ketuvim* written as *tav, nun, kaf*).[63] Jacob Samuel Bik, a disciple of Mendel Lefin's who later rejected the Haskalah and embraced Hasidism, employed the same wordplay in a letter to Nachman Krochmal (1785–1840) in which Bik juxtaposed Kantian ethics, with its attendant secularization and rejection of heteronomy as a basis for ethics, to traditional Jewish morality:

> You said that in my letter I turned from the path of truth, God forbid, and I realized that this idea came to you and to our wise friend . . . because you run after the teachings of the Christian [Kant]. Instead of taking hold of his philosophic teachings and shattering them on the rocks of the Torah and the commandments, you wholeheartedly entrust yourselves to him, "because to him your souls yearn" (an allusion to Ps 42:2, which reads in the original, '*Ken Nafshi Ta'arog (kaf, nun, tav) elekhah elohim*' ("for my soul yearns toward you, God"), spelling KaNT).[64]

Lefin selectively appropriated those elements in Kant's thought that served his vision of a moderate Jewish Enlightenment. He thus rejected the Kantian conclusion that ethics derived from the activity of the autonomous human mind, and not from the supra-sensible world, in order to remain firmly grounded within a traditional Jewish understanding of heteronomous ethical behavior. Nothing in his writings even hints at an acceptance of Kant's autonomous, human-centered moral system, although Lefin, like Kant, disavowed the idea that reward in the world-to-come should be the motivation for ethical behavior.[65] In formulating his epistemological and ethical system, Lefin took only the delimiting of human apprehension from Kant, which he then validated by his reading of Maimonides. Dependent upon

---

[63]   Jay Harris, "The Image of Maimonides in Nineteenth-Century Jewish Historiography," *PAAJR* 54 (1987): 122. Luzzatto was also known for his harsh critique of Maimonides, who he believed had ossified Jewish law in the *Mishneh torah* and whose extreme rationalism paved the way for the influence of non-Jewish ("Atticist," in Luzzatto's terminology) ethics upon traditional Jewish culture. See Emil L. Fackenheim, *Encounters Between Judaism and Modern Philosophy* (New York: Basic Books, 1973), 40–44 and Morris B. Margolies, *Samuel David Luzzatto: Traditionalist Scholar* (New York: KTAV, 1979), 11–12, 14–15, 76–77, 147, 194–7.

[64]   Cited in Ephraim Kupfer, "Jacob Samuel Bik in Light of New Documents," *Gal-Ed* 4–5 (1978): 539. Krochmal later shared the letter with Samson Bloch ha-Levi (1784–1845) and Solomon Judah Rapoport, indicating that Galician *maskilim* were well aware of the Kantian challenge to traditional Jewish Law. For Kant as a religious thinker, see Adina Davidovich, "Kant's Theological Constructivism," *The Harvard Theological Review* 86:3 (1993): 323–51.

[65]   Cassirer, *Kant's Life and Thought*, 86.

God's command, ethical behavior was best learned by *imitatio dei*, imitating God's attributes, not through a non- or atheocentric philosophy:

> Indeed, the most perfect of teachers is the Divine himself, may he be blessed. Therefore we are commanded, "You shall walk in his ways" (Deut 28:9) and [we should] cleave to his virtues. This is one of the foundations of the Torah. From it we are commanded to recognize his ways from his actions, meaning, that through this we learn to do good for other creatures, as Maimonides wrote, may his memory be blessed, in [the *Guide*] 3:54 about the verse, "I am the Lord who exercises lovingkindness, judgment, and righteousness in the earth." (Jer 9:23) Meaning, [we best learn through *imitatio dei*], *not through philosophic knowledge that brings no benefit in the matter of doing good for one's fellow creatures.*[66]

The metaphysical world inhabited by celestial beings and God presented a closed book to Lefin. He could, however, read the soul, which he considered part of the natural world, a component of physics, not metaphysics, although its immateriality was incontestable. Lefin's division of knowledge into two separate spheres was not solely due to his desire to protect traditional Jewish heteronomy against the challenge of Kantian ethics. His psychology, as well as his epistemology, were inextricably connected to his overarching polemic against Hasidism.

Training the Rational Soul

The eighteenth century witnessed a spread in the publication and dissemination of traditional rabbinic ethical literature (*musar*), texts devoted to instructing a Jew how to live a pious life beyond the explicit prescriptions set in legal (halakhic) writings, but within its boundaries, and of medieval kabbalistic works, many of which focused on the destructiveness of sin for both the individual in particular and the cosmos as a whole.[67] This *musar* literature counselled asceticism as the corrective to a sinful life and did not hesitate to use fear as a goad to repentence. The ninth "gate" of Bahya ibn Pakuda's *Ḥovot halevavot* charged that contemporary generations were in greater need of asceticism because their "evil inclinations" were powerful — unlike those of their biblical predecessors — and distracted them from the essential religious attitudes and practices necessary to earn a place in the

---

[66]   The Joseph Perl Archive, JNULA, 4° 1153/130, 55. Emphasis is mine.

[67]   On the literary genre of *musar*, see Joseph Dan, *Sifrut hamusar vehaderush* (Jerusalem: Magnes Press, 1975) and Isaiah Tishby and Joseph Dan, *Mivḥar sifrut hamusar* (Jerusalem: Magnes Press, 1970). One of the most prominent features of ethical literature of the eighteenth century was a critique of the traditional rabbinate, an inner condemnation of its corruption and ineffectualness. This internal critique, according to Chimen Abramsky, had a "profound influence" on the rabbinate's decline. Chimen Abramsky, "The Crisis of Authority within European Jewry in the Eighteenth Century," in *Studies in Jewish Religious and Intellectual History* (ed. Siegfried Stein and Raphael Loewe; Tuscaloosa, Ala.: The University of Alabama Press, 1979), 13–28.

world-to-come.[68] Although Bahya did not urge extreme abstinence as a form of normative religious behavior, East European Jews engaged in fasting, self-flagellation, and other forms of ascetic behavior throughout the eighteenth century.[69] Kabbalistic ethical literature, too, enjoyed a wise renaissance in the wake of the Sabbatian heresies, beginning with republication of the works of the medieval pietists (*Hasidei Ashkenaz*), and continuing with Elijah de Vidas's *Reshit hokhmah*, Isaiah ha-Levi Horowitz's *Shenei luhot haberit*, Zevi Hirsch Koidnover's *Qav hayashar* (1705) and Elijah ben Avraham Cohen's *Shevet musar* (1712). Yiddish translations of many of these works were also widely circulated. Both the Hebrew and Yiddish *musar* works were adapted for widespread circulation and took the form of pocket chapbooks, disseminating kabbalistic theology, concepts, and rituals to a broad audience.[70]

While both traditional Jewish *musar* and mystical writings saw an inextricable connection between the human soul and the supernal realm, enlightened European thinkers conceived of the soul independently, and strove to detach ethics and morality from metaphysics. The enlightened goals of cultivating and reforming the human soul became a cornerstone of the concept of *Bildung*, which believed in the possibility of individual cultivation of virtue and personal self-improvement independent of religious dogma. Thinkers such as Christian Thomasius (1655–1728), Christian Wolff (1679–1754), Wilhelm von Humboldt, Jean-Jacques Rousseau, J. B. Basedow, and his fellow philanthropists, like Joachim Heinrich Campe, all believed in the individual pursuit of virtue and morality.[71] *Maskilim*, drawing on their medieval Jewish heritage and on the contemporary Enlightenment's engagement with the cultivation of *Bildung*, also turned to writing original ethical works and to translating classics of that genre from antiquity, including Aristotle's *Ethics*.[72] For example, Isaac Satanów and Naftali Herz Wessely (1725–1805), *maskilim* situated in Prussia, wrote modern ethical works in Hebrew, both entitled *Sefer hamiddot* (*Ethics*).[73] Enlightened Jews also penned treatises on the soul's

---

[68] Bahya ibn Pakuda, *Sefer torat hovot halevavot* (trans. Shmuel Yerushalmi; Jerusalem: Me'ori Yisra'el, 1972), 230–47.
[69] Harris Bor, "Moral Education in the Age of the Jewish Enlightenment" (Ph.D. diss, University of Cambridge, 1996) and Arthur Green, "Typologies of Leadership and the Hasidic Zaddiq," in *Jewish Spirituality: From the Sixteenth Century Revival to the Present* (ed. Arthur Green; New York: Crossroad, 1987), 133.
[70] Moshe Rosman, *Founder of Hasidism: A Quest for the Historical Ba'al Shem Tov* (Berkeley: University of California Press, 1996), 19.
[71] W. H. Bruford, *The German Tradition of Self-Cultivation: "Bildung" from Humboldt to Thomas Mann* (Cambridge: Cambridge University Press, 1975) and David Sorkin, "Wilhelm von Humboldt: The Theory and Practice of Self-Formation (Bildung), 1791–1810," *Journal of the History of Ideas* 44 (1983): 55–73.
[72] Bor, "Enlightenment Values, Jewish Ethics."
[73] See Isaac Satanów, *Sefer hamiddot* (Berlin, 1784) and Naftali Herz Wessely, *Sefer hamiddot*

immortality, a theme that resonated with both enlightened natural religion and classical rabbinic theology. Mendelssohn's *Phädon oder über die Unsterb-lichkeit der Seele in drey Gesprächen* (*Phaedon, or Regarding the Immortality of the Soul in Three Dialogues*, 1767), arguably the preeminent treatment of the sub-ject in the late eighteenth century, reworked Plato's original text, striving to show the possibility of perfecting the human soul and to prove its immortal-ity using modern philosopical concepts.[74] In 1769, Mendelssohn also penned a Hebrew work, *Sefer hanefesh* (*The Soul*). Comprised of two sections, "The Soul" and "Discourse on the Soul's Connection with the Body," *Sefer hanefesh* endeavored to harmonize medieval Jewish and Wolffian philosophy, much like Mendelssohn would do for politics in his *Jerusalem*.[75] Following Mendels-sohn's lead, Lefin penned two essays on the soul's immortality, which will be discussed below.

To address the specific circumstances of East European Jewry, Mendel Lefin, too, turned to the writing of enlightened *musar*.[76] He penned *Sefer ḥeshbon hanefesh* (*Moral Accounting*), a detailed, behaviorist guide to moral education and self-improvement, in an effort to protect the souls of contem-porary Eastern European youths, a group whom he felt were particularly vulnerable to the allure of the new movement, from falling victim to the spiritual and psychological snares of Hasidism. He expressed this particular concern in the *Essai d'un plan de réforme*:

[The repeated printing of the *Zohar*] vitalized the new sect [Hasidism], which makes *enthusiasm and faith* the fundamental principle of religion and has become almost universal in Poland *because it always recruits young people, who, in view of their credulity and*

(Berlin, 1786).
[74] Altmann, *Moses Mendelssohn: A Biographical Study*, 149. Other discussions of the soul's immorality included Johann Gustav Reinbeck, *Philosophical Thoughts on the Rational Soul and its Immortality* (1740) and Hubert Hayer, *La Spiritualité et l'immortalité de l'âme* (1757). In his autobiography, Mordecai Aaron Günzburg described the formative influence Mendels-sohn's *Phaedon* had on his intellectual development. See Israel Bartal, "Mordecai Aaron Günzberg: A Lithuanian Maskil Faces Modernity," in *From East and West: Jews in a Changing Europe, 1750–1870* (ed. Frances Malino and David Sorkin; London: Oxford University Press, 1990), 129.
[75] *Sefer hanefesh* was only published in 1787, shepherded to press by David Friedländer. See Sorkin, *Moses Mendelssohn*, 23–24.
[76] The primacy of ethics for Lefin can be seen from the comment in his unpublished journal that the commandment, "'You shall love your God,' was given for the purpose of the commandment, 'You shall love your neighbor as yourself.' We learn from this that the commandments that are between man and God were given generally for the purpose of the commandments between man and man, thus the blessings of enjoyment (*al hamezonot*) were established, as were the commandments, the redemptions (*ge'ulot*), and the miracles that were done for our ancestors and us, to compel man to internalize the quality of recognition [of others in order] to do good for his fellow man." The Joseph Perl Archive, JNULA, 4° 1153/130, 53.

their passionate age easily fall into the traps of the Hasidim. . . . [Youth], which has neither learned to economize nor to be economically self-sufficient, is inclined toward prodigality, which suits their [the Hasidim's] views.[77]

Lefin's awareness that Hasidism had an exceptional appeal for young men was shared by his maskilic contemporaries, including Hayim Malaga in his Yiddish satire, *Gedules reb volf metscharne ostrakhah* (*R. Wolf of Czarny Ostróg's Glories*), as well as by later generations of *maskilim* in Austrian Galicia, all of whom must have intuitively sensed the demographic basis of Hasidism's allure for Jewish youths in the eighteenth century.[78] Between 1648 and 1765, the Jewish population of the Polish-Lithuanian Commonwealth increased threefold to more than half a million.[79] Coupled with this population explosion was a decrease in viable economic opportunities for Jewish youths. Jewish communal authorities were well aware of the swelling of the ranks of unemployed Jewish teens and called for the establishment of more institutions for higher learning (yeshivot) as a means of coping with their great numbers. Already in 1662, the supra-communal administrative body of Lithuania in an effort to spur the creation of new schools commented that "boys and youths turn to idleness."[80] *Sefer ḥeshbon hanefesh* strove to encourage young Jewish men to train their impetuous adolescent souls to act virtuously without resorting to either classical or mystical approaches to moral self-reform.

Lefin's *Sefer ḥeshbon hanefesh* is both a work of enlightened *musar* and an anti-Hasidic polemic disguised as a traditional ethical text.[81] Printed with the

---

[77]　[Lefin], "*Essai d'un plan de réforme*," 411 and 419, footnote 4. Emphasis is mine, although Lefin underlined the words "enthusiasm and faith" in the original. Other examples of Lefin's concern with the vulnerability of the adolescent can be found in the Joseph Perl Archive, JNULA, 4° 1153/123, 1b, 4° 1153/128e, paragraph 7, and 4° 1153/134b, 1a.

[78]　Shmuel Werses, "Hasidism in the Perspective of Haskalah Literature: From the Polemics of Galician Maskilim," in *Megammot vetsurot besifrut hahaskalah* (Jerusalem: Magnes Press, 1990), 103.

[79]　David Biale, "Childhood, Marriage, and the Family in the Eastern European Jewish Enlightenment," in *The Jewish Family: Myths and Reality* (ed. Steven M. Cohen and Paula E. Hyman; New York: Holmes & Meier, 1986), 46 and David Biale, *Eros and the Jews: From Biblical Israel to Contemporary America* (Berkeley: University of California Press, 1997), 127–30.

[80]　Cited in Gershon David Hundert, "Approaches to the History of the Jewish Family in Early Modern Poland-Lithuania," in *The Jewish Family: Myths and Reality* (ed. Steven M. Cohen and Paula E. Hyman; New York: Holmes & Meier, 1986), 19. See, too, Gershon David Hundert, "The Conditions in Jewish Society in the Polish-Lithuanian Commonwealth in the Middle Decades of the Eighteenth Century," in *Hasidism Reappraised* (ed. Ada Rapoport-Albert; London: The Littman Library of Jewish Civilization, 1996), 45–50.

[81]　This chapter is an expansion of my earlier essay, Nancy Sinkoff, "Benjamin Franklin in Jewish Eastern Europe: Cultural Appropriation in the Age of the Enlightenment," *Journal of the History of Ideas* 61, no. 1 (2000): 133–52. See, too, Hillel Levine, "Between Hasidism and Haskalah: On a Disguised Anti-Hasidic Polemic," in *Peraqim betoldot haḥevrah hayehudit biymei*

literary apparatus typical of a traditional rabbinic work, such as approbations, biblical citations, and rabbinic prooftexts, and structured around thirteen virtues resonant of the "gates" in *Hovot halevavot*, Lefin clearly hoped
that its form would appeal to traditionally-educated East European Jewish
youths. For Lefin, traditional *musar* was insufficient to meet the spiritual
demands of the hour, a sentiment shared by the numerous eighteenth-
century Jewish authors who wrote new forms of ethical treatises in this
period, because it depended upon an antiquated system of external rewards
and punishments.[82] He rejected fear of punishment as the basis of morality;
authentic virtue in an enlightened soul had to be a voluntary acceptance of
Jewish law, autonomously arrived at by a sentient human being. Love, not
fear, of God should be the basis of morality. Moreover, traditional ethical
writings assumed the soul's metaphysical essence, while Lefin, employing the
contemporary science of his day, believed in the soul's naturalness. Finally,
traditional *musar*, Lefin wrote, did not provide a concrete framework by
means of which the individual could change his behavior. As he succinctly
stated, "*musar* without advice is not sufficient at all."[83]

Repudiating the efficacy of traditional *musar*, Lefin turned to Benjamin
Franklin's "Rules of Conduct" — principles outlined by the American
natural philosopher in the second part of his memoirs — as the basis for his
program of moral self-reform in *Sefer heshbon hanefesh* and seamlessly incorporated them into a Jewish literary genre.[84] Lefin's general familiarity with
Franklin derived from his distinguished reputation in Eastern Europe and
specifically from Adam Kazimierz Czartoryski's personal acquaintance with

---

habeinayim uva'et hahadashah (ed. Immanuel Etkes and Joseph Salmon; Jerusalem: Zalman
Shazar Center, 1980), 182–91.
[82] Lefin, *Sefer heshbon hanefesh*, paragraphs 12–14, 18, and 19. In his work on the origins of
compulsory schooling in Prussia and Austria, James Van Horn Melton makes a similar point
about the breakdown of the efficacy of external forms of social control in eighteenth-
century Central Europe and argues that the movement for compulsory school arose as a
means of providing internalized methods of social control. See James Van Horn Melton,
Absolutism and the Eighteenth-Century Origins of Compulsory Schooling in Prussia and Austria
(Cambridge: Cambridge University Press, 1988). See, too, Locke's essay, "Some Thoughts
Concerning Education" (1693), where he criticized corporeal punishment and advocated
the internalization of "*esteem* and *disgrace.*" Emphasis in the original. John Locke, *Some
Thoughts Concerning Education* (ed. Ruth Grant and Nathan Tarcov; Indianapolis, Ind.:
Hackett, 1996), 36.
[83] Lefin, *Sefer heshbon hanefesh*, paragraph 49.
[84] Benjamin Franklin, *The Autobiography of Benjamin Franklin: A Genetic Text* (ed. J. A. Leo
Lemay and P. M. Zall; Knoxville: The University of Tennessee Press, 1981), xix, xlvii,
footnote 69. A complete French translation of Franklin's work was made in 1791 by Louis
Guillaume Le Veillard, Franklin's close friend, but the second section was published only in
1798. Lefin, *Sefer heshbon hanefesh*, paragraphs 12–14 and 19.

his fellow freemason.[85] The focus on the autonomy of the soul in *Sefer heshbon hanefesh* also displays Lefin's debt to other contemporary psychological theorists; Helvétius's belief that "self-love" was the basis of morality directly informed Lefin's understanding of the soul.[86] Like Helvétius, Lefin felt that the human soul was natural and could be understood through scientific experiment and observation. Yet, given his commitment to traditional Jewish life and his belief in the obligatory power of heteronomous Jewish law, however, self-love did not mean liberation from divine authority for Lefin, as it did for Helvétius and more radical exponents of the Enlightenment.[87] Self-love was rather an aspect of God-given morality. "*Self-love* (*ahavat ha'adam et atsmo*) is the strongest of the loves that God planted in the bestial soul . . . so he [man] could repel the various frequent spurts of lust and trouble that disturb the health of his body."[88] In *Sefer heshbon hanefesh*, Lefin hoped to present a method of moral reform based completely on the efforts of the individual Jew that would prove more attractive to East

---

[85]   Personal correspondence between Adam Kazimierz and his son, Adam Jerzy, attests to the friendship between the two men, both of whom were members of the masonic lodge, Les Neuf Soeurs, in Paris. See Nicholas Hans, "UNESCO of the Eighteenth Century: *La Loge des Neuf Soeurs* and its Venerable Master, Benjamin Franklin," *Proceedings of the American Philosophical Society* 97 (1953): 513–24 and Adam Kazimierz to Adam Jerzy Czartoryski, October, 23, 1776[?]. See 6285 II, EW 1046, the Czartoryski Library, Cracow. The letter, copied in the late nineteenth century from the original, is misdated. Adam Jerzy first went abroad with his mother, Izabela Fleming Czartoryska, in 1786, the year in which the letter, I believe, was written. For Adam Jerzy's itinerary, see Adam Jerzy Czartoryski, *Memoirs of Prince Adam Czartoryski and His Correspondence with Alexander I* (ed. Adam Gielgud; Orono, Me.: Academic International, 1968), 1:45–49. See, too, Arthur A. Chiel, "Benjamin Franklin and Menachem Mendel Lefin," *Conservative Judaism*, Summer 1979, 50–55, although Chiel believes that Lefin had access to all of Franklin's memoirs in 1791.

Tolstoy's autobiographical story, "Recollections of a Billiard Maker" and an unfinished work, "A History of Yesterday," attest to the influence of Franklin's system on East European *intelligenti*. Tolstoy, like Franklin, concluded that "pride is the principle and most dangerous of all human vices." See Jayme A. Sokolow, "'Arriving at Moral Perfection': Benjamin Franklin and Leo Tolstoy," *American Literature* 48, no. 3 (November 1975): 427–32 and Eufrosina Dvoichenko-Markov, "Benjamin Franklin and Leo Tolstoy," *Proceedings of the American Philosophical Society* 46, no. 2 (1952): 119–28.

[86]   Lefin's interest in Helvétius also stemmed from their shared criticism of fanaticism and belief that legislation and education were agents of moral progress, dogmas for the men of the Enlightenment. Lefin began his plan for the rationalization of the rabbinate in Prince Adam Czartoryski's lands with a paraphrased quote from Helvétius's *De l'Esprit*, "Virtues are the work of good laws." Mss. 2253, the Czartoryski Library, Cracow, 28. See, too, the Joseph Perl Archive, JNULA, 4° 1153/6 and 128d; Abraham Schwadron Collection of Jewish Authographs, Mendel Lefin Papers, JNULA. Solomon Maimon also reported that he was a proponent of Helvétius's system of self-love. See Solomon Maimon, *An Autobiography* (trans. J. Clark Murray; Urbana: University of Illinois Press, 1954), 217.

[87]   Gay, *The Enlightenment*, 1:3–8.

[88]   Lefin, *Sefer heshbon hanefesh*, paragraphs 87–88, 90. Emphasis is mine.

European adolescents than Hasidic methods and techniques for inculcating virtue and expiating sin.

Employing the vocabulary of the medieval Jewish tradition that divided the human soul into bestial (*nefesh habahamit*) and rational (*nefesh hasikhlit*) constituent parts, Lefin nonetheless wrested the human soul — comprised of both bestial and rational components — from the metaphysical realm. In *Sefer ḥeshbon hanefesh*, Lefin presented a carefully structured plan for teaching an individual to control his bestial soul, to strengthen his moral virtues, and to lead a rational life devoted to God without recourse to the supernal realm. Lefin compared the bestial soul to a reed or a bullrush standing in the wind without internal means of support, subject to the direction of the wind.[89] On its own, the bestial soul had no connection to divine commandment, either positive or negative; it was driven by instinct, experience, and habit.[90] In a manuscript fragment, Lefin compared the bestial will (*der bestialische Willen*) to the rational will (*der rationale Willen*): "The bestial will is always instantaneously propelled by a sensation, but the rational will blocks the action until it deliberates and considers its motives."[91] Essentially inert, the bestial soul could be disciplined and controlled by the rational soul if an individual followed the method outlined in *Sefer ḥeshbon hanefesh*.[92]

The rational faculty corresponded to the rational soul, capable of reining in the passions of the bestial soul and changing its course.[93] It "can distinguish and examine how thoughts are connected. Its strength of will means that it is not subservient to the external images. It can connect ideas to feelings or separate those that are conjoined for another purpose. . . . It can instruct the bestial soul through study and habit."[94] Lefin compared the training of human behavior to animal husbandry, citing the example of teaching a sharp-eyed bird to hunt, and commenting that a conscientious owner treated his animals well. So, too, should the initiate in Lefin's method treat his bestial soul well.[95]

Eighteenth-century moral philosophers, Lefin among them, believed that adolescence presented a unique developmental opportunity for the moral

---

[89] Lefin's use of the image of a reed may have derived from two sources, one internal to Judaism, the other external. *b. Ta'anit 20b* reads: "A man should always be as pliable as a reed, not rigid like a cedar." Pascal defined mankind as a "thinking reed," weak, but endowed with the ability to think, which was the basis of morality. See Blaise Pascal, *Pensées* (ed. and trans. A. J. Krailsheimer; Harmondsworth, UK: Penguin Books, 1966), 95.

[90] Lefin, *Sefer ḥeshbon hanefesh*, paragraphs 7, 8, and 90.

[91] The Joseph Perl Archive, JNULA, 4° 1153/133.

[92] Lefin, *Sefer ḥeshbon hanefesh*, paragraphs 2, 3, and 96.

[93] Ibid., paragraph 15.

[94] Ibid., footnote to paragraph 97.

[95] Ibid., paragraphs 3 and 4.

educator.[96] Puberty posed the greatest obstacle to moral self-reform, yet was the most opportune time for education because the full powers of both the faculties of imagination and rationality blossomed in this stage of human development.[97] In Kantian terms, it was in adolescence that the individual could be liberated from his nonage. A manuscript fragment of Lefin's *Nachlaß* discussed:

> The tender childhood of man [as] an almost completely animal condition. During the development of the powers of reason and free will, all of his bestial fallacies [*"paralogisms"* in Kant's terminology] remain subject to his parents' judgment; his impulses submit to their [his parents'] superiority for correction. This superiority actually dwindles very quickly, but is maintained by the habit of obedience for a fairly long time until the one who has matured finally completely escapes from the tutelage of his parents, and trusts the tutelage of his very own mind.[98]

With maturation came not only the ability to train one's bestial soul to be rational, but an "ennobling" of one's tastes and interests from the "common sensuousness" and extremism of childhood passions for intense sweets, dark colors, crude music, and obstinacy.[99]

Lefin's selective appropriation of Franklin's method and his familiarity with the writings of Rousseau, the philanthropists, and other eighteenth-century thinkers interested in the cultivation of virtue and moral education, reflected his belief in the legitimacy of using non-Jewish writings and ideas in the cultivation of the modern East European Jew. He employed Benjamin Franklin's method because it provided a concrete, pragmatic system by which the individual could monitor and train his behavior. Franklin himself had despaired of changing his own behavior merely through contemplation

---

96   In *Émile*, the classic of eighteenth-century pedagogy, Rousseau posited that formal education should begin only in puberty, when the child's emotional, moral, and aesthetic faculties were mature and the "natural" essence of the child could not be corrupted. See Jean-Jacques Rousseau, *Émile* (trans. Barbara Foxley; London: Dent, 1966), xxix–xxx and 207. For Lefin's interest in Rousseau, see the Abraham Schwadron Collection of Jewish Autographs and Portraits, papers of Mendel Lefin (1749–1826), and the Joseph Perl Archive, JNULA, 4° 1153/128d. Other *maskilim* like Naftali Herz Wessely and the *me'assefim* were also inspired by *Émile* and other Enlightenment educational writings. See Shmuel Werses, "Between Two Worlds: Jacob Samuel Bik between Haskalah and Hasidism — A Reassessment," in *Megammot vetsurot besifrut hahaskalah* (Jerusalem: Magnes Press, 1990), 128. For the Enlightenment's focus on the education of youth, see Gay, *The Enlightenment*, 2:497–552 and Ernst A. Simon, "Pedagogic Philanthropism and Jewish Education (Hebrew Section)," in *Jubilee Volume in Honor of Mordecai Kaplan* (ed. Moshe Davis; New York, 1953), 149–87. Even Helvétius, who disagreed with the timing of Rousseau's educational program, felt that adolescence was a unique stage in human development. See Mordecai Grossman, *The Philosophy of Helvetius* (New York: Teachers College, Columbia University, 1926), 137–38.
97   Lefin, *Sefer ḥeshbon hanefesh*, paragraphs 9, 10 and 82.
98   The Joseph Perl Archive, JNULA, 4° 1153/128e, paragraph 7.
99   The Joseph Perl Archive, JNULA, 4° 1153/128b, paragraph 5.

of his wrongdoing, and devised his "Rules of Conduct" to increase the possibility of personal growth and success.[100] Lefin affirmed Franklin's conclusion that self-improvement required a structured plan of behavior modification, which, if properly implemented, would result in the inculcation of habitually moral behavior: "[Behavior modification could result in moral habits] like the case of a Greek wrestler who trained himself to carry a newborn calf on his shoulder every day for several hours until it was three years old. It never became too heavy for him . . . because his habit [of carrying it] had so increased his strength."[101]

Franklin's method was predicated on his belief that the repetition and cultivation of good habits would result in consistently ethical behavior. He believed that in order to "acquire the *habitude*" of all the desirable virtues an individual was best served by short-term concentration on one virtue at a time.[102] He thus devised a personal accounting system in which the individual would start with thirteen virtues (i.e. temperance, silence, order, resolution, frugality, industry, sincerity, justice, moderation, cleanliness, tranquility, chastity, and humility) and devote one week to the development of each. Franklin ordered his virtues in a progression such that temperance or "coolness and clearness of head" would make the cultivation of "silence" easier, which, in turn, would allow him to "order" his day and make it more productive, etc. Franklin's behaviorist innovation lay in his design of a moral accounting book, in which each page was devoted to one virtue. On each page, he created a grid with the vertical columns representing the seven days of the week and the horizontal columns representing the thirteen virtues. During the week devoted to justice, for example, Franklin would strive to be as just as possible, "leaving the other virtues to their ordinary chance," and make a mark in the corresponding box of that day's failings in the category of justice. At the end of the week, Franklin examined the markings to see how he had progressed, or lapsed, in the cultivation of that week's particular virtue. The thirteen-week cycle of weekly reflection and accounting repeated four times to round out the year. In this manner, Franklin hoped to have "the encouraging pleasure of seeing on my pages the progress I made in virtue, by clearing successively my lines of their spots, till in the end, by a number of courses, I should be happy in viewing a clean book, after thirteen weeks' daily examination."[103]

Lefin borrowed Franklin's accounting system in its entirety for *Sefer ḥeshbon hanefesh*. He appropriated Franklin's suggestions that the individual

---

[100] Franklin, *The Autobiography of Benjamin Franklin*, 78.
[101] Lefin, *Sefer ḥeshbon hanefesh*, paragraph 21. See, too, the footnote to paragraph 97.
[102] Franklin, *The Autobiography of Benjamin Franklin*, 80. Emphasis is mine.
[103] Ibid., 82.

select a "short precept" (in Lefin's words, a "short *musar*") that would encapsulate the week's virtue and create a special accounting book with the aforementioned grid. Lefin specified that the journal (*pinqas*) should be nine pages with eighteen sides and that the individual should use a lead pencil for the daily marks, but should write the sums at the end of the week using a pen. He even borrowed the majority of Franklin's virtues; Lefin's original list of thirteen virtues included calmness (*menuhah*), patience (*savlanut*), order (*seder*), stubbornness (*aqshanut*),[104] cleanliness (*neqiyut*), humility (*anavah*), justice (*tsedeq*), frugality (*qimmuts*), diligence (*zerizut*), silence (*shetiqah*), tranquility (*nihuta*), truth (*emet*), and asceticism (*perishut*). Lefin added two additional lines in the grid, one for the sums of the particular week and one for a yearly summation and accounting, hopeful that the sins of the skilled practitioner, "with God's help," would decrease over time, resulting in a book "wiped clean of all spots."[105]

Lefin did not hesitate to incorporate Franklin's technique into *Sefer heshbon hanefesh* although he concealed the Gentile provenance of the method from his traditional readers. Franklin's commitment to the principles of natural religion and his avowed ecumenicism, both of which he affirmed in his memoirs, made his work palatable for Lefin, who would have been suspicious of any overtly Christian overtones.[106] Lefin's profound regard for Franklin helped to shape the latter's image as a defender of religious tolerance in later works by Galician *maskilim*. Nachman Krochmal translated into Hebrew Franklin's paraphrase of a Persian parable in which Abraham is rebuked by God for being inhospitable to a pagan, and Jacob Samuel Bik, prior to turning his back on the Haskalah, praised Lefin's use of Franklin's method by citing *m. Shabbat 16:8*, "Israel can make use of a light [on the Sabbath] kindled by a Gentile."[107]

The Dangers of Enthusiasm and Imagination

Historians have tended to regard Mendel Lefin's use of Franklin's technique as a confirmation of their view that the sole impetus for the Haskalah among

---

104 In later editions of *Sefer heshbon hanefesh*, the virtue of "stubbornness" was replaced by "industry" (*haritsut*). See, for example, Mendel Lefin, *Sefer heshbon hanefesh* (Warsaw: J. Levenson, 1852).
105 Lefin, *Sefer heshbon hanefesh*, paragraph 26.
106 Franklin, *The Autobiography of Benjamin Franklin*, 76, 88, and 92.
107 George Alexander Kohut, "Abraham's Lesson in Tolerance," *The Jewish Quarterly Review* 15 (1903): 104–11; Joseph Klausner, "'Ethical Fable' of R. Nachman Krochmal," *Tarbiz* 1, no. 1 (1930): 131–35; Shmuel Werses, "The Original, Unknown Version of Jacob Samuel Bik's letter to Tobias Feder," in *Megammot vetsurot besifrut hahaskalah* (Jerusalem: Magnes Press, 1990), 350–51.

East European Jewry lay in its exposure to the West in general, and to the Berlin Haskalah's Western orientation in particular; they have regarded *Sefer ḥeshbon hanefesh* as merely a translation of yet another text of the European and American Enlightenments into Hebrew.[108] Implicit in their view is an uncritical acceptance of a unidirectional influence of a Western text such as Benjamin Franklin's *Autobiography* on a *maskil* like Mendel Lefin. This view ignores the Polish-Jewish context in which Lefin adapted Franklin's work and misses a critical theoretical point. Translation is never mere imitation. Even the most literal line-by-line translation is an interpretation or adaptation of one text to a new historical context. The newness of the context is fundamental, underscoring the active appropriation of a given text by the translator or adaptator to his or her own specific historical purposes.[109] While Lefin clearly shared with Franklin the primary goal of anchoring morality in the development of the individual and the consonant ability to change behavior within the rational power of the self, the broader concerns of the two writers belies the apparent similarity of their works. Franklin conceived of his behaviorist technique as an innovative way to improve individual character for the creation of an international political party (the United Party of Virtue) of virtuous men who would "act with a view to the good of mankind."[110] He had no clear adversary, antagonist, or religious authority to oppose. In contrast, Lefin appropriated Franklin's method to address the spiritual crisis of eighteenth-century Polish Jewry, to provide it with a new method of moral self-reform to replace traditional *musar*, and to counter the appeal of Hasidism.

Lefin formulated his campaign against Hasidism systematically and, as in most of his other works written in Jewish languages, covertly.[111] *Sefer ḥeshbon*

---

[108] Hillel Levine pointed out the disguised anti-Hasidism in *Sefer ḥeshbon hanefesh* and showed that most literary historians erred in regarding it as either a translation of Franklin's *Poor Richard's Almanac* or of the entire *Autobiography*. See Levine, "Menachem Mendel Lefin," 56, footnote 59 and Eisig Silberschlag, "The Anglo-Saxon Factor in Our Modern Literature: First Contacts," *Divrei hakongres ha'olami ha'revi'i lamada'ei hayahadut* 2 (1969): 71–75.

[109] Roger Chartier, *On the Edge of the Cliff: History, Language, and Practices* (trans. Lydia G. Cochrane; Baltimore: The Johns Hopkins University Press, 1997) and Roger Chartier, *Cultural History: Between Practices and Representations* (trans. Lydia G. Cochrane; Ithaca, New York: Cornell University Press, 1988).

[110] Franklin may have seen the United Party of Virtue as a political extension of the goals of his Junto group, a club he created in 1726 devoted to the discussion of popular morality. Although Franklin kept Junto alive for over thirty years, he only shared his idea about his more ambitious plans with two friends. See Franklin, *The Autobiography of Benjamin Franklin*, 88, 91–92.

[111] Levine, "Between Hasidism and Haskalah," 182–91; Chone Shmeruk, "On Several Principles in Mendel Lefin's Translation of Proverbs," in *Sifrut yidish befolin: mehqarim ve'iyyunim historiyyim* (Jerusalem: Magnes Press, 1981), 165–83; Nancy Sinkoff, "Strategy and Ruse in the Haskalah of Mendel Lefin of Satanów (1749–1826)," in *New Perspectives on the Haskalah*

hanefesh's program of moral self-reform began with the assumptions of eighteenth-century faculty psychology and predicated, as we saw above, the existence of three faculties of the human mind or soul (sensual, imaginative, and rational), but couched this cultural borrowing in medieval Jewish philosophical terminology. Unlike his predecessors and contemporary traditionalists, Lefin's psychology was anthropocentric; he rejected belief in the divine origin of the soul, and the practical system of moral self-reform in *Sefer ḥeshbon hanefesh* assumed the ability of the practitioner to control his soul without appeal to the supernal realm. For Lefin, habitual self-reflection through Franklin's personal accounting book provided a means for the rational soul to control its bestial antithesis. A key to this mastery was rational command of the "association of ideas" that stimulated the mind through the senses, and influenced the bestial soul, even in a state of complete repose.[112] The immature, untrained rational soul was incapable of controlling the relentless absorption of external stimuli, of making sense of the confused connection of one idea to another, and of reining in the passions and "concatenations of images" of the bestial soul.[113] The success of Lefin's psychological anthropocentrism required developmental maturity and guidance by a traditional rabbinic figure to strengthen the youthful practitioner's rational soul.[114]

Fear of the passions of the faculty of imagination, which reached their height in adolescence, lay at the root of Lefin's critique of Hasidism. In his view, the imaginative faculty's wantonness led to psychological problems, which produced epistemological and metaphysical errors. These errors, in turn, produced religious distortions and cultural perversions. Lefin's understanding of the imaginative faculty as the source of Hasidic lack of restraint parallels the European-wide critique of enthusiasm in the early modern period. As Michael Heyd has argued, "enthusiasm" became associated with anyone claiming to have direct divine intervention, and critics — particularly the Protestant clergy — charged a disparate group, including millenarians, sectarians, prophesizers of various stripes, and alchemists with "enthusiasm" in their campaign to protect their own unmediated relationship to Scripture

---

(ed. Shmuel Feiner and David Sorkin; London: Littman Library of Jewish Civilization, 2001), 86–102.

[112] Lefin, *Sefer ḥeshbon hanefesh*, paragraph 96 and 97.

[113] Ibid., footnote to paragraph 97. See, too, the Joseph Perl Archive, 4° 1153/133, 2.

[114] Because adolescents were likely to delay improving their behavior, it was the duty of their rabbi to spur them toward the process of self-reflection and self-control. The mature adult should begin to observe his young charges at the age of thirteen, taking notes on their individual moral blemishes for five years, and then instructing them in *musar tiqqun hamiddot* (the ethics of character improvement). See Lefin, *Sefer ḥeshbon hanefesh*, paragraphs 39, 40 and 46.

and to fight against radical atheism.[115] For example, as part of the medical critique of enthusiasm articulated in his *Enthusiasmus Triumphatus* (1656), Henry More focused attention on the imaginative faculty and its configuration of "animal spirits," whose function, indebted to Galen's physiology, was to transmit external sensations to the soul. In an inverse relationship to the faculties of reason and understanding, the imaginative faculty could persuade the soul that the unreal was real. "This happens in sleep, when we dream, as well as in the case of mad and melancholic men," wrote More.[116] As we saw above, Lefin, too, saw sleep as the playground of the unrestrained imaginative faculty, which was capable of combining the possible with the impossible, a proof with its contradiction.[117] By nature intemperate and immoderate, the imaginative faculty led to fantasy.

Lefin's critique of the reckless license of the imaginative faculty had epistemological consequences, just as it had for Kant, whose *Dreams of a Spirit-Seer* was inspired, in great part, by his complex relationship with Emmanuel Swedenborg, a well-known religious enthusiast of the period. Kant pushed the faculty of the imagination out of his epistemology because he saw it as intimately connected with the bestial aspect of humanity, and associated it with all of the limitations of the body (death, sexuality, illness, and madness).[118] Lefin, too, rejected the imaginative faculty as a source of knowledge. Reasonable men knew that their knowledge of the world, both temporal and supernal, was delimited by their sense perception, and did not aspire to apprehend the metaphysical realm. Unreasonable men were those who believed themselves capable of understanding the realm of the Divine, but their "knowledge" had no empirical basis. The imaginative faculty's "knowledge" of the supernal realm could not be proven and was, thus, a fabrication of those who professed it.

Lefin argued that kabbalistic and Hasidic hermeneutics, which strove to apprehend the supernal realm through the complex theosophic structure first expressed in *Sefer habahir* and then fully articulated in the *Zohar*, pushed the boundaries of the empirically true and theologically sound. Hasidic exegesis was an act of imaginative "fantasy," which, in the terminology of the eighteenth century, was unequivocally derogatory. Lefin believed that

---

[115] Michael Heyd, *'Be Sober and Reasonable': The Critique of Enthusiasm in the Seventeenth and Early Eighteenth Centuries* (New York: E. J. Brill, 1995). See, too, Cragg, *Reason and Authority in the Eighteenth Century*, 30.

[116] Cited in Heyd, *'Be Sober and Reasonable,'* 95–96.

[117] The Joseph Perl Archive, JNULA, 4° 1153/127d, 3a. See, too, the Joseph Perl Archive, 4° 1153/71a, for Lefin's association of fever with an over-active imaginative faculty.

[118] Hartmut and Gernot Böhme, "The Battle of Reason with the Imagination," in *What Is Enlightenment? Eighteenth-Century Answers and Twentieth-Century Questions* (ed. James Schmidt; Berkeley: University of California Press, 1996), 437–41.

contemporary Hasidim arrogantly assumed that they could apprehend the true nature of the Divine by contemplation and investigation of the *sefirot*, the divine emanations, from the Godhead. He protested that unlike Maimonides, who proved and explained his views through reason, the Hasidim merely asserted the veracity of what they believed, appealing to "closed secrets (*sodot*)" that could not be subjected to rational proofs. Their self-confidence struck Lefin as overweening pride. The great King David himself had admitted his epistemological limitations, "My heart is not haughty, nor my eyes lofty, nor do I exercise myself in great matters or in things too exalted for me" (Prov 131:1), cited Lefin, "so how did the commoner [the average Hasid generally, or, more specifically, the Besht] leap to the top of the height, adorning the firmaments?"[119] Inquiry into the metaphysical realm, which was beyond the pale of human knowledge, could lead only to antinomian despair, insanity, or sexual deviance. Job's insistence upon understanding God's attribute of judgment resulted in grief. Ben Zoma's insatiable desire to explore the supra-temporal world led to dementia.[120] Mystical speculations about the unions and couplings of the divine emanations had led to the "sexual abominations" in the days of Sabbatai Zevi and Jacob Frank. The implications of unlimited epistemological speculation were clear: Hasidism's theosophic inquiry into the nature of the Divine led to worship of other gods and to antinomian behavior.[121]

While acknowledging the existence of an esoteric tradition, Lefin decried the contemporary Hasidic practice of communicating that tradition to the masses of East European Jews, whose limited grasp of metaphysics could only lead to misapprehension of the meaning of the Torah.[122] Lefin cavilled against the popularization of the esoteric allusions in the Bible, what he termed its "riddles," because they were likely to be misinterpreted by the majority of Jews. Linguistic confusion, in turn, could easily lead to idolatry, as evidenced by the spiritual regression of the generations after Noah, and of the Egyptians and Greeks, all of whom "erred by mixing together stars and

---

[119] Lefin, "*Elon moreh*," 8. *Maskilim*, followed later by nineteenth-century historians, viewed the Besht as an *am ha'arets* (ignoramus), one unschooled in higher Jewish learning. See, for example, Heinrich Graetz, *History of the Jews* (Philadelphia: The Jewish Publication Society of America, 1891), 374–94 and Dubnow, *Toldot hahasidut*, 1:44.

[120] Lefin assumes a reading of the Talmudic narrative in *b. Hagigah 14a* that attributes Ben Zoma's insanity to his desire to unlock the mysteries of the esoteric world.

[121] Lefin, "*Elon moreh*," 7 and 15. The *ga'on* of Vilna and other *mitnaggedim* also criticized the Hasidim associated with Shneur Zalman of Lady (Liady) for their zeal in practicing *hitbonenut* (intense scrutiny of the Divine). See Nadler, *The Faith of the Mithnagdim*, 22.

[122] Lefin valorized instead the historical King Solomon as a model of ethical, spiritual, and educational leadership. Like other *maskilim*, he turned to Ecclesiastes as the literary example *par excellence* of responsible teaching. See Lefin, *Sefer qohelet*, and his references to King Solomon in Lefin, "*Elon moreh*."

planets and the forms of their images, until in the end they, too, worshipped all kinds of beasts, animals, birds, and frogs, and made graves, mausoleums, and enormously huge altars for them as a memorial until today."[123] Early Christians, too, had erred in interpreting the transubstantiation of Christ as the actual transformation of bread and wine into his body and blood. Contemporary Hasidim had taken the *keruvim* (cherubs) out of their esoteric "storehouses" and "discussed them in front of the masses, who [were] likely to believe in metallic bodies, which are actually only metaphors and allusions to lofty matters, and to project these embodiments of metal onto divine matters, as is known from [the biblical case of] the brass serpent."[124] Lefin believed that contemporary Hasidism's debt to kabbalistic hermeneutics, founded on a psychology that predicated the divinity of the human soul and on an epistemology that strove toward total apprehension of the supernal realm, which Hasidism believed effected a theurgic response by the Divine, was a subversion of all that was sacred in rabbinic Judaism. Criticizing both the techniques of and the erotic language and symbolism encoded within the practical Kabbalah, Lefin censured contemporary Hasidim:

> Who connect letters and make word combinations with their secrets (*mitqasherim otiyyot vetserufim im sitreihem*), [beholding] thousands of worlds burgeoning from the flame of a fire and all kinds of male and female creations encoded in every jot and tittle, which are all connecting to, copulating with, hugging, and kissing one another. The initiate who knows how to effect those very unions is able to create thousands of [imaginary] worlds.[125]

Never reluctant to cast blame on the gullibility of his contemporary Polish-Jewish brethren for foolishly believing in the fabrications of Hasidism, Lefin nevertheless reserved his greatest ire for the zaddik (rebbe in Yiddish), the new type of leader among East European Jewry who viewed himself and was viewed by his followers as an intercessor with the Divine. He had already expressed the belief in the *Essai d'un plan de réforme* that Hasidism,

---

[123]   The Joseph Perl Archive, 4ᵒ 1153/72, JNULA, 1a.
[124]   The Joseph Perl Archive, 4° 1153/72, 2a. Rabbinic tradition, based on the biblical account in 2 Kgs 18:4, credited King Hezekiah with destroying Moses' brass serpent out of fear that future generations would regard the physical shape as the actual embodiment of God. See *b. Berakhot 10b* and *b. Hullin 6b.*
[125]   Lefin, "*Elon moreh,*" 7. Lefin alluded to what he believed were deliberately obfuscating methods of Hasidic exegesis when he criticized "the transgressors (*hato'im*) [who] heap obscure, tenuous interpretations upon the mind to obscure the understanding of those who seek their [the traditional texts'] wisdom, filling their bellies with exaggerations and false talk that has no meaning at all." Lefin, *Sefer ḥeshbon hanefesh,* paragraph 117. On Hasidism's debt to both the exegetical tradition of theosophic Kabbalah and the techniques of practical Kabbalah, see Moshe Idel, *Kabbalah: New Perspectives* (New Haven, Conn.: Yale University Press, 1988) and Moshe Idel, *Hasidism: Between Ecstasy and Magic* (Albany: State University of New York Press, 1995).

particularly through the institution of the zaddik, unfairly and deceitfully arrogated a unique relationship to God for its own initiates. In a later archival fragment, he described the zaddikim as follows:[126]

> A distorted and crooked generation has arisen. Their leaders, in particular, ingratiate themselves to the people through all kinds of endearments and cajolery. They ask how they are doing and inquire after their well-being, all in order to turn them into faithful lovers, to obligate them to recognize their goodness, and to make them their future disciples, with all of their hearts and money. [This leadership] also pecks out their eyes from understanding a book or any explicit reason in Scripture and they slander the pleasant *musar* of the Sages, may their memories be blessed, and turn their words into wormwood. Instead, they fill their prayer books with the names of [Hasidic] men and women and of their mothers. . . . They assure an individual or even entire communities that they see an edict about to befall them, and that they [the zaddikim] have already begun to pray for them with all of their might, which permits them to accept their financial tribute (*pidyoneihem*).[127]

Scholarship on Hasidism has long been preoccupied with the figure of the zaddik, the Hasidic rebbe, and with whether or not the Besht, in his lifetime, fostered the concept of a gap between the superior spiritual prowess of the zaddik and the inferior powers of his followers. Early scholarly advocates of Hasidism interpreted the movement as a democratic revolt against the oligarchy of the institutionalized Jewish community and thus argued that the cult of the zaddik resulted from later distortions of the Besht's original egalitarian impulses.[128] More recent scholarship, however, argues that the ontological distinction between zaddik and Hasid existed from the very beginning of the Besht's teachings, and that later generations of Hasidim merely made explicit what had been implicit in the early years of the

---

[126] On the doctrine of the zaddik in Hasidic thought, see Green, "Typologies of Leadership and the Hasidic Zaddiq." See, too, Ada Rapoport-Albert, "God and the Zaddik as the Two Focal Points of Hasidic Worship," in *Essential Papers on Hasidism* (ed. Gershon David Hundert; New York: New York University Press, 1991), 299–329; Isaiah Tishby and Joseph Dan, "Hasidic Thought and Literature," in *Peraqim betorat haḥasidut uvetoldoteihah* (ed. Avraham Rubinstein; Jerusalem: Zalman Shazar Center, 1977), 263–69; Joseph Weiss, "The Saddik — Altering the Divine Will," in *Studies in Eastern European Mysticism* (ed. David Goldstein; London: Oxford University Press, 1985), 183–93; Immanuel Etkes, "The Zaddik: The Interrelationship between Religious Doctrine and Social Organization," in *Hasidism Reappraised* (ed. Ada Rapoport-Albert; London: The Littman Library of Jewish Civilization, 1996), 159–67.

[127] The Joseph Perl Archive, JNULA, 4° 1153/55, 1b. Part of this manuscript is in Lefin's hand, the other in Joseph Perl's.

[128] See Dubnow, *Toldot haḥasidut* and Dinur, *Bemifneh hadorot.* For assessments of the early historiography on Hasidism, see Arthur Green, "Early Hasidism: Some Old/New Questions," in *Hasidism Reappraised* (ed. Ada Rapoport-Albert; London: The Littman Library of Jewish Civilization, 1996), 441–46 and Immanuel Etkes, "The Study of Hasidism: Past Trends and New Directions," in *Hasidism Reappraised* (ed. Ada Rapoport-Albert; London: The Littman Library of Jewish Civilization, 1996), 447–64.

148 CHAPTER THREE

eighteenth century. In this view, only the zaddik could achieve communion
(*devequt*) with the Divine. The Hasid's role was to "cleave" to a zaddik, an
individual endowed with spectacular spiritual powers, who served as a channel between the temporal and supernal worlds in the delivery of prayers and
the expiation of sin. In Ada Rapoport-Albert's words: "Hasidism, right from
the start . . . blocked entirely and *a priori* the direct route of ordinary people
to God by placing the righteous or perfect men, the men of form, spirit,
knowledge, or understanding or eventually, the zaddikim, in the middle of
that route."[129] This view of the zaddik's exceptional relationship to the
Divine, which explicitly relegated other Jews to lower spiritual status, found
its fullest expression in the works of Elimelekh of Leżajsk (Lizensk), who
dedicated most of his book, *No'am elimelekh* (*Elimelekh's Pleasantness*, 1788), to
the obligations of the "practical zaddik" as a privileged intercessor between
the mundane and supernal realms.[130]

Lefin and other maskilic critics decried the Hasidic principle that followers accept the sanctity and power of the zaddikim unequivocally and argued
that the imposition of "fabricated" new religious obligations upon their
credulous flock assured their hegemony. Lefin railed against the "bundles
upon bundles of new commandments" created through the Hasidic hermeneutic of "secrets (*sodot*)":

> [The Hasidim] perform miracles and deeds of heroism and write books of secrets. One is
> obligated to believe in them as a principle of faith. . . . They make up new [command-
> ments] at their pleasure, [including] purity commandments and commandments regard-
> ing the ritual bath. One is commanded to publicize their miracles and wonders within
> the secret of the "account of the chariot" (*ma'aseh hamerkavah*) constantly. (I heard how
> they prattle in this manner: "the zaddikim are called the *patriarchs*, and the *patriarchs* are
> the *chariot*, therefore, the tales of the miracles of the zaddikim are 'the account of the
> chariot'").[131] [They fabricated] a fee for blessing guests, a fee for prayer on account of
> the sick based on the golden secret . . . [and made] merrymaking an obligatory

[129] Rapoport-Albert, "God and the Zaddik," 314.
[130] Isaiah Tishby and Joseph Dan, "Hasidic Thought and Literature," 267 and Etkes, "The
Zaddik." Writing to Lefin in 1811 on the occasion of the marriage of his daughter, Hinde,
Jacob Samuel Bik regaled his mentor with the anti-Hasidic jesting that had taken place at
the nuptials, which revealed the antipathy of the *maskilim* to the institution of the zaddik.
"One of the [Beshtian stories that the jesters related was] that neither the Torah, the commandments, nor good deeds are useful in acquiring the world-to-come; [rather, the world-
to-come can only be attained by] snatch[ing] merit from a zaddik who has merit in the
world-to-come. When the learned men in attendance heard this they were very alarmed. But
Israel Bodek said to them that this [view of the power of the zaddik] was already written in
R. [Eli]melekh [of Leżajsk]'s book." Published in Weinlös, "Mendel Lefin of Satanów: A
Biographical Study," 342.
[131] Both the midrash *Bereshit Rabbah* 47:8 and the *Zohar* 1: 213b, gloss Gen 17:22 with the
comment, "The patriarchs are the chariot," a comment Shneur Zalman elaborates on in the
Tanya 1, chapter 23. See Naftali Loewenthal, *Communicating the Infinite: The Emergence of the
Habad School* (Chicago: The University of Chicago Press, 1990), 59–60.

commandment. There is always a feast. It is obligatory to please their great men with money and words so that they will bestow upon [the individual Hasid] the holy spirit of delight. [They made] smoking tobacco [obligatory] and [assumed] permission to annul or to innovate tradition (for example, it is commanded to bake unleavened bread a week before Passover, and to eat a loaf made of legumes on Passover . . . to [wear a] white shtreimal, [for] mourners standing by the doorway to smoke tobacco in the synagogue and in the house of study, [for] the mourner to wear Sabbath clothing on the Sabbath and to walk past the elevated platform where the Torah is read during the additional service for the Sabbath, [to resurrect] old melodies for welcoming the Sabbath and for the evening service . . . to immerse in the ritual bath for the sin of a nightly emission on the eve of Yom Kippur . . . and a thousand more examples like this.[132]

The economics of the zaddik's mediating relationship to his disciples was yet another aspect of the new Hasidic leadership that particularly galled Lefin. The practice of *pidyonot*, by which a Hasid gave money to his zaddik to ensure that his entreaty would find its way to Heaven, struck Lefin as outright exploitation. He illustrated this in the eighth chapter of *Sefer ḥeshbon hanefesh*, ironically called *qimmuts* (frugality) by citing the midrash on the phrase *re'ut ruaḥ* in Eccl 4:6 ("Better is a handful with quietness, than both hands full of labor and striving after wind/*re'ut ruaḥ*"): "Better that one does a small amount of his own *tsedaqah* (charity) than to steal, perpetrate violence and oppression, and do more *tsedaqah* than others."[133] Lefin warned his readers to be wary of those (unnamed) individuals whose virtues were often extolled, but whose words were, in fact, a web of lies, flattery, and hypocrisy, oft-quoted maskilic epithets for the Hasidic leaders.[134] The profligacy of these predators led them to invent new customs related to clothes and jewelry, and to create new charities, which only served to embarrass the poor and glorify those who had impoverished them. In *"Teshuvah,"* Lefin wrote that the classical Sages called someone a *rama'i* (charlatan) who extorted charity from others for his own use and enjoyment. In Lefin's view, the zaddikim of his period, who "dress and sleep in expensive fine silks from the donations for the redemption of souls (*pidyon hanefashot*)," were guilty of this appellation. Even worse was their deceitful manipulation of exegetical strategies to justify their greed. When asked why they were dependent upon *pidyonot*, contemporary zaddikim, lampooned Lefin, responded, "Behold, there are several hidden reasons."[135] In *Sefer ḥeshbon hanefesh*, Lefin admonished his readers to be suspicious of the lavish courts of the zaddikim, to

---

[132] The Joseph Perl Archive, 4° 1153/72, 3b. See, too, the Joseph Perl Archive, JNULA, 4° 1153/127d.

[133] Lefin, *Sefer ḥeshbon hanefesh*, paragraph 92. See *Qohelet Rabbah* (Vilna), *parashah* 3 for the gloss on the biblical phrase.

[134] Lefin, *Sefer ḥeshbon hanefesh*, paragraph 91.

[135] The Joseph Perl Archive, JNULA, 4° 1153/72, 2a–3b. Note the irony in Lefin's reference to the esoteric, hidden reasons for Hasidic practice.

avoid large assemblies of people, and to select one honest friend with whom to compare their moral progress, all as a means of directing the vulnerable young yeshivah boy away from the Hasidic view of the zaddik as an obligatory mediator for a Jew's spiritual and ethical quest.[136]

In his unpublished journal, Lefin copied what he felt was evidence for the divine-like glorification of the zaddikim by contemporary Hasidism from their own literature, a literary strategy that Joseph Perl took up in his *Über das Wesen der Sekte Chassidim* (*Regarding the Essence of the Hasidic Sect*):[137]

> In the book *Judah's Staff*, page 11, I heard in the name of the *ga'on*, the Hasid, Dov Ber of Międzyrzec (Mezhirech), an interpretation of the phrase, "The master of the universe who rules before everything was created" (*adon olam asher malakh beterem kol yetsir nivra*), etc. 'It is known that a zaddik is called "*all*" (*kol*), and this is his interpretation of the phrase "the master of the universe who rules," *by himself*, meaning, before the zaddik was created (*beterem kol yetsir nivra*). But from the time that the zaddik was created "with all of his desire" [*beheftso kol*], the zaddik rules as is God's desire.' And from the book *No'am elimelekh*, page 22a, this is a direct quote, "'A storekeeper is exempt, but a homeowner is obligated,' meaning, that the essence of the obligation is on the zaddik, who is obligated to activate everything (*kol*). He [the zaddik] is called the homeowner who emanates eternally, as does a homeowner who influences his sons. Because of the holy deeds of the zaddik alone, who can activate everything, as it were, the obligation does not fall on the Holy One, blessed is he." And from the same reference, page 11b, this is a direct quote, "'God's eyes are toward the righteous ones (zaddikim),' meaning, God supervises Israel through the zaddikim."[138]

Lefin further elaborated his critique of Hasidism's penchant to view the zaddik in a quasi-divine manner in *Sefer ḥeshbon hanefesh*'s seventh chapter, cannily entitled *tsedeq* (justice) to pun with his adversaries' title. For Lefin, a truly righteous man (zaddik) performed God's will by fulfilling the commandment, "You shall love your neighbor as yourself" (Lev 19:18), which he interpreted to mean respecting his fellow Jews (if not rational non-Jews) and doing good for all of Creation, particularly man. Lefin stated that the Sages considered this commandment to be "the foundation of the whole Torah."[139] Appreciating one's fellow Jews and treating them honestly was the essence of authentic Jewish faith (*emunah*) intended by the prophet

---

[136] Lefin, *Sefer ḥeshbon hanefesh*, paragraph 45. He also stressed the efficacy of the traditional *ḥavruta* (study partnership) for moral training, even going so far as to suggest that a man's wife made the most ideal partner for his technique of moral self-improvement. See paragraphs 34 and 44.

[137] [Joseph Perl], *Über das Wesen der Sekte Chassidim* (ed. Avraham Rubinstein; Jerusalem: Publications of the Israel Academy of Sciences and Humanities, 1977). The full title of the work is *Über das Wesen der Sekte Chassidim. Aus ihren eigenen Schriften gezogen* (*Regarding the Essence of the Sect of the Hasidism, taken from their own Writings*).

[138] The Joseph Perl Archive, JNULA, 4° 1153/130, 17.

[139] Reference to Lev 19:18 as an essential principle of the Torah can be found attributed to R. Akiba in *Sifre Qiddushin, 2:4* and midrash *Bereshit Rabbah*, chapter 24.

Habakkuk, when he expressed that "a righteous man (zaddik) shall live by his faith (*emunah*)" (Hab 2:4). Lefin unquestionably knew of the Hasidic interpretation of this verse from Habakkuk, in which the intransitive *yihyeh* (will live) was read as a transitive verb *yeḥayeh* (will vitalize). In the Hasidic reading, the verse emphasized the zaddik's singular power to mediate his followers' spiritual life: "a zaddik will vitalize [his followers] through his faith."[140] Lefin believed that Hasidism violated the "commandments between man and his fellow man, such as the prohibition against stealing, robbery, injustice, trickery, jealousy, hatred, gossip, etc." Reliance on the zaddik's monopoly on faith was antithetical, wrote Lefin consciously alluding to his enemies, to the positive commandment of *gemilut ḥasidim* (being charitable to others). Lefin parodied what he believed was the "true" meaning of *tsedeq* (justice/charity) to the false exploitation of the zaddik by penning his critique in the book's ninetieth paragraph. When rendered in Hebrew, the number 90 is written simply with the eighteenth letter of the alphabet (*tsadi* or *zaddik*).[141]

Lefin employed Franklin's technique for moral self-reform because it firmly secured the process of controlling one's appetite and perfecting one's morals in the individual. He dedicated *Sefer ḥeshbon hanefesh* to critically examining matters that are "between man and himself," the first category in Wolffian psychology that Lefin assumed in his letter in *Hame'assef* in 1789.[142] Lefin's emphasis on individual self-examination, what one historian has called "introspective psychology,"[143] represented a radical break from the *musar* tradition of medieval Jewish ethical writing and posed an alternative to the Hasidic understanding of the soul, which, in turn, redounded to the social realm.[144] If the human soul did not possess a divine essence, then its rehabilitation in the case of sin did not require recourse to the divine realm or to individuals with unique abilities to affect the Divine. Disconnecting the

---

140   Isaiah Tishby and Joseph Dan, "Hasidic Thought and Literature," 267.
141   Lefin, *Sefer ḥeshbon hanefesh*, paragraph 90.
142   Lefin, *Hame'assef* 5 (1789): 86.
143   Levine, "Menachem Mendel Lefin," 60.
144   Lefin's psychology found a surprising ally in Israel Salanter (1810–1883), founder of the modern, nineteenth-century *musar* movement. Boldly breaking with his mentors, Hayim of Wołożyn (Volozhin) and Zundel of Salant, Salanter divorced an individual's evil tendencies from the metaphysical realm of the Kabbalah's *sitra aḥra* (other side) and placed responsibility for them squarely within the individual's soul. Salanter, indebted to Lefin, believed that lust could be controlled by the individual Jew through a program of ethical education directed by reason. Salanter was so influenced by Lefin's stress on the autonomy of the individual to deal with his evil inclination that he reprinted *Sefer ḥeshbon hanefesh* in 1845, a posthumous imprimatur that ironically guaranteed its acceptance by the traditional Jewish community and the republication, up until today, of Lefin's work. See Immanuel Etkes, *R. Yisra'el Salanter vereshitah shel tenu'at hamusar* (Jerusalem: Magnes Press, 1982), 133–35, 142, and 145–46.

soul from the metaphysical realm therefore directly challenged the fundamental assumption of Hasidism: that the average Jew could not successfully
atone for his sin without submitting to the authority of a zaddik.

Lefin's appropriation of Franklin's method obviated the requirement for
a spiritual and ethical mediator in the life of an average rabbinic Jew.
Individual introspection and sentience, reinforced through a daily program
of rigorous behavior modification, could be effective. Rooting moral
transformation in the individual underscored Lefin's commitment to the
autonomy of the soul and of the self, and he did not hesitate to identify
contemporary zaddikim with idols and the Hasidim who turned to them for
intercession with God as idol worshipers, "Our Sages, may their memories be
blessed, said, 'Don't turn to idols (Lev 19:4),' 'to that conceived in your own
minds.'[145] And if you incline after them, the result will be to turn them into
the Divine . . . because when they [the Hasidim] turn intentionally toward
[false idols], even toward bars of metal, they are likely to be made divine."[146]
Joseph Perl recorded and saved a maskilic prayer in his archive that underscored the maskilic belief in individual autonomy, what the text calls da'at
ha'enoshit (human understanding), as God's greatest gift to the Jews and the
sole tool to negate the idolatrous claim of contemporary Hasidism that their
zaddikim were "gods and prophets [who believe they may] interpret and
resolve [exegetical issues in] the [Written and Oral] Torahs as [they]
desire."[147] The prayer's accusation that the Hasidim considered their zaddikim to be prophets followed a litany about earlier false prophets, Sabbatai
Zevi, Nathan of Gaza, Baruchiah Russo, Nehemiah Hayon, and Jacob Frank,
underscoring the maskilic view that Hasidism's valorization of the zaddik
would result in antinomianism and sexual deviance.[148]

---

[145] b. Sabbath 149a.

[146] The Joseph Perl Archive, JNULA, 4° 1153/72, 1a and 2a.

[147] The Joseph Perl Archive, JNULA, 4° 1153/5. It is not clear who authored the prayer,
although the handwriting is Perl's. The text makes specfic reference to the writer's advanced
age, but the second side of the page mentions the year 1818, when Perl would have been
only forty-six years old, yet Lefin sixty-nine. Lefin's almost complete blindness led him to
rely frequently on his disciples for writing, proofreading, and copyediting, in which case the
prayer may be his in its entirety. See the Appendix for a transcription and translation of the
text. See, too, Lefin's equation of Hasidic devotion to the zaddik to idolatrous worship. The
Joseph Perl Archive, JNULA, 4° 1153/127d, 8a.

[148] Similar connections between the power of the imaginative faculty and false prophecy
were drawn by the Cambridge Platonist, John Smith (1618–1652). See Heyd, 'Be Sober and
Reasonable,' 186. Maskilim did not hesitate to suspect the Hasidim of homosexuality, which
they condemned. See Simha Katz, "Letters of Maskilim Debasing Hasidim," Moznayim 10
(1944): 266–76. On sexual tensions in anti-Sabbatian polemics, see Elisheva Carlebach, The
Pursuit of Heresy: Rabbi Moses Hagiz and the Sabbatian Controversies (New York: Columbia
University Press, 1990), 9.

Sefer ḥeshbon hanefesh not only presented a comprehensive program of moral self-reform that addressed the fundamental distinction between Hasidic and modern psychology. It also incorporated a direct critique of Hasidic techniques for expiating sin. The first virtue enumerated in Lefin's work, *menuḥah* (calmness), or in Franklin's terminology "temperance," permeates the work. Emotional balance and the development of moderate temperament was necessary to fulfill Lefin's program of ethical development and imperative to render proper service to God in accordance with the traditional, rabbinic model that he favored: "There is no question that the majority of cases of [moral] illnesses can only be healed through moderation."[149] Lefin's reiteration of terms such as *metinut* (moderation), *yishuv hada'at* (consideration), as well as *menuḥah* and *menuḥat hanefesh*, throughout *Sefer ḥeshbon hanefesh* illustrate his belief that the cultivation of these virtues represented an antidote to the Hasidic emphasis on unbridled emotion and ecstatic worship, known by the Hebrew term *hitlahavut* (ecstasy or ardor).[150] In their denunciations of the new movement, *mitnaggedim* frequently criticized the Hasidic claim that awe and ardor in prayer were more important than habitual prayer at the appointed times.[151] For the Hasidim, *hitlahavut* was necessary to stimulate the supernal realm's role in the rectification of sin. In a parable early in the pages of *Sefer ḥeshbon hanefesh*, Lefin, in contrast, illustrated the dangers of mistaking extreme ardor for appropriate forms of devotion:[152]

> Two young men, both of whom were God-fearing sons of Torah, decided to pray with the intention of expressing the meaning of the words. One had a sharp mind and a *strong temperament*, and was his parents' only son. The *awe* blazed in his heart suddenly to compel his soul to complete his prayers with all of his might, without any speck of a *sinful thought* (*maḥashavah zarah*). [But] his evil inclination rebelled against him, and he became even more infuriated at it. The struggle within his soul continued and increased for several months until he became crazy. Each time that he arrived at a place in the prayer to mention God's name, he became confused and mentioned instead the name of an idol. Thus he became crazy, rebelled against his parents, threw himself from the roof, and died. The second [youth] was of *moderate intelligence* [and] *settled in temperament*, [yet] an ignoramus at the time of his adolescence. He began to train himself in Torah and divine service [*avodah*] slowly as he became older. He studied a lot of Torah and became famous as an important scholar in his city. He was pure and truthful in his negotiations with other men, and his prayer was free of sinful thoughts. . . . When he was asked how he merited this [to pray without the interruption of a sinful thought], he responded: 'I decided over these past many years to accustom my mind to focus on one thought

149 Lefin, *Sefer heshbon hanefesh*, paragraph 70.
150 On *hitlahavut* in Hasidic prayer, see Gershom Scholem, "Hasidism: The Latest Phase," in *Major Trends in Jewish Mysticism* (Jerusalem: Schocken Books, 1941), 335 and Loewenthal, *Communicating the Infinite*, 110–14.
151 Wilensky, *Hasidim umitnaggedim*, 1:38–41, 45, 50, 54, and 75.
152 See Levine, "Between Hasidism and Haskalah," 188 for his discussion of the parable.

(either a thought of Torah or a prayer) for a specific period of time, and thus I learned how to concentrate (uninterrupted) for at least one hour, if not more' [thus making it possible for him to focus on his prayers]. He died with a good reputation, having written a pleasant work on the *Shulḥan arukh*. . . . [Yet,] due to our great sins, it is common today for precious young people to be scorched in the fire of awe when they rush *to uproot and to eradicate* the evil inclination quickly and to destroy its trace from within the inner creases of their hearts. The result is that they are drowned in black bitterness and in the dullness of the intellect, meaning, the death of their rational soul.[153]

The parable underscores Lefin's familiarity with and criticism of Hasidic techniques for coping with *maḥashavot zarot* (pl. of *maḥashavah zarah*), the "foreign," "strange," or "evil" thoughts, understood to be sexual, that interrupted a Jew in prayer from remaining focused on the Divine.[154] Eighteenth-century Hasidism's preoccupation with coping with *maḥashavot zarot* was due perhaps to the population explosion in Poland that resulted in an abundance of young adolescent boys. As early as the period of the Besht, techniques for "elevating" as opposed to "negating" sinful thoughts became widely disseminated. These "sinful" thoughts could be elevated, and purified in the process, because their source was divine. The Beshtian revolution, as Joseph Weiss calls it, asserted that God's omnipresence included residing in "sinful thoughts," thus allowing the Hasid to feel that his most base thoughts derived from goodness, and could be returned to their source through proper technique and intention. The second and third generation of Hasidic masters also faced the question of "sinful thoughts" and responded to their existence in a variety of ways. Menachem Mendel of Witebsk (Vitebsk) and Meshullam Feibush of Międzybóż (Medzibozh), disagreeing with the Beshtian innovation that blurred the distinction between good and evil, did not feel capable of elevating "sinful thoughts" to their divine root. In their teachings, they returned to traditional *musar* literature to guide their followers in the expiation of sin.[155] Soon after, however, a new school of expiating "sinful thoughts" arose, spread by Menachem Mendel's young disciple, Shneur Zalman of Lady (Liady) (1745–1812), after his teacher's death in 1788.

By the end of the century, Shneur Zalman became the undisputed leader of Hasidism in White Russia and the founder of a distinct movement within Hasidism known as Habad, based on the Hebrew acronym of the words *ḥokhmah* (wisdom), *binah* (understanding) and *da'at* (knowledge). In 1797, he published what would become his most influential work, *Liqqutei amarim*, which to this day is known simply as the *Tanya*, in an anonymous edition.

---

153 Lefin, *Sefer heshbon hanefesh*, paragraphs 16 and 17. The emphasis is mine.
154 Joseph Weiss, "The Beginnings of Hasidism," in *Peraqim betoldot haḥasidut uvetoldoteihah* (ed. Avraham Rubinstein; Jerusalem: Zalman Shazar Center, 1977), 122–82.
155 Isaiah Tishby and Joseph Dan, "Hasidic Thought and Literature," 274.

The work, which is divided into two sections, a) *Sefer shel beinonim* (*The Book of the Intermediate Men*) and b) *Sha'ar hayihud veha'emunah* (*The Gate of Unity and Faith*), is a systematic and popular presentation of Shneur Zalman's Hasidic teachings, including treatments of the respective status of the zaddik and the *beinoni* and of techniques for meeting the challenge of "sinful thoughts."[156] Published simultaneously with *Taqqanot liozna* (*Edicts of Lady*), which circumscribed the amount of time Shneur Zalman would devote to *yihudim*, the private confessional meetings between Hasid and zaddik that had characterized his school of Hasidism, the *Tanya* provided Shneur Zalman's followers with a clear presentation of an alternative system to traditional *musar's* method of moral training and a clear exposition of techniques for coping with "sinful thoughts."[157]

Shneur Zalman's psychology began with the assumption that there were two souls within each Jew, one whose essence was goodness, the other's evil. Employing kabbalistic terminology from Hayim Vital's *Ets hayim*, Shneur Zalman described the evil, bestial soul's provenance as the outer covering, the husk (*qelippah*), of the emanation of *nogah* (brilliance) from the *sitra ahra* ("the other side"). The divine soul (*nefesh ha'elohit*), in contrast, embodied pure goodness, yet Habad doctrine emphasized the paradoxical and reciprocal dimension of the relationship between the two souls. Both souls were divine in origin, the bestial soul representing a process of separation from the supernal realm, the divine soul representing a return to it. Rachel Elior describes the Habad doctrine of the two souls as "two types of consciousness."[158] The goal of the Hasidic worldview was to transform individual consciousness to transcend everything in the concrete, mundane world associated with the bestial soul through awareness of the only truth, the divine soul. In the *Tanya*, Shneur Zalman outlined three categories of Jews in relationship to their position in the battle of the souls: the zaddik (righteous man), the *beinoni* (intermediate man), and the *rasha* (evil man). The zaddik represented the rare individual in whom the struggle between the two souls was absent; he achieved a total transformation of his soul so that it returned fully to its divine source. The *rasha* was the individual in whom the bestial soul, derived from the husk of *nogah*, was triumphant. The *Tanya* trained its

---

156 On *Liqqutei amarim*, see Dubnow, *Toldot hahasidut*, 2:232–41, Immanuel Etkes, "R. Shneur Zalman of Lady's Manner as a Hasidic Leader," *Zion* 50 (1985): 321–54, Rachel Elior, *The Paradoxical Ascent to God: The Kabbalistic Theosophy of Habad Hasidism* (Albany State University of New York Press, 1993), and Loewenthal, *Communicating the Infinite*.

157 In the foreword to *Sefer shel habeinonim*, Shneur Zalman criticized works of traditional *musar* as inherently limited because of their human origin, while the system he outlined in the *Tanya*, because it was divine, was thus uncontestable and infallible. See Shneur Zalman of Lady, *Liqqutei amarim [Tanya]* (trans. Nissan Mindel; New York, 1969), 9–11.

158 Elior, *The Paradoxical Ascent to God*, 104–07.

teachings on the third type of individual, the *beinoni*, in whom the two souls were locked in eternal battle, "each one wishing and desiring to rule over him and pervade his mind exclusively." The *beinoni*, despite his struggle, ultimately mastered self-control, but could not transform the "sinful thoughts." In the *Tanya*, Shneur Zalman, following the teachings of Mena-chem Mendel, advised the *beinoni* to use traditional methods, subjugation and repression, of banishing the "sinful thoughts" from his mind, while the pure zaddik, who only received "sinful thoughts" from other worshippers, effected their transformation through Hasidic techniques. The *Tanya* asser-ted that only the zaddik had the power to engage the "sinful thoughts" and to annihilate the *sitra ahra* without succumbing to the bestial soul.[159] The zad-dik's special responsibility to engage the *mahashavot zarot* of the sinful men of his generation by "descending" to the *sitra ahra* and elevating the sinful thoughts is generally referred to in Hasidic literature as *nefilat hatsadiq* ("de-scent of the zaddik").[160] The implication, given the mediating relationship between zaddik and Hasid, was that the full elevation and transformation of "sinful thoughts" could only occur through faith in the zaddik's power. The *Tanya* thus implicitly counseled the average Jew, the *beinoni*, to find a zaddik to whom he could "cleave," whose singular powers and connection to the Divine provided an incontestable means to atonement.

The *Tanya*'s accessible elaboration of a systematic theory of the soul and its relationship to ethical behavior enjoyed broad popularity among East European Jews at the end of the eighteenth and beginning of the nineteenth centuries. Hillel Levine justly argued that Lefin's appropriation of Franklin's technique of triumphing over the bestial soul was a direct response to the success of the *Tanya*, which was published three times between 1797 and 1808.[161] Lefin wrote *Sefer heshbon hanefesh* to compete directly with the Habad system of repressing "sinful thoughts" in order to elevate and purify them.[162]

---

[159] Shneur Zalman of Lady, *Liqqutei amarim [Tanya]*, 1, chapters 27 and 28. Joseph Dan and Isaiah Tishby argue for an exoteric and esoteric reading of Shneur Zalman's approach to "sinful thoughts," positing that the *Tanya*, which dissuaded the *beinoni* from attempting to elevate the "sinful thoughts," is more conservative than his later sermons, which posited the possibility of the *beinoni* to transform the "coverings" (*levushim*) of the thoughts toward the purity of the supernal realm. See Isaiah Tishby and Joseph Dan, "Hasidic Thought and Literature," 275–78. For other interpretations of Shneur Zalman's teachings, see Dubnow, *Toldot hahasidut*, 2:239 and Loewenthal, *Communicating the Infinite*, 238–39, footnote 108.

[160] Isaiah Tishby and Joseph Dan, "Hasidic Thought and Literature," 263–64, 266. See Rivka Schatz Uffenheimer, *Hasidism as Mysticism: Quietistic Elements in Eighteenth Century Hasidic Thought* (Jerusalem: Magnes Press, 1993), 367–68, footnote 43, on the psychological dimensions of the doctrine of the "descent of the zaddik" in Hasidic thought.

[161] See Levine, "Between Hasidism and Haskalah," 189 and Levine, "Menachem Mendel Lefin," 38, 64, and 188–95.

[162] Shneur Zalman's view on the obligation of the individual Jew and of the zaddik, respec-tively, in the elevation and purification of "strange thoughts" was not monolithic. In the

In his unpublished journal, he interpreted the Mishnaic phrase, "Know what is above you, a seeing eye . . . and that all your deeds are written in a book" (*m. Avot 2:1*), by citing Ps 31:20, "I place God before me," as a means of explaining his view of the correct demeanor for prayer. The prooftext had been adduced by Moses Isserles, arguably the most authoritative rabbinic decisor in early modern Ashkenaz, in his commentary to the *Shulḥan arukh* (*Oraḥ ḥayim*, 1:1). Isserles, in turn, referred to Maimonides's *Guide* 3:52, to underscore the proper deportment of a pious Jew during prayer. Lefin posited that one engaged in prayer should endeavor to implant the thought of God in his soul, to guard it before him, as if God were by his side, in order to remain focused on the liturgy, just as one should try to inculcate other qualities in the soul that would be activated when one performed an action related to them. Lefin solicited the support of classic rabbinic texts (Maimonides and Isserles) in order to contrast what he viewed to be a normative posture for prayer and the performance of the commandments with the *Tanya*'s method of repression and elevation:

> Those who say that it is a commandment to compel, force, and strengthen the [sinful] thought with constant vigilance, that it should not move from our concentration for even a minute, err. Not only does this method contradict the kind of knowledge that the Divine, may he be blessed, implanted in the soul of man [through] the "process of ideas" that, like a river, never ceases. But, this manner [of controlling thoughts] will result in carelessness and boredom, as in the case of R. Joshua ben Levi, who, like a fool, investigated a chicken for three hours [and fell asleep][163] . . . and the action of R. Ishmael [b. Elisha] who said, "I will read [by the light of a lamp on the Sabbath] and I will not tilt it," and he inadvertently [tilted the lamp, thus sinning],[164] and like the gnat of Titus. Once it [the gnat] began [to knock against Titus's brain], there was no stopping it (like the act [of the intemperate youth] that will be explained in *Sefer ḥeshbon hanefesh*).[165]

Repression and elevation of "sinful thoughts" were not only against God's will in implanting human understanding in the soul of men. These techniques were destined to backfire psychologically, creating lackluster practitioners of Judaism at best, and unintentional sinners at worst. Even more profoundly, Lefin believed that the techniques of Habad Hasidism subverted

---

Tanya, Shneur Zalman presented two views on the importance of elevating evil thoughts. He both advised the average Jew (*habeinoni*) besieged with an impure thought during prayer to simply divert his attention from it *and* to wage an active war against it through repression and subjugation. His sermons, published after his death, placed a much stronger emphasis on the elevation of evil/strange thoughts as fundamental to the service of God than did the *Tanya*. See Isaiah Tishby and Joseph Dan, "Hasidic Thought and Literature," 275–76.

163 *b. Berakhot 7a* and *b. Avodah Zarah 4b.*

164 *b. Shabbat 12b.*

165 The Joseph Perl Archive, JNULA, 4° 1153/130, 53. According to Talmudic legend, a gnat entering the head of Titus (Flavius Vespasian, captor of Jerusalem, later Emperor of Rome) through his nose plagued him for seven years and swelled to the size of a two-pound dove. See *b. Gittin 56b* and *Midrash Bereshit Rabbah* (Albeck), *parashah* 10.

the rational tradition of Maimonides and the authentic inheritance of Ashkenazic rabbinic Judaism. Directly criticizing the glorification of the zaddik in Habad Hasidism, Lefin began the eighth chapter of *Sefer heshbon hanefesh* with the three words that form Habad's acronym, wisdom (*hokhmah*), understanding (*binah*), and knowledge (*da'at*), condemned the movement's profligacy, and concluded that "the spirit of *true Sages* are not comfortable with it."[166]

Lefin's appropriation of Franklin's "Rules of Conduct" with their emphasis on moderation reflected his interest in finding a pragmatic, accessible means to rival the appeal of Hasidic enthusiasm, particularly the emphasis on *hitlahavut* that accompanied the repression and elevation of "sinful thoughts" during prayer. The risks of extreme enthusiasm were fatal in Lefin's view and he urged his readers instead to approach prayer in a moderate, conventional fashion. In one of Lefin's later works, an imaginary description of the world-to-come, a righteous man bemoans the pressures from unnamed adversaries that he has had to withstand in the mundane world. From the complaints, "Some wanted to persuade me with very dazzling ardor (*hitlahavut*)," it is obvious that his fictitious pursuers were Hasidim.[167] Lefin's concerns about the dangers of *hitlahavut* were shared by other anti-Hasidic Polish Jews. Writing to Lefin from Bar, a Podolian town south of Międzybóz, Benjamin Reich, the son of Lefin's friend and fellow *maskil*, Meir ha-Cohen Reich, delighted in regaling the older *maskil* with absurd Hasidic homilies on the need for ecstasy in prayer:

I was in Międzybóz before the New Year with the rebbe from Most, and I heard things from him that delight the heart of the listener. I will transcribe one of the things that he said in his [own] pure language, *because exegetical riddles are dear to me*.

"Our brothers in Israel, this is the rule, take into your heart that there are two kinds of service [prayer] to God, may he be blessed. One is the characteristic of enthusiasm (*lahav*) and one is the characteristic of standing (*nitsav*). [The first kind] is the man who is enthusiastic during the time of his prayer and performs a commandment with ardor, and the second [type] is the one who stands in one place, praying according to the guidelines stipulated in the *Shulhan arukh* and the *Seder hayom*. Clearly, the level of the second is lower than the first. Sometimes it is possible that the second will attain the level of the first . . . if he behaves himself this way for several days until his prayer becomes completely intuitive. Then it is possible that he will obtain the levels of the first. [But] in my opinion he is in need of aid from Heaven and the merit of the patriarchs. Then, he, too, will approach the level achieved by service performed with enthusiasm. This is what was intended by the verse (Judg 3:22): 'and the haft (*nitsav*) went in *after* the blade (*lahav*)].'"[168]

---

166 Levine, "Between Hasidism and Haskalah," 189.
167 The Joseph Perl Archive, JNULA, 4° 1153/127d, the section entitled "The Fate of the Righteous," 5a.
168 Benjamin Reich to Mendel Lefin, undated, but sent to Lefin in Tarnopol, Austrian

Meir ha-Cohen Reich, concerned lest his son be influenced by the Hasidic practice of lengthening prayers, warned him in a letter in 1823 to pray succinctly and with intention, echoing Lefin's implicit critique of Hasidic prayer as a deviation from the carefully structured liturgical formulae of traditional rabbinic Judaism.[169] Despite the perception of the *maskilim* that traditional *musar* was no longer efficacious for moral self-reform, they still believed that prayer performed according to what had been customary rabbinic practice in Poland prior to the efflorescence of Hasidism could guide a young Jew toward an ethical life and appropriate service devoted to the Divine.

Given the conservatism of East European Jewry, Lefin always anchored his use of non-Jewish ideas within authoritative Jewish sources. The method of moderation outlined in *Sefer ḥeshbon hanefesh* echoed Maimonides's concerns in *Eight Chapters*, a commentary on the mishnaic tractate *Avot* devoted to the problems of the soul. In the *Eight Chapters*, Maimonides articulated his renowned harmonization of Aristotelian philosophy with rabbinic Judaism, focusing on Jewish law as the equivalent of the philosopher's "golden mean."[170] Daily repetition of the commandments demanded by Jewish law vouchsafed a virtuous life because the rabbinic system was equivalent to the "golden mean" and ensured that practitioners' behavior did not deviate toward the extremes of exaggeration or deficiency. Rabbinic Judaism practiced according to its traditional Ashkenazic formulation almost assuredly guaranteed the practitioner a life of equanimity and virtue.[171] Although

---

Galicia (second decade of the nineteenth century). The Joseph Perl Archive, JNULA, 4° 1153/70. Emphasis is mine. The homily puns on the word *lahav* (blade) and its similarity to *hitlahavut* (ecstasy).

[169] See Meir ha-Cohen Reich to Benjamin Reich, Bar, 1823. Jacob Samuel Bik copied the letter into his private journal. See Merzbacher manuscript, found in the municipal library of Frankfurt-on-the-Main, 64, Ms. hebr. fol. 11, 39b; a microfilm of the manuscript is held in the Department of Photographed Manuscripts and Archives, JNULA. In 1808, Lefin sent Meir ha-Cohen Reich a copy of *Sefer ḥeshbon hanefesh* for his opinion. See the letter to Jacob Meshullam Orenstein, the head of the rabbinical court in Lemberg, the Abraham Schwadron Collection of Jewish Autographs and Portraits, papers of Mendel Lefin (1749–1826), JNULA.

[170] Maimonides, however, did not have a consistent view of the ethics of the "middle path." While *Eight Chapters* and the *Mishneh torah* generally counseled moderation and only occasionally argued that deviation from the mean was necessary as a kind of "corrective therapy" to its opposite extreme, the *Guide* offers a startling contradiction to the Aristotelian mean. In the *Guide*, Maimonides often rejects the middle path, excoriates the body and the practical world, and subordinates ethics to the ultimate perfection, intellectual apprehension of the Divine. See Davidson, "The Middle Way in Maimonides' Ethics."

[171] See Isadore Twersky, ed., *A Maimonides Reader* (New York: Behrman House, 1972), 367–68. Lefin revealed his debt to Maimonides already in 1789, when in his *Iggerot haḥokhmah* he counseled moderation as the key to control of the body: "In the first section it will be explained how to control all the powers of the body and use every single limb *to restore and to*

Lefin does not specifically mention Maimonides in the body of *Sefer ḥeshbon hanefesh*, the influence of the medieval master on his thought is indisputable. Like Maimonides, Lefin made frequent analogies between bodily illness and moral illness, between doctors and moralists, and appropriated his predecessor's frequent warnings against the medieval palliatives of asceticism and physical chastisement as a cure for moral ills.[172] Maimonides's influence on Lefin was literary, as well. In the *Eight Chapters*, Maimonides cited Ps 19:8 as a prooftext for the rejection of asceticism, physical chastisement, and flight from society:

> The perfect law which leads us to perfection, as one who knew it well testifies by the words, 'the Law of the Lord is perfect, restoring the soul; the testimonies of the Lord are faithful making wise the simple (*maḥkimat peti*)' (Ps 19:8), recommends none of those things [such as self-torture, flight from society, etc.]. On the contrary, it aims at man's following the path of moderation in accordance with the dictates of nature, eating, drinking, enjoying legitimate sexual intercourse, all in moderation.[173]

As Shmuel Werses has shown in his study of a manuscript bearing on Lefin's unpublished Yiddish anti-Hasidic parody, *Maḥkimat peti* (*Making Wise the Simple*), Lefin made ironic and caustic use of the same verse from Psalms to form the title of his work. Alluding to Isaiah Horowitz's gloss in his *Shenei luḥot haberit* (*Two Tablets of the Covenant*), in which the mystic interpreted Ps 19:8 as an attack on the study of philosophy and an encouragement to study Kabbalah, Lefin used it to rebut the authority of the *Zohar* and the spread of mysticism.[174]

In his battle against Hasidism as a movement that subverted the authentic

---

strengthen them with a moderate effort, meaning, not to damage them by arduous labor, and not to immobilize or damage them through laziness." Emphasis in the original. See Lefin, *Hame'assef* 5 (1789): 86. Isaac Michael Monies, a long-time Talmud teacher in Joseph Perl's school in Tarnopol cited the moderation of *Eight Chapters* in his maskilic responsum on custom. See Isaac Michael Monies, "Responsum on the Custom of Lighting Candles on Lag Ba'omer in Memory of R. Shimon bar Yochai," *Yerushalayim* 1 (1844): 17.

[172] Lefin also used a medical analogy in the introductory paragraph of *Liqqutei kelalim*. See N. M. Gelber, "Mendel Lefin of Satanów's Proposals for the Improvement of Jewish Community Life presented to the Great *Sejm* (1788–1792)," in *The Abraham Weiss Jubilee Volume* (ed. Samuel Belkin; New York: Shulsinger Brothers, 1964), 287. He had already affirmed his interest in medicine in the translation of Tissot's *Avis au Peuple sur sa Santé* into Hebrew. Couching the translation of the medical text in terms of providing East European Jewry with the means of fulfilling the commandment of visiting the sick, Lefin hoped it would be an effective antidote to medical charlatans and to the Hasidim who rejected the use of medicine. See Chone Shmeruk, "Moses Markuse and his Book, *Ezer yisroel*," in *Sifrut yidish: peraqim letoldoteihah* (Tel Aviv: The Porter Institute for Poetics & Semiotics, 1978), 190 and 196.

[173] Cited in Twersky, *A Maimonides Reader*, 371.

[174] Shmuel Werses, "Regarding the Lost Pamphlet, *Maḥkimat peti*," in *Megammot vetsurot besifrut hahaskalah* (Jerusalem: Magnes Press, 1990), 326.

tradition of Ashkenazic Judaism, Lefin used Franklin's technique and selectively employed the ideas of other eighteenth-century Enlightenment thinkers who sought to liberate the self from what Kant called "man's self-incurred tutelage."[175] At all times, Lefin attempted to balance the innovation of the Enlightenment's emphasis on the self with the continuity of traditional rabbinic Judaism. *Sefer ḥeshbon hanefesh* thus satirized Hasidism while offering an individualized program for moral self-improvement consonant with traditional values of devotion to God and to Jewish law. Through an accessible, individualized program of moral reflection, Lefin hoped to turn the masses of East European Jewry toward the right path, one guided by rationalism and moderation, which he attributed to Maimonides, and away from the Hasidic path of irrationalism, superstition, and extremism, in order to lead them to a revitalized traditional Jewish life.[176]

The Immortality of the Enlightened Soul

Although Lefin opposed speculation into God's essence and the structure of the supra-sensible world, he upheld — as did most eighteenth-century thinkers — the belief in the immortality of the soul as a principle of the natural world. On the question of the soul's immateriality, Lefin followed Moses Mendelssohn. Lefin penned two essays on the soul's immortality, one in German, *Los der abgeschiednen Seelen* (*The Fate of the Departed Souls*), the other in Yiddish, *Ma'amar olam hagemul* (*Essay on the Afterlife*), and devoted chapter five of his *Nachlaß* to a discussion of Mendelssohn's *Phaedon*.[177] All three essays remained in manuscript, the last irretrievably lost. Unlike Mendelssohn, who was later criticized by Kant for his argument, Lefin did not endeavor to prove the immortality of the soul.[178] As one of Maimonides's

---

[175] Immanuel Kant, "What is Enlightenment?" in *Foundations of the Metaphysics of Morals* (trans. Lewis White Beck; New York: Macmillan, 1990 (c. 1959)), 85.

[176] See Lefin's comment on Eccl 12:11, in Lefin, *Sefer qohelet*. See, too, the Joseph Perl Archive, JNULA, 4° 1153/128e, paragraph 9, where Lefin refers to King Solomon's ability to find only one wise man among a thousand people (Eccl 7:28) who would "be able to graze these human animals on wisdom."

[177] Weinlös, "R. Menachem Mendel of Satanów," 800, where he transcribes the outline for Lefin's *Nachlaß*; the fifth essay is called "Summary of Mendelssohn's Phaedon." *Los der abgeschiednen Seelen* is an incomplete version of *Ma'amar olam hagemul*. See the Joseph Perl Archive, JNULA, 4° 1153/68 and 127d, respectively.

[178] Altmann, *Moses Mendelssohn: A Biographical Study*, 179. Kant's objections to the *Phaedon* appeared in the second and revised edition of *Critique of Pure Reason* (1787). In the section "On the Paralogisms of Pure Reason," Kant disagreed with Mendelssohn's proofs for the soul's incorruptibility. Even if the soul were simple (and thus not subject to annihilation or corruption), Kant argued, it had to have an "intensive quality," which could diminish. Thus, he reasoned, the soul could not disappear into nothingness in one instant, but could lose its powers slowly over time. Nevertheless, Kant, too, believed in the soul's immortality. See

thirteen articles of faith and a cardinal principle of traditional rabbinic theology, the immortality of the soul was, for Lefin, an unassailable fact. His essays on the immortality of the soul are descriptions of the world-to-come reported by a righteous man who has experienced the liberation of death. They can be seen as maskilic manifestos of an imagined paradise, and owe an implicit debt to Maimonides's vision (in the *Guide*) of the beatific joy experienced by the disembodied soul capable of attaining intellectual perfection in the higher world, as well as to Mendelssohn's *Phaedon*, and to the eighteenth-century literary convention of the heavenly dialogue.[179]

Lefin began *Ma'amar olam hagemul* with an outline of his faculty psychology. He underscored the essential difference between the sensual and pictorial faculties of the soul, which were bound to a human being's corporeal condition, and its rational faculty, which was independent of, but imprisoned by, the body. Like Mendelssohn, and Maimonides before him — who based his dichotomy between the body and the soul on his Greek predecessors — Lefin believed that death meant only the physical demise of an individual. In the Maimonidean afterlife, the soul, freed from the chains of the body, would be free to achieve intellectual perfection and to apprehend God.[180] Mendelssohn had argued, through an "enlightened" Socrates who welcomed death, that philosophers desired a complete break with their sensual passions in order to apprehend God without the fetters of the "terrestrial contagion" called the body: "Death is never terrible to a true philo-

---

Immanuel Kant, *Critique of Pure Reason* (trans. Norman Kemp Smith; New York: St. Martin's, 1929), 373–74. See, too, François Fénelon's modern dialogue between Ulysses and Gryllus (who had been changed into a pig by the sorcerer Circe), in which Gryllus rejects the idea that there is anything in the body that is not subject to corruption. François de Salignac de La Mothe Fénelon, *Dialogues of the Dead* (Glasgow: Robert and Andrew Foulis, 1754), 1:29–30. Lefin mentioned Fénelon's descriptions of the world-to-come in *The Fate of the Departed Souls*. See the Joseph Perl Archive, JNULA, 4° 1153/68, 2b.

[179] Dialogues in the afterlife were a common literary genre during the Enlightenment. See the discussion in Chapter Four.

[180] See Moses Maimonides, *Mishneh torah*, The Book of Knowledge, Laws of Repentence, 8:2, 8:4, 8:6; *Guide* 1:31, 2:15; *Commentary on the Mishnah*, Tractate Sanhedrin, 10:1. Maimonides's emphasis on the world-to-come in contrast to bodily resurrection in his writings led to accusations against him, which he defended in his "The Essay on Resurrection" (*Ma'amar tehiyat hametim*). See Moses Maimonides, *Crisis and Leadership: The Epistles of Maimonides* (ed. David Hartman and trans. Hillel Halkin; Philadelphia: The Jewish Publication Society of America, 1985), 211–45. Lefin wrote an essay on the *Mishneh torah* that he hoped to edit even in 1826, the last year of his life, but which is no longer extant, and mentioned Maimonides's "Essay on Resurrection" in his introductory remarks to his translation of the *Guide*. See the Joseph Perl Archive, JNULA, 4° 1153/67 and Maimonides, *Sefer moreh nevukhim*. See, too, Harry Blumberg, "The Problem of Immortality in Avicenna, Maimonides and St. Thomas Aquinas," in *Wolfson Jubilee Volume*, vol. 1 (ed. Saul Lieberman; Jerusalem: American Academy for Jewish Research, 1965), 165–85.

sopher, but always welcome."[181] In death, Lefin concurred, the intellect, untrammeled by the sensual perceptions and imaginative associations, would alone guide the association of ideas in the human understanding.[182] Lefin described how the rational faculty of the soul, once "released from the bodily prison" and unburdened by worries about how to protect and provide for the body, which he termed "the mortal *Camera Obscura* (dark chamber),"[183] would be free to contemplate the individual's past and to apprehend God.[184]

Despite Lefin's fidelity to traditional rabbinic theology, his conception of paradise had a distinctly universalist cast, a hallmark of the Enlightenment's optimism.[185] Lefin's maskilic Heaven knew no parochial boundaries of nationality or temporality; one who had merited the world-to-come could enjoy the company of "all of the sages and righteous men from all the nations and all the generations," individuals whom one only knew formerly through their writings. Paradise would reverse the Tower of Babel and return human society to a pristine stage of language in which all men could understand one another; no dialects would obscure universal comprehension. In mutual admiration, the sages from all the nations would discuss their pasts and all of the obstacles that they had faced in the mundane world. They would laugh among themselves about the fictive misconceptions they had held about the afterlife when they were alive. The discussions among the disembodied intellects could go on endlessly and effortlessly, augmented by newly deceased souls joining the paradisiacal convocation.[186]

Among the topics that would be discussed by the circle of bodiless souls was the variety of religious conceptions of service to God. In this section Lefin betrayed, once again, his preoccupation with Hasidism. Writing in the voice of a disembodied soul in paradise, Lefin's protagonist recalled beseeching those who had tried to trap him in the temporal world into forsaking classical rabbinic worship for fealty to "human idols" surrounded by

---

181   Moses Mendelssohn, *Phädon, or the Death of Socrates* (London: J. Cooper, 1789), 42.

182   The Joseph Perl Archive, JNULA, 4° 1153/127d, 4b–5a. See, too, 4° 1153/71a, 2a and 4° 1153/130, 69.

183   Note Lefin's use of the Lockian phrase, "dark chamber," itself a reference to a recent scientific invention. The *camera obscura*, a four-sided black box with a convex lens and one internal white surface, was an eighteenth-century ancestor of the contemporary camera capable of representing images that, in Euler's words, "were more accurate descriptions than [those] a pencil [was] capable of producing." See Euler, *Letters of Euler*, 317–18. In *Mishlei assaf*, 2:5–16, Isaac Satanów also used the camera to illustrate his epistemology. See Bor, "Moral Education in the Age of the Jewish Enlightenment."

184   The Joseph Perl Archive, JNULA, 4° 1153/68, 2a. See, too, 4° 1153/127d, 6b–7a.

185   See Lefin's introduction to his Yiddish translation of Psalms, published in Simha Katz, "Menachem Mendel Lefin of Satanów's Bible Translations," *Kiryat sefer* 16 (1939): 129.

186   The Joseph Perl Archive, JNULA, 4° 1153/127d, 7a–8a and 4° 1153/68, 2b.

"jewels, foods, liquors, and splendid homes." While many of his contemporaries were tricked into believing that the world-to-come could only be attained by following the teachings of these men, who posed as "gods, or at least as God's prophets," Lefin's imaginary righteous soul resisted, rejecting their glories, prophecies, and secrets (sodot)."[187] The essay affirmed the perception of the maskilim that only a small elite could withstand the persecution of their Hasidic foes. Resolute adherence to the right, meaning rabbinic, manner to worship God came with a price of social isolation.[188] Lefin ended Ma'amar olam hagemul with his protagonist lamenting the fact that he could not share his knowledge about the world-to-come with friends who were still imprisoned in their bodies on the earth. Were he to try, his mortal friends would probably feel that their dreams, stimulated by the imaginative faculty, were mocking them. The essay thus affirmed Lefin's epistemology. Only death and the merit of the world-to-come would open the door to metaphysical knowledge.[189]

Lefin's interest in the study of nature, in contemporary theories of psychology, particularly sensationalism, and in the debates over the nature of the soul illustrate how he drew from the world of non-Jewish eighteenth-century thought to shape his vision of the Jewish Enlightenment in Eastern Europe. In light of the conservative political and religious environment in which he lived, Lefin was always careful to justify his appropriation of non-Jewish materials by appealing to authoritative Jewish hermeneutic methods and genres. He frequently cited the classical sayings of the Rabbinic Sages, "'Who is wise?' 'The one who learns from every man'[190] . . . 'whether from a non-Jew or from Israel or from a slave or from a handmaid, the Holy Spirit rests upon him according to his deeds,'"[191] as justification for his cultural

---

[187] The Joseph Perl Archive, JNULA, 4° 1153/127d, 8a.

[188] If Lefin projected those feelings onto his image of paradise, he did so because of his own sense of isolation in Podolia and later in Austrian Galicia. The introduction to the second edition of Nachlaß ended with a statement that the author had "finally moved beyond the borders of Abdera," and no longer had to be considered a crank for doing scholarly work. Published in Weinlös, "Mendel Lefin of Satanów: A Biographical Study," 348. The name "Abdera" had at least two meanings. It functioned in Greek folklore much the way Chełm did in Polish-Jewish folklore, as a synonym for a city inhabited by simpletons. Joseph Klausner and Jacob Birnbaum also argued that it represented Brody, the "enlightened" city in which Lefin finally finished editing his philosophic work, because Abdera and Brody are spelled with the same letters of the Hebrew alphabet. Klausner, Historyah shel hasifrut, 1:201 and Jacob Birnbaum, "Lefin (Levin), Menachem Mendel," in Leksikon fun der nayer yidisher literatur, (eds. Samuel Niger and Jacob Shatzky; vol. 5, eds. Ephraim Euerbach, Isaac Charlash, and Moses Starkman; New York: Marstin Press, 1963), 351. Brody as Abdera can be found in [Joseph Perl], Bohen tsaddiq (Prague, 1838), 57.

[189] The Joseph Perl Archive, JNULA, 4° 1153/127d, 8b–9a.

[190] m. Avot 4:1.

[191] Seder Eliyahu Rabbah, 10:1.

borrowing.[192] Incorporating classical Jewish dicta not only gave Lefin's work a traditional imprimatur, but also expressed his ardent belief that there was nothing incompatible between a rationalized, renewed Judaism and the universal values common to all men. This effort at justification betrays the self-consciousness of Lefin's efforts to transform Polish Jewry and his embrace of an ideology of modernity. Fundamental to this new consciousness was his sincere conviction that a revitalized Polish-Jewish rabbinic culture could be open to the universal values inherent in the experiences and knowledge of enlightened Gentiles.

Lefin believed that only one obstacle stood in the way of his desire to balance his commitment to the traditional rabbinic culture of Ashkenazic Jewry with openness to the intellectual creativity of eighteenth-century Europe: the seemingly intractable hold that Hasidism had on the youth of Polish Jewry. All of Lefin's efforts at the appropriation, adaptation, and dissemination of West European ideas were weapons in his lifelong struggle against Hasidism, whose forms of leadership, prayer, communal organization, and relationship to the non-Jewish world thwarted his attempts, and that of other moderate *maskilim* in Eastern Europe, to fashion an enlightened Jewish future. Lefin's tolerant attitude toward non-Jewish learning and non-Jews as a preeminent value of modern Jewish life contrasted sharply with what he believed to be Hasidic intolerance expressed by the Zoharic demonization of the Gentile soul popularized in Shneur Zalman of Lady's *Tanya*.[193] Intolerance of Gentiles was an extension of Hasidism's hierarchy of spiritual prowess among Jews that assumed the unique powers of the zaddik, giving him an exclusive relationship to the Divine.

Despite Lefin's avid interest in the intellectual ferment of his contemporary world, his reluctance to internalize the challenge of transcendental philosophy's autonomous system of ethics illustrates the limits of his conception of the Enlightenment. His claims of being a follower of Kant notwithstanding, Lefin conflated the most conservative reading of Maimonides's epistemology with Kant's, ignoring the latter's revolutionary implications for the obligatory and heteronomous character of traditional Jewish law. When

---

[192] See the Joseph Perl Archive, 4° 1153/124, the unpublished introduction to Lefin's *Masa'ot hayam* (*Journeys by Sea*, Żółkiew, 1818), 130, 55, and 134a, for these prooftexts.
[193] The Hasidic master's psychology expanded upon the Zohar's demonization of Gentiles. In the *Tanya*, Shneur Zalman equated Gentiles with the *sitra ahra*, the demonic, evil force in life: "Therefore, also the evil impulse and the force that strains after forbidden things is a demon of non-Jewish demons, which is the evil impulse of the [Gentile] nations whose souls are derived from the three unclean *qelippot* [thought, speech, and action]." See Shneur Zalman of Lady (Liady), *Liqqutei amarim [Tanya]*, 31–32 and Dubnow, *Toldot hahasidut*, 2:236. Lefin's recoiling at Hasidism's denigration of non-Jews found fulsome expression in Perl's *Über das Wesen der Sekte Chassidim* (*Regarding the Essence of the Hasidic Sect*). See [Perl], *Über das Wesen der Sekte Chassidim*, 46–48.

challenged by non-Jewish views that threatened the rabbinic worldview that he wanted to maintain, Lefin held steadfast to the bifurcation of knowledge into two realms, metaphysics and physics, which he believed was consonant with the medieval Jewish rationalist tradition that he was eager to transmit to his East European Jewish audience. In his translation of *The Guide of the Perplexed*, Lefin further elaborated on the opposition between metaphysical knowledge, which he called *hokhmah* (wisdom), and scientific and mathematical knowledge, which he called *da'at* (knowledge), a distinction that provided him with a means of harmonizing a traditional Jewish conception of the continuous decline in understanding ever since the moment of Revelation with contemporary, eighteenth-century beliefs in the intellectual progress of humanity over time. There could be cumulative human progress in matters of reason, argued Lefin, but not in matters of metaphysics, where there had been no qualitative advance since the period of the patriarchs.[194] As "wisdom" became more and more distant from Revelation, "knowledge," increased over time, a gloss he justified by the prooftext, "For the earth shall be full of knowledge (*de'ah*) of the Lord, as the waters cover the sea" (Isa 11:9).[195] The cumulative knowledge of the natural world, including the autonomous realm of the human soul, constituted Lefin's definition of Enlightenment (*Aufklärung*),[196] which ultimately served a Jew's higher purpose: to recognize, love, and fear God within the limits of human epistemology, and to delight God's creatures with the discoveries of that knowledge.

Lefin's artful construction of *Sefer heshbon hanefesh* as an enlightened *musar* text with a camouflaged anti-Hasidic message illustrates the didactic objectives of the moderate Haskalah, whose proponents, like all the activists within the European Enlightenments, strove to influence a broad audience. Wresting education from traditional authorities, whether it be the Jesuit order or Hasidic-influenced *hadarim* (Jewish elementary schools), creating new literary media such as the moral weekly to disseminate enlightened ideas, and popularizing contemporary psychology and scientific theories shaped the educational goals of all of Europe's enlightened activists. Lefin likewise endeavored to disseminate his cultural program of the moderate Haskalah as widely as possible, an effort that resulted from the elite perspective he shared with other *maskilim* that the East European Jewish masses, due to their own ignorance and failings, were desperately in need of enlightened leadership

---

194 Lefin, "*Elon moreh*," 13 and Levine, "Menachem Mendel Lefin," 68–69, and 75.

195 The Joseph Perl Archive, JNULA, 4° 1153/23, "Key to the Pamphlet, *Elon moreh*," chapter 3. See, too, Hillel Levine, "'Dwarfs on the Shoulders of Giants': A Case Study in the Impact of Modernization and the Social Epistemology of Judaism," *JSS* 40, no. 1 (Winter 1978): 63–72.

196 "*Die Summe menschlicher Entdeckungen macht die Aufklärung aus und die jenige der Produkte ihrer physischen Kräfte ihrer Staats macht.*" The Joseph Perl Archive, JNULA, 4° 1153/133.

to save them from the clutches of Hasidism. Recognizing that the message of the Haskalah would be lost on the Jewish masses of Poland without the creation of an accessible literature, Lefin turned to Yiddish, the vernacular of Ashkenazic Jewry, a strategy that underscores the Polish-Jewish context of his program of the moderate Haskalah. Lefin's linguistic innovation and instrumentalism, exemplified by his translation of Scripture into Yiddish, is the subject of the next chapter.

CHAPTER FOUR

THE LINGUISTIC BOUNDARIES OF ENLIGHTENMENT: REVISITING THE LANGUAGE POLEMIC IN EASTERN EUROPE

> The [Yiddish] language is a mix of rabbinism, Aramaic, and Chaldaic, mixed with Arabic and Greek words, elaborate idioms that cannot be forced into any grammatical rules.[1]
>
> David Friedländer, *Über die Verbesserung der Israeliten im Königreich Pohlen* (1816)

The previous three chapters have stressed the "Polishness," the culture, society, and politics of pre-partitioned Poland, as well as the rich religious tradition of medieval and early modern Polish Judaism, that shaped Mendel Lefin's encounter with modernity and his formulation of the Jewish Enlightenment. We have seen that the Sabbatian and Frankist legacy in Podolia and the distinctive relationship between the Jewish community and the Polish magnate class in the southeastern Polish borderlands informed Lefin's conception of the Haskalah as religiously and politically moderate. Lefin's selective appropriation of contemporaneous European theories of psychology and natural philosophy, in turn, informed his design of a behaviorist program of moral self-reform to combat the appeal of Hasidism, a native-born Podolian religious movement within Judaism. In turning to another aspect of Lefin's Enlightenment activism, his use of Yiddish, we find too that his Podolian origins and resettlement in the southeastern Polish borderlands after his sojourn in Berlin defined the linguistic parameters of his conception of the Haskalah.

Because it has become a historiographic truism to identify the rise of a vernacular literature as an essential feature of modern political nationalism, Lefin's turn to writing and translating in Yiddish, the vernacular of East European Jews, already at the end of the 1780s, raises the question of the relationship of the Haskalah to the origins of Jewish nationalism, whether in

---

[1] David Friedländer, *Über die Verbesserung der Israeliten im Königreich Pohlen. Ein von der Regierung daselbst im Jahr 1816 abgefordertes Gutachten* (Berlin: Nicolaische Buchhandlung, 1819), 22.

its Diaspora-nationalist or Zionist-territorialist form, to the fore.[2] Even before the emergence of mass political movements within East European Jewry, *maskilim* interpreted Lefin's use of Yiddish as an expression of his putative populist sentiment, which they often termed "democratic" and juxtaposed negatively to their image of the linguistic and social elitism of his Prussian brethren. Abraham Baer Gottlober, Lefin's biographer, and Mordecai Suchostober, a disciple who edited Lefin's translation of the *Guide of the Perplexed* into mishnaic Hebrew from Ibn Tibbon's medieval Hebrew translation, depicted Lefin as particularly attuned to the needs of the Jewish masses of Eastern Europe.[3] Both Gottlober and Suchostober correctly point to Lefin's innovations in language as one of the signs of his originality. But, the hagiographic quality of the words of *maskilim* later in the nineteenth century should not be read uncritically, as did Yiddishist ideologues, individuals dedicated to a form of modern Jewish nationalism that valorized the Yiddish language as an expression of the modern Diaspora-centered nationhood of the Jews, in the early twentieth century.[4] Max Erik, N. M. Gelber, Israel Weinlös, and others concluded that Lefin's reaction against *melitsah*, the Hebrew style comprised of conjoined biblical phrases and neologisms formed from biblical roots, and a hallmark of the early Berlin

---

[2]   On the varieties of political movements that defined themselves in modern Jewish nationalist terms, see Ezra Mendelsohn, *On Modern Jewish Politics* (Oxford: Oxford University Press, 1993). Regarding vernacularity as the sine qua non of modern nationalism, see Benedict Anderson, who concluded, "The new middle-class intelligentsia of nationalism had to invite the masses into history; and the invitation-card had to be written in a language they understood." Benedict Anderson, *Imagined Communities: Reflections on the Origin and Spread of Nationalism* (New York: Verso, 1983): 80. On the implicit "nationalism" of the *maskilim* who wrote in Hebrew, in contrast to the "anti-nationalists" who wrote in German, see Isaac E. Barzilay, "National and Anti-National Trends in the Berlin Haskalah," *JSS* 21, no. 3 (July 1959): 165–92. Adrian Hastings, an outspoken critic of Anderson and others who root nationalism in the eighteenth century and to the rise of the modern nation-state, nonetheless also sees the rise of a vernacular literature as "the most important and widely present factor" in the "development of nationhood from one or more ethnicities." See Adrian Hastings, *The Construction of Nationhood: Ethnicity, Religion, and Nationalism* (Cambridge: Cambridge University Press, 1997), 2–3.

[3]   Abraham Baer Gottlober, *Hamaggid* 17 (1873): 356 and Suchostober's comments in Moses Maimonides, *Sefer moreh nevukhim* (trans. Mendel Lefin; Żółkiew, 1829).

[4]   The 1908 International Conference on the Yiddish Language held in Czernowitz gave full expression to the marriage of modern Jewish nationalism and Yiddishism when delegates declared Yiddish to be *a* national language of the Jewish people. This declaration represented a compromise with the Hebraists in attendance who opposed recognition of the vernacular as *the* national language of the Jewish people. Many also rejected any parity between Yiddish, the language of the Diaspora, and Hebrew, which they viewed as the eternal national language of the Jews. Chaim Zhitlowsky (1865–1943), a Yiddish philosopher and writer, is considered the architect of Diaspora nationalist Yiddishism. On Zhitlowsky, see David H. Weinberg, *Between Tradition and Modernity: Haim Zhitlowski, Simon Dubnow, Ahad Ha-Am, and the Shaping of Modern Jewish Identity* (New York: Holmes & Meier, 1996).

Haskalah, was "created by explicit democratic justifications," when, in fact, there was no democracy, in either political or social terms, in late eighteenth-century East European Jewish society.[5] Although Lefin wrote in a popular style, we should not confuse the medium of his Haskalah with its message, and retrospectively project onto Lefin a Romantically-inspired "national" vision. Lefin's turn to Yiddish, mishnaic Hebrew, and popular literature all resulted from the didactic agenda he shared with all enlightened *intelligenti* that the masses, whether Jewish or not, needed enlightened leadership.[6] Lefin's innovation was his recognition, long before the rise of political and cultural Yiddishism, that without the creation of an accessible and comprehensible literature, the message of the Haskalah would be lost on the Jewish masses of Poland. His use of Yiddish was, thus, a utilitarian step to reach as wide an audience as possible among East European Jews.[7] By employing the vernacular of Polish Jews, Lefin boldly asserted the need for *maskilim* to recognize the East European setting of the future of the Haskalah. Lefin's Prussian compatriots, writing in the context of a modernizing German nation-state that sought to impose linguistic homogeneity on its new subjects through its bureaucracy and new educational system, and who themselves eagerly sought to be integrated into the

---

[5] Raphael Mahler, *A History of Modern Jewry, 1780–1815* (New York: Schocken Books, 1971), 79. See, too, Israel Weinlös's depiction of Lefin in Israel Weinlös, "Mendel Lefin of Satanów: A Biographical Study from Manuscript Material," *YIVO bleter* 1 (1931): 334–57, particularly 344: "As we mentioned earlier, Lefin was by nature a democrat and conceived of benefiting the broad masses [through his turn to Yiddish]." His translations were "important national work." See, too, Israel Weinlös, "R. Menachem Mendel of Satanów," *Ha'olam* 13 (1925): 819; N. M. Gelber, *Arim ve'imahot beyisra'el: Brody* (Jerusalem, 1955), 179 and 224. Despite Max Erik's venomous opinions about Weinlös's Zionism, he, too, regards Lefin's Hebrew style as democratic. See Max Erik, *Etiudn tsu der geshikhte fun der haskole* (Minsk, 1934), 147. Raphael Mahler vacillates in his assessment of Lefin's (as well as Perl's and Isaac Baer Levinsohn's) decision to write in Yiddish. He concludes that the decision was both utilitarian, "a necessary evil without which the broad masses could not be approached with the slogans of enlightenment," and ideological, a reflection of the warm opinions of the common people and their language held by the *maskilim*. See Raphael Mahler, *Hasidism and the Jewish Enlightenment: Their Confrontation in Galicia and Poland in the First Half of the Nineteenth Century* (Philadelphia: The Jewish Publication Society of America, 1985), 39 and Raphael Mahler, *Divrei yemei yisra'el* (Rehavia: Worker's Library, 1956), 1:79, 82.

[6] Lefin made no secret of his belief that East European Jewry required the leadership of *maskilim* like himself. See, for example, his famous rebuke of Nachman Krochmal's alleged philosophic retreat from the responsibility of engaging and enlightening the Jewish masses. The letter to Krochmal (1785–1840) was first published in Meir Letteris, ed., *Mikhtavim* (Lemberg, 1827), 33–35. See, too, Avraham Rubinstein, "Mendel Lefin's 'Prayer of Thanksgiving'," *Kiryat sefer* 42 (1966/67): 403–04, based on the Joseph Perl Archive, JNULA, 4° 1153/127, for the first part of the letter that Letteris did not include, although Rubinstein's transcription erred in a few places.

[7] See Dan Miron, *A Traveler Disguised: The Rise of Modern Yiddish Fiction in the Nineteenth Century* (New York: Schocken Books, 1973), 40–41.

social and political life of the nation-state in formation, consequently abandoned using a distinctly Jewish language by the end of the eighteenth century.[8] Polish and Russian *maskilim*, in contrast, employed Hebrew and Yiddish, as well as Gentile languages (French, Polish, German, and Russian) in their works from the late eighteenth and well into the nineteenth century, a polylingualism that reflected the multinational, multiconfessional, and multilingual Imperial contexts in which they lived. Lefin's linguistic move therefore acknowledged the linguistic regionalism and traditionalism of the environment from which he hoped to draw his audience. Although writing from post-partition Austrian Galicia, where the Habsburgs — the ruling power since 1772 — also aspired to linguistic uniformity for official, bureaucratic documents and institutions, Lefin nonetheless rejected both the new state's demand and the maskilic formula that modernity and enlightenment, respectively, required subordination of all dialects to German's hegemony.[9]

The decision to write in German and to envision it as the future language of the Jews was taken for granted by most eighteenth-century *maskilim*, just as the disparagement of Yiddish became a constitutive element in their program for the transformation of Jewish identity. Although select German-Jewish *maskilim* wrote in Yiddish in the late eighteenth and early nineteenth centuries,[10] Mendel Lefin's decision to translate the Bible into Yiddish

---

[8] See Eric A. Blackall, *The Emergence of German as a Literary Language, 1700–1775* (Cambridge: Cambridge University Press, 1959) for the Prussian context and Robert A. Kann, *A History of the Habsburg Empire, 1526–1918* (Berkeley: University of California Press, 1974), 183–91, 203, for the Habsburg Empire. On the Jacobin campaign to standardize the use of French, see Andrzej Walicki, *The Enlightenment and the Birth of Modern Nationhood: Polish Political Thought from Noble Republicanism to Tadeusz Kosciuszko* (Notre Dame, Ind.: University of Notre Dame Press, 1989), 73. In Poland, patriots like Hugo Kołłątaj exhorted reformers to standardize Polish as a means to unify the crumbling Commonwealth, for "only that country can truly be called a nation that understands one language and whose language suffices for education, law, and government." Cited in Walicki, *The Enlightenment and the Birth of Modern Nationhood*, 73. On the efforts of Prussian Jews to integrate into the modern nation-state in formation, see David Sorkin, *The Transformation of German Jewry, 1780–1840* (New York: Oxford University Press, 1987).

[9] The Habsburgs promulgated a language ordinance in 1784 that made German the official state language. Nonetheless, the linguistic and ethnic heterogeneity of Habsburg lands meant linguistic polyglotism in many parts of the Empire well into the twentieth century. On the language edict and the political, social meaning of absolutism, see Chapter Five.

[10] Two maskilic plays with large Yiddish components were published before the turn of the eighteenth century, Isaac Euchel's *R. Henekh oder vos tut me damit* (1793) and Aaron Wolfsohn-Halle's *Leichtsinn und Frömmelei* (1796). In both cases the Yiddish was used as a means to portray the East Europeanness of specific characters in the play, not as the language of the production as a whole. The first entirely Yiddish play, the anonymous *Di genarte velt* (*The Duped World*), appeared in the second decade of the nineteenth century. See Meir Wiener, *Tsu der geshikhte fun der yidisher literatur in nayntsnt yorhundert* (Kiev, 1940), 38.

Even when *maskilim* wrote in Yiddish, they rarely attempted to publish their works or

resulted in the first major polemic over the language question among East European *maskilim*, an issue that continued to resonate among enlightened Jews throughout the nineteenth century.[11] The furor ignited by Lefin's use of Yiddish illustrates that the language question represented larger issues in the articulation of what East European *maskilim* meant by becoming modern. To what extent should European Jews acculturate into their host countries and what relationship should language have to the process of acculturation? What were the linguistic parameters of the responsibility the *maskilim* had toward making the message of the Haskalah accessible? How strong or tenuous was the Haskalah movement, and could it withstand a plurality of means to enlighten the broad Jewish public? Last, what role did Yiddish play in the formation of both modern German and modern East European Jewish identity? These questions, and others, shaped the language polemic, giving voice to the ways in which Lefin and other East European *maskilim* sought to make Polish Jews modern.

Jeffrey Grossman has argued persuasively that Yiddish became a synedoche of the "Otherness" of Jewish culture that German Jews sought to detach themselves from in the period of the Enlightenment.[12] Yet Grossman's focus on the debate over Yiddish in Germany misses the relationship East European Jews had to German culture and the role they played in the construction of the discourse about Yiddish. In the period of the Enlightenment, the German language represented the values of *Bildung*, such as inward moral cultivation and self-improvement, so central to the Haskalah. For most East European *maskilim* in the early nineteenth century, the disavowal of Yiddish became a litmus test of their distance from the insular, "baroque" culture of early modern Polish Jewry, the very Jews they hoped to transform. The polemic thus illuminates the ways in which modernizing

---

only did so anonymously. Traditionalist suspicion of the cultural orientation of the *maskilim*, coupled with self-censorship, resulted in a paucity of published works in Yiddish before the mid-nineteenth century. Under Tsar Nicholas I in Russia, for example, only two Jewish printers, one in Vilna, the other in Żytomierz, were allowed to operate (a restriction originally and ironically initiated by *maskilim*) and both were dominated by Hasidim. Moreover, the Hasidim did not hesitate to destroy maskilic works that they believed were anti-Hasidic (many of them were); it is no accident that in many cases only one copy, often in disrepair, of a particular Yiddish maskilic text is extant. Miron, *A Traveler Disguised*, 15, 35, 43–44 and Chone Shmeruk, *Sifrut yidish: peraqim letoldoteihah* (Tel Aviv: The Porter Institute for Poetics & Semiotics, 1978), 238–39, 242.

[11] See Ahad Ha'am's essay, "*Riv haleshonot*," in Asher Zevi Ginsburg, *Al parashat haderakhim: qovets ma'amarim* (Berlin: Yidisher Ferlag, 1930); Benjamin Harshav, *Language in the Time of Revolution* (Berkeley: University of California Press, 1993); David Patterson, *A Phoenix in Fetters: Studies in Nineteenth and Early Twentieth Century Hebrew Fiction* (Savage, Md.: Rowman & Littlefield, 1988).

[12] Jeffrey A. Grossman, *The Discourse on Yiddish in Germany: From the Enlightenment to the Second Empire* (Rochester, N.Y.: Camden House, 2000).

Prussian Jews — and East European Jews who modelled their Haskalah on the Berlin exemplar — created an "Other" in the Polish Jews from whose culture and language they recoiled.[13] It also underscores the individuality of Lefin's vision of the Haskalah, which he conceived of as a modernizing ideology for Polish Jews that was inspired by, but not subservient to, the model articulated in Berlin.

Wisdom and the Turn to Yiddish

Moses Mendelssohn began his monumental project to translate all of Hebrew scripture into German with the book of Ecclesiastes, a natural starting point for *maskilim* interested in issues of the individual, the soul, and divine reward and punishment, cardinal tenets of the natural religion he believed to be harmonious with traditional Judaism.[14] Mendelssohn accepted the rabbinic attribution of the book to King Solomon, whom he revered as a master teacher of universal truths in a popular, easily readable style. Following Judah ha-Levi's assessment of Solomon as the source of all sciences that were later transmitted to the Gentile world of antiquity, Mendelssohn imagined Solomon as the model *maskil*, a master of practical knowledge and natural religion with a biblical and rabbinic pedigree.[15]

Lefin followed directly in Mendelssohn's footsteps when he began his Yiddish translation of Scripture, first translating Ecclesiastes, which he accompanied with a short Hebrew commentary, sometime before 1788.[16]

---

[13]   The classic work on the German-Jewish construction of an East European mirrored "Other" is Steven E. Aschheim, *Brothers and Strangers: The East European Jew in German and German Jewish Consciousness, 1800–1923* (Madison: University of Wisconsin Press, 1982). See, too, Steven E. Aschheim, *Brothers and Strangers* Reconsidered (Rome: Archivio Guideo Izzi, 1998) and Ismar Schorsch, "The Myth of Sephardic Supremacy," in *From Text to Context: The Turn to History in Modern Judaism* (Hanover, N.H.: University Press of New England, 1994), 71–92.

[14]   Moses Mendelssohn, *Sefer megillat qohelet im bi'ur qatsar umaspik lehavanat haketuv al-pi peshuto leto'elet hatalmidim* (Berlin, 1770). Mendelssohn wrote the translation and commentary as early as 1768. See David Sorkin, *Moses Mendelssohn and the Religious Enlightenment* (Berkeley: University of California Press, 1996), 36–45. On Ecclesiastes, see Robert Gordis, *Koheleth — The Man and His World* (New York: Schocken Books, 1968).

   Mendelssohn's German translation of the Pentateuch, *Netivot hashalom (vehaḥibur kolel ḥamishat ḥumshei hatorah im tiqqunei soferim vetargum ashkenazi uvi'ur*, Berlin, 1780), is colloquially known by the name of its Hebrew commentary, the *Bi'ur*. On the *Bi'ur*, see Edward Breuer, *The Limits of Enlightenment: Jews, Germans and the Study of Scripture in the Eighteenth-Century* (Cambridge, Mass.: Harvard University Press, 1996).

[15]   Sorkin, *Moses Mendelssohn*, 43.

[16]   Lefin's Yiddish translation of Ecclesiastes first appeared in Odessa in 1873, published by Zevi Cohen Reich (the nephew of Meir ha-Cohen Reich, Lefin's close friend from Bar) and Yehuda Kari, although Alexander Sender (Zevi) Margoliot, head of the rabbinical court in Satanów, reported, in his approbation for Lefin's *Sefer refu'at ha'am*, that he had seen Lefin's

Abraham Baer Gottlober recalled in his memoirs that Lefin, inspired by Mendelssohn's work, had already decided to translate the entire Hebrew Bible into Yiddish while in Berlin in the early 1780s. Aware of the ineffectiveness of using German as a vehicle for communicating Haskalah ideology to Polish Jewry, "He [Lefin]," in Gottlober's words, "decided . . . to speak to them in their language [Yiddish], for all non-Jewish languages and books were inaccessible to them. He girded up his loins to translate the books into the people's language [Yiddish]."[17] Like Mendelssohn and Judah Leib Ben Ze'ev (1764–1811) before him, Lefin believed King Solomon to be the author of Ecclesiastes, whose pithy insights into the human condition affirmed the universal values of the Enlightenment in a Jewish key.[18] While the radical skepticism and indifference to God and the commandments (Eccl 11:9b and 12:12–14 are considered later additions by biblical scholars) had proved troublesome to the Rabbis in their own historical period, Lefin assumed a reading of Ecclesiastes that affirmed what had become the normative rabbinic understanding of God's Providence in early modern Ashkenaz.[19] When the ancient writer observed that both the righteous and the wicked are doomed (Eccl 3:17), Lefin's Hebrew commentary assured his readers that there was a world-to-come where God's justice would be effected.[20] To Ecclesiastes' view that there is no ontological distinction between the condition and fate of humanity and that of the animal kingdom, Lefin responded by echoing the liturgy to assert his belief in the essential difference between the human and animal worlds, "*We are obligated to praise*

"pleasant and accessible commentary on Ecclesiastes with its translation into our language [Yiddish]," already in 1788. See Mendel Lefin, *Sefer qohelet im targum yehudit uvi'ur* (Odessa, 1873); Mendel Lefin, trans., *Sefer refu'at ha'am* (Żółkiew, 1794) and Simha Katz, "Menachem Mendel Lefin of Satanów's Bible Translations," *Kiryat sefer* 16 (1939): 116.

[17]   Abraham Baer Gottlober, "Russia," *Hamaggid* 17 (1873): 363.

[18]   Lefin's debt to Mendelssohn can also be felt in his effort at writing a theory of translation, much like Mendelssohn had done in the introduction, *Or linetivah* (*Light for the Path*), to *Netivot hashalom*. Lefin's essay on translation was never published and is no longer extant. Fragments of it are contained in the introduction to his translation of the *Guide*: "We know that one must always select words that are known to the listeners and to limit as much as possible the use of words that are strange, and to use them only if they convey a particular syntactical distinctiveness, particularly of an unfamiliar word, because every unfamiliar word burdens the speaker and weighs heavily upon the listener. If [the use of the unfamiliar word] does not have a specific goal, it will result in incomprehension." See Lefin's introduction to Maimonides, *Sefer moreh nevukhim*, 2.

[19]   On the biblical text, see H. L. Ginsburg, ed., *The Five Megillot and Jonah* (Philadelphia: The Jewish Publication Society of America, 1969). Although *b. Bava Batra 16a* attributes Ecclesiastes to King Hezekiah (727–689 B.C.E.), the Rabbinic view is that the content of the book is King Solomon's (tenth century B.C.E.). See Jay Harris, *Nachman Krochmal: Guiding the Perplexed of the Modern Age* (New York: New York University Press, 1991), 172–92 for a discussion of the canonicity and periodization of Ecclesiates.

[20]   Lefin's decision to write his commentary in Hebrew will be discussed below.

him, may he be blessed, *for not placing our portion* with the animal world, which is not conscious of its mortality and therefore lives without law; therefore, you, human beings, *know and take to heart* that you are surely mortal and will be judged in the future, as is written above."[21]

Affirming rabbinic Judaism's and eighteenth-century natural religion's belief in the immortality of the soul, a conception unknown to the third century B.C.E. author of Ecclesiastes,[22] Lefin concluded:

> Thus, it is true that I [Ecclesiastes] also considered the opinions of the philosophic heretics who are pressed to resolve this difficulty [Eccl 3:18–21, "Humanity has no superiority over beast"] by denying the very existence of good and evil for they see no distinction [between human beings] and beasts. They believe that there is no ethical or moral law; rather "might is right" [in the law of nature].[23] The wolf preys on the lamb and the eagle preys on the dove. They accept only those things that we know with certainty, [such as] the common mortality of the human and animal worlds. They query, "Who says that a human soul rises afterwards [after death] to another world and stands on trial in a world completely different than theirs [the beasts]? Rather, humanity is included in the category of beasts, and beasts are in the category of plants, and all were [created] from dust and will return to dust, etc." I, too, [Ecclesiastes] almost wavered and doubted [the distinction between humans and animals] like them.[24]

Lefin's religious moderation led him to elide the radical implications of a *peshat* (contextual) reading of Ecclesiastes and instead to assume the accepted midrashic reading.[25] As part of his didactic agenda, shaped in the crucible of eighteenth-century Podolia, Lefin used his Hebrew commentary to Ecclesiastes to contrast the ancient author's unadorned commitment to wisdom with the benighted world of superstition, a thinly veiled allusion to Lefin's contemporary critique of Hasidism. Moreover, as he had articulated

---

[21] Lefin, *Sefer qohelet*, Hebrew comment on Eccl 9:11–12. Emphasis is mine to underscore the allusions to the Aleinu prayer, recited thrice daily.

[22] On the emergence of the idea of the immortality of the soul in the Second Temple Period, see Shaye Cohen, *From the Maccabees to the Mishnah* (Philadelphia: Westminster, 1987).

[23] Although unmentioned, Lefin appears familiar with Hobbesian political theory in which the impetus for civil society is the sovereign's power to protect human beings from the inherent beastliness and anarchy of the state of nature. Mendelssohn began *Jerusalem*, which Lefin undoubtedly knew well, with a critique of Hobbes's theory of the state. See Moses Mendelssohn, *Jerusalem, or, On Religious Power and Judaism* (Hanover, N.H.: Brandeis University Press, 1983), 33–37.

[24] Lefin, *Sefer qohelet*, Hebrew comment on Eccl 3:18–21.

[25] Nachman Krochmal would later reject this conservative posture in his towering *The Guide of the Perplexed of Our Time* (*Moreh nevukhei hazeman*), arguing, in contrast to Lefin and others, that the Rabbis knew of Ecclesiastes' late authorship, but concealed the knowledge as part of a didactic strategy appropriate to their time. In his time, however, argued Krochmal, it was imperative that the Rabbis' esoteric strategy be revealed. Only then could traditional Judaism withstand the assault of modernity with any kind of intellectual integrity. See Harris, *Nachman Krochmal*, 171.

in *Sefer ḥeshbon hanefesh* and his other philosophic works, God's bestowal of the rational faculty upon human beings was circumscribed, and speculation about the metaphysical world was inaccessible to human comprehension. To verses 11:1–6, Lefin concluded:

> Don't hasten to fortune-tellers [who divine] with numbers or with time or by the passage of the clouds or by the falling of trees, *because God did not bestow wisdom upon you to discern these things.* Is it not certain that there is nothing in them for your benefit? Woe unto the one who is meticulous over these vanities, for they will always turn out to be meaningless for him. . . . *Furthermore, don't demand [to know] that which is inconceivable to you.* Like the fetus in his mother's belly, so, too, is the seed within the earth. [God] did not bequeath to human beings the ability to understand [the creation of life].[26]

Berlin Rears Its Head

We know little of the contemporary response to Lefin's Yiddish translation of Ecclesiastes because it remained in manuscript. However, an uproar greeted the publication of his translation of Proverbs, *Sefer mishlei shelomo im perush qatsar veha'ataqah ḥadashah bilshon Ashkenaz leto'elet aḥeinu beit yisra'el be'artsot Polin* (*The Book of Solomon's Proverbs, with a Short Commentary and a New Translation in the Language of Ashkenaz [Yiddish] for the Use of Our Brothers in the Lands of Poland*), which appeared in Tarnopol in 1814.

Lefin's decision to translate Proverbs into Yiddish was motivated by the same ideological concerns as his earlier work on Ecclesiastes: to bring the universalist wisdom tradition, attributed to King Solomon, to the masses of East European Jewry who were ill-equipped to read the text's biblical Hebrew and incapable of understanding the felicitous German translations rendered by his Prussian compatriots. Isaac Euchel (1756–1804) clearly expressed the maskilic interest in the books of the Hagiographa in the introduction to his German translation of Proverbs (Berlin, 1790), "I have chosen to translate and interpret the Book of Proverbs because it is a book of morals appropriate for every human being . . . a book meant for the education of man as such. . . . Most of its proverbs deal with human relations and are not concerned with religion."[27] Moreover, like Mendelssohn's translation efforts and Naftali Herz Wessely's programmatic appeal in *Divrei shalom ve'emet* (*Words of Peace and Truth,* Berlin, 1782), Lefin's translation of Proverbs sought to assert the primacy of the Biblical canon in the Haskalah's project of revitalizing Jewish education. In the short introduction to Proverbs, Lefin justified his Yiddish translation in the context of the Haskalah's preoccupation with the loss of Hebrew literacy and the concomitant abandonment of the Bible among the Jews of Eastern Europe:

---

[26] Lefin, *Sefer qohelet,* Hebrew comment on Eccl 11:1–6. Empahses are mine.
[27] Barzilay, "National and Anti-National Trends," 180.

After the holy language was divided into seventy confusing languages, it remained as an unblemished inheritance to the descendants of Jacob until they were exiled from their land and scattered among the Gentiles. [Then] their language was corrupted by the languages of their enemies. We now have only twenty-four books that were transmitted to us [in the original Hebrew]. The morphology of the letters, the form of the words and their syllabification, as well as vernacular synonyms for the original text, were transmitted orally in the vernacular to all the communities of Israel in the Diaspora. Commentators and translators of the Hebrew Bible arose to serve the needs of the Jews no matter where they lived so the Torah would not be forgotten. But, recently, migrations and neglect [of the language] have increased, and we no longer understand [the Torah] properly from the old commentaries.[28]

In the introduction, Lefin expressed hope that his new Yiddish translation would supersede a contemporaneous Yiddish translation known as *Maggishei minhah* (*Presenters of an Offering*), then widespread among Polish Jewry.[29] Written by Jacob ben Isaac of Janów, the author of the *Tsena urena* (the popular Yiddish rendition of the Pentateuch composed in the sixteenth century), *Maggishei minhah* contained a translation of the books of the Prophets and the Hagiographa. The popular homiletic rendition of Proverbs in *Maggishei minhah* conflated the content of Rashi's midrashic commentary with the simple, or contextual, meaning of the biblical text, thus superimposing a specific Jewish message upon an explicitly universalist book. Aware that his effort to replace the ubiquitous *Maggishei minhah* might raise the possibility of the rejection of his translation by the East European public he hoped to reach, Lefin sought and received approbations — just as he had done with *Sefer heshbon hanefesh* and his Yiddish translation of Ecclesiastes — from respected Polish rabbinical figures to introduce the book and assured his readers that the small size of the book would make it "comfortable for everyone to carry in his pocket and *tefillin* pouch."[30] Because maskilic works associated with the Berlin circle were viewed with suspicion in Eastern Europe, Lefin hedged his bets and published his translation of Proverbs anonymously.[31]

---

[28]   [Mendel Lefin], *Sefer mishlei shelomo im perush qatsar veha'ataqah hadashah bilshon Ashkenaz leto'elet aheinu beit yisra'el be'artsot Polin* (Tarnopol, 1814), introduction.

[29]   Twenty-one editions of the work were published by 1821, four of which were extant in Eastern Europe in Lefin's time (Slavita, 1807; Lemberg, 1808; Slavita, 1815; Ostróg, 1821). See Chone Shmeruk, "On Several Principles in Mendel Lefin's Translation of Proverbs," in *Sifrut yidish beFolin: mehqarim ve'iyyunim historiyyim* (Jerusalem: Magnes Press, 1981), 168.

[30]   See the introduction to [Lefin], *Sefer mishlei shelomo*, and the approbations of Joshua Heschel, the head of the rabbinical court in Tarnopol, and of Mordecai ben Eleazer Sender Margoliot, the head of the rabbinical court in Satanów.

[31]   The work's anonymity was noticed only by Simha Katz. See Simha Katz, "Additions to the List of Publications in Tarnopol," *Kiryat sefer* 15 (1938): 515–16. On the circulation of Lefin's Yiddish manuscripts prior to 1814, see Yehudah Friedlander, "The Language Battle in Eastern Europe at the Beginning of the Nineteenth Century," *Min haqatedrah* (1981): 5–34.

Yet, despite the thematic consonance with the earlier German translations of the Hagiographa, Lefin's selection of Yiddish as the language of translation signalled a departure from the Mendelssohnian path, and it was his assertion of the need to modify the Prussian model that set off the debate about language among *maskilim* in the period of the Enlightenment. In the second decade of the nineteenth century, Tobias Gutmann Feder (1760–1817), a Polish-born itinerant *maskil* known for his mastery of Hebrew grammar and Bible launched a frontal attack against Lefin's use of Yiddish in his Hebrew satire, *Qol meḥatsetsim* (*The Archers' Voice*).[32] In the work, Feder condemned the turn to Yiddish as a language worthy of the Enlightenment as "madness" and concluded that Lefin had degraded himself to the level of beasts with the translation. *Qol meḥatsetsim* circulated in manuscript among *maskilim* in the second decade of the nineteenth century, but was first published only in 1853 in an expurgated version. The original and most complete version of *Qol meḥatsetsim* is replete with scatological and defamatory remarks, beginning with the title page:[33]

The Archers' Voice

Three Arrows To One Side of It
And a Circle of Truth to Those Who Know It:

An arrow of victory[34] for the father of the German translators, Moses ben Maimon, may the memory of a wise man be blessed.
An arrow of victory for his disciples.
An arrow of victory for the elucidators of sacred texts in the correct way.

Insult and Disgrace

Upon the new translation of Proverbs that befouled it. Its foulness will ascend and its ill savour will rise,[35] all who see it will flee from it[36] and will extract it piece by piece[37] and it will be burned, consumed in fire, and its name will no longer be remembered.

---

[32] Judg 5:11.
[33] The most authentic version of *Qol meḥatsetsim* was copied in Humań (Uman) in 1830. See Yehudah Friedlander, "Tobias Gutmann Feder: 'The Archers' Voice,'" *Zehut*, May 1981, 275–303; Katz, "Menachem Mendel Lefin of Satanów's Bible Translations," 114, footnote 3; Moshe Pelli, "'Otherwordly Voices'," *HUCA* 54 (1983): 1–15.
[34] 2 Kgs 13:17.
[35] Joel 2:20.
[36] Nah 3:7.
[37] Ezek 24:6.

Vomit and Excrement

From the body of Mendel Satanów, a man who in his youth was *enlightened* and in his old age *became foolish*,[38] who arranged words with the taste of the white of an egg,[39] to find favor in the eyes of concubines and young women. But they, too, despise it completely,[40] saying, "Are we short of crazy men that this one comes to play the madman?[41] Have you seen this rash man, for surely he attempts to defy the systems of the translators?[42] Pursue him as far as Shevarim!"[43] It will be a shame and a dreadful disgrace. His advice has perished and his wisdom has vanished.[44] His hair turned white and he did not know.

In the Year
But Woe to the Man who gives Birth to Vanity in his Old Age
According to the minor reckoning [1814][45]

Feder's *Qol meḥatsetsim* owed a conscious debt to Aaron Wolfsohn-Halle's *Siḥah be'erets haḥayim* (*Dialogue in Heaven*), which, published in *Hame'assef* in 1794–1797, concluded with a critique of non-German translations of the Bible.[46] Both satires used the literary convention of situating their maskilic protagonists in Heaven, meting out judgments on the lower world.[47] In Feder's heavenly tribunal, Hebrew masters such as Moses Mendelssohn, Menasseh ben Israel (1604–1657), Moses Hayim Luzzatto, Naftali Herz Wessely, Isaac Euchel, Joel Brill (1760–1802) and Judah Leib Ben Ze'ev find themselves incapable of deciphering Lefin's Yiddish translation of Proverbs. Mendelssohn could not understand even one of the 1,000 words while Luzzatto and Menasseh ben Israel, concurring that the language was neither Italian nor Arabic, could not resolve its mysterious origins. Despairing of ever solving the linguistic riddle on their own, the *maskilim* finally seek the aid of the author of *Melammed siah* (*The Teacher of Discourse*), a Yiddish text explaining the words of the Pentateuch and of the five scrolls in the Hagiographa, which appeared in Amsterdam in 1710.[48] Only he is able to read and understand Lefin's translation.

---

38 A pun on the homonyms להשכיל (to enlighten) and להסכיל (to make foolish). The emphasis is mine.
39 Job 6:6.
40 Ezek 15:57.
41 1 Sam 21:16.
42 1 Sam 17:25.
43 Josh 7:5.
44 Jer 49:7.
45 See Friedlander, "Tobias Gutmann Feder," 279 on the *gematriyah* of this phrase.
46 Friedlander, "The Language Battle in Eastern Europe," 28–31.
47 Judah Leib Mieses's *Qinat ha'emet* (Vienna, 1828), one of the most important texts of the later, virulently anti-Hasidic Galician Haskalah, employed the same scenario. On Mieses, see Chapter Five.
48 Elikim ben Jacob of Komarno authored *Melammed siah* in 1710 and also translated Menasseh ben Israel's Spanish version of *Miqveh yisra'el* into Hebrew in 1681.

Like all of the *maskilim* who idealized Moses Mendelssohn and considered his writings exemplary, Feder saw Lefin's turn to Yiddish as an abandonment of the Mendelssohnian method, "the correct way," of translating Scripture, which required translation into German: "Why now do you abandon the source of life [Mendelssohn's example] to dig wells for yourself, wells that are broken? One who drinks from them will die prematurely."[49] Feder expressed bitter disappointment that Lefin, who knew German and French, had chosen to work in Yiddish, which, Feder claimed for polemical effect, was neither Lefin's mother tongue, nor the language of his ancestors and teachers.[50] Feder's disillusionment with Lefin was rendered all the more palpable by his depiction of Lefin as the *maskil* who, prior to his translation of Proverbs into Yiddish, could have guided the Jewish people in an epoch bereft of Mendelssohn, Wessely, and Euchel.[51] In Mendelssohn's closing soliloquy, the great philosopher consoled his fellow *maskilim* with the hope that, despite Lefin's betrayal, there was still a remnant among the Jews who would disseminate his German translation of Scripture and honor it by continuing to translate into German.[52]

Feder's critique of Lefin's turn to Yiddish included all of the touchstones that comprised the creation of the Polish-Jewish "Other" in the eyes of

---

[49] Friedlander, "Tobias Gutmann Feder," 280. On the image of Mendelssohn among the *maskilim*, see James Lehmann, "Maimonides, Mendelssohn, and the *Me'assfim*: Philosophy and Biographical Imagination in the Early Haskalah," *LBIYA* 20 (1975): 87–108 and Shmuel Feiner, "Mendelssohn and 'Mendelssohn's Disciples': A Re-examination," *LBIYA* 40 (1995): 133–67.

[50] Friedlander, "Tobias Gutmann Feder," 280. The maskilic denial of knowing Yiddish can also be seen in the claim by Moses Markuse, Lefin's contemporary and fellow petitioner to the Polish *Sejm*, that he had to debase his German in order to write in the "jargon" of Polish Jewry in his Yiddish translation of Tissot's *Book of Popular Healing*. Yiddish was Markuse's mother tongue. See Chone Shmeruk, "Moses Markuse from Słonim and the Source of His Book, *Ezer yisroel*," in *Sifrut yidish beFolin: meḥqarim ve'iyyunim historiyyim* (Jerusalem: Magnes Press, 1981), 185 and Chapter Two.

[51] Friedlander, "The Language Battle in Eastern Europe," 286.

[52] Ibid., 293. Mendelssohn's opposition to Yiddish, however, has been misunderstood in the literature. Based on his comment, made in the context of a proposal to revise the Jewish oath in Prussian courts, that "this jargon has contributed not a little to the immorality of the common man," many historians have concluded that Mendelssohn was implacably hostile to Yiddish. In fact, despite his extraordinary command of High German, Mendelssohn used Yiddish in his private correspondence throughout his life. He opposed mixing German and Hebrew in the Jewish oath, which he abhorred, because such an amalgam did justice to neither language; part of his problem with using Yiddish as a literary language was that Mendelssohn viewed it as "corrupt" German, not as a language on its own terms. He did not want Yiddish to become the official language of Prussian Jewry, but did not make a conscious effort to eradicate its use. See Werner Weinberg, "Language Questions relating to Moses Mendelssohn's Pentateuch Translation," *HUCA* 55 (1984): 197–242. Weinberg's position notwithstanding, Mendelssohn did not view Yiddish as capable of transmitting the values of *Bildung*. See Grossman, *The Discourse on Yiddish in Germany*, 74–88.

German-oriented *maskilim*, which will be explored below, but one aspect, its alleged effeminacy, deserves attention here because of its central position on the title page. Feder accused Lefin of seeking to please "concubines and young women" with the Yiddish translation, and later criticized him for discarding German for an unintelligible language of peasants and women.[53] Feder's comment about the gendered aspect of Yiddish literacy affirms a historical reality. Both ritualistic and non-ritualistic Yiddish writings that flourished in the fifteenth through seventeenth centuries in Eastern Europe were primarily addressed to women, or to men illiterate in Hebrew, and were viewed in the cultural hierarchy of Jewish letters only as a literary sub-genre.[54] The disparagement of Yiddish and its association with women illustrates, too, the gendered nature of the Haskalah; all *maskilim*, to a man, directed their intellectual energies at other men, and expressed strong reservations about transforming the status of women within Jewish society.[55] Feder saw Lefin's employment of Yiddish as an emasculation of the true path of the Jewish Enlightenment.[56]

Defending and Transforming Early Modern Poland

Lefin's contemporaries, including younger *maskilim* living in Brody, Austrian Galicia, such as Jacob Samuel Bik, Solomon Judah Rapoport (1790–1867) and Nachman Krochmal, the heir apparents to the Haskalah in East Central Europe, became deeply involved with the language polemic initiated by

---

[53]   Friedlander, "Tobias Gutmann Feder," 280. The reference to peasants alludes to Lefin's use of Slavic-component words in his Yiddish.
[54]   Shaul Stampfer, "What Did 'Knowing Hebrew' Mean in Eastern Europe," in *Hebrew in Ashkenaz* (ed. Lewis Glinert; London: Oxford University Press, 1993), 129–40.
[55]   Joseph Perl's daughter, Sheindel, was the exception that proved the gendered rule of the Haskalah. Several letters in the Perl archive refer to Sheindel as an *ishah maskelet* (an "enlightened woman"), meaning a woman who had mastered the texts and language (Hebrew) necessary to participate in the Haskalah's "republic of letters." Much later in the nineteenth century, the female Hebraist, Miriam Markel-Mosessohn (1839–1920), too, would correspond with major figures of the Russian-Jewish Haskalah. On Markel-Mosessohn, see Carole Balin, *'To Reveal Our Hearts': Russian-Jewish Women Writers in Imperial Russia* (Cinncinnati, Ohio: Hebrew Union College Press, 2001), 13–50. For references to Sheindel Pineles, see the letter from Benjamin Reich to Mendel Lefin, undated, 4° 1153/70, and that of Hayim Malaga to Mendel Lefin, 1821, 4° 1153/135a, both in the Joseph Perl Archive, JNULA. See, too, N. M. Gelber, "The History of the Jews of Tarnopol," in *Entsiqlopedyah shel galuyyot: Tarnopol*, vol. 3 (ed. Phillip Krongruen; Jerusalem, 1955), 88, footnote 154.
[56]   On the relationship of language and gender in nineteenth-century Jewish letters, see Naomi Seidman, *A Marriage Made in Heaven: The Sexual Politics of Hebrew and Yiddish* (Berkeley: University of California Press, 1997); on the gendered conservatism of the Haskalah, see Shmuel Feiner, "The Modern Jewish Woman: Test Case in the Relationship between the Haskalah and Modernity," *Zion* 58, no. 4 (1993): 453–99.

Feder. The issues raised by Feder's assault on Lefin and his translation of Proverbs into Yiddish were still very much a part of their formulations, which were not fully resolved, for modernizing Polish Jewry.

The first *maskil* to enter the fray over Feder's composition was Bik, who wrote to Feder on January 1, 1815, urging him not to publish *Qol mehatsetsim.* Bik, taking on the role of intercessor in the controversy, defended Lefin on five points: 1) criticism of Lefin would harm the already vulnerable Haskalah movement; 2) Feder had not only criticized Lefin's writing in his vitriolic satire, but had attacked him *ad hominem*; 3) despite Feder's claim that Yiddish was not Lefin's mother tongue nor the language that his ancestors and teachers had spoken, Yiddish was, in fact, the linguistic inheritance of Ashkenazic Jewry's great sages; 4) even Gentiles considered Yiddish to be a real language, not an illegitimate linguistic mélange. It could be developed into a literary language by men of letters, as had been done with other dialects; and 5) enlightened members of society had a responsibility to speak to the lower classes in a language that the latter could understand.[57]

Bik's appeal to Feder provoked a half-hearted apology on April 30, 1815, in which he expressed regret for unintentionally blemishing Lefin's honor, but expressly refused to backpedal on his denunciation of Yiddish.[58] Comparing himself at the very least to Socrates' "weakest students,"[59] Feder insisted that he had to stand by his words and the truth:

> Your friend knew us [the other *maskilim*]. [He knew] that all of the excuses we used to improve his [Lefin's] translation in order to refine it seven times into silver would result in nothing but vanity. Its outcome will be the drosses of a [chamber] pot with eternal refuse.[60] So let me be slain by one of the zealots, but I will not bow down to a lie and prostrate myself to vanity. . . . With my last breath, I will speak out to the multitudes that

---

[57] Bik's letter to Feder was first published in an incomplete version in *Kerem ḥemed*, 1 (1833), the maskilic Hebrew journal published in Vienna from 1833–1843. The complete text, found in Bik's personal journal, was published by Shmuel Werses. See Shmuel Werses, "The Original, Unknown Version of Jacob Samuel Bik's letter to Tobias Feder," in *Megammot vetsurot besifrut hahaskalah* (Jerusalem: Magnes Press, 1990), 338–55. For a comprehensive look at Bik's life, see, too, Shmuel Werses, "Between Two Worlds: Jacob Samuel Bik Between Haskalah and Hasidism — A Reassessment," in *Megammot vetsurot besifrut hahaskalah* (Jerusalem: Magnes Press, 1990), 110–59. On *Kerem ḥemed*, see Jacob Toury, *Die jüdische presse im österreichischen Kaiserreich: ein Beitrag zur Problematik der Akkulturation 1802–1918* (Tübingen: Mohr, 1983), 7, footnote 17 and Bernhard Wachstein, *Die hebräische Publizistik in Wien* (Vienna: Selbstverlag der Historischen Kommission, 1930).

[58] Feder's response was first published by Letteris in *Mikhtavim*, 17–23, in an incomplete version and then in *Kerem ḥemed*, 1 (1833), 99–102. A version of the letter, with several points of difference from the published editions, can also be found in the Joseph Perl Archive, JNULA, 4° 1153/136.

[59] In Letteris, *Mikhtavim*, 20, in *Kerem ḥemed*, 100. Feder was, no doubt, alluding to Mendelssohn's *Phaedon or Regarding the Immortality of the Soul in Three Dialogues* (Berlin, 1767).

[60] Ezek 24:6.

Mendel Lefin destroyed the world's harmony for a lie. His enlightenment had sent forth precious teachings. But, [now] he has defiled himself with the filthy translation of Proverbs. . . . The ink and the journal will scream at him! For he completely destroyed them. I, however, will not deviate either right or left from the path of truth.[61]

Then, Feder begged Bik and the other *maskilim* in Brody to send him 100 Polish zlotys to cover the expenses incurred by the printer and publisher of *Qol meḥatsetsim*. Once paid, they would not publish the work and Feder would throw the pages of his satire "upon the logs on the fire; they will not be remembered or noticed anymore." Should the 100 zlotys not be forthcoming, Feder threatened, he would go ahead with the publication of *Qol meḥatsetsim*.[62]

Determined to stop publication of the satire, Bik enlisted the *maskilim* of Brody to come up with the necessary funds. In a series of letters to Rapoport and Krochmal, Bik also took the opportunity to discuss his defense of Lefin and clarify his position on the use of Yiddish as a language of Enlightenment. His letters affirm his commitment to defend Lefin as a point of respect and are not due to his belief in the efficacy of using Yiddish as a vehicle for enlightenment.[63] Bik also informed Rapoport that he had not hidden his reservations about the translation from Lefin himself, one of many signs that Lefin and Bik were engaged in an ongoing discussion about language and the Enlightenment in the second decade of the nineteenth century.[64] Although there is some historical speculation that an edition of *Qol meḥatsetsim* was published in Berdyczów in 1816, where Feder resided at the time, no historian has ever seen such an early printed version of the satire.[65] Thus

---

61   Tobias Gutmann Feder to Jacob Samuel Bik, the fourth day of the Intermediate Days of Passover (April 30), 1815, the Joseph Perl Archive, JNULA, 4° 1153/136, 1b. In Letteris, *Mikhtavim*, 20.
62   The Joseph Perl Archive, JNULA, 4° 1153/136, 1b and 2a.
63   See Bik's letter to Rapoport, May 7, 1815, a copy of which appears in Bik's personal journal, which is held in the Merzbacher collection in the municipal library of Frankfurt-on-the-Main. A microfilm of this manuscript, #26448, is held in the Department of Microfilmed Hebrew Manuscripts, JNULA. See page 15b for Bik's letter to Rapoport. See, too, Werses, "The Original, Unknown Version," 341–42. On May 26, 1815, Bik sent a letter to Nachman Krochmal in which he mentioned both the letter of defense that he had sent to Rapoport and Feder's response to his initial letter. He also attached a copy of *Qol meḥatsetsim* for Krochmal's perusal.
64   Werses, "The Original, Unknown Version," 341–42. See, too, Bik's letter to Lefin on March 12, 1819, published in Philip Friedman, "The First Battles between the Haskalah and Hasidism," *Fun noentn ovar* 4 (1937): 260–62.
65   Simha Katz, Joseph Klausner, and A. M. Haberman believed that there was basis to the speculation that *Qol meḥatsetsim* was published in Berdyczów, as early as 1816, despite Bik's intervention. See Katz, "Menachem Mendel Lefin of Satanów's Bible Translations," 114, footnote 3 and Joseph Klausner, *Historyah shel hasifrut ha'ivrit haḥadashah* (Jerusalem: The Hebrew University, 1952), 1:218. See, too, Bernhard Friedberg, *Toldot hadefus ha'ivri beFolonyah* (Tel Aviv: N.p., 1950), 143 and Erik, *Etiudn tsu der geshikhte fun der haskole*, 158.

it appears that Bik's effort to halt publication of *Qol meḥatsetsim* was effective.

Yet, as the existence of the 1830 version of *Qol meḥatsetsim* illustrates, Bik was unsuccessful in preventing manuscript copies of the satire from circulating among East European *maskilim*. Moreover, it appears that Lefin himself knew of the satire and of the epistolary fireworks it had produced.[66] He may even have known of Feder's intention to write *Qol meḥatsetsim* before Proverbs went to press, as evidenced by an unusual phrase in Joshua Heschel's approbation to his work. Citing Prov 1:11, the traditional prooftext for approbations, Heschel wrote that the author of the translation of Proverbs had asked him to remind the readers that anyone encroaching upon the copyright of his work transgressed both a biblical and rabbinic injunction. While there is nothing peculiar in this standard admonition, Heschel added the phrase "lest a strange man raise his hand against the work . . . and harm him [the author] with *arrows* [*veyaziq oto beḥitsav*]," which appears to be a veiled allusion to *Qol meḥatsetsim*.[67] Lefin knew that most, if not all, *maskilim* opposed using Yiddish for enlightening the Jews of Poland in general, and specifically recoiled at the translation of the Bible into a language they considered little more than a "jargon." It is thus likely that his decision to publish his translation of Proverbs anonymously was due as much to his anticipation of the censure of his fellow *maskilim*, who undoubtedly had seen his other Yiddish translations in manuscript and had already discouraged him from undertaking the project, as to his fear of the rejection of the "modern" commentary by traditional East European Jews.

Two recently discovered documents, both in Lefin's hand, demonstrate definitively that Lefin was well aware of Feder's satire.[68] On the front page of the first document, a satiric title page of a work designed as a literary echo of Feder's pamphlet, the text reads:

---

[66] On later historical references to the polemic, see Katz, "Menachem Mendel Lefin of Satanów's Bible Translations," 114–16; Mahler, *Divrei yemei yisra'el*, 1:84–87; Klausner, *Historyah shel hasifrut*, 1:246; Zalman Reizen, *Fun Mendelson biz Mendele* (Warsaw: Kultur-Lige, 1923), 1:156. Isaac Baer Levinsohn defended Lefin in 1880 in his *Eshkol hasofer*, saying to Feder, "Your tongue is not of wine, it cleaved to the roof of your mouth," even though he disparaged Yiddish in Isaac Baer Levinsohn, *Te'udah beyisra'el* (ed. Immanuel Etkes; Vilna, 1828), 30–36. Cited in Friedlander, "The Language Battle in Eastern Europe," 12 and 17.

[67] [Lefin], *Sefer mishlei shelomo*, the first approbation, unpaginated. The emphasis is mine. Note, too, that the *gematriyah* in the letter that the author of *Melammed siaḥ* sends to Lefin at the end of *Qol meḥatsetsim* equals the year 1811, perhaps signalling that Feder had composed his satire at least three years prior to the publication of Lefin's Proverbs. See Friedlander, "Tobias Gutmann Feder," 293.

[68] The Joseph Perl Archive, JNULA, 4° 1153/136.

Barbs to the Archer

Two parts

1) *Voice of the Thorns.*[69] Letters from So-and-So to So-and-So with an introduction, commentary, and abridgment that weakens every one of them. With the addition of glosses to the books that have been published for the benefit of his orphaned generation in order to confirm his limited intelligence and base personality. As the arrogance of his countenance broadens,[70] his mouth becomes impudent. Each epistle is certified with the signature of the writer except for those that have been published.

2) *A Thorn in the Hand of a Drunkard.*[71] Endless parables and poems. The wail of a frog composing poetry and of a mouse who appoints himself lord. The crown of pride of a drunkard,[72] whose pleasure is his wine. The delight of the swine in the mud of his house.[73] Together all of them will totter, but still sing. Turn away from a toothless frog and from a mousehole that aspires to Heaven. What will the lame-footed drunkard and the pig, like a battering ram without horns, boast about in evil?[74]

In the Year
'Tobias is a Drunk' according to the minor reckoning [1815]
His grave is in his throat[75]
Berlin
("tit for tat," but not like it)

The *gematriyah* that appears at bottom of the document locates Lefin in Berlin in 1815, shortly after Feder wrote *Qol meḥatsetsim,* although we know that Lefin then resided in Austrian Galicia.[76] He composed the text to appear as if it were written in Berlin, the geographic center of the German-Jewish Enlightenment and the mythic pinnacle to which Feder aspired and in whose ideological mantle he cloaked his own work. Lefin entitled his fictive pamphlet *Qotsim lameḥatsets* (*Barbs to the Archer*), a deliberate allusion to the title of Feder's satiric work, *Qol meḥatsetsim* (*The Archers' Voice*). He called the first section *Qol hasirim,* a reference to Eccl 7:6: "For as the crackling of nettles (*qol hasirim*) under a pot, so is the laughter of a fool: this also is vanity." Here, Lefin sarcastically conveys that his critic's laughter, at Lefin's own expense, was the vain laughter of a fool. The title *Qol hasirim* of the first section is also a reproach to the claim articulated by Feder in his response to Jacob Samuel Bik that Lefin's translation, no matter how great

---

69   Eccl 7:6.
70   Ps 10:4.
71   Prov 26:9.
72   Isa 28:1 and 28:3.
73   Isa 66:17.
74   2 Sam 4:4.
75   Ps 5:10.
76   According to a list of materials from the Joseph Perl Archive in Tarnopol catalogued in the inter-war years by Philip Koffler, Lefin was in both Tarnopol and Sieniawa in 1815. See the Koffler appendix to the Joseph Perl Archive, JNULA.

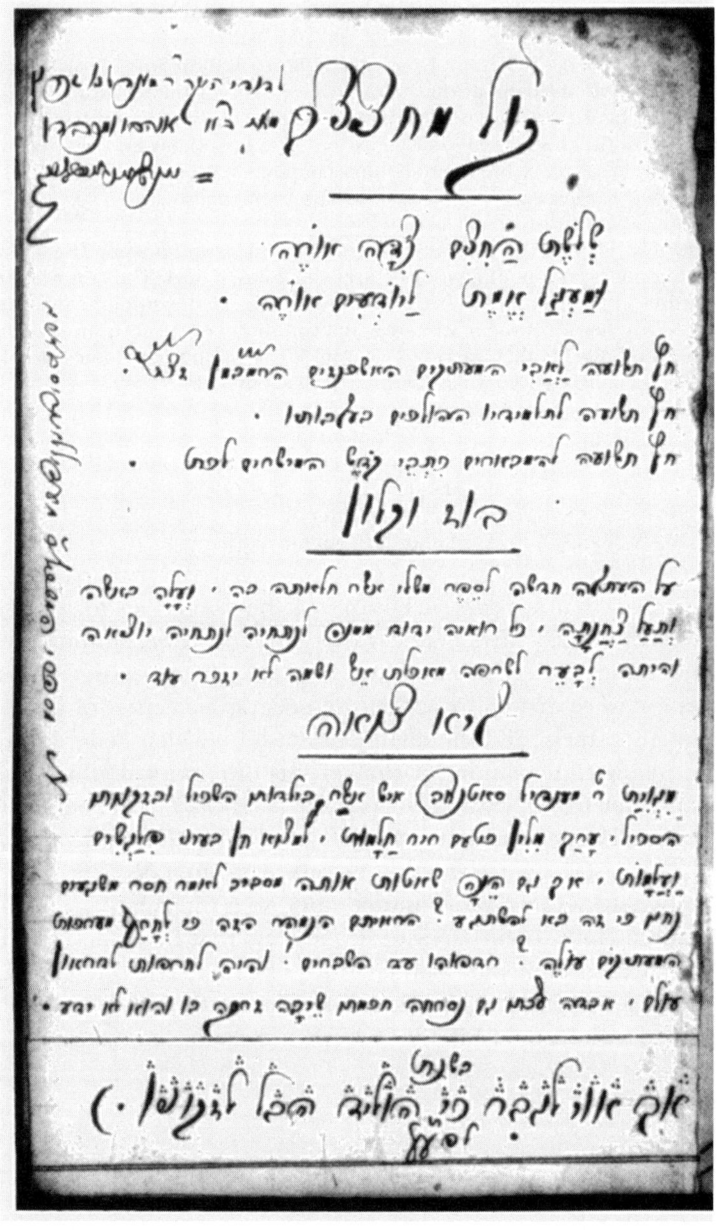

Illustration 5

The title page of *Qol meḥatsetsim* (*The Archers' Voice*)
(NYPL, *ZP 482)

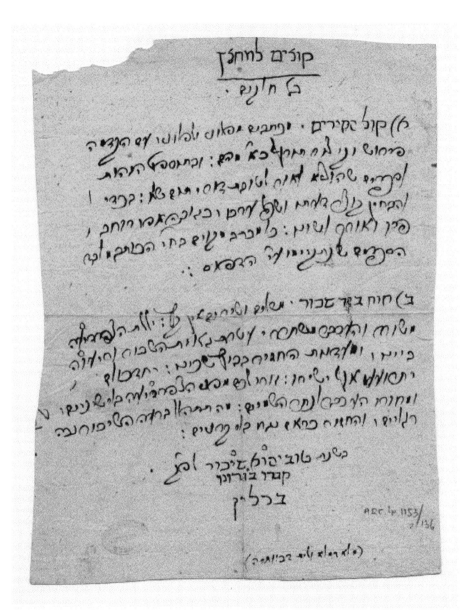

Illustration 6

The title page of *Qotsim lameḥatsets* (*Barbs to the Archer*)
(The Joseph Perl Archive, JNULA, 4° 1153/136)

the effort to purify its language, would remain "nothing but vanity (*re'ut ruaḥ*), [whose] outcome will be the drosses of a [chamber] *pot* (*sir*) with eternal refuse."[77] The second part of the text, written in a choppy style of strung-together biblical verses, is a parody of *melitsah*, the Hebrew style for which Feder was renowned. Part two of *Qotsim lameḥatsets* mocks Feder's literary style, comparing it to the "wailing of a frog," a charge that parallels his characterization of Lefin's Yiddish as the language of animals, and equates him with those in Isa 66:17 who will perish at God's hand. The *gematriyah* at the bottom of the page, decrying Feder as a drunk, corresponds to the *gematriyah* on the title page of *Qol meḥatsetsim*. The structure of Lefin's response, indicating two discrete sections, suggests that Feder's *Qol meḥatsetsim* may have originally been penned in two parts, an implication supported by Feder's own comments in his letter to Jacob Samuel Bik.[78]

On the back of the page is a separate text, also written in Lefin's hand.[79] The second text, satirically written as if it had been penned by Feder on the same day that he had written to Bik, reads:

> With God's help, Berdyczów, the fourth day of the Intermediate Days of Passover [April 30], 1815, from the time since the creation of the world.
> "I will put iron on my neck and brass on my forehead, etc."[80]
> And This Weakens the Words of the Letter:
>
> My signature below will testify that I am poor and insolent like all my friends who go begging, saying: "Take pity, weak men and have compassion upon me because I am poor. I am expiring at your feet and am kissing the ends of your buttocks. Surely have compassion! Among the refugees from a burning city, I am a priest who has converted and my wife is having difficult labor. Take my daughter, who has matured, for ransom money. Upon whom can I depend? And if you do not listen to my supplication, then I will have to curse, insult, vilify, and make you contemptible in the eyes of everyone, (or) then your heart will weaken and you will flee from the voice of the besmirched pig's shout of your persecutors, (or) then you will implore me to accept your ransom."

---

[77] Ezek 24:6. Tobias Gutmann Feder to Jacob Samuel Bik, the fourth day of the Intermediate Days of Passover (April 30), 1815, the Joseph Perl Archive, JNULA, 4° 1153/136, 1a. In Letteris, *Mikhtavim*, 19. The emphases are mine.

[78] To Bik, Feder threatened: "Wait until the day that the second part of *Qol meḥatsetsim* is published, then you will know the truth. . . . The first part that you saw is still hidden in my tent!" The Joseph Perl Archive, JNULA, 4° 1153/136, 1b. In Letteris, *Mikhtavim*, 21.

[79] A second version of this text also appears on the second side of a copy of Feder's original letter to Bik; see the Joseph Perl Archive, JNULA, 4° 1153/136. The existence of the copy of the letter itself suggests that Lefin was privy not only to Feder's response to Bik, but also to Bik's original letter to Feder. This copy of the letter may have been Lefin's own, perhaps sent to him by Jacob Samuel Bik in the midst of the controversy over the publication of Proverbs. See Werses, "The Original, Unknown Version," 347.

[80] Isa. 48:4. Feder's letter to Bik begins with "I will put iron on my neck and brass on my forehead," and is dated "Berdyczów, the fourth day of the Intermediate Days of Passover [April 30], 1815, from the time since the creation of the world."

Lefin's response to Feder mocked his compatriot for blackmailing the *maskilim* of Brody to prevent the publication of *Qol meḥatsetsim*.[81] Although the text remained in manuscript, it is significant in illustrating Lefin's rejection of Feder's assertion that there could only be one linguistic path for the Haskalah.

Lefin's commitment to writing in and translating into Yiddish in order to enlighten the Jews of Poland was a hallmark of his regional version of the Haskalah and a conscious adaptation of the Mendelssohnian model of translation for the Jews of Poland. Historians have long lamented the fact that Lefin either never wrote a programmatic statement about this commitment or that a German essay, "*Über die Kultur der polnisch-jüdischen Sprache als unfehlbars Mittel zu ihrer Aufklärung*," mentioned in a partial list of Lefin's unpublished manuscripts, was irretrievably lost.[82] Yet, a six-page letter written by Lefin in maskilic German (German written in Hebrew characters) that discusses the issue of using Yiddish as a means to enlighten the Jews of Poland is extant, and is undoubtedly the German essay in question.[83] The body of the letter is not composed in Lefin's handwriting, but there is no question of the letter's authorship.[84] Lefin often resorted to having his works

---

[81]   Feder had pleaded poverty in his letter to Bik. See Tobias Gutmann Feder to Jacob Samuel Bik, the fourth day of the Intermediate Days of Passover (April 30), 1815. The Joseph Perl Archive, JNULA, 4° 1153/136, 1b and 2a, and in Letteris, *Mikhtavim*, 21.

[82]   See Shmeruk, "On Several Principles," 167, footnotes 5 and 6, Miron, *A Traveler Disguised*, 278, footnote 19, Friedlander, "The Language Battle in Eastern Europe," 9, and Weinlös, "R. Menachem Mendel of Satanów," 819. Weinlös transcribed a letter of Lefin's (undated and without an addressee) in which he catalogued several of his unpublished writings, including "a German essay on the importance of popular literature in the Yiddish language for the culture and Enlightenment of the Jewish inhabitants of Poland." Lefin also mentioned the essay in a "list of still-to-be-edited essays" written in 1826. See the Joseph Perl Archive, JNULA, 4° 1153/67.

[83]   The Joseph Perl Archive, JNULA, 4° 1153/134a.

[84]   The manuscript contains the sentence, "*so sind wir denn endlich zum ersten Gesuchtspunkte wovon wir ausgegangen sind, das ist, von der Kultur der polnisch-jüdishen Sprache als Mittel zu ihrer Aufklärung. Nun wider herausgenommen*," which resonates directly with the title of the essay alluded to by Lefin in his list of unedited works. See the Joseph Perl Archive, JNULA, 4° 1153/134a, 3b and 67. Other evidence supporting Lefin's authorship of the unsigned letter is that it quotes one of his favorite rabbinic maxims, "Who is wise? The one who learns from every man" (*m.* Avot 4:1), which he cited in his unpublished introduction to *Masa'ot hayam* (*Journeys by Sea*, Żółkiew, 1818), Hebrew translations of two of the German writer Joachim Heinrich Campe's travelogues. On Jewish interest in Campe, see Zohar Shavit, "From Friedländer's Lesebuch to the Jewish Campe — The Beginning of Hebrew Children's Literature in Germany," *LBIYA* 33 (1988): 385–415 and Moshe Pelli, "The Literary Genre of the Travelogue in Hebrew Haskalah Literature: Shmuel Romanelli's *Masa Barav*," *Modern Judaism* 11 (1991): 241–60. For an analysis of *Masa'ot hayam*'s role in Lefin's anti-Hasidic campaign, see my "Strategy and Ruse in the Haskalah of Mendel Lefin of Satanów (1749–1826)," in *New Perspectives on the Haskalah* (ed. Shmuel Feiner and David Sorkin; London: Littman Library of Jewish Civilization, 2001), 86–102. Last, although the manuscript was not

transcribed by friends and disciples because of his age and ill health, even complaining bitterly in the introduction to his translation of the *Guide of the Perplexed* that his fellow *maskilim* had disappointed him by not giving him "assistants to ease the burden of my aging eyes," as they had promised.[85] The letter forms part of an ongoing exchange with one of Lefin's unnamed maskilic friends over the role of the intelligentsia in creating a literary language from a dialect.[86] This was an issue at the heart of Enlightenment efforts to standardize language, particularly in the context of the nation-state's drive to centralize communication, which became transparent in the Royal Prussian Academy of Sciences and Belles-Lettres of Berlin's 1784 essay questions that challenged the hegemony of French as the universal language of Europe, a topic posed to assert the possibility that German might wrest French from its pedestal.[87]

Lefin uncategorically placed the responsibility of creating a literary language from a regional dialect into the hands of a nation's educated elite. Basing his conclusions on the transformation of High German from a dialect into the literary language of the German Empire, Lefin argued that Yiddish, too, could be transformed into a literary language if members of the Jewish intelligentsia endeavored to write interesting and scholarly works in it: "From whence was the German language able to boast today of so many master-pieces in all different fields? Did not the enlightened men of High Germany

---

written by Lefin, there are four places in the text where Lefin's own hand can be discerned. On page 5a, Lefin himself wrote the words *polnisch-jüdische* and *dazumals*; on page 5b, he wrote the words *fanatischer* and *von*.

[85] See Maimonides, *Sefer moreh nevukhim*, 1a–1b.

[86] Bik, who told Lefin that his translations of Benjamin Franklin's essays had made him rethink the issue of provincial languages and their relationship to a unified national audience, was undoubtedly the "dear friend" to whom the letter is addressed. For the comments about Franklin's essays, see Jacob Samuel Bik to Mendel Lefin, March 12, 1819, published in Friedman, "The First Battles," 260–62. Although the manuscript is not dated, the earliest possible date of its composition is 1811, the date alluded to by the author of *Melammed siah* of Feder's first composing *Qol mehatsetsim*. The undated German letter penned by Lefin in which the essay on the use of Yiddish for the Enlightenment of the Jews of Poland is mentioned must have been written between the publication of *Sefer heshbon hanefesh* in 1808 and the Proverbs translation in 1814. See Weinlös, "R. Mendel Lefin of Satanów," 819. Whether or not Lefin wrote several versions of the essay, or reworked it in the form of the letter after the polemic with Feder, cannot be known at this juncture. Bik wrote his letter to Lefin regarding their correspondence about provincial languages in 1819, making 1819 the latest possible date of Lefin's response.

[87] One of the contest's winners, Johann Christoph Schwab (1743–1821), pointed out that the political decentralization of Germany, in contrast to France, had hindered the development of the German language. See Edwin H. Zeydel, "A Criticism of the German Language by a German of the Eighteenth Century," *Modern Language Notes* 38, no. 4 (April 1923): 193–201.

first take the trouble to write something interesting in their dialect?"[88] Lefin's views are confirmed by the explosion of materials for an emergent readership literate in German, including Bible translations, philosophy (such as Christian Wolff's *German Logic*, which appeared in fourteen editions between 1713–1754), moralistic periodical literature, novels, and popular scientific works.[89] Lefin's attitude toward the possibility of cultivating Yiddish as a tool of Enlightenment is derived from his comparison with what he terms "the natural, cultural history of most of the European nations," an allusion to the contemporary theoretical work on nationalism and language circulating among the enlightened circles of Europe and in the German cultural sphere in particular.[90] The intellectual leadership of a nation should write edifying works in its mother tongue in order to produce a general literary emulation among the non-elite, which, in turn, would both stimulate the refinement of the language and the spread of the Enlightenment. The authors of such works would be encouraged when they saw their works "finally ennobling the spirit and hearts of their brethren," from the most educated "to the lowest class of the rabble."[91] Despite Lefin's emphasis on the priority of written literature in the development and refinement of language, he conceded that in the right circumstances, when a nation experienced auspicious economic growth, language could grow and develop from an oral context as well. Lefin argued that enlightened writers in German lands had developed High German from an earlier proto-standardized oral language. But Yiddish could claim neither favorable political circumstances nor auspicious national economic development to spur its cultivation. Its development depended upon the concerted efforts of the enlightened Jewish intelligentsia.

Lefin had earlier used his Hebrew commentary to Ecclesiastes to develop his assertion of the *intelligenti*'s vanguard role in the dissemination of Enlightenment values to the Jewish masses, and the choice of language

---

88 The Joseph Perl Archive, JNULA, 4° 1153/134a, 1b.

89 On the evolution of High German into a literary language, see Blackall, *The Emergence of German* and Hans Eggers, *Deutsche Sprachgeschichte* (Reinbeck: Rowohlts Enzyklopädie, 1986).

90 The work of Johann Gottfried Herder (1744–1803), arguably one of the most important theoreticians on the origins of language and the relationship of language to national development, had enormous impact throughout eighteenth-century Europe. All of his works, including *Ideas for a Philosophy of the History of Mankind* (1784–1791), *Another Philosophy of History in the Development of Humanity* (1774), *Origin of Language* and *About the Activity of Poetry upon the Morals of Nations [Völker] in the Past and Present* (1781) sought to uncover the "national spirit" implicit in the language and poetry of the German people. See Grossman, *The Discourse on Yiddish in Germany*, 28–51 and Carlton J. H. Hayes, "Contributions of Herder to the Doctrine of Nationalism," *The American Historical Review* 32, no. 4 (July 1927): 719–36. The Czartoryskis, both father and son, knew Herder personally. See W. H. Zawadzki, *A Man of Honour: Adam Czartoryski as a Statesman of Russia and Poland, 1795–1831* (Oxford: Clarendon Press, 1993), 19–21, 67, and 147.

91 The Joseph Perl Archive, JNULA, 4° 1153/134a, 2a.

(Hebrew) spoke as loud as its content.[92] He intended the mishnaic Hebrew of the commentary for his maskilic compatriots, the "select individuals . . . endowed with knowledge," who, as in Ecclesiastes' period, were few and far between, and bore a special responsibility to enlighten the benighted.[93] Glossing the enigmatic phrasing in Eccl 12:11, "The sayings of the wise are like goads, like nails fixed in prodding sticks," Lefin wrote, "This was the method of the 'wise' from time immemorial: to craft their words decisively and tactically (*betaḥbulot nimratsot*) in order to turn the people's understanding (lit. *nefesh*/soul) toward the straight path."[94] *Maskilim* reading the Hebrew commentary would well understand Lefin's message; their task was to emulate the great Solomon himself, to persuade "those with little reason"[95] through didactic ethical writings to aspire to the maskilic values of *Bildung* that they projected onto the teachings of Ecclesiastes. Like his *Sefer ḥeshbon hanefesh*, Lefin's Hebrew commentary to Ecclesiastes functioned as an enlightened *musar* text designed to cultivate internal moral self-improvement; on Eccl 9:17–18, Lefin commented, "The wise are indeed capable of directing the people's hearts through suasion, which is more effective than a fool's assertive rebuke." Moral suasion penned in German, however, would fall on deaf ears in Jewish Poland. Lefin's positioning of a Hebrew commentary to accompany his Yiddish translations of Ecclesiastes, Proverbs, and Psalms is further evidence of the sophisticated understanding of audience he revealed when writing his *Essai d'un plan de réforme* in French and *Entwurf eines Rabinersystems* in German. Different language strategies were necessary for reaching different audiences. While *maskilim* read the Hebrew commentaries, the Jewish masses would be uplifted by accessible Yiddish translations of the works in their sacred canon that affirmed the values of the Enlightenment.

The first task of the *intelligenti* was to wean the Jews of Poland away from their traditional literary canon, the older Yiddish translations and petitionary prayers (*tekhines*) that Lefin and his fellow *maskilim* viewed as ungrammatical, exegetically flawed, and culturally backward.[96] Lefin's critique of the older

---

[92] All of Lefin's extant Yiddish translations of Scripture are accompanied by short Hebrew commentaries.

[93] See Lefin's gloss to Eccl 2:26.

[94] Shmuel Leib Goldenberg, editor of *Kerem ḥemed,* used the same verse as the first volume's epigraph. Goldenberg actually edited *Kerem ḥemed* with Solomon Judah Rapoport (Shir), whom Ezra Spicehandler considered the real force behind the journal. Ezra Spicehandler, "Joshua Heschel Schorr: Maskil and Eastern European Reformist," *HUCA* 31: 181–222 and 40–41: 503–528 (1960): 194. On Lefin's use of the term *taḥbulah* (pl. *taḥbulot*) to flag a maskilic literary strategy, see my "Strategy and Ruse in the Haskalah of Mendel Lefin of Satanów (1749–1826)."

[95] Lefin's gloss to Eccl 12:9.

[96] The Joseph Perl Archive, JNULA, 4° 1153/134a, 6a.

Yiddish translations reflected his fidelity to the Mendelssohnian perspective on translation. Mendelssohn conceived of the German translation in the *Bi'ur* in order to supplant the word-for-word method of the older Judeo-German Bible translations, such as that found in *Melammed siaḥ*. The German-Jewish audience he hoped to reach with his translation was already reading and speaking German and the word-for-word translations of Scripture at their disposal were often syntactically incorrect.[97] Similarly, Lefin conceded that "steering the Jewish masses away from their harmful, obsolete 'little Bibles' in the 'Polish-Jewish language'" would not be easy, for they "have been indispensable to the Jewish rabble here [in Poland] for a long time," either relentlessly smuggled in from abroad or indigenously produced in Poland.[98] Yet, because Yiddish was the "living language" of the Jews of Poland, a phrase he employed three times in the letter, it could be cultivated to enjoy the same advantages that translations and popular literature had acquired in Germany. Yiddish could be made relevant for modernizing Polish Jews.[99]

Defending his position on writing popular literature in Yiddish for the Jews of Poland as a legitimate extension of the Mendelssohnian path, Lefin implicitly rebutted Tobias Feder's accusation that he had forsaken the Mendelssohnian literary heritage. Mendelssohn, Lefin wrote, succeeded in two important missions when composing his German translation of the Bible with its accompanying Hebrew commentary: the elevation of literary culture and the Enlightenment of his brethren. Lefin also praised David Friedländer's translation efforts and concluded that, "inspired by a living language," they were extraordinarily impressive, stimulating great interest among their readers by "intruding upon their feelings . . . with their sanctity . . . [and] sublime beauty."[100] A vital, living language was a malleable tool that could express a multitude of sentiments and ideas to a variety of readers in the hands of a capable writer. Yiddish translations and writings crafted with the

---

97 Weinberg, "Language Questions," 228–31 and Shmeruk, "On Several Principles," 171.
98 The Joseph Perl Archive, JNULA, 4° 1153/134a, 6a. Mahler affirms Lefin's despair about the permeability of the borders between Russia and Galicia despite the "rigorous surveillance" of the Habsburg authorities. Mahler, *Hasidism and the Jewish Enlightenment*, 107–08. See, too, Alan Sked, *The Decline and Fall of the Habsburg Empire, 1815–1918* (London: Longman Group, 1989), 47–51 for an interpretation of the censorship under Metternich as a "nuisance" rather than as a harsh prohibition.
99 The Joseph Perl Archive, JNULA, 4° 1153/134a, 6a.
100 Ibid., 4a. In 1786, David Friedländer published a translation of the traditional prayer-book, *Gebete der Juden auf das ganze Jahr*, which he followed two years later with his translation of Ecclesiastes (*Der Prediger. Aus dem Hebräischen nebst einer vorangeschickten Abhandlung, über den besten Gebrauch der heiligen Schrift, in pädigogischer Rücksicht*, Berlin, 1788). While praising Mendelssohn's and Friedländer's translations, Lefin was nonetheless dismayed at the alacrity with which certain sectors of Berlin Jewry discarded traditional rabbinic texts.

same talent and sensitivity of a Mendelssohn or Friedländer could uplift the
Jews of Poland. The responsibility lay with the writer or translator.[101]
    Lefin was not satisfied with merely an implicit response to Tobias Feder.
Rather, he issued an unambiguous challenge to Feder's contention that the
writing of Enlightenment works for the masses of East European Jewry would
be in vain. The Jews of Poland would remain stuck in their base condition,
Lefin asserted:

> Until Providence finally delivers a competent Redeemer on their account.[102] He looks
> after it [Polish Jewry] zealously, studies their language and manners of thinking, and
> searches for the right path to their hearts. Now he tackles the arduous task of composing
> with the utmost care a fair number of beneficial works, which appeal to their taste, in
> their language. *The weak minds of the "enlightened" ridicule his undertaking in the beginning.*
> [But] his audience's praise and the desired progress from his effort is suffcient reward
> for the steadfast until the time when truly deserving men who support his work appear
> . . . and the importance of popular writing is finally generally recognized. Then the
> common people will cautiously take a chance with this reading matter, finding it
> harmless, reasonable, edifying, and useful, and abandon their aversion to the "polished"
> world. [In turn, they will] disdain ignorance, enjoy the pleasures of the beautiful, noble,
> and natural, learn the scholarly language of books, and acquire various advice, comfort,
> and instruction from it.[103]

Despite Mendelssohn's commanding influence, Mendel Lefin defined his
Haskalah as an adaptation of the Berlin path and shaped his program for the
transformation of Polish Jewry in the cultural context from which he came,
the world of Podolian Jewry. His assertion of the legitimacy of regional
distinctiveness found expression in his choice of Yiddish, and also in his
cultivation of the Podolian dialect of Yiddish in his translations. He explicitly
supported the retention of a dialect of Yiddish by employing expressions

---

[101] Lefin continued his conceptualization of the issue of writing styles and audience in his
introduction to his Yiddish translation of Psalms: "It is known that there is a great difference
between simple speech and the language of poetry and prose. When one has to do some
general matter with one's peers — all the more so when one has to give orders to a servant
— then [one uses] language in its simplest form. But if one has an important matter to
discuss, particularly with someone of a higher social status, then the language will be
constructed completely differently. All the more so when [the language] is between man
and God (for example, in prayers of praise, such as "the Heavens tell of God's honor,"
hallelujahs, petitions, and requests, or thanks for the goodness that we have received from
him, may he be blessed), then the language must reflect its most elevated, purified, and
adorned [form]." Cited in Katz, "Menachem Mendel Lefin of Satanów's Bible Translations,"
129.
[102] Lefin used the German word, *Erlöser*, for "redeemer," a choice that may be an indirect
refutation of Feder's charge in *Qol meḥatsetsim* to Lefin to "be diligent, to restore the
precious languages [Hebrew and German] that have not had a more fitting *redeemer [go'el]*
than you since Mendelssohn's death." See Friedlander, "Tobias Gutmann Feder," 280.
[103] The Joseph Perl Archive, JNULA, 4° 1153/134a, 2a. The emphasis, referring directly to
Feder, is mine.

specific to Podolian Jewry and by deliberately avoiding German-component Yiddish words, when he had the syntactical choice. In so doing, he affirmed his contention that a vernacular language, particularly in its "living" dialect form, would reach its intended audience.[104] Writing in a Yiddish that was native to the Jews of Podolia would redress the problem of comprehension created by maskilic translations into *melitsah* Hebrew, which in its fidelity to biblical syntax ignored the reality of a population who no longer understood the original biblical language. Lefin concluded in the introduction to his Yiddish translation of Psalms that clear and direct language was preferable to "comments from thousands of phrases that are conjoined like a braid of gold," and that "the best remedy to rectify the aforementioned failings, it seems, is to prepare a complete translation of several Psalms . . . in our Yiddish language as it is spoken by us today."[105] A Haskalah program imported from Berlin without modification, which imposed a "foreign" language and culture upon Polish Jewry, was predestined to fail. Undaunted by the fracas that his translation of Proverbs into Yiddish created and despite his isolation, Lefin persisted in writing in and translating into Yiddish, even after the Feder debacle, hoping perhaps that his fellow *maskilim* would finally recognize the efficacy of writing in the mother tongue of East European Jewry.[106]

---

[104] Although Lefin's use of Yiddish was instrumental, his own literary aspirations resulted in a translation that is universally praised. See Mahler, *Divrei yemei yisra'el*, 1: 82–83; Miron, *A Traveler Disguised*, 41; Reizen, *Fun Mendelson biz Mendele*, 157–58.

[105] Published in Katz, "Menachem Mendel Lefin of Satanów's Bible Translations," 129–30.

[106] Besides Proverbs and Ecclesiastes, Lefin completed translations of Lamentations, and worked on Psalms and Job. In a letter to a maskilic contemporary, Lefin mentioned, "Several manuscripts are ready for publication, [including] a translation of the Psalms from the preacher Solomon, the Book of Job, Jeremiah's Lamentations, all to uplift the Jewish vernacular [literally: "folk language"]." Published in Weinlös, "R. Menachem Mendel of Satanów," 800. Gottlober also claimed to have seen manuscript copies of all five scrolls of the Hagiographa in Bar in Meir ha-Cohen Reich's possession. See Gottlober, "Russia," *Hamaggid* 17, no. 40 (1873): 363. For a transcription of part of manuscript 8°/1053, which is held in the Division of Microfilmed Manuscripts in the Jewish National and University Library, Jerusalem, and which includes all of Lamentations, Psalms 1–62, (including an introduction in Yiddish) and Job 1–16, 1–18:15, 28:6–37:12 and 38:12–41:5, see Katz, "Menachem Mendel Lefin of Satanów's Bible Translations." Lefin's anti-Hasidic satire, *Der ershter khosed* (*The First Hasid*), which is no longer extant, was also written in Yiddish, as was a version of his essay on the immortality of the soul.

It is also probable that Lefin was the author of the very rare *Oniyyah so'arah* (*The Raging Boat*), an anonymous bilingual (Hebrew and Yiddish) translation of Wilhelm Y. Bontekoe's tale of his voyage to the East Indies, which also appeared sometime in the second decade of the nineteenth century. Bontekoe's journey appeared in the fifth volume of Joachim Heinrich Campe, *Sammlung interessanter und durchgängig zweckmässig abgefasster Reisebeschreibungen für die Jugend* (Reutlingen: J. Grözinger, 1786). Catalog information about *Oniyyah so'arah* is contradictory and vague, although Samuel Poznanski claimed definitively that Lefin was its translator. See Samuel Poznanski, "Wiener's 'Bibliotheca Friedlandiana'," *JQR* 9 (1897): 159. For the best bibliographic discussion of the book, see Isaac Yudlov, *The Israel*

Lefin's persistence in the use of Yiddish in particular, and the continuous Hebraism of the East European Jewish Enlightenment in general, under-scores the difference between the nation-state and Imperial contexts in the dissemination and articulation of Enlightenment attitudes toward language. Although the European Enlightenment had challenged the legitimacy of dialects and enlightened absolutist states had imposed state languages on linguistically heterogenous populations, polylingualism remained the norm in the Imperial contexts of East Central and Eastern Europe in the eight-eenth century, persisting through the interwar years of the twentieth cen-tury.[107] The natural bilingual landscape inhabited by the Jews of the Polish-Lithuanian Commonwealth in the eighteenth century, using Yiddish as their vernacular and *leshon haqodesh* (liturgical/ritual Hebrew) for all aspects of religious life, continued later when they lived under the Russian and Habs-burg Empires.[108] The Jewish Enlightenment challenged this natural pre-modern diglossia among the Jews of Eastern Europe, but did not end it. As Israel Bartal has argued, East European *maskilim* directed their linguistic efforts "at *replacing* the two component languages: the state language or a European language (most commonly, German) for Yiddish, and biblical Hebrew for *leshon ha-kodesh*."[109] By insisting on the efficacy of Yiddish for

---

Mehlman Collection in the Jewish National and University Library (Jerusalem: Beit hasefarim, 1984), 208, who cites 1818, but with a question, as the date of publication. Evidence point-ing to Lefin's hand in *Oniyyah so'arah* was its (probable) publication in Żółkiew, where *Masa'ot hayam* and *Di genarte velt* first appeared, its joint publication with one of the travel-ogues from *Masa'ot hayam* in the Vilna 1823 edition of that same title, its use of Slavic words in the Yiddish translation, and its being translated from the same source as those in *Masa'ot hayam*. The earliest extant edition of *Oniyyah so'arah* is held in the Jewish National and University Library and is missing the title page and the first few pages, making it extremely difficult to attribute the work. Unusual words known to a German reader, but not to a Hebrew or Yiddish reader, appear in parentheses. Linguistic features of the translation include the use of Slavic-component Yiddish words and of hypercorrections to make the Yiddish appear more "western," for example, hypercorrecting and thus mistranslating the German word for "ship" as *shuf* instead of *shif*. These features were characteristic of the Yiddish of East European *maskilim* who wanted their words to appear more "enlightened," and less "eastern" (Polish). I am indebted to Professor Chava Turniansky of the Hebrew University for her linguistic and literary insights into this text.

[107] The linguistic homogenity of post-World War Two Poland is only one of the conse-quences, banal in comparison to the murder of one-third of its citizenry, of its political incarnation as a nation-state. See Norman Davies, *God's Playground: A History of Poland* (New York: Columbia University Press, 1984) and Michael Steinlauf, *Bondage to the Dead: Poland and the Memory of the Holocaust* (Syracuse, N.Y.: Syracuse University Press, 1997).

[108] This natural bilingualism, however, should not be understood as two completely distinct linguistic spheres. Spoken Yiddish includes many Hebrew-component words and communal edicts were penned in a scribal mixture of Hebrew and Yiddish. Moreover, liturgical Hebrew is comprised of Aramaic phraseology and terminology.

[109] Israel Bartal, "From Traditional Bilingualism to National Monolingualism," in *Hebrew in Ashkenaz* (ed. Lewis Glinert; New York: Oxford University Press, 1993), 141–50.

enlightening East European Jewry, Lefin qualified the Berlin Haskalah's replacement of the traditional diglossia (*leshon haqodesh*/Yiddish) with an enlightened diglossia (biblical Hebrew/German) and rejected the monolingualism that modernity in the nation-state heralded. His conception of the Haskalah thus rephrased both the European Enlightenment's and the Berlin Haskalah's articulation of the language question.

No discussion of Mendel Lefin's writings can escape the anti-Hasidism that was central to his enlightened worldview. The campaign of the *maskilim* against older medieval Yiddish translations of Scripture that conflated rabbinic midrashic interpretation with Scripture itself led Lefin to retain the original Hebrew word of Scripture as a Hebrew-component word in his Yiddish translations as a matter of principle. In so doing, Lefin fulfilled the maskilic emphasis upon the centrality of Hebrew and the importance of *peshat* exegetically.[110] But Lefin's anti-Hasidic stance, born from the regional context in which he lived and worked, demanded a qualification of his own Hebraist and modern exegetical penchants. Lefin did not use the Hebrew-component Yiddish word as a translation of the original biblical Hebrew in cases of words burdened with ideological significance, such as the term zaddik, which appears sixty-five times in Proverbs and would likely be read by nineteenth-century Polish Jews not as "a righteous man," as a contextual translation would render it, but as "Hasidic rebbe." In all but three cases in his translation of Proverbs, Lefin did not retain the word zaddik, but utilized the Yiddish *erlikh* (honest) as part of his campaign against the new Hasidic leadership as, for example, in Prov 10:11, "The source of life is the word (lit. "mouth") of a zaddik, but the word of fools cloaks violence," which Lefin rendered as "*Akval fin leben iz dos moyl fin ayn* **erlikhn**, *ober dos moyl fun* **hultayis** *badekt rabunig*"/"The source of life is the word of an honest man, but the word of rogues cloaks violence," ensuring that the translation kept the meaning of Proverbs in the ethical realm.[111] He employed the same ideological strategy in his translation of Eccl 9:1, "For all this I noted, and I ascertained all this: that the actions of even the righteous (zaddikim) and the wise are determined by God," by *retaining* the word zaddik in the Yiddish in order to emphasize that God, not the Hasidic rebbe, determines the course

---

[110] Like his maskilic peers in Berlin, Lefin articulated the hope that Hebrew would be restored to its former glory in the messianic age. See the introduction to his Yiddish translation of Psalms, where he prayed for a swift restoration of the Temple, where the "Levites [will] sing their songs in *our sweet, holy language.*" Emphasis is mine. Cited in Katz, "Menachem Mendel Lefin of Satanów's Bible Translations," 130.

[111] [Lefin], *Sefer mishlei shelomo*, on Prov 10:11. Lefin's spelling of the Yiddish word for "honest" as *erlikh* not *erlekh* — as well as *fin* instead of *fun*, and *hultayis* instead of *hultayes* — reflects the regional dialect of Podolia.

of history and was the highest authority in the life of a pious Jew.[112] Moreover, Lefin's letter on the efficacy of using Yiddish for the Enlightenment of East European Jewry echoed his call in *Essai d'un plan de réforme* to censor kabbalistic works as a means to stem the spread of Hasidism. He complained that the feckless censors did not bar entry of "idolatrous and kabbalistic literary material (*schriftlichen Ausarbeitung von Schwärmerei und Kabbalah*) . . . from Beshtian libraries in Russia, which are even more dearly prized by their followers because they are [officially] forbidden."[113] Because Lefin's target audience, the Jews of Podolia now living under Austrian authority in the province of Galicia, showed no signs of attenuating their devotion to Hasidism in the early nineteenth century, his translation of Scripture into Yiddish became another salvo in his anti-Hasidic arsenal.

The Role of Yiddish in the Shifting Borders of Ashkenaz

Mendel Lefin's singularity with regard to Yiddish and Tobias Feder's attack upon it point to a major shift in the cultural boundaries of the elite Ashkenazic Jewish world inaugurated by the Enlightenment. By the 1740s, the Jews of Berlin, who were already speaking German, had begun to use High German instead of Yiddish as their written language, and German *maskilim* aspired to a complete linguistic replacement of the latter by the former.[114] Here it is important to emphasize that the *maskilim* of Berlin did not represent a majority of either Berlin or German Jewry. Regionalism within German Jewry persisted into the twentieth century, but Berlin was the center of Jewish modernization — both real and imagined — in the early nineteenth century.[115] The significance of the language polemic lies in its being a benchmark of the ideology of self-consciously modernizing Jews of Askkenaz who looked to the Berlin Haskalah as a model of modernization. The battle over Yiddish thus became a symbolic battleground in the definition of modern Jewish culture by German and East European *maskilim*. Both German *maskilim*, and East European *maskilim* oriented toward German culture,

---

[112] Shmeruk, "On Several Principles," 180–81.

[113] The Joseph Perl Archive, JNULA, 4° 1153/134a, 5b.

[114] Literary change lagged behind oral shifts, themselves subject to dialect influences well into the nineteenth century; Prussian Jews continued to write High German with Hebrew characters until the Emancipation Law of 1812. See Steven M. Lowenstein, *The Berlin Jewish Community: Enlightenment, Family, and Crisis, 1770–1830* (New York: Oxford University Press, 1994), 22, 46–48, and 85. See, too, Ya'akov Shavit, "A Duty Too Heavy To Bear: Hebrew in the Berlin Haskalah, 1783–1819: Between Classic, Modern and Romantic," in *Hebrew in Ashkenaz* (ed. Lewis Glinert; New York: Oxford University Press, 1993), 111–28.

[115] Werner J. Cahnman, "The Three Regions of German-Jewish History," in *German Jewry: Its History and Sociology* (ed. Joseph B. Maier, Judith Marcus, and Zoltán Tarr; New Brunswick, N.J.: Transaction Books, 1989), 3–14.

based their rejection of Yiddish on educational, cultural, and social grounds, surpassed only by a deep antipathy that was primarily aesthetic. Condemned as a dialect or impure linguistic mixture, Yiddish represented the antithesis of the maskilic ideal of *dabber tsahot*, a clear, orderly, grammatically correct, and elegant way of speaking and writing.[116] Yiddish was the literary and aesthetic antithesis of *Bildung* and embodied the insularity of "baroque Judaism" that adherents of the Haskalah sought to end by learning German.

Qol mehatsetsim reveals that Feder expected Lefin, who had drunk from the Mendelssohnian well, to return to Poland and pen German works in an effort to redirect Polish Jews away from their linguistic dependence upon Yiddish, German's poor and much-hated cousin. Lefin's turn to Yiddish thus represented a betrayal of all of the ideals of the Berlin Haskalah. Feder deliberately crafted his portrait of the author of *Melammed siah*, the only character capable of deciphering Lefin's Yiddish translation, as the antithesis of the decorous, bourgeois, modernizing German Jew:

> [Stationed] . . . at the beginning of the third level that is in Hell . . . [the author of *Melammed siah*] lies there with those who are unintelligible and steal their language from their neighbor.[117] He was a terribly old man, whose height was a span. Spittle ran down his beard, which descended to his navel. Hunchbacked and bruised in the testicles, he walks stooped over.[118] In his locks of wavy, raven-black hair were countless small and large insects.[119]

The Yiddish teacher's long, dirty beard, which Feder later contrasted with the clean-shaven faces of German speakers, is illustrative of the image of acculturated distance modernizing German Jewry had travelled from traditional Polish Jews. As we explored earlier with regard to Lefin's resistence to the assumption on the part of certain Polish reformers during the Four-Year *Sejm* that modernization of the Jews of Poland required a change in their pre-modern costume, by the last quarter of the eighteenth century the beard came to mark the Jewish male as either modern or "backward," German or Polish, enlightened or benighted. *Maskilim* were often characterized by traditional Jews as "Germans who shaved their beards and sidecurls."[120] In Feder's

---

[116] For this interpretation of *dabber tsahot*, see Miron, *A Traveler Disguised*, 43.

[117] Here Yiddish, seen as a thief of other languages, is pitted against German, pure and honest, untainted by influences from other languages.

[118] The bruised masculinity of the author of *Melammed siah* is further evidence of the imputation of femininity and weakness onto Yiddish.

[119] Friedlander, "Tobias Gutmann Feder," 292.

[120] Later scholars of Polish Jewry continued to use the beard as a marker of maskilic consciousness. See the comments in David Flinker, *Arim ve'imahot beyisra'el: Warsaw* (Jerusalem: The Kook Institute, 1948), 61. Jacob Shatzky, who argued for the conservatism of East European *maskilim*, described them as "*mitnaggedim* without beards and sidecurls." Both references are cited in Mordechai Zalkin, "The Jewish Enlightenment in Poland: Directions for Discussion," in *Qiyyum veshever: yehudei Polin ledoroteihem*, vol. 2 (ed. Israel Bartal and

Qol meḥatsetsim, Yiddish and beardedness were inextricably linked to the Jewish Enlightenment's new construct of the "baroque" East European Jew.
Despite his uncompromising rejection of Lefin's turn to Yiddish, Feder's
own satire illustrates the complexity of the dissociation of elite Prussian Jews
from Polish Jews in the course of the eighteenth and nineteenth centuries.
In *Qol meḥatsetsim,* Feder uses the word "Ashkenaz" twice, once to depict the
lands and language of Germany, when he describes Moses Mendelssohn as
"the father of the *Ashkenazic* [German] translators,"[121] and once to refer to
Polish Jewry, when the pathetic Yiddish teacher from Amsterdam ecstatically
declaims after reading Lefin's Proverbs, "I am an *Ashkenazi* [a Yiddish
speaker] in the unwalled cities, and in the cities of fortresses/With this
merit, I will grasp paradise, I will be a free man."[122] Feder's use of the word
"Ashkenaz" to mean both German lands and contemporary Yiddish-speaking
Polish Jewry highlights the ambivalence inherent in the disjunction between
the two communities, which, prior to the Enlightenment, had been naturally
joined.[123] Feder's linguistic Germanocentrism denied the linguistic and
cultural rupture that occurred between modernizing German and Polish
Jewries at the turn of the century, while his debasement of Yiddish and
pejorative depiction of Polish Jewry was part of the cultural distancing
engaged in by enlightened Jews in the German sphere from what would later
be called the *Ostjude,* the "Oriental" Jew, and, simply, the "Polish Jew."[124]

Israel Gutman; Jerusalem: Zalman Shazar Center, 2001), 406.

[121] Friedlander, "Tobias Gutmann Feder," 279.

[122] Ibid., 292.

[123] The halakhic division of *minhag Ashkenaz* (the customs of German lands) and *minhag
Polin* (the customs of Poland), marked by the Elbe River, anteceded the Enlightenment, but
the distinctions in customary law or folk practice of Judaism were still more similar than
different between medieval German and Polish Jews when compared to other Jewish communities. See Steven M. Lowenstein, "The Shifting Boundary between Eastern and Western
Jewry," *JSS* (new series) 4, no. 1 (Fall 1997): 61–78. See, too, the discussion in Joseph Davis,
"The Reception of the Shulhan 'Arukh and the Formation of Ashkenazic Jewish Identity,"
AJS Review 26, no. 2 (November 2002): 271, where the phrase *leshon Ashkenaz* was employed
in the sixteenth and seventeenth centuries to refer to the common linguistic bond between,
and hence shared halakhic destiny of, German and Polish Jews. According to Joshua Falk
(ca. 1550–1614), speakers of *leshon Ashkenaz,* whether German or Yiddish, viewed Isserles's
glosses on the *Shulḥan arukh* as authoritative.

   Israel Bartal has argued that Feder's assault on Lefin's translation of Proverbs into
Yiddish may be seen as an expression of a pre-Haskalah "consciousness of the bond with
Germany" among Polish Jews. In this reading, Feder's insistence on the primacy of German
as the language of the *maskilim* and the Jewish future is an attempt to preserve Polish Jewry's
connections to its past in medieval Ashkenaz (northern France and German lands). See
Israel Bartal, "The Image of Germany and German Jewry in East European Jewish Society
During the Nineteenth Century," in *Danzig: Between East and West* (ed. Isadore Twersky;
Cambridge, Mass.: Harvard University Press, 1985), 1–17, particularly page 7.

[124] This cultural distancing, continuing throughout the nineteenth and twentieth centu-

Lefin's stubborn insistence on the need for and effectiveness of writing in Yiddish indicated that he recognized and accepted the real cultural and linguistic gap that existed between the two communities. His turn to Yiddish, and its defense by Bik and others, also confirms that several East European *maskilim* conceived of the Haskalah as inspired by, but not blindly imitative of, the *Weltanschauung* of Berlin Jewry. They wanted to transform Polish Jewry in order to redirect it away from the baroque stamp of the early modern period and from the conscious Hasidic rejection of modernity. East European *maskilim* like Lefin, and later Bik, Rapoport, Krochmal, and Joseph Perl, did not seek to "improve" Polish Jews by thoroughly erasing their culture. Rather they strove to transform selectively those elements in the premodern Polish Jewish past that they believed stood in the way of modernization. Bik's letter defending Lefin's turn to Yiddish was explicit: Yiddish, not German, *was* the language of a glorious Polish-Jewish past, and thus ably suitable for Enlightenment purposes. Nonetheless, the aesthetic elevation of the languages spoken and written by Jews was an essential component of the maskilic program, affirmed by Lefin's frustration about the low level of oral and literary communication exhibited by his brethren living on the Czartoryski estates:

> It is . . . a special trait of the people of our faith in Poland, may God protect it [Poland], that they conduct their affairs rashly. They are accustomed to hurrying and being as curt [in their business affairs with others] as they are among themselves. Their casual conversations are brief and marked by the winking of their eyes and swinging gesticulations of their heads, hands, and bodies, etc. Therefore, most of them are very lazy with regard to writing and only do so under duress. Most of their letters begin with one accepted variant [of salutation], such as 'May abundant peace [be with you], etc.' and conclude with a similarly accepted closing, 'On account of urgent matters, I must conclude,' and they only get to the point of their request [somewhere] in the middle.[125]

Yet, for Lefin, linguistic transformation did not need to be linguistically exclusive. Whether written in German, French, Hebrew, or Yiddish, maskilic

---

ries, is due, in great part, to the ongoing migrations of East European Jews westward. The constant influx of East European Jews into German society and an upsurge in anti-Semitism in the late nineteenth century forced several sectors within German Jewry to reassess their own identities and relationship to a shared Ashkenazic Jewish past. The turn inward has been termed "dissimulation" by Shulamit Volkov and others. See Shulamit Volkov, "The Dynamics of Dissimulation: *Ostjuden* and German Jews," in *The Jewish Response to German Culture* (ed. Jehudah Reinharz and Walter Schatzberg; Hanover, N.H.: University Press of New England, 1985), 195–211.

[125] Mendel Lefin, *Liqqutei kelalim*, in N. M. Gelber, "Mendel Lefin of Satanów's Proposals for the Improvement of Jewish Community Life presented to the Great *Sejm* (1788–1792)," in *The Abraham Weiss Jubilee Volume* (ed. Samuel Belkin; New York: Shulsinger Brothers, 1964), 289.

works should be penned with the highest literary standards.[126] Lefin's goals as a translator in general and his commitment to writing in Yiddish in particular was instrumental, a tactic based on an assessment of the cultural and social reality of the audience, the masses of Polish Jewry, whom he hoped to reach. His turn to Yiddish was consistent with his belief that the success of the Haskalah in Eastern Europe depended upon adapting it to its regional and cultural context. Just as he had conceived of his efforts to thwart Hasidism as a preservation of an earlier rational form of pre-modern Polish-Jewish life, Lefin believed that the goals of the Haskalah could be articulated in Yiddish, the vernacular voice of Polish Jewry.

Like Mendelssohn before him, Lefin viewed the Haskalah as a modern intellectual posture that *maskilim* would spread through literary works of suasion and edification. All of Lefin's efforts presupposed that the masses of Polish Jews, having undergone the same epiphany in consciousness that the *maskilim* had experienced — in great part because of their exposure to maskilic works — would turn to the Haskalah voluntarily. Lefin's labors were not in vain if measured in terms of his influence on later generations of East European Jewish *maskilim* in whom his formulation of the Haskalah found an audience. But their engagement with Lefin's version of the moderate Haskalah took place in a radically different political context. The partitions of Poland in 1772, 1793, and 1795 divided the province of Podolia, thrusting residents in the southern and western region under Austrian sovereignty. The Polish-Jewish *maskilim* born under Habsburg rule would have to grapple with the demands of living in an absolutist state with its top-down political pressures to centralize authority and thwart local, communal privilege, the very external interventions into Jewish communal and cultural autonomy that Lefin had been suspicious of his entire life. Lefin's disciple, Joseph Perl, who saw himself as carrying the standard of his teacher's moderate legacy, now had to contend directly with the politics of a modernizing absolutist state, and with the concomitant heightened cultural stakes within Polish Jewry between those who embraced, and those who rejected, modernity.

---

[126] In a letter to Jacob Orenstein, the head of the rabbinical court in Lwów, Lefin expressed his surprise that Orenstein did not "feel the need for grammar in the Holy Language as with all other languages, for a distorted style disgraces the speaker and confounds the listener." See Mendel Lefin to Jacob Meshullam Orenstein, 1808. The Abraham Schwadron Collection of Jewish Autographs and Portraits, Mendel Lefin Papers, JNULA.

CHAPTER FIVE

AFTER PARTITION:
THE HASKALAH IN AUSTRIAN GALICIA

> While the majority of the men of your country [Galicia] have deviated
> from the blessed middle path (*ha'orah hamemutsah hame'ushar*), embrac-
> ing instead the imperfect extremes (*haqetsot mafsidei hashelemut*), you,
> God's chosen one, have not. [They have turned], on the one hand, to
> the Beshtians, who are ignorant, idolatrous false visionaries, and on the
> other hand, to the Karaites, who lack the authentic, luminous tradition.
> You, [in contrast,] have succeeded in guiding [others] on the middle
> path without arrogance. This is a sign of the suppleness of your mind
> and of the uprightness of your heart.[1]
>
> Isaac Samuel Reggio to Samuel Leib Goldenberg,
May 26, 1829.

Joseph Perl, arguably Lefin's most eminent disciple in Austrian Galicia,
endeavored to solidify the moderate Haskalah by founding and supporting
modern institutions, such as a school, synagogue, and archive, and by continuing his predecessor's campaign against Hasidism, in the very same geographic region, the southeastern Polish borderlands, that Lefin inhabited.[2]
Yet Perl's activism, although continuous with Lefin's program in many ways,
responded to a profoundly new political context, the dismemberment of the
Poland-Lithuanian Commonwealth, the creation of the new province of

---

[1] Published in *Kerem ḥemed*, 1 (1833): 70. Isaac Samuel Reggio (1784–1855), an Italian
Jewish participant in the Haskalah and *Hokhmat yisra'el*, the academic study of Judaism, in
Central Europe, used the word "Karaite," a term referring to ninth-century opponents of
rabbinic Judaism, as an epithet against modernizing Jews of his period who abandoned
rabbinic law. As he stated later in the letter, "The principle difference between them [the
modern Karaites] and us is the Babylonian Talmud, specifically the Amoraic teaching
regarding their methods of legal exegesis; they [the Karaites] have rebelled and raised their
voices against this issue." See 71. On the analogy between Karaites and nineteenth-century
reformers, see Ezra Spicehandler, "Joshua Heschel Schorr: Maskil and Eastern European
Reformist," *HUCA* 31 (1960): 201.
[2] Institutionalization marks the maturation of the Haskalah. See Shmuel Feiner, "The
Early Haskalah among Eighteenth-Century Jewry," *Tarbiz* 67, no. 2 (1998): 189–240; David
Sorkin, *The Transformation of German Jewry, 1780–1840* (New York: Oxford University Press,
1987); Immanuel Etkes, "The Question of the Precursors of the Haskalah in Eastern
Europe," in *Hadat vehaḥayim: hahaskalah be'eiropa hamizraḥit* (ed. Immanuel Etkes; Jerusalem:
Zalman Shazar Center, 1993), 25–44.

Galicia and Lodomeria, and its subordination to absolutist Habsburg rule. As I have argued, the partitions of Poland and the subsequent control of partitioned Polish lands by the absolutist states of Europe were the central historical events of the region at the end of the eighteenth and beginning of the nineteenth centuries. Perl's construction of Jewish modernity was indelibly shaped by the new form of the state that was now sovereign in the southeastern Polish borderlands.

While Lefin labored intellectually under the patronage of a Polish republican aristocratic family and within the context of the decentralized political structure of the Commonwealth, Perl worked within a spiritually and politically charged new environment. The partitions of Poland changed the political stakes of the Haskalah by subsuming the activism of the *maskilim* under the aegis of a centralizing tutelary state.[3] Perl appealed directly to both the Imperial Viennese and the provincial Galician authorities in his efforts to foster the growth of a modern and religiously observant Galician Jewry that was not steeped in mysticism. Although the Habsburgs took control of Perl's region in 1772 under Maria Theresa's reign, major transformations in the state's attitude toward its Galician subjects occurred only with the ascension of Joseph II to the throne as sole regent from 1780–1790. Joseph's commitment to reforming activism, which will be explored in detail below, both encouraged the efforts of modernizing Jews like Perl and directly threatened the autonomy of the traditional Jewish community. Joseph II's successors, rather than continuing his efforts to rationalize the administration of his lands, retreated from intervening into the social structure of Galicia, including the organization of the Jewish community, and bolstered the traditional features of the province. Restoration Austria's political conservatism thus thwarted the goals of the *maskilim*. This chapter explores Perl's undaunted efforts to make Galician Jews modern, with or without the alliance of the state.

Like Lefin, however, Perl's conception of the Haskalah was shaped not only by state politics. This chapter's assertion that the era of the partitions is the critical turning point in European Jewish history also highlights an internal dimension of the history of Polish Jews that was simultaneous with the dismemberment of the Commonwealth: the consolidation of Hasidism and the crystallization of its opposition. 1772, the year of the first partition, marks the promulgation of the first public ban against the Hasidim and the emergence of the *mitnaggedim* as a religious stream within traditional Ashkenazic Judaism.[4] Hasidism's spiritual conquest of most of Galician Jewry

---

3   On the Prussian case, see Sorkin, *The Transformation of German Jewry.*
4   Mordecai Wilensky, *Hasidim umitnaggedim: letoldot hapulmus shebeineihem bashanim 1772–1815* (Jerusalem: The Bialik Institute, 1970) and Mordecai Wilensky, "Hasidic-Mitnaggedic

by Perl's lifetime made the objects of his reformist energy impervious, if not hostile, to his work.[5] The chapter will investigate Perl's dogged lifelong campaign against Hasidism and focus on the way in which his anti-Hasidic polemic invigorated his critique of Ashkenazic Jewry's attachment to religious custom (*minhag*). Religious custom, more than Jewish law (*halakhah*), had created the stumbling block, Perl asserted, to his efforts to transform Polish Jewry. Perl's critique of Hasidism, like Lefin's, rested on his conviction that the new spirituality subverted the traditional rabbinic culture of Ashkenazic Judaism. As a moderate *maskil*, he sought to protect that culture from what he believed to be its further debasement. Perl's formulation of the Haskalah in Austrian Galicia can thus be understood only through an examination of the complementary and necessary dependence of the inner dynamics of Jewish culture with the host environment.[6] In other words, modernizing Jews like Joseph Perl shaped their conception of modernity in two contexts: the new politics of Austrian absolutism and the triumph of Hasidic piety among Polish Jews.

The Creation of Galicia

When Maria Theresa (reign: 1740–1780) participated in the first partition of Poland she claimed as Habsburg territory the lands of the medieval Galicia-Volhynian Kingdom, which the Hungarian royal house had considered part of its historic legacy since the thirteenth century. In 1772, the Habsburgs renamed these lands the Kingdom of Galicia and Lodomeria (the Latin form of Volhynia) and absorbed them as a province of the Monarchy. Military presumption defined the boundaries of the freshly-created province, which did not parallel the borders of the medieval Ukrainian-Ruthenian Principality-Kingdom of Halych-Volyn (Galicia-Volhynia). The new province actually included little of Volhynia, but incorporated the former Polish palatinates of Rus' (minus the northern half of the palatinate of Chełm), Bełz, and the section of Podolia west of the Zbrucz River (see map 2). The province's geographic area comprised 83,000 kilometers and 2,797,000 inhabitants. In 1774, the Habsburgs acquired Bukovina from the Ottomans, and formally

---

Polemics in the Jewish Communities of Eastern Europe: The Hostile Phase," in *Tolerance and Movements of Religious Dissent in Eastern Europe* (ed. Béla K. Király; New York: Columbia University Press, 1975), 89–113. An excerpt of the writ of excommunication from Vilna is reprinted in Paul Mendes-Flohr and Jehuda Reinharz, eds., *The Jew in the Modern World* (Oxford: Oxford University Press, 1995), 390.

[5] Jacob Katz, ed., *Toward Modernity: The European Jewish Model* (New Brunswick, N.J.: Transaction Books, 1987), 9.

[6] On this point, see Amos Funkenstein, "The Dialectics of Assimilation," *JSS* (new series) 1, no. 2 (1995): 1–14.

added its territory to Galicia in 1797. Maria Theresa did not participate in the second partition, but doubled the size of Galicia and Lodomeria after the third. The Napoleonic Wars represented a setback to the Habsburgs' imperial ambitions when, in 1809, a section of Austrian Galicia was lost to the French, becoming the Duchy of Warsaw, and later fixed at the Congress of Vienna, as the Congress Kingdom of Poland. The Tarnopol region, too, became Russian during the Napoleonic conflict, but was returned to Austrian rule in 1815. Cracow, an independent city-state since 1815, was formally subordinated under Habsburg rule only in 1847.[7]

Much like the eleven eastern provinces of the former Polish-Lithuanian Commonwealth (including Belorussia and eastern Ukraine) taken by Catherine the Great in the partitions, and later designated as the "Pale of Settlement," the new province of Galicia and Lodomeria was home to one of the most densely populated areas of Jewish settlement in Europe. Horst Glassl estimates that there were 225,000 Jews in Galicia in 1773;[8] other historians state that 260,000 Jews had become subjects of the Habsburg Monarchy by 1795.[9]

A comparison between the policies of the Russian and Austrian authorities toward their new territorial acquisitions and residents underscores the claim that the form of state, not a preoccupation with the Jews themselves, was the most decisive factor informing the legislation or government edicts regarding the Jewish community. The creation of the Pale of Settlement, although viewed by most traditional Jewish historiography as an act of anti-Jewish geographic restriction was, as Richard Pipes has shown, continuous with previous Russian legislation regarding the Jews. Catherine the Great issued an order in 1772 affirming prior privileges for the Jewish community now under her authority to continue living where they had always lived and practicing the professions they had always practiced. Jewish requests to settle in the Russian interior, which had always been denied them, remained on the books, but Jews could move to "New Russia," the newly conquered areas around the Black Sea. Catherine's primary concern after the partitions of Poland was in augmenting her tax base through levies on her new subjects, whom she attempted to categorize based on socio-economic gradations.[10] As

---

[7]   Paul Robert Magocsi, *Galicia: A Historical Survey and Bibliographic Guide* (Toronto: University of Toronto Press, 1983), 92–94.

[8]   Horst Glassl, *Das österreichische Einrichtungswerk in Galizien (1772–1790)* (Wiesbaden: In Kommission bei Otto Harrassowitz, 1975), 191.

[9]   Arnold Springer, "Enlightened Absolutism and Jewish Reform: Prussia, Austria, and Russia," *California Slavic Studies* 11 (1980): 241.

[10]   For the traditional view of the "Pale of Settlement," see S. M. Dubnow, *History of the Jews in Russia and Poland* (Philadelphia: The Jewish Publication Society of America, 1916); Salo W. Baron, *The Russian Jew under Tsars and Soviets* (New York: Schocken Books, 1987); and

we saw earlier, Alexander I's Edicts of 1804 had minimal impact on the Jewish community in the Pale. There was no major change in the life of the Jews resident in Russian Poland until the ascension of Tsar Nicholas I and the beginning of universal military conscription of the Jews.[11] In contrast to the former Polish Jews now living in the Pale of Settlement, whom the Tsars (until Nicholas I) basically ignored, former Polish Jews living in the new province of Galicia and Lodomeria faced an activist absolutist state with a clear political agenda to centralize political authority under the Crown and with relatively more bureaucratic tools to effect its goals. While most historiography on the Jews of Austrian Galicia has emphasized the pernicious anti-Jewish sentiment of the new authorities, examination of Habsburg policy shows that the Jewish population of the southeastern borderlands constituted only one of many simmering political issues for the new authorities, including the explosive "peasant question"[12] and what would later be considered its "nationalities question:" how to rule over an ethnically, religiously, and nationally heterogenous population.[13] In contrast to its

Louis Greenberg, *The Jews in Russia: The Struggle for Emancipation* (New Haven, Conn.: Yale University Press, 1944), 8. For the revisionist view, see Richard Pipes, "Catherine II and the Jews: The Origins of the Pale of Settlement," *Soviet Jewish Affairs* 5, no. 2 (1975): 3–20.
[11] Michael Stanislawski, "Russian Jewry, the Russian State, and the Dynamics of Jewish Emancipation," in *Paths of Emancipation: Jews, States and Citizenship* (ed. Pierre Birnbaum and Ira Katznelson; Princeton, N.J.: Princeton University Press, 1995), 262–83 and Michael Stanislawski, *Tsar Nicholas I and the Jews: The Transformation of Jewish Society in Russia, 1825–1855* (Philadelphia: The Jewish Publication Society of America, 1983). See, too, Olga Litvak, "Authority and Individual in the Russian-Jewish Literature on Conscription" (Ph.D. diss., Columbia University, 1999).
[12] For the problem of the Polish (and Ukrainian) peasantry under partitioned rule, see Stefan Kieniewicz, *The Emancipation of the Polish Peasantry* (Chicago: University of Chicago Press, 1969), J. Leskiewicz, "Land Reforms in Poland (1764–1870)," *Journal of European Economic History* 1 (1972): 435–48, and Keely Stauter-Halstead, *The Nation in the Village: The Genesis of Peasant National Identity in Austrian Poland, 1848–1914* (Ithaca, N.Y.: Cornell University Press, 2001).
[13] In 1815, the Habsburg Monarchy, which stretched west to the border between Bavaria and Bohemia and between Tyrol and Switzerland and east to the border between Galicia and Russian Poland, included Germans, Poles, Lithuanians, Ukrainians (Ruthenians), Armenians, Wallachs, Magyars, Slovaks, Tatars, Karaites, Jews, Scots, and Italians. See D. Dombrovska, Abraham Wein, and Aharon Vais, eds., *Pinqas haqehillot. Polin: entsiqlopedyah shel hayishuvim hayehudiyyim lemin hivasdam ve'ad le'ahar sho'at milhemet ha'olam hasheniyyah, galit-syah hamizrahit* (Jerusalem: Yad Va-Shem, 1980), 10; Andrei Markovits and Frank E. Sysyn, eds., *Nationbuilding and the Politics of Nationalism: Essays on Austrian Galicia* (Cambridge, Mass.: Harvard University Press, 1982); R. J. W. Evans, "Joseph II and Nationality in the Habsburg Lands," in *Enlightened Absolutism: Reform and Reformers in Later Eighteenth-Century Europe* (ed. H. M. Scott; London: Macmillan, 1990), 209–19; István Deák, *Beyond Nationalism: A Social and Political History of the Habsburg Officer Corps, 1848–1918* (New York: Oxford University Press, 1992).
A "national triangle" of Poles, Jews and Ukrainians existed in the southeastern Polish borderlands now under Austrian rule, finding social and political expression in peasant

neighbor in the East, Habsburg policy in Galicia and Lodomeria strove almost immediately to cope with its new Jewish population. It did so, however, not as a result of anti-Jewish animus, but as part of a general policy to centralize its authority.

Absolutism and Habsburg Policy for the Jews of Galicia

I take as my starting point that absolutism defined the modernization of East Central European states. Absolutism meant the state's assertion of its authority as the *preeminent* authority in society, which directly conflicted with older forms of social and political organization, such as the ecclesiastical and noble orders. From the Thirty Years War forward, the state, often in the form of the Emperor or King, initiated policies to centralize and to bureaucratize its control over its subjects and to reduce its dependence on the nobility and Church. While orders came from the person of the King or Emperor, the abstract interests of the state were affirmed as superior to the leader's personal needs, expressed famously in Frederick the Great's dictum, "The King is the first servant of the State." The political processes of centralization informed the state's attitude toward the economy, the educational system, and the power of the Church. Culturally, a whole new host of ideas, such as the "felicity" or general welfare of its subjects and the "utility" of a particular policy for the benefit of the collective whole, accompanied the state's assertion of its authority. The political drive to utilize, even exploit, all of the Monarchy's subjects equally resulted in an implicit toleration of ethnic and religious difference, which, in turn, became ideological hallmarks of the Enlightenment.[14] Cameralism, the belief that national wealth and military strength were the key to a state's power, informed the policies of the

uprisings and contested elections throughout the nineteenth century, and literary representation in the works of the Hebrew writers Asher Barash and Samuel Joseph Agnon, both Jewish sons of Galicia. See John-Paul Himka, "Dimensions of a Triangle: Polish Ukrainian-Jewish Relations in Austrian Galicia," *Polin: Focusing on Galicia: Jews, Poles, and Ukrainians, 1772–1918* 12 (1999): 25–48 and Shmuel Werses, "The National Triangle: Jews, Poles, and Ruthenians in Eastern Galicia in the Stories of Asher Barash," *Gal-Ed* 13 (1993): 155–80.

14   There is a continuing debate among early modern European historians about which came first, absolutism or Enlightenment. Mark Raeff argued that the political transformations of absolutism produced the ideas of the Enlightenment, an ideological justification for the profound changes in society that absolutism had wrought. See Marc Raeff, "The Well-Ordered Police State and the Development of Modernity in Seventeenth- and Eighteenth-Century Europe: An Attempt at a Comparative Approach," *American Historical Review* 80, no. 5 (December 1975): 1221–43. For a critique of Raeff, see H. M. Scott, "Introduction: The Problem of Enlightened Absolutism," in *Enlightened Absolutism: Reform and Reformers in Later Eighteenth-Century Europe* (ed. H. M. Scott; London: Macmillan, 1990), 15.

absolutist state, which strove to unify civic life, trade, occupations, morals, and health under the overarching control of the central authorities.[15] While there were important distinctions among the absolutist policies of Maria Theresa, Joseph II, Frederick the Great, and Catherine the Great, all of them shared a commitment to top-down centralization of their control over society and to subordination of competing local sources of authority. Penetration of Enlightenment ideas infused the policies of the Habsburg and Prussian Emperors to a much greater degree than they did those of the Russian Tsars.

While absolutist centralism and control informed the policies of Maria Theresa, "enlightened" or "reforming" absolutism defined those of her son, Joseph II.[16] The terms "enlightened" and "reforming" connote the crafting of the state's policies in the spirit of the progressive, optimistic, and rationalizing trends of the European Enlightenments that valorized individual self-cultivation and morality (*Bildung*) while still professing a belief in an omnipotent and omniscient Creator and the just arrogation of power by one ruler.[17] Enlightened absolutism was not democratic. Rather, Joseph II strove to prevent the spread of revolutionary and democratic ideas of the French Revolution and endeavored to thwart social unrest through his own top-down, state-initiated juridical, educational, economic, and peasant policies. Joseph II's statecraft was indebted to cameralist theory, which advocated rationalizing and professionalizing the state's bureaucracy, creating a secular civil realm, and subjugating the clergy to its authority. Vienna under Joseph's sole rule was, in many ways, a paradigm for the centralizing, interventionist, tutelary absolutist state.[18]

The encounter between the state and the Jewish communal governing body, the kahal, with its broad local privileges that embodied Jewry's autonomous and privileged status, became the defining interaction in the transition from medievalism to modernity for Europe's Jews. As Salo Baron long ago argued, its corporate existence could not be tolerated in the modern nation-state.[19] The process of "emancipation," the granting of civic

---

15 On the term "cameralism," see Adam Żółtowski, *Border of Europe: A Study of the Polish Eastern Provinces* (London: Hollis & Carter, 1950), 71; Joachim Whaley, "The Protestant Enlightenment in German Lands," in *The Enlightenment in National Context* (ed. Roy Porter and Mikuláš Teich; Cambridge: Cambridge University Press), 113; Roy Porter, *The Enlightenment* (London: Macmillan, 1990), 29; Robert A. Kann, *A History of the Habsburg Empire, 1526–1918* (Berkeley: University of California Press, 1974), 173–77.
16 T. C. W. Blanning, *Joseph II* (Essex: Longman Group, 1994), 80.
17 Scott, "Introduction: The Problem of Enlightened Absolutism."
18 Lois C. Dubin, *The Port Jews of Habsburg Trieste: Absolutist Politics and Enlightenment Culture* (Stanford, Calif.: Stanford University Press, 1999), 8.
19 Salo Baron, "Ghetto and Emancipation," *The Menorah Journal* 14 (June 1928): 515–26 and Zosa Szajkowski, "Jewish Autonomy Debated and Attacked During the French

status, naturalization, national equality, and equal political rights to the Jews occurred in direct relationship to the state's transformation into a modern nation-state founded on the rule of law and informed by Enlightenment principles (religious toleration, secularization, scientific thought, reason, and individualism).[20] In the centralizing absolutist states of Central Europe, however, the kahal continued to exist throughout the nineteenth century, representing both an obstacle to modern state-building and a symptom of their incomplete modernization.[21]

Raphael Mahler (1899–1977), the Galician-born historian whose work on nineteenth-century Polish and Galician Jewry is still profoundly influential thus rightly focused on the relationship of the absolutist state to the formal Jewish community.[22] For Mahler, an avowed Jewish nationalist, the absolutist state's drive toward centralization, which required the dissolution of all local privileges, including the authority of the kahal, was a deliberate attack on the "national" component of Jewish life in Galicia. Positioning himself as a materialist historian against the dominant school of cultural and literary history represented by the Russian-Jewish historian, Simon Dubnow (1860–1941), Mahler asserted that the Haskalah represented the cultural expression of the rising Jewish bourgeoisie and Hasidism that of the oppressed Jewish masses.[23] As a proponent of Ber Borochovian Zionism, a variant of Marxist-Zionism, Mahler sought to uncover the "true" teleological forces

---

Revolution," in *Jews in the French Revolutions of 1789, 1830, and 1848* (New York: KTAV, 1970), 576–91.

[20] Pierre Birnbaum and Ira Katznelson, "Emancipation and the Liberal Offer," in *Paths of Emancipation: Jews, States, and Citizenship* (ed. Pierre Birnbaum and Ira Katznelson; Princeton, N.J.: Princeton University Press, 1995), 4–23.

[21] The organized Jewish community also continued to exist in France, the model for full political equality, albeit in an attenuated form and supervised by the state. See Phyllis Cohen Albert, *The Modernization of French Jewry: Consistory and Community in the Nineteenth Century* (Hanover, N.H.: Brandeis University Press, 1977).

[22] Raphael Mahler, *Hasidism and the Jewish Enlightenment: Their Confrontation in Galicia and Poland in the First Half of the Nineteenth Century* (Philadelphia: The Jewish Publication Society of America, 1985).

[23] For his critique of Dubnow, see Raphael Mahler, *A History of Modern Jewry, 1780–1815* (New York: Schocken Books, 1971), xi–xii. Mahler believed that Hasidism and Haskalah were dialectical opposites, representing fundamental contradictions in the socio-economic foundations of Polish-Jewish society. Hasidism was the ideological manifestation of the disenfranchised, Jewish petty bourgeoisie that was still dependent upon the feudal economy. In contrast, the Haskalah movement, "in its political view and *Weltanschauung . . .* adhered to the ruling absolutism" and its "progressiveness . . . [could be] measured by the degree of progressiveness of the bourgeoisie, the class that carried on the struggle against social and political feudalism." See Eugene Orenstein's introduction to Mahler, *Hasidism and the Jewish Enlightenment*, xiv–xvi. See, too, Immanuel Etkes, "The Study of Hasidism: Past Trends and New Directions," in *Hasidism Reappraised* (ed. Ada Rapoport-Albert; London: The Littman Library of Jewish Civilization, 1996), 449.

within history that would lead to the liberation of Diaspora Jewry from the tutelage of the Gentile state.[24] He therefore excoriated the loyalty of the *maskilim* to the non-Jewish state, whether Polish, Russian, Austrian, or German. Although the political allegiance of the *maskilim* to the absolutist state was an inexorable necessity of scientific Marxism's reading of history, Mahler's ideological commitments to Jewish "autoemancipation" meant that he anathematized their activism as opportunistic toadyism.

More recently, David Biale, continuing in Mahler's nationalist tradition, argued that the *maskilim* "glorified" the modern state and harnessed themselves to its power as they made a bid to replace the traditional leadership of the Jewish community (the lay leaders of the kahal and the rabbinic authorities). While Biale correctly noted that many *maskilim* evoked the rabbinic dictum, *dina dimalkhuta dina* ("the law of the land [the Gentile hosts] is the law") as a rationale for their political allegiance to the politics of absolutism,[25] his interpretation, like Mahler's before him, is problematic for several reasons. First, it anachronistically projects a nineteenth- and twentieth-century nationalist agenda onto the whole of Jewish history. Second, it posits the political powerlessness of the medieval Jewish community as a strawman against whom the *maskilim* battled. As Ismar Schorsch has persuasively argued, medieval Jewry was not confined to a non-political existence characterized by oppression, defamation, persecution, and martyrdom.[26] Rather, the stewards of the Jewish community employed a whole host of strategies, including knowledgeable and sophisticated intercession, tax negotiation, and well-positioned bribery, to assure the security of their people. Third, it limits the Haskalah to its politics, diminishing the cultural dimensions of its vision of Jewish life in the modern period. The etatism of the *maskilim* of Galicia, including that of Joseph Perl, is inarguable, but it was only one component in their efforts to transform Galician Jewry. In other words, the ideas of the Haskalah should not be reduced to the ways the ideology of the

---

[24]   On Ber Borochov, see Mitchell Cohen, *Zion and State: Nation, Class and the Shaping of Modern Israel* (New York: Columbia University Press, 1992). For a critique of Marxist approaches to "enlightened absolutism," see Scott, "Introduction: The Problem of Enlightened Absolutism," 14.

[25]   David Biale, *Power and Powerlessness in Jewish History* (New York: Schocken Books, 1986), particularly Chapter Four, "Absolutism and Enlightenment." In its original Talmudic context (*b. Nedarim 28a, b. Baba Kamma 113ab*), the dictum referred specifically to issues related to taxation, but was adduced to express various political postures toward Gentile authority in subsequent Jewish history. See Gerald Bildstein, "A Note on on the Function of 'The Law of the Land is the Law'," *Jewish Journal of Sociology* 15 (1973): 213–19.

[26]   Ismar Schorsch, "On the Political Judgment of the Jew," in *From Text to Context: The Turn to History in Modern Judaism* (Hanover, N.H.: Brandeis University Press, 1994), 118–32. Schorsch's interpretation owes much to Salo Baron's critique of this characterization of medieval Jewry as "lachrymose." See Baron, "Ghetto and Emancipation."

maskilim and their relationship to the non-Jewish state did or did not thwart Jewish national self-awareness.[27]

Habsburg administration of the new province began officially in December 1773, but Empress Maria Theresa had already initiated her rule through the creation of fifty-nine administrative districts (*Bezirke*) within six regions (*Kreise*). The Crown directly administered the province from Vienna and installed provincial governing councils (*Gubernium*) that *Kreise* officials oversaw. Such state activism was necessary given the unwillingness of Galicia's noble class, Poles all, to submit at this early stage to Viennese rule. The *Kreise* and *Bezirke* appointees supervised the judicial and administrative matters of the manorial estates that dominated Galicia's socio-economic landscape. Vienna appointed a governor of the province to be its first bureaucratic address and in 1776 the office of the governor was given control over all departments of provincial authority. Maria Theresa named Count Auersperg as provincial governor in 1774 and he served until 1780. Centralization of authority continued in 1782, when the financial and administrative authorities of Bohemia (which included Galicia, Moravia, and Silesia) were merged into the United Bohemian-Austrian Court Chancery.[28]

On July 16, 1776, Empress Maria Theresa promulgated the Galician Jewish Ordinance (*Galicienjudenordnung*) in order to begin formal rule of her realm's new Jewish subjects. Personally, Maria Theresa vacillated between her Counter-Reformation religious animus against the Jews, which resulted in the expulsion of the Jews from Prague in 1744–1745, and mercantilist aspirations that sought to exploit the Jews economically.[29] In Galicia, subordination of the Jewish community defined her statecraft. The Ordinance divided the Jewish community into six regions that corresponded to the *Kreise*. It reaffirmed medieval Jewish privileges, e.g. self-government and

---

[27] Yet historiography has its own inner dialectic. For a contemporary critique of the preoccupation with the ideology of the Haskalah, see Mordechai Zalkin, *Ba'alot hashaḥar: hahaskalah hayehudit ba'imperyah harusit bame'ah hatesha-esreh* (Jerusalem: Magnes Press, 2000) and Mordechai Zalkin, "The Jewish Enlightenment in Poland: Directions for Discussion," in *Qiyyum veshever: yehudei Polin ledoroteihem*, vol. 2 (ed. Israel Bartal and Israel Gutman; Jerusalem: Zalman Shazar Center, 2001), 391–413.

[28] Samuel T. Myovich, "Josephism at its Boundaries: Nobles, Peasants, Priests and Jews in Galicia, 1772–1790" (Ph.D. diss., Indiana University, 1994), particularly Chapter Two.

[29] Robert S. Wistrich, *The Jews of Vienna in the Age of Franz Joseph* (New York: Oxford University Press, 1990), 15. The conflict between Maria Theresa's values meant that in Trieste, the Habsburg port on the Adriatic, mercantilist considerations overruled her staunch rejection of the principle of civic toleration of the Jews. On April 19, 1771, she extended to Triestine Jewish merchants an exceptional privilege, for which they paid handsomely, to live, work, and form a Jewish community in the city, civic toleration by any other name. See Dubin, *The Port Jews of Habsburg Trieste*, 41–63.

communal autonomy, but also introduced a greater measure of government supervision than under Polish rule, including the creation of a Jewish Directorate (*General-Directorate*) that was to be the collective representative of Galician Jewry to Vienna. The Jewish Directorate, comprised of a chief rabbi (*Landesrabin*) and six elders, was to oversee the merging of smaller Jewish communities into larger ones, and to supervise their financial transactions, particularly issues related to kahal indebtedness. The Imperial election commission supervised the election of the chief rabbi, who was elected by twelve sages (two from each *Kreis*) and six delegates (one from each *Kreis*) who had taken an oath that they were not related to the candidates. Three names were then sent to the Empress, who made the final selection. The chief rabbi's jurisdiction was both religious, which in and of itself meant all matters related to Jewish life, and administrative.[30]

Maria Theresa's subordination of the power of local Jewish authorities, whether economic or spiritual, to the rule of the state, paralleled her general policy toward all local privileges, including Christian religious education.[31] The Empress's desire to create a uniform set of educational requirements for her populace was encouraged in July 1773, when Pope Clement XIV dissolved the Society of Jesuits, freeing up monies and property for the state. Maria Theresa received roughly thirteen million florins of income to bolster her educational reform efforts, which she spurred by the creation of a new school commission comprised of enlightened thinkers and reform Catholics. On December 6, 1774, she promulgated a school edict, the *Allgemeine Schulordnung*, endeavoring to make elementary education compulsory for her vast population. Under the personality of Johann Ignaz Felbiger, the Habsburgs embarked on a broad campaign to instill in their subjects loyalty to the state as the embodiment of the best values of the Church. Uniformity of instruction throughout Habsburg lands was the goal. In 1776, the school commission created a network of *Normalschule*, most of which were established in former Jesuit *gymnasia*, whose graduates were intended to fill the ranks of teachers for newly created primary schools. By 1779, 546 of them were teaching in Viennese and Lower Austrian primary schools. While universal literacy in German was a goal of the school reform, the Monarchy's linguistic diversity was an impediment to the school reform's goal of universal literacy. In 1780, the Court Chancellory conceded that Polish might still be used to "instill religion and morality" in Galicia.[32] Educational

---

30 Glassl, *Das österreichische Einrichtungswerk*, 196–202.

31 H. M. Scott, "Reform in the Habsburg Monarchy, 1740–1790," in *Enlightened Absolutism: Reform and Reformers in Later Eighteenth-Century Europe* (ed. H. M. Scott; London: Macmillan, 1990), 145–87, particularly 161–167.

32 James Van Horn Melton, *Absolutism and the Eighteenth-Century Origins of Compulsory Schooling in Prussia and Austria* (Cambridge: Cambridge University Press, 1988), 225.

reform of the Jewish community of Galicia would also be addressed by Vienna, as we shall see below, but with less success. Because Maria Theresa's primary interest in the Jews was economic, to assure that they continued to provide much-needed tax revenue from the poor province, she increased taxes on meat, candles, marriage, and toleration under her rule. Despite the state's incipient intervention in local Jewish privilege, little else changed in the lives of Galician Jews under her reign.[33]

The ascension of Joseph II as sole regent in 1780 marked the beginning of a concerted Habsburg effort to reform the social structure of the province from above and center. His policy toward Galician Jewry was part of an overarching commitment to integrate the Jewish community throughout the Monarchy, an effort embodied in a series of edicts, known as the *Toleranz-patente* (October 18, 1781, Bohemia; December 15, 1781, Silesia; January 2, 1782, Lower Austria; February 3, 1782, Moravia; March 31, 1783, Hungary; May 7, 1789, Galicia). Joseph II sought to incorporate the Jewish community into the Monarchy by subsuming Jewish law under the civil law of the state, redirecting the economic behavior of the Jews away from lease-holding and trade and toward agricultural and artisanal crafts, and broadening the educational program in Jewish schools. Jewish schools were required to use German, since 1784 the official state language, and to provide instruction of secular subject matter, such as arithmetic and geography, necessary for participation in civil society.[34] The edicts embodied Joseph II's activist politics, which sought to strengthen and modernize the state by dissolving all prior medieval corporate privileges and institutions in order to make the peoples of the Monarchy "useful" and loyal subjects. Despite the overarching general goals that informed all of the edicts, however, each edict was shaped to suit the province or city for which it was intended, and requires a specific investigation.[35]

Galicia posed very specific and difficult obstacles for the Emperor that caused a delay in the promulgation of the province's edict. Pervasive social problems characterized the region. Over seventy percent of the province's

---

[33] Springer, "Enlightened Absolutism" and Dombrovska, Wein, and Vais, *Pinqas haqehillot,* 13.

[34] Artur Eisenbach, *The Emancipation of the Jews in Poland, 1780–1870* (ed. Antony Polonsky and trans. Janina Dorosz; London: Basil Blackwell, 1991), 55, Mahler, *Hasidism and the Jewish Enlightenment,* 3–6, and Raphael Mahler, *Divrei yemei yisra'el* (Rehavia: Worker's Library, 1956), 1:69–71. The *Toleranzpatent* (Edict of Toleration) issued for Lower Austria on January 2, 1782 is the edict most often cited in the historiography on Habsburg Jewry. Translated excerpts of it can be found in Paul Mendes-Flohr and Jehuda Reinharz, *The Jew in the Modern World,* 36–40. See, too, Blanning, *Joseph II,* 70–72.

[35] See Dubin, *The Port Jews of Habsburg Trieste,* 72, on this point. For the dismayed reaction of some members of Triestine Jewry, for whom the official edicts represented a curtailment of their privileges, see 143–48.

2,000,000 inhabitants were enserfed peasants required to perform labor duties (*robot*) for the nobility, to whom they were completely subject. Noble privilege dictated the ability of a serf, who could be bought, sold, or leased at the noble's discretion, to marry and pursue a trade. The grain-based manorial system resulted in the laws known as *propinacja*, which required peasants to purchase alcohol distilled in noble breweries and led to widespread alcohol abuse.[36] The province was also home to a larger, poorer, and more traditional Jewish population than all the other Habsburg territories combined. Vienna's efforts in Galicia focused on reforming the productive relations in the countryside in order to stimulate the development of cities, trade, and manufacture, and to make the province more productive and its residents more useful to the state as a whole.[37]

In 1782, after several trips to the new province, Joseph II reorganized Galicia, raising the number of *Kreise* to eighteen from six, hopeful that the new structure would give the state more control over the region, particularly over the noble manors (*dominia*).[38] Austrian legislation soon replaced the Polish system, curtailing noble privilege. Their local parliaments (*dietines*) were abolished and the much-vaunted "equality" cherished by the Polish nobility was challenged by their designation into two separate estates, magnates and gentry. What little burgher influence existed was impeded when the Habsburgs removed their urban councils. The Imperial Governor (*Gubernator/Naczelnik*), located in Lemberg (formerly Polish Lwów), the administrative center of the province, was now its official central authority. These administrative and legal reforms were motivated by Joseph II's centralizing aims. His policies on church-state relations and religious toleration were informed by his Enlightenment commitments.[39]

On May 27, 1785, the Emperor issued a provisional general edict for Galician Jewry (*Judensystem in Galizien*).[40] The new law sought to dissolve

---

[36] Myovich, "Josephism at its Boundaries," 93–100.

[37] Joseph's first act in the province was the issuance of a circular in the spirit of Christian Wilhelm Dohm's *Über die bürgerliche Verbesserung der Juden* (Berlin, 1781), which urged the economic productivization of the Jewish community, its "uplift" and "improvement" through secular education and Germanization, and which hindered Jewish migration to the western lands of the Empire. This constricted view of the utility of Joseph II's Jewish subjects would subsequently change. See Myovich, "Josephism at its Boundaries," 249.

[38] On Joseph II's visits to Galicia, in 1773, 1780, 1783 and 1786, see Derek Beales, *Joseph II: In the Shadow of Maria Theresa, 1741–1780* (Cambridge: Cambridge University Press, 1987), 301–02, 359–66.

[39] Magocsi, *Galicia*, 94 and Scott, "Reform in the Habsburg Monarchy."

[40] Joseph Karniel argues that the 1785 legislation was not actually a *Patent*, which would have removed restrictions, but an *Ordnung* that extended privileges to the Jews equivalent to those held by other subjects. The Jews of Galicia were never subject to the discriminations applicable to the Jewries in the western part of the Empire. See Joseph Karniel, "Das Toleranzpatent Kaiser Joseph II. für die Juden Galiziens und Lodomeriens," *Jahrbuch des Instituts*

medieval Jewish privileges in order to subordinate the Jewish community under the authority of the centralizing state. Toward these ends, Joseph II eliminated Maria Theresa's Jewish Directorate, subjecting the rabbinate and its scribes and courts to the state's control. The provisional law reformed the tax structure toward a more progressive, less onerous burden, but nonetheless maintained special taxes for the Jews, forbade peddling, and encouraged them to work in agriculture.[41] The provisional edict also attempted to redirect Jewish economic behavior away from the professions, leasing, liquor distillation, and tavern keeping, which had defined the economic interdependence of the Jewish community and their Polish noble hosts for centuries.[42] The edict's fourth paragraph expressed Joseph II's bald economic agenda:

> In order to stimulate Galician Jewry toward agriculture and other useful crafts and occupations, freedom to purchase land and pursue trade will be granted. Those who lease or buy land are permitted during the first three years to employ qualified Christian workers, from whom they can acquire agricultural knowledge. Those Jews who assiduously pursue useful crafts should not be hindered in their work and trading of guild products if they contribute their share to these guilds as Christians do.[43]

Standardizing the language of his administration became critical to Joseph II's cameralist aims because no centralized authority could function effectively without a common language. Paragraph five of the provisional legislation for Galicia demanded that Jewish businessmen and shopkeepers maintain all their books and registers in German or Polish (a temporary concession to the dominant vernacular of the province) and forbade their extending credit according to past Jewish business practices and credit customs.[44] Disseminating German as the official state language became policy and, in turn, informed Joseph II's educational goals in the official edict, issued four years later, on May 7, 1789.

---

für deutsche Geschichte 11 (1982): 55–91, particularly 55.

[41]   Karniel, "Das Toleranzpatent Kaiser Joseph II." and Myovich, "Josephism at its Boundaries," 262–69. Joseph II had visited Karaite settlements in Poland and Crimea and viewed their subsistence from agriculture as a model for a new Jewish economic profile. In *Bohen tsaddiq* (*The Test of the Righteous*), the sequel to Perl's anti-Hasidic novel, *Megalleh temirin* (*Revealer of Secrets*), the protagonist Ovadiyah ben Pesakhiyah discovers a Jewish agricultural paradise in New Russia and Crimea. See [Joseph Perl], *Bohen tsaddiq* (Prague, 1838), 98–119.

[42]   For example, Jacob Leczinski calculated that of a population of 3,690 in Żytomierz in 1789, 39.1 percent of the Jewish population, which comprised 23.9 percent of the population as a whole, was engaged in tavern keeping. Jacob Leczinski, "The Condition of Ukrainian Jewry at the End of the Eighteenth and the Beginning of the Nineteenth Centuries," *He'avar* 7 (1960): 6–14.

[43]   Published in Karniel, "Das Toleranzpatent Kaiser Joseph II.," 72.

[44]   Ibid.

The 1789 Edict of Toleration

Habsburg policy toward the Jews of Galicia as embodied in the Edict of Toleration for Galicia was first and foremost informed by its general etatist aims; parity and utility were the guiding principles of Joseph II's reform efforts toward the Jews, the Roman Catholic and Eastern Churches, the nobility, burghers, and peasants. The Emperor was quoted as saying, "National and religious differences must not make the slightest difference in all this and all must feel themselves to be brothers in a single monarchy, all striving to be useful to each other."[45] While the Galician provincial authorities, embodied by the Galician Court Chancellory that represented noble interests, resisted Vienna's effort to equalize the privileges and duties of the Jews, the final version of the edict reflected Joseph II's enlightened principles.[46] Its preamble stressed parity between the state's treatment of Jew and Christian, and emphasized the desire to remove any legal distinction (*Unterschied*) between Christian and Jewish subjects. It claimed as its aim the bestowal of "all of the benefits and privileges" (*alle Begünstigungen und Rechte*) enjoyed by other subjects upon the Jews and to regard them "in the same way as other subjects."[47] The edict outlined the state's cameralist expectations in the following areas of public life: religion, education, communal organization, population levels, economic behavior, political and legal authority within the Jewish community, and duties toward the state.

The very first paragraph under the section on Religion affirmed the "free and unhindered practice of [the Jewish] religion provided [it was] not in conflict with the state's law." However, the independent communal autonomy of the Jews, embodied in the Jewish municipality with its extensive internal administration that guaranteed the autonomy of Judaism as defined by the traditional rabbinate, could not but conflict with the state's centralizing aims. Subsequent paragraphs abolished the kahal rabbinate and

---

[45] Cited in Blanning, *Joseph II*, 59. On Joseph II's debt to natural law theories as the basis of his reformist policies, see Scott, "Reform in the Habsburg Monarchy."

[46] The edict for Galicia affected the largest Jewish community in Europe. Its neglect in the historiography is part and parcel of the preoccupation with the stunning full political emancipation gained by French Jewry in 1791, the lingering imperialism of Russian historiography over Polish, and the general disregard for matters Polish in European historiography. See Piotr S. Wandycz, "Historiography of the Countries of Eastern Europe: Poland," *The American Historical Review* 97, no. 4 (1992 October): 1011–25.

Polish noble landlords in Galicia resented and opposed Austrian centralization that threatened their economic power, and strove to retain control over the peasants and Jewish administrators living on their lands. See Glassl, *Das österreichische Einrichtungswerk* and N. M. Gelber, "The History of the Jews of Tarnopol," in *Entsiqlopedyah shel galuyyot: Tarnopol*, vol. 3 (ed. Phillip Krongruen; Jerusalem, 1955), 41.

[47] Karniel, "Das Toleranzpatent Kaiser Joseph II.," 75.

stipulated that only the *Kreis* rabbis, representing the large regional cities, were to be authoritative. Jews living in smaller communities could be served by "religious servants" and cantors supervised by the regional rabbinate, whose salaries were to be standardized under the state. The regional authorities (*Kreisamt*) were to oversee the election of the regional rabbi. Itinerant preachers and cantors were not to be tolerated; private religious services could be held, but only with payment of a tax. By 1795, all of the regional rabbis were to know German.[48] From the Habsburg perspective, subordination and standardization of an official, state-sanctioned rabbinate was merely part of its overarching goal to dissolve all vestigial structures of feudal privilege. It had done the same with its Christian population in Galicia by circumventing the power of the Pope in Roman Catholic affairs and by bolstering the status of the Greek Orthodox (Ruthenian) Church through its dependence on state support. Habsburg enlightened reform was not anti-religious, although it was anti-clerical and interventionist; Joseph II believed in promoting religious values and confessional education in the service of the state.[49] Vienna viewed its efforts on behalf of the Jewish community to be an equitable quid pro quo of granting unhindered religious expression in exchange for the Jewish community's unequivocal commitment to the state's centralizing aims.[50]

The edict's section on education attested to Vienna's goals of making the Jewish community of Galicia useful to the state by creating a network of German schools modelled after the *Normalschulen*. Teachers literate in German were to translate the state's oaths of duty to the students, ensure that graduates knew German, and prevent marriages of those untutored in the state's language. Jews who wanted to teach in these schools were required to attend a regional teachers' seminary in Lemberg under the supervision of the state's education directorate. The establishment of these German schools for the Jewish community, and their subsequent failure, will be discussed below.

Jewish communal organization was now to be conjoined with the political communities, and Jews could be counted as members of those communities with their fellow Christians. Despite this erosion of the kahal's independence *de jure*, the Jewish municipality still raised communal taxes and provided for the community's social and religious needs *de facto*. Paragraphs 19 and 20 of the edict read:

---

[48]   Ibid., 75–76.
[49]   Myovich, "Josephism at its Boundaries," 137–94 and Springer, "Enlightened Absolutism," 244.
[50]   Blanning, *Joseph II*, 72–74.

The duties of the [communal] leadership are: to represent their communities when necessary, to speak in their names, to plead their cases, to worry about provisioning poor Jews, to raise the contributions for communal expenses if there is an unforeseen communal expenditure, to utilize the regional authority, and, overall, to take care of and handle that which aims at the welfare of the community. . . . Each community, according to the ratio of its power and assets, will designate a yearly loan of money or another benefit — confirmed by the regional authority — to the heads of the community. The poll taxes however are to be totally overhauled by them.[51]

In contrast to the historiographic assessments of these paragraphs of the edict as abrogating Jewish communal autonomy in order to erode Jewish identity,[52] comparison with the dissolution of the *va'ad de'arba artsot* (Council of the Four Lands) in the Polish-Lithuanian Commonwealth in 1764 and of the kahal in Russian lands in 1844 reveals a different interpretation. While King August Poniatowski dissolved the Council of Four Lands in mid-century, the municipal structure of Polish Jewry, the local kahal, continued to exist, which explains why the condition of the Jews' municipal govern-ment and civil status was so hotly contested during the Four-Year *Sejm*.[53] As Michael Stanislawski has argued, the dissolution of the executive agency of the Jewish community in the Pale of Settlement did not attack the "legal integrity and autonomy of the Jewish community." Until the Provisional Government emancipated Russian Jewry in 1917, most Jews continued to be recognized as belonging to their local Jewish communities.[54] The state's incursion into the autonomy of the Jewish community without the concomi-tant granting of full political rights in the context of the total dissolution of all pre-modern privileges meant that Jewish communal autonomy continued to exist. In Galicia, the persistence of a communal tax on the Jews, as well as the continuity of religious authority in the areas of marriage and divorce (which the 1789 legislation, as well as the earlier empire-wide *Ehepatent*

---

[51]   Published in Karniel, "Das Toleranzpatent Kaiser Joseph II.," 79–80.

[52]   On this point, see Myovich, "Josephism at its Boundaries," 204. For the view that Joseph II's 1789 legislation was designed to undermine Jewish identity, see Mahler, *A History of Modern Jewry*, 332; William O. McCagg Jr., *A History of Habsburg Jews, 1670–1918* (Blooming-ton, Ind.: Indiana University Press, 1989), 18–30; Stanisław Grodziski, "The Jewish Question in Galicia: The Reforms of Maria Theresa and Joseph II, 1772–1790," *Polin* 12: Focusing on Galicia: Jews, Poles, and Ukrainians, 1772–1918 (1999): 61–72.

[53]   Adam Teller, "The Legal Status of the Jews on the Magnate Estates of Poland-Lithuania in the Eighteenth Century," *Gal-Ed* 15–16 (1997): 61. On the debates in the *Sejm*, see Chap-ter Two. Eli Lederhendler, however, argued for the decisive shift in Russian-Jewish political life, and the emergence of the *maskilim* as filling a key leadership position in the rudderless Jewish community after the official dissolution of the Jewish municipality and the initiation of the Crown Enlightenment. See Eli Lederhendler, *The Road to Modern Jewish Politics: Political Tradition and Political Reconstruction in the Jewish Community of Tsarist Russia* (New York: Oxford University Press, 1989).

[54]   See Stanislawski, "Russian Jewry, the Russian State, and the Dynamics of Jewish Emanci-pation," 267–68.

maintained) illustrates the incomplete state-building inherent in the official edict.[55] Joseph II was an enlightened absolutist reformer, not a revolutionary, and the 1789 law for Galicia reflected his commitment to an evolutionary, top-down reform of society, which maintained many components of his *ancien regime*. In the late eighteenth century, Galician Jewry certainly faced a more activist state than when they resided in the Polish-Lithuanian Commonwealth or than did their brethren in Russian lands. Yet, although standardized and regulated by the state, the Jewish municipality continued to guide the official internal life of Galicia's Jews.[56]

The issues of population and economics were intimately connected and the edict strove to keep Galician Jews in Galicia while making them both more productive economically and reducing tension with the indigenous peasantry.[57] In contrast to the edicts for Lower Austria, Bohemia, and Moravia, the Galician edict did not strive to decrease the population of the Jews, and therefore rescinded the marriage tax entirely. The census of the Jewish population was to be conducted by the army, with the same standards that had been applied to the Christian population.[58] Freedom of movement within Galicia for Galician Jews was guaranteed, although emigration to and settlement in the province required proof that the newcomers would sustain themselves by agricultural production. An exit tax and documentation of the resolution of all debts was mandatory for those Jews seeking to leave Galicia. To maintain order, the holy grail of the absolutist state, all Jews were required to take surnames and "to maintain an accurate register in German of births, weddings, and deaths, in precisely the manner as these registers are maintained by the parishes of the Christian communities."[59]

The edict's economic provisions for Galicia's Jews illustrate the singular economic condition of the province. No restrictions were placed on Jewish involvement with trade and Jews could be equal members of guilds, as well as sell their products to Christians. But Jews were expressly forbidden to hold leases on taverns, noble properties, and mills. They could no longer lease a tenth (*Zehent*) of a manorial farm or hold the leases on market stalls, meadows, paths, and roads owned by the nobility. The edict's preeminent

---

[55] On the tax classes in the edict, see paragraph 22 in Karniel, "Das Toleranzpatent Kaiser Joseph II.," 80. On the *Ehepatent* (Marriage Edict), see below.

[56] As we have explored earlier, and as we will see below, Hasidism had sorely tested Jewish communal authority before the partitions and would continue to do so under Austrian sovereignty.

[57] Myovich, "Josephism at its Boundaries," 262.

[58] Karniel, "Das Toleranzpatent Kaiser Joseph II.," 80.

[59] Published in ibid., 81. On the metrical books in Russian-Jewish society as a source for the social history of Jewish marriage and divorce, see ChaeRan Freeze, *Jewish Marriage and Divorce in Imperial Russia* (Hanover, N.H.: Brandeis University Press, 2002).

concern, which it euphemistically referred to as "necessary for the welfare of Galicia's subjects," was the nexus between alcohol consumption, innkeeping, and the peasants. Although the nobility owned the lands, distilleries, and taverns throughout Galicia, the Jewish community had long been the middlemen administering this critical aspect of the economy. Weaning the peasants from alcohol consumption was a way to loosen the noble stranglehold on the province. Incapable of confronting the Polish nobility head on, the Habsburgs sought to weaken their economy by delimiting the permissable leases their Jewish administrators could hold. Paragraph thirty-two of the edict forbade Jews to hold leases on taverns and mandated that both the Jewish arrendator and the noble owner were liable for financial penalities should the law be broken. The third time the law was broken meant noble forfeit of the land. The only tavern-keeping permitted to the Jews was private.[60]

Although Galicia's edict, in contrast to those of the other Habsburg territories, did not prohibit Jewish involvement with trade, it nevertheless urged Jewish settlement on the land. While the regional authorities were to determine the number and location of the Jewish colonists, their "promotion toward productive labor," however, was to be at the expense of the Jewish community itself. Jews who could prove that they sustained themselves and their families from agriculture were exempt from paying the protection tax (*Schutzsteuer*).[61]

The edict strove to constrict the autonomy of the Jewish municipality (the kahal) and to subordinate the adjudication of political disputes to the authority of the state. This meant that a Jew, "like other subjects," was to bring a complaint of a political nature first to his local authority, second to the regional authority, and last to the Imperial authority. The complaint registered with the local authority could be in a provincial vernacular, but any higher political authority would only hear a petition addressed in German. The Jewish community as an administrative unit was not to be involved with any political disputes; the edict singled out the prohibition on rabbinic *ḥerem* as a means of Jewish political and social control. The state's courts, not the Jewish communal courts, were to adjudicate all legal disputes between Jews and Christians and among the Jews themselves. The Habsburg state's concern with the means of social control within the Jewish community contrasts with the benign neglect that characterized Polish magnate treatment of the internal politics of the kahal; the institution of *ḥerem* posed

---

[60] Karniel, "Das Toleranzpatent Kaiser Joseph II.," 82 and Gelber, "The History of the Jews of Tarnopol." The 1789 edict thus anticipated Tsar Alexander I's concerns with reducing Jewish control of taverns and distilleries in 1804. See Chapter Two.
[61] Karniel, "Das Toleranzpatent Kaiser Joseph II.," 87.

no threat to magnate authority, whose sole concern was to elevate the fees for the rabbinic office as much as possible. The Jews living on the private lands of pre-partitioned Poland could police themselves as they wished. Habsburg subordination of the judicial authority of the kahal was stipulated in the spirit of parity, to equalize the legal treatment of all the Emperor's subjects (according to social class); the principle of parity also informed the stipulation that no outward signs of difference in terms of specific dress and clothing for the Jews were to remain on any legal books. Only the rabbinate was to be permitted to distinguish itself by its costume.[62]

The last section of the edict, entitled "Duties toward the State," asserted that Jews were entitled to the same civil protection afforded to Christian subjects, in exchange for which they were equally bound by civil duties and particular payments. Now considered part of the general political communities in which they lived, the Jews were obligated, "like Christians," to provide services to the state, including building roads, supplying horses and cattle for the military, and securing labor for dam construction. By far the most important duty now mandatory for the Jewish community was military conscription, an issue with far-reaching implications for Jewish communal autonomy and life.[63] In recognition, however, of their special religious needs, Jewish recruits were kept together in purveying and transportation units, "where they can eat together communally according to their religious conceptions and customs," and consideration was to be given "not to press them to do any other work on the Sabbath than that which necessity demands and for which Christians are urged to do on Sunday and [Christian] holidays as well."[64] This religious consideration undoubtedly allowed the state to control the desire of those Jews who wanted to advance in the military, but also established the Habsburg army as a vehicle for Jewish integration in the nineteenth century.[65]

The desired key to the edict's success was not only the state's muscle, but the inner transformation of Galicia's Jews, their *Verbesserung*, regeneration, and improvement in the spirit of the tutelary absolutist's state's quid pro quo through education and linguistic uniformity. The 1789 edict required the Jews of Galicia, like other Habsburg subjects, to teach German in their schools, use it in their communal and economic registers, and master it in

---

[62] Ibid., 84.

[63] The most notorious case of obligatory military conscription of the Jewish community occurred in Russian Poland, in the Pale of Settlement. There, the state's quota for conscripts was filled by the Jewish municipal council itself, exacerbating pre-existing socio-economic divisions within and undermining the age-old cohesion of the Jewish community. See Stanislawski, *Tsar Nicholas I and the Jews*.

[64] Published in Karniel, "Das Toleranzpatent Kaiser Joseph II.," 84–87.

[65] Myovich, "Josephism at its Boundaries," 286 and Deák, *Beyond Nationalism*.

order to obtain a civil marriage certificate. To help effect his goals of making the Jewish community useful and productive subjects who employed the language of the state, Joseph II turned to Naftali Herz Homberg (1749–1841), a traditionally-educated Central European Jew who embraced educational reform as the key to the Polish-Jewish community's transformation.[66]

A student of Ezekiel Landau, chief rabbi of Prague, and graduate of traditional Central European yeshivot, Homberg received his enlightened education among the circle of early *maskilim* in Breslau, Hamburg, and Berlin. Homberg tutored Mendelssohn's son and contributed to his Hebrew commentary on Deuteronomy in *Netivot hashalom*. In 1782, Homberg moved to Vienna, and in 1787 he was appointed superintendent of the German-Jewish language schools in Galicia and assistant censor of Jewish books. Uncritical support of Habsburg cameralism distinguished Homberg's worldview. He founded 107 schools and classes in Galicia, including the teacher's seminary in Lemberg, which advocated a European education and condemned study of the Talmud. As assistant censor he drew up a list of Jewish books that should be prohibited, most of which were kabbalistic and mystical in nature. Homberg rejected the Herderian conception of nationalism that valorized subjective national folkways, traditions, and language,[67] including traditional Jewish messianic aspirations for the return of the Jews to the Land of Israel. Instead, he subscribed to the utilitarian conception of nationalism outlined in Joseph von Sonnenfels's *Über die Liebe des Vaterlandes* (1771), a programmatic essay describing the beneficence of the tutelary absolutist state that could stimulate the economy, help resolve the peasant problem, and be a catalyst for universal societal good.[68] The traditional Jewish prayerbook, with its frequent petitions for the end of the exilic condition, therefore also earned Homberg's opprobrium and a place on his list of censored books.

Homberg embodied the state's modernizing bureaucracy; he was clean-shaven, university-educated, and critical of local privilege that was an obstacle to centralization. Besides his educational role, Homberg also became the collector of the hated candle tax initiated in 1787 that required every

---

66   On Homberg, see Majer Bałaban, "Herz Homberg in Galizien," *Jahrbuch für jüdische Geschichte und Literatur* 19 (1916): 189–221; Ruth Kestenberg-Gladstein, *Neuere Geschichte der Juden in den böhmischen Ländern* (Tübingen: Mohr, 1969); Wolfgang Häusler, *Das galizische Judentum in der Habsburgermonarchie: im Lichte der zeitgenössischen Publizistik und Reiseliteratur von 1772–1848* (Munich: R. Oldenbourg, 1979); Michael A. Meyer, *Response to Modernity: A History of the Reform Movement* (New York: Oxford University Press, 1988), 152–3.
67   Carlton J. H. Hayes, "Contributions of Herder to the Doctrine of Nationalism," *The American Historical Review* 32, no. 4 (July 1927): 719–36 and Isaiah Berlin, *Vico and Herder: Two Studies in the History of Ideas* (New York: Viking, 1976).
68   On Sonnenfels, see Robert A. Kann, *A Study in Austrian Intellectual History from Late Baroque to Romanticism* (London: Thames & Hudson, 1960).

married Jewish woman to pay a fee for two candles per week, regardless of whether or not she could afford the levy. Charges of embezzlement of candle tax money forced Homberg to leave Galicia in 1802. He moved back to Vienna and became a censor of Hebrew books, although he never succeeded in gaining permanent residency there. His 1812 catechism, *Benei tsiyyon* (*Sons of Zion*), became the basis for the German exam required for a Jewish couple seeking to be married civilly, a caveat that remained on the books until 1918. Because of Homberg's efforts, the traditional Jewish community in Galicia feared Habsburg engagement with any of their privileges (communal autonomy, exemption from military service, a separate educational system) as a pernicious threat to their way of life. The schools originally under his authority were closed in 1806 because of the Jewish community's lack of attendance. Homberg's defeat in Jewish Galicia adumbrated that of Max Lilienthal's in Vilna in the 1840s, and underscored the ever-widening gulf between the values of modernizing German Jewry and their traditional brethren in Eastern and Central Europe.[69] Homberg's failure to gain the trust of the traditional Jewish community highlights the complexity of transforming a culture and society that had been thoroughly transfigured by Hasidism and rejected the activism of the centralizing state.

Joseph II's 1789 *Toleranzpatent* for Galicia embodied the optimistic ideals of reforming absolutism. The edict represented an effort to emancipate the Jewish community in Galicia *civilly* without the Monarchy's transformation into a modern nation-state that would necessitate the *political* emancipation of the Jews. Dismantling the Jewish corporation would have required a full commitment to reforming all of the Galician society, including emancipating the serfs, a radical social shift not yet on Vienna's agenda and vigorously opposed by the still-powerful Polish *szlachta*.[70] The kahal thus was left intact, although many of its functions were now subordinate to the state. Illustrative of the incompleteness of Habsburg state-building, which meant only a partial erosion of the social and legal boundaries between Jews and other subjects, was provision 50 in the edict that required Galician Jewry to continue paying a "protection" tax to the state, as well as a tax on kosher meat to fund its communal expenses.

---

[69] Meyer, *Response to Modernity*, 152. Tsar Nicholas I brought Lilienthal to Russia to head the government's educational reforms and was greeted with suspicion by both *mitnaggedim* and Hasidim. On Lilienthal, see Stanislawski, *Tsar Nicholas I and the Jews*, 69–96.

[70] On Joseph II's agrarian policy, see Scott, "Reform in the Habsburg Monarchy," 177–87. The Polish *szlachta* would pay dearly for their political intransigence. In 1846, Galician peasants erupted in a violent *jacquerie* against their Polish overlords, an event that prodded Vienna to proffer them emancipation in exchange for loyalty to the Crown.

The enlightened cameralist ethos of the edict foundered after Joseph II's death in 1790 and the radicalization of the French Revolution. His successors disavowed his reformist agenda and sought to maintain order in the province by a realliance with its conservative elements, the clergy and the nobility. Despite the state's abandonment of its optimistic efforts to create a rational, tolerant society subservient to a reasonable Crown, the forward-looking, confident ethos of Josephinian reform continued to guide those Jews in the Austrian partition of Poland who sought to harmonize modernity and Jewish tradition. Joseph Perl was the most articulate spokesman of that effort.[71]

Joseph Perl and the Moderate Haskalah

Joseph Perl was born in 1773 in Tarnopol, a private city belonging to the Sobieski family that became an important trade center after the partitions, to a family of wholesale wine merchants and kosher meat leesees. Given a traditional East European Jewish education, and married at 14, Perl's early years were characterized by study (he was supported by his father-in-law in the *kest* system typical of Ashkenazic Jewry) and apprenticeship in the world of business. Following in the footsteps of both his father, Todros, and father-in-law, Isaac Leib Atlas, Perl became a successful merchant, travelling to Pest, Vienna, and cities in Prussia, where he sold wine and other agricultural products. Perl was attracted to the ideas of the Haskalah, perhaps stimulated by his encounters with *maskilim* like Dov Ber Ginsburg of Brody (1776–1811), who had been involved with *Hame'assef* and was a personal friend of the *maskil* Judah Leib ben Ze'ev.[72] Ginsberg moved to Tarnopol for three years, during which time Perl expanded his traditional studies to include German, French, Latin, mathematics, history, natural science, and medieval Jewish philosophy, the curricular impetus for the turn to the Haskalah. In 1792, Perl already identified himself as a *maskil* when he visited the provincial rabbi, Shmuel ben Moses Pinhas Falkenfeld, at the home of Franczisek Koritowski (later the magnate owner of Tarnopol), and asked about Galician Jewry's lack of interest in the Jewish Enlightenment.[73]

---

[71]   Joseph Perl's handwritten copy of the 1789 edict, penned in maskilic German, is still extant. See the Joseph Perl Archive, JNULA, 4° 1153/101.

[72]   On the significance of Brody as a free trade city that stimulated the open exchange of both commerce and ideas, see Mahler, *Hasidism and the Jewish Enlightenment*, 31, Israel Weinlös, *Yosef Perls lebn un shafn* (Vilna: YIVO, 1937), 9–11, and N. M. Gelber, *Arim ve'imahot beyisra'el: Brody* (Jerusalem, 1955), 9–11.

[73]   Weinlös, *Yosef Perls lebn un shafn*, 7–9 and Gelber, "The History of the Jews of Tarnopol," 41–47. For the query to Falkenfeld, see the letter in Israel Weinlös, *Historishe schriftn* (Vilna, 1937), 811.

By 1809, Perl had begun his maskilic activities, travelling to Vienna to seek permission to found a modern Jewish school in Tarnopol. Well aware of Homberg's failure to win the sympathy of Galicia's Jews toward the state's and the Haskalah's commitment to modernity, Perl endeavored to shape his school in the spirit of the moderate Haskalah.[74] These early efforts were interrupted by the outbreak of the Napoleonic Wars, when Tarnopol and its region fell under Russian sovereignty. This change in political fortunes required Perl to shift his address for petitioning state support. Tsar Alexander I had created a new Ministry of Education in 1802, sharing with other enlightened autocrats of the period an interest in education reform.[75] The edicts of 1804 that grappled with the massive Jewish population in Russia resulting from the partitions included provisions regarding education, but the financing of any new Jewish schools had to come from the Jewish community itself.[76] As under the Austrians, the Russian government stipulated that the Jewish community use a vernacular language for instruction; "Germanization" was halted as Polish was restored as the language of the Tarnopol region. In 1810, the Jews of Tarnopol expressed their loyalty to the Russian Tsar in the synagogue, illustrating their acknowledgment of the new Gentile authority. No fundamental administrative changes occurred to inform Jewish life in this period and the Polish nobility was empowered to retain their social and economic control.[77]

Under the Russians, Perl continued his efforts to found a modern Jewish school. In 1812, he made a public speech announcing that he had obtained financial backing for his school from the Koritowski family. He also penned a memorandum to the Russian authorities articulating his critique of traditional Jewish education. The memo echoed the maskilic judgment of traditional Jewish education sounded by Naftali Herz Wessely (whom Perl mentioned by name) in *Divrei shalom ve'emet*, which the Prussian *maskil* had written in support of Joseph II's Edict of Toleration for Lower Austria. Wessely's pamphlet established the maskilic critique of traditional Jewish education as imbalanced, educating the Jewish child solely in "divine knowledge" (*torat ha'elohim*), which focused on Jewish law and behavior, at the expense of "human knowledge" (*torat ha'adam*), which was comprised of the whole

---

[74]   Homberg had established a school in 1788 in Tarnopol, Perl's city, but it, like his other schools, was closed in 1806.
[75]   By the end of Alexander I's reign, the Empire boasted six universities, forty-eight secondary schools, and 337 improved primary schools. See Nicholas Riasanovsky, *A Parting of the Ways: Government and the Educated Public in Russia, 1801–1855* (Oxford: Clarendon, 1976).
[76]   Shmuel Ettinger, "The Edicts of 1804," *He'avar* 22 (1977): 97–110, particularly clause six. See, too, Mordechai Zalkin, "Trends in the Development of Haskalah Education in the Russian Empire at the Beginning of the Nineteenth Century," *Zion* 62 (1997): 133–71.
[77]   Gelber, "The History of the Jews of Tarnopol," 43–45.

spectrum of secular studies (mathematics, geography, history, language study, rhetoric). *Divrei shalom ve'emet* urged the creation of a new cultural ideal within Ashkenazic Jewry to replace the valorization of the *talmid ḥakham* (the Torah Sage) with the moral man. In the pamphlet, Wessely insisted that *torat ha'adam* precede *torat ha'elohim* in the developmental education of the Jewish child; without the foundation of "human knowledge," the teachings of "divine knowledge" would be inaccessible and incomprehensible. An education shaped solely by *torat ha'elohim*, even though Wessely insisted it was ontologically superior to the teachings of *torat ha'adam*, would render the Jewish student both useless to his people and for participation in European civil society.[78] Guided by Wessely's formula for Jewish education, Jewish youth would be fully capable of integrating into modern Europe as productive, useful members of society without abandoning Hebrew literacy, knowledge and love of the Bible, or observance of Jewish law.[79] Wessely presented his program as continuous with traditional Jewish pedagogy, but its revolutionary transvaluation of the early modern Ashkenazic Jewish curriculum and its direct appeal to the Enlightenment's valorization of autonomous ethics and morality was met with swift opposition from traditional circles.[80]

Perl's memorandum described the *ḥeder* (lit. "room," the name for the traditional Jewish elementary school) as unnatural, morally problematic, educationally restrictive, and physically unhealthy for Jewish children.[81] Echoing Wessely's argument against Ashkenazic Jewry's exclusive focus on *torat ha'elohim*, Perl criticized the instruction in the *ḥeder* for its concentration on rabbinic law, commandments, and edicts, while neglecting the ethical education

---

[78] Naftali Herz Wessely, *Divrei shalom ve'emet* (Berlin, 1782), 3–5.
[79] On Wessely, see Lois C. Dubin, "The Social and Cultural Context: Eighteenth-Century Enlightenment," in *History of Jewish Philosophy* (ed. Daniel H. Frank and Oliver Leaman; London: Routledge, 1997), 636–59; Edward Breuer, *The Limits of Enlightenment: Jews, Germans and the Study of Scripture in the Eighteenth-Century* (Cambridge, Mass.: Harvard University Press, 1996); Etkes, "The Question of the Precursors of the Haskalah in Eastern Europe."
[80] On the controversy surrounding *Divrei shalom ve'emet*, see Jacob Katz, *Out of the Ghetto: The Social Background of Jewish Emancipation, 1770–1870* (Cambridge, Mass.: Harvard University Press, 1973), 65–68, 124–28, 151; Alexander Altmann, *Moses Mendelssohn: A Biographical Study* (Tuscaloosa, Ala.: The University of Alabama Press, 1973), 57–70, 142–60; Mordechai Eliav, *Hahinukh hayehudi begermanyah biymei hahaskalah veha'imantsipatsyah* (Jerusalem: The Jewish Agency, 1960), 39–51; Moshe Shraga Samet, "Moses Mendelssohn, Naftali Herz Wessely and the Rabbis of their Generation," in *Meḥqarim betoledot am yisra'el ve'erets yisra'el lezekher Tsevi Avneri* (ed. Akiba Gilboa and Oded Bustenay; Haifa: The University of Haifa, 1970), 233–57.
[81] Perl's memo is published in Philip Friedman, "Joseph Perl as an Educational Activist and His School in Tarnopol," *YIVO bleter* 31–32 (1948): 188–89. On maskilic criticism of the *ḥeder*, see Steven J. Zipperstein, "Transforming the Heder: Maskilic Politics in Imperial Russia," in *Jewish History: Essays in Honour of Chimen Abramsky* (ed. Ada Rapoport-Albert and Steven J. Zipperstein; London: The Littman Library of Jewish Civilization, 1988), 87–109.

so prized by the *maskilim*.[82] Its teachers, the much-scorned *melammedim* drawn from the poorest classes, were unprepared, immoral, and fond of corporeal punishment.[83] Their assistants were equally dreadful. The fecklessness of the *ḥeder* system led students, accustomed as they were to indolence and idle chatter, into the arms of the Hasidim. For Perl, as for many *maskilim*, East European Jewry's custom of early marriage was singled out for opprobrium as leading to early sexuality and stunted intellectual growth, often to the particular detriment of the male partner in the marriage. The *ḥeder*, concluded Perl, was particularly guilty of promoting this behavior and causing its deleterious results because it introduced Jewish boys to the Talmudic laws of marriage and conjugal relations while they were still developmentally immature.[84] Perl's acerbity toward the traditional *ḥeder* notwithstanding, his 1812 memo also took pains to distinguish his educational program from that of Homberg. The memo concluded that Homberg's schools, guided by teachers who were superficially enlightened (*afteraufgeklärt*), had been overzealous in their abandonment of traditional Jewish praxis and done more harm than good in the cause of modernizing Galician Jewry.[85]

Perl sought to establish his school in the spirit of the moderate Haskalah, in which Jewish tradition provided the foundation of the curriculum. Classes held in Perl's home began already in 1813, even before the erection of the school building. The school instructed children of both sexes between the ages of five and thirteen. First graders learned how to read German and Hebrew and understand the prayerbook. Writing in both languages, as well as the addition of Russian, mathematics, and written Yiddish, were introduced

---

[82]　Perl illustrated his debt to Wessely in a manuscript fragment for his Hebrew prose almanacs, *Luaḥ halev*, that he appended to the calendars he published between 1814–1816. Perl cited Prov 22:6, "Educate a youth according to his way, thus when he ages, it will not depart from him," the same biblical prooftext that Wessely used to urge the reform of traditional Jewish education. See Wessely, *Divrei shalom ve'emet*, 1. For Perl's citation, see the Joseph Perl Archive, 4° 1153/96a. On Perl's calendars, see Mahler, *Hasidism and the Jewish Enlightenment*, 149–67.

[83]　See Lefin's criticism of corporeal punishment in Mendel Lefin, *Sefer ḥeshbon hanefesh* (Lemberg, 1808), paragraph 18.

[84]　Friedman, "Joseph Perl as an Educational Activist," 134. For other maskilic critiques of early marriages, see Meir Letteris, *Nosafot leme'assef* (1784): 97–98 and Shimshon Bloch, *Shevilei olam* (Warsaw: Natan Schriftgisser, 1882), 18–21. See, too, David Biale, *Eros and the Jews: From Biblical Israel to Contemporary America* (Berkeley: University of California Press, 1997), Chapter Seven: "Eros and the Enlightenment;" Israel Bartal, "'Potency' and 'Impotency': Between Tradition and the Jewish Enlightenment," in *Eros, erusin ve'issurim: miniyyut umishpaḥah bahistoryah* (ed. Israel Bartal and Isaiah Gafni; Jerusalem: Zalman Shazar Center, 1998), 225–37; on the impotence of both the *ḥeder* and early marriage in the Vilna *maskil* Mordecai Aaron Günzberg's Hebrew autobiography, *Aviezer*, see Alan Mintz, "Banished from Their Father's Table": *Loss of Faith and Hebrew Autobiography* (Bloomington Indiana University Press, 1989), 25–29.

[85]　Friedman, "Joseph Perl as an Educational Activist," 137.

in second grade.[86] These children also began formal study of the Hebrew Bible, "according to the best commentary and German translation," a clear reference to Mendelssohn's translation and *Bi'ur*. The next class added accounting, Mishnah, and Talmud, as well as "religion and ethics" drawn from these traditional sources. Fourth graders studied the principles of business and agriculture, history, natural science, geography, aesthetics, and rhetoric, subject matters taken almost directly from Wessely's programmatic pamphlet. Perl's curriculum also encouraged higher Jewish learning under the tutelage of talented Talmudists for those students with aptitude. Polish, French, and Italian were also suggested as options for the students. Girls studying at Perl's school received a gendered curriculum, learning handicrafts deemed appropriate for homemaking, foreign languages suitable for interaction with Gentile society, and *tekhines*, the Yiddish prayers typical of the East European female library.[87]

The Russian governor, Ignacy Theils, granted Perl permission to build the school building and Perl himself helped to fund and oversee its construction. It was ready on Shavuot 1815, by which time, because of the new borders decided upon by the Congress of Vienna, Tarnopol was once again under Austrian rule.[88] The Austrian governor of the province, Baron Franz von Hauer, replaced Theils, who left Tarnopol on August 22, 1815. Simultaneously, Nachman Pineles, a local printer and friend of Perl's, and Jacob Neumann, the school's first principal, went to Lemberg to secure a

---

[86]   Perl shared with Lefin the disdain for Yiddish and the belief in its efficacy for enlightening Galician Jewry. He wrote a version of his anti-Hasidic masterpiece, *Megalleh temirin*, a parodic sequel to the tales of the Hasidic master, Nachman of Bracław (Bratslav), entitled "The Tale of the Lost Prince," translated Fielding's *Tom Jones*, and penned a historical novel, *Antigonus*, situated in the Second Temple period, all in Yiddish. Perl turned to Yiddish not only to caricature Hasidism in the Jewish vernacular of Eastern Europe, but also to create an alternative library for that public who, in Perl's words, "unfortunately, have nothing to read, particularly on the Sabbath and Holidays . . . and either violate the holy days or read irrational [Hasidic] chapbooks." However, Perl never published any of these Yiddish materials. The citation is from Chone Shmeruk, *Sifrut yidish: peraqim letoldoteihah* (Tel Aviv: The Porter Institute for Poetics & Semiotics, 1978), 257 and see, too, 234–260. If students in his school were to speak and read Yiddish, which they undoubtedly were, then Perl's curriculum endeavored to instruct them how to employ the language properly.

[87]   Vocational training was an essential component of the school to insure that graduates could be gainfully employed. Separate "rooms for industry" for both boys and girls were established. See Weinlös, *Yosef Perls lebn un shafn*, 19. On gendered expectations for East European Jewish girls in both Europe and the American Diaspora, see Paula E. Hyman, *Gender and Assimilation in Modern Jewish History* (Seattle: University of Washington Press, 1995); Shmuel Feiner, "The Modern Jewish Woman: Test Case in the Relationship between the Haskalah and Modernity," *Zion* 58, no. 4 (1993): 453–99; and my "Educating for 'Proper' Jewish Womanhood: A Case Study in Domesticity and Vocational Training, 1897–1926," *American Jewish History* (June 1988): 572–99.

[88]   Perl's work in education was recognized a year later by Tsar Alexander I.

permanent certificate for Perl's educational institution. Perl received permission to open a school from the Imperial-Royal School Commission in October 1815, with the provisions that it meet the province's educational standards. Because Perl had funded the school largely out of his own pockets, he hoped that the government, with its commitment to school reform, would help alleviate some of his financial burden and the school's debts.[89] He was initially disappointed with the state's response and drafted a financial plan for the school, which depended upon donating the school building and synagogue to the Tarnopol kahal, whose members in that period were sympathetic to Perl's modernizing efforts. The kahal was to reimburse Perl over a period of three years and the remaining part of the school's budget was to be financed by tuitions and the tax on kosher meat.

That same year, the principal, Jacob Neumann, published the school's guiding principles, *Kurze Übersicht des in der Tarnopoler Israelitische Freischule eingeführten Lehrplan* (*A Short Outline of the Lesson Plans adopted in the Tarnopol Israelite Free School*).[90] The *Kurze Übersicht*'s first principle not only echoed Restoration Austria's concern with religion as the glue of a conservative social order, but also affirmed Perl's debt to Lefin's conception of the moderate Haskalah: "A Jewish school cannot exist where the pillarstone is not religion."[91] Neumann's pamphlet illuminates Perl's effort to harmonize traditional Judaism with the Enlightenment's precepts of natural religion. The *Kurze Übersicht* asserted that *torat ha'elohim* was an essential component of the school's curriculum, but Talmud was to be taught with a modern pedagogical outlook, not only emphasizing *halakhah*, but also ethics.[92] The school

---

[89] Perl's financial independence allowed him a great degree of political and cultural license. Most *maskilim* were not part of the economic elite, but dependent upon it. As Steven Lowenstein has shown for the Berlin Haskalah, there were two groups of Jews engaged in modernization, the economic elite (silk manufacturers, financiers, bankers, and others associated with the Prussian court) and the *maskilim*, many of East European origin, who frequently worked as tutors in the homes of their wealthy patrons. See Steven M. Lowenstein, *The Berlin Jewish Community: Enlightenment, Family, and Crisis, 1770–1830* (New York: Oxford University Press, 1994), 34–39.

[90] The full title was *Kurze Übersicht des in der Tarnopoler Israelitische Freischule eingeführten Lehrplans, nach dem der Unterricht, in allen Classen dieser Schule, ertheilt wird. Zur Befriedigung derjenigen, die von dieser Lehranstalt eine genauere Kenntniss zu haben wünschen* (*A Short Outline of the Lesson Plans adopted in the Tarnopol Israelite Free School that Guide the Instruction of all the Classes in the School, for Those who Wish to Have Accurate Knowledge of this School*).

[91] See the first sentence of [Mendel Lefin], *"Essai d'un plan de réforme ayant pour objet d'éclairer la Nation Juive en Pologne et de redresser par là ses moeurs,"* in *Materiały do dziejów Sejmu Czteroletniego* (ed. Arthur Eisenbach et al.; Wrocław: Instytut Historii Polskiej Akademii Nauk, 1969), 410.

[92] The contract between the parents and the school stipulated that instruction in Mishnah, Talmud, and *midrash* would be developmentally appropriate for children "according to their understanding and in a straight-forward manner." The same pedagogical approach would guide instruction in *halakhah* and Jewish customs. The contract is published as an appendix

combined Jewish and general subjects in a split-day schedule, and all instruction was in "purified German." The lesson plans considered "Religion" a separate subject for which a textbook was to be written.[93] Duty was its guiding principle: it included man's obligation (*Pflicht*) to God, himself, other men, his superiors, the government, the ruler of the country, and the fatherland. Weekly hours of *Bildung*, the inner moral development of the pupil, were part of every class's curricular requirements. In the spirit of educational philanthropism, Perl's school rejected corporeal punishment and instead urged verbal warnings and didactic lectures on ethics.[94] Positive incentives included public announcements of the best students at the mid-year examinations.[95] The official government letter recognizing the school as an official state institution responsible for teachers' salaries, the participation of the kahal of Tarnopol and others in the surrounding region in its financing, and Perl's directorship in perpetuity, was sent on September 12, 1818.[96] East Central Europe's first modern Jewish school, initiated and financed by individual *maskilim*, now boasted official state sponsorship, a full thirty years before Tsar Nicholas I's Crown Enlightenment.[97]

---

in Friedman, "Joseph Perl as an Educational Activist," 189.

In contrast, there was no Talmud instruction in the Berlin *Freischule*, which, founded in 1778 by David Friedländer and Isaac ben Daniel Itzig, considered introducing Jewish subject matter in only 1783. See *Hame'assef* (1784): 161 and Simha Assaf, *Meqorot letoldot hahinukh beyisra'el* (Tel Aviv: Devir, 1954), 251.

[93] The emergence of "Religion" as a separate subject in the German-Jewish schools of the early nineteenth century is illustrative of the confessionalization of Judaism that occurred as a byproduct of both the Enlightenment's commitment to the moral autonomy of the individual and the separation of Church and State that followed in the wake of the French Revolution. Although Perl's social context was far more conservative than that of his West European brethren, he was nonetheless shaped by their ideology.

[94] Ernst A. Simon, "Pedagogic Philanthropism and Jewish Education (Hebrew Section)," in *Jubilee Volume in Honor of Mordecai Kaplan* (ed. Moshe Davis; New York, 1953), 149–87.

[95] A German-Hebrew bilingual diploma from the school required the following subjects for graduation: Hebrew Language; Bible with a "pure" German translation; Religion; Reading (German); Writing/Penmanship (German); Writing/Dictation (German); Language (German); Mathematics; Natural History; Earth Science; Reading (French); Writing (French); Language (French); Mishnah, with the commentary of R. Ovadiyah of Bertinoro; Talmud with *Tosafot* and Commentaries; Independent Understanding of the Talmud by the Student; Biblical Grammar; Hebrew Letter Writing (Dictation); Hebrew penmanship; Letter Writing with Regard to Communal life. See Illustration 7. The Abraham Schwadron Collection of Jewish Autographs and Portraits, Joseph Perl Collection.

[96] Friedman, "Joseph Perl as an Educational Activist," 164–66.

[97] On Tsar Nicholas I's "Crown Enlightenment," see Immanuel Etkes, "The 'Crown Enlightenment' and the Change in the Status of the Jewish Enlightenment Movement in Russia," *Zion* 43 (1978): 264–313; on late eighteenth- and early nineteenth-century educational efforts in "New" Russia and Russian Poland, see Zalkin, "Trends in the Development of Haskalah Education."

SCHULZEUGNISS.

De   Schüler   der   Classe welche
die TARNOPOLER Israelitische F R E Y S C H U L E   be-
sucht , und die darin vorgeschriebenen Lehrgegenstände in dem   Curse
folgender Massen gelernt hat :

Sprachlehre	)		
Bibel mit rein deutscher Uebersetzung	) hebräisch	
Religionslehre	)	
Lesen	)	
Schönschreiben	) deutsch	
Rechtschreibung und Dictando	)	
Sprachlehre	)	
Rechnen		
Naturgeschichte		
Erdbeschreibung		
Lesen	)	
Schreiben	) französisch	
Sprachlehre	)	

Da diese Schüler nebst diesen erlernten Gegenständen sich immer   sitt -

sam betragen hat ; so ist ih   hiemit die   Fortgangs = Classe mit

zu erkannt worden .

Tarnopol den   18ι

Schulvorsteher   Director

Illustration 7

The bilingual diploma of the *Israelitische Freischule* in Tarnopol
(The Abraham Schwadron Collection of Jewish Autographs and Portraits,
the Joseph Perl papers, JNULA)

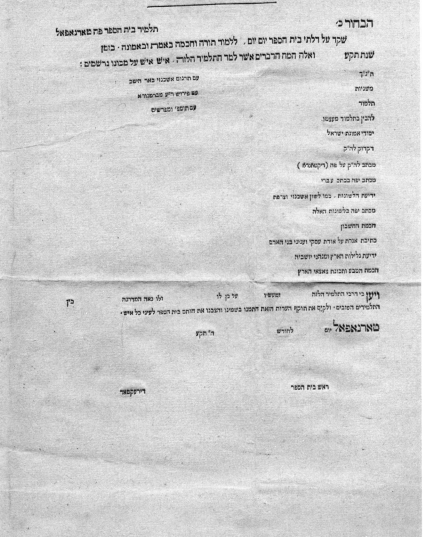

Illustration 7

The bilingual diploma of the *Israelitische Freischule* in Tarnopol
(The Abraham Schwadron Collection of Jewish Autographs and Portraits,
the Joseph Perl papers, JNULA)

As part of his efforts to ground the Haskalah within the culture of Ashkenazic Jewry, Perl stipulated that a synagogue be built next to the school for worship, to insure that "the essentials of Tradition" not be lost, and to provide income for the fledgling educational institution. The synagogue's construction, with approximately 113 places for men and sixty-three for women, occurred simultaneously with that of the school. A library and archive were also part of the complex.[98] An 1815 précis for the synagogue, *Allgemeine Ordnung und Vorschriften für das mit der Tarnopoler Israelitischen Lehranstalt vereinigte Bethaus* (*General Rules and Provisions for the Synagogue attached to the Tarnopol Israelite School*), now lost, detailed the behavior appropriate for prayer, giving honors in the synagogue to its leadership (rabbis, preachers, communal prayer leaders), Torah reading, the synagogue servants, and the *gabbai* (*Haushofmeister*).[99] The synagogue's services were to be marked by the decorousness characteristic of the earliest "reform" synagogue in Seesen.[100]

Perl also drafted an enlightened trilingual prayerbook, *Sheva tefillot* (*Seven Blessings*), for his students.[101] Printed in maskilic German, Hebrew, and

[98] Gelber, "The History of the Jews of Tarnopol," 50 and Friedman, "Joseph Perl as an Educational Activist," 147. Perl mandated in his will that the institutions remain connected in perpetuity. Much to the dismay of the Yiddish writer Mendele Mokher Sforim and the Hebrew poet Hayim Nachman Bialik, who wanted to take the archival riches out of Europe already by the late nineteenth century, Perl's wish was honored by the state and later generations of Galician Jews. See Shmuel Werses, "The Joseph Perl Archives and their Peregrinations," *Ha'universitah* 19, no. 1 (1974): 38–52. Perl's efforts to create a kind of Jewish communal center, with synagogue, school, and library/archive, anticipates Mordecai Kaplan's conception of the "synagogue center," an institution that would fulfill the communal, as well as the religious needs of East European Jews on U.S. soil. On Kaplan, see Jeffrey Gurock, *A Modern Heretic and a Traditional Community: Mordecai M. Kaplan, Orthodoxy, and American Judaism* (New York: Columbia University Press, 1997) and Deborah Dash Moore, *At Home in America: Second Generation New York Jews* (New York: Columbia University Press, 1981), 131–34.

[99] The full title is *Allgemeine Ordnung und Vorschriften für das mit der Tarnopoler Israelitischen Lehranstalt vereinigte Bethaus. Nebst einem Anhange von Instructionen und Weisungen für alle bei dieser Betschule dienenden Personen, welche immer die Richtschnur ihres Verhaltens bleiben muß.* Cited in Friedman, "Joseph Perl as an Educational Activist," 147, footnote 38. Many of the early pamphlets associated with Perl's school and synagogue were printed on a maskilic press in Tarnopol run by Nachman Pineles. Pineles published both maskilic and traditional works, including Lefin's Yiddish translation of Proverbs, but could not make the press economically viable, even after moving it under the auspices of Perl's school. It shut down in 1817. See A. M. Haberman, "Hebrew Printing and the List of Books published in Tarnopol," *Alim lebibliografyah veqorot yisra'el* 2, no. 1 (1935): 24–31 and Simha Katz, "Additions to the List of Publications in Tarnopol," *Kiryat sefer* 15 (1938): 515–16.

[100] On the reforms in Seesen, see Meyer, *Response to Modernity*, 38–43.

[101] Joseph Perl, *Sheva tefillot* (Tarnopol, 1814). Between 1782–1884, 160 textbooks devoted to systematizing Judaism appeared among West European Jews. Liturgical reforms within the European Jewish community first occurred in Napoleon-dominated states and cities (in the Duchy of Westphalia and in Seesen), and then later in Prussia, in the Berlin and Hamburg Temples. On prayerbook reform in Western Europe in the age of the Enlightenment,

Polish, illustrating the natural multilingualism of Galicia's Jewish population, Perl intended his *Sheva tefillot* to be a supplement to the traditional prayer-book, a collective catechism to bolster the social environment of the school. The prayers, a kind of maskilic *shirei shel yom* (daily morning psalms), were to be declaimed every morning by the pupils:

> Dear Children! For now, here are seven prayers for the seven days of the week, presented to you in Hebrew and German. . . . The rationale, goals, and use of prayer, all of that is well-known to you from the first paragraph in the school statutes. Since the discussion there is only about prayer in general, the [discussion] here is to call your attention to the purpose and use of these particular school prayers. Their purpose is to broaden our souls with great and comforting thoughts in order to create a good disposition toward studying so that the lessons that are presented will make the deepest and most enduring impression upon us. So mark my words well, children! The purpose of prayer in this case is above all to facilitate the process of learning. For without this strong purpose and active effort to harmonize and practice [prayer with] good teachings, prayer would be abject prattle![102] Thus taught the wisest King with these magnificent words (Prov 28:9): "The prayers of one who does not heed Torah will not be heard."

> [Reciting the prayers,] the students all stand. One student prays loudly and slowly, the others with a soft undertone. Every day another student prays so that all of the students steadily acquire, through the loud declamation of these prayers, internal mastery and fluency, which is pleasing to God.[103]

Perl's preamble to *Sheva tefillot* depicts the instrumentality of prayer that characterized Jewish modernizers, who desired the liturgy to be useful in instilling moral virtue, as well as his familiarity with Jewish religious innovation in the West.[104] The school prayers were intended to ready the students

---

see Jakob J. Petuchowski, "Manuals and Catechisms of the Jewish Religion in the Early Period of Emancipation," in *Studies in Nineteenth-Century Jewish Intellectual History* (ed. Alexander Altmann; Cambridge, Mass.: Harvard University Press, 1964), 47–64. *Sheva tefillot* was printed in Tarnopol, on Nachman Pineles's press, and included a Hebrew introduction to the book's Polish translation by Jacob Tugenhold (1794–1871). Tugendhold, a *maskil* from Galicia, established a modern Jewish school in Warsaw in 1819 and was later the vice-censor of Hebrew books in the Congress Kingdom of Poland.

[102] Perl, in contrast to David Friedländer, who referred to Hebrew prayer as "empty prattle" in his famous letter to Pastor Teller (*Sendschreiben an Seine Hochwürden Herrn Obers-consistorialrath und Probst Teller zu Berlin von einigen Hausvätern judischer Religion*, Berlin, 1788), considered it efficacious toward the goal of making his students receptive to his broader educational goals. The comment from Friedländer is cited in Eliav, *Hahinukh hayehudi beGermanyah*, 64.

[103] Perl, *Sheva tefillot*, unpaginated. In the 1786 issue of *Hame'assef*, Elijah Morpurgo (1740–1830), an Italian-Jewish disciple of Wessely's, recommended that students not move during studies or prayer. The liturgy, he argued, should be standardized with attractive melodies. See *Hame'assef* (1786), 66–78 and the discussion in Eliav, *Hahinukh hayehudi beGermanyah*, 53–55.

[104] See Michael A. Meyer, "Reflections on Jewish Modernization," in *Jewish History and Memory: Essays in Honor of Yosef Hayim Yerushalmi* (ed. Elisheva Carlebach, John M. Efron, and David N. Myers; Hanover, N.H.: Brandeis University Press, 1998), 369–77.

for their day of study and the booklet was imbued with all of the features of the natural religion espoused by the *maskilim*. The prayer for Sunday affirmed God as Creator and humanity's special relationship with him through his bequest of reason and wisdom. Monday's prayer extolled the childrens' parents. Tuesday's praised the political authorities, soliciting God's favor for the ruler, "who is like a father to us."[105] On Wednesdays, the children were to pray on behalf of their teachers. Thursday's text petitioned God to hear the prayers of the school as a collective "social society" that exemplified humanity's cooperative nature.[106] On Friday, the children beseeched God to take care of the poor and unfortunate. On the Sabbath, *Sheva tefillot* echoed Lefin's affirmation of the natural world, particularly the perfection of the celestial realm, as proof of God's creative power. The prayer for the seventh day also asserted the immortality of the soul and the distinction between "this world" and "the world to come," illustrating Perl's debt to both classical rabbinic theology and the tenets of natural religion. Engravings in the chapbook supported the text's universalist moral tone; at the end of Jacob Tugendhold's translation, an owl ("Wisdom") perched on an oil lantern ("Enlightenment") that was balanced on an olive branch ("Peace"). A cornucopia ("Nature's bounty") faced the text on the adjacent page.[107]

Although *Sheva tefillot* reverberates with some of the language and many of the themes of early reform prayerbooks in Prussia, it was designed as an addition to, not a replacement for, the traditional prayerbook. Perl introduced some aesthetic reforms into his school and synagogue, such as a German sermon, a boys' choir, and an organ, yet his school always considered Talmud an essential part of its curriculum. His paeans to natural religion were similar, "reasonable" supplements to traditional Jewish theology, which he never criticized and which he tried to insulate and protect from the continued growth of Hasidism and the efflorescence of *minhag* in the region. A sustained critique of the Talmud within East Central European Jewry found

---

[105] Here Perl is seeking God's favor for the Russian Tsar in maskilic German while in the Hebrew introduction to the Polish translation of the prayers, which Jacob Tugendhold called "the language of our motherland," the latter explained Tuesday's prayer as a request for the "welfare of Poland, where we dwell, and from which we derive many benefits." Both of their petitions illustrate the multivalent identity (German-speaking, Russian subjects, and Polish loyalty) of Jews in the southeastern Polish borderlands in the era of the partitions through the Congress of Vienna. Tugendhold's words also illustrate the abiding "Polishness" of Galicia's Jews in the nineteenth century. See Perl, *Sheva tefillot*, unpaginated.

[106] The school's *Verhaltungsmaßregeln für die Schüler des Tarnopoler israelitischen Freiinstituts, wie solche sich in ihrem ganzen Betragen, sowohl zu Hause als beim Gebete, wie auch in der Schule, vor, während und nach dem Unterrichte aufzuführen haben. Gezogen aus den Schulgesetzen, zur bequemen Übersicht der Schüler aller Classen*, published in 1815 by Nachman Pineles, emphasized the social component in the school's statutes. I don't believe the statutes are extant.

[107] Perl, *Sheva tefillot*, unpaginated.

an audience only after mid-century, in the Galician *maskil* Joshua Heschel Schorr's *Hehaluts* (*The Pioneer*), which he published intermittently between 1851–1887.[108]

The Battle against Hasidism is Pitched

Perl remained the director of the Tarnopol Israelite Free School until his death in 1839. Throughout these years, he endeavored to solidify support for his school and program of modernizing the Jews of Galicia. He did so within a political climate that was increasingly conservative and that unwittingly bolstered the already emboldened Hasidim, whose social separatism, new patterns of leadership, and proliferation of new customs to which they were especially devoted represented for Perl, as they had for his mentor, Mendel Lefin, a betrayal of traditional Ashkenazic Jewish piety and culture. Perl's anti-Hasidism was comprised of several components. He criticized *minhagim* that had been long observed by Polish Jewry — and were still observed by the Hasidim — as part of their cultural-religious inheritance, which, measured against the rational spirit of the age, he deemed ridiculous. He polemicized against the efflorescence of new customs specific to the Hasidic revolution. Finally, Perl cavilled against Polish-Jewry's penchant toward supererogation, or "going beyond that which is commanded,"[109] in its observance of traditional Jewish law. Perl saw Hasidism's creation of new customs as an extension of Polish-Jewry's historical tendency to valorize the more stringent position (*humra*) regarding a particular religious observance. All three of these components colluded, in Perl's view, to make Galician Jewry hostile to the Haskalah's program of cultural transformation. Hasidism's valorization of "irrational" religious customs, its creation of many new customs, and its inclination toward stringency in its interpretation of Jewish law combined to subvert Perl's conception of the traditional rabbinic culture of Ashkenazic Judaism. As a moderate *maskil* he sought to protect that culture from further decline. Perl regarded his battle against Hasidism, which he waged by writing satiric epistolary novels and voluminous memoranda to Vienna and Lemberg, as well as by spearheading the appointment of Solomon Judah Rapoport/Shir, a moderate *maskil*, as rabbi of Tarnopol, as a battle for the cultural soul of Ashkenazic Jewry.

---

[108] Ezra Spicehandler, "Joshua Heschel Schorr: Maskil and Eastern European Reformist," *HUCA* 31 (1960): 181–222 and 40–41 (1960): 503–528.

[109] On the rabbinic critique of voluntary supererogation in antiquity, see Sara Epstein Weinstein, *Piety and Fanaticism: Rabbinic Criticism of Religious Stringency* (London: Jason Aronson, 1997).

Perl's first published literary salvo against the Hasidim was *Megalleh temirin* (*Revealer of Secrets*, Vienna, 1819), a brilliant and vitriolic epistolary satire based on a Hasidic protagonist who finds and publishes 151 letters that relate to his Hasidic brethren's search for a German book denouncing Hasidism. The novel's scenario involves a hapless Hasid, Ovadiyah ben Pesakhiyah, whose name is a numerological word play on Joseph Perl's name, who strives to locate and destroy a German exposé, which the characters merely call "the *bukh* (book),"[110] of his movement and its leadership.[111] The fictional *bukh* disparaging Hasidism was, indeed, fact, not fiction. Perl had already written an anonymous work, *Über das Wesen der Sekte Chassidim aus ihren eigenen Schriften gezogen (Regarding the Essence of the Hasidic Sect, taken from their own Writings)*, in 1816 and sent it to von Hauer, the Galician governor, whose censorship officer, Count Sedlnitzky, rejected it for publication.[112] In *Megalleh temirin*, the German book has been published, sent from Galicia to the Russian ambassador, and serves as a pretext for the government's persecution of the Hasidim. Like *Über das Wesen der Sekte Chassidim*, *Megalleh temirin* seeks to expose Hasidic secrets, the inner practices, hermeneutics, and rites to which only its initiates were privy. *Megalleh temirin* lampoons the Hasid's dependence upon the zaddik (rebbe in Yiddish), ridicules the new piety's preoccupation with the "secrets (*sodes* in the Yiddish pronunciation of the period)" of their Torah, and generally depicts the Hasidim as benighted and lazy fools. Perl's disdain for the ungrammatical Yiddish-Hebrew speech of the Hasidim, and their inattention to Hebrew grammar, shaped the vocabulary and syntax he put into the mouths of the novel's characters, a direct expression of the Haskalah's preoccupation with the aesthetics of language.[113]

Perl's literary and political anti-Hasidic strategies, including his employment of satire, use of anonymity, and appeal to the Gentile authorities to clamp down on Hasidic publication of kabbalistic and mystical books,

---

[110] For traditional East European Jewry, the word *bukh* in German or Yiddish connoted a secular book. The Hebrew word *sefer* (Yiddish, *seyfer*) conveyed the meaning of a traditional religious text.

[111] Avraham Rubinstein, "Joseph Perl's Interpretation of Names," *Tarbiz* 43 (1973): 205–16.

[112] In 1977, Avraham Rubinstein published a bi-lingual edition of *Über das Wesen der Sekte Chassidim* with a comprehensive introduction detailing its literary, source, and publication history. [Joseph Perl], *Über das Wesen der Sekte Chassidim* (ed. Avraham Rubinstein; Jerusalem: Publications of the Israel Academy of Sciences and Humanities, 1977).

[113] Ovadiyah ben Pesakhiyah begged his readers in *Megalleh temirin*'s prologue to trust that "whoever reads this composition not . . . think that I made — G-d forbid! — any change of language in the letters I reproduced. . . . I have reproduced all the tales and the letters in the very same language as I have them from the correspondents." The translation is Dov Taylor's. See Joseph Perl, *Joseph Perl's Revealer of Secrets: The First Hebrew Novel* (trans. Dov Taylor; Westview Press, 1997), 15.

illustrate his debt to Mendel Lefin.[114] Lefin's *Essai d'un plan de réforme* had urged *maskilim* to combat Hasidism on the literary battlefield, particularly through the art of satire, and he composed *Maḥkimat peti*, his Hebrew anti-Hasidic satire, in epistolary form, with letters exchanged between a young Italian Jew visiting Poland and a Karaite in Constantinople.[115] Lefin's work, probably influenced by Montesquieu's *Lettres persanes* (1754) and D'Argens's *Lettres juives, chinoises et cabalistiques* (1736 and 1738), both of which were translated from French into German in the mid-eighteenth century, also included letters from the Hasidim themselves.[116] Perl, like Lefin, published *Megalleh temirin* and its sequel, *Bohen tsaddiq* (*The Test of the Righteous*), anonymously. Perl's anonymous submission of *Über das Wesen der Sekte Chassidim* to the Austrian authorities, and *Megalleh temirin*'s literary aspiration that the *bukh* had, in fact, influenced them to bear down on the Hasidic movement, attests to Perl's confidence that the state's and his political and cultural interests were harmonious. Lefin, too, we recall, had appealed directly to Prince Adam Czartoryski to stem the growth of Hasidism on the magnate's lands and had suggested in his *Essai d'un plan de réforme* that the Polish government censor kabbalistic and Hasidic books.[117]

While *Megalleh temirin* illuminates Perl's debt to Lefin, the context of centralizing absolutism in which Perl wrote transformed and politicized Lefin's ideology. Lefin's trust in Czartoryski and Perl's in the Austrian and Galician authorities represent a similar politics, the Jewish community's age-old alliance with the highest political authority, but the historical context in which they were effected bespeak a world of difference. The political context

---

[114] Avraham Rubinstein, "Haskalah and Hasidism: Joseph Perl's Activities," *Bar Ilan, Sefer hashanah* 12 (1974): 166–78 and his introduction to [Perl], *Über das Wesen der Sekte Chassidim.*

[115] The Italian Jewish community, as Lois Dubin points out, was an important model of moderate acculturation and tradition for Prussian *maskilim*. Lefin's construction of *Maḥkimat peti* (*Making Wise the Simple*) with an Italian character, and, as will be discussed below, Perl's eye toward Italian-Jewish *halakhah*, underscores this point for East European *maskilim* as well. See Lois C. Dubin, "The Rise and Fall of the Italian Jewish Model in Germany: From Haskalah to Reform, 1780–1820," in *Jewish History and Jewish Memory: Essays in Honor of Yosef Hayim Yerushalmi* (ed. Elisheva Carlebach, John M. Efron, and David N. Myers; Hanover, N.H.: Brandeis University Press, 1998), 271–95.

[116] *Maḥkimat peti* discussed the origin of the *Zohar*, using Jacob Emden as a source, and the authenticity of *Shivḥei haBesht* (*In Praise of the Ba'al Shem Tov*), which first appeared in 1815. Lefin probably started writing *Maḥkimat peti* shortly after 1815, and it subsequently influenced Perl's shaping of *Megalleh temirin*, which ultimately saw the light of day while Lefin's work did not. See Shmuel Werses, "Regarding the Lost Pamphlet, *Maḥkimat peti*," in *Megammot vetsurot besifrut hahaskalah* (Jerusalem: Magnes Press, 1990), 319–37.

[117] Chone Shmeruk also noted that Perl employed Lefin's Yiddish terminology (*ehrlikh* for zaddik and *hultay* for *rasha*) in his unpublished Yiddish epistles. See Chone Shmeruk, "On Several Principles in Mendel Lefin's Translation of Proverbs," in *Sifrut yidish beFolin: meḥqarim ve'iyyunim historiyyim* (Jerusalem: Magnes Press, 1981), 183. See, too, Max Erik, *Etiudn tsu der geshikhte fun der haskole* (Minsk, 1934), 150, 170–71.

of decentralized pre-partition Poland allowed Lefin to seek Gentile support
for his campaign against the Hasidim while maintaining his commitment to
internal Jewish communal autonomy. Lefin, like Perl after him, had an
immoderate political stance toward the Hasidism, but he was suspicious of
absolutism, and strove to protect the kahal from dissolution.[118] In contrast,
Perl's appeal to Vienna in the context of the centralizing ethos of absolutist
Austria articulated his desire that Gentile authority directly intervene in Jewish communal life, even at the expense of its legendary autonomy.[119] Hoping
to persuade the Austrian authorities that Hasidism was dangerous not only
for the Jewish community, but for the state's general welfare and aims, Perl
was unrelenting in his solicitation of the Habsburgs.[120] In *Über das Wesen der
Sekte Chassidim*, he argued that Judaism had an historical development and
contemporary Hasidism represented its nadir. Rather than progressing from
the period of medieval rationalism, embodied by the Sephardic codifiers
Isaac Alfasi (the "Rif"), Maimonides, and Joseph Karo, who had refined
earlier Judaism by ridding it of its mystical accretions, Hasidism had ossified
those accretions with its attachment to the exegesis of new commandments
derived through mystical interpretations and the whims of the zaddikim,
who sought to control the Jewish community and make it impenetrable to
the state's political requirements.[121] Perl's cultural message of the Haskalah
was moderate; he never advocated the abandonment of Jewish law. But his
immoderate politics toward the Hasidim, which impelled him to use the
tutelary state's arrogation of authority for his own maskilic ends, radicalized
his program for the transformation of Galician Jewry.

Concluding that Perl's politics embraced the state as a positive element in
the transformation of the Jewish community of Galicia still leaves open the
question of what he hoped would result from its intervention. Examination

---

[118] See Chapter Two.

[119] Rubinstein, "Haskalah and Hasidism." Perl had earlier expressed this political posture
in the maskilic dream that closed his parody, "The Tale of the Lost Prince," of the tales of
Nachman of Bracław (Bratslav). The parody was written before *Megalleh temirin* and only
published posthumously. See Joseph Perl, *Ma'asiyyot ve'iggerot mitsaddiqim amittiyim ume'anshei
shelomeinu* (ed. Chone Shmeruk and Shmuel Werses; Jerusalem: Publications of the Israel
Academy of Sciences and Humanities, 1969), 38–41.

[120] Rubinstein describes how denouncing a member of the Jewish community to the
Gentile authorities, known as *malshinut* (slander) in the world of traditional Jewry, was a
natural extension of the etatism of the *maskilim* under absolutism. He also points out that at
the height of the Jewish culture wars at the end of the eighteenth and beginning of the nineteenth century, other subcultures within Ashkenazic Jewry (e.g. *mitnaggedim* v. Hasidim,
Hasidim v. Hasidim) also willingly resorted to slander. Rubinstein, "Haskalah and
Hasidism," 172.

[121] [Perl], *Über das Wesen der Sekte Chassidim*, 63–68. On Perl's historical treatment of Jewish
religious development, see Shmuel Feiner, *Haskalah vehistoryah: toldotav shel hakarat-ever
yehudit modernit* (Jerusalem: Zalman Shazar Center, 1998), 135.

of Perl's many memoranda to the Austrian and Galician authorities illustrates that he hoped that an alliance with the state would thwart the spread of Hasidism, reign in the influence of customary law, and allow a reasonable, moderate rabbinic Judaism to reestablish itself within Galician Jewry, unmaking its increasingly "baroque" culture and paving the way toward Polish-Galician Jewry's smooth transition to full participation in modern European society.

Haminhag kehalakhah hu ("Custom is as Binding as Law")

Minhag (customary law) was always a central component of Jewish law, representing the non-elite anonymous practice of the Jewish community over time. Rabbinic leaders themselves debated and appealed to customary law, whose authority was based on the statement, "Go and see how the people behave," which appears in both Talmuds (*b. Berakhot 45a* and *y. Pesahim 54a*); they also monitored the development of customary law in order to ensure that it was not erroneous, too burdensome, or illogical, and that it was in accordance with the inherited principles of rabbinic authority. Customary law was particularly effective in the area of monetary law, in which it had the rabbinically-sanctioned authority to annul certain *halakhot* based on the principle *minhag mevattel halakhah* (custom overrides *halakhah*).[122] Galician Jewry, the heirs to the Polish-Jewish rabbinic tradition, had always valorized *minhag* as an independent source of religious authority. Scholars such as Haym Soloveitchik, Elimelech Westreich, Avraham Grossman, Israel Ta-Shma, and others have detailed the power of customary law and its pietist penchant in medieval Ashkenazic Jewish culture.[123] Ta-Shma argues that ancestral custom was the decisive component in determining behavior for Ashkenazic Jews already by the eleventh century, its influence subsiding somewhat in the subsequent two centuries, but experiencing a renewal by

---

[122] Menachem Elon argued that *minhag*'s authority to annul written law did not extend to other areas of religious practice. See Menachem Elon, *Hamishpat ha'ivri: toldotav, meqorotav, eqronotav* (Jerusalem: Magnes Press, 1973), 2:713–77. Ruth Langer, however, concluded that in cases of tension between top-down juridical *halakhah* and practiced customary law in the use of liturgical poetry (*piyyut*) and its incorporation into "normative" liturgy, custom often won out. See Ruth Langer, *To Worship God Properly: Tensions Between Liturgical Custom and Halakhah in Judaism* (Cincinnati, Ohio: Hebrew Union College Press, 1998), 253.

[123] Elimelech Westreich, "The Ban on Polygamy in Polish Rabbinic Thought," in *Polin: The Jews in Early Modern Poland*, vol. 10 (ed. Gershon David Hundert; The Littman Library of Jewish Civilization, 1997), 66–84; Haym Soloveitchik, "Religious Law and Change: The Medieval Ashkenazic Example," *AJS Review* 12, no. 2 (Fall 1987): 205–21; Israel Ta-Shma, "Law, Custom, and Tradition among Ashkenazic Jews in the Eleventh and Twelfth Centuries," *Sidra* 3 (1987): 85–161.

the fourteenth.[124] In the sixteenth century, when the Cracow-born Ashkenazic *poseq* (decisor) Moses Isserles glossed his Sephardic confrere Joseph Karo's decisions in the *Shulḥan arukh*, the great post-Talmudic compendium of Jewish law, he underscored the centrality of *minhag* for Ashkenazic Jewry. Referring to *minhag Ashkenaz* on the title page of the code's first edition, all of Isserles's comments reflect the singularity of Ashkenazic practice due to its adherence to customary law. Isserles was overwhelmingly loyal to custom as it had developed in Poland and often cited *b. Berakhot 45a* as a prooftext for his halakhic decisions.[125]

The centrality of *minhag* to Ashkenazic Jewish culture can also be heard in the critique of Hasidism voiced by the Lithuanian rabbinic elite, the *mitnaggedim*, in the late eighteenth century. The *mitnaggedim* were concerned that Hasidic religious practice, with its numerous new rituals and customs, undermined both normative Jewish religious practice (*halakhah*) and specific Ashkenazic religious behavior that had been shaped by custom. The bans and writs promulgated against the Hasidim in the late eighteenth century reverberated with both concerns. The writ of excommunication against the Hasidim that the kahal of Brody issued in 1772 criticized their transgression of the halakhic requirements for the time and length of daily prayers. It also warned the larger Jewish community of the new Hasidic customs of using the Sephardic prayerbook, donning the white *kittel* (robe) on the Sabbath in addition to its customary use on the Day of Atonement, and changing the accepted standards for kosher slaughtering (*shehitah*).[126] Abraham Katzenellenbogen, the head of the rabbinical court of Brześć Litewski (Brisk, Lithuania), charged in a 1784 letter to the Hasidic figure, Levi Isaac of Berdyczów, that the Hasidim do not follow "God's chosen leadership, the powerful founders of the tradition, the famous *ge'onim*, the rabbinic princes," [who established] "good *laws* and upright *customs*."[127] The kahal of Cracow in 1786

---

[124] Ta-Shma, "Law, Custom, and Tradition among Ashkenazic Jews," 90.

[125] Moses A. Shulvass, *Jewish Culture in Eastern Europe: The Classical Period* (New York: KTAV, 1975), 58. See Isserles's introduction to the Laws of the Sin Offering (*Torat haḥatat*), where he warned his Ashkenazic readers that should they follow Joseph Karo's decisions regarding the dietary laws they would "contradict all of the customs that are upheld in these lands." Joseph Davis observed that Isserles introduced his glosses to the *Shulḥan arukh* by disassociating himself from Karo's *minhagim*: "Without [the *mappa*], the table which he [Karo] laid before the Lord is not yet ready for the men of these lands, for in the majority of customs (*minhagim*) of these lands, we do not follow his opinions." Cited in Joseph Davis, "The Reception of the Shulhan 'Arukh and the Formation of Ashkenazic Jewish Identity," *AJS Review* 26, no. 2 (November 2002): 263. See, too, note 50 on that same page. Davis notes, however, that Isserles was not specific about which lands actually comprised *medinut eilu* ("these lands").

[126] The text of the Brody ḥerem is published in Wilensky, *Ḥasidim umitnaggedim*, 1:44–49.

[127] Ibid., 1:123. Emphasis is mine.

accused the Hasidim of attempting to change "the standard liturgy (*nusaḥ*) of prayer that was established in Ashkenaz by R. Moses Isserles," and warned, "Who knows where these things [Hasidic customs] will lead?"[128] Customs that were supererogatory also became the targets of rabbinic censure. Solomon Kluger (1785–1869), the head of the rabbinical court in Brody, Austrian Galicia, from the 1820s on, wrote a responsum in 1849 to Isaac Eisek Seferin, a Hasidic zaddik from Komarno in which he argued that individuals who wished to wear an additional set of phylacteries for morning prayers — a Hasidic custom that had spread in Galicia — were permitted to do so. Yet, he concluded, their voluntary supererogation was not to be seen as binding on the Jewish public as a whole for there was a difference between "customs that have been observed from the time of the Sages of the Talmud and more recent customs." The latter were not obligatory for the majority of the people.[129] The traditional rabbinate, whether they were avowed *mitnaggedim* in Lithuania or heads of rabbinical courts in Galicia, feared above all that Hasidism's triumph would mean the loss of their authoritative power both to adjudicate the inherited corpus of Jewish law and to channel customary practice into normative halakhic praxis.

Yet Hasidism's victory was full of paradoxes. In contrast to the fears of the *mitnaggedim* that Hasidism's innovations would lead inexorably to heresy, mass disillusionment, and a sectarian splintering of the Jewish community, the eighteenth-century spiritual revolution became a further impetus to the cultural retrenchment of Ashkenazic Jewry. The numerous writs of excommunication against the Hasidim proved powerless. Hasidism had already conquered most of East European Jewry by the time its move north to Lithuania aroused the ire of Vilna's rabbinate. Thus, while Hasidism's triumphant penetration into Polish Jewish life by 1772 initiated a cultural war among *mitnaggedim*, Hasidim, and *maskilim* over the place of *minhag* and religious authority in Jewish religious life, it ultimately served to make Polish Jewry even more attached to religious custom, both inherited practices and Hasidic innovations.[130] Moreover, the Hasidic spiritual landscape gave rise to

[128] Ibid., 1:138.
[129] On Kluger and his relationship to Hasidism, see Hayim Gertner, "The Rabbinate and Hasidism in Nineteenth-Century Galicia: R. Solomon Kluger and the Hasidim," in *Bema'aglei ḥasidim: qovets meḥqarim lezikhro shel profesor Mordekhai Vilenski* (ed. Immanuel Etkes et al.; Jerusalem: Bialik Institute, 1999), 51–74. Regarding the custom of laying four sets of phylacteries, see 60–61.
[130] Traditionalists threatened by innovations in Jewish law initiated by West European Jews appealed directly to age-old Ashkenazic custom in their efforts to stay change, just as had the *mitnaggedim* in their struggle with the Hasidim. *Eleh divrei haberit*, the pamphlet produced by traditionalist critics of the Hamburg Temple, exhorted the reformers not to disregard the *minhag* of Ashkenazic worship and employed the Talmudic *memra* in order to censure the reformers. Rebbe Hayim Halberstam of Sądz (1793–1876), reacting to the construction of a

the efflorescence of numerous new customs associated with various zaddikim, which soon became as binding as religious practices derived from
inherited legislation. As Jacob Katz concluded, Hasidism ultimately made the
majority of Galicia's Jews impervious to the rational influences of the
Enlightenment. It also made them implacably hostile to the cameralist
ambitions of the absolutist state.

By the early nineteenth century, modernizing Jews like Joseph Perl
interested in transforming the culture of Galician Jewry thus confronted a
Jewish population even more resolute in its commitment to Jewish law and
minhag according to Ashkenaz. His critique of *minhag* was both distinct and
directly related to his polemic against Hasidism, which he blamed as a
contemporary font of new, illegitimate customs. Were Galician Jewry able to
wean itself from those elements of customary law that had no basis in
halakhah, and that served to isolate the Jews by steeping them in irrationality,
it would be open to those aspects of *torat ha'adam* Perl and other *maskilim*
believed were the sine qua non of a productive, useful, and modern Jewish
life.

The apparently limitless explosion of Hasidic custom that deviated from
traditional Jewish law as it had been practiced in Poland alarmed other members of Perl's circle, most notably Isaac Michael Monies (d. 1844),[131] the first
Talmud teacher in Perl's school, who wrote a maskilic responsum in 1825
criticizing the contemporary Hasidic custom of lighting candles on Lag
Ba'omer in memory of Shimon bar Yochai, and Judah Leib Mieses (d. 1831),
who devoted his *Qinat ha'emet (Truth's Zeal*, Vienna, 1828) entirely to the
issue of customary law.[132] Monies admitted the binding nature of customary

---

synagogue that had a place for a cantor and choir, warned: "*God forbid if we change something
from the custom of our ancestors*, [we will] destroy, God forbid, the entire religion, 'go and see'
what the new sect that despises the words of the Sages has done. [They] are so far removed
from the people of Israel and deliberately transgress several commandments." Emphasis is
mine. Cited in Shmuel Shilo, "The War against Reform in the *Responsa* of Polish and Russian
Sages in the Nineteenth Century," *Dinei yisra'el* 20–21 (2000): 419–33.
[131] Isaac Michael Monies, "Responsum on the Custom of Lighting Candles on Lag Ba'omer
in Memory of R. Shimon bar Yochai," *Yerushalayim* 1 (1844): 9–21. Monies taught Talmud in
Perl's school for twenty-five years, translated four of Euler's letters for *Kerem ḥemed*, wrote an
article on prayer, and a book on aesthetics that never saw the light of day. See Gelber, "The
History of the Jews of Tarnopol," 50, footnote 63 and Bernhard Wachstein, *Die hebräische
Publizistik in Wien* (Vienna: Selbstverlag der Historischen Kommission, 1930), 150–51. Isaac
Baer Levinsohn corresponded with Joseph Perl about Monies's work, *Megalleh sod (Revealer of
[the] Secret*), and other anti-Hasidic literary matters, including his lending Monies a copy of
Jacob Emden's *Mitpaḥat sefarim (Covering of the Scrolls of the Law*).
[132] Judah Leib Mieses, *Sefer qinat ha'emet* (Vienna: Anton von Schmid, 1828) and Feiner,
Haskalah vehistoryah, 137–44. Perl asked Mieses, who travelled frequently to Vienna and
Prague, and was in contact with maskilic circles there, to guard the fact that he had shared
Über das Wesen with Peter Beer (1758–1838), a Bohemian *maskil*, and with Isaac Marcus Jost

law in Judaism, but distinguished between those customs erected as a fence around the commandments, and those that had evolved through history and had "occurred unintentionally, through circumstance or chance, and continued [to be upheld] without reason until the masses came to consider them as binding as a commandment."[133] These customs were periodically reviewed by the sages of a given generation, who had the power to annul them, particularly if they derived from a Gentile or idolatrous source. In Monies's view, this was the case with the practice of lighting candles on Lag Ba'omer, which had no precedent in traditional Jewish culture.[134] He averred, "There is absolutely no mention of the village of Meron in Scripture. . . . The villagers of Meron received it [the custom] from the Arabs, [who] are accustomed to seeing great sanctity in the graves of the holy Tannaites and to kindling lights on the graves of holy men." For Monies, the new Hasidic custom was a foreign accretion that dishonored the earlier prophets, particularly Moses — at whose (unknown) grave no candles are lit — and damaged traditional Judaism. Monies's responsum also claimed that Israel's great sages did not valorize stringency (humra), even though it was a necessary counterweight to the category of leniency (qula) in the rabbinic legal ethos.[135] Citing Maimonides's *Eight Chapters*, which, as we have seen, became a maskilic prooftext adduced to counter Hasidism, Monies asserted

---

(1793–1860), a Prussian *maskil*, both of whom were early practitioners of *Wissenschaft des Judentums* and whose works of Jewish history reflect Perl's influence. See the correspondence published in Philip Friedman, "The First Battles between the Haskalah and Hasidism," *Fun noentn ovar* 4 (1937): 259–73. On Beer and Jost's debt to Perl, see Michael A. Brenner, "Between Haskalah and Kabbalah: Peter Beer's History of Jewish Sects," in *Jewish History and Jewish Memory: Essays in Honor of Yosef Hayim Yerushalmi* (ed. Elisheva Carlebach, John M. Efron, and David N. Myers; Hanover, N.H.: Brandeis University Press, 1998), 389–404.

[133] Monies, "Responsum on the Custom of Lighting Candles on Lag Ba'omer," 10.

[134] In the introduction to his translation of the *Guide of the Perplexed*, Mendel Lefin also pointed to this custom as evidence of the accretion of commandments by the Hasidim: "Behold, [I know the case of] an upstanding (*kasher*) man who argued against the innovation of lighting candles on the Lag Ba'omer festival at Mt. Meron. A certain Hasidic apostate jumped out at him and angrily screamed, 'Oy, cursed is the apostasy [of not lighting the candles], [it is] fit for Amraphel's oven [referring to a midrashic reading that drew an analogy between Amraphel and Nimrod, who pushed Abram into an oven]." Mendel Lefin, "*Elon moreh*," *Hamelits* (1867): 6. On the name Amraphel, see Gen 14:1 and Rashi's comment on the verse.

[135] On the penchant toward stringency in Ashkenazic Jewish culture at the end of the Middle Ages, see Haym Soloveitchik, "Rupture and Reconstruction: The Transformation of Contemporary Orthodoxy," in *Jews in America: A Contemporary Reader* (ed. Roberta Rosenberg Farber and Chaim I. Waxman; Hanover, N.H.: Brandeis University Press), 320–76. On the tension within *halakhah* between the merit of "going beyond the letter of the law" and solely observing its letter, see Joshua Halberstam, "Supererogation in Jewish *Halakhah* and Islamic *Shari'a*," in *Studies in Islamic and Judaic Traditions* (ed. William M. Brinner and Stephen D. Ricks; Atlanta, Ga.: Scholars Press, 1986), 85–99.

that moderation between two extremes was fundamental to rabbinic teaching, and decried the extremism inherent in the Hasidic proliferation of
customs. All those concerned with the distortion of Judaism and protection
of its reasonableness should labor to uproot the custom of kindling candles
in memory of Shimon bar Yochai.[136]

Mieses's *Qinat ha'emet* was a far more expansive treatment of customary law
than was Monies's, but his goal was the same: to combat the multiplication of
Hasidic customs that he believed were foreign to normative Ashkenazic
rabbinic Judaism. In *Qinat ha'emet*, Mieses used the well-worn literary form of
the dialogue in the afterlife, in which the protagonists sit in Heaven, judging
their brethren below. In Mieses's work, Maimonides and Solomon of Chełm,
author of *Sefer mirkevet mishneh* (Frankfurt-on-the-Main, 1751) and a vocal
early critic of Hasidism, use historical thinking to explain the contemporary
crisis among Polish Jewry, and squarely place the blame for its ignorance on
the Besht, who in their opinion was the most recent link in the insidious
chain of foreign mystical influences that began with the *Zohar*.[137] It was the
task of the progressive elite, the *maskilim*, to combat these foreign accretions,
unmask the exploitative Hasidic leadership that preyed on the people
through their manipulation of these foreign customs, and restore Judaism to
its pre-mystical glory. Mieses demonized the Hasidim, but, like Perl, never
attacked the centrality of the Talmud or rabbinic law.[138]

Perl began his political activism against *minhag* in general and Hasidic
minhag in particular in 1829 with a series of letters against the proliferation
of collection boxes in the name of Meir Ba'al ha-Nes, a second-century *tanna*
who was believed to be buried on the shores of the Sea of Galilee.[139] East
European Jews had long given charity in memory of Meir Ba'al ha-Nes much
as they had commissioned and worn amulets to ward off physical danger, to

---

[136] Monies, "Responsum on the Custom of Lighting Candles on Lag Ba'omer," 14–21.

[137] Mieses's Maimonides is not only a thorough-going rationalist, but a Copernican, as well,
and in the course of the satire informs Solomon of Chełm of his support of the Polish
scientist's heliocentric theories. See Yehuda Friedlander, "Hasidism as the Image of
Demonism: The Satiric Writings of Judah Leib Mieses," in *From Ancient Israel to Modern
Judaism: Intellect in Quest of Understanding, Essays in Honor of Marvin Fox* (ed. Jacob Neusner,
Ernst S. Frerichs, and Nahum M. Sarna; Atlanta, Ga.: Scholars' Press, 1989), 165.

[138] On Mieses's critique of Hasidism, see Friedlander, "Hasidism as the Image of Demonism." and Yehuda Friedlander, "The Struggle of the Mitnagedim and Maskilim against
Hasidism: Rabbi Jacob Emden and Judah Leib Mieses," in *New Perspectives on the Haskalah*
(ed. Shmuel Feiner and David Sorkin; London: The Littman Library of Jewish Civilization,
2001), 103–12. For Mieses's commitment to the Talmud, see Mahler, *Hasidism and the Jewish
Enlightenment*, 41.

[139] In his earlier *luḥot*, Perl criticized the contemporary custom of spitting during the
Aleinu at the mention of non-Jewish worship, and cited Isaiah Horowitz's comment in his
Shenei luḥot haberit that the custom was outdated. See Mahler, *Hasidism and the Jewish
Enlightenment*, 150.

induce the return of some lost beloved item, and to show their bond with the Land of Israel. Perl undoubtedly knew of this well-established folk tradition of Polish Jewry, but his zeal in uprooting Hasidism led him to conclude that the increase in the number of collection boxes had been encouraged by Hasidic zaddikim. Perl's epistolary pamphlet, *Ketit lama'or* (*Beaten Oil for the Eternal Light*), argued against the collection boxes, concluding that the custom of raising money for Meir Ba'al ha-Nes derived from a censored Hasidic work, *Keter shem tov* (*Crown of the Good [God's] Name*, Żółkiew, 1795). The Austrian authorities accepted the argument in Perl's cover letter to the epistles and granted him permission to publish the work. When *Ketit lama'or* finally appeared in 1836 in the Viennese maskilic Hebrew journal, *Kerem ḥemed*, the collection boxes had already been removed. Perl evidently concluded that the Austrian government supported his campaign against superstitious *minhag* because he continued to petition the non-Jewish authorities.[140]

Perl's offensive against the general role of customary law in Jewish life, which he believed had become particularly ossified among Ashkenazic Jews, found its fullest expression in an unpublished manuscript, *Über die Modifikation der mosaischen Gesetze* (*Regarding the Modification of Mosaic Laws*), which he wrote some time before 1831.[141] Addressed to the Galician authorities (*Kreisamt*), Perl argued that Jewish law had developed historically and had always reflected the *Zeitgeist* of its historical context: "Jewish laws — particularly the ceremonial — always underwent modification. . . . The teachers in the past always made a consistent effort to improve the laws in the *spirit of the times*."[142] For Perl, the contemporary, debased state of Polish Jewry, made

---

140 Avraham Rubinstein, "Joseph Perl's Pamphlet, *Ketit lama'or*," *Alei sefer* 3/4 (1976): 140–57.

141 The Joseph Perl Archive, 4° 1153/144, henceforth *Über die Modifikation*. The manuscript is written in Perl's German script, with occasional use of Hebrew citations. It is comprised of eighty-three pages with an introduction and is listed in Philip Koffler's appendix to the Perl archive, which he compiled during the interwar years. Avraham Rubinstein briefly noted the existence of the manuscript in his edition of [Perl], *Über das Wesen der Sekte Chassidim*, 4, footnote 17, but no other scholarly mention, let alone analysis, of the manuscript exists. The Austrian censor rejected the manuscript for publication on February 17, 1831. See number six in the Koffler appendix. See, too, "Comments or corrections to the book dealing with Jewish Law," the Joseph Perl Archive, JNULA, 4° 1153/131, and manuscript 38.7075, JNULA.

As he had done with *Über das Wesen*, Perl sought the aid of his former student, Bezalel Stern, then the head of the new Jewish school in Odessa, in the preparation of the manuscript. On Stern's editorial help to Perl, see [Perl], *Über das Wesen der Sekte Chassidim*, 6 and Friedman, "The First Battles."

142 Perl, *Über die Modifikation*, 82. In one of his seminal early essays on the Haskalah, Immanuel Etkes argued that the *maskilim* exhibited a sharpened consciousness about the historical development of *halakhah* and *minhag*, often criticizing the latter as "additions" to

even more obscurantist by the efflorescence of Hasidism, no longer reflected, and was an obstacle to, "the spirit of the times." Perl's treatise, imbued
with the optimistic cameralist ethos of a Josephian Austria long past, sought
to convince the Galician authorities that only customary law, and not essential religious law, was the source of Galician Jewry's opposition to the
cameralist program of the state. Perl's strategy in *Über die Modifikation*, in
contrast to his many other memos, was not to attack the Hasidim directly,
although they were the most obvious opponents of modernity in Galicia.[143]
Rather, he strove to expose the general tendency within Ashkenazic jurisprudence of viewing customary law as tantamount to *halakhah*. For Perl, one
of the outstanding contemporary obstacles within Galician Jewish society to
his program of modernization was the complicity of the Ashkenazic rabbinate and its public in elevating *minhag* over *halakhah*. He thus surveyed and
analyzed the pietist penchant indigenous to medieval Ashkenazic Jewish
culture well before the birth of Hasidism in the eighteenth century, as well as
scrutinized the history of the Ashkenazic rabbinate. Perl believed that if he
could successfully prove that Jews had adapted and modified their religious
behavior based on time and circumstances (*Zeit und Ümstände*) and that
much of what was currently practiced was due to customary and not revealed
law, then contemporary Galician Jews, without impugning their commitment
to rabbinic authority and to rabbinic law, could modify certain contemporary
practices.[144]

---

the core of Jewish law. Immanuel Etkes, "Immanent Factors and External Influences in the
Development of the Haskalah Movement in Russia," in *Toward Modernity: The European Jewish
Model* (ed. Jacob Katz; New Brunswick, N.J.: Transaction Books, 1987), 27.

[143] Perl's later work, *Bohen tsaddiq*, begins with a jab at customary law. Perl apologizes for
not writing an introduction to his book, with the explanation that the custom of writing
obsequious introductions is relatively new and, like virtues and religious behavior, is historically conditioned. He continues, "It is known that ethics and behavior change with time:
there are those [virtues] that our predecessors upheld, which we don't, and vice-versa.
Recent generations observe bad practices that earlier generations did not uphold, such as
eating before morning prayers, which are [now] intentionally delayed. *Now, it is bad to pray at
dawn, but considered a venerable, old custom to do so afterwards.*" Emphasis is mine. [Perl], *Bohen
tsaddiq*, 4. The comments about the time of prayer are directed at followers of Beshtian
Hasidism, who were criticized by their opponents for flagrantly violating the prescribed time
for prayer.

[144] In her study of the tension between Jewish practice derived from legislation and that
derived from custom, Ruth Langer concluded, "Under certain circumstances, rabbinic
authorities — utterly convinced that it was absolutely wrong and even dangerous for the
community to continue in its errant ways — attempted and succeeded in overthrowing
minhag." However, she also notes that the balance between liturgical *halakhah* and *minhag*
was never fixed historically; in certain time periods and under certain circumstances, custom
had more weight than decreed *halakhah* and vice-versa. Migrations and other geographic
ruptures, as well as the growth of philosophy and mysticism, played a central role in the
dynamics of liturgical development. Langer, *To Worship God Properly*, 247 and 251.

Perl presented four cases to the Austrian authorities to prove his belief in the flexibility and historically-conditioned nature of Jewish law and custom: the permissibility of shaving, the halakhic requirement that a converted male Jew give his estranged Jewish wife a Jewish writ of divorce (a *get*), the question of the legality of moneylending by Jews to both Jews and Christians, and the obligation to release debts in the Sabbatical Year. Perl treated each issue to a brief historical survey and endeavored to show that Jewish law had never ceased to develop according to the "spirit of the times."

As we saw earlier, Lefin's defense of the Jewish beard at the Four-Year *Sejm* and Tobias Gutmann Feder's employment of male facial hair as a metonym for the alleged lack of refinement or anti-aestheticism of early modern Polish Jewry illustrated that the issue of how male East European Jews looked remained a preoccupation for modernizing Jews well into the nineteenth century.[145] Wearing a trimmed beard himself, Perl chose to address the permissibility of shaving as the first issue in his treatise on the impediments to the integration of Ashkenazic Jews into Habsburg society.[146] Through a discussion of the statements in the Bible, Mishnah, and the Babylonian Talmud, and by means of such legal luminaries as Maimonides, Abraham ibn Ezra, Joseph Karo, and various kabbalistic thinkers, Perl strove to demonstrate that the halakhic prohibition on shaving was always defined by historical context. In the ancient Near East, the practice of idolatrous priests to round the beards of their dead during cultic worship led to the original prohibition in the Bible, Perl reasoned, following Ibn Ezra and Maimonides.[147] Medieval Kabbalists, however, depending on the customs of the nations among whom they lived, adopted different practices. Isaac Luria, the sixteenth-century Kabbalist living in "Eastern lands, where the beard is regarded as sacred, attributed a mystical sanctity to every beard hair, [and] stated that the plucking of even one beard hair was an enormous transgression deserving of cruel punishment."[148] In contrast, Menachem Asaria, a seventeenth-century Italian Kabbalist, made a practice of trimming his beard

---

[145] The issue still has resonance. See Henry Goldschmidt, "Suits and Souls: Trying to Tell a Jew When You See One in Crown Heights," in *Jews of Brooklyn* (ed. Ilana Abramowicz and Seán Gavin; Hanover, N.H.: University Press of New England, 2002), 214–23.

[146] Perl, however, continued to wear sidecurls. See the image reproduced in Perl, *Joseph Perl's Revealer of Secrets*, xvii.

[147] Perl, *Über die Modifikation*, 1. Ibn Ezra's comment on Lev 19:27 discourages shaving on two grounds: to distinguish Jews from Gentiles, who shave, and to prevent Jews from engaging in cultic idolatrous practices. See Abraham ibn Ezra, *Commentary on the Torah*, Lev 19:27. Maimonides forbids the shaving of the edges of the hairline (*peyotei harosh*) because it was a custom of idolators. See Maimonides, *Mishneh torah*, Laws of Idolatry, 12:7. See, too, Moses Maimonides, *The Guide of the Perplexed* (trans. Shlomo Pines; Chicago: University of Chicago Press, 1963), 3:37.

[148] Perl, *Über die Modifikation*, 65.

every Friday "to honor the Sabbath, and his students followed his example." Perl concluded, "Each of these Kabbalists wrote [his opinion] according to the customs of his country."[149]

Although Perl presented his comparison of Luria's and Asaria's practices without judgment, his preference for Italian tonsorial fashion could not have been clearer.[150] Perl, like other *maskilim,* valorized Italian Jewry as exemplifying the Haskalah's aspirations toward creating a Jewish culture that balanced the demands of Jewish tradition with the claims of modernity; in an 1839 letter to Shmuel Goldenberg, the editor of *Kerem ḥemed,* Perl decried Polish Jewry's fear of "wisdom," in contrast to contemporary Italian-Jewry, which produced the legal encylopedia, *Paḥad yitsḥaq* (published between 1750 and 1840), and other more scientific halakhic *responsa,* such as the *Shemesh tsedaqah* (Venice, 1743).[151] The Italian-Jewish symbiosis between devotion to Jewish law and integration into non-Jewish society became even more appealing and politically useful for a *maskil* like Perl because the partitions of

---

[149] Ibid., 67.

[150] Ironically, Perl included a vignette from a report by Joseph August Schultes (1773–1831), professor of botany at Cracow University, about his journey through Galicia, in his 1814 calendar, which praised the beards of Galician Jewish men: "The Jewish inhabitants of Galicia are practically the only ones who are engaged with commerce and industry in the whole region and who think about the needs and good of society. They alone sew the clothes that we wear and make the shoes that cover our feet. They make products of glass, gold, silver, bronze, and every kind of metal, and they also know how to engrave magnificently and to crush stones. If they lease the fields and meadows from the nobility, then they develop and work the land wisely and industriously. God is blessed through the work of their hands because he gave them the earth and its bounty [Ps 24:1]. You will find inns, places to sleep, to eat, and to restore yourselves, in the homes of the Jews. The Jews' physical appearance is pleasing to the eye and mind. Their foreheads are high and broad, their eyes bright like lanterns; most of them have long and crooked noses, and their hair is golden yellow. *All of this is pleasant enough, but it is the majesty of their beards that gives them the appearance of wise and brilliant men."* Joseph Perl, *Luaḥ halev* (Tarnopol, 1814), section 1, unpaginated. Emphasis is mine. On Schultes, see Mahler, *Hasidism and the Jewish Enlightenment,* 154. For a classic positive image of the Jewish beard from a Polish source, see Adam Mickiewicz's *Pan Tadeusz,* an excerpt of which is translated in Harold Segal, *Stranger in Our Midst: Images of the Jew in Polish Literature* (Ithaca, N.Y.: Cornell University Press, 1986), 71–75.

[151] Perl, writing under his pseudonym, Ovadiyah, in *Kerem ḥemed,* 3 (1838): 53–61. Isaac Hezekiah ben Samuel Lampronti (1679–1756), a rabbi, physician, and educator, authored the comprehensive *Paḥad yitsḥaq* encompassing halakhic materials from the Mishnah, the Talmuds, the decisors, the Tosafists, and later *responsa.* His own rabbinic *responsa* were collected by his contemporary, Samson Morpurgo, in *Shemesh tsedaqah.*

Isaac Euchel, who also admired Italian Jewry, specifically noted the beardlessness of his brethren from Leghorn (Livorno), "The Jews in Leghorn live together in calm and security in fine homes amidst the nobles of the land. . . . Most of them shave their beards and style their hair." Cited in Dubin, "The Rise and Fall of the Italian Jewish Model in Germany," 273. See, too, Lois Dubin, "Trieste and Berlin: The Italian Role in the Cultural Politics of the Haskalah," in *Toward Modernity: The European Jewish Model* (ed. Jacob Katz; New Brunswick, N.J.: Transaction Books, 1987), 189–224.

Poland brought Galicia and northern Italy under the same Imperial rule. Indeed, eager to convince the state that fulfillment of its cameralist aims posed no fundamental threat to Jewish law, Perl proffered Italian Jewry as a living prooftext of the possibility of transforming Galicia's Jews.[152] Perl's position on the beard, however, was informed less by the state's dress requirements for its subjects than by his own *Weltanschauung*. Restoration Austria made no sartorial demands on Galicia's Jews, and Joseph II's position on toleration had earlier meant the rescinding of the requirement that all married and widowed Jewish men wear beards.[153] The desire for the Hasidim and other traditional Jews to trim their beards came solely from Perl. He considered his worldview consistent with traditional Ashkenazic Jewish culture and labored to show in *Über die Modifikation* that any modifications in Jewish law that he suggested were grounded in the halakhic process and consonant with traditional rabbinic authority. His treatise, he claimed, strove to familiarize his Gentile readership with the "spirit of the Talmudists in relation to the exegesis of law" and to address two questions:

---

[152] Perl closed his treatise by adducing the historicism in Leone Modena's *Beit yehudah*: "I end this work with the wish of R. Judah of Modena, [the] author of comments to the *Ein ya'aqov* and of the commentary, [called] *Haboneh*, [who is] known to the Jewish nation, 'We learn from this to evaluate all Rabbinic edicts regarding virtues, trade, or habit according to the peoples [to] and places [in which they were given].' We find this [consideration for context] in several places in the Talmud." Perl, *Über die Modifikation*, 83. I have used the English translation of Modena's comment in Bezalel Safran, "Leone da Modena's Historical Thinking," in *Jewish Thought in the Seventeenth Century* (ed. Isadore Twersky and Bernard Septimus; Cambridge, Mass.: Harvard University Press, 1987), 381–98. The early reformer, Eliezer Lieberman, also cited Modena's *Haboneh* in his *Nogah hatsedeq*, which he adduced in his defense of using an organ during prayers. See Dubin, "The Rise and Fall of the Italian Jewish Model in Germany," 281.

[153] Scott, "Reform in the Habsburg Monarchy," 169. Maria Theresa upheld medieval tonsorial requirements for married and widowed male Jews as a means of discouraging the public appearances of affluent Viennese Jews who had begun to attend theaters, dance halls, restaurants, and other public places under her reign. See Myovich, "Josephism at its Boundaries," 222. Habsburg tolerance of traditional Jewish dress contrasts starkly with the position of the Jacobins during the French Revolution and of the 1844 Russian law. On the French case, see Zosa Szajkowski, *Jews and the French Revolutions of 1789, 1830 and 1848* (New York: KTAV, 1970), 785–807; on the Vilna-based *maskil* Rashi Fuenn's favorable response to the 1844 Russian edict prohibiting traditional Jewish dress, which he did not see as threatening the core of Judaism, as many of his brethren did, see his letter of May 18, 1845 published in Shmuel Feiner, *Mehaskalah lohemet lehaskalah meshammeret: nivḥar mikhtevei Rashi Fin* (Jerusalem: Dinur Center, 1993), 189–92.

After 1848, the Habsburgs *would* however make sartorial demands on the Jews in order to encourage integration. Traditional Jews of all ideological stripes reacted negatively to these edicts. See Jacob Katz, *A House Divided: Orthodoxy and Schism in Central European Jewry in the Nineteenth Century* (trans. Ziporah Brody; Hanover, N.H.: University Press of New England, 1998) and Gertner, "The Rabbinate and Hasidism in Nineteenth-Century Galicia," 63–68.

"1. Did the Jews, or actually their teachers, allow themselves to make changes in Mosaic law, and, [if so,] on what grounds? If this question should be answered in the affirmative, then one must ask 2. Whether or not the changes in the law [that occurred] were grounded in its very own spirit, or not?" He concluded that a "quick look at Mosaic Law and at the behavior of contemporary Jews" showed that the "foundation" of Jewish law had "another form." Analysis of the Talmud illustrated that "Jewish law generally — except for several key elements — was constantly subject to change. At first, many a law was altered a little bit; later, completely."[154]

As he had done with the beard, Perl sketched the history of Jewish divorce law for the Galician authorities to demonstrate its evolution over time. Yet, in contrast to the question of male facial hair, Perl's desire to make Jewish divorce law compatible with the state had a basis in new Habsburg legislation. Consonant with Josephinian cameralism, the state desired to create a civil sphere to control marriage, which it endeavored to effect with the promulgation of a new *Ehepatent* (Marriage Edict) on January 16, 1783. The marriage edict, however, produced a law that blurred the authority for the performance and dissolution of marriage. Marriages were to be contracted according to civil procedure, but the state maintained the clergy's role as religious functionaries and recordkeepers.[155] The 1785 provisional edict for Galicia, in the spirit of equalizing Jewish status under the law and encouraging productivization of the Jewish economy, eliminated the marriage tax for Jews living on the land and made marriage contracts and divorce proceedings subject to the civil courts.[156] When the *Toleranzpatent* for Galicia was issued in 1789, all marriage taxes were abolished, although the requirement that married couples pass a German exam remained on the books.[157] Later Habsburg legislation reflected the same kind of ambiguity toward the absolute separation of Church and State in matters of marriage and divorce.

---

[154] Perl, *Über die Modifikation*, 5–6.
[155] On the efforts of Jewish couples whose liaisons violated traditional Jewish law to appeal to the state, see Dubin, *The Port Jews of Habsburg Trieste*, 174–97 and Lois C. Dubin, "Les Liaisons dangereuses. Mariage juif et État moderne à Trieste au XVIIIe siècle," *Annales: Histoire, Sciences Sociales* 49, no. 5 (Septembre-Octobre 1994): 1139–70. On the desire of a famous Austrian Catholic to divorce and remarry, see Ulrike Hermat, "Divorce and Remarriage in Austria-Hungary: The Second Marriage of Franz Conrad von Hötzendorf," *Austrian History Yearbook* 32 (2001): 69–104.
[156] Myovich, "Josephism at its Boundaries," 262–69.
[157] The response of the Jewish commuity of Galicia spoke volumes about its assessment of the value of civil and religious spheres; nine years after the promulgation of the first Habsburg law on marriage, the Jews of Galicia avoided civil marriages, married religiously, and gave their children their mothers' surnames. Avoidance of civil marriage remained the norm for Galician Jewry until 1848. See A. Y. Brawer, *Galitsyah viyehudeihah: mehqarim betoldot Galitsyah bame'ah hashemoneh-esreh* (Jerusalem: Bialik Institute, 1965), 149, 202, and 280.

The *Allgemeines Bürgerliche Gesetzbuch* of 1811 (*ABGB*) affirmed denomina-
tional difference and empowered the clergy to uphold the practices of their
respective faiths with regard to marriage and divorce. Catholics, following
the Church's doctrine of the indissolubility of the marital sacrement, could
not divorce, but Protestants and Jews could, according to their religious
law.[158] While Jews could sunder their marital ties under the Habsburg code,
they could do so only according to the stipulations of traditional Jewish law,
which required that the husband give his estranged Jewish wife a written bill
of divorce to enable her to remarry. According to Jewish law, this requirement applied, as well, to a male convert from Judaism to Christianity.

Perl's treatise directly addressed the singular problematic within Jewish
law in which a woman seeking to remarry must still obtain a writ of divorce
from her converted husband, illustrating his concern with both the autonomy of the individual and the plight of the *agunah* (grass widow).[159] He
surveyed the history of divorce, beginning with biblical times, and compared
it to the ritual of *ḥalitsah*, the ceremony releasing a man from the obligation
of marrying his deceased brother's widow. Perl concluded that the goals of
both ceremonies in the biblical period were to enable a woman to remarry,
but that the public performance of *ḥalitsah* distinguished it from the private
ritual of divorce, in which a man simply wrote a bill of divorce and handed it
to his wife.[160] He sought to convince the Galician authorities that contemporary converts need not be required to fulfill the demands of a rabbinic court
in order to dissolve their marriages with their Jewish wives. Divorce, Perl
argued, had been private in biblical times, only becoming public and subject
to the supervision of a rabbinical court that demanded the fulfillment of a
myriad legal requirements because the rabbinate, informed by "time and
circumstances (*Zeit und Ümstande*)," sought to protect women from irresponsible husbands who might divorce them at will.[161]

---

[158] The *ABGB* permitted Protestants to divorce, but forbade Catholic converts to Protest-
antism from divorcing or remarrying. In the course of the nineteenth century, the Catholic
view of divorce steadily informed all divorce law affecting Christians, becoming the definitive
influence on the civil code by 1855. Absolute civil marriage and intermarriage only became
law in 1938. See Hermat, "Divorce and Remarriage in Austria-Hungary."

[159] See Rashi's famous responsum regarding the marital status of women whose husbands
had been forcibly converted during the Crusades, cited in *The Jew in the Medieval World: A
Source Book, 315–1791* (ed. Jacob Radar Marcus; Cincinnati, Ohio: Hebrew Union College
Press, 1938), 301–02, and the discussion in Jacob Katz, "Although He Has Sinned, He Remains a Jew," *Tarbiz* 27 (1958): 203–17. For the tensions between converts and the Jewish
community in Germany over marital issues in the early modern period, see Elisheva Carlebach, *Divided Souls: Converts from Judaism in Germany, 1500–1750* (New Haven, Conn.: Yale
University Press, 2001), 25, 138–39.

[160] Perl, *Über die Modifikation*, 10.

[161] See his discussion in ibid., 7–28.

The role of historical context and *Zeitgeist* in shaping Jewish law became even more apparent to Perl when he compared the ways in which Jewish legal codifiers living in different cultural spheres addressed the status of women and the legal requirements for divorce. Contrasting Joseph Karo's decisions in both his *Beit yosef* and *Shulḥan arukh* with Moses Isserles's glosses to the latter, Perl concluded that Ashkenazic custom had developed historically to be more stringent than had Sephardic custom. Karo, living in a polygamous society in which divorce was less of a taboo for a woman, wavered as to whether or not a man should be permitted or allowed to write the *get* by himself, as the Torah explicitly states, "He [the husband] writes her a bill of divorce (Deut 24:103)." Yet, Isserles, living in Ashkenaz, where monogamy had been normative Jewish marital practice since the twelfth century, included this stringency in his comments to the *Shulḥan arukh*.[162] In Perl's view, Isserles's legal culture erred in its excessive pietism and the creation of innumerable rituals that were not part of the original intent of Mosaic Law. In the case of divorce, however, Isserles's strictness resulted from a desire to protect women from cruel and punitive husbands.[163] Isserles's concern for reducing the cases in which women remained as *agunot* (plural of *agunah*), remarked Perl, led him to dispense with several conditions for the proper writing of the *get*. Even a brief survey of the rabbinic attitude toward Jewish divorce law illustrated that reasonableness and historical context informed their decisions. Perl's unstated conclusion was that rationality and decency should inform the contemporary problem of a convert seeking to divorce his Jewish wife. No longer a member of the Jewish community, a convert should be able to divorce his wife privately and prevent her from becoming a grass widow without impugning the integrity of Jewish law.

Perl's treatment of interest and the release of debts in the Sabbatical Year in the second and third sections of his treatise also appealed to history and *Zeitgeist*. His engagement with the religious legality of extending credit, an issue that had long preoccupied halakhists and the Church — and one that had also been long resolved — speaks legions about the preoccupation of *maskilim*, and the modernizing state, with redirecting the economic behavior of Ashkenazic Jews away from moneylending, petty trade, and commerce toward agriculture.[164] In *Über die Modifikation*, Perl analyzed the dominance of

---

[162] On the ban on polygamous marriage in Ashkenaz and its attribution to Gershom ben Judah, "Light of the Diaspora," (960–1028), see Ze'ev W. Falk, *Jewish Matrimonial Law in the Middle Ages* (Oxford: Oxford University Press, 1966), 13.

[163] Perl, *Über die Modifikation*, 26.

[164] All of the early modern petitions urging Jewish resettlement in western Europe or protecting Jewish privileges in Italian city-states emphasized the positive role of Jewish mercantile activity, including the extension of credit. See the discussion in Jonathan I. Israel, *European Jewry in the Age of Mercantilism, 1550–1750* (Oxford: Clarendon, 1985). On Simone

Jews in trade despite the biblical prohibition on lending with interest to a fellow Jew. While the productivization of the poor Jews of Galicia was central to both the *maskilim* and the state,[165] Perl's discussion of moneylending had a distinctly apologetic tone. The concentration of Jews in professions of trade and commerce had been historically conditioned. Surveying the Bible's repeated injunctions against lending on interest, Perl concluded, "The great and magnificent plan of the Lawgiver — who expresses himself so often and clearly in the Pentateuch — [was] to make the Jewish nation into farmers."[166]

Luzzatto's petition to the Venetian authorities to prevent the expulsion of the Jews, see "A Discourse on the Status of the Jews, and in Particular of those Living in the Illustrious City of Venice," in Benjamin C. I. Ravid, *Economics and Toleration in Seventeenth Century Venice: The Background and Context of the Discorso of Simone Luzzatto* (New York: American Academy for Jewish Research, 1977) and Benjamin Ravid, "Moneylending in Seventeenth Century Jewish Vernacular Apologetica," in *Jewish Thought in the Seventeenth Century* (ed. Isadore Twersky and Bernard Septimus; Cambridge, Mass.: Harvard University Press, 1987), 257–83. For the role of economic behavior in shaping Jewish identity and non-Jewish attitudes toward the Jews in modern Europe, see Derek Jonathan Penslar, *Shylock's Children: Economics and Jewish Identity in Modern Europe* (Berkeley: University of California Press, 2001).

As in the case of intermarriage, the issue of moneylending between Jew and non-Jew touched the critical issue of whether or not Jews, invited into the modern European state, would treat their non-Jewish co-citizens and co-subjects by the same standard as they treated their own. The Napoleonic Sanhedrin crystallized this concern in its eighth question: "Does Jewish law forbid Jews from taking interest from their own? What about from Gentiles?" In response, the notables of the Sanhedrin dissimulated, assuring Napoleon that Mosaic Law did not permit the extension of interest to Gentiles. See M. Diogene Tama, trans., *Transactions of the Parisian Sanhedrim, or Acts of the Assembly of Israelitish Deputies of France and Italy* (New York: University Press of America, 1985), 197–207; Simon Schwarzfuchs, *Napoleon, the Jews and the Sanhedrin* (London: The Littmann Library of Jewish Civilization, 1979), 69, 203, footnote 22; Gil Graff, *Dina de-Malkhuta Dina in Jewish Law, 1750–1848* (Tuscaloosa, Ala.: The University of Alabama Press, 1985). Ishmael ben Abraham Isaac ha-Kohen of Modena, too old to travel to Paris, rejected the political accomodationism of the notables, claiming that their denial of Jewish law's sanction of lending money with interest to Gentiles contradicted the Bible, the Talmud, and the Talmud's decisors. See Judah Rosenthal, "R. Ishmael of Modena's Responses to the Emperor Napoleon's Twelve Questions," *Talppiyyot* 4 (1950): 565–87, particularly 583. Jay Berkovitz argues in a forthcoming article that the notables' positive attitude toward Gentiles exhibited in their responses to Napoleon reflects a more open-minded attitude to Christians and Christianity on the part of several important traditional eighteenth-century European Jews than has usually been assumed. See Jay Berkovitz, "Changing Conceptions of Gentiles at the Threshold of Modernity: The Napoleonic Sanhedrin," forthcoming in *Orthodox Forum*. I would like to thank Professor Berkovitz for sharing his work with me.

On the question of how the medieval Ashkenazic rabbinate balanced their commitment to the principles of Jewish law with the exigencies of daily life that required negotiating with Gentile authority and surviving economically, see Haym Soloveitchik, "Pawnbroking and a Study of *Ribbit* and of the Halakhah in Exile," *PAAJR* 38–39 (1970): 203–68.

165 Springer, "Enlightened Absolutism."

166 Perl, *Über die Modifikation*, 30.

With the passage of time and the context of historical circumstance, the prohibitions against extending credit could no longer be upheld. As Jewish economic opportunity was constricted because of the enmity of the government authorities and the gradual shift away from agriculture as the dominant mode of production in the economy of ancient Israel, trade began to monopolize Jewish life. Surveying the economic profile of medieval Ashkenazic Jewry, Perl made a sweeping claim, "What the great-grandfather was forced to do out of material need, the grandsons continued out of custom, and so all of Jewry — save a small part — became businessmen, negociants, and speculators, so that Jew and Commerce, which was inextricably bound up with profit, became, indeed, inseparable *objects.*"[167]

Incapable of fighting economic realia, rabbinic leaders derived legal constructs to protect biblical law and allow extension of loans with interest. Preeminently concerned with maintaining the sanctity of divine law and the legitimacy of rabbinic authority to interpret the law, the rabbis created the legal category known as the *heter isqa,*[168] by which the creditor became an associate in business with the debtor, who managed the "business" and paid his associate, the lender, a fixed amount of profit they had previously agreed upon. Perl conceded to his Gentile audience that this legal loophole might appear implausible, but insisted that it was not:

> While now the scoffer delights in condemning this manner [of circumventing the law], I confess my weakness that in this case I admire the vision and knowledge of the teachers of that period for the spirit of their time (*ihrem Zeitgeiste*). The businessmen were given an easy means to insure they could deal with cash any way they could without running into collision with interest law. The law maintained its authority; the non-commerical [Jews] or the poor received what little they needed without interest; [and] usury was sufficiently controlled.[169]

Defending rabbinic prerogative, even while criticizing its historical intransigence as it had developed in Ashkenaz, Perl appears as an apologist for Jewish legal argumentation.[170]

Regarding the Torah's command to leave fields fallow and remit debts in the seventh year, Perl concluded that biblical Israel upheld the law until Nehemiah's period, but that the exigencies of Jewish accommodation to

---

[167] Ibid., 42. The emphasis is Perl's.

[168] In letter seventeen of *Boḥen tsaddiq,* in which Ovadiyah ben Pesakhiyah criticizes the merchants of Brody, an important Galician border city, for their immoral business practices, he points specifically to their extending interest without the *heter isqa.* See [Perl], *Boḥen tsaddiq,* 75–78. Perl's depiction of Brody aroused the ire of the *maskilim* in Brody. See Spicehandler, "Joshua Heschel Schorr," 31:198.

[169] Perl, *Über die Modifikation,* 45–46.

[170] See, too, Perl's defense of the traditional non-Hasidic rabbinate in [Perl], *Über das Wesen der Sekte Chassidim,* 66.

Persian, Greek, and Roman rule led to the commandment's disregard and transgression.[171] The Jewish religious leadership in the late Second Temple Period felt compelled both to protect the Torah's original intention to absolve all debts in the Sabbatical Year and to protect the members of the Jewish community whose livelihoods depended upon "lending and borrowing." Various legal maneuverings, including Hillel's initiation of the institution of the *Prosbul*, which prevented the remission of debts in the Sabbatical Year, ensued to honor the spirit of the law, to prevent bankruptcy, and to provide moderate loans to the poor in the years before the Sabbatical.[172] The Rabbis' consideration for economic and political pressures resulting from a new historical context in which the Jews had become a "trade-oriented nation" induced them to avail "themselves of a means by which to be able to circumvent, [for] they could not abolish, this law [*shemitah*]."[173] Perl concluded that the classical Sages "could make the effort to lighten or to circumvent laws that could be disadvantageous given the political conditions of the nation." The abrogation of laws that had fallen into disuse was also part of their purview.[174]

---

[171] Perl, *Über die Modifikation*, 49. In his footnote, Perl explicitly appealed to the rabbinic adage *dina dimalkhuta dina* ("the law of the land [the Gentile hosts] is the law") cited in *b. Gittin 10b* to explain why ancient Israelites accommodated to non-Jewish law and abandoned observance of the laws of the Sabbatical Year.

[172] See the prooftexts cited by Perl, *m. Shevi'it 10:1–2* and *b. Gittin 36a*, in which the discussion adduces biblical justification for the *Prosbul* based on Deut 15:2 and 15:9.

[173] Perl, *Über die Modifikation*, 51–52.

[174] Ibid. Suggestively, Perl chose the case of ritual immersion required by the Torah for a man's involuntary nocturnal emission (*qeri*) as the prooftext for rabbinic flexibility regarding the law. The Torah's original requirement, reasoned Perl, had fallen into disuse in the Babylonian exile and was reinstituted and modified by Ezra at the beginning of the Second Temple period. According to *b. Bava Qamma 82a*, Ezra required that immersion occur *only* for recitation of the Shema and reading of the Torah because, in Perl's view, he "realized that unconditional purification could not be required from a slavish, broken nation as it had been from a free, independent [nation]." By the period of the Talmud, ritual immersion for *qeri* was no longer common practice. Perl's fascination with the laws governing involuntary emission, although he did not belabor the point in his treatise to the Galician *Kreisamt*, was no doubt conditioned by the Hasidic preoccupation with the subject. Shneur Zalman of Lady (Liady) devoted chapter seven of the *Tanya* to the question of masturbation, which he considered more heinous than other kinds of sexual infractions involving a man and his wife because the semen was wasted, unabsorbed by the "husks" of the *sitra ahra*. Rectifying the sin of involuntary emission dominated books of popular Jewish spirituality in the eighteenth century. See Gershon David Hundert, "Jewish Popular Spirituality in the Eighteenth Century," *Polin* 15 (2002): 93–103, Biale, *Eros and the Jews*, chapter 6, "The Displacement of Desire in Eighteenth-Century Hasidism," and my earlier discussion of *mahashavot zarot* in Chapter Three. See, too, Lefin's brief comment on the Hasidic innovation of immersing on the eve of the Day of Atonement to atone for *qeri* in the Joseph Perl Archive, JNULA, 4° 1153/72, 3b.

After answering his treatise's first question to his satisfaction, concluding that the leaders and teachers of the Jewish community had allowed themselves to make changes in Mosaic legislation, Perl continued with an examination of the second issue: the "basis" (*Grund*) upon which the rabbinic leadership in the past had modified Jewish law. He concluded that the rabbinic leadership, both Talmudic and post-Talmudic, had always taken time and circumstances into their interpretation of Jewish law, but had always done so in a manner to maintain the law's integrity, authority, and sanctity. The rabbis in the past had "tried to derive modifications from the law itself, and were very cautious about changing the law, so as not to diminish its authority in the people's eyes."[175] Concern for the integrity of the halakhic process meant that the rabbinate was assiduous in modifying or deriving law from its internal "orthography, grammar, and logic."[176] Rabbinic exegesis, for Perl, resulted from an effort to produce an *a priori* desired legal result, but from within the law itself.[177] Authority was vested in the rabbinic teachers, whose duty it was to interpret the law in the spirit of God's original intention, and to prevent "a swindler or an imposter" from arising and leading "the people away from the true belief in divine law through erroneous interpretations of the laws."[178] An exegetical system that allowed the occasional error in rabbinic judgment to creep in was still preferable to the disunity that could ensue without the recognition of one authority guided by the religion's fundamental principles.[179]

Religious authority in Judaism, however, Perl argued, was vested not only in religious personalities, like the biblical prophet Samuel, but also at certain historical junctures in temporal leaders, like Jephthah, an ancient Israelite judge whose authority derived from his military prowess. Indeed, the Rabbis of the Talmud themselves expressed the view that the Jewish people should not discriminate between obedience to "temporal rulers and leaders in matters of law" in their adage, "What Jephthah was in his time, Samuel was in his" (*b. Rosh Hashanah 25b*).[180] Implicit in Perl's use of this Talmudic

---

[175] Perl, *Über die Modifikation*, 62–63.
[176] Ibid., 55.
[177] For a full study of the development of *midrashei halakhah*, see Jay M. Harris, *How Do We Know This?: Midrash and the Fragmentation of Modern Judaism* (Albany: State University of New York Press, 1995).
[178] Perl, *Über die Modifikation*, 56.
[179] Ibid., 58.
[180] In the course of his discussion of temporal and religious leadership, Perl also cited Ps 99:6, the same biblical prooftext that Zecharias Frankel (1801–1875), rebutting Abraham Geiger's support of the vernacularization of the liturgy at the 1845 Reform Convention held in Frankfurt-on-the-Main, adduced to argue that the Bible, and later the Talmud, rejected the centralization of religious authority in the hands of the priests. For Frankel, Hebrew was to remain the language for all Jews and all prayer in order to prevent a separation between a

prooftext was a point he would develop later in the treatise: that at certain historical moments the Jews could be legitimately guided by their temporal Jewish leaders who were to be considered as authoritative as any religious leadership.[181]

Perl's treatise next addressed the conundrum facing all reformist *maskilim*: how to account for the character of cultural pietism that had enveloped Ashkenazic Jewry, making it hostile to what he felt was its natural legal tradition, one open to modification? The current state of Ashkenazic rabbinic culture, in Perl's reading, was a betrayal of the original legitimacy of rabbinic authority. In consonance with Perl's defense of rabbinic culture on a theoretical level, he did not cast all the blame on the rabbis themselves, and opined that "as a group — there are always exceptions in every class of men — they are overall deeply moral and virtuous; their virtues do not permit a conscious tyranny over the people. If we see them perform actions of this kind, then we must attribute their origin to ignorance that has sanctified custom through time and marked it with holiness."[182]

The proclivity of the Ashkenazic rabbinate to adjudicate Jewish law in the direction of legal stringencies, argued Perl, lay in the economic history of the Jews. The inconsistency of rabbinic income in Ashkenazic Jewish society led to the professionalization of the rabbinate, making it dependent upon the will and needs of the people, who were often ignorant of the highest principles of Jewish law.[183] As he had done in the case of the beard and divorce, Perl examined the historical development of Judaism's attitude toward rabbinic income and explored the difference between Sephardic and Ashkenazic custom. The prohibition in the Mishnah against receiving an income from rabbinic adjudication and teaching could be upheld in ancient times

---

priestly caste literate in Hebrew and a laity literate in German. Frankel's comments are translated in Paul Mendes-Flohr and Jehuda Reinharz, *The Jew in the Modern World*, 180.

[181] Perl was clearly influenced by Judah Leib Mieses's republication of David Caro's *Tekhunat harabbanim* (*Die Pflichten den Rabbiner*) in 1823. Caro (1782–1839), a Polish *maskil*, had penned *Tekhunat harabbanim* as the third section of his *Berit emet* (*The True Covenant*, Dessau, 1820), which defended the aesthetic and liturgical changes of the Hamburg Temple and criticized the traditionalist pamphlet, *Eleh divrei haberit* (*These Are the Words of the Covenant*), that attacked the reformers. *Tekhunat harabbanim* addressed five issue of rabbinic authority: "(1) What was the designation of the rabbi in the earliest times and what is it now? (2) Is it essential for the Jews to have a rabbi? And how is a Jew appointed and chosen for this sacred work? (3) What are the obligations of a rabbi that he must do and uphold? (4) How did the Sages of old fulfill their obligations and how do they fulfill them now? (5) If the teachers and leaders of the Jews do not do what is good and right, what happens?" See Judah Leib Mieses, *Tekhunat harabbanim* (Vienna: Anton Strauss, 1823).

[182] Perl, *Über die Modifikation*, 68.

[183] On the perception of the decline in standards in the German-Jewish rabbinate and the abuse of rabbinic fees, see Sorkin, *The Transformation of German Jewry*, 48–49.

because most of the Sages and the people were engaged with agriculture. With the passage of time, and the shift in Jewish economic activity away from farming and toward trade, the Sages found themselves in a quandary. If they sustained themselves economically, they had no time "to remain true to their calling as jurists [*Casuisten*]." They gradually chose to remove themselves from worldly affairs and to devote themselves to divine service. Concerned with protecting the spirit of the Mishnah's prohibition on deriving income from their rabbinic legal work, Perl explained, the Sages of Talmud derived a means by which to protect the law and support themselves economically. A rabbi, the Talmud reasoned, could be paid for the loss of time (which he might have used for a trade), not for his teaching and learning.[184] This became common practice, but opposition to this legal circumvention arose by medieval times. Perl cited Maimonides's *Commentary on the Mishnah*, *Avot 4:6*, in which the medieval codifier railed against the practice of compensating rabbis, and cited both biblical and rabbinic precedents to support his claim. In contrast to Maimonides's position against rabbinic remuneration, Perl adduced the case of the Ashkenazic codifier, Asher ben Jehiel (the Rosh), who endorsed rabbinic compensation: "He [the Rosh] was a German Jew who at the time of the expulsion of the Jews from France came to Toledo [Spain], where he had to live as a rabbi from his Talmudic expertise. Experience confirms very well that the majority of [Ashkenazic] rabbis, having no stable livelihood, [found] the opinion of R. Asher preferable to that of Maimonides."[185] In time, rabbinic compensation also included a wide spectrum of fees for the performance of religious ceremonies, such as

---

[184] See the discussion in *b. Ketubbot 105a* cited by Perl.

[185] Perl, *Über die Modifikation*, 71. In his footnote, Perl pointed his readers to Asher ben Jehiel's comments on *m. Bekhorot 4:5*, on the Mishnah that begins "one who receives compensation for adjudication." Perl's historical knowledge of the Rosh comes from *Seder hadorot* (Karlsruhe, 1769), a traditional bibliography compiled by Jehiel ben Solomon Heilprin (1660–1746), a Lithuanian rabbinic figure. Shir, too, employed *Seder hadorot*, as well as the *Arukh* by Solomon ibn Parhon (1160) and Abraham Zacuto's *Yuhasin*. On Shir's historical method, see Gerson Cohen, "The Reconstruction of Gaonic History," in *Texts and Studies in Jewish History and Literature*, vol. 1 (ed. Jacob Mann; New York: KTAV, 1942), 15.

Perl also added: "R. Ovadiyah [Ovadiyah ben Avraham Bertinoro, c. 1450–before 1516], commentator on the Mishnah, and R. Moses Isserles, both of whom lived in the sixteenth century, among others, provide more proof for [the difference between Ashkenazic and Sephardic positions on rabbinic remuneration]; the first was not provided with a rabbinic position, thus he railed against the rabbis who were paid for their efforts in assisting at religious ceremonies (see his comments on *m. Bekhorot 4:6*), while R. Moses Isserles, who, as already mentioned, was provided with a rabbinic position, rejected anew the position of R. Ovadiyah." Perl, *Über die Modifikation*, 71. Isserles's rejection of Bertinoro's position is with regard to the payment of scribes and rabbis drawing up writs of divorce, which Isserles did not consider to belong to the category of adjucation. See Isserles's comments to *Shulḥan arukh, seder haget*, section 4.

circumcisions, betrothals, and marriages. Gifts at Chanukah[186] and Purim became normative.[187]

Asher ben Jehiel's position and the historically-conditioned restrictions on Jewish economic activity informed Ashkenazic-Jewish culture's attitude toward rabbinic compensation. Polish-Jewish families consciously instructed their sons to be knowledgeable in Talmud, and nothing else, leaving them only the rabbinate, membership on a rabbinic court, and teaching as means of subsistence. The devotion to Talmud and the retreat from society's economic demands worked together to create the economic "baroqueness" of early modern Polish Jewry, whose rabbinic class's ability to sustain itself merely through the collection of fees increasingly caught the attention of their Polish lords.[188] In time, the Polish overseers "took the rabbinate into their power . . . and imposed a rent for one or more rental periods upon it [the rabbinate], as they did with the liquor vendors."[189] Here we find Perl echoing a well-known complaint in early modern Polish-Jewish history: the purchase of rabbinic offices.[190] Perl's critique of the Polish-Jewish rabbinate thus encompassed seemingly contradictory complaints: contempt for its retreat from the world and disdain for its corruption at the behest of the Polish nobility.

Finally, Perl decried the Polish-Jewish rabbinate's dependence upon the Polish-Jewish masses for economic support. Rather than lead the Jewish public, the Polish-Jewish religious leadership followed the unlettered people, who:

> Just like those of any nation, have no conception of genuine religion and morality. Since they are an oppressed people, they were accustomed only to concocting impiety, fanaticism, and superstition. . . . This people naturally wanted to determine the worth of

---

[186] Perl used the word *Weihnachtsgeschenke* (literally, Christmas gifts) for his Austrian readers, perhaps because the two holidays often fall promixate to one another on the calendar.

[187] In his footnote, Perl complained about a wealthy rabbi from his childhood who demanded that the author give him a gift for Purim. Perl, *Über die Modifikation*, 72.

[188] Israel ben Moshe Zamość voiced a similar critique in his *Netsaḥ yisra'el* (1741). See Harris, *How Do We Know This?* 139.

[189] Perl, *Über die Modifikation*, 74–75.

[190] On the *konsensy rabinostwa*, the arenda for rabbinic office, see Chapter Two, M. J. Rosman, *The Lords' Jews: Magnate-Jewish Relations in the Polish-Lithuanian Commonwealth during the Eighteenth Century* (Cambridge, Mass.: Harvard Ukranian Research Institute, 1990), 200, and Teller, "The Legal Status of the Jews," 57–59. Perl's indignation at the purchase of rabbinic offices was articulated earlier by David Caro, who commented that "in most cases [of rabbinic appointment] in Poland a wealthy man purchases a rabbinic seat for his son or son-in-law like a man buys an apple for his small son, even though he is dull, young, and stupid." Caro cited, and Perl alluded to, *y. Bikkurim*, chapter 3, 65d, in which the prayershawl on a man who purchases his rabbinic office is compared to a donkey's saddle. See Caro's text, reprinted by Mieses, *Tekhunat harabbanim*, 11, footnote on the bottom of the page.

its teachers according to no other measure than those whose actions flattered their [the people's] mentality. The more a teacher behaved according to the sense and taste of the this superstitious people, the better became his reputation and the more productive were his revenues.[191]

A man who wanted to retain his position of rabbinical leadership had to "feign piety, withdraw into his cell, and retreat as much as possible from the world and the spirit of the times."[192] With the passage of time, the Polish-Jewish rabbinate used its erudition not to bolster existing *halakhah* and customs, but to create "new customs and ceremonies from which a Talmudist of antiquity would recoil with shrieks."[193] The mindless will of the people, who idolized the pietist and stigmatized the rationalist, had gotten the best of sincere members of the rabbinate who were incapable of uprooting an accepted popular custom. "Thus," Perl concluded, even "the Rashba (Solomon ibn Adret, a thirteenth-century rabbinic figure), despite his great authority, could not bring the people to give up a custom as dumb as it was superstititous: the slaughtering of a sin offering on the day before the Day of Atonement."[194]

Minhag, *Rabbinic Authority, and Modernity*

Treating the issue of *minhag* and its effect on Jewish religious praxis cuts to the heart of the Haskalah's effort to transform Polish Jewry and to the much more fundamental issue of rabbinic authority and its continuity in the modern period.[195] Perl believed that he had proven that the classical Sages had both taken the "spirit of the times" into consideration when adjudicating Jewish law and modified *halakhah* only if able to maintain the integrity of the

---

[191] Perl, *Über die Modifikation*, 75–76.

[192] Ibid., 76.

[193] Ibid., 77.

[194] Ibid. The ritual of *kapparah*, in which a rooster or hen to whom the sins of a penitent Jew are transferred is swung over the penitent's head and then slaughtered, dates from the seventh century. *Kapparah* was not universally accepted; Maimonides, Joseph Karo, and Solomon ibn Adret, were against the custom, calling it "the ways of the Amorites." Moses Isserles allowed it and *kapparah* became normative practice among Ashkenazic Jews. See Jacob Z. Lauterbach, "The Ritual for the Kapparot Ceremony," in *Studies in Jewish Law, Custom and Folklore* (ed. Jacob Z. Lauterbach; New York: KTAV, 1970), 133–43. On the persistence of the ritual among contemporary Ashkenazic Jewish communities, see Aviva Weintraub, "Poultry in Motion: The Jewish Atonement Ritual of Kapores," in *Jews of Brooklyn* (ed. Ilana Abramovitch and Seán Galvin; Hanover, N.H.: University of New England Press, 2002), 209–13.

[195] For an important analysis of contemporary Orthodoxy's devaluation of customary law, see Soloveitchik, "Rupture and Reconstruction." See, too, the discussion in Dan Miron, "Folklore and Antifolklore in the Yiddish Fiction of the Haskalah," in *Studies in Jewish Folklore* (ed. Frank Talmage; Cambridge, Mass.: Association for Jewish Studies, 1980), 219–49.

halakhic process and the authority of the law itself. In his effort to historicize Jewish law, Perl positioned himself as a legitimate successor to internal Jewish traditions of rabbinic critique.[196] He defined himself as a moderate *maskil* when it came to the question of Jewish law and rabbinic authority, although his negative attitude toward Hasidism was unrestrained. For Perl, the Hasidim were the fullest expression of a more fundamental problem in Jewish culture in Eastern Europe: the penchant toward supererogation. Perl wanted to create a modern Polish-Jewish culture within what he considered to be the reasonable boundaries of the law. Thus, in his treatise and other memos Perl never explicitly challenged the authority of the Oral Law, but rather focused on the cultural insularity that Ashkenazic Jewry's fidelity to custom had created, and that produced resistance to their integration into the Habsburg state. He hoped to transform Galician Jewry by combatting its supererogation from within the sources of rabbinic Judaism, and from within the culture of pre-modern Polish Jewry. In *Über die Modifikation*, Perl wished to make a principled commitment to the ability of contemporary rabbinic authorities to adjust Jewish law to the spirit of the times.

Perl's critique of *minhag* was culturally specific. He wanted the contemporary Polish-Galician rabbinate to assert its authority to rein in the uncontrollable growth of new customary laws that Polish-Galician Jewry now considered binding. The entrenchment of customary law not only created an obstacle for contemporary Galician Jews to become upstanding modern subjects of the Habsburg Monarchy, but it also distanced them from the authentic traditions of their Polish Jewish ancestors.[197] Perl's efforts to historicize the supererogation of Polish Jewry as a means to thwart the efflorescence of Hasidic custom and to counter the cultural insularity that Ashkenazic Jewry's fidelity to custom had engendered was thus part of a crusade to restore his image of Polish Jewry's past glory. Although fascinated with Sephardic and Italian Jewry, Perl's vision of the Haskalah for Galician Jewry did not entail, as it did for many of his Prussian brethren, an "unhinging," to use Ismar Schorsch's pointed phrase, "from the house of Ashkenazic Judaism."[198] Or at

---

196 For a discussion of internal rabbinic critique of Jewish law, see Talya Fishman, *Shaking the Pillars of Exile: 'Voice of a Fool,' an Early Modern Jewish Critique of Rabbinic Culture* (Stanford, Calif.: Stanford University Press, 1997). On Moses Mendelssohn's and Naftali Herz Wessely's conservative attitude toward rabbinic authority and biblical exegesis, see Breuer, *The Limits of Enlightenment.*

197 On the ancestral traditions of Polish Jews, see [Perl], *Boḥen tsaddiq*, 34.

198 Ismar Schorsch explored Prussian Jewry's romantic fascination with what they believed to be Sephardic Jewry's exemplary balance of Jewish tradition and non-Jewish learning and culture in Ismar Schorsch, "The Myth of Sephardic Supremacy," in *From Text to Context: The Turn to History in Modern Judaism* (Hanover, N.H.: University Press of New England, 1994), 71–92. Many East European *maskilim*, too, valorized the culture of Sephardic Jewry and looked toward it as an model of the desired harmony between faith and reason, Hebraism

least not from the entire house of Ashkenaz. Like his German-Jewish peers, who created an image of themselves by imaging a benighted, East European "Other," Perl, as Lefin had before him, engaged in a similar act of typological distancing. Viewing the Hasidic aesthetic as the antithesis of the values of *Bildung* that he aspired to, Perl projected "Otherness" primarily onto the Hasidim, who he believed intentionally fostered their *Unbildung*.[199] The rest of his Galician-Jewish brethren were merely weak and misguided. He also maintained that although there was historic precedent for the Ashkenazic penchant toward stringency in the adjudication of Jewish law, the unwillingness of the contemporary Polish-Jewish rabbinate to decide law in "the spirit of the times" contradicted the intent of both biblical and rabbinic legislation.[200] Contemporary Hasidism's love affair with superfluous custom burdened an already "baroque" culture and represented a usurpation of traditional rabbinic authority.[201]

By the end of *Über die Modifikation*, Perl felt he had made his case to the state for the urgent need to supervise the creation of a reasonable rabbinate to guide Galician Jewry. In keeping with his concern to distance himself from Herz Homberg's failed attempt to transform Galician Jewry, Perl reminded the *Kreisamt* to allow the Jewish community to be involved with the selection of the *religious affairs* administration that would empower and salary the rabbinate, for its goals were "to affect the Jews and no one else."[202] If the selection took place among that part of the Jewish community that understood the "true principles of religion" and not the group that represented the "[fanatical] spirit of the people," the new rabbinate would liberate Galician Jewry "from the intense pressure of [being obligated by the] voluntary legal adornments of their ignorant teachers [e.g. the Hasidic zaddikim]."[203] A

---

and knowledge of Gentile languages, expertise in traditional Jewish sources and in the Gentile fields of philosophy, philology and poetry, and devotion to Jewish law and participation in the Gentile state. See Shmuel Werses, "Judah ha-Levi in the Mirror of the Nineteenth Century," in *Megammot vetsurot besifrut hahaskalah* (Jerusalem: Magnes Press, 1990), 50–89.

[199] For the use of the term *Unbildung*, see Steven E. Aschheim, *Brothers and Strangers: The East European Jew in German and German Jewish Consciousness, 1800–1923* (Madison: University of Wisconsin Press, 1982), 8.

[200] Perl, *Über die Modifikation*, unpaginated introduction. See, too, David Caro's critique of stringency, published in Mieses, *Tekhunat harabbanim*, 32.

[201] Perl remained loyal to some *minhagim* practiced in Ashkenaz, despite his general campaign against customary law. According to Israel Bartal, the literary historian Chone Shmeruk frequently repeated that Perl punished his servants for forgetting to spread straw on the threshold of his synagogue in Tarnopol on the eve of Yom Kippur in order to flagellate sinners. See Israel Bartal, "Chone Shmeruk — In Memoriam," *Gal-Ed* 15–16 (1997): 18.

[202] Perl, *Über die Modifikation*, 80. Emphasis is Perl's.

[203] Ibid.

short while after he penned his treatise, Perl endeavored to effect this transformation in the rabbinate by his campaign to install Shir (Solomon Judah Rapoport) as head of the rabbinical court in Tarnopol.[204]

Perl's final effort, penned shortly before his death, to redirect Galician Jewry away from the appeal of what he believed to be Hasidic supererogation and superstitiousness was a long memorandum to the authorities in Tarnopol regarding state supervision of rabbis, *shohatim* (kosher slaughterers), and *mohalim* (circumcisers), three critical areas of Jewish communal life that he felt had been usurped by the Hasidim.[205] In the cover letter to the memorandum, Perl described the goals of the state as the antithesis of the culture of the Hasidim, who wanted, in Perl's view, "to strip the Jews of all *Bildung*," and to prevent them from making any steps toward integration into Galician society. Worse, and here echoing Lefin's own concerns, Perl asserted that the goal of the Hasidic leadership was complete authority over every aspect of the lives of Galician Jewry, from whom they demanded total loyalty at the expense of any allegiance to God or the state.[206] The memo's content detailed how the Hasidim slowly, yet inexorably, came to dominate Galician-Jewish society by intimidating the non-Hasidic rabbinate, harassing the non-Hasidic *shohatim* out of business,[207] and assuring that no male Jewish infants were circumcized by *mohalim* not subject to Hasidic control.[208] If the government did not intervene immediately to quash the relentless subjugation of Galician Jewry by these "Janissaries," there would be "no force on earth able to bring the Jews closer to general society and to integrate (*assimiliren*) them with the rest of Galicia's residents."[209] The "sect's" separatism and intoler-

---

[204] See Simon Bernfeld, *Toldot Shir [R. Shelomoh Yehudah Rapoport]* (Berlin: Zevi Hirsch bar Yizhak Izkowski, 1898), 78–90 and Isaac Barzilay, *Shlomo Yehudah Rapoport [Shir] (1790–1867) and His Contemporaries* (Jerusalem: The American Academy for Jewish Research, 1969), 93.

[205] Philip Friedman relates, without questioning the authenticity of the account, that when Joseph Perl died in 1839 (on Simhat Torah), the Hasidim of Tarnopol danced in the streets to celebrate. Given that the holiday of Simhat Torah encourages dancing, it would not be surprising that Hasidim celebrating the festival would have danced in the streets, whether or not their enemy, Perl, had died. See Friedman, "Joseph Perl as an Educational Activist," 179.

[206] The cover letter is published in Raphael Mahler, *Haskole un hsides: der kampf tsvishn haskole un hsides in galitsye in der ershter helf fun nayntsnt yorhundert* (New York: YIVO Institute, 1942), 238–39. See, too, Perl's comments about Hasidism's rejection of any obligations to the state in [Perl], *Über das Wesen der Sekte Chassidim*, 133–40.

[207] On the economic underpinnings of the conflict between Hasidic *shehitah* and the Jewish communal authorities, see Chone Shmeruk, "The Social Significance of Hasidic Ritual Slaughter," *Zion* 20 (1955): 47–72.

[208] Raphael Mahler, "Joseph Perl's Memo to the Authorities regarding the System of Appointing Rabbis, Ritual Slaughterers, and Circumcisers," in *Sefer hayovel mugash likhvod Dr. N. M. Gelber leregel yovelo hashivim* (ed. Israel Klausner, Raphael Mahler, and Dov Sadan; Tel Aviv: Olameinu, 1963), 85–104.

[209] Published in ibid., 89 and 91. I have translated Perl's term *assimilern* as "to integrate" to avoid the contemporary connotation of "communal and self-liquidation," which he did not

ance had already created insuperable barriers to the state's efforts. The bald
etatism revealed in this memo derived from Perl's effort, which he believed
to be moderate, to separate his commitment to Jewish law from loyalty to a
cowed rabbinate or, worse from his point of view, to corrupt Hasidim who
arrogated the authority to derive new laws and customs in opposition to the
values of classical rabbinic Judaism.

Perl's treatise on Jewish law and his last memo to the provincial authorities reveal the struggle of the moderate *maskilim* in Eastern Europe to define
what they believed to be the legitimate parameters of rabbinic authority.
Although penned a half-century after Mendelssohn's *Jerusalem*, Perl's comments show the commanding stamp of his predecessor's efforts to retain the
sanctity of the Talmud and rabbinic exegesis, while asserting the primacy of
individual conscience.[210] In both *Über die Modifikation* and his last memo, Perl
argued that Judaism's "true" principles denied its rabbinic leadership the
authority to punish and emphasized instead its role as educator:

> Those who understand Judaism know that rabbis are not regarded as clergy in any way;
> that Jewish law does not require the presence of a rabbi [for the performance of rituals];
> that no single religious ceremony exists that can be performed exclusively by the rabbi.
> [They know] that the rabbi is, above all, only a man who becomes familiar with that
> which is legally correct and incorrect — particularly in the case of the dietary laws — in
> order to resolve the doubts of the uninformed Jew, who turns to him in various cases.
> [They also know] that these [doubts] could be resolved by every other [ordinary] Jew, as
> well, if he tried.[211]

> According to Jewish religious principles, rabbis are to be considered and treated not like
> ordinary people, nor as servants of the Church, but as normal religious individuals.
> Rabbis and religious functionaries are, according to the true sense of Judaism, only
> teachers of the people; their responsibility is to teach the people religious and moral
> principles, to preach, and to supervise their [the people's] practice, without, indeed,
> being able to exercise any kind of authority against transgressors.[212]

In both texts, Perl, serving as vernacular interpreter of Judaism to a non-
Jewish audience, underscored his commitment to individual moral autono-

---

intend. On the nineteenth-century meaning of the word "assimiliation," see Hyman, *Gender
and Assimilation*, 10–49.

[210] For Mendelssohn, the rabbinate's historic authority to punish, particularly to excommunicate, was illegitimate, denying Judaism's true principles. As he detailed in the first
section of *Jerusalem*, which argued for the total separation of Church and State, only the state
had the right to police *actions*; religion's purview included solely the edification and instruction of *principles*. For Mendelssohn, "true" religion did not have the power of coercion. See
Moses Mendelssohn, *Jerusalem, or, On Religious Power and Judaism* (Hanover, N.H.: Brandeis
University Press, 1983), 33–75. In his words, "The right to our own convictions is inalien-
able," 61. See, too, David Sorkin, *Moses Mendelssohn and the Religious Enlightenment* (Berkeley:
University of California Press, 1996), 120–25.

[211] Perl, *Über die Modifikation*, unpaginated introduction.

[212] Published in Mahler, "Joseph Perl's Memo to the Authorities," 98.

my, even in the case of Jewish law. More activist than philosopher, Perl did not write a sophisticated philosophic treatment of how Jewish law could be binding individually, while denying the rabbinate coercive power, as Mendelssohn had done. But, like Mendelssohn, Perl strove to show his respect for the theory of rabbinic authority, while rejecting the praxis of Rabbinic authority.[213] His insistence that the true role of the rabbi was teacher, not judge and jury, revealed his modern sensibilities and the diminution of Jewish corporate autonomy and rabbinic authority in the Habsburg sphere, even in the period of the Restoration.[214]

By focusing his frustration on *minhag* and supererogation, as did other East European *maskilim*, and not on *halakhah*, Perl asserted that the Haskalah, while reformist, did not attack the foundation of Jewish law, the Talmud. Perl's effort to preserve rabbinic authority while making it reasonable distinguishes moderate *maskilim* from their counterparts, particularly those in contemporaneous Prussia and later in Galicia, whose commitment to modernization entailed a full-scale embrace of civil law and the separation of Synagogue and State. Abraham Geiger (1810–1874), Samuel Holdheim (1806–1860), and Joshua Heschel Schorr (1818–1895) regarded Talmudic law, not religious custom, as the primary impediment to the modernization and rationalization of Judaism.[215] Perl looked toward the state to support his campaign against *minhag*, but shaped his program of the Haskalah to fit a context in which the social and political process of full modernization had not yet occurred. Despite his etatism, Perl never articulated the political desire to subordinate all of Jewish law under the civil law of the state. He hoped to wean Galician Jewry from its dependence on religious custom generally, and from its submission to Hasidic custom particularly, thus making it possible for them to make a transition into the modern world that would be still faithful to what Perl felt was the core of traditional rabbinic culture.

Perl's vision of the Haskalah was marked by a dualism, as it had been for Mendel Lefin before him and for the moderate *maskilim* who subsequently

---

[213] Perl, even more than the circle of *maskilim* in late eighteenth century Prussia, appears here as a disciple of Mendelssohn. On the question of Mendelssohn's influence and mentorship, see Shmuel Feiner, "Mendelssohn and 'Mendelssohn's Disciples': A Re-examination," *LBIYA* 40 (1995): 133–67.

[214] On the transformation of the rabbinate, see Ismar Schorsch, "Emancipation and the Crisis of Religious Authority: The Emergence of the Modern Rabbinate," in *Revolution and Evolution: 1848 in German-Jewish History* (ed. Werner Mosse, Arnold Paucker, and Reinhard Rurup; Tubingen: Mohr, 1981), 206–54.

[215] On Geiger and Holdheim, see Meyer, *Response to Modernity*, 80–119. On Heschel Schorr, see Spicehandler, "Joshua Heschel Schorr." For Geiger's own attitude toward the Talmud, see Max Wiener, *Abraham Geiger and Liberal Judaism* (Philadelphia: The Jewish Publication Society of America, 1962).

walked the paths they paved.[216] He worked to make Galician Jews active and upright participants in Habsburg society without sacrificing their knowledge of and commitment to Judaism's classical texts and principle beliefs. Liberty of conscience was a hallmark of his modern commitments, but he endeavored to preserve a realm for the continuity of traditional Judaism's legal and religious obligations. As it did for Lefin, the battle against Hasidism shaped all of Perl's efforts to transform Galician Jewry. Hasidism's new form of religious leadership, devotion to esoteric hermeneutics, ardor for supererogatory religious behavior, and rejection of what Perl believed to be the state's well-intentioned reforms represented a vision of Jewish life that was diametrically opposed to that envisaged by the *maskilim*. The Hasidim, who according to Perl were accustomed to condemning anything contrary to their pietist dicta, "campaign[ed] particularly viciously against *Wissenschaft*, culture, and Enlightenment."[217] Jewish life in Galicia, if guided by a reasonable rabbinate, could fulfill the aspirations of Wessely's *Divrei shalom ve'emet*, transforming an insular, supererogatory, Hasidic-oriented, in a word, "baroque" Jewish population, into a modern Jewish community literate in and obligated by its classical tradition and sources.

Perl's efforts to transform Galician Jewry in the spirit of the moderate Haskalah failed. Opposition to his school from traditional rabbinic circles erupted as early as 1816, when a *herem* against Shir, Isaac Erter, Zevi Natkes, and Judah Pastor, "those who pursue sciences (*hokhmot*) and [study] non-Jewish languages," was issued in Lemberg under the direction of Jacob Meshullam Orenstein and specifically mentioned the maskilic schools of Brody and Tarnopol.[218] Orenstein, pressured by the Austrians who clearly

---

[216] On the dualism of the *maskilim*, see Shmuel Feiner, "Toward a Historical Definition of the Haskalah," in *New Perspectives on the Haskalah* (ed. Shmuel Feiner and David Sorkin; London: The Littman Library of Jewish Civilization, 2001), 184–219. See, too, David Caro's preface to *Tekhunat harabbanim*, in which he took pains to define the term *maskil* as "a lover of truth who studies a great deal of wisdom and science . . . and moderates all of his behavior and actions according to the laws of reason and wisdom," but not, as the masses think, a self-promoting, self-interested man, who is more swindler than *maskil*. Caro also contrasted the false zaddik, "who was only fastidious with regard to upholding unreasonable and baseless *minhagim* [and] not to the true and essential commandments" to the real zaddik, "an upright man, who, although unlearned in wisdom and science, conducts himself with righteousness and treats all men justly." Both definitions illustrate the middle path that *maskilim* endeavored to walk between religious pietism and the "false" Enlightenment.

[217] [Perl], *Über das Wesen der Sekte Chassidim*, 147.

[218] Friedman, "Joseph Perl as an Educational Activist," 169 and Weinlös, *Yosef Perls lebn un shafn*, 31–32, footnote 1, for selections of the text of the writ, which does not mention the names of the *maskilim*. Weinlös, in contrast to Mahler, suggests that Judah Leib Mieses was included in the ban. Jacob Samuel Bik related the events of the *herem* against Shir in an 1818 letter to Nachman Krochmal. See Ephraim Kupfer, "Jacob Samuel Bik in Light of New

supported instruction of German for the Jews of Galicia, ultimately had to repeal the *herem* in a public ritual reading outside the synagogue in Lemberg. Emboldened by the state's intervention into the Jewish culture war, the *maskilim* of Brody, with Perl's intercession, were able to pressure Zevi Hirsch of Żydaczów, a Hasidic zaddik, out of the city. This raised the stakes of the *Kulturkampf* even higher and the Żydaczower Hasidim responded by putting the *maskilim* of Tarnopol in *herem* in 1822.[219] In 1827, when the same rebbe wanted to spend the Sabbath in Zbaraż, Perl drafted a memo to the local authorities, who prevented him from leaving his home village of Podkamień.[220] Yet Perl's other efforts to stem the growth and influence of Hasidism on Galician Jewry foundered. Even his campaign to secure a rabbi predisposed to the moderate Haskalah for Tarnopol's rabbinic court collapsed. Although Shir won the majority of the kahal electors' votes and was installed in 1838, the victory was pyrrhic. The traditional Jewish community in Tarnopol, both Hasidic and non-Hasidic, rejected Rapoport, who served in Galicia for only three years and then left for Prague.[221]

In a letter written to Samuel Leib Goldenberg at the end of his life, Perl raised the white flag of surrender. Imploring Goldenberg to make sure that *Kerem hemed*, the journal under his editorship, represent the best values of the moderate Haskalah despite the extremism within Galician-Jewish culture, Perl wrote:

> In our country now there are no men who combine Torah and Wisdom. [No one] has a reputation in both [fields]. When even a speck of [secular] knowledge is seen in someone, everyone distances himself from that individual and heaps abuse upon him. Their opinion is that a Torah scholar must separate himself from the affairs of this world. . . . Therefore, when a Polish Jew even begins to learn some kind of Gentile language or writing, or to be engaged in any kind of non-Jewish knowledge, he abandons both the Torah and the commandments. They [those interested in *hokhmot*] no longer have anything to do with God-fearing Jews committed to the Torah, who distance themselves from them, for they [those interested in *hokhmot*] see that the men who are considered men of Torah hate and pursue them almost to their deaths.[222]

Documents," *Gal-Ed* 4–5 (1978): 544–45. Non-Hasidic opposition to Shir would continue, particularly from Solomon Kluger, the head of the rabbinical court in Brody. See Gelber, "The History of the Jews of Tarnopol," 75–76. On Kluger, see Shilo, "The War against Reform," and Gertner, "The Rabbinate and Hasidism in Nineteenth-Century Galicia."

[219] Gelber, *Arim ve'imahot beyisra'el: Brody*, 195–97.

[220] Friedman, "The First Battles," 263.

[221] Bernfeld, *Toldot Shir [R. Shelomoh Yehudah Rapoport]* and Weinlös, *Yosef Perls lebn un shafn*, 55–65.

[222] Joseph Perl's letter to Samuel Leib Goldenberg, *Kerem hemed* 3 (1838): 57.

While Perl could only imagine the Hasidim as the cause of what he believed to be Galician Jewry's unrelenting obscurantism, Hasidic piety was not the only impediment to his program of the moderate Haskalah. The conservatism of Restoration Austria also colluded against Perl's activism, for the very state to whom he addressed his memoranda had long ceased to push for radical changes in Galician society, both Jewish and general. Ultimately, without the state's support, the moderate *maskilim* were no match for Galician Jewry's tenacious traditionalism, which, even after the dramatic political events of the second half of the nineteenth century, retained its power and meaning for a large sector of the Jewish population, well into the twentieth century. Although the revolution of 1848 emancipated Galician Jewry, post-revolutionary forces repealed the legal steps granting Jews equality under the law, and full political emancipation was only achieved in 1867. Complete legal equality then created its own political and cultural paradox: Jewish traditionalists who had earlier rejected the state's intervention into Jewish life quickly learned how to employ the state for their own ends in order to protect, as best they could, the borders of their traditional culture against the onslaught of modernity.[223]

---

[223] When traditional Galician Jewry organized Orthodox political parties for representation in the regional and national Diet, a right garnered after 1867, they did so as a political expedience. Their tactic of allying with the state was ideologically pre-modern, even if the tools they employed (voting, mass parties) were distinctly modern. See Gershon C. Bacon, *The Politics of Tradition: Agudat Yisrael in Poland, 1916–1939* (Jerusalem: Magnes Press, 1996); Rachel Manekin, "Politics, Religion, and National Identity: The Galician Jewish Vote in the 1873 Parliamentary Elections," in *Polin 12: Focusing on Galicia: Jews, Poles, and Ukrainians, 1772–1918* (ed. Israel Bartal and Antony Polonsky; London: The Littman Library of Jewish Civilization, 1999), 100–19; Piotr Wróbel, "The Jews of Galicia under Austrian-Polish Rule, 1869–1918," *Austrian History Yearbook* 25 (1994): 97–138. See Israel Bartal, "Early Modern Jewish Politics: 'The Council of the Four Lands' in Eastern Europe," in *Hatsiyyonut vehahazarah lahistoryah: ha'arakhah mehadash* (ed. S. N. Eisenstadt and Moshe Lisk; Jerusalem: Yad Yitzhak ben Zevi, 1999), 194, for a discussion of the "early modern politics" of contemporary *haredim* ("God-fearers, or "ultra-Orthodox") who pragmatically utilize the political system of the modern state of Israel, a state they consider theologically illegitimate. See, too, Katz, *A House Divided* and Michael K. Silber, "The Emergence of Ultra-Orthodoxy: The Invention of a Tradition," in *The Uses of Tradition: Jewish Continuity in the Modern Era* (ed. Jack Wertheimer; New York: The Jewish Theological Seminary of America, 1992), 23–84 for the "modernity" of self-consciously anti-modern religious movements in Judaism.

EPILOGUE

THE LEGACY OF THE MODERATE HASKALAH

This book has argued that while Mendel Lefin's and Joseph Perl's program of the moderate Haskalah failed to sway the majority of East European Jews to the maskilic movement, their significance lies in being the most important Polish-Jewish proponents of a vision of modern Jewish life that harmonized European culture with traditional rabbinic Judaism in the fateful age of the partitions.[1] Both Lefin and Perl feared that traditional Polish-Jewish society, threatened by modernity's areligious rationalism and Hasidism's obscurantism, was at a critical juncture at the end of the eighteenth century. In response, they offered their version of a moderate Jewish Enlightenment as a pathway through the shoals of atheistic modernity and Hasidic piety. For both Lefin and Perl, and for other moderate *maskilim* after them, the Haskalah meant transition, not crisis.

The parochial image of Poland and of its benighted Jews in particular has obscured the significance of Lefin's and Perl's ideology and has reduced it to a local, secondary Jewish response to modernity. This book has asserted, however, that because of the partitions of the Polish-Lithuanian Commonwealth, which made Poland's Jews Europe's Jews, no history of modern European Jewry can be written without understanding its Polish antecedents. Europe and European Jewry were transformed in the years 1772–1795 by the partitions, which thrust a demographically massive community of Ashkenazic Jews defined by a singular tradition of communal, legal, and religious autonomy into an encounter with the European state that sought, throughout the modern period, to integrate this community as its subjects, and then citizens. Opposition to integration came not only from traditional anti-Jewish forces within European society (the clergy, competitive burghers, certain elements in the nobility, the peasantry), but also from within the culture of Polish Jewry, which had long defined itself by its steadfast commitment to Jewish law and devotion to religious custom. Eighteenth-century Hasidism, which revolutionized traditional Ashkenazic Jewish culture, deepened these

---

1   Lefin's and Perl's formulation of the moderate Haskalah anticipates by a half century, for example, Judah Leib Gordon's wrestling with fealty to Hebraism and the rabbinic tradition and the desire for the unconditional integration of East European Jewry into modern European society. On Gordon, see Michael Stanislawski, *For Whom Do I Toil?: Judah Leib Gordon and the Crisis of Russian Jewry* (New York: Oxford University Press, 1988).

earlier cultural tendencies, inoculating Polish Jewry from the modernization efforts of the state, whether Polish, Russian, or Austrian.

Although regionally specific, Mendel Lefin's and Joseph Perl's conception of the moderate Jewish Enlightenment addressed the critical issues that the majority of Europe's Jews would encounter throughout the nineteenth and into the twentieth century. Even with the shift toward nationalist forms of identity,[2] most of the world's Jews until World War II were eastern Ashkenazic Jews, the descendants of Polish Jews, who had to define their relationship to the non-Jewish state, decide the parameters of rabbinic authority and rabbinic exegesis in their lives, assess whether or not the command of a Jewish language was necessary for the production of Jewish culture, and clarify their relationship to non-Jews and to Jews of divergent religious attitudes and behaviors. For many contemporary Jews, these negotiations — as well as the solutions offered by the moderate Polish *maskilim* — are still relevant.

In interpreting the Haskalah as moderate, reasonable, and religiously-informed, Jewish scholars of the Haskalah in both the United States and Israel share the search for a "usable past."[3] It would be disingenuous of me to suggest that, despite the historian's credo to write the past in as dispassionate and objective manner as possible, I am divorced from my own historical context and subjectivity. Clearly Lefin's and Perl's high degree of Jewish literacy, religious moderation, and unrepentant modernity appeal to me personally. But what I have tried to do in this book is not to evaluate whether or not their conception of the Haskalah was favorable or unfavorable for the shaping of modern Jewish identity. Rather, I have endeavored to understand and explain the historical forces that led Polish *maskilim* to define the Haskalah in the ways they did and, in so doing, to shift the gaze of the historian of modern European Jewry eastward.

Yet, given the current postmodern critique of the Enlightenment as univocal, essentialist, and static[4] — and thus an unsuitable exemplar for

---

[2]   In the nineteenth century, self-proclaimed nationalists, such as Perez Smolenskin (1840 or 1842–1885), savaged Mendelssohn and his peers for their alleged betrayal of Judaism and the Jewish people. On Smolenskin, see Joseph Klausner, *Historyah shel hasifrut ha'ivrit hahadashah* (Jerusalem: The Hebrew University, 1952), 1: 74–75 and Azriel Shohat, *Im hillufei tequfot* (Jerusalem: The Bialik Institute, 1960), last chapter.
[3]   On the subjectivity of Jewish historiography, see David N. Myers and David B. Ruderman, eds., *The Jewish Past Revisited: Reflections on Modern Jewish Historians* (New Haven, Conn.: Yale University Press, 1998).
[4]   See Steven D. Kepnes's introduction in Steven Kepnes, ed., *Interpreting Judaism in a Postmodern Age* (New York: New York University Press, 1996), 2. Michel Foucault's work initiated the theoretical critique of the Enlightenment and of western "rationality" as a veil for power. See, for example, Philip Barker, ed., *Michel Foucault: An Introduction* (Edinburgh: Edinburgh University Press, 1998); Hugo A. Meynell, *Postmodernism and the New Enlightenment*

contemporary behavior — and the blossoming in both the academy[5] and in Jewish communal life of the pietism or enthusiasm that the *maskilim* battled against, Lefin's and Perl's conception of the Haskalah may indeed present a viable paradigm for a self-conscious, religiously moderate, and textually literate modern Jewish identity.

(Washington, D.C.: The Catholic University of America Press, 1999); Christopher Fox, "Introduction: How to Prepare a Noble Savage: The Spectacle of Human Science," in *Inventing Human Science: Eighteenth-Century Domains* (ed. Christopher Fox, Roy Porter, and Robert Wexler; Berkeley, Calif.: University of California Press, 1989), 1–30.

[5] Current scholarship in the fields of Jewish mysticism, Kabbalah, and Hasidism provides an important corrective to the overly rational reading of the Jewish past offered by the founding fathers of *Wissenschaft des Judentums*. Gershom Scholem first articulated his critique of *Wissenschaft des Judentums* in his seminal essay, "Reservations about *Hokhmat yisra'el*," in *Luah ha'arets* (1945) and reprinted in Gershom Scholem, "Reservations about *Hokhmat yisra'el*," in *Devarim bego: pirqei morashah utehiyyah* (Tel Aviv: Am Oved, 1976), 385–403. A shorter and less forceful version can be found in Gershom Scholem, "The Science of Judaism — Then and Now," in *The Messianic Idea in Judaism and Other Essays on Jewish Spirituality* (New York: Schocken, 1971), 304–13.

APPENDIX

Prayer Against the Hasidim
Joseph Perl Archive, JNULA, 4° 1153/5

בא"י או"א האל הגדול והנורא האל הקדוש אתה חונן לאדם דעת האנושית
אתה חוננתנו למדע תורתך שבכתב וגם אתה הנחלת לאבותינו תורה
שבע"פ ותתן לנו מורים אמת ומפרשי צדק להאיר עינינו בהם בכן רוממתנו
מכל החיים קרבתנו לעבודתך ושמך הקדוש עלינו קראת ומפני חטאינו
וברוב אולתינו תכפו עלינו צרות רבות ארוכות ורעות לקצוי ארץ נדחנו
לאלפי שנים ואין שיור בידינו עוד זולתי מתנותיך היקרות האלה ולולא הם
נחמתי כבר אבדתי בעני ואך עתה לעת זקוני צמחה בי זרע דורות אנשים
כחשים דור אביו יקלל וכו" דור טהור בעיניו ומצואתו לא רוחץ דור רמו
עיניו וכו" דור חרבות שניו לאכול עניים מארץ וכו" קמו לגנוב לבות עמך
בית ישראל ולגזול גם נחלת מורשה זאת מידיהם כי הנה על עמך יערימו
סוד להשכיחם תורותיך ואף גם להעבירם על דעת האנושי[ן]ת אז יבואו
שץ [ש"צ] נתן ברכיה חיון ופרענק ימ"ש לבדות להם שמות רזים ורמזים אין
מספר לחייב את העם להאמין בהם באלהותם ובנביאיהם העוזבים אורחות
יושר ללכת בדרכי חושך וחלקלקות לאמור אלוהים אנו ונביאים ובידינו
התורות לפרשם ולפותרם כחפצינו ואתה ברחמיך הפרת את עצתם איבדת
זכרם ואת ריבוי ספריהם ביערת מקרב עמך ועתה קמו תרבות אנשים רעים
וחטאים תחתיהם אלה הם נביאי הבעל (ש"ט) שתילי קוציהם ומפיחי מפרי
פגוליהם אה"ה ד" אל תשליכנו לעת זקנה רצה בשארית עמך ישראל
ובתפלתם להשיב עבודתך אל מכונה ותורתך לתיקונה ימחו כזבים מן הארץ
האלילים כרות יכרתון כל הרשעה כלה כעשן תכלה ואנחנו עמך נודה שמך
לעולם לדור ודור נספר תהלתך.

"Blessed are you, God, God of our ancestors, the great, awesome, and holy
God. You have bequeathed *human understanding* (*da'at ha'enoshit*) to humanity.[1] You have gifted us with the knowledge of your Written Torah and you
have also bequeathed the Oral Torah to our ancestors. You gave us truthful
teachers and just commentators to enlighten us with [their teachings]. Thus
you elevated us above all life[2] and brought us closer to your divine service.

---

[1] The language of the prayer alludes to the Amidah, qualifying God's gift of wisdom with
the word *ha'enoshit* (human) to emphasize the autonomy of the human faculty of reason that
was a hallmark of the Enlightenment.

[2] The phrase substitutes the word *haḥayim* (life) for *haleshonot* (the [Gentile] languages),

Your holy name called us. But because of our many sins and the vastness of our iniquities, many lengthy evil troubles befell us. We were exiled to the ends of the earth for thousands of years. We have nothing else except these precious gifts [the two Torahs], and were it not for them, I would have already lost all hope because of my misery. Indeed, now, in my old age, the seed of generations of liars has blossomed, a generation "who will curse its fathers" (Prov 30:11), a generation pure in its own eyes, but who will never be clean of its own filth, an "arrogant generation" (Ps 131:1 and Prov 30:13), "a generation whose sword-like teeth will eat the poor from the land" (Prov 30:14) has arisen to deceive your people, the House of Israel, and also to plunder this inheritance from their hands. For, behold, they will plot against your people to make them forget your Torahs and even to make them negate human understanding. Then Sabbatai Zevi, Nathan [of Gaza], Baruchiah [Russo], [Nehemiah] Hayon and [Jacob] Frank, may their names be blotted out, will come to fabricate never-ending names, secrets, and allusions in order to obligate the people to believe in them, in their divinity, and in their prophets, who abandon [the] paths of righteousness to walk in dark, crooked roads, saying, "We are gods and prophets and we may interpret and resolve [exegetical issues in] the Torahs as we desire." You, in your compassion, obstructed their design[s], destroyed their memory, and prevented the proliferation of their books from your people's midst. Now, in their stead, a culture of sinning, evil men, has arisen; they are the prophets of the Ba'al [Shem Tov], the sprouts of their thorns, the disseminators of the fruit of their filth.[3] God and God of our ancestors, do not forsake us in [our] old age. Favor your remnant in Israel and [hear] their prayer to return your divine service to its dwelling place and your Torah to its rightful interpretation. May lies be wiped out from the earth, idolatry extirpated,[4] and all of the evil be destroyed like smoke,[5] and we, your people, will praise your name forever. We will sing your praise for generations.

---

which follows the phrase *atah beḥartanu miqol ha'amim* ("you have chosen us from among all the other nations") in normative rabbinic liturgy, expressing the ambivalence of the *maskilim* toward Jewish national particularism. Instead, the prayer affirms the universal distinction between the human and animal worlds.

[3]   The Hebrew in this phrase is awkward. The author might have meant to write סְפִיחֵי, meaning, "the products of the fruit of their filth," but the manuscript has מְפִיחֵי. The author deliberately punned on the name Ba'al as an allusion to biblical Israel's idolatrous worship of Baal (Num 22:41, Num 25:1–9, and Deut 4:3). See the note below.

[4]   This line quotes directly from the second paragraph of the Aleinu, thereby underlining the analogy the *maskilim* drew between Beshtian Hasidism and idolatry.

[5]   Cited from the liturgy for Rosh haShanah.

BIBLIOGRAPHY

Primary Sources:

Archives

The Department of Manuscripts and Archives of the Jewish National and University Library (JNULA), Jerusalem.

The Joseph Perl Archive, 4° 1153.
The Abraham Schwadron Collection of Jewish Autographs and Portraits, including the papers of Jacob Samuel Bik, Joseph Perl, and Mendel Lefin.
Heb. 38.7075. "Notes to Joseph Perl's Literary Work."

The Department of Microfilmed Hebrew Manuscripts of the Jewish National and University Library, Jerusalem.

Jacob Samuel Bik's diary, a xerox of Merzbacher manuscript, the municipal library of Frankfurt-on-the-Main, 64, Ms. hebr. fol. 11.
Mendel Lefin's Yiddish translations of Psalms (1–56; 91–99), Job (1–18), and Lamentations, Jerusalem.

The Central Archives of the Jewish People, Jerusalem.

Letters of Sheindel Pineles, Joseph Perl's daughter, the N. M. Gelber Archive.

The Czartoryski Family Archive and Library, Cracow, Poland.

MS 2253, "Entwurf eines Rabinersystems in den Gutern Ihrer Durchlaucht des Fursten Adam Czartoryski General von Podolien," April 4, 1794.
MS EW 3267, Adam Jerzy Czartoryski to Adam Kazimierz Czartoryski, August 10, 1803.
MS EW 3267, Adam Jerzy Czartoryski to Izabela Czartoryska, March 2, 1804.
6032 III, EW 819. Adam Jerzy Czartoryski to Adam Kazimierz Czartoryski, May 4, 1789.
6096 II, EW 1089 [copy]. May 18, 1782, May 26, 1785; August 10 and 17, 1787; June 28, 1792 [copied later in 1884 by Róza Zamoyska.] Adam Jerzy Czartoryski to Izabela Fleming Czartoryska.
6030 III, EW 623. Izabela Fleming Czartoryska to Adam Kazimierz Czartoryski, September 1,1804/1805, and September 16, 1805.
6285 EW 1046, Adam Kazimierz Czartoryski to Adam Jerzy Czartoryski, October 23, 1776 [should be 1786] and March 19, 1803.
6338 IV, EW 1503, June 28, 1802; 6338 IV, EW 1503, July 3, 1802; 6338 IV, MS EW 1503, March 19, 1803; May 16, 1803; May 26, 1803. Adam Kazimierz to Adam Jerzy Czartoryski.

Printed Materials

Abramovitsh, S. Y. *Tales of Mendele the Book Peddler.* Edited by Dan Miron and Ken Frieden. Translated by Ted Gorelick and Hillel Halkin. New York: Schocken Books, 1996.

Abu'av, Isaac. *Menorat hama'or.* Edited by Yehudah F. Horev. Jerusalem: The Kook Institute, 1961.

Agnon, Shmuel Joseph. *Ir umelo'ah.* Jerusalem: Schocken Books, 1986.

———. *A Book that Was Lost and Other Stories.* Edited by Alan Mintz and Anne Golumb Hoffman. New York: Schocken Books, 1995.

Assaf, Simha. *Meqorot letoldot haḥinukh beyisra'el.* Tel Aviv: Devir, 1954.

Barash, Asher. *Pictures from a Brewery.* Translated by Katie Kaplan. New York: Bobbs-Merrill, 1971.

Batowski, Zygmunt, ed. *Z korespondencyi Norblin.* Lwów, 1911.

Ben-Ya'akov, Yitsak Eisik. *Otsar hasefarim.* Vilna: Romm Publishers, 1880.

Bloch, Shimshon. *Shevilei olam.* Warsaw: Natan Schriftgisser, 1882.

Bolechów, Ber. *The Memoirs of Ber Bolechow, (1723–1805).* Edited and translated by M. Vishnitzer. New York: Oxford University Press, 1922. Repr., New York: Arno, 1973.

Bontekoe, Willem Ysbrandsz. *Oniyyah so'arah.* Translated by Mendel Lefin? Żółkiew? 1818.

———. *Memorable Description of the East Indian Voyage 1618–25.* Translated by Pieter Beyl and C. B. Bodde-Hodgkinson. London: George Routledge & Sons, 1929.

Campe, Joachim Heinrich. *Sammlung interessanter und durchgängig zweckmässig abgefasster Reisebeschreibungen für die Jugend.* Reutlingen: J. Grözinger, 1786–93.

———. *Sämmtliche Kinder- und Jugendschriften: neue Gesammtausgabe der letzen Hand.* Braunschweig: Kinderbibliotek, 1830.

———. *Über einige verkannte wenigstens ungenützte Mittel zur Beförderung der Industrie, der Bevölkerung und des öffentliche Wohlstandes.* Wolfenbüttel (Frankfurt/Main): Verlag Sauer & Auvermann KG, 1786.

Cohen, Mark, ed. and trans. *The Autobiography of a Seventeenth-Century Rabbi: Leon Modena's Life of Judah.* Princeton, N.J.: Princeton University Press, 1988.

Cooper, Anthony Ashley, Third Earl of Shaftesbury. *Characteristics of Men, Manners, Opinions, Times.* Hildesheim: Georg Olms Verlag, 1978.

Coxe, William. *Travels in Poland and Russia.* London, 1802. Repr., New York: Arno, 1970.

Czartoryski, Adam Jerzy. *Memoirs of Prince Adam Czartroyski and His Correspondence with Alexander I.* Edited by Adam Gielgud. Orono, Me.: Academic International, 1968.

———. *Pamiętniki i Memoriały Polityczne, 1776–1809.* Edited by Jerzy Skowronek. Warsaw: Instytut Wydawniczy Pax, 1986.

Da Modena, Leone. *Beit yehudah.* Venice, 1635.

Döblin, Alfred. *Journey to Poland.* Edited by Heinz Graber. Translated by Joachim Neugroschel. New York: Paragon House Publishers, 1991.

Euler, Leonhard. *Letters of Euler on Different Subjects in Physics and Philosophy addressed to a German Princess.* Translated by Henry Hunter. London: Murray & Highley, 1802.

Feder, Tobias Gutmann. *Qol meḥatsetsim (o siah be'olam hanefashot).* Lemberg: Jacob Ehrenpreis, 1875.

Fénelon, François de Salignac de La Mothe. *Dialogues of the Dead.* Glasgow: Robert and Andrew Foulis, 1754.

Fleckeles, Eliezer ben David. *Ahavat david.* Prague, 1800.

Franklin, Benjamin. *The Autobiography of Benjamin Franklin: A Genetic Text.* Edited by J. A. Leo Lemay and P. M. Zall. Knoxville: The University of Tennessee Press, 1981.

Friedlander, Yehudah. "Tobias Gutmann Feder: 'The Archers' Voice.'" *Zehut* (May 1981): 275–303.

Friedländer, David. *Lesebuch für jüdische Kinder zum Besten der jüdischen Freischule.* Berlin, 1779.

———. *Sendschreiben an die deutsche Juden.* Berlin, 1788.

———. *Über die Verbesserung der Israeliten im Königreich Pohlen. Ein von der Regierung daselbst im Jahr 1816 abgefordertes Gutachten.* Berlin: Nicolaische Buchhandlung, 1819.

Fuenn, Samuel Joseph. *Qiryah ne'emanah.* Vilna, 1860.

Gellert, Christian Fürchtegott. *Fabeln und Erzählungen.* Tübingen: Max Niemeyer Verlag, 1966.

Glückel of Hameln. *The Memoirs of Glückel of Hameln.* Translated by Marvin Lowenthal. New York: Schocken Books, 1977.

Gottlober, Abraham Baer. "Russia." *Hamaggid* 17, no. 38–40 (1873): 347, 355–56, 364–64.

———. "Memoirs." Pages 250–59 in *Di yudische folksbibliotek.* Edited by Sholom Aleichem. Kiev, 1888.

———. *Zikhronot umasa'ot.* Edited by Reuben Goldberg. Jerusalem: Bialik Institute, 1976.

Hartley, David. *Observations on Man, His Frame, His Duty and His Expectations.* London: T. Tegg & Son, 1834.

Heller, Aryeh Leib ben Joseph. *Avnei milu'im.* Lemberg, 1815.

Helvétius, Claude-Adrian. *De l'Esprit or Essays on the Mind and its Several Faculties.* Translated by William Mudford. New York: Albion, 1810.

Herder, Johann Gottfried. "Essay on the Origin of Language." Pages 87–166 in *On the Origin of Language.* Edited by John H. Moran and Alexander Cope. New York: Frederick Ungar Publishing, 1966.

Horowitz, Isaiah. *The Generations of Adam.* Translated by Miles Krassen. Mahwah, N.J.: Paulist Press, 1996.

Horowitz, Zevi ha-Levi Ish. *Letoldot haqehillot beFolin.* Jerusalem: The Kook Institute, 1978.

Hunt, Lynn, ed. and trans. *The French Revolution and Human Rights: A Brief Documentary History.* Boston: Bedford, 1996.

Ibn Pakuda, Bahya. *Hovot halevavot.* Edited by Moses Hyamson. Jerusalem: Feldheim Publishers, 1978.

———. *Sefer torat hovot halevavot.* Translated by Shmuel Yerushalmi. Jerusalem: Me'ori Yisra'el, 1972.

A Jewish Life under the Tsars: The Autobiography of Chaim Aronson, 1825–1888. Translated by Norman Marsden. Totowa, N.J.: Allanheld, Osmun & Co., 1983.

Kant, Immanuel. *Critique of Pure Reason.* Translated by Norman Kemp Smith. New York: St. Martin's, 1929.

———. "What is Enlightenment?" Pages 83–90 in *Foundations of the Metaphysics of Morals.* Translated by Lewis White Beck. New York: Macmillan, 1990 (c. 1959).

Kobler, Franz, ed., *Jüdische Geschichte in Briefen aus Ost und West.* Vienna: Im Saturn-Verlag, 1938.

Labaree, Leonard W., ed. *The Papers of Benjamin Franklin.* New Haven, Conn.: Yale University Press, 1959.

Lefin, Mendel. "*Elon moreh.*" *Hamelits* (1867): 1–28.

[Lefin, Mendel]. *"Essai d'un plan de réforme ayant pour objet d'éclairer la Nation Juive en Pologne et de redresser par là ses moeurs."* Pages 409–21 in *Materiały do dziejów Sejmu Czteroletniego.* Edited by Arthur Eisenbach, Jerzy Michałski, Emanuel Rostworowski, and Janusz Woliński. Wrocław: Instytut Historii Polskiej Akademii Nauk, 1969.

——. *"Liqqutei kelalim."* Pages 287–301 in N. M. Gelber, "Mendel Lefin of Satanów's Proposals for the Improvement of Jewish Community Life presented to the Great *Sejm* (1788–1792)." Pages 287–305 in *The Abraham Weiss Jubilee Volume.* Edited by Samuel Belkin. New York: Shulsinger Brothers, 1964.

——. *Masa'ot hayam.* Żółkiew: Gershon Letteris, 1818; Lemberg: 1859.

——. *Moda levinah.* Berlin, 1789.

——. *Sefer ḥeshbon hanefesh.* Lemberg, 1808; Warsaw: J. Levenson, 1852; Jerusalem: The book Center, 1988.

[Lefin, Mendel]. *Sefer mishlei shelomo im perush qatsar veha'ataqah ḥadashah bilshon Ashkenaz leto'elet aheinu beit yisra'el be'artsot Polin.* Tarnopol, 1814.

——. trans., *Sefer moreh nevukhim.* Żółkiew, 1829.

——. *Sefer qohelet im targum yehudit uvi'ur.* Odessa, 1873.

——. trans., *Sefer refu'at ha'am.* Żółkiew, 1794.

Letteris, Meir, ed. *Mikhtavim.* Lemberg, 1827.

——. *Zikaron basefer.* Vienna, 1868–69.

Levinsohn, Isaac Baer. *Te'udah beyisra'el.* Edited by Immanuel Etkes. Vilna, 1828.

Locke, John. *An Essay Concerning Human Understanding.* Edited by Alexander Campbell Fraser. New York: Dover, 1959.

——. *Some Thoughts Concerning Education.* Pages 7–161 in *Some Thoughts Concerning Education and an Essay on Human Understanding.* Edited by Ruth Grant and Nathan Tarcov. Indianapolis, Ind.: Hackett, 1996.

Löw, Leopold. *Gesammelte Schriften.* Edited by Immanuel Löw. 2d edition. Hildesheim: Georg Olms Verlag, 1979.

Maimonides, Moses. *Crisis and Leadership: The Epistles of Maimonides.* Edited by David Hartman and translated by Hillel Halkin. Philadelphia: The Jewish Publication Society of America, 1985.

——. *The Guide of the Perplexed.* Edited and translated by Shlomo Pines. Chicago: University of Chicago Press, 1963.

Maimon, Solomon. *An Autobiography.* Translated by J. Clark Murray. Urbana: University of Illinois Press, 1954.

Marcus, Jacob Radar, ed., *The Jew in the Medieval World: A Source Book, 315–1791.* Cincinnati, Ohio: Hebrew Union College Press, 1938.

Mendelssohn, Moses. *Jerusalem, or, On Religious Power and Judaism.* Edited by Alexander Altmann and translated by Allan Arkin. Hanover, N.H.: Brandeis University Press, 1983.

——. *Phädon, or the Death of Socrates.* London: J. Cooper, 1789.

——. *Sefer megillat qohelet im bi'ur qatsar umaspik lehavanat haketuv al-pi peshuto leto'elet hatalmidim.* Berlin, 1770.

Mendes-Flohr, Paul and Jehuda Reinharz, eds. *The Jew in the Modern World.* Oxford: Oxford University Press, 1995.

Mieses, Judah Leib. *Sefer qinat ha'emet.* Vienna: Anton von Schmid, 1828.

——. *Tekhunat harabbanim.* Vienna: Anton Strauss, 1823.

Modena, Leone. *The History of the Rites, Customes, and Manner of Life, of the Present Jews, throughout the World.* Translated by Edmund Chilmead. London, 1650.

Monies, Isaac Michael. "Responsum on the Custom of Lighting Candles on Lag Ba'omer in Memory of R. Shimon bar Yochai." *Yerushalayim* 1 (1844): 9–21.

Montesquieu, Charles de Secondat. *Persian Letters*. Translated by C. J. Betts. New York: Penguin, 1986.

Pascal, Blaise. *Pensées*. Edited and translated by A. J. Krailsheimer. Harmondsworth, UK: Penguin Books, 1966.

Pasek, Jan Chryzostom. *Memoirs of the Polish Baroque*. Edited and translated by Catherine S. Leach. Berkeley: University of California Press, 1976.

[Perl, Joseph]. *Boḥen tsaddiq*. Prague, 1838.

———. *Joseph Perl's Revealer of Secrets: The First Hebrew Novel*. Translated by Dov Taylor. Westview Press, 1997.

———. *Luaḥ halev*. Tarnopol, 1814.

———. *Ma'asiyyot ve'iggerot mitsaddiqim amittiyyim ume'anshei shelomeinu*. Edited by Chone Shmeruk and Shmuel Werses. Jerusalem: Publications of the Israel Academy of Sciences and Humanities, 1969.

———. *Megalleh temirin*. Vienna, 1819.

———. *Sheva tefillot*. Tarnopol: Nachman Pineles, 1814.

———. *Tsir ne'eman*. Tarnopol: Nachman Pineles, 1814–16.

———. *Über das Wesen der Sekte Chassidim*. Edited by Avraham Rubinstein. Jerusalem: Publications of the Israel Academy of Sciences and Humanities, 1977.

Pribram, A. François, ed. *Urkunden und Akten zur Geschichte der Juden in Wien*. 2 vols. Vienna: Wilhelm Braumüller, 1918.

Rapoport, Solomon Yehudah. *Toledot*. Warsaw, 1913.

Reggio, Isaac Samuel. *Iggerot yashar*. Vienna, 1834.

Rousseau, Jean-Jacques. *Émile*. Translated by Barbara Foxley. London: Dent, 1966.

———. *The Government of Poland*. Translated by Wellmoore Kendall. Indianapolis, Ind: Hackett Publishing Company, 1985.

Segal, Harold B., ed. *Stranger in Our Midst: Images of the Jew in Polish Literature*. Ithaca, N.Y.: Cornell University Press, 1986.

The Shipwreck of the Antelope East-India Packet, H. Wilson, Esq. Commander, on the Pelew Islands . . . in August 1783. London: D. Brewman, 1788.

Tishby, Isaiah, ed. *The Wisdom of the Zohar*. London: Oxford University Press, 1989.

Transactions of the Parisian Sanhedrim, or Acts of the Assembly of Israelitish Deputies of France and Italy. Edited by M. Diogene Tama. New York: University Press of America, 1985.

Van Doren, Carl ed., *Benjamin Franklin's Autobiographical Writings*. New York: The Viking Press, 1945.

Wessely, Naftali Herz. *Divrei shalom ve'emet*. Berlin, 1782.

Wilensky, Mordecai. *Ḥasidim umitnaggedim: letoldot hapulmus shebeineihem bashanim 1772–1815*. Jerusalem: Bialik Institute, 1970.

Zalman of Lady, Shneur. *Liqqutei amarim [Tanya]*. Translated by Nissan Mindel. New York, 1969.

Secondary Sources:

Abbreviations:

HUCA: *Hebrew Union College Annual*
JQR: *Jewish Quarterly Review*
JSS: *Jewish Social Studies*
LBIYA: *Leo Baeck Institute Yearbook*
PAAJR: *Publications of the American Academy for Jewish Research*

Abramsky, Chimen. "The Crisis of Authority within European Jewry in the Eighteenth Century." Pages 13–28 in *Studies in Jewish Religious and Intellectual History*. Edited by Siegfried Stein and Raphael Loewe. Tuscaloosa, Ala.: The University of Alabama Press, 1979.

Adelman, Howard Ernest. "Success and Failure in the Seventeenth Century Ghetto of Venice: The Life and Thought of Leon Modena, 1571–1648." Ph.D. diss., Brandeis University, 1985.

Ain, Abraham. "'Swislocz': Portrait of a Jewish Community in Eastern Europe." Pages 22–50 in *East European Jews in Two Worlds: Studies from the YIVO Annual*. Edited by Deborah Dash Moore. Evanston, Ill.: Northwestern University Press, 1990.

Albert, Phyllis Cohen. *The Modernization of French Jewry: Consistory and Community in the Nineteenth Century*. Hanover, N.H.: Brandeis University Press, 1977.

Alter, Robert. *The Invention of Hebrew Prose: Modern Fiction and the Language of Realism*. Seattle: University of Washington Press, 1988.

Altmann, Alexander. *Moses Mendelssohn: A Biographical Study*. Tuscaloosa, Ala.: The University of Alabama Press, 1973.

Anderson, Benedict. *Imagined Communities: Reflections on the Origin and Spread of Nationalism*. New York: Verso, 1983.

Applebaum, Anne. *Between East and West: Across the Border Lands of Europe*. New York: Pantheon Books, 1994.

Appleby, Joyce, and Lynn Hunt, ed. *Telling the Truth About History*. New York: W.W. Norton, 1994.

Aschheim, Steven E. *Brothers and Strangers: The East European Jew in German and German Jewish Consciousness, 1800–1923*. Madison: University of Wisconsin Press, 1982.

———. *Brothers and Strangers* Reconsidered. Rome: Archivio Guideo Izzi, 1998.

Ash, Timothy Garton. "The Puzzle of Central Europe." *The New York Review of Books* (March 18, 1999): 18–23.

Assaf, David. *Breslav: bibliografyah mu'eret, R. Nahman Mibreslav, toldotav umorashato hasifrutit: sifrei talmidav vetalmidei talmidav: ḥasidut Breslav usevivoteihah*. Jerusalem: Zalman Shazar Center, 2000.

Avineri, Shlomo. "Marx and Jewish Emancipation." *Journal of the History of Ideas* 25, no. 3 (September 1964): 445–50.

Åkerman, Susanna. "The Forms of Queen Christina's Academies." Pages 165–88 in *The Shapes of Knowledge from the Renaissance to the Enlightenment*. Edited by Donald R. Kelley and Richard H. Popkin. Dordrecht: Kluwer, 1991.

Bacon, Gershon C. *The Politics of Tradition: Agudat Yisrael in Poland, 1916–1939*. Jerusalem: Magnes Press, 1996.

Baer, Yitzhak. *A History of the Jews in Christian Spain*. 2 vols. Philadelphia: The Jewish Publication Society of America, 1978.

———. *Galut*. Translated by Robert Warshow. Lanham, Md.: University Press of America, 1988.

Bałaban, Majer. *Dzieje Żydów w Galicyi i w Rzeczpospolitej Krakowskiej, 1772–1868*. Lwów: Nakl. Ksiej. Polskiej B. Polonieckiego, 1914.

———. "Herz Homberg in Galizien." *Jahrbuch für jüdische Geschichte und Literatur* 19 (1916): 189–221.

———. *Letoldot hatenu'ah hafranqit*. Tel Aviv: Devir, 1934.

———. "Mendel Lewin i książę Adam Czartoryski." *Chwila*, 7–8, no. 5313–14 (Stycznia 1934): 10–12.

Balin, Carole. *'To Reveal Our Hearts': Russian-Jewish Women Writers in Imperial Russia*. Cinncinnati, Ohio: Hebrew Union College Press, 2001.

Barker, Philip, ed. *Michel Foucault: An Introduction.* Edinburgh: Edinburgh University Press, 1998.

Barnavi, Eli, ed. *A Historical Atlas of the Jewish People.* New York: Schocken Books, 1992.

Baron, Salo. *A Social and Religious History of the Jews.* Philadelphia: The Jewish Publication Society of America, 1976.

———. "Ghetto and Emancipation." *The Menorah Journal* 14 (June 1928): 515–26.

———. "The Eichmann Trial." Pages 3–53 in *American Jewish Yearbook.* Edited by Morris Fine and Milton Himmelfarb. New York: The American Jewish Commitee and the Jewish Publication Society of America, 1962.

———. *The Russian Jew under Tsars and Soviets.* New York: Schocken Books, 1987.

Bartal, Israel. "Chone Shmeruk – In Memoriam." *Gal-Ed* 15–16 (1997): 15–22.

———. "Early Modern Jewish Politics: 'The Council of the Four Lands' in Eastern Europe." Pages 186–94 in *Hatsiyyonut vehaḥazarah lahistoryah: ha'arakhah meḥadash.* Edited by S. N. Eisenstadt and Moshe Lisk. Jerusalem: Yad Yitzhak ben Zevi, 1999.

———. "From Traditional Bilingualism to National Monolingualism." Pages 141–50 in *Hebrew in Ashkenaz.* Edited by Lewis Glinert. New York: Oxford University Press, 1993.

———. "Mordecai Aaron Günzberg: A Lithuanian Maskil Faces Modernity." Pages 126–47 in *From East and West: Jews in a Changing Europe, 1750–1870.* Edited by Frances Malino and David Sorkin. London: Oxford University Press, 1990.

———. "'Potency' and 'Impotency': Between Tradition and the Jewish Enlightenment." Pages 225–37 in *Eros, erusin ve'issurim: miniyyut umishpaḥah bahistoryah.* Edited by Israel Bartal and Isaiah Gafni. Jerusalem: Zalman Shazar Center, 1998.

———. "'The Heavenly City of Germany' and Absolutism à la Mode d'Autriche: The Rise of the Haskalah in Galicia." Pages 14–32 in *Toward Modernity: The European Jewish Model.* Edited by Jacob Katz. New Brunswick, N.J.: Transaction Books, 1987.

———. "The Image of Germany and German Jewry in East European Jewish Society During the Nineteenth Century." Pages 1–17 in *Danzig: Between East and West.* Edited by Isadore Twersky. Cambridge, Mass.: Harvard University Press, 1985.

———. "The *Pinkas* of the Council of the Four Lands." Pages 110–18 in *The Jews in Old Poland, 1000–1795.* Edited by Antony Polonsky, Jakub Basista, and Andrzej Link-Lenczowski. London: I. B. Tauris, 1993.

———. "'The Second Model': France as a Source of Influence in the Processes of Modernization of East European Jewry, 1772–1863." Pages 271–85 in *Hamahppekhah hatsarfatit verishumah.* Edited by Richard Cohen. Jerusalem: Zalman Shazar Center, 1991.

Bartal, Israel and Antony Polonsky. "Introduction: The Jews of Galicia under the Habsburgs." Pages 3–24 in *Polin: Focusing on Galicia: Jews, Poles, and Ukrainians, 1772–1918.* Vol. 12. Edited by Israel Bartal and Antony Polonsky. London: The Littman Library of Jewish Civilization, 1999.

Bartov, Omer. *Murder in Our Midst: The Holocaust, Industrial Killing, and Representation.* New York: Oxford University Press, 1996.

Barzilay, Isaac. "National and Anti-National Trends in the Berlin Haskalah." *JSS* 21, no. 3 (July 1959): 165–92.

———. "The Enlightenment and the Jews: A Study in Haskalah and Nationalism." Ph.D. diss., Columbia University, 1955.

———. "The Italian and Berlin Haskalah." *PAAJR* 29 (1960–61): 17–54.

——. *Shlomo Yehudah Rapoport [SHIR] (1790–1867) and His Contemporaries.* Jerusalem: The American Academy for Jewish Research, 1969.

——. "The Treatment of the Jewish Religion in the Literature of the Berlin Haskalah." *PAAJR* 24 (1955): 39–68.

——. *Yoseph Shlomo Delmedigo (Yashar of Candia): His Life, Works and Times.* Leiden: E. J. Brill, 1974.

Beales, Derek. *Joseph II: In the Shadow of Maria Theresa, 1741–1780.* Cambridge: Cambridge University Press, 1987.

——. "Social Forces and Enlightened Policies." Pages 37–53 in *Enlightened Absolutism: Reform and Reformers in Later Eighteenth-Century Europe.* Edited by H. M. Scott. London: Macmillan, 1990.

Beauvois, Daniel. *Lumières et Societé en Europe de l'Est: L'Université de Vilna et les Ecoles Polonaises de l'Empire Russe (1803–1832).* Lille: Université de Lille, 1977.

——. "Polish-Jewish Relations in the Territories Annexed by the Russian Empire in the First Half of the Nineteenth Century." Pages 78–90 in *The Jews in Poland.* Edited by Chimen Abramsky, Maciej Jachimczyk, and Antony Polonsky. London: Basil Blackwell, 1986.

Beinart, Haim, ed. *The Sephardi Legacy.* Jerusalem: Magnes Press, 1992.

Berger, Michael. *Rabbinic Authority.* New York: Oxford University Press, 1998.

Berger, Peter L. *The Sacred Canopy: Elements of a Sociological Theory of Religion.* New York: Doubleday & Company, 1969.

Berlin, Isaiah. *Vico and Herder: Two Studies in the History of Ideas.* New York: Viking, 1976.

Bernfeld, Simon. *Toldot Shir [R. Shelomoh Yehudah Rapoport].* Berlin: Zevi Hirsch bar Yizhak Izkowski, 1898.

Biale, David. "Childhood, Marriage, and the Family in the Eastern European Jewish Enlightenment." Pages 45–62 in *The Jewish Family: Myths and Reality.* Edited by Steven M. Cohen and Paula E. Hyman. New York: Holmes & Meier, 1986.

——. *Eros and the Jews: From Biblical Israel to Contemporary America.* Berkeley: University of California Press, 1997.

——. *Power and Powerlessness in Jewish History.* New York: Schocken Books, 1986.

Biber, Menachem Mendel. *Mazkeret legedolei Ostrahah.* Berdyczów: Hayim Jacob Sheftil, 1907.

Bickerman, Elias. *Four Strange Books of the Bible.* New York: Schocken Books, 1967.

Bildstein, Gerald. "A Note on the Function of 'The Law of the Land is the Law'." *Jewish Journal of Sociology* 15 (1973): 213–19.

Birnbaum, Jacob. "Lefin (Levin), Menachem Mendel." Page 351 in *Leksikon fun der nayer yidisher literatur.* Edited by Samuel Niger and Jacob Shatzky. Vol. 5 edited by Ephraim Euerbach, Isaac Charlash, and Moses Starkman. New York: Marstin Press, 1963.

Birnbaum, Pierre and Ira Katznelson, eds. *Paths of Emancipation: Jews, States, and Citizenship.* Princeton, N.J.: Princeton University Press, 1995.

Blackall, Eric A. *The Emergence of German as a Literary Language, 1700–1775.* Cambridge: Cambridge University Press, 1959.

Blanning, T.C.W. *Joseph II.* Essex: Longman Group, 1994.

Blejwas, Stanislaus. *Realism in Polish Politics: Warsaw Positivism and National Survival in Nineteenth Century Poland.* New Haven, Conn.: Yale Concilium on International and Area Studies, 1984.

Bloch, Marc. *The Historian's Craft.* New York: Vintage Books, 1953.

Blumberg, Harry. "The Problem of Immortality in Avicenna, Maimonides and St. Thomas Aquinas." Pages 165–85 in *Wolfson Jubilee Volume.* Vol. 1. Edited by Saul Lieberman. Jerusalem: American Academy for Jewish Research, 1965.

Blum, Jerome. "Russia." Pages 68–97 in *European Landed Elites in the Nineteenth Century*. Edited by David Spring. Baltimore: The Johns Hopkins University Press, 1977.

Bogucka, Maria. "Polish Towns between the Sixteenth and Eighteenth Centuries." Pages 138–56 in *A Republic of Nobles: Studies in Polish History to 1864*. Edited by J. K. Federowicz. Cambridge: Cambridge University Press, 1982.

Bor, Harris. "Moral Education in The Age of the Jewish Enlightenment." Ph.D. diss., University of Cambridge, 1996.

———. "Enlightenment Values, Jewish Ethics: The Haskalah's Transformation of the Traditional *Musar* Genre." Pages 48–63 in *New Perspectives on the Haskalah*. Edited by Shmuel Feiner and David Sorkin. Oxford: The Littman Library of Jewish Civilization, 2001.

Böhme, Hartmut and Gernot. "The Battle of Reason with the Imagination." Pages 426–52 in *What Is Enlightenment? Eighteenth-Century Answers and Twentieth-Century Questions*. Edited by James Schmidt. Berkeley: University of California Press, 1996.

Brawer, A. Y. *Galitsyah viyehudeihah: mehqarim betoldot Galitsyah bame'ah hashemoneh-esreh*. Jerusalem: Bialik Institute, 1965.

Brenner, Michael. "Between Haskalah and Kabbalah: Peter Beer's History of Jewish Sects." Pages 389–404 in *Jewish History and Jewish Memory: Essays in Honor of Yosef Hayim Yerushalmi*. Edited by Elisheva Carlebach, John M. Efron, and David N. Myers. Hanover, N.H.: Brandeis University Press, 1998.

Breuer, Edward. *The Limits of Enlightenment: Jews, Germans and the Study of Scripture in the Eighteenth-Century*. Cambridge, Mass.: Harvard University Press, 1996.

Brock, Peter. "Polish Nationalism." Pages 310–72 in *Nationalism in Eastern Europe*. Edited by Peter Sugar and Ivo Lederer. Seattle: University of Washington Press, 1969.

Bruford, W. H. *The German Tradition of Self-Cultivation: "Bildung" from Humboldt to Thomas Mann*. Cambridge: Cambridge University Press, 1975.

Buber, Solomon, ed. *Anshei shem: ge'onei yisra'el, adirei torah, rabbanim asher shimshu baqodesh ba'ir Lwów mishenat 1500 ve'ad 1890*. Cracow, 1895.

Butterwick, Richard. *Poland's Last King and English Culture: Stanisław August Poniatowski, 1732–1798*. Oxford: Oxford University Press, 1998.

———. "The Enlightened Monarchy of Stanisław August Poniatowski (1764–1795)." Pages 193–218 in *The Polish-Lithuanian Monarchy in European Context, c. 1500–1795*. Edited by Richard Butterwick. New York: Palgrave, 2001.

Cahnman, Werner J. "The Three Regions of German-Jewish History." Pages 3–14 in *German Jewry: Its History and Sociology*. Edited by Joseph B. Maier, Judith Marcus, and Zoltán Tarr. New Brunswick, N.J.: Transaction Books, 1989.

Carlebach, Elisheva. *The Pursuit of Heresy: Rabbi Moses Hagiz and the Sabbatian Controversies*. New York: Columbia University Press, 1990.

———. *Divided Souls: Converts from Judaism in Germany, 1500–1750*. New Haven, Conn.: Yale University Press, 2001.

Carsten, F. L. "The Court Jews: A Prelude to Emancipation." *LBIYA* 3 (1958): 140–56.

Cassirer, Ernst. *Kant's Life and Thought*. Translated by James Haden. New Haven, Conn.: Yale University Press, 1981.

———. *The Philosophy of the Enlightenment*. Boston, Mass.: Beacon Press, 1962.

Chartier, Roger. *Cultural History: Between Practices and Representations*. Translated by Lydia G. Cochrane. Ithaca, New York: Cornell University Press, 1988.

———. *On the Edge of the Cliff: History, Language, and Practices*. Translated by Lydia G. Cochrane. Baltimore: The Johns Hopkins University Press, 1997.

Chiel, Arthur A. "Benjamin Franklin and Menachem Mendel Lefin." *Conservative Judaism* (Summer 1979): 50–55.

Cohen, Gerson. "The Reconstruction of Gaonic History." Pages 13–96 in *Texts and Studies in Jewish History and Literature*. Vol 1. Edited by Jacob Mann. New York: KTAV, 1942.

Cohen, Mark. "Leone da Modena's *Riti*: A Seventeenth-Century Plea for Social Toleration of the Jews." Pages 429–73 in *Essential Papers on Jewish Culture in Renaissance and Baroque Italy*. Edited by David B. Ruderman. New York: New York University Press, 1992.

Cohen, Mitchell. *Zion and State: Nation, Class and the Shaping of Modern Israel*. New York: Columbia University Press, 1992.

Cohen, Richard I. *Jewish Icons: Art and Society in Modern Europe*. Berkeley: University of California Press, 1998.

Cohen, Shaye. *From the Maccabees to the Mishnah*. Philadelphia: Westminster, 1987.

Cott, Nancy. *Public Vows: A History of Marriage and the Nation*. Cambridge, Mass.: Harvard University Press, 2000.

Cragg, Gerald R. *Reason and Authority in the Eighteenth Century*. Cambridge: Cambridge University Press, 1964.

Cumming, Ian. *Helvétius: His Life and Place in the History of Educational Thought*. London: Routledge, 1955.

Cygielman, Shmuel. "Regarding the Suggestions of Mateusz Butrymowicz, a Representative of the Great *Sejm*, for the Reform of the Jewish Community of Poland and Lithuania at the End of the 1780s and R. Hershel Józefowicz of Chełm's Response." Pages 87–100 in *Bein yisra'el la'amim: sefer mugash leShmuel Ettinger*. Edited by Shmuel Almog. Jerusalem: Zalman Shazar Center, 1987.

Czapliński, Władysław and Tadeusz Ładigórski, eds. *The Historical Atlas of Poland*. Warsaw: Państwowe Przedsiębiorstwo Wydawnictw Kartograficznych, 1986.

Dan, Joseph. *Sifrut hamusar vehaderush*. Jerusalem: Magnes Press, 1975.

Darnton, Robert. *The Great Cat Massacre and Other Episodes in French Cultural History*. New York: Basic Books, 1984.

Davidovich, Adina. "Kant's Theological Constructivism." *The Harvard Theological Review* 86:3 (1993): 323–51.

Davidson, Herbert. "The Middle Way in Maimonides' Ethics." *PAAJR* 54 (1987): 31–72.

———. "Maimonides on Metaphysical Knowledge." *Maimonidean Studies* 3 (1992–93): 49–103.

Davies, Norman. *God's Playground: A History of Poland*. 2 vols. New York: Columbia University Press, 1984.

Davis, Joseph. "The Reception of the Shulhan 'Arukh and the Formation of Ashkenazic Jewish Identity." *AJS Review* 26, no. 2 (November 2002): 251–76.

Davis, Natalie Zemon. "Religion and Capitalism Once Again? Jewish Merchant Culture in the Seventeenth Century." *Representations*, no. 59 (Summer 1997): 56–84.

Dawidowicz, Lucy. *The Golden Tradition: Jewish Life and Thought in Eastern Europe*. Boston: Beacon Press, 1967.

Deák, István. *Beyond Nationalism: A Social and Political History of the Habsburg Officer Corps, 1848–1918*. New York: Oxford University Press, 1992.

De Grazia, Margreta. "The Secularization of Language in the Seventeenth Century." *Journal of the History of Ideas* 41, no. 2 (June 1980): 319–29.

De Madariaga, Isabel. "The Russian Nobility in the Seventeenth and Eighteenth Centuries." Pages 223–73 in *The European Nobilities in the Seventeenth and Eighteenth Centuries*. Vol. 2. Edited by H. M. Scott. New York: Longman, 1995.

Dinur, Benzion. *Bemifneh hadorot.* Jerusalem: Bialik Institute, 1955.

——. "The Historic Path of Polish Jewry." Pages 193–201 in *Dorot ureshumot: Meḥqarim ve'iyyunim bahistoriografyah hayisraelit beve'ayoteha uvetoldoteihah.* Edited by Benzion Dinur. Jerusalem: Bialik Institute, 1978.

Dobrzycki, Jerzy. "The Scientific Revolution in Poland." Pages 150–57 in *The Scientific Revolution in National Context.* Edited by Roy Porter and Mikuláš Teich. Cambridge, Cambridge University Press, 1992.

Doren, Carl Van. *Benjamin Franklin.* New York: The Viking Press, 1939.

Dec, Dorota, Krystyna Moczulska, Marek Rostworowski, eds. *Żydzi – Polscy.* Cracow: Drukarnia Narodowa w Krakowie, 1989.

Dorff, Elliot N. "Custom Drives Jewish Law on Women." Pages 82–106 in *Gender Issues in Jewish Law: Essays and Responsa.* Edited by Walter Jacob and Moshe Zemer. New York: Berghahn Books, 2001.

Dubin, Lois C. "Les Liaisons dangereuses: Mariage juif et État moderne à Trieste au XVIIIe siècle." *Annales: Histoire, Sciences Sociales* 49, no. 5 (Septembre-Octobre 1994): 1139–70.

——. "Researching Port Jews and Port Jewries: Trieste and Beyond." Edited by David Cesarani. *Jewish Culture and History* 4, no. 2 (Winter 2001): 47–58.

——. *The Port Jews of Habsburg Trieste: Absolutist Politics and Enlightenment Culture.* Stanford, Calif.: Stanford University Press, 1999.

——. "The Rise and Fall of the Italian Jewish Model in Germany: From Haskalah to Reform, 1780–1820." Pages 271–95 in *Jewish History and Jewish Memory: Essays in Honor of Yosef Hayim Yerushalmi.* Edited by Elisheva Carlebach, John M. Efron, and David N. Myers. Hanover, N.H.: Brandeis University Press, 1998.

——. "The Social and Cultural Context: Eighteenth-Century Enlightenment." Pages 636–59 in *History of Jewish Philosophy.* Edited by Daniel H. Frank and Oliver Leaman. London: Routledge, 1997.

——. "Trieste and Berlin: The Italian Role in the Cultural Politics of the Haskalah." Pages 189–224 in *Toward Modernity: The European Jewish Model.* Edited by Jacob Katz. New Brunswick, N.J.: Transaction Books, 1987.

Dubnow, Simon. *History of the Jews in Russia and Poland.* Philadelphia: The Jewish Publication Society of America, 1916.

——. *Toldot haḥasidut.* Tel Aviv: Devir, 1930.

Dukes, Paul. "The Russian Enlightenment." Pages 176–91 in *The Enlightenment in National Context.* Edited by Roy Porter and Mikuláš Teich. Cambridge: Cambridge University Press, 1981.

Dvoichenko-Markov, Eufrosina. "Benjamin Franklin and Count M. A. Benyowski." *Proceedings of the American Philosophical Society* 49, no. 6 (1955): 405–17.

——. "Benjamin Franklin and Leo Tolstoy." *Proceedings of the American Philosophical Society* 46, no. 2 (1952): 119–28.

Eddie, Scott. "Galician Jews as Migrants: An Alternative Hypothesis." *Austrian History Yearbook* 11 (1975): 59–63.

Efron, John. *Medicine and the German Jews: A History.* New Haven, Conn.: Yale University Press, 2001.

Efron, Noah J. "Jewish Thought and Scientific Discovery in Early Modern Europe." *Journal of the History of Ideas* 58, no. 4 (1997): 719–32.

Efros, Israel. *Philosophical Terms in the Moreh Nebukim.* New York: AMS Press, 1966.

Eggers, Hans. *Deutsche Sprachgeschichte.* Reinbeck: Rowohlts Enzyklopädie, 1986.

Eisen, Arnold. "Constructing the Usable Past: The Idea of Tradition in Twentieth-Century American Judaism." Pages 429–28 in *The Uses of Tradition: Jewish Continuity in the Modern Age.* Edited by Jack Wertheimer. Cambridge, Mass.: Harvard University Press, 1992.

———. "Divine Legislation As 'Ceremonial Script': Mendelssohn on the Commandments." *AJS Review* 15, no. 2 (1990): 239–67.
———. "Rethinking Jewish Modernity." *JSS* (new series) 1, no. 1 (Fall 1994): 1–21.
Eisenbach, Artur. *The Emancipation of the Jews in Poland, 1780–1870*. Edited by Antony Polonsky. Translated by Janina Dorosz. London: Basil Blackwell, 1991.
Elbaum, Ya'akov. *Petihut vehistagrut: hayetsirah haruhanit, hasifrutit beFolin uve'artsot Ashkenaz beshilhei hame'ah hashesh-esreh*. Jerusalem: Magnes Press, 1990.
Elias, Norbert. *The Court Society*. Translated by Edmund Jephcott. Oxford: Basil Blackwell, 1983.
———. *The History of Manners*. Translated by Edmund Jephcott. New York: Pantheon, 1978.
Eliav, Mordechai. *Hahinukh hayehudi beGermanyah biymei hahaskalah veha'imantsipatsyah*. Jerusalem: The Jewish Agency, 1960.
Elior, Rachel. *Heirut al haluhot: hamahashavah hahasidit, meqoroteihah hamistiyyim viyesodoteihah haqabbaliyyim*. Tel Aviv: The Defense Institute, 1999.
———. *The Paradoxical Ascent to God: The Kabbalistic Theosophy of Habad Hasidism*. Albany: State University of New York Press, 1993.
Elon, Menachem. *Hamishpat ha'ivri: toldotav, meqorotav, eqronotav*. Jerusalem: Magnes Press, 1973.
Elukin, Jonathan M. "Jacques Basnage and *The History of the Jews*: Anti-Catholic Polemic and Historical Allegory in the Republic of Letters." *Journal of the History of Ideas* 53, no. 4 (Oct.-Dec.1992): 603–30.
Emch-Dériaz, Antoinette. *Tissot: Physician of the Enlightenment*. American University Series. New York: Peter Lang, 1992.
Endelman, "Introduction." Pages 1–19 in *Jewish Apostasy in the Modern World*. Edited by Todd Endelman. New York: Holmes & Meier, 1987.
———. *The Jews of Georgian England, 1714–1830: Tradition and Change in a Liberal Society*. Philadelphia: The Jewish Publication Society of America, 1979.
———. "The Legitimization of the Diaspora Experience in Recent Jewish History." *Modern Judaism* 11, no. 2 (May 1991): 195–209.
Erik, Max. *Etiudn tsu der geshikhte fun der haskole*. Minsk, 1934.
Etkes, Immanuel. *Ba'al hashem: haBesht–magyah, mistiqah, hanhagah*. Jerusalem: Zalman Shazar Center, 2000.
———. ed. *Hadat vehahayim: hahaskalah be'eiropah hamizrahit*. Jerusalem: Zalman Shazar Center, 1993.
———. "Hasidism as a Movement: The First Stage." Pages 1–26 in *Hasidism: Continuity or Innovation*. Edited by Bezalel Safran. Cambridge, Mass.: Harvard University Press, 1988.
———. "Immanent Factors and External Influences in the Development of the Haskalah Movement in Russia." Pages 13–32 in *Toward Modernity: The European Jewish Model*. Edited by Jacob Katz. New Brunswick, N.J.: Transaction Books, 1987.
———. "R. Shneur Zalman of Lady's Manner as a Hasidic Leader." *Zion* 50 (1985): 321–54.
———. *R. Yisra'el Salanter vereshitah shel tenu'at hamusar*. Jerusalem: Magnes Press, 1982.
———. "The 'Crown Enlightenment' and the Change in the Status of the Jewish Enlightenment Movement in Russia." *Zion* 43 (1978): 264–313.
———. "The Study of Hasidism: Past Trends and New Directions." Pages 447–64 in *Hasidism Reappraised*. Edited by Ada Rapoport-Albert. London: The Littman Library of Jewish Civilization, 1996.
———. "The Vilna Gaon and the Haskalah: Image and Reality." Pages 192–217 in *Peraqim betoldot hahevrah hayehudit biymei habeinayim uva'et hahadashah*. Jerusalem: Magnes Press, 1980.

———. "The Zaddik: The Interrelationship between Religious Doctrine and Social Organization." Pages 159–67 in *Hasidism Reappraised*. Edited by Ada Rapoport-Albert. London: The Littman Library of Jewish Civilization, 1996.

Ettinger, Shmuel. "Hasidism and the *Kahal* in Eastern Europe." Pages 63–75 in *Hasidism Reappraised*. Edited by Ada Rapoport-Albert. London: The Littman Library of Jewish Civilization, 1996.

———. "The Council of the Four Lands." Pages 93–109 in *The Jews in Old Poland, 1000–1795*. Edited by Antony Polonsky, Jakub Basista, and Andrzej Link-Lenczowski. London: I. B. Tauris, 1993.

———. "The Edicts of 1804." *He'avar* 22 (1977): 97–110.

———. "The Participation of the Jews in the Settlement of Ukraine (1569–1648)." Pages 107–43 in *Bein Polin leRusya*. Edited by Israel Bartal and Jonathan Frankel. Jerusalem: Zalman Shazar Center, 1994.

———. "The Role of the Jews in the Settlement of the Ukraine in the Sixteenth and Seventeenth Centuries." Pages 143–49 in *Bein Polin leRusya*. Edited by Israel Bartal and Jonathan Frankel. Jerusalem: Zalman Shazar Center, 1994.

Evans, R. J. W. "Joseph II and Nationality in the Habsburg Lands." Pages 209–19 in *Enlightened Absolutism: Reform and Reformers in Later Eighteenth-Century Europe*. Edited by H. M. Scott. London: Macmillan, 1990.

Everett, Leila P. "The Rise of Jewish National Politics in Galicia, 1905–1907." Pages 149–77 in *Nationbuilding and the Politics of Nationalism: Essays on Austrian Galicia*. Edited by Andrei S. Markovits and Frank E. Sysyn. Cambridge, Mass.: Harvard University Press, 1982.

Fabre, Jean. *Stanislas-Auguste Poniatowski et l'Europe des Lumières*. Strasbourg: Publications de la Faculté des Lettres de l'Université de Strasbourg, 1952.

Fackenheim, Emil L. *Encounters between Judaism and Modern Philosophy*. New York: Basic Books, 1973.

Fagan, Brian M. *Clash of Cultures*. New York: W.H. Freeman and Company, 1983.

Falk, Ze'ev W. *Jewish Matrimonial Law in the Middle Ages*. Oxford: Oxford University Press, 1966.

Feiner, Shmuel. "Between the French Revolution and the Changes in the 'Berlin Haskalah'." *Zion* 57, no. 1 (1992): 89–92.

———. *Haskalah vehistoryah: toldotav shel hakarat-ever yehudit modernit*. Jerusalem: Zalman Shazar Center, 1998.

———. *Mehaskalah lohemet lehaskalah meshammeret: nivhar mikhtevei Rashi Fin*. Jerusalem: Dinur Center, 1993.

———. "Mendelssohn and 'Mendelssohn's Disciples': A Re-examination." *LBIYA* 40 (1995): 133–67.

———. "The Early Haskalah among Eighteenth-Century Jewry." *Tarbiz* 67, no. 2 (1998): 189–240.

———. "The Modern Jewish Woman: Test Case in the Relationship between the Haskalah and Modernity." *Zion* 58, no. 4 (1993): 453–99.

———. "The Pseudo-Enlightenment and the Question of Jewish Modernization." *JSS* (new series) 3, no. 1 (Fall 1996): 62–86.

———. "'The Rebellion of the French' and 'The Freedom of the Jews' – the French Revolution in the Image of the Past of the East European Jewish Enlightenment." Pages 215–47 in *Hamahppekhah hatsarfatit verishumah*. Edited by Richard Cohen. Jerusalem, 1991.

———. "Toward a Historical Definition of the Haskalah." Pages 184–219 in *New Perspectives on the Haskalah*. Edited by Shmuel Feiner and David Sorkin. London: The Littman Library of Jewish Civilization, 2001.

Fine, Lawrence, ed. *Safed Spirituality*. New York: Paulist Press, 1984.

Fishman, David. "A Polish Rabbi Meets the Berlin Haskalah: The Case of R. Barukh Schick." *AJS Review* 12 (1987): 95–121.
——. *Russia's First Modern Jews: The Jews of Shklov.* New York: New York University Press, 1995.
Fishman, Talya. *Shaking the Pillars of Exile: 'Voice of a Fool,' an Early Modern Jewish Critique of Rabbinic Culture.* Stanford, Calif.: Stanford University Press, 1997.
Flinker, David. *Arim ve'imahot beyisra'el: Warsaw.* Jerusalem: R. Kook Institute, 1948.
Fox, Christopher. "Introduction: How to Prepare a Noble Savage: The Spectacle of Human Science." Pages 1–30 in *Inventing Human Science: Eighteenth-Century Domains.* Edited by Christopher Fox, Roy Porter, and Robert Wexler. Berkeley: University of California Press, 1989.
Fram, Edward. *Ideals Face Reality: Jewish Law and Life in Poland, 1550–1655.* Cincinnati, Ohio: Hebrew Union College Press, 1997.
Frankel, Jonathan. "Assimilation and the Jews in nineteenth-century Europe: Towards a New Historiography?" Pages 1–37 in *Assimilation and Community: The Jews in Nineteenth-Century Europe.* Edited by Jonathan Frankel and Steven J. Zipperstein. Cambridge: Cambridge University Press, 1992.
Freeze, ChaeRan. *Jewish Marriage and Divorce in Imperial Russia.* Hanover, N.H.: Brandeis University Press, 2002.
Freeze, Gregory L. "The *Soslovie* (Estate) Paradigm and Russian Social History." *American Historical Review* 20 (1986): 11–26.
Fridberg, Hayim David. *Beit eqed sefarim.* Tel Aviv, 1952.
Friedberg, Bernhard. *Toldot hadefus ha'ivri beFolonyah.* Tel Aviv: N.p., 1950.
Friedlander, Yehuda. "Hasidism as the Image of Demonism: The Satiric Writings of Judah Leib Mieses." Pages 159–77 in *From Ancient Israel to Modern Judaism: Intellect in Quest of Understanding, Essays in Honor of Marvin Fox.* Edited by Jacob Neusner, Ernst S. Frerichs, and Nahum M. Sarna. Atlanta: Scholars' Press, 1989.
——. "The Language Battle in Eastern Europe and the Beginning of the Nineteenth Century." *Min haqatedrah* (1981), 5–34.
——. "The Struggle of the Mitnagedim and Maskilim against Hasidism: Rabbi Jacob Emden and Judah Leib Mieses." Pages 103–12 in *New Perspectives on the Haskalah.* Edited by Shmuel Feiner and David Sorkin. London: The Littman Library of Jewish Civilization, 2001.
Friedman, Philip. *Die galizischen Juden im Kampfe um ihre Gleichberechtigung.* Frankfurt-on-the-Main: J. Kauffman, 1929.
——. "Joseph Perl as an Educational Activist and His School in Tarnopol." *YIVO bleter* 31–32 (1948): 131–90.
——. "The First Battles between the Haskalah and Hasidism." *Fun noentn ovar* 4 (1937): 259–73.
Friesel, Eviatar. *Atlas of Modern Jewish History.* New York: Oxford University Press, 1990.
Frost, Robert I. "The Nobility of Poland-Lithuania, 1569–1795." Pages 183–222 in *The European Nobilities in the Seventeenth and Eighteenth Centuries.* Vol. 2. Edited by H. M. Scott. London: Longman, 1995.
Fuks, Leib. "The Social and Economic Background of the Two Yiddish Translations of the Bible Published in Amsterdam, 1676–1679." *Gal-Ed* 1 (1973): 31–50.
Funkenstein, Amos. "Passivity as a Sign of Diaspora Jewry: Myth and Reality." Pages 232–42 in *Tadmit vetoda'ah historit bayahadut uvesevivatah hatarbutit.* Tel Aviv: Am Oved, 1991.
——. *Perceptions of Jewish History.* Berkeley: University of California Press, 1992.
——. "The Dialectics of Assimilation." *JSS* (new series) 1, no. 2 (1995): 1–14.

Gay, Peter. *The Enlightenment: An Interpretation.* 2 vols. New York: Alfred A. Knopf, 1966–69.

Gelber, N. M. *Aus zwei Jahrhunderten.* Vienna: R. Löwit, 1924.

———. "Ksiądz Piattoli a Sprawa Żydowska na Sejmie Wielkim." *Nowe Życie* 1, no. 6 (Grudzień 1924): 321–33.

———. *Arim ve'imahot beyisra'el: Brody.* Edited by Y. L. Ha-Kohen. Jerusalem, 1955.

———. "Mendel Lefin of Satanów's Proposals for the Improvement of Jewish Community Life presented to the Great Polish Sejm (1788–1792), (Hebrew Section)." Pages 271–305 in *The Abraham Weiss Jubilee Volume.* Edited by Samuel Belkin. New York: Shulsinger Brothers, 1964.

———. "The History of the Jews of Tarnopol." Pages 21–108 in *Entsiqlopedyah shel galuyyot: Tarnopol.* Vol. 3. Edited by Phillip Krongruen. Jerusalem, 1955.

Gertner, Hayim. "The Rabbinate and Hasidism in Nineteenth-Century Galicia: R. Solomon Kluger and the Hasidim." Pages 51–74 in *Bema'aglei ḥasidim: qovets meḥqarim lezikhro shel profesor Mordekhai Vilenski.* Edited by Immanuel Etkes, David Assaf, Israel Bartal, and Elchanan Reiner. Jerusalem: Bialik Institute, 1999.

Gilman, Sander. "Introduction: The Frontier as a Model for Jewish History." Pages 1–25 in *Jewries at the Frontier: Accomodation, Identity, Conflict.* Edited by Sander L. Gilman and Milton Shain. Urbana: University of Illinois Press, 1999.

———. *The Jews' Body.* New York: Routledge, 1991.

Ginsberg, H. Louis. *Studies in Koheleth.* New York: The Jewish Theological Seminary of America, 1950.

Ginsburg, Asher Zevi. *Al parashat haderakhim: qovets ma'amarim.* Berlin: Yidisher Ferlag, 1930.

Ginsburg, H. L., ed. *The Five Megillot and Jonah.* Philadelphia: The Jewish Publication Society of America, 1969.

Glassl, Horst. *Das österreichische Einrichtungswerk in Galizien (1772–1790).* Wiesbaden: In Kommission bei Otto Harrassowitz, 1975.

Goldberg, Jacob. *Jewish Privileges in the Polish Commonwealth.* Jerusalem: The Israel Academy of Sciences and Humanities, 1985.

———. "The Changes in the Attitude of Polish Society toward the Jews in the Eighteenth Century." *Polin* 1 (1986): 35–48.

———. "The Privileges Granted to Jewish Communities of the Polish Commonwealth as a Stabilizing Factor in Jewish Support." Pages 31–54 in *The Jews in Poland.* Edited by Chimen Abramsky, Maciej Jachimczyk, and Antony Polonsky. London: Basil Blackwell, 1986.

Goldscheider, Calvin and Alan S. Zuckerman. *The Transformation of the Jews.* Chicago: The University of Chicago Press, 1986.

Goldschmidt, Henry. "Suits and Souls: Trying to Tell a Jew When You See One in Crown Heights." Pages 214–23 in *Jews of Brooklyn.* Edited by Ilana Abramowicz and Seán Gavin. Hanover, N.H.: University Press of New England, 2002.

Gordis, Robert. *Koheleth – The Man and His World.* New York: Schocken Books, 1968.

Graetz, Heinrich. *History of the Jews.* Philadelphia: The Jewish Publication Society of America, 1891.

Graff, Gil. *Dina de-Malkhuta Dina in Jewish Law, 1750–1848.* Tuscaloosa, Ala.: The University of Alabama Press, 1985.

Grafton, Anthony. "Introduction: Notes from Underground on Cultural Transmission." Pages 1–7 in *The Transmission of Culture in Early Modern Europe.* Edited by Anthony Grafton and Ann Blair. Philadelphia: University of Pennsylvania Press, 1990.

Green, Arthur. "Early Hasidism: Some Old/New Questions." Pages 441–46 in *Hasidism Reappraised*. Edited by Ada Rapoport-Albert. London: The Littman Library of Jewish Civilization, 1996.
——. *Tormented Master: A Life of Rabbi Nahman of Bratslav*. Tuscaloosa, Ala.: The University of Alabama Press, 1979.
——. "Typologies of Leadership and the Hasidic Zaddiq." Pages 127–56 in *Jewish Spirituality: From the Sixteenth Century Revival to the Present*. Vol. 2. Edited by Arthur Green. New York: Crossroad, 1987.
Greenberg, Louis. *The Jews in Russia: The Struggle for Emancipation*. 2 vols. New Haven, Conn.: Yale University Press, 1944.
Greenblatt, Stephen. *Marvelous Possessions: The Wonder of the New World*. Oxford: Clarendon Press, 1991.
Greenstein, Edward L. "Medieval Bible Commentaries." Pages 213–59 in *Back to the Sources*. Edited by Barry W. Holtz. New York: Summit, 1984.
Grochulska, Barbara. "The Place of the Enlightenment in Polish Social History." Pages 239–57 in *A Republic of Nobles: Studies in Polish History to 1864*. Edited by J. K. Fedorowicz. Cambridge: Cambridge University Press, 1982.
Grodziski, Stanisław. "The Jewish Question in Galicia: The Reforms of Maria Theresa and Joseph II, 1772–1790." Pages 61–72 in *Polin: Focusing on Galicia: Jews, Poles, and Ukrainians, 1772–1918*. Vol. 12. Edited by Israel Bartal and Antony Polonsky. London: The Littman Library of Jewish Civilization, 1999.
Grossman, Jeffrey A. *The Discourse on Yiddish in Germany: From the Enlightenment to the Second Empire*. Rochester, N.Y.: Camden House, 2000.
Grossman, Mordecai. *The Philosophy of Helvetius*. New York: Teachers College, Columbia University, 1926.
Guldon, Zenon and Jacek Wijaczka. "The Accusation of Ritual Murder in Poland, 1500–1800." *Polin* 10 (1997): 99–140.
Gurock, Jeffrey. *A Modern Heretic and a Traditional Community: Mordecai M. Kaplan, Orthodoxy, and American Judaism*. New York: Columbia University Press, 1997.
Guterman, Alexander. "The Suggestions of Polish Jews toward the Reforms of Their Legal, Economic, Social, and Cultural Status in the Period of the Great Sejm (1788–1792)." M.A. thesis, The Hebrew University of Jerusalem, 1975.
Haberman, A. M. "Hebrew Printing and the List of Books Published in Tarnopol." *Alim lebibliografyah veqorot yisra'el* 2, no. 1 (1935): 24–31.
——. "Toward a History of Menachem Mendel Lefin of Satanów." Pages 461–63 in *Sefer Klausner*. Tel Aviv: The Jubilee Commitee and the Society "*Omanut*," 1937.
Habermas, Jürgen. *The Philosophical Discourse of Modernity*. Cambridge, Mass.: MIT Press, 1987.
Halberstam, Joshua. "Supererogation in Jewish *Halakhah* and Islamic *Shari'a*." Pages 85–99 in *Studies in Islamic and Judaic Traditions*. Edited by William M. Brinner and Stephen D. Ricks. Atlanta: Scholars Press, 1986.
Halpern, Israel. *Yehudim veyahadut bemizrah eiropah: mehqarim betoldoteihem*. Jerusalem: Magnes Press, 1963.
Hans, Nicholas. "UNESCO of the Eighteenth Century: *La Loge des Neuf Soeurs* and its Venerable Master, Benjamin Franklin." *Proceedings of the American Philosophical Society* 97 (1953): 513–24.
Harris, Jay. *How Do We Know This?: Midrash and the Fragmentation of Modern Judaism*. Albany: State University of New York Press, 1995.
——. *Nachman Krochmal: Guiding the Perplexed of the Modern Age*. New York: New York University Press, 1991.
——. "The Image of Maimonides in Nineteenth-Century Jewish Historiography." *PAAJR* 54 (1987): 117–29.

Harshav, Benjamin. *Language in the Time of Revolution*. Berkeley: University of California Press, 1993.

Hastings, Adrian. *The Construction of Nationhood: Ethnicity, Religion, and Nationalism*. Cambridge: Cambridge University Press, 1997.

Hatfield, Gary. "Remaking the Science of the Mind: Psychology as Natural Science." Pages 184–231 in *Inventing Human Science*. Edited by Christopher Fox, Roy Porter, and Robert Wokler. Berkeley: University of California Press, 1995.

Hauptman, Judith. *Rereading the Rabbis: A Woman's Voice*. New York: Westview Press, 1998.

Hayes, Carlton J. H. "Contributions of Herder to the Doctrine of Nationalism." *The American Historical Review* 32, no. 4 (July 1927): 719–36.

Hayes, John H. *An Introduction to Old Testament Study*. Nashville, Tenn.: Abingdon Press, 1979.

Häusler, Wolfgang. *Das galizische Judentum in der Habsburgermonarchie: im Lichte der zeitgenössischen Publizistik und Reiseliterature von 1772–1848*. Munich: R. Oldenbourg, 1979.

Heilbron, J. L. "Experimental Natural Philosophy." Pages 358–87 in *The Ferment of Knowledge: Studies in the Historiography of Eighteenth-Century Science*. Edited by G. S. Rousseau and Roy Porter. Cambridge: Cambridge University Press, 1980.

———. "Franklin as an Enlightened Natural Philosopher." Pages 196–220 in *Reappraising Benjamin Franklin: A Bicentennial Perspective*. Edited by J. A. Leo Lemay. Cranbury, N.J.: Associated University Presses, 1993.

Heimann, P.M. "'Nature is a Perpetual Worker': Newton's Aether and Eighteenth-Century Natural Philosophy." *Ambix* 20 (March 1973): 1–25.

Hermat, Ulrike. "Divorce and Remarriage in Austria-Hungary: The Second Marriage of Franz Conrad von Hötzendorf." *Austrian History Yearbook* 32 (2001): 69–104.

Hertzberg, Arthur. *The French Enlightenment and the Jews*. New York: Columbia University Press, 1968.

Hertz, Deborah. *Jewish High Society in Old Regime Berlin*. New Haven, Conn.: Yale University Press, 1988.

Heyd, Michael. *'Be Sober and Reasonable': The Critique of Enthusiasm in the Seventeenth and Early Eighteenth Centuries*. New York: E. J. Brill, 1995.

Himka, John-Paul. "Dimensions of a Triangle: Polish-Ukrainian-Jewish Relations in Austrian Galicia." Pages 25–48 in *Polin: Focusing on Galicia: Jews, Poles, and Ukrainians, 1772–1918*. Vol. 12. Edited by Israel Bartal and Antony Polonsky. London: The Littman Library of Jewish Civilization, 1999.

Hinz, Henryk. "The Philosophy of the Polish Enlightenment and its Opponents: The Origins of the Modern Polish Mind." *Slavic Review* 30, no. 2 (June 1971): 340–49.

Hirszowicz, Lukasz. "The Jewish Issue in Post-War Communist Politics." Pages 199–208 in *The Jews in Poland*. Edited by Chimen Abramsky, Maciej Jachimczyk, and Antony Polonsky. Oxford: Basil Blackwell, 1986.

Hobsbawm, E. J. *Nations and Nationalism since 1780*. Cambridge: Cambridge University Press, 1990.

Home, Roderick Weir. "Scientific Links Between Britain and Russia in the Second Half of the Eighteenth Century." Pages 213–19 in *Electricity and Experimental Physics in Eighteenth-Century Europe*. Edited by Roderick Weir Home. Hampshire: Variorum, 1992.

Horn, Maurycy. *Żydzi na Rusi Czerwonej w XVI i pierswzej połowie XVII w*. Warsaw: Państwowe Wydawnicto Naukowe, 1975.

Horowicz, Zevi Hirsch. *Kitvei hage'onim*. Pietrkov, 1828 (repr. New York: Menorah, 1959).

Horowitz, Elliot. "The Early Eighteenth Century Confronts the Beard: Kabbalah and Jewish Self-Fashioning." *Jewish History* 8 (1994): 95–115.

——. "The Rite to Be Reckless: On the Perpetration and Interpretation of Purim Violence." *Poetics Today* 15, no. 1 (Spring 1994): 11–54.

Hroch, Miroslav. "'Central Europe': The Rise and Fall of an Historical Region." Pages 21–34 in *Central Europe: Core or Periphery?* Edited by Christopher Lord. Prague: Copenhagen Business School Press, 2000.

——. *Social Preconditions of National Revival in Europe.* Cambridge, Cambridge University Press, 1985.

Hundert, Gershon. "Approaches to the History of the Jewish Family in Early Modern Poland-Lithuania." Pages 17–28 in *The Jewish Family: Myths and Reality.* Edited by Steven M. Cohen and Paula E. Hyman. New York: Holmes & Meier, 1986.

——. "Jewish Life in the Eighteenth-Century Polish-Lithuanian Commonwealth." Pages 225–41 in *Qiyyum veshever: yehudei Polin ledoroteihem.* Edited by Israel Bartal and Israel Gutman. Jerusalem: Zalman Shazar Center, 1997.

——. "Jewish Popular Spirituality in the Eighteenth Century." *Polin* 15 (2002): 93–103.

——. "Jews, Money and Society in the Seventeenth-Century Polish Commonwealth: The Case of Kraków." *JSS* 43 (1981): 161–74.

——. "Some Basic Characteristics of Jewish Life in Poland." *Polin* 1, no. 1 (1986): 28–34.

——. "The Conditions in Jewish Society in the Polish-Lithuanian Commonwealth in the Middle Decades of the Eighteenth Century." Pages 45–50 in *Hasidism Reappraised.* Edited by Ada Rapoport-Albert. London: The Littman Library of Jewish Civilization, 1996.

——. "The Implications of Jewish Economic Activities for Christian-Jewish Relations in the Polish Commonwealth." Pages 55–63 in *The Jews in Poland.* Chimen Abramsky, Maciej Jachimczyk, and Antony Polonsky. Oxford: Basil Blackwell, 1986.

——. *The Jews in a Polish Private Town: The Case of Opatów in the Eighteenth Century.* Baltimore: The Johns Hopkins University Press, 1992.

Hyman, Paula E. *Gender and Assimilation in Modern Jewish History.* Seattle: University of Washington Press, 1995.

——. *The Emancipation of the Jews of Alsace: Acculturation and Tradition in the Nineteenth Century.* New Haven, Conn.: Yale University Press, 1991.

Idel, Moshe. *Hasidism: Between Ecstasy and Magic.* Albany: State University of New York Press, 1995.

——. *Kabbalah: New Perspectives.* New Haven, Conn.: Yale University Press, 1988.

Israel, Jonathan I. *European Jewry in the Age of Mercantilism, 1550–1750.* Oxford: Clarendon, 1985.

Jacob, Margaret. *Living the Enlightenment: Freemasonry and Politics in Eighteenth-Century Europe.* Oxford: Oxford University Press, 1991.

——. "The Crisis of the European Mind: Hazard Revisited." Pages 251–71 in *Politics and Culture in Early Modern Europe: Essays in Honor of H.G. Koenigsberger.* Edited by Phyllis Mack and Margaret C. Jacob. Cambridge: Cambridge University Press, 1987.

Jacobs, Louis. "The Uplifting of the Sparks in Later Jewish Mysticism." Pages 22–50 in *Jewish Spirituality: From the Sixteenth Century Revival to the Present.* Edited by Arthur Green. New York: Crossroad, 1987.

Jedlicki, Jerzy. *A Suburb of Europe: Nineteenth-Century Polish Approaches to Western Civilization.* Budapest: Central European University Press, 1999.

Jedynak, Barbara and Stanisław. "Die philosophische und gesellschaftlichen An-schauungen Stanisław Leszczyńskis." Pages 229–47 in *Frühaufklärung in Deutsch-land und Polen*. Edited by Karol Bal, Siegfried Wollgast, and Petra Schellen-berger. Berlin: Akademie Verlag, 1991.

Jones, G. Gareth. "Novikov's Naturalized *Spectator*." Pages 149–65 in *The Eighteenth Century in Russia*. Edited by J. G. Garrard. Oxford: Clarendon Press, 1973.

Kagan, Berl. *Sefer haprenumeranten*. New York: The Jewish Theological Seminary of America, 1975.

Kalik, Judith. *Ha'atsulah hapolanit viyehudeihah bemamlekhet Polin-Lita bere'i hatehiqqah bat hazeman*. Jerusalem: Magnes Press, 1997.

Kalir, Joseph. "The Jewish Service in the Eyes of Christian and Baptized Jews in the Seventeenth and Eighteenth Centuries." *JQR* 56 (1965–66): 51–80.

Kann, Robert A. *A History of the Habsburg Empire, 1526–1918*. Berkeley: University of California Press, 1974.

———. *A Study in Austrian Intellectual History from Late Baroque to Romanticism*. London: Thames & Hudson, 1960.

Karniel, Joseph. "Das Toleranzpatent Kaiser Joseph II. für die Juden Galiziens und Lodomeriens." *Jahrbuch des Instituts für deutsche Geschichte* 11 (1982): 55–91.

Kassow, Samuel D. "Communal and Social Change in the Polish Shtetl." Pages 56–85 in *Jewish Settlement and Community in the Modern Western World*. Edited by Ronald Dotterer, Deborah Dash Moore, and Steven M. Cohen. London: Associated University Presses, 1991.

Katz, Jacob. *A House Divided: Orthodoxy and Schism in Central European Jewry in the Nineteenth Century*. Translated by Ziporah Brody. Hanover, N.H.: University Press of New England, 1998.

———. "'Alterations in the Time of the Evening Service': An Example of the Rela-tionship between Religious Custom, Law and Society." *Zion* 35 (1970): 35–60.

———. "Although He Has Sinned, He Remains a Jew." *Tarbiz* 27 (1958): 203–17.

———. *Jews and Freemasons in Europe, 1723–1939*. Translated by Leonard Oschry. Cambridge, Mass.: Harvard University Press, 1970.

———. "Orthodoxy in Historical Perspective." *Studies in Contemporary Jewry* II (1986): 3–17.

———. *Out of the Ghetto: The Social Background of Jewish Emancipation, 1770–1870*. Cambridge, Mass.: Harvard University Press, 1973.

———. "Rabbinical Authority and Authorization in the Middle Ages." Pages 41–56 in *Studies in Medieval Jewish History and Literature*. Edited by Isadore Twersky. Cambridge, Mass.: Harvard University Press, 1979.

———. "Regarding the Connection of Sabbatianism, Haskalah, and Reform." Pages 83–101 in *Studies in Jewish Religious and Intellectual History*. Edited by Siegfried Stein and Raphael Loewe. Tuscaloosa, Ala.: University of Alabama Press, 1979.

———. "The Term 'Emancipation:' Its Origin and Historical Impact." Pages 1–25 in *Studies in Nineteenth-Century Jewish Intellectual History*. Edited by Alexander Altmann. Cambridge, Mass.: Harvard University Press, 1964.

———. *Tradition and Crisis: Jewish Society at the End of the Middle Ages*. Translated by Bernard Dov Cooperman. New York: New York University Press, 1993.

———. ed., *Toward Modernity: The European Jewish Model*. New Brunswick, N.J.: Trans-action Books, 1987.

Katz, Simha. "Additions to the List of Publications in Tarnopol." *Kiryat sefer* 15 (1938–39): 515–16.

———. "Letters of Maskilim Debasing Hasidim." *Moznayim* 10 (1944): 266–76.

———. "Menachem Mendel Lefin of Satanow's Bible Translations." *Kiryat sefer* 16 (1939–40): 114–33.

——. "New Materials from the Perl Archive." *YIVO bleter* 13 (1938): 557–76.

Kemlein, Sophia. *Die posener Juden, 1815–1848: Entwicklungsprozesse einer polnischen Judenheit unter preussischer Herrschaft.* Hamburg: Dolling und Galitz, 1997.

Kepnes, Steven, ed. *Interpreting Judaism in a Postmodern Age.* New York: New York University Press, 1996.

Kestenberg-Gladstein, Ruth. *Neuere Geschichte der Juden in den böhmischen Ländern.* Tübingen: Mohr, 1969.

Kieniewicz, Stefan. *The Emancipation of the Polish Peasantry.* Chicago: University of Chicago Press, 1969.

——. "Polish Society and the Jewish Problem in the Nineteenth Century." Pages 70–79 in *The Jews in Poland.* Edited by Maciej Jachimczyk, Chimen Abramsky, and Antony Polonsky. Oxford: Basil Blackwell, 1986.

Kieval, Hillel J. "Caution's Progress: The Modernization of Jewish Life in Prague, 1780–1830." Pages 71–105 in *Toward Modernity: The European Jewish Model.* Edited by Jacob Katz. New Brunswick, N.J.: Transaction Books, 1987.

Kirshenblatt-Gimblett, Barbara. "Introduction." Pages 12–38 in *Life Is with People.* Mark Zborowski and Elizabeth Herzog. New York: Schocken Books, 1995.

Klatzkin, Jacob. *Otsar hamunahim hafilosofiyyim ve'antologyah filosofit.* Berlin, 1928.

Klausner, Joseph. "'Ethical Fable' of R. Nachman Krochmal." *Tarbiz* 1, no. 1 (1930): 131–35.

——. *Historyah shel hasifrut ha'ivrit hahadashah.* Jerusalem: The Hebrew University, 1952.

Klier, John Doyle. *Russia Gathers Her Jews: The Origins of the 'Jewish Question' in Russia, 1772–1825.* Dekalb, Ill.: Northern Illinois University Press, 1986.

Klimowicz, Mieczysław. "Die Frühaufklärung der Jahre 1733–1763 und die Aufklärung der Periode des Königs Stanisław August im Lichte der deutsch-polnischen literarischen Beziehungen." Pages 163–73 in *Frühaufklärung in Deutschland und Polen.* Edited by Rainer Riemenschneider. Braunschweig: Georg-Eckert-Institut für Internationale Schulbuchforschung, 1981.

Klimowicz, Mieczysław. "Polnische Literatur und Kunst im Zeitalter der Aufklärung." Pages 97–107 in *Polen und Deutschland im Zeitalter der Aufklärung.* Edited by Karol Bal, Siegried Wollgast, and Petra Schellenberg. Berlin: Akademie Verlag, 1991.

Kohut, George Alexander. "Abraham's Lesson in Tolerance." *The Jewish Quarterly Review* 15 (1903): 104–11.

Kornberg, Jacques, ed. *The Golden Age and Beyond: Polish-Jewish History.* Toronto: University of Toronto Press, 1997.

Kupfer, Ephraim. "Concerning the Cultural Image of Ashkenazic Jewry and its Sages in the Fourteenth and Fifteenth Centuries" *Tarbiz* 42 (1973): 113–47.

——. "From Far and Near." Pages 217–19 in *Sefer zikaron mugash leDr. N. M. Gelber leregel yovelo hashivim.* Edited by Israel Klausner, Raphael Mahler, and Dov Sadan. Tel Aviv: Olameinu, 1963.

——. "Jacob Samuel Bik in Light of New Documents." *Gal-Ed* 4–5 (1978): 535–47.

Lamm, Norman. "The Phase of Dialogue and Reconciliation." Pages 89–113 in *Tolerance and Movements of Religious Dissent in Eastern Europe.* Edited by Béla K. Király. New York: Columbia University Press, 1975.

Langer, Ruth. *To Worship God Properly: Tensions Between Liturgical Custom and Halakhah in Judaism.* Cincinnati, Ohio: Hebrew Union College Press, 1998.

Lauterbach, Jacob Z. "The Ritual for the Kapparot Ceremony." Pages 133–43 in *Studies in Jewish Law, Custom and Folklore.* Edited by Jacob Z. Lauterbach. New York: KTAV, 1970.

Leczinski, Jacob. "The Condition of Ukrainian Jewry at the End of the Eighteenth and the Beginning of the Nineteenth Centuries." *He'avar* 7 (1960): 6–14.

Lederhendler, Eli. *The Road to Modern Jewish Politics: Political Tradition and Political Reconstruction in the Jewish Community of Tsarist Russia.* New York: Oxford University Press, 1989.

Lehmann, James. "Maimonides, Mendelssohn, and the *Me'assfim*: Philosophy and Biographical Imagination in the Early Haskalah." *LBIYA* 20 (1975): 87–108.

Leskiewicz, J. "Land Reforms in Poland (1764–1870)." *Journal of European Economic History* 1 (1972): 435–48.

Levine, Hillel. "Between Hasidism and Haskalah: On a Disguised Anti-Hasidic Polemic." Pages 182–91 in *Peraqim betoldot hahevrah hayehudit biymei habeinayim uva'et hahadashah.* Edited by Immanuel Etkes and Joseph Salmon. Jerusalem: Zalman Shazar Center, 1980.

———. "'Dwarfs on the Shoulders of Giants': A Case Study in the Impact of Modernization and the Social Epistemology of Judaism." *JSS* 40, no. 1 (Winter 1978): 63–72.

———. "Menahem Mendel Lefin: A Case Study of Judaism and Modernization." Ph.D. diss., Harvard University, 1974.

———. "Paradise Not Surrendered: Jewish Reactions to Copernicus and the Growth of Modern Science." Pages 203–25 in *Epistemology, Methodology, and the Social Sciences.* Edited by Robert S. Cohen and Marx W. Wartofsky. Dordrecht, Holland: D. Reidel Publishing Company, 1983.

Levine, Hillel, ed. and trans. *'Hakroniqa:' te'udah letoldot Ya'aqov Franq utenu'ato.* Jerusalem: Publications of the Israel Academy of Sciences and Humanities, 1984.

Liberles, Robert. *Religious Conflict in Social Context: The Resurgence of Orthodox Judaism in Frankfurt am Main, 1838–1877.* Westport, Conn.: Greenwood Press, 1985.

Lichten, Joseph. "Notes on the Assimilation and Acculturation of Jews in Poland, 1863–1943." Pages 106–29 in *The Jews in Poland.* Edited by Maciej Jachimczyk, Chimen Abramsky, and Antony Polonsky. Oxford: Basil Blackwell, 1986.

Lieberman, Haim. *Ohel rahel.* New York: Empire Press, 1980.

Liebes, Yehudah. "New Light on the Matter of the Besht and Sabbatai Zevi." *Mehqerei Yerushalayim bemahashevet yisra'el* 3 (1983): 564–69.

Litinski, Menahem Nahum. *Sefer qorot Podolyah veqadmoniyyut hayehudim sham.* Odessa: A. Belinson, 1895.

Litvak, Olga. "Authority and Individual in the Russian-Jewish Literature on Conscription." Ph.D. diss., Columbia University, 1999.

Loewenthal, Naftali. *Communicating the Infinite: The Emergence of the Habad School.* Chicago: The University of Chicago Press, 1990.

Lovejoy, David S. *Religious Enthusiasm in the New World.* Cambridge, Mass.: Harvard University Press, 1985.

Lowenstein, Steven. *The Berlin Jewish Community: Enlightenment, Family, and Crisis, 1770–1830.* New York: Oxford University Press, 1994.

———. "The Jewishness of David Friedländer." *Braun Lectures in the History of the Jews of Prussia* (1997), 5–30.

———. "The Readership of Mendelssohn's Bible Translation." *HUCA* 53 (1982): 179–213.

———. "The Shifting Boundary between Eastern and Western Jewry." *JSS* (new series) 4, no. 1 (Fall 1997): 61–78.

Lukowski, Jerzy. *Liberty's Folly: The Polish-Lithuanian Commonwealth in the Eighteenth Century, 1697–1795.* London: Routledge, 1991.

———. *The Partitions of Poland, 1772, 1793, 1795.* London: Longman, 1999.

———. "Recasting Utopia: Montesquieu, Rousseau and the Polish Constitution of 3 May 1791." *The Historical Journal* 37, no. 1 (March 1994): 65–87.

Maccoby, Hyam, ed. *Judaism on Trial: Jewish-Christian Disputations in the Middle Ages.* Rutherford, N.J.: Fairleigh Dickinson Press, 1981.

Mączak, Antoni. "From Aristocratic Household to Princely Court: Restructuring Patronage in the Sixteenth and Seventeenth Centuries." Pages 315–27 in *Princes, Patronage, and the Nobility: The Court at the Beginning of the Modern Age c. 1450–1650.* Edited by Ronald G. Asch and Adolf M. Birke. Oxford: Oxford University Press, 1991.

Magocsi, Paul Robert. *Galicia: A Historical Survey and Bibliographic Guide.* Toronto: University of Toronto Press, 1983.

———. *Historical Atlas of East Central Europe.* Seattle: University of Washington Press, 1993.

Mahler, Raphael. *A History of Modern Jewry, 1780–1815.* New York: Schocken Books, 1971.

———. *Divrei yemei yisra'el.* Rehavia: Worker's Library, 1956.

———. *Hasidism and the Jewish Enlightenment: Their Confrontation in Galicia and Poland in the First Half of the Nineteenth Century.* Philadelphia: The Jewish Publication Society of America, 1985.

———. *Haskole un hsides: der kampf tsvishn haskole un hsides in galitsye in der ershter helf fun nayntsnt yorhundert.* New York: YIVO Institute, 1942.

———. "Joseph Perl's Memo to the Authorities regarding the System of Appointing Rabbis, Ritual Slaughterers, and Circumcisers." Pages 85–104 in *Sefer hayovel mugash leDr. N. M. Gelber leregel yovelo hashivim.* Edited by Israel Klausner, Raphael Mahler, and Dov Sadan. Tel Aviv: Olameinu, 1963.

———. "The Economic Background of Jewish Emigration from Galicia to the United States." *YIVO Annual of Jewish Social Science* 7 (1952): 256–57.

Malino, Frances. *A Jew in the French Revolution: The Life of Zalkind Hourwitz.* Cambridge, Mass.: Blackwell Publishers, 1996.

———. "The Right to be Different: Zalkind Hourwitz and the Revolution of 1789." Pages 85–106 in *From East and West: Jews in a Changing Europe, 1750–1870.* Edited by Frances Malino and David Sorkin. London: Basil Blackwell, 1990.

———. *The Sephardic Jews of Bordeaux: Assimilation and Emancipation in Revolutionary and Napoleonic France.* Tuscaloosa, Ala.: University of Alabama Press, 1978.

Manekin, Rachel. "Politics, Religion, and National Identity: The Galician Jewish Vote in the 1873 Parliamentary Elections." Pages 100–19 in *Polin: Focusing on Galicia: Jews, Poles, and Ukrainians, 1772–1918.* Vol. 12. Edited by Israel Bartal and Antony Polonsky. London, The Littman Library of Jewish Civilization, 1999.

Manuel, Frank E. *The Broken Staff: Judaism through Christian Eyes.* Cambridge, Mass.: Harvard University Press, 1992.

Margolies, Morris B. *Samuel David Luzzatto: Traditionalist Scholar.* New York: KTAV, 1979.

Markovits, Andrei, and Frank E. Sysyn, eds. *Nationbuilding and the Politics of Nationalism: Essays on Austrian Galicia.* Cambridge, Mass.: Harvard University Press, 1982.

Marinelli-König, Gertraud. *Polen und Ruthenen in den wiener Zeitschriften und Almanachen des Vormärz (1805–1848).* Vienna: Verlag der Oesterreichischen Adademie der Wissenschaften, 1992.

Mark, Rudolf A. *Galizien unter österreichischer Herrschaft: Verwaltung-Kirche-Bevölkerung.* Historische und Landeskundliche Ostmitteleuropa-Studien. Marburg: Herder-Institut, 1994.

Marrus, Michael R. *The Holocaust in History.* New York: New American Library, 1987.

May, Henry F. *The Enlightenment in America.* New York: Oxford University Press, 1976.

McCagg Jr., William O. *A History of Habsburg Jews, 1670–1918.* Bloomington: Indiana University Press, 1989.

Melton, James Van Horn. *Absolutism and the Eighteenth-Century Origins of Compulsory Schooling in Prussia and Austria.* Cambridge: Cambridge University Press, 1988.

Mendelsohn, Ezra. "From Assimilation to Zionism in Lvov: The Case of Alfred Nossig." *Slavonic and East European Review* 49 (October 1971).

———. "Jewish Assimilation in L'viv: The Case of Wilhelm Feldman." Pages 94–110 in *Nationbuilding and the Politics of Nationalism: Essays on Austrian Galicia.* Edited by Andrei S. Markovits and Frank E. Sysyn. Cambridge, Mass.: Harvard University Press, 1982.

———. *On Modern Jewish Politics.* Oxford: Oxford University Press, 1993.

———. "The Dilemma of Jewish Politics in Poland: Four Responses." Pages 203–15 in *Jews and non-Jews in Eastern Europe, 1918–1945.* Edited by Bela Vago and George L Mosse. New Brunswick, N.J.: Transaction Books, 1974.

———. *The Jews of East Central Europe Between the Wars.* Bloomington: Indiana University Press, 1983.

———. *The Origins of the Modern Jew.* Detroit, Mich.: Wayne State University Press, 1979.

Meyer, Michael A. *Response to Modernity: A History of the Reform Movement.* New York: Oxford University Press, 1988.

———. "Reflections on Jewish Modernization." Pages 369–77 in *Jewish History and Memory: Essays in Honor of Yosef Hayim Yerushalmi.* Edited by Elisheva Carlebach, John M. Efron, and David N. Myers. Hanover, N.H.: Brandeis University Press, 1998.

———. "Where does the Modern Period of Jewish History Begin?" *Judaism* 24 (1975): 329–38.

Meynell, Hugo A. *Postmodernism and the New Enlightenment.* Washington, D.C.: The Catholic University of America Press, 1999.

Mintz, Alan. *'Banished from Their Father's Table': Loss of Faith and Hebrew Autobiography.* Bloomington: Indiana University Press, 1989.

Miron, Dan. *A Traveler Disguised.* New York: Schocken Books, 1973.

———. "Folklore and Antifolklore in the Yiddish Fiction of the Haskalah." Pages 219–49 in *Studies in Jewish Folklore.* Edited by Frank Talmage. Cambridge, Mass.: Association for Jewish Studies, 1980.

———. "The Literary Image of the Shtetl." Pages 1–48 in *The Image of the Shtetl and Other Studies of Modern Jewish Literary Imagination.* Syracuse, N.Y.: Syracuse University Press, 2000.

Miron, Dan and Anita Norich. "The Politics of Benjamin III: Intellectual Significance and its Formal Correlatives in Sh.Y. Abramovitsh's *Masoes Benyomin Hashlishi.*" Pages 1–115 in *The Field of Yiddish: Studies in Language, Folklore, and Literature.* Edited by Barbara Kirschenblatt-Gimblett, Marvin I. Herzog, Dan Miron, and Ruth Wisse. New York: Institute for Human Issues, Inc., 1980.

Molik, Witold. "Residenten als ein Relikt der Magnatenklientel auf polnischen Boden im 19tn Jahrhundert." Pages 83–94 in *Patronage und Klientel: Ergebnisse einer polnisch-deutschen Konferenz.* Edited by Hans-Heinrich Nolte. Cologne: Böhlen Verlag, 1989.

Moore, Deborah Dash. *At Home in America: Second Generation New York Jews.* New York: Columbia University Press, 1981.

Moran, Bruce T., ed. *Patronage and Institutions: Science, Technology, and Medicine at the European Court, 1500–1750.* Suffolk: The Boydell Press, 1991.

Morley, Charles. "Czartoryski as a Polish Statesman." *Slavic Review* 30, no. 3 (September 1971): 606–14.

Myers, David N. and David B. Ruderman, eds. *The Jewish Past Revisited: Reflections on Modern Jewish Historians.* New Haven, Conn.: Yale University Press, 1998.

Muir, Edward. *Ritual in Early Modern Europe.* Cambridge: Cambridge University Press, 1997.

Mundschein, Joshua. *Migdal oz.* Jerusalem: Lubavich Institute, 1980.

Myovich, Samuel T. "Josephism at its Boundaries: Nobles, Peasants, Priests and Jews in Galicia, 1772–1790." Ph.D. diss., Indiana University, 1994.

Nadler, Allan. *The Faith of the Mithnagdim.* Baltimore: The Johns Hopkins University Press, 1997.

Nolte, Hans-Heinrich. "Patronage und Klientel: das Konzept in der Forschung." Pages 1–17 in *Patronage und Klientel: Ergebnisse einer polnisch-deutschen Konferenz.* Edited by Hans-Heinrich Nolte. Cologne: Böhlan Verlag, 1989.

Opalski, Magdalena and Israel Bartal. *Poles and Jews: A Failed Brotherhood.* Hanover, N.H.: Brandeis University Press, 1992.

Oron, Michal. "Dr. Samuel Falk and the Eibeschuetz-Emden Controversy." Pages 243–56 in *Mysticism, Magic and Kabbalah in Ashkenazi Judaism.* Edited by Karl Erich Grözinger and Joseph Dan. Berlin: Walter de Gruyter, 1995.

——. "Mysticism and Magic in Eighteenth-Century London: Samuel Falk, the 'London Ba'al Shem'." Pages 7–20 in *Sefer Yisra'el Levin.* Vol. 2. Edited by Re'uven Zur and Tova Rosen. Tel Aviv: The University of Tel Aviv, 1995.

Parry, J. H. *The Age of Reconnaissance.* Berkeley University of California Press., 1981.

Patterson, David. *A Phoenix in Fetters: Studies in Nineteenth and Early Twentieth Century Hebrew Fiction.* Savage, Md.: Rowman & Littlefield, 1988.

Pekacz, Jolanta. "To What Extent did Prince Adam Czartoryski Influence Alexander I's 'Jewish' Statute of 1804?" *The Polish Review* 40, no. 4 (1995): 403–41.

Pelli, Moshe. "The Literary Genre of the Travelogue in Hebrew Haskalah Literature: Shmuel Romanelli's *Masa Barav.*" *Modern Judaism* 11 (1991): 241–60.

——. "Otherworldly Voices." *HUCA* 54 (1983): 1–15.

Penrose, Boies. *Travel and Discovery in the Renaissance, 1420–1620.* Cambridge, Mass.: Harvard University Press, 1955.

Penslar, Derek Jonathan. *Shylock's Children: Economics and Jewish Identity in Modern Europe.* Berkeley: University of California Press, 2001.

——. "The Origins of Jewish Political Economy." *JSS* (new series) 3, no. 3 (Spring/Summer 1997): 26–60.

Petuchowski, Jakob J. "Manuals and Catechisms of the Jewish Religion in the Early Period of Emancipation." Pages 47–64 in *Studies in Nineteenth-Century Jewish Intellectual History.* Edited by Alexander Altmann. Cambridge, Mass.: Harvard University Press, 1964.

——. *Prayerbook Reform in Europe.* New York: The World Union for Progressive Judaism, 1968.

Piekarz, Mendel. *Biymei tsemiḥat haḥasidut: megammot ra'ayoniyyot besifrei derush umusar.* Jerusalem: Magnes Press, 1978.

——. *Hahanagah haḥasidut: samkhut ve'emunat tsaddiqim be'aspaklaryat sifrutah shel haḥasidut.* Jerusalem: Bialik Institute, 2000.

Pines, Shlomo. "The Limitations of Human Knowledge According to Al-Farabi, Ibn Bajja, and Maimonides." Pages 82–109 in *Studies in Medieval Jewish History and Literature.* Edited by Isadore Twersky. Cambridge, Mass.: Harvard University Press, 1979.

Pinqas haqehillot. Polin: entsiqlopedyah shel hayishuvim hayehudiyyim lemin hivasdam ve'ad le'aḥar sho'at milḥemet ha'olam hasheniyyah, Galitsyah hamizraḥit. Edited by D.

Dombrovska, Abraham Wein, and Aharon Vais. Jerusalem: Yad Va-Shem, 1980.

Pipes, Richard. "Catherine II and the Jews: The Origins of the Pale of Settlement." *Soviet Jewish Affairs* 5, no. 2 (1975): 3–20.

——. "'Intelligentsia' from the German 'Intelligenz'?" *Slavic Review* 30, no. 3 (September 1971): 615–18.

Popkin, Jeremy D. "Periodical Publication and the Nature of Knowledge in Eighteenth-Century Europe." Pages 203–14 in *The Shapes of Knowledge from the Renaissance to the Enlightenment.* Edited by Donald R. Kelley and Richard H. Popkin. Dordrecht: Kluwer, 1991.

Popkin, Richard H. "Medicine, Racism, Anti-Semitism: A Dimension of Enlightenment Culture." Pages 405–42 in *The Languages of Psyche: Mind and Body in Enlightenment Thought.* Edited by G. S. Rousseau. Berkeley: University of California Press, 1990.

——. "Newton and Maimonides." Pages 216–29 in *A Straight Path: Studies in Medieval Philosophy and Culture, Essays in Honor of Arthur Hyman.* Edited by Ruth Link-Salinger. Washington, D.C.: The Catholic University of America Press, 1988.

Porter, Roy. *The Enlightenment.* London: Macmillan, 1990.

Porter, Roy and Mikuláš Teich, eds. *The Enlightenment in National Context.* Cambridge: Cambridge University Press, 1981.

Poznanski, Samuel. "Wiener's 'Bibliotheca Friedlandiana'." *JQR* 9 (1897): 17–161.

Prokopówna, Eugenia. "The Image of the *Shtetl* in Polish Literature." *Polin* 4 (1989): 129–42.

Racevskis, Karlis. *Postmodernism and the Search for the Enlightenment.* Charlottesville: University Press of Virginia, 1993.

Raeff, Marc. "The Enlightenment in Russia and Russian Thought in the Enlightenment." Pages 25–47 in *The Eighteenth Century in Russia.* Edited by J. G. Garrard. Oxford: Clarendon, 1973.

——. "The Well-Ordered Police State and the Development of Modernity in Seventeenth- and Eighteenth-Century Europe: An Attempt at a Comparative Approach." *American Historical Review* 80, no. 5 (December 1975): 1221–43.

——. "Transfiguration and Modernization: The Paradoxes of Social Disciplining, Paedagogical Leadership, and the Enlightenment in Eighteenth-Century Russia." Pages 99–115 in *Alteuropa – Ancien Régime – Frühe Neuzeit: Probleme und Methoden der Forschung.* Edited by Hans Erich Bödecker and Ernst Hinrichs. Stuttgart-Bad Cannstatt: Friedrich Frommann Verlag, 1991.

Raisin, Jacob. *The Haskalah Movement in Russia.* Philadelphia: The Jewish Publication Society of America, 1913.

Rapoport-Albert, Ada. "God and the Zaddik as the Two Focal Points of Hasidic Worship." Pages 299–329 in *Essential Papers on Hasidism.* Edited by Gershon David Hundert. New York: New York University Press, 1991.

——. "On Women in Hasidism, S. A. Horodecky and the Maid of Ludmir Tradition." Pages 495–525 in *Jewish History: Essays in Honour of Chimen Abramsky.* Edited by Ada Rapoport-Albert and Steven J. Zipperstein. London: Peter Halban, 1988.

——. ed. *Hasidism Reappraised.* London: Vallentine Mitchell & Co. Ltd., 1996.

Ravid, Benjamin. "Moneylending in Seventeenth Century Jewish Vernacular Apologetica." Pages 257–83 in *Jewish Thought in the Seventeenth Century.* Edited by Isadore Twersky and Bernard Septimus. Cambridge, Mass.: Harvard University Press, 1987.

——. *Economics and Toleration in Seventeenth Century Venice: The Background and Context of the Discorso of Simone Luzzatto.* New York: American Academy for Jewish Research, 1977.

Rayner, John D. "Gender Issues in Jewish Divorce." Pages 33–57 in *Gender Issues in Jewish Law: Essays and Responsa*. Edited by Walter Jacob and Moshe Zemer. New York and Oxford: Berghahn Books, 2001.

Reddaway, William Fiddian, et al. *Cambridge History of Poland*. New York: Octagon, 1971.

Reiner, Elchanan, ed. *Kroke – Kazimierz – Cracow: Studies in the History of Cracow Jewry*. Tel Aviv: The Center for the History of Polish Jewry, 2001.

——. "The Yeshivas of Poland and Germany during the Sixteenth and Seventeenth Centuries and the Debate over *Pilpul*." Pages 9–80 in *Keminhag Ashkenaz uFolin: sefer yovel leChone Shmeruk*. Edited by Israel Bartal, Chava Turniansky, and Ezra Mendelsohn. Jerusalem: Zalman Shazar Center, 1993.

——. "Wealth, Social Status and *Talmud Torah*: The *Kloiz* in the East European Jewish Community in the Seventeenth and Eighteenth Centuries." *Zion* 58, no. 3 (1993): 287–328.

Reizen, Zalman. "Campe's 'Entdeckung von Amerika' in Yiddish." *YIVO bleter* 5, no. 1 (1933): 29–40.

——. *Fun Mendelson biz Mendele*. Warsaw: Kultur-Lige, 1923.

Riasanovsky, Nicholas. *A Parting of the Ways: Government and the Educated Public in Russia, 1801–1855*. Oxford: Clarendon, 1976.

Richarz, Monika, ed. *Jewish Life in Germany: Memoirs from Three Centuries*. Translated by Stella P. Rosenfeld and Sidney Rosenfeld. Bloomington: Indiana University Press, 1991.

Riley, Glenda. *Divorce: An American Tradition*. New York: Oxford University Press, 1991.

Ringelblum, Emmanuel. "Hasidism and Haskalah in Warsaw in the Eighteenth Century." *YIVO bleter* 13 (1938): 124–32.

Robinson, Ira. "Kabbala and Science in *Sefer haberit*: Modernization Strategy for Orthodox Jews." *Modern Judaism* 9, no. 3 (October 1989): 275–88.

Rosen, Abraham, H. Sarig. *Kaminits – Podolsk and Its Environs*. Translated by Bonnie Schooler Sohn. Bergenfield, N.J.: Avotaynu Foundation, Inc., 1999.

Rosenthal, Judah. "R. Ishmael of Modena's Responses to the Emperor Napoleon's Twelve Questions." *Talppiyyot* 4 (1950): 565–87.

Rose, William J. *Stanislas Konarski: Reformer of Education in Eighteenth-Century Poland*. London: Jonathan Cape, 1929.

Roskies, David. *The Jewish Search for a Usable Past*. Bloomington: Indiana University Press, 1999.

——. "The Medium and the Message of the Maskilic Chapbook." *JSS* 41 (1979): 275–90.

Rosman, Moshe [M. J.]. "A Minority Views the Majority: Jewish Attitudes towards the Polish Lithuanian Commonwealth and Interaction with Poles." *Polin* 4 (1989): 31–41.

——. *Founder of Hasidism: A Quest for the Historical Ba'al Shem Tov*. Berkeley: University of California Press, 1996.

——. "Jewish Perceptions of Insecurity and Powerlessness in 16th–18th Century Poland." *Polin* 1 (1986): 19–27.

——. "Międzybóż and R. Ba'al Shem Tov." *Zion* 52 (1987): 177–89.

——. "Rebbe Israel Rubinowicz-Ritfin – An Aquaintance of the Polish Ruler in the Eighteenth Century." Pages 107–15 in *Ha'umah vetoldoteihah*. Vol. 2. Edited by Shmuel Ettinger. Jerusalem: Zalman Shazar Center, 1984.

——. *The Lords' Jews: Magnate-Jewish Relations in the Polish-Lithuanian Commonwealth during the Eighteenth Century*. Cambridge, Mass.: Harvard Ukranian Research Institute, 1990.

——. "Toward the History of a Historical Source: *In Praise of the Ba'al Shem Tov* and its Editing." *Zion* 58, no. 2 (1993): 2–40.

Rostworowski, Emanuel. "Polens Stellung in Europa im Zeitalter der Aufklärung." Pages 11–21 in *Polen und Deutschland im Zeitalter der Aufklärung.* Edited by Rainer Riemenschneider. Braunschweig: Georg-Eckert-Institut für Internationale Schulbuchforschung, 1981.

Roth, Cecil. "The Cabalist and the King." Pages 139–64 in *Essays and Portraits in Anglo-Jewish History.* Edited by Cecil Roth. Philadelphia: The Jewish Publication Society of America, 1962.

Rozenblit, Marcia. "The Jews of the Dual Monarchy." *Austrian History Yearbook* 13 (1992): 160–80.

Rubinstein, Avraham. "Haskalah and Hasidism: Joseph Perl's Activities." *Bar Ilan, Sefer hashanah* 12 (1974): 166–78.

——. "Joseph Perl's Interpretation of Names." *Tarbiz* 43 (1973–74): 205–16.

——. "Joseph Perl's Pamphlet, *Ketit lama'or.*" *Alei sefer* 3/4 (1976–77): 140–57.

——. "Mendel Lefin's 'Prayer of Thanksgiving'." *Kiryat sefer* 42 (1966/67): 403–04.

Ruderman, David B. *Jewish Enlightenment in an English Key: Anglo-Jewry's Construction of Modern Jewish Thought.* Princeton, N.J.: Princeton University Press, 2000.

——. *Jewish Thought and Scientific Discovery in Early Modern Europe.* New Haven, Conn.: Yale University Press, 1995.

——. ed. *Essential Papers on Jewish Culture in Renaissance and Baroque Italy.* New York: New York University Press, 1992.

Safran, Bezalel. "Leone da Modena's Historical Thinking." Pages 381–98 in *Jewish Thought in the Seventeenth Century.* Edited by Isadore Twersky and Bernard Septimus. Cambridge, Mass.: Harvard University Press, 1987.

Samet, Moshe Shraga. "Moses Mendelsohn, Naftali Herz Wessely and the Rabbis of their Generation." Pages 233–57 in *Mehqarim betoledot am yisra'el ve'erets yisra'el lezekher Tsevi Avneri.* Edited by Akiba Gilboa and Oded Bustenay. Haifa: The University of Haifa, 1970.

Sarna, Jonathan. "Jewish Prayers for the U.S. Government: A Study in the Liturgy of Politics and the Politicsof Liturgy." Pages 201–21 in *Moral Problems in American Life: New Perspectives on Cultural History.* Edited by Karen Halttunen and Lewis Perry. Ithaca, N.Y.: Cornell University Press, 1998.

Schacter, Jacob Joseph. "Rabbi Jacob Emden: Life and Major Works." Ph.D. diss., Harvard University, 1988.

Schaffer, Simon. "Natural Philosophy." Pages 55–91 in *The Ferment of Knowledge: Studies in the Historiography of Eighteenth-Century Science.* Edited by G. S. Rousseau and Roy Porter. Cambridge: Cambridge University Press, 1980.

Schiper, Ignacy. "Die galizische Judenschaft in den Jahren 1772–1848 in wirschafts-statistischer Beleuchtung." *Jüdische Monatshefte* 9–10 *(1918).*

Schneider, Herbert W. "The Significance of Benjamin Franklin's Moral Philosophy." Pages 298–304 in *Studies in the History of Ideas.* Vol. 2. New York: Columbia University Press, 1925.

Scholem, Gershom. *Major Trends in Jewish Mysticism.* Jerusalem: Schocken Books, 1941.

——. *On the Kabbalah and Its Symbolism.* New York: Schocken Books, 1969.

——. "Reservations about *Hokhmat Yisra'el.*" Pages 385–403 in *Devarim bego: pirqei morashah utehiyyah.* Tel Aviv: Am Oved, 1976.

——. *Sabbatai Sevi: The Mystical Messiah, 1626–1676.* Translated by R. J. Werblowsky. Princeton, N.J.: Princeton University Press, 1973.

——. *The Messianic Idea in Judaism and Other Essays in Jewish Spritiuality.* Schocken Books, 1971.

——. "The Sabbatian Movement in Poland." Pages 68–140 in *Mehqarim umeqorot letoldot hashabta'ut vegilguleihah.* Jerusalem: Bialik Institute, 1974.

Schorsch, Ismar. "Emancipation and the Crisis of Religious Authority: The Emergence of the Modern Rabbinate." Pages 206–54 in *Revolution and Evolution: 1848 in German-Jewish History.* Edited by Werner Mosse, Arnold Paucker, and Reinhard Rurup. Tubingen: Mohr, 1981.

——. *From Text to Context: The Turn to History in Modern Judaism.* Hanover, N.H.: University Press of New England, 1994.

——. *Jewish Reactions to German Anti-Semitism, 1870–1914.* New York: Columbia University Press, 1972.

Schwarzfuchs, Simon. *Napoleon, the Jews and the Sanhedrin.* London: The Littmann Library of Jewish Civilization, 1979.

Scott, H. M., ed. *Enlightened Absolutism: Reform and Reformers in Later Eighteenth-Century Europe.* London: Macmillan, 1990.

——. ed. *The European Nobilities in the Seventeenth and Eighteenth Centuries.* London: Longman, 1995.

Seidman, Naomi. *A Marriage Made in Heaven: The Sexual Politics of Hebrew and Yiddish.* Berkeley: University of California Press, 1997.

Sepinwall, Alyssa Goldstein. "Regenerating France, Regenerating the World: the Abbé Grégoire and the French Revolution, 1750–1831." Ph.D. diss., Stanford University, 1998.

Shandler, Jeffrey. "Heschel and Yiddish: A Struggle with Signification." *The Journal of Jewish Thought and Philosophy* 2: 245–99.

——. "Szczuczyn: A *Shtetl* Through a Photographer's Eye." Pages 19–27 in *Lives Remembered: A Shtetl Through A Photographer's Eye.* New York: Museum of Jewish Heritage: A Living Memorial to the Holocaust, 2002.

Shatzky, Jacob. "Recensions: Review of A. Friedkin's *Avraham Baer Gottlober un zayn epokhe.*" *Pinkas* 1 (1927–28): 162–68.

Shavit, Ya'akov. "A Duty Too Heavy To Bear: Hebrew in the Berlin Haskalah, 1783–1819: Between Classic, Modern and Romantic." Pages 111–28 in *Hebrew in Ashkenaz.* Edited by Lewis Glinert. New York: Oxford University Press, 1993.

Shavit, Zohar. "From Friedländer's Lesebuch to the Jewish Campe – The Beginning of Hebrew Children's Literature in Germany." *LBIYA* 33 (1988): 385–415.

——. "The Function of Yiddish Literature in the Development of Hebrew Children's Literature." *Hasifrut* 3–4, no. 35–36 (1986): 148–53.

Shilo, Shmuel. "The War against Reform in the *Responsa* of Polish and Russian Sages in the Nineteenth Century." *Dinei yisra'el* 20–21 (2000–01): 419–33.

Shmeruk, Chone. "Investigations into Jacob Frank's Childhood Memoirs." *Gal-Ed* 15–16 (1997): 35–42.

——. *Sifrut yidish beFolin: mehqarim ve'iyyunim historiyyim.* Jerusalem: Magnes Press, 1981.

——. *Sifrut yidish: peraqim letoldoteihah.* Tel Aviv: The Porter Institute for Poetics & Semiotics, 1978.

——. "The Social Significance of Hasidic Ritual Slaughter." *Zion* 20 (1955): 47–72.

——. "Yiddish Literature and Collective Memory: The Case of the Chmielnicki Massacres." *Polin* 5 (1990): 173–83.

Shohat, Azriel. *Im hillufei tequfot.* Jerusalem: Bialik Institute, 1960.

Shulvass, Moses. *From East to West: The Westward Migration of Jews from Eastern Europe during the Seventeenth and Eighteenth Centuries.* Detroit, Mich.: Wayne State University Press, 1971.

——. *Jewish Culture in Eastern Europe: The Classical Period.* New York: KTAV, 1975.

Silber, Michael K. "The Emergence of Ultra-Orthodoxy: The Invention of a Tradition." Pages 23–84 in *The Uses of Tradition: Jewish Continuity in the Modern Era.* Edited by Jack Wertheimer. New York: The Jewish Theological Seminary of America, 1992.

Silbershlag, Eisig. "Hebrew Literature in Vienna 1782–1939." Pages 29–44 in *The Great Transition: The Recovery of the Lost Centers of Modern Hebrew Literature.* Edited by Glenda Abramson and Tudor Parfitt. Rowman & Allanheld Publishers, 1985.

———. "Parapoetic Attitudes and Values in Early Nineteenth-Century Hebrew Poetry." Pages 117–39 in *Studies in Nineteenth-Century Jewish Intellectual History.* Edited by Alexander Altmann. Cambridge, Mass.: Harvard University Press, 1964.

———. "The Anglo-Saxon Factor in Our Modern Literature: First Contacts." *Divrei hakongres ha'olami harevi'i lamada'ei hayahadut* 2 (1969): 71–75.

Simon, Ernst A. "Pedagogic Philanthropism and Jewish Education (Hebrew Section)." Pages 149–87 in *Jubilee Volume in Honor of Mordecai Kaplan.* Edited by Moshe Davis. New York, 1953.

Sinkoff, Nancy. "Benjamin Franklin in Jewish Eastern Europe: Cultural Appropriation in the Age of the Enlightenment." *Journal of the History of Ideas* 61, no. 1 (2000): 133–52.

———. "Educating for 'Proper' Jewish Womanhood: A Case Study in Domesticity and Vocational Training, 1897–1926." *American Jewish History* 77, no. 4 (June 1988): 572–99.

———. "Strategy and Ruse in the Haskalah of Mendel Lefin of Satanów (1749–1826)." Pages 86–102 in *New Perspectives on the Haskalah.* Edited by Shmuel Feiner and David Sorkin. London: Littman Library of Jewish Civilization, 2001.

Sked, Alan. *The Decline and Fall of the Habsburg Empire, 1815–1918.* London: Longman Group, 1989.

Slomka, Jan. *From Serfdom to Self-Government: Memoirs of a Polish Village Mayor, 1842–1927.* William John Rose. Glasgow: The University Press, 1941.

Sokolow, Jayme A. "'Arriving at Moral Perfection': Benjamin Franklin and Leo Tolstoy." *American Literature* 48, no. 3 (November 1975): 427–32.

Soloveitchik, Haym. "Pawnbroking and a Study of *Ribbit* and of the Halakhah in Exile." *PAAJR* 38–39 (1970–72): 203–68.

———. "Religious Law and Change: The Medieval Ashkenazic Example." *AJS Review* 12, no. 2 (Fall 1987): 205–21.

———. "Rupture and Reconstruction: The Transformation of Contemporary Orthodoxy." Pages 320–76 in *Jews in America: A Contemporary Reader.* Edited by Roberta Rosenberg Farber and Chaim I. Waxman. Hanover, N.H.: Brandeis University Press.

Sorkin, David. "Emancipation, Haskalah, and Reform: The Contribution of Amos Funkenstein." *JSS* (new series) 6, no. 1 (Fall 1999): 98–110.

———. "From Context to Comparison: The German Haskalah and Reform Catholicism." *Tel Aviver Jahrbuch für deutsche Geschichte* 20 (1991): 23–58.

———. *Moses Mendelssohn and the Religious Enlightenment.* Berkeley: University of California Press, 1996.

———. "Religious Reforms and Secular Trends in German-Jewish Life: An Agenda for Research." *Leo Baeck Institute Yearbook Annual* 40 (1995): 169–84.

———. "The Case for Comparison: Moses Mendelssohn and the Religious Enlightenment." *Modern Judaism* 14 (1994): 121–38.

———. "The Early Haskalah." Pages 9–26 in *New Perspectives on the Haskalah.* Edited by Shmuel Feiner and David Sorkin. London: Littmann Library, 2001.

———. "The Spirit of Prussian Jewry: The Dual Legacy of Berlin." *Braun Lectures in the History of the Jews of Prussia* 2 (1993): 1–13.

——. *The Transformation of German Jewry, 1780–1840*. New York: Oxford University Press, 1987.

——. "Wilhelm von Humboldt: The Theory and Practice of Self-Formation (Bildung), 1791–1810." *Journal of the History of Ideas* 44 (1983): 55–73.

Spicehandler, Ezra. "Joshua Heschel Schorr: Maskil and Eastern European Reformist." *HUCA* 31 (1960): 181–222 and 40–41 (1960): 503–528.

Springer, Arnold. "Enlightened Absolutism and Jewish Reform: Prussia, Austria, and Russia." *California Slavic Studies* 11 (1980): 237–67.

Stampfer, Shaul. "What Did 'Knowing Hebrew' Mean in Eastern Europe." Pages 129–40 in *Hebrew in Ashkenaz*. Edited by Lewis Glinert. London: Oxford University Press, 1993.

Stanislawski, Michael. *For Whom Do I Toil?: Judah Leib Gordon and the Crisis of Russian Jewry*. New York: Oxford University Press, 1988.

——. *Psalms for the Tsar: A Minute-Book of a Psalms Society in the Russian Army, 1864–1867*. New York: Yeshiva University Library, 1988.

——. "Russian Jewry, the Russian State, and the Dynamics of Jewish Emancipation." Pages 262–83 in *Paths of Emancipation: Jews, States and Citizenship*. Edited by Pierre Birnbaum and Ira Katznelson. Princeton, N.J.: Princeton University Press, 1995.

——. "The Tsarist Mishneh Torah: A Study in the Cultural Politics of the Russian Haskalah." *PAAJR* 50 (1983): 165–83.

——. "The Yiddish *Shevet Yehudah*: A Study in the 'Ashkenization' of a Spanish-Jewish Classic." Pages 134–49 in *Jewish History and Jewish Memory: Essays in Honor of Yosef Hayim Yerushalmi*. Edited by Elisheva Carlebach, John M. Efron, and David N. Myers. Hanover, N.H.: Brandeis University Press, 1998.

——. *Tsar Nicholas I and the Jews*. Philadelphia: The Jewish Publication Society of America, 1983.

Stauter-Halstead, Keely. *The Nation in the Village: The Genesis of Peasant National Identity in Austrian Poland, 1848–1914*. Ithaca, N.Y.: Cornell University Press, 2001.

Steinlauf, Michael. *Bondage to the Dead: Poland and the Memory of the Holocaust*. Syracuse, N.Y.: Syracuse University Press, 1997.

Stone, Daniel. "Jews and the Urban Question in Late Eighteenth Century Poland." *Slavic Review* 50, no. 3 (Autumn 1991): 531–41.

——. *Polish Politics and National Reform, 1775–1788*. New York: Columbia University Press, 1976.

Sysyn, Frank E. *Between Poland and the Ukraine: The Dilemma of Adam Kysil, 1600–1653*. Cambridge, Mass.: Harvard University Press, 1985.

Szabo, Frank A. J. "'Austrian' First Impressions of Ethnic Relations in Galicia: The Case of Governor Anton von Pergen." Pages 49–60 in *Polin Volume Twelve: Focusing on Galicia: Jews, Poles, and Ukrainians, 1772–1918*. Vol 12. Edited by Israel Bartal and Antony Polonsky. London: The Littman Library of Jewish Civilization, 1999.

Szajkowski, Zosa. *Jews and the French Revolutions of 1789, 1830 and 1848*. New York: KTAV, 1970.

——. *The Economic Status of the Jews in Alsace, Metz and Lorraine (1648–1789)*. New York: Editions Historiques Franco-Juives, 1954.

Ta-Shma, Israel. "Law, Custom and Tradition among Ashkenazic Jews in the Eleventh and Twelfth Centuries." *Sidra* 3 (1987): 85–161.

Teller, Adam. "The Economic Activity of Polish Jewry in the Second Half of the Seventeenth Century and early Eighteenth Century." Pages 209–24 in *Qiyyum veshever: yehudei Polin ledoroteihem*. Edited by Israel Bartal and Israel Gutman. Jerusalem: Zalman Shazar Center, 1997.

——. "The Legal Status of the Jews on the Magnate Estates of Poland-Lithuania in the Eighteenth Century." *Gal-Ed* 15–16 (1997): 41–63.

Tishby, Isaiah and Joseph Dan. "Hasidic Thought and Literature." Pages 250–315 in *Peraqim betorat hahasidut uvetoldoteihah*. Edited by Avraham Rubinstein. Jerusalem: Zalman Shazar Center, 1977.

——. *Mivhar sifrut hamusar*. Jerusalem: Magnes Press, 1970.

Toury, Jacob. *Die jüdische presse im österreichischen Kaiserreich: ein Beitrag zur Problematik der Akkulturation 1802–1918*. Tübingen: Mohr, 1983.

Tsamriyon, Tsemah. *Hame'assef: ketav ha'et hamodernit harishon be'ivrit*. Tel Aviv: University Publishing Projects, Ltd., 1988.

Twersky, Isadore, ed. *A Maimonides Reader*. New York: Behrman House, 1972.

——. "The Shulhan 'Aruk: Enduring Code of Jewish Law." Pages 322–43 in *The Jewish Expression*. Edited by Judah Golden. Bantam: New York, 1970.

Uffenheimer, Rivka Schatz. *Hasidism as Mysticism: Quietistic Elements in Eighteenth Century Hasidic Thought*. Jerusalem: Magnes Press, 1993.

Ury, Scott. "Who, What, When, Where, and Why Is Polish Jewry? Envisioning, Constructing, and Possessing Polish Jewry." *JSS* (new series) 6, no. 3 (2000): 205–28.

Vinograd, Yeshayahu. *Ivrit mereshit hadefus ha'ivri beshenat 1469 ve'ad shenat 1863*. Otsar hasefer ha'ivri: Jerusalem, 1993.

Volkov, Shulamit. "The Dynamics of Dissimulation: *Ostjuden* and German Jews." Pages 195–211 in *The Jewish Response to German Culture*. Edited by Jehudah Reinharz and Walter Schatzberg. Hanover, N.H.: University Press of New England, 1985.

Wachstein, Bernhard. *Die hebräische Publizistik in Wien*. Vienna: Selbstverlag der Historischen Kommission, 1930.

Walicki, Andrzej. *The Enlightenment and the Birth of Modern Nationhood: Polish Political Thought from Noble Republicanism to Tadeusz Kosciuszko*. Notre Dame, Ind.: University of Notre Dame Press, 1989.

Walker, Mack. "Jewish Identity in a World of Corporations and Estates" in *In and Out of the Ghetto: Jewish-Gentile Relations in Late Medieval and Early Modern Germany*. Edited by R. Po-Chia Hsia and Hartmut Lehmann. Cambridge: Cambridge University Press, 1995.

Wandycz, Piotr S. "Historiography of the Countries of Eastern Europe: Poland." *The American Historical Review* 97, no. 4 (1992 October): 1011–25.

——. *Lands of Partitioned Poland, 1795–1918*. Seattle: University of Washington, 1974.

——. "The Poles in the Habsburg Monarchy." *Austrian History Yearbook* 32 (1967): 287–313.

——. *The Price of Freedom: A History of East Central Europe from the Middle Ages to the Present*. London: Routledge, 1992.

Wegner, Judith Romney. *Chattel or Person? The Status of Women in the Mishnah*. New York: Oxford University Press, 1988.

Weinberg, David H. *Between Tradition and Modernity: Haim Zhitlowski, Simon Dubnow, Ahad Ha-Am, and the Shaping of Modern Jewish Identity*. New York: Holmes & Meier, 1996.

Weinberg, Werner. "Language Questions Relating to Moses Mendelssohn's Pentateuch Translation." *HUCA* 55 (1984): 197–242.

Weiner, Miriam. *Jewish Roots in Poland: Pages from the Past and Archival Inventories*. New York: YIVO, 1997.

Weinlös, Israel. *Historishe schriftn*. Vilna, 1937.

——. "Mendel Lefin of Satanów: A Biographical Study from Manuscript Material." *YIVO bleter* 1 (1931): 334–57.

——. "R. Menachem Mendel of Satanów." *Ha'olam* 13 (1925): 39: 778–79; 40: 799–800; 41: 819–20; 42: 839–40.

——. *Yosef Perls lebn un shafn.* Vilna: YIVO, 1937.

Weinlös, Israel and Zelig Kalmanowicz. *Yosef Perls yidishe kesovim.* Vilna: YIVO, 1937.

Weinreich, Max. *History of the Yiddish Language.* Translated by Shlomo Noble. Chicago: The University of Chicago Press, 1980.

Weinryb, Bernard D. "The Beginnings of East-European Jewry in Legend and Historiography." Pages 445–502 in *Studies and Essays in Honor of Abraham A. Neuman.* Edited by Meir ben-Horin, Bernard Weinryb, and S. Zeitlin. Leiden: E. J. Brill, 1962.

——. *The Jews of Poland.* Philadelphia: The Jewish Publication Society of America, 1976.

Weinstein, Sara Epstein. *Piety and Fanaticism: Rabbinic Criticism of Religious Stringency.* London: Jason Aronson, 1997.

Weintraub, Aviva. "Poultry in Motion: The Jewish Atonement Ritual of Kapores." Pages 209–13 in *Jews of Brooklyn.* Edited by Ilana Abramovitch and Seán Galvin. Hanover, N.H.: University of New England Press, 2002.

Weiss, Joseph. "The Beginnings of Hasidism." Pages 122–82 in *Peraqim betoldot hahasidut uvetoldoteihah.* Edited by Avraham Rubinstein. Jerusalem: Zalman Shazar Center, 1977.

——. "The Hasidic Way of Habad." Pages 194–201 in *Studies in Eastern European Jewish Mysticism.* Edited by David Goldstein. London: Oxford University Press, 1985.

——. "The Saddik – Altering the Divine Will." Pages 183–93 in *Studies in Eastern European Mysticism.* Edited by David Goldstein. London: Oxford University Press, 1985.

Weissberg, M. "Die neuhebräische Aufklärungsliteratur in Galizien." *Monatsschrift für Geschichte und Wissenschaft des Judentums* 21, 35, 36 (1913 and 1927–1928): 513–26, 735–49; 54–62, 100–09; 71–88, 184–201.

Weissler, Chava. *Voices of the Matriarchs: Listening to the Prayers of Early Modern Jewish Women.* Boston: Beacon Press, 1998.

Werses, Shmuel. "An Unknown Satirical Writing of Joseph Perl." *Hasifrut* 1 (1968): 206–07.

——. *Haskalah veshabta'ut: toldotav shel ma'avaq.* Jerusalem: Zalman Shazar Center, 1988.

——. "The French Revolution in the Perspective of the Haskalah." *Tarbiz* 63, no. 3–4 (1989): 483–521.

——. "The Joseph Perl Archives and their Peregrinations." *Ha'universitah* 19, no. 1 (1974): 38–52.

——. *Megammot vetsurot besifrut hahaskalah.* Jerusalem: Magnes Press, 1990.

——. "The National Triangle: Jews, Poles, and Ruthenians in Eastern Galicia in the Stories of Asher Barash." *Gal-Ed* 13 (1993): 155–80.

Wertheimer, Jack. *Unwelcome Strangers: East European Jews in Imperial Germany.* New York and Oxford: Oxford University Press, 1987.

Westfehling, Uwe. *Jean-Pierre Norblin: ein Künstler des Revolutionszeitalters in Paris und Warschau.* Cologne: Wallraf-Richartz-Museum, 1989.

Westreich, Elimelech. "The Ban on Polygamy in Polish Rabbinic Thought." Pages 66–84 in *Polin: The Jews in Early Modern Poland.* Vol. 10. Edited by Gershon David Hundert. The Littman Library of Jewish Civilization, 1997.

Whaley, Joachim. "The Protestant Enlightenment in German Lands." Pages 106–17 in *The Enlightenment in National Context.* Edited by Roy Porter and Mikuláš Teich. Cambridge: Cambridge University Press.

Whitfield, Peter. *New Found Lands: Maps in the History of Exploration.* New York: Routledge, 1998.

Wiener, Max. *Abraham Geiger and Liberal Judaism.* Philadelphia: The Jewish Publication Society of America, 1962.

Wiener, Meir. *Tsu der geshikhte fun der yidisher literatur in nayntsnt yorhundert.* Kiev, 1940.

Wilensky, Mordecai. "Hasidic-Mitnaggedic Polemics in the Jewish Communities of Eastern Europe: The Hostile Phase." Pages 89–113 in *Tolerance and Movements of Religious Dissent in Eastern Europe.* Edited by Béla K. Király. New York: Columbia University Press, 1975.

Wisse, Ruth R. *I. L. Peretz and the Making of Modern Jewish Culture.* Seattle: University of Washington Press, 1991.

Wistrich, Robert. "The Modernization of Viennese Jewry: The Impact of German Culture in a Multi-Ethnic State." Pages 43–70 in *Toward Modernity.* Edited by Jacob Katz. New Brunswick, N.J.: Transaction Books, 1987.

———. *The Jews of Vienna in the Age of Franz Joseph.* New York: Oxford University Press, 1990.

Wolff, Larry. *Inventing Eastern Europe: The Map of Civilization on the Mind of the Enlightenment.* Stanford, Calif.: Stanford University Press, 1994.

Wróbel, Piotr. "The Jews of Galicia under Austrian-Polish Rule, 1869–1918." *Austrian History Yearbook* 25 (1994): 97–138.

Wunder, Meir. *Entsiqlopedyah leḥakhmei Galitsyah.* Jerusalem: Institute for Commemoration of Galician Jewry, 1986.

Wyrobisz, Andrzej. "The Arts and Social Prestige in Poland between the Sixteenth and Eighteenth Centuries." Pages 153–78 in *A Republic of Nobles: Studies in Polish History to 1864.* Edited by J. K. Fedorowicz. Cambridge: Cambridge University Press, 1982.

Yerushalmi, Yosef Hayim. "Assimilation and Racial Anti-Semitism: The Iberian and the German Models." *Leo Baeck Memorial Lecture* 26 (1982): 3–38.

———. *The Lisbon Massacre and the Royal Image in the Shebet Yehudah.* Cinncinnati, Ohio: Hebrew Union College Press, 1976.

———. *Zakhor: Jewish History and Jewish Memory.* Seattle: University of Washington Press, 1982.

Yudlov, Isaac. *The Israel Mehlman Collection in the Jewish National and University Library.* Jerusalem: Beit hasefarim, 1984.

Zafren, Herbert F. "Variety in the Typography of Yiddish: 1535–1635." *HUCA* 53 (1982): 137–63.

Zalkin, Mordechai. *Ba'alot hashaḥar: hahaskalah hayehudit ba'imperyah harusit bame'ah haleshu-esreh.* Jerusalem: Magnes Press, 2000.

———. "The Jewish Enlightenment in Poland: Directions for Discussion." Pages 391–413 in *Qiyyum veshever: yehudei Polin ledoroteihem.* Vol. 2. Edited by Israel Bartal and Israel Gutman. Jerusalem: Zalman Shazar Center, 2001.

———. "Trends in the Development of Haskalah Education in the Russian Empire at the Beginning of the Nineteenth Century." *Zion* 62 (1997): 133–71.

Zawadzki, W. H. *A Man of Honour: Adam Czartoryski as a Statesman of Russia and Poland, 1795–1831.* Oxford: Clarendon Press, 1993.

Zeitlin, William. *Qiryat sefer bibliotheca hebraica post-Mendelssohniana.* Leipzig: K. F. Koehler's Antiquarium, 1891–1895.

Zeydel, Edwin H. "A Criticism of the German Language by a German of the Eighteenth Century." *Modern Language Notes* 38, no. 4 (April 1923): 193–201.

Zienkowska, Krystyna. "'The Jews have Killed a Tailor:' The Socio-Political Background of a Pogrom in Warsaw in 1790." *Polin* 3 (1988): 78–102.

Zinberg, Israel. *A History of Jewish Literature*. New York: KTAV, 1975.

Zipperstein, Steven J. *Imagining Russian Jewry: Memory, History, Identity*. Seattle and London: University of Washington Press, 1999.

———. *The Jews of Odessa: A Cultural History, 1794–1881*. Stanford, Calif.: Stanford University Press, 1986.

———. "Transforming the Heder: Maskilic Politics in Imperial Russia." Pages 87–109 in *Jewish History: Essays in Honour of Chimen Abramsky*. Edited by Ada Rapoport-Albert and Steven J. Zipperstein. London: The Littman Library of Jewish Civilization, 1988.

Żółtowski, Adam. *Border of Europe: A Study of the Polish Eastern Provinces*. London: Hollis & Carter, 1950.

INDEX

hitlahavut (ecstasy or ardor in Hasidic
    prayer), 113, 158, 158n
Hobbes, Thomas, 175n
ḥokhmat haneshamot. See psychology
Ḥokhmat yisra'el, 203n
Holdheim, Samuel, 267
Holland (Netherlands), 18–19
Holocaust, influence on historiography of
    Polish Jewry, 1, 13, 107n
Homberg, Naftali Herz, 37n, 83, 223–24,
    226n, 228, 264
Horowitz, Isaiah ha-Levi; his *Shenei luḥot
    haberit*, 133, 160
Horowitz, Yehudah, 40
Hourwitz, Zalkind, 5n, 75–77, 79
Human (Uman), 178n
ḥumra (stringency), 237, 245
Hungary; Hungarians; Magyars, 15, 207n,
    214
Hurwitz, Phinehas Elijah, his *Sefer haberit*,
    125n
Husiatyn, 28

Ibn Adret, Solomon (Rashba), 262, 262n
Ibn Ezra, Abraham, 249
Ibn Parhon, Solomon, his *Arukh*, 260n
Ibn Pekuda, Bahya; his *Ḥovot halevavot*,
    122, 132, 133n
Ibn Tibbon, Samuel, 128–29, 129n, 169
Imperial-Royal School Commission
    (Prussia), 230
Imperial Statute Concerning the Jews
    (Russia, 1804), 4, 49, 106–12, 207,
    221n, 226
Inländer, Moses, 33n
International Conference on the Yiddish
    Language, 169n
Isaac of Acco, 42, 42n
Isaac of Drohobycz, 34
Israel of Międzybóż. *See* Ba'al Shem Tov
Israel, Land of, 119
Israelitische Freischule in Tarnopol. *See*
    educational reform
Isserles, Moses, 22, 122, 126, 157, 242,
    242n, 254, 260n, 262n
Islam, 15, 16n, 25
Italian Jews; Italians, 15, 207n, 239n, 250–
    51, 254n, 263
Itzig, Isaac ben Daniel, 231n

Jacob Joseph of Połonna (Polonnoye), 33–
    34
Jagielnica, 28
Jawornicki, Jan, 66
Jephthah, 258
Jericzów, 104
Jezierzany, 28

Jesuit order, 64
Jewish Directorate (Galicia), 213, 216
Jewish nationalism, 2, 210–211, 223
'Jewish Question,' 4, 55, 71–83, 105–06
Jezierski, Jacek, 74
Job, 130, 145
Joseph II, 54n, 91, 98, 204, 209, 214–25,
    217n
Joshua, 125
Jost, Isaac Marcus, 244n, 245n
Judah Leib of Połonna (Polonnoye), 34
Judah Loewe of Prague, 122, 126
Junto group. *See* Franklin, Benjamin

Kabbalah; kabbalistic teachings and
    writings, 2, 22, 41n, 43n, 88, 125n, 133,
    145, 160, 198, 249–250
kahal (Jewish municipality), 72n, 73, 76–
    78, 95–99, 101, 105, 108, 111, 209–211,
    231, 242, 269
Kamieniec Podolski, 24, 27–28, 85n
Kant, Immanuel, 116, 127–128, 127n, 130–
    132, 131n, 139, 144, 1161, 161n, 165
Kaplan, Mordecai, 234n
kapparah, 262n
Karaites, 32, 203, 203n, 207n, 216n, 239
Karniel, Joseph, 215n
Karo, Joseph; his *Shulḥan arukh*, 22, 46,
    154, 158, 240, 242, 242n, 249, 254, 262n
Katz, Jacob, 10, 37, 244
Katz, Simha, 177n, 185n
Katz, Tobias, 125n
Katzenellenbogen, Abraham, 242
Katznelson, Ira, 13n, 70n
Kerem ḥemed, 184n, 244n, 250, 269
Khazar kingdom; 'Khazar theory of
    origins,' 16, 16n
Kiev; Kievan state, 16, 17, 23, 34
kittel (prayer robe), 242
Klausner, Joseph, 37n, 164n, 183n
Klewań, 103
kloizim (mystical study groups), 22
Kluger, Solomon, 243, 269n
Knights' School (Polish; *also* Cadets
    Corps), 63–64, 65n
Kniaznin, Franciszek, 66
Koblanski, Józef, 66
Kochubey, Victor, 107, 108
Koffler, Philip, 247n
Koidnover, Zevi Hirsch; his *Qav hayashar*,
    133
Kołłątaj, Hugo, 73–74, 85, 95, 171n
Komarno, 79, 179n, 243
Konarski, Stanisław, 63
Königsberg, 80
konsensy rabinostwa (rabbinic license or
    rent), 96, 102–104, 261n